Niels Bohr's Times,
In Physics, Philosophy, and Polity

Frontispiece Niels Bohr and the author in Amsterdam, 1953.

Niels Bohr's Times,

In Physics, Philosophy, and Polity

ABRAHAM PAIS

CLARENDON PRESS · OXFORD
1991

Oxford University Press, Walton Street, Oxford OX2 6DP

Oxford New York Toronto
Delhi Bombay Calcutta Madras Karachi
Petaling Jaya Singapore Hong Kong Tokyo
Nairobi Dar es Salaam Cape Town
Melbourne Auckland

and associated companies in
Berlin Ibadan

Oxford is a trade mark of Oxford University Press

Published in the United States
by Oxford University Press, New York

A catalogue record for this book is available from
the British Library

Library of Congress Cataloging-in-Publication Data
Pais, Abraham, 1918–
Niels Bohr's times: in physics, philosophy, and polity/Abraham Pais.
Includes bibliographical references and indexes.
1. Nuclear physics—History.   2. Bohr, Niels, 1885–1962.
I. Title.
QC773. P35   1991   530'.092—dc20   90-27248
ISBN 0-19-852049-2

Phototypeset by Cotswold Typesetting Ltd, Gloucester
Printed in the United States of America

To the reader

The life of Niels Bohr spans times of revolutionary change in science itself as well as in its impact on society. As the curtain rises, the reality of atoms is still under debate, the structure of atoms still a matter of conjecture, the atomic nucleus is not yet discovered, practical applications of atomic energy, for good or evil, are not even visible on the far horizon. All that changed during Bohr's life, much of it under his own influence. He was the first to understand how atoms are put together, he played a leading role in the development of the theory of the atomic nucleus, and he was the godfather of nuclear medicine. He was also the first to bring to the attention of leading statesmen the need for openness between West and East, a need resulting from the advent of formidable new weapons developed during and after World War II. Time and again he would stress that openness was essential for political world stability.

Even more profound than new discoveries and perceptions regarding the structure of matter are new physical laws discovered in that same period. Here the key concepts are relativity theory and quantum theory. Bohr was the principal figure in elucidating the revisions of the philosophical foundations of physics needed for a comprehension of quantum phenomena.

I have been told that Vladimir Horowitz once commented on Mozart's music that it is too easy for beginners and too hard for experts. The same can be said of quantum physics. In this book I attempt to outline for beginners how most experts think about quantum theory. This undertaking demands that I suppress mathematical details as much as possible. (In spite of my efforts at simplicity, a phrase from a preface by Bertrand Russell will also apply here: 'There are several sentences in the present volume which some unusually stupid children of ten might find a little puzzling.') I hope that the present account will serve to counteract the many cheap attempts at popularizing this subject, such as efforts by woolly masters at linking quantum physics to mysticism.

After years of preparatory work, the Niels Bohr Archive was officially established on 7 October 1985, the centenary of Bohr's birth, as an independent self-governing institution under the Danish Ministry of Education. It is housed in the Niels Bohr Institute in Copenhagen. There one finds Bohr's scientific correspondence, 6000 letters and drafts to and from 400 correspondents, and 500 manuscripts, all in round numbers; also housed are his general and personal correspondence (the latter mostly in Danish), both of which occupy about the same amount of space as the scientific correspondence. Bohr's political and family correspondence have also been deposited in the archive but remain closed for the time being.

In addition one finds in the archive a collection of transcripts of interviews with Bohr and others that deal with recollections of earlier times. These, too, are rich in information, though every user must face the delicate question of how reliable such memories are.

All these archival materials have of course served me as major sources for the present book. Even more important to me have been personal contacts, first and foremost with Bohr's sons, Hans, Erik (recently deceased), Ernest, and most particularly Aage, who have encouraged me in my efforts and helped me with comments. Each of them appreciated my offer to show them parts of the manuscript. All of them refused, essentially because they felt that mine should be an independent view and assessment. This work therefore does not carry their seal of approval. May they not find too much fault.

Two good friends did read the entire manuscript: Res Jost and Sam Treiman. I am deeply grateful for their criticisms and counsel. Res's recent death is a great personal loss to me.

I am also much indebted to the staff members of the Niels Bohr Archive. Erik Rüdinger and Finn Aaserud were always ready to help with my endless questions. So was Hilde Levi, whom I thank particularly for her advice on issues in biology. Helle Bonaparte, Felicity Pors, and Judith Hartbro helped me in practical matters and added cheer to my labors. I also thank the archivists of the Rockefeller Foundation and the Ford Foundation for their kind help.

I gratefully record the assistance I received regarding specific subjects. Knud Max Møller shared with me his astounding knowledge of Danish archival sources. Rigsantikvar Olaf Olsen answered many questions about Denmark's history. Ms Isobel Mordy F.S.G. helped me in tracing the ancestry of Jenny Raphael, Bohr's maternal grandmother. Discussions with Jens Lindhard on statistical mechanics, with Ben Mottelson on nuclear physics, and with David Favrholdt on philosophical issues were very useful. I enjoyed numerous exchanges with Jørgen Kalckar and Stefan Rozental on Bohr's personality and philosophy.

I am pleased to thank those who briefed me on issues concerned with experimental physics: Torben Huus and Niels Ove Lassen on the Niels Bohr Institute in Copenhagen; Hans Bjerrum Møller and Klaus Singer on the National Laboratory at Risø; Sven Bjornholm on the Niels Bohr Institute at Risø. Correspondence with John Krige added to my understanding of Bohr's relations with CERN. I further thank Nobel committees in Stockholm for making available to me documents concerning Nobel Prize nominations for Niels Bohr and for his father.

This book was written partly in New York, partly in Copenhagen, which has become my second home. My improved awareness of the Danish ambiance has been of great help in a better understanding of Bohr. I am greatly beholden to the Alfred P. Sloan Foundation for an important grant that helped me in many phases of preparation. I thank Marie Grossi for her excellent help in preparing the manuscript.

My dear Ida's care sustained me throughout my labors.

New York   A.P.
July 1990

A note on the references

When in the text of this book I refer at one place to a point made somewhere else I use the shorthand (5f) to denote Chapter 5, section (f).

Each chapter has its own set of references.

The following abbreviations have been used for entries that occur frequently:

CW   Niels Bohr, *Collected works*; North-Holland, Amsterdam 1972 onwards.

NBA Niels Bohr Archive, Copenhagen.

NBR *Niels Bohr, his life and work as seen by his friends and colleagues,* Ed. S. Rozental, North-Holland, Amsterdam 1967.

IB   *Inward bound: of matter and forces in the physical world,* A. Pais, Oxford University Press 1986.

SL   *Subtle is the Lord . . . ,* A. Pais, Oxford University Press 1982.

He utters his opinions like one perpetually groping and never like one who believes he is in possession of definite truth.

ALBERT EINSTEIN
on Niels Bohr

To Ida, Joshua, and Lisa

Og til alle mine gode venner i Danmark

Contents

If you find those sections marked with an asterisk (*) too technical, then just skip them and read on.

1 **A Dane for all seasons**   1

  (a) Themes   1
  (b) Some personal recollections   4
  (c) A tour through this book   14

2 **'In Denmark I was born . . .'**   32

3 **Boyhood**   42

4 **Toward the twentieth century: from ancient optics to relativity theory**   52

  (a) 1903   52
  (b) The nature of light; beginnings   53
  (c) Particles or waves?   56
  (d) Color, visible and invisible   60
  (e) Of Maxwell's theory, Hertz's experiment, and the definition of classical physics   63
  (f) Trouble with the aether: the Michelson–Morley experiment   66
  (g) In which classical physics comes to an end and Einstein makes his first appearance   68

5 *Natura facit saltum*: **the roots of quantum physics**   74

  (a) The age of continuity   74
  (b) Kirchhoff's law   75
  (c) 1860–1896   77
  (d) 1896: physics takes a bizarre turn   78
  (e) Introducing Max Planck   79
  (f) A brief digression on statistical mechanics   80
  (g) In which Planck stumbles on a new law that ushered in the physics of the twentieth century   82
  (h) Particles or waves?   87

6 **Student days**   92

  (a) Physics in Denmark, from a college for the clergy to the epoch of Ørsted   92
  (b) In which Bohr begins his university studies and starts mobilizing help in writing   97
  (c) The atom: status in 1909   103
  (d) Niels Bohr, M.Sc., Ph.D.   107
  (e) Death of father. Bohr becomes engaged   111

7   In which Bohr goes to England for postdoctoral research   117

(a) Cambridge: Thomson, father of the electron   117
(b) Manchester: Rutherford, father of the nucleus   121

8   Bohr, father of the atom   132

(a) Young man in a hurry   132
(b) In which Bohr leaves the church and gets married   133
(c) The Rutherford memorandum   135
(d) 'The language of spectra . . . a true atomic music of the spheres'   139
(e) In which Bohr hears about the Balmer formula   143
(f) Triumph over logic: the hydrogen atom(*)   146
(g) Reactions, including Bohr's own   152

9   How Bohr secured his permanent base of operations   160

(a) The early schools in quantum physics   160
(b) In which Bohr returns to Manchester and then becomes
     Denmark's first professor of theoretical physics   163
(c) In which Bohr acquires his own institute   166

10   'It was the spring of hope, it was the winter of despair'   176

(a) Mathematics in physics   176
(b) The old quantum theory 1913–1916: sketches(*)   179
     1. Introductory. 2. How order was brought in the periodic
     table of elements. 3. The Stark effect. 4. The Franck–Hertz
     experiment. 5. New quantum numbers; the fine structure of
     the hydrogen spectrum
(c) In pursuit of principles: Ehrenfest, Einstein, and Bohr   189
     1. Ehrenfest on adiabatics. 2. Einstein on probability.
     3. Bohr on correspondence
(d) The crisis   196
     1. Helium. 2. The Zeeman effect. 3. The fourth quantum
     number. 4. Enter Pauli
(e) Bohr and the periodic table of elements   202
     1. From electron rings to electron shells. 2. The mystery of
     the rare earths. 3. Bohr's quantum number assignments.
     4. The exclusion principle. 5. The discovery of hafnium
(f) The Nobel Prize   210
     1. The Prize and the press. 2. Who nominated Bohr? 3. The
     ceremonies. 4. Who did Bohr nominate?

11   Bohr and Einstein   224

(a) Comparisons   224
(b) First encounters   227
(c) More on Einstein and the light-quantum   230
(d) 'The culmination of the crisis': the BKS proposal   232
(e) The new era dawns: de Broglie   239
(f) Spin   241

12 'A modern Viking who comes on a great errand'   249

   (a) Bohr & Sons   249
   (b) International recognition   251
   (c) First trip to America   253
   (d) Bohr as fund raiser   255
   (e) The institute up till mid-1925. Introducing Heisenberg   260

13 'Then the whole picture changes completely': the discovery of quantum mechanics   267

   (a) A last look back: Bohr as 'director of atomic theory'   267
   (b) Kramers in 1924   270
   (c) Heisenberg in 1924   272
   (d) 1925: how quantum mechanics emerged 'quite vaguely from the
       fog'(*)   275
   (e) Bohr's earliest reactions   279
   (f) Early 1926: the second coming of quantum mechanics   280
   (g) The summer of 1926: Born on probability, causality, and
       determinism   284
   (h) Appendix. c- and q-numbers for pedestrians   289

14 The Spirit of Copenhagen   295

   (a) The Copenhagen team in 1926. Heisenberg resolves the helium
       puzzle   295
   (b) In which Schrödinger comes on a visit   298
   (c) Prelude to complementarity. The Bohr–Heisenberg dialog   300
   (d) The uncertainty relations, with a look back at the
       correspondence principle   304
   (e) Complementarity: a new kind of relativity   309
   (f) Solvay 1927. The Bohr–Einstein dialog begins   316

15 Looking into the atomic nucleus   324

   (a) Beginnings of a new direction for Bohr and his school   324
   (b) Theoretical nuclear physics: the prehistoric era   325
   (c) Great progress: the first artificial transmutation of chemical
       elements and the first signs of a new force. Great confusion: the
       proton–electron model of the nucleus   327
   (d) In which quantum mechanics reveals nuclear paradoxes and the
       neutron is discovered   330
   (e) In which the Bohrs move to the Residence of Honor   332
   (f) In which Bohr takes nuclear matters in hand   335
   (g) Being a brief prelude to the war and the years thereafter   341

16 Toward the edge of physics in the Bohr style, and a bit
   beyond   346

   (a) Particles and fields   346
   (b) QED(*)   350
   (c) Spin (continued). The positron. The meson(*) 352
   (d) Bohr on QED(*)   358
   (e) Bohr and the crisis of 1929. The neutrino   364

17 How Bohr orchestrated experimental progress in the 1930s, in physics and in biology 375

(a) Four fateful factors 375
(b) The first accelerators 375
(c) Weaver at the helm 379
(d) Troubles in Germany 381
(e) Bohr and the Rockefeller foundation's emergency program 383
(f) The discovery of induced radioactivity 386
(g) Four fateful factors fit 387
(h) How Hevesy introduced isotopic tracers in biology 388
(i) Bohr as fund raiser (continued) 394
(j) Denmark's first accelerators and the fifth fateful factor 398

18 Of sad events and of major journeys 407

(a) Days of sorrow 407
(b) Times of travel 413

19 'We are suspended in language' 420

(a) Bohr and philosophy: 'It was, in a way, my life' 420
(b) Complementarity (continued). More on the Bohr–Einstein dialog. A new definition of 'phenomenon' 425
(c) Bohr on statistical mechanics 436
(d) Complementarism 438
    1. Introductory. 2. Psychology. 3. Biology. 4. Human cultures. 5. Conclusion: language

20 Fission 452

(a) The early days, including Bohr's discovery of the role of uranium 235 452
(b) Fission in Copenhagen 458
(c) Atomic energy? Atomic weapons? 460
(d) Bohr as president of the *Kongelige Danske Videnskabernes Selskab* 464

21 Bohr, pioneer of 'glasnost' 473

(a) Introduction 473
(b) Denmark and Germany, from 16 November 1864 until 4 May 1945 474
(c) Bohr's war years, the Scandinavian episode 479
    1. Keeping the work going. 2. Heisenberg's visit. 3. A letter from England. 4. The Swedish interlude. 5. The fate of the institute
(d) Bohr's war years, the Anglo-American episode 490
    1. On to Britain. 2. Anglo-American efforts up till October 1943. 3. From London to New York. 4. Bohr's role in the weapons program
(e) Bohr, Churchill, Roosevelt, and the atomic bomb 497
    1. Glasnost 1944. 2. Meetings with Ambassador Halifax and Justice Frankfurter. 3. The Kapitza letter. 4. Bohr meets Churchill. 5. Bohr meets Roosevelt. 6. Coda. 7. Going home

22 In which Bohr moves full steam into his later years   509

    (a) Prolog   509
    (b) The later writings, 1945–1962   510
          1. Physics, research. 2. Physics, discussions of complementarity. 3. Complementarity outside physics. 4. Occasional addresses. 5. Writings in memoriam
    (c) Glasnost 1950: Bohr's open letters to the United Nations   513
    (d) CERN   519
    (e) Nordita   521
    (f) Risø   523
          1. The National Laboratory. 2. A new part of the Niels Bohr Institute. 3. Risø in 1989
    (g) The later travels   528
    (h) The final half year   529

23 Epilog   534

    Appendix   A synopsis of this book in the form of a chronology   538

    Index of names   547

    Index of subjects   553

1

A Dane for all seasons

(a) Themes

In October 1957 man entered the space age.

On 5 October the *New York Times* carried a headline spanning the entire front page: 'Soviet fires earth satellite into space; it is circling the globe at 18000 mph; sphere tracked in 4 crossings over US.' Sputnik I had gone into orbit.

When newspapers asked a number of distinguished personalities to comment on this momentous event, it was only natural that the seventy-two year old Niels Bohr, the most prominent living physicist, would be among them. In his reply Bohr struck a plea for openness between the West and the USSR, the theme that had dominated his life ever since 1943: 'Professor Niels Bohr, the Danish physicist and Nobel Prize winner, said yesterday that the Soviet accomplishment pointed up the need to bring about understanding and confidence among nations.'[1]

Two more major space events followed soon afterwards. On 3 November 1957 the *New York Times* came out with another banner headline: 'Soviet fires new satellite carrying dog; half ton sphere is reported 900 miles up.' On the following 7 December the same paper reported on the first US attempt: Vanguard I, weighing 4 pounds, the size of a grapefruit or softball, had risen 2 to 4 feet – and then exploded. 'This spectacular failure increased the hysteria and embarrassment in the United States and the ridicule abroad. In England the press reveled in [calling] Vanguard Puffnik, Flopnik, Kaputnik.'[2]

President Eisenhower, collected but concerned from the time of the first Russian space shot, decided something had to be done. He invited James Killian, president of MIT, for a breakfast at the White House which took place[3] on 24 October. At that meeting Eisenhower offered Killian an appointment (the first of its kind) as full-time special assistant to the President for science and technology, to help in mobilizing the best scientific talent. Killian accepted. The two men parted.

On the afternoon of that day they met again.

On the morning of that same 24 October, Robert Oppenheimer and I took an

early train from Princeton to Washington. We were on our way to the Great
Hall of the National Academy of Sciences, where, that afternoon, the first
Atoms for Peace Award was to be presented to Niels Bohr. It was a festive
event. The meeting was called to order by Killian, its presider and chairman
of the awards committee. The first speaker was John Wheeler who in 1939
had collaborated with Bohr on a major paper concerning the theory of
nuclear fission. Thereafter Killian read the award citation, from which I
quote:

Niels Henrik David Bohr, in your chosen field of physics you have explored the
structure of the atom and unlocked many of Nature's other secrets. You have
given men the basis for greater understanding of matter and energy. You have
made contributions to the practical uses of this knowledge. At your Institute for
Theoretical Physics at Copenhagen, which has served as an intellectual and
spiritual center for scientists, you have given scholars from all parts of the world
an opportunity to extend man's knowledge of nuclear phenomena. These scholars
have taken from your Institute not only enlarged scientific understanding but also
a humane spirit of active concern for the proper utilization of scientific
knowledge.
In your public pronouncements and through your world contacts, you have
exerted great moral force in behalf of the utilization of atomic energy for peaceful
purposes.
In your profession, in your teaching, in your public life, you have shown that the
domain of science and the domain of the humanities are in reality of single realm.
In all your career you have exemplified the humility, the wisdom, the humaneness,
the intellectual splendor which the Atoms for Peace Award would recognize.

Killian then presented the award (a gold medal and a check for $75000) to
Bohr, with a smiling Eisenhower looking on.[4] In his brief response Bohr
stressed the need for international understanding: 'The rapid advance of
science and technology in our age ... presents civilization with a most
serious challenge. To meet this challenge ... the road is indicated by that
worldwide cooperation which has manifested itself through the ages in the
development of science.'
Next, the President addressed Bohr, calling him 'a great man whose mind
has explored the mysteries of the inner structure of atoms, and whose spirit
has reached into the very heart of man.'[5] The meeting was concluded with a
speech by Arthur Compton, one of the administrative leaders in the US
scientific efforts during World War II.[6]
After the ceremonies I had a chance to congratulate Bohr and to tell him
how much I was looking forward to his forthcoming visit to the Institute for
Advanced Study in Princeton, of which I was then a faculty member. I also
recall greeting Supreme Court Justice Felix Frankfurter. We briefly
chatted about how bittersweet a moment in Bohr's life this occasion had to
be.

More about that much later (see chapter 22, section (c)).

Killian's citation eloquently describes that combination of qualities we find in Bohr and only in Bohr: creator of science, teacher of science, and spokesman not only for science *per se* but also for science as a potential source for the common good.

As a creator he is one of the three men without whom the birth of that uniquely twentieth century mode of thought, quantum physics, is unthinkable. The three, in order of appearance, are: Max Planck, the reluctant revolutionary, discoverer of the quantum theory, who did not at once understand that his quantum law meant the end of an era in physics now called classical; Albert Einstein, discoverer of the quantum of light, the photon, founder of the quantum theory of solids, who at once realized that classical physics had reached its limits, a situation with which he never could make peace; and Bohr, founder of the quantum theory of the structure of matter, also immediately aware that his theory violated sacred classical concepts, but who at once embarked on the search for links between the old and the new, achieved with a considerable measure of success in his correspondence principle.

How different their personalities were. Planck, in many ways the conventional university professor, teaching his courses, delivering his Ph.D.'s. Einstein, rarely lonely, mostly alone, who did not really care for teaching classes and never delivered a Ph.D., easily accessible yet so apart, ever so friendly yet so distant. And Bohr, always in need of other physicists, especially young ones, to help him clarify his own thoughts, always generous in helping them clarify theirs, not so much a teacher of courses nor a supervisor of Ph.D.'s but forever giving inspiration and guidance to so many engaged in post-doctoral and senior research, father figure extraordinary to physicists belonging to several generations, including this writer's.

Bohr's researches, his teachings, his endeavours in the political sphere, and his relations with other major figures of his time – these are among the themes to be developed in this book. But there are more. There is also Bohr the philosopher, the administrator, the fund raiser, the catalyst in promoting physical applications to biology, the helper of political refugees, the co-founder of international physics institutes as well as the nuclear power projects in Denmark, and, last but not least, the devoted family man. A composite picture will emerge of a life so full and dedicated that one wonders how a single individual could have managed so much. The beautiful title chosen by Westfall[7] for his biography of Newton, *Never at rest* (a quotation from Newton himself), applies to Bohr as well.

Bohr's spectrum of activities was broad; the intensity with which he attacked whatever task lay before him was high. All who knew him well were aware of his immense powers of concentration which one could often note simply by looking at him. Two stories will illustrate this.

Bohr's aunt Hanna Adler once told me of an experience she had long ago when she sat in a Copenhagen streetcar together with Bohr's mother and the two young sons, Harald and Niels. The boys were hanging on their mother's lips as she was telling them a story. Apparently there was something peculiar about these two young faces in concentration, for Miss Adler overheard one lady in the streetcar remark to her neighbour, '*Stakkels mor*' (that poor mother).

James Franck, colleague and friend of Bohr through many years, later had similar experiences: 'One thinks of Bohr when one had a discussion with him. Sometimes he was sitting there almost like an idiot. His face became empty, his limbs were hanging down, and you would not know this man could even see. You would think that he must be an idiot. There was absolutely no degree of life. Then suddenly one would see that a glow went up in him and a spark came, and then he said: "Now I know." It is astonishing, this concentration ... You have not seen Bohr in his early years. He could really get an empty face; everything, every movement was stopped. That was the important point of concentration. I am sure it was the same with Newton too.'[8]

(b) Some personal recollections

I knew Niels Bohr from 1946 until shortly before his death in 1962. Thereafter I continued to keep in touch with his wife Margrethe, with whom I exchanged letters every Christmas until 1984, when she too passed away. I also knew Niels' brother Harald and 'Moster Hanna', Miss Hanna Adler, Niels' mother's sister, during the last years of their respective lives. During the Bohr centenary celebrations in Copenhagen in 1985, I had much pleasure in meeting again with Niels' sons, Hans, Erik, Aage, and Ernest. Through more than forty years I have kept in touch with my friend Aage, the physicist. Although I shall draw on these various experiences in later chapters, this biography is not by any means merely a series of personal recollections.

As I have been told time and again, those who have read recollections and biographies of Bohr often tend to come away with the overall reaction that his life story is too good to be true. I, too, believe that his was a wonderful life and that he was a good man, capable of both bringing and receiving happiness. I do not consider him, however, as an angelic figure to whom struggle, ambition, disappointment, and personal tragedy were alien.

It has been said that traces of the storyteller cling to his story. This certainly applies to the present instance because of my very good fortune to have known the Bohr family for many years. My familiarity with Bohr and his environment will of course introduce subjective elements in what I shall have to tell. This troubles me not one bit, since I believe that all biography, indeed all history, is subjective in character. I do think, however, that in order for the reader to get some appreciation of the relation between the author and his subject it may be of use to share right away with her or him some personal recollections. Before I turn to these,* it may be well to state that I loved Bohr. I have tried to exercise restraint in regard to these sentiments, which may or may not shine through in what follows.

In January 1946 I came for the first time to Copenhagen from my native Holland. I was the first of the post–World War II generation to come to Bohr's institute from abroad for a longer period of study. The morning after my arrival I went to the secretary, Mrs Betty Schultz, who told me to wait in the journal room adjoining the library where she would call me as soon as Professor Bohr was free to see me. I had sat there reading for a while, when someone knocked at the door. I said come in. The door opened. It was Bohr. My first thought was, what a gloomy face.

Then he began to speak.

Later I have often been puzzled about this first impression. It vanished the very moment Bohr started to talk to me that morning, never to return. True, one might correctly describe Bohr's physiognomy as unusually heavy or rugged. Yet his face is remembered by all who knew him for its intense animation and its warm and sunny smile.

I did not see much of Bohr during the next month or so. After a brief trip to Norway he was very busy with plans for the extension of his institute. However, I was soon invited for Sunday dinner at the Bohr home in Carlsberg and that evening I had my first opportunity to talk physics with Bohr in his study. I told him of things I had worked out during my years in hiding in Holland. These concerned certain problems in quantum electro-dynamics, the quantum theory of electric and magnetic fields and of their interactions with matter. While I was telling him about what I had done, he smoked his pipe; he looked mainly at the floor and would only rarely look up at the blackboard on which I was enthusiastically writing down various formulae. After I finished, Bohr did not say much, and I felt a bit disheartened with the impression that he could not care less about the whole subject. I did not know him well enough at the time to realize that this was not entirely true. At a later stage I would have known right away that his curiosity was aroused, as he had neither remarked that this was very very interesting nor said that we agreed much more than I thought – his favourite ways of expressing that he did not believe what he was told.

After this discussion we went back to the living room to rejoin the

_____

* The rest of this section is taken from what I wrote in 1963, the year after Bohr's death.[9]

company. Then, as on later occasions, I felt fortunate to be for a while in the invigorating atmosphere of warmth and harmony that Mrs Bohr and her husband knew how to create wherever they were in the world, but above all in their Copenhagen home. The conversation now turned to more general topics, and that evening I caught a first glimpse of Bohr's intense preoccupation with the problems of the international political scene. In this area all his thoughts were focused on one central idea, the unique opportunities for an open and peaceful world due to the advent of atomic weapons, a subject to which I shall return at length later on. Here I shall only record the deep impression which Bohr's sense of urgency on this issue made on a young man who had just emerged from life in occupied Europe. 'The release (by the US) of atomic data for purely scientific purposes is but a side issue. The essential point is the political issue. The current political problems of Poland, Iran, etc., however important, are but side issues.' Such remarks may now seem obvious. They were not at all so widely accepted then. On such topics, as in matters scientific, Bohr's strength lay in the single-minded pursuit of one given theme. At the time he was still optimistic that in not more than a year or two such views as he then expressed would find acceptance by the governments most vitally concerned.

It would be wrong to suppose, however, that evenings at the Bohrs were entirely filled with discussions of such weighty matters. Sooner or later, for the purpose of illustrating some point, or just for the pleasure of it, Bohr would tell one or more stories. I believe that at any given time he had about half a dozen favorite jokes. He would tell them; we would get to know them. Yet he would never cease to hold his audience. For me, to hear again the beginning of such a familiar tale would lead me to anticipate not so much the denouement as Bohr's own happy laughter upon the conclusion of the story.

Shortly thereafter, on 3 March, the 25th anniversary of the institute was celebrated. True to Bohr's style it was an intimate occasion, the high point of which came as Bohr reminisced about the people and the events of that heroic period. There was no pomp, only a few brief speeches. It was my pleasant task to express the gratitude of the first installment of post-war visitors from abroad. And, of course, that evening there was a feast held by Parentesen, the graduate students' club. It was the time I learned to sing *Videnskabens Fædre* (the Fathers of Science), of which the last verse is to be rendered while the participants stand on their chairs, beer in hand: *'Nobelmanden Niels Bohr ved vej blandt alle vildspor . . .'* (. . . knows the way amidst all false tracks). It gave us all a sense of pride to have Bohr in our midst at that moment, also standing on his chair.

During the following weeks it became clear that Bohr had become quite interested in the problems of quantum electrodynamics which I had mentioned to him. Every now and then he would call me to his office to have me explain one or other aspect of them. He was particularly intrigued by those arguments which showed that many elementary particle problems are fundamentally quantum problems which cannot be dealt with by the methods of classical physics. It may be noted that this view did not have as wide an acceptance at that time as was to be the case two years later when the modern version of the theory known as the renormalization program started to develop.

Meanwhile, I had become involved in several other enterprises that went on at the institute. I would like to mention one of them, an investigation with Lamek Hulthén of neutron–proton scattering, as it is interesting to recall how bold we felt in extending the numerical work to the then unheard of energy of 25 million electronvolts (eV). (These days one can accelerate particles to energies a billion times higher.)

Then, one day in May, Bohr asked me whether I would be interested in working with him on a daily basis during the coming months. I was thrilled and accepted. The next morning I went to Carlsberg. The first thing Bohr said to me was that it would only be profitable to work with him if I understood that he was a dilettante. The only way I could react to this unexpected statement was with a polite smile of disbelief. But evidently Bohr was serious. He explained how he had to approach every new question from a starting point of total ignorance. It is perhaps better to say that Bohr's strength lay in his formidable intuition and insight rather than in erudition. I thought of his remarks of that morning some years later, when I sat at his side during a colloquium in Princeton. The subject was nuclear isomers. As the speaker went on, Bohr got more and more restless and kept whispering to me that it was all wrong. Finally, he could contain himself no longer and wanted to raise an objection. But after having half-raised himself, he sat down again, looked at me with unhappy bewilderment, and asked, 'What is an isomer?'

The first subject of work was the preparation of Bohr's opening address to the International Conference on Fundamental Particles to be held in July 1946 in Cambridge, England. It was the first meeting of its kind in the post-war era. Bohr planned to make a number of comments on the problems of the quantum theory alluded to earlier. I must admit that in the early stages of the collaboration I did not follow Bohr's line of thinking a good deal of the time and was in fact often quite bewildered. I failed to see the relevance of remarks such as, for example, that Erwin Schrödinger was completely shocked in 1926 when he was told of the probability interpretation of quantum mechanics, or references to some objection by Einstein in 1927 which apparently had no bearing whatever on the subject at hand. It did not take very long before the fog started to lift, however. I began to grasp not only the thread of Bohr's arguments but also their purpose. Just as in many sports players go through warming-up exercises before entering the arena, so Bohr would relive the struggles which took place before the content of quantum mechanics was understood and accepted. I can say that in Bohr's mind this struggle started afresh every single day. This, I am convinced, was Bohr's inexhaustible source of identity. Einstein appeared forever as his leading spiritual sparring partner: even after Einstein's death he would argue with him as if he were still alive.

I can now explain the principal and lasting inspiration that I derived from the discussions with Bohr. In Holland I had received a solid training as a physicist. It is historically inevitable that men of my generation received quantum mechanics served up ready made. While I may say that I had a decent working knowledge of the theory, I had not fathomed, and indeed could hardly have, how very profoundly the change from the classical to the quantum mechanical way of thinking affected both the architects and the close witnesses of the revolution in physics which took place in 1925–7. Through steady exposure to Bohr's 'daily struggle' and his ever repeated emphasis on 'the epistemological lesson which quantum mechanics has taught us', to use a favorite phrase of his, my understanding not only of the history of physics but of physics itself deepened. In fact, the many hours which Bohr spent talking to me about complementarity have had a liberating effect on every aspect of my thinking.

Of course, the purpose of the foregoing remarks is hardly to edify the reader with what goes on in the mind of the present author. Rather, they are meant to exemplify the way in which the direct close contact with Bohr affected physicists of the post–quantum mechanical era. To earlier generations he had been a leader in battle at the frontiers of knowledge. This was no longer so in the times I am referring to and thereafter; such is destiny. To those of us who knew him then, Bohr had become the principal consolidator of one of the greatest developments in the history of science. It is true that, to the end, Bohr was one of the most open-minded physicists I have known, forever eager to learn of new developments from younger people and remaining faithful to his own admonition always to be prepared for a surprise. (In these respects he was entirely different from Einstein.) But inevitably his role in these quite new developments shifted from actor to spectator. Bohr created atomic quantum physics and put his stamp on nuclear physics. With particle physics, the next chapter, the post-Bohr era begins. The Cambridge paper of 1946 actually represents Bohr's furthest penetration into the more modern problems.

At about that time Bohr suggested to me to 'lay aside titles', as the Danes say, which means that one addresses the other person in the familiar 'thou' form. I recall how in the beginning I twisted sentences around in the most awkward ways, to avoid the formal form of address; but I got used to it in the end. (Today the familiar form has come in almost universal use, somewhat to my regret.)

Sometime later the Bohr family went to their summer house in Tisvilde. I was invited to stay with them, so that the work could continue. It was a wonderful experience. A good deal of the day was spent working in a separate little pavilion on the grounds. All during this period, Aage Bohr joined in as well. We would go for a swim in the afternoon and often work more at night. In fact after Aage and I had retired, Bohr would still come in sometimes, in a shoe and a sock, to impart to us just one further thought that had occurred to him that very minute and would keep talking for an hour or so.

Other evenings were spent in the family circle, and sometimes Bohr would read one or more of his favorite poems. I marked them in my own books: Goethe's 'Zueignung', Schiller's 'Sprüche des Konfuzius', 'Breite und Tiefe', 'Mädchens Klage', etc. Bohr liked especially to quote the following lines by Schiller:

> ... Wer etwas Treffliches leisten will,
> Hätt' gern etwas Grosses geboren,
> Der sammle still und unerschlafft
> Im kleinsten Punkte die höchste Kraft.

These lines have been translated[10] as

> Ah! he who would achieve the fair,
> Or sow the embryo of the great,
> Must hoard – to wait the ripening hour –
> In the least point the loftiest power.

Like everything Bohr did, large or small, he was able to put his whole being into it and he could convey beautifully how small the point was and how lofty the power.

Bohr was an indefatigable worker. When he was in need of a break in the discussions, he would go outside and apply himself to the pulling of weeds with what can only be called ferocity. At this point I can contribute a little item to the lore about Bohr the pipe smoker. It is well known that to him the operations of filling a pipe and lighting it were interchangeable but the following situation was even more extreme. One day Bohr was weeding again, his pipe between his teeth. At one point, unnoticed by Bohr, the bowl fell off the stem. Aage and I were lounging in the grass, expectantly awaiting further developments. It is hard to forget Bohr's look of stupefaction when he found himself holding a thoughtfully lit match against a pipe without bowl.

Bohr devoted tremendous effort and care to the composition of his articles. However, to perform the physical act of writing, pen or chalk in hand, was almost alien to him. He preferred to dictate. On one of the few occasions that I actually did see him write himself, Bohr performed the most remarkable act of calligraphy I shall ever witness.

It happened during that summer in the pavilion in Tisvilde, as we were discussing the address Bohr was to give on the occasion of the tercentenary celebration of Newton's birth. Bohr stood in front of the blackboard (wherever he dwelt, a blackboard was never far) and wrote down some general themes to be discussed. One of them had to do with the harmony of something or other. So Bohr wrote down the word *harmony*. It looked about as follows:

However, as the discussion progressed, Bohr became dissatisfied with the use of harmony. He walked around restlessly. Then he stopped and his face lit up. 'Now I've got it. We must change *harmony* to *uniformity*.' So he picked up the chalk again, stood there looking for a moment at what he had written before, and then made the single change:

with one triumphant bang of the chalk on the blackboard.

Then came the time to return to Copenhagen. We went by car. It was an act of faith to sit in an automobile driven by Bohr. On that particular occasion he complained that he felt too hot and actually let go of the wheel to take off his jacket. Mrs Bohr's rapid intervention saved the situation. Shortly afterwards Bohr went to England. I saw him on his return, and then left Denmark.

I stopped in the Netherlands on my way to the United States, and had occasion to call on Adriaan Fokker in Haarlem. I mentioned to him some recent experiences in Denmark. This led Fokker to tell me of his own contact with Bohr in a much earlier period. He had some interesting things to say. In 1913–14 he studied with Einstein in Zürich and there he gave the first colloquium on Bohr's theory of the hydrogen atom (to which I shall come back at length later on). Einstein, Max von Laue, and Otto Stern were among the audience. Einstein did not react immediately, but kept a meditative silence. In 1914 Fokker spent six weeks with Rutherford, when he met Bohr. Bohr asked everyone: 'Do you believe it?'

I met Bohr again two months later, at the celebration of the bicentennial of Princeton University. He asked me to spend some time with him on the preparation of a talk for that occasion. I did so and I know how well prepared Bohr was with carefully structured arguments. However, I recall my amazement at the talk which Bohr actually gave, which was done without a worked out manuscript before him. I should say that this amazement was due to the fact that till then I had never heard Bohr speak publicly.

In attempting to describe the experience of listening to Bohr in public, I am reminded of a story about the violinist Eugène Ysaye, who at one time had a member of a royal family as his pupil. Another musician of great renown (to whom I owe this tale) once asked Ysaye how this pupil was doing. Whereupon Ysaye lifted his hands heavenwards and sighed: 'Ah, her royal highness, she plays divinely bad.'

However different the background was in the two cases, these are the words which best characterize the situation. Bohr was divinely bad as a public speaker.* This was not due to his precept never to speak more clearly than one thinks. Had he done so, the outcome would have been quite different, as he was a man of the greatest lucidity of thought. Nor was it entirely due to the fact that Bohr's voice did not carry far, which made it impossible to hear him at the back of a large audience. The main reason was that he was in deep thought as he spoke. I remember how that day he had finished part of the argument, then said 'And . . . and . . . ,' then was silent for at most a second, then said, 'But . . . ,' and continued. Between the 'and' and the 'but' the next point had gone through his mind. However, he simply forgot to say it out loud and went on somewhere further down his road. To me, the story was continuous as I knew precisely how to fill in the gaps Bohr had left open. And so it has come to pass more than once that I have seen an audience leave a talk by Bohr in a mild state of bewilderment, even though he had toiled hard in preparing himself in great detail. Still, when he would come up to me afterwards with the characteristic question: *'Jeg håber det var nogenlunde'* (I hope it was tolerable), I could assure him that it was much more than that. In spite of all the linguistic shortcomings, this unrelenting struggle for truth was a powerful source of inspiration.

At the same time, it should be emphasized that Bohr's best way of

* Bohr mght not have agreed. Léon Rosenfeld was sitting next to him at the Maxwell celebrations in Cambridge in 1931 when one of the speakers commented on Maxwell's reputation as a poor lecturer, and then added: 'So perhaps with our friend Bohr: he might want to instruct us about the correlation of too many things at once.' Whereupon Bohr whispered to Rosenfeld: 'Imagine, he thinks I am a poor lecturer!' [11]

communicating actually was the spoken word, but with just one or at most a few persons present. Bohr's need for verbal expression was great, as the following occurrence may illustrate. On a later occasion (1948) Bohr arrived in Princeton after a trip by sea from Denmark. For about a week he had had no opportunity to discuss scientific matters; he was quite pent up. Wolfgang Pauli and I were walking in a corridor of the Institute for Advanced Study when Bohr first came in. When he saw us, he practically pushed us into an office, made us sit down, said, 'Pauli, *schweig*' (P., shut up), and then talked for about two hours before either of us had a chance to interrupt him. Had Bohr's words been recorded, it would have constituted a fascinating document on the development of quantum theory.

My own first direct experience of the impact of Einstein on Bohr happened a few weeks later, when Bohr came to my office at the Institute of which I then was a temporary member. He was in a state of angry despair and kept saying 'I am sick of myself,' several times. I was concerned and asked what had happened. He told me he had just been downstairs to see Einstein. As always, they had got into an argument about the meaning of quantum mechanics. And, as remained true to the end, Bohr had been unable to convince Einstein of his views. There can be no doubt that Einstein's lack of assent was a very deep frustration to Bohr. It is our good fortune that this led Bohr to keep striving at clarification and better formulation. And not only that: it was Bohr's own good fortune too.

Bohr left the US in late November 1946. In February 1948 he returned to the institute in Princeton, of which he was then a permanent member.

During that time I saw a lot of Bohr, as he and his wife lived at 14 Dickinson Street, the same house in which I occupied the top floor. When I came home at night, the following charming little comedy would often be enacted. As I opened the door, Bohr would always just be walking in the corridor, his back towards me, on his way to the kitchen. In that way he would let me notice him first. He would then turn around in apparent surprise and ask if I would not care for a glass of sherry. And then we would settle down to talk about political problems. For at that period Bohr had become disillusioned with the official reactions to the atom. It was now his desire to make a direct attempt to get his views considered by those in positions of responsibility, and he was preparing a memorandum to this effect, which was discussed over and over during those evenings. It formed the basis for Bohr's Open Letter to the United Nations in 1950, to be discussed later on.

During that same period I was witness to an amusing incident which involved both Bohr and Einstein. One morning Bohr came into my office and started as follows: '*Du er så klog . . .*' (you are so wise). I started to laugh (no formality or solemnity was called for with Bohr) and said: 'All right, I understand.' Bohr wanted me to come down to his office and talk. We went there, and it should be explained that Bohr at that time used Einstein's own office in Fuld Hall. At the same time, Einstein himself used the adjoining small assistant's office; he had a dislike of the big one, which he did not use anyway. (A photograph in the Einstein anniversary issue of the *Reviews of Modern Physics*, 1949, shows Einstein sitting in the asistant's office.) After we had entered, Bohr asked me to sit down ('I always need an origin for the coordinate system') and soon started to pace furiously around the oblong table in the center of the room. He then asked me if I could note down a few sentences as they emerged during his pacing. It should be explained that, at such sessions, Bohr never had a full sentence ready. He would often dwell on one word, coax it, implore it, to find the continuation. This could go on for several minutes. At that moment the word was 'Einstein'. There was Bohr, almost running around the table and repeating: 'Einstein . . . Einstein . . .'. It would have been a curious sight for someone not familiar with him. After a little while he walked to the window, gazed out, repeating every now and then: 'Einstein . . . Einstein . . .'.

At that moment the door opened very softly and Einstein tiptoed in. He indicated to me with a finger on his lips to be very quiet, an urchin smile on his face. He was to explain a few minutes later the reason for his behavior. Einstein was not allowed by his doctor to buy any tobacco. However, the doctor had not forbidden him to steal tobacco, and this was precisely what he set out to do now. Always on tiptoe he made a beeline for Bohr's tobacco pot, which stood on the table at which I was sitting. Meanwhile Bohr, unaware, was standing at the window, muttering 'Einstein . . . Einstein . . .'. I was at a loss what to do, especially because I had at that moment not the faintest idea what Einstein was up to.

Then Bohr, with a firm 'Einstein' turned around. There they were, face to face, as if Bohr had summoned him forth. It is an understatement to say that for a moment Bohr was speechless. I, myself, who had seen it coming, had felt distinctly uncanny for a moment, so I could well understand Bohr's own reaction. A moment later the spell was broken when Einstein explained his mission and soon we were all bursting with laughter.

The periods of closest contact which I had with Bohr are those described above. In subsequent years I saw him often, either in Denmark or in the US, but no longer for protracted periods of time.

In the fall of 1961 we were both present at the Solvay congress in Brussels. It was the 50th anniversary of the first one, and Bohr gave an account, both charming and fascinating, of the developments during that period.[12] He was present at the report I gave at that meeting, after which we talked in the corridor and spoke of the future of particle physics. It was the last time I spoke to him.

(c) A tour through this book

As a guide to the reader I conclude this introductory chapter with a nontechnical outline of what is to follow. Note also that a detailed chronology can be found at the end of this book. From here on I use the notation (4f) to refer to Chapter 4, section (f).

To set the stage I begin by relating three stories widely separated in time.

In 1923 Max Born, distinguished physicist from the Bohr–Einstein generation submitted a letter to the Göttingen Academy of Sciences in which he proposed both Einstein and Bohr for nomination as foreign members. In recommending Bohr, he wrote: 'His influence on theoretical and experimental research of our time is greater than that of any other physicist.'[13] Note that Born's personal relations with Einstein were closer than those with Bohr. At about that same time Percy Bridgman from Harvard wrote to an acquaintance that Bohr was now idolized as a scientific god through most of Europe.[14]

In 1963 Werner Heisenberg, a physicist of the next generation, wrote in an obituary of Bohr: 'Bohr's influence on the physics and the physicists of our century was stronger than that of anyone else, even than that of Albert Einstein.'[15]

My third story concerns a conversation that took place in the early 1980s between myself and a friend of mine, one of the best and best-known physicists of my own generation, the one following Heisenberg's.

'You knew Bohr well,' he said.

'I did,' I said.

'Then tell me,' he asked, 'what did Bohr really do?'

'Well,' I replied, 'first and foremost he was one of the founding fathers of the quantum theory.'

'I know,' he answered, 'but that work was superseded by quantum mechanics.'

'Of course,' I said, and then proceeded to explain Bohr's role in quantum mechanics, in particular his introduction of complementarity. This, I found out, had not been clear to him.

What did Bohr really do? How could it happen that two generations would accord Bohr's influence the highest praise while the next one hardly knew why he was a figure of such great significance? Also, why is it that complementarity – a concept defined and discussed at length in (14e) and (19b) – which Bohr himself considered to be his main contribution, is not mentioned in some of the finest textbooks on physics, such as the one on quantum mechanics[16] by Paul Dirac, the historically oriented quantum mechanics text[17] by Sin-itiro Tomonaga, or the lectures[18] by Richard Feynman? It has taken me the writing of this biography to give, to the best of my ability, the answers to such central questions.

In order to understand Bohr, it is imperative to place him in the context of Danish society. I begin to do so in Chapter 2, where his ancestry from his father's side is traced back to a German soldier, and from his mother's side to a wealthy Danish Jewish family with roots in London and Frankfurt. Several members of these preceding generations had been devoted to teaching and research. Niels' father had been proposed for a Nobel Prize and had at one time been rector of Copenhagen University. It may be said that the Bohr family belonged to the Danish élite at the time of Niels' birth.

Chapter 3 deals with Bohr's happy childhood. It begins with a description of the mood in Denmark resulting from the disastrous 1864 war with Prussia. This chapter includes an account of Niels' very close relationship with his younger brother Harald, and of his baptism in the Lutheran church.

The next two chapters are devoted to a sketch of the status of physics by the time Bohr began his university studies. In Chapter 4 I give a brief outline of the evolution of optics and of electricity and magnetism from their beginnings to Einstein's discovery of relativity theory in 1905, when Bohr was an undergraduate student. Bohr, of course, became thoroughly conversant with this major advance. Relativity played a minor role in his own researches, however. The only glimpse of relativistic reasoning we find are: in his papers of 1915, one on the so-called fine structure of the hydrogen spectrum (10b) and the other on the stopping of electrons traversing matter (7b); in his discussion (1930) of Einstein's 'clock-in-the-box' experiment (19b); and in his joint work with Léon Rosenfeld on quantum electrodynamics, published in 1933 (16d), in which Rosenfeld was responsible for the mathematical aspects of relativity theory. Bohr's admiration for these contributions by Einstein was profound. Thus, in 1920, when he made his first nomination for a Nobel Prize, he chose Einstein, 'first and foremost' for his work on relativity (10f).

In Chapter 5 I give an account of the origins of the quantum theory, with emphasis on Planck's discovery of the first quantum law in 1900 (5g) – when Bohr was still in high school – and of Einstein's proposal in 1905 that under certain circumstances a light bundle behaves as a stream of particles, photons (5h).

Of all the major figures in twentieth century science, I regard Planck as the most unusual one and his law as the most bizarre of fundamental discoveries. I therefore felt it necessary to mention something about Planck's background (5e), emphasizing that nothing was further from his mind than causing a scientific revolution, which in fact he did. It should also be stressed that Planck made many wrong theoretical moves, but retraced his steps time and again until finally he got it right (5g). It is less surprising that he would err so often in trying to reach a goal where existing logic was powerless, than that he kept persisting. The clues which would ultimately save him were in essence twofold: a theoretical result that by 1900 was 40 years old (Kirchhoff's law (5b)) and experimental data obtained in that very year 1900 (5g).

Neither Planck nor anyone else fully appreciated at once how revolutionary his discovery was – with the exception of Einstein, whose particle picture of light was, like Planck's law, extremely radical for its time. Nineteenth century physicists had developed a successful theory of light as consisting of waves (4c). But a wave and a particle picture mutually exclude each other! In 1909 Einstein suggested that a new theory was called for which should incorporate this particle–wave duality (11c). In 1923 Louis de Broglie suggested that not only light but also matter should exhibit this same duality (11e), another daring idea amply confirmed later. The theory which does fuse particles and waves, quantum mechanics, was born in 1925. But I am running ahead of my story.

The discoveries of the quantum theory and of relativity set the stage for the physics of the twentieth century in general and of the Bohr era in particular. In loose terms, quantum and relativistic phenomena are those where extrapolations from everyday experience about the world around us fail, where the kinds of visualizations of events, so successful in earlier times, are no longer adequate. The physics of those earlier times is now most often called 'classical physics', a term defined precisely in (4g). I note, however, that Bohr included relativity in what *he* called classical physics. For example, in a radio address* to the Danish people on Einstein's seventieth birthday (14 March 1949), Bohr said: 'He [E.] extended and completed the system which one now calls classical physics,' a usage of the word 'classical' which I can understand, though mine is different.

After these digressions about the upheavals in physics in the earliest years of the twentieth century, I return to Bohr.

Continuing my endeavor to illuminate the life and times of Bohr in a Danish setting, I preface my account of his student years with a sketch of the evolution of physics in Denmark up to the time he entered university (6a), noting the primitive state of local laboratory facilities at that time (6b). Bohr's main achievements in that period were a prize essay, which won a gold medal (6b), and his master's and doctor's theses (6d). Just before obtaining his doctor's degree, Bohr suffered the loss of his beloved father (6e). The year before he had become engaged to Margrethe Nørlund (6e). They married two years later, right after Bohr had left the Lutheran church (8b). It was a splendid union.

After obtaining his Dr. Phil. degree, Bohr went to England for postdoctoral studies. He worked first with J. J. Thomson in Cambridge, an

* Manuscript in NBA.

experience that was not a success (7a). From there he went to Manchester, to work with Ernest Rutherford, who had discovered the atomic nucleus just one year earlier. Bohr's contacts with Rutherford set a stamp on the whole of his later scientific life. For an understanding of Bohr the scientist, it is important to note that this influence stems very little from what Rutherford taught Bohr by way of physics. Rather, it was Rutherford's way of combining his own active research program with leadership in guiding younger physicists that made a lasting impression on Bohr and determined his own style from then on (7b). Note also that his Manchester period must have made a strong impression on him because it was the first occasion on which he came close to the frontiers of physics, in contrast to his prior experiences in Denmark, where research interests centered on more old-fashioned subjects.

In 1913, eight months after returning from England to Denmark, Bohr made his most important scientific discovery of his career: the decoding of the atomic spectrum of hydrogen. This achievement marks him out as the founder of the quantum dynamics of atoms (Chapter 8). In the course of this research he also became the first to show that β-radioactivity is a process originating in the atomic nucleus (8f).

As a result of this work Bohr became recognized almost immediately as a leading figure in physics, even before his academic position had been settled. Even before his work on the hydrogen atom, he had had the audacity to apply for a full professorship, but without success (8a). In 1914 he applied again (9b), but at first nothing happened. As a result he accepted a position as lecturer in Manchester (9b). Finally, in 1916, he received the hoped for appointment in Copenhagen (9b).

At that time the university there did not yet have its own physics institute, so Bohr was housed in cramped quarters in Copenhagen's Institute of Technology (9c). In 1917, therefore, he petitioned the authorities to establish a university physics institute (9c). After much travail that Institute was officially opened in 1921.

Bohr, then 35 years old, had already spent much time and energy on administrative responsibilities. He managed to combine these activities with important research of his own (to which I shall turn in a while). No wonder then that he became overworked, in spite of his formidable physical strength, and was forced to take some weeks of absolute rest (9c). The same was to be necessary several times later in his life, as in 1924 (12e) and 1935 (17j).

With the opening of Bohr's institute, there were now three European centers where quantum physics was vigorously pursued, the others being in Munich and Göttingen (9a). It would be fair to say that the Copenhagen institute was the world's leading center for theoretical physics in the 1920s and 1930s. In those years Bohr was known as the 'director of atomic theory'

(13a). Copenhagen attracted physicists, especially young ones, from all over the world. Between 1916 and 1961, the year before Bohr's death, 444 visitors from 35 countries spent at least a month in Copenhagen.[19] During Bohr's lifetime about 1200 physics papers were published from Copenhagen (among them about 200 by Bohr himself), including such gems as Heisenberg's papers on the uncertainty relations (14d) and on the quantum mechanics of the helium atom (14a), and young Dirac's on the transformation theory as well as his first paper on quantum electrodynamics (14a, 16b). It should be emphasized that along with his own research work and his administrative duties Bohr was an inspiring teacher to many of the visitors. From 1924 on he was permanently relieved of the obligation to teach courses for students, however (12e).

Bohr's style of conducting physics showed two main characteristics. First, an emphasis on youth, which he already stressed in his address at the institute's opening (9c). Secondly, 'to the vigorous growth of the international work on the advancement of science', the toast he proposed at the dinner on 10 December 1922, the day on which he received his Nobel prize (10f) – one of the numerous high honors bestowed on him from early on (12b). From the 1920s Bohr was not only a man of renown in scientific circles but also a national hero. 'There is a story that a young man arrived in Copenhagen and took a taxi to Bohr's institute; and the taxi man wouldn't take any money because it was to Bohr's that he had driven.'[20]

What was it like for those young men Bohr would choose to work with him on a day-to-day basis? It was a wonderful experience, but it was also an exercise in endurance to collaborate with someone as indefatigable as Bohr. Without any ill intent from Bohr, it was difficult to find the time and energy for one's own research. For example, Oskar Klein, one of Bohr's early co-workers, has said that he did his own most original and daring work when Bohr was away from Copenhagen.[21]

When Bohr argued with his co-workers, he would never impose his views but would always attempt to convince the others of his opinions, as the following story illustrates. At one time Bohr tried to win over two young men to a conviction of his. After long discussions he failed to persuade them. So next he talked to each of them separately. When that did not help either he asked them in despair: 'But don't you agree *a little bit* with me?' Some time later he came back to tell them he had been wrong.[22]

The most renowned instances of Bohr's teaching and leadership are the international theoretical physics conferences he organized at his institute. Beginning in 1929[23] these were annual affairs through 1938. They are remembered as the world's most outstanding gatherings of their kind during that period. Some of them included a jocular session, the most famous one being a parody on Faust performed in 1932.[24]

The Copenhagen institute's name was initially the Institute for Theoretical Physics (until 1965 when it was renamed the Niels Bohr Institute). This was perhaps somewhat of a misnomer since from the start Bohr laid great emphasis on the need for having theory and experiment pursued under the same roof (9c). Accordingly, in the early 1920s several instruments were installed for doing various kinds of spectroscopic experiments. When in the 1930s the institute's focus shifted to nuclear physics (15a,17), several types of high-energy accelerators were installed, all these activities being personally directed by Bohr. These various instruments were quite expensive. Moreover, their acquisition demanded enlargement of the institute's laboratory space, also expensive. In addition there were ever pressing requirements for room to accommodate the stream of visiting physicists, and for their financial support.

Clearly, then, Bohr needed a lot of money, far more than he could expect from his government. (His university was and is a state university.) So Bohr, never at a loss, decided to become his own fund raiser, at which he showed himself to be particularly adept. His ever growing stature in the world of science helped him greatly. He needed foundations to provide Kroner or dollars; foundations needed him as evidence for grants well disbursed.

Bohr's principal Danish source of financial support through the years was the Carlsberg Foundation, endowed by revenues of the Carlsberg breweries (12d). Other Danish money came from the Rask Ørsted Fund (12d), and later also from the Thrige Foundation (17i). His principal foreign support initially came from the International Education Board, founded in 1923 as a branch of the Rockefeller philanthropy (12d). As luck would have it, that was the same year in which Bohr made his first trip to the United States so that he could make personal contact with that board, with the result that Bohr became the first to receive from them an institutional grant in physics (12d). Incidentally, Bohr's American lecture tour brought atomic physics for the first time to the attention of wider circles (12c). Later American support also included grants from the Ford Foundation (22a).

The principal uses to which Bohr put the various grants were acquisition of equipment and a series of extensions to his institute, in the years 1925–6 (12e,14a), 1935–8 (17j), and 1946–50 (22a).

Physics also ultimately benefited from a grant of 150000 Kroner (about $30000) awarded by the Carlsberg Foundation on 2 May 1929 for establishing an institute of mathematics, on the occasion of the 450th anniversary of Copenhagen University. The original plan to situate this institute in the Skindergade did not work out, so in 1932 Bohr wrote to the minister of education[25] proposing they build it next to his own institute. That is how it came to be. The mathematics institute was opened on 8 February 1934, with Harald Bohr as director, and with Niels giving an address of welcome. In 1964 the mathematicians moved to other quarters; their previous quarters were taken over by Nordita, a joint Scandinavian physics institute (22c).

Quite another need for grant funds arose as the result of the terrible events in Germany after the Nazis came to power in 1933. Bohr was quite active in aiding the refugees, mostly Jewish, who came to Denmark. He was a board member of the Danish committee for help to refugee intellectuals.[26] Aided by grants from various foundations, he was able to offer temporary hospitality at his institute to physicists in trouble (17d,e).

To conclude this brief survey of outside support, I mention the one instance which was to Bohr's personal benefit. The founder of the Carlsberg breweries had willed his beautiful residence on the brewery grounds free for life to the Dane most prominent in science, literature, or the arts (12d). In 1932 Bohr was elected occupant of this 'Residence of Honor' (15e). He and his family forever hospitably opened their home to guests, from royalty to young physics students (22a).

Having made our first acquaintance with Bohr as the founder of modern physics in Denmark, as teacher, administrator, and fund raiser, let us now turn next to further aspects of his own research.

It is essential to recall that the evolution of the quantum theory is divided into two sharply distinct periods. The first, from 1900 to 1925, now known as the time of the old quantum theory, spanned the most unusual years in the entire history of physics. Quantum laws and regularities were discovered, which, experiment showed, had to be taken very seriously, yet which violated the fundamental logic of classical physics on which the science of that period rested. A prime example of this bizarre state of affairs is Bohr's work, beginning in 1913, which for the first time made atomic structure into a subject of scientific inquiry.

Bohr's papers on the structure of atoms unleashed a veritable flood of activity in many research centers, including contributions by Bohr himself. A major tool he developed for dealing with quantum problems, and which no one better than he knew how to apply, was the correspondence principle (8f, 10c), which establishes links between predictions of the classical theory and expectations for the quantum theory.

In those early years one finds a variety of mathematical analyses in Bohr's work, at which he was adept. Later, formulae vanish almost entirely from his papers. I comment in (10a) on Bohr's somewhat ambivalent attitude toward mathematics in physics.

Although in the next few lines I use a number of technical terms, be assured that these will be explained in the chapters and sections indicated. Bohr's achievements of that period include the discovery of the principal quantum number (8f, 10b); his interpretation of the Franck–Hertz experiment (10b); his introduction of selection rules in atomic transitions (10c); his work on the ground states of complex atoms, which laid the foundations of quantum chemistry (10e), which influenced Pauli to introduce the exclusion principle (10d), and which, in turn, led Uhlenbeck and Goudsmit to the discovery of electron spin (11f). All this, as well as the discoveries of the Bose–Einstein and Fermi statistics (13a), belongs to the era of the old quantum theory. In retrospect these many successes are all the more fabulous and astounding because they are based on analogies – atomic orbits similar to the motions of the planets around the sun, and spin similar to the rotation of the planets while orbiting – which are in fact false. No wonder, then, that the old quantum theory also showed capital flaws, most notably its failure to explain all atomic spectra beyond the simplest one, that of hydrogen (10d), and to explain the behavior of most kinds of atoms when exposed to a magnetic field. As Hendrik Kramers, Bohr's closest collaborator in those years (9c, 13b), once put it: 'The quantum theory has been very like other victories; you smile for months and then weep for years.'[27]

Also dating back to the era of the old quantum theory are the earliest encounters between Bohr and Einstein (11b). These meetings had a profound impact on both men. In 1922 Einstein wrote to a friend about Bohr: 'He is truly a man of genius. It is fortunate to have someone like that. I have full confidence in his way of thinking.'[28] Their relations were marked not only by profound mutual respect but also by great affection, if not love,[29] none of which changed when in later years they found themselves at odds about issues of scientific principle (14e, 19b). (More about that shortly.) In (11a) I endeavor to make a comparison between their personalities.

I now turn to the quantum theory's second phase which began with the birth of quantum mechanics. (Just prior to this, Bohr had made a futile attempt at evading Einstein's photons (11d).) Quantum mechanics was actually discovered twice. First, in 1925, came Heisenberg (13d), one of Bohr's disciples, though the most independent one of the lot. (As Kramers once said of Bohr and Heisenberg, they both were 'tough, hard nosed, uncompromising, and indefatigable'.[21]) His version, matrix mechanics, demanded the use of a mathematical algorithm rather unfamiliar to physicists. One deals with quantities, call them a and b, where $a \times b$ does not equal $b \times a$. (I have added a do-it-yourself section (11h) for the benefit of those who would like to learn how this can come about.) Next, in 1926, Erwin Schrödinger discovered another version, wave mechanics, which looked quite different. It took little time to realize that the two versions are in fact identical (13f).

Also from 1926 dates Max Born's recognition (13g) that quantum mechanics marks the end of the general validity of causality in the strict sense of classical physics, a situation foreseen by Einstein (10c). Stated briefly (and not in all generality), classical causality means the following:

Premise. I give you the positions and velocities of particles at a given time.

Deduction. This information together with Newton's laws enables you to tell me their positions and velocities at a later time.

Born made clear that in quantum mechanics one can only answer the question, What are the *probabilities* for certain values of position and velocity at a later time.

For a variety of reasons (13a) Bohr himself did not contribute to the revolutionary theories created in 1925–6. He was delighted with these new developments, however (13e). The year 1927 marks the start of Bohr's own contributions to the foundations of quantum mechanics.

The beginnings of this new phase in Bohr's scientific career can be traced to his discussions in the fall of 1926 with Schrödinger in Copenhagen, discussions in which Heisenberg also participated. During these heated talks, no one present was able to offer a coherent interpretation of the new mechanics (14b). After Schrödinger's departure Bohr and Heisenberg continued arguing about foundational issues, Bohr focusing on an interpretation of particle–wave duality, Heisenberg contenting himself with his matrix mechanics, essentially a particle picture (14c). After the two of them became thoroughly exhausted, Bohr took off by himself to Norway, to ski and to think.

In Bohr's absence Heisenberg discovered his uncertainty relations. These say that the law of causality is not valid in quantum mechanics because the premise (just mentioned) is false. The general laws of quantum mechanics imply that, as a matter of first principle, one cannot know all the determining elements of the present with unlimited accuracy (14d).

Meanwhile Bohr, in Norway, had begun to formulate his views on the philosophical basis of quantum mechanics that have become known as complementarity.

It is one of the several remarkable confluences in Bohr's life that the central question he addressed – What are the means by which we communicate physical information obtained in the laboratory? – is intimately related to a philosophical problem that had preoccupied him since his student days – How do we avoid ambiguity in the use of language? (19a). Philosophizing was part of Bohr's nature, from early on until the end of his life.

Briefly stated, Bohr's main points are these (14e). Quantum mechanics renders meaningless the question: Does light or matter *consist* of particles or waves? Rather, one should ask: Does light or matter *behave* like particles or waves? That question has an unambiguous answer if and only if one specifies the experimental arrangement by means of which one makes observations. The outcome of observations, even those dealing with *quantum* phenomena, is necessarily expressed in *classical* language; physicists have no other way of recording experimental results than with the same sort of instrument readings used in the classical era. This curious relationship between quantum *phenomena* and classical *language* is discussed in more detail in (14e) and (19b,d).

What, then, is complementarity? It is the realization that particle and wave behavior are mutually exclusive, yet that both are necessary for a complete description of all phenomena (14e). What is a phenomenon? According to Bohr, it is an account of observations which includes the specification of the tools of detection (19b).

Bohr's formulation of the complementarity concept, which he kept refining from 1927 on, makes him one of the most important twentieth century philosophers. As such he must be considered the successor to Kant who had considered causality as a 'synthetic judgement a priori', not derivable from experience. Causality is, in Kant's own words, 'a rule according to which phenomena are sequentially determined. Only by assuming that rule is it possible to speak of experience of something that happens.'[30] This view must now be considered *passé*. Since Bohr, the very definition of what constitutes a phenomenon has wrought changes that, unfortunately, have not yet sunk in sufficiently among professional philosophers.

Again according to Kant, constructive concepts are intrinsic attributes of the *Ding an sich*, a viewpoint desperately maintained by Einstein, but abandoned by quantum physicists. In Bohr's words: 'Our task is not to penetrate into the essence of things, the meaning of which we don't know anyway, but rather to develop concepts which allow us to talk in a productive way about phenomena in nature.' (19d).

Bohr's usage of 'phenomenon' is the one now subscribed to by nearly all physicists. Not by Einstein, however. Until his death he kept insisting that one should look for a deeper level of theory in which, as in classical physics, one can talk of phenomena independently of observational details. He did eventually accept the results of quantum mechanics, but believed that these should emerge by some effective averaging process applied to the deeper theory. Bohr tried hard, and often, to convince him of the complementarity view (14f, 19b). He never succeeded.

I can now answer a question raised at the beginning of this section: Why do some textbooks not mention complementarity? Because it will not help in quantum mechanical calculations or in setting up experiments. Bohr's considerations are extremely relevant, however, to the scientist who occasionally likes to reflect on the meaning of what she or he is doing.

Do I believe that Bohr's are the last words on the meaning of quantum mechanics? For my answer turn to the end of (19b). Here I only note that those who accept Bohr's way of thinking speak of the spirit of Copenhagen – an expression coined by Heisenberg (14f) – while those who are critical speak of the Copenhagen orthodoxy.

Complementarity can be formulated without explicit reference to physics, to wit, as two aspects of a description that are mutually exclusive yet both necessary for a full understanding of what is to be described. Bohr attempted to apply complementarity in this broad sense to other fields, such as psychology,* biology, and anthropology. The most interesting among these discussions are, it seems to me, his comments on instinct and reason, on free will, and on love and justice (19d). Personally I have found the complementary way of thinking liberating.

Since I am touching here on Bohr's interests outside physics, this may be an appropriate place to say something about his acquaintance with culture in a broad sense.

First, I should note that Bohr never cared much for, nor knew much of, what professional philosophers had to say (19a). Occasional attempts to trace the origins of Bohr's complementarity to their writings are without basis in fact (19a). In particular the occasionally expressed belief that Bohr's views on physics were influenced by oriental philosophy is unfounded. These speculations have an amusing origin. In 1947 Denmark's highest distinction, knighthood in the Order of the Elephant, was conferred on Bohr (9c, 20d). Tradition demanded that he now acquire a coat of arms. So he consulted others about a choice of emblem. One friend reported[31] that he had browsed without success in the Royal Library. Then Hanna Kobylinski, an expert on Chinese history, the wife of Bohr's close co-worker Stefan Rozental, had an idea:[32] use the Yin–Yang symbol. Formally known[33] as Tai-Ji-Tu. This is the diagram of the supreme poles: Yang, the active, male, and Yin the receptive, female, principle. Bohr thought that this was a great idea. And that is how Yin–Yang was chosen, with the added motto: *Contraria sunt complementa* (opposites are complementary).**

Bohr's parents were not religious. As a child he did not receive education in religious matters. He could appreciate religious feelings but not what one might call its philosophy. His wife once said: 'He was sorry for the role religion played . . . He thought it was not good for human beings to hold on to things which were, as nearly as one could see, not true.'[34] (See also (8b).)

Bohr was an avid reader (and crossword-puzzle solver). He would never thank an author for the gift of a book until after he had read it. From early

---

* Bohr was never much interested in psychoanalysis.

** You can see Bohr's coat of arms by visiting Frederiksborg castle near Hillerød, entering its chapel, then going upstairs to a gallery where at the south end are hung the coats of arms of all Knights of the Order of the Elephant.

on he had great talents for retaining and reciting poetry (Chapter 3) and loved reading aloud to others from his favourite authors. To my regret, my knowledge of what Bohr has read is scanty. This is what I do know.[35] From boyhood onward Bohr was very fond of the Icelandic sagas (Chapter 3), which he first heard when his father read them to him (Chapter 2). In later years Niels would take particular delight in introducing foreign visitors to those tales, from which stem one of his very favorite quotations: 'He went out to gather together words and thoughts.' On his seventieth birthday his sons dedicated a saga[36] to him which they themselves had written in old Icelandic style.

Among the Danish classics Bohr was fond of the plays by Ludvig Holberg (19b) and the stories by Hans Christian Andersen and Poul Martin Møller (19d). He admired Søren Kierkegaard's mastery of the Danish language, though not his philosophy (19a). Among Danish contemporaries he appreciated Georg Brandes and Isak Dinesen both of whom he knew personally. He also corresponded with Dinesen.[37] He was friends with the Danish poet Hans Seedorff (12a, 18a). Among other Scandinavian authors he liked the Norwegians Henrik Ibsen, Bjørnsterne Bjørnson, and Hermann Wildenvey.[38]

Bohr knew little English when aged 26 he went to Cambridge for his postdoctoral studies. He made up for that (7a) by reading, with a dictionary at hand, *The Pickwick Papers* by Charles Dickens, an author of whom he remained fond all his life. He liked Shakespeare, especially *Othello*. I further know of his fondness for Mark Twain and for Richard Wright's *Native son*. In a lighter vein he enjoyed reading detective stories and the writings of Stephen Leacock and of P. G. Wodehouse, in particular the latter's *The man who gave up smoking*.

Bohr's knowledge of French was poor. I have it from an eyewitness that he once greeted the French ambassador to Denmark with a cordial *aujourd'hui*. He was quite at home with the German language and literature, however. His knowledge of and admiration for Goethe's poems and dramas were profound (Goethe's theory of colors interested him less), as we learn particularly from Jørgen Kalckar's sensitive monograph[39] on Bohr and Goethe. He was likewise fond of Schiller's writings, particularly his epigrams. More can undoubtedly be said about Bohr and German literature, but the only further comment I can make is that Bohr met Thomas Mann in Princeton, who found him a stimulating personality.[40]

Music played no role to speak of in Bohr's life (Chapter 3), but he had a great feeling for painting. 'Bohr was vitally interested in the new ground so swiftly broken by modern painting during his lifetime . . . He knew that it was an art to be a scientist and that there is science in creating art . . . "It is for the painters to find something new," he said.'[41] Among the paintings hanging in his house was one by a founder of cubism (15e).

As yet another manifestation of Bohr's wide-ranging interests, it may be mentioned that in 1925 he was the youngest member of the *Store Fem* (Big Five), a committee of Denmark's most prominent men of learning which organized the collection of funds for improving the poor conditions of Denmark's National Museum.[42]

Next topic: the changes in Bohr's life and in the scientific program at his institute during the 1930s.

Regarding personal matters Bohr and his family experienced much sorrow: the deaths of Niels' mother and his sister Jenny; the suicide of his friend Paul Ehrenfest; his mentor Rutherford did not survive an operation. Bohr's greatest grief was to see his oldest son drown before his eyes in a sailing accident (18a). In addition Bohr was deeply concerned with the fates of friends and colleagues in Nazi Germany and Austria (17d).

Also on the personal side I mention the move by Bohr and his family to the Residence of Honor (15e), and his elections to chairman of the Danish society to combat cancer (1935, (17i)) and to president of the Royal Danish Academy of Sciences and Letters (1939, (20d)).

During the 1930s Bohr made his most extensive journeys, two trips to the United States, his first visit to the Soviet Union, and a trip around the world with longer stops in the US, Japan, China, and the USSR (18b).

With regard to science, the focus of Bohr's institute changed from atomic physics to nuclear physics and biology. The roots of nuclear physics date back to the beginning of the twentieth century (15b). After the arrival of quantum mechanics it became clear that many early ideas about the nucleus were incorrect (15c,d). Theoretical nuclear physics (the first book on that subject was written in Copenhagen (15a)) came into its own after the discovery of the neutron in 1932 (15d). Bohr's liquid drop model of the nucleus was a significant contribution to this subject (15f). The most important consequences of this model were the interpretation (20a) by Robert Frisch and Lise Meitner (published in a paper written at Bohr's institute) of the fission of uranium (the name fission is another Copenhagen contribution), and Bohr's realization that slow neutron fission of uranium must be attributed to the rare isotope with atomic weight 235 (20a). During the war years Bohr's liquid drop model was a main guide to theorists working at the atomic weapons laboratory, Los Alamos (15g).

The 1930s also witnessed major strides forward in the design and use of accelerators, machines that speed up particles such as electrons or protons to high energies, after which they are made to smash into targets, a process that generates nuclear reactions (17b). Under Bohr's guidance, and with important support from foundations (17i), three accelerators were constructed at his institute (17j), among them one of Europe's first cyclotrons. (Germany's first cyclotron went into operation five years after Denmark's

(21c).) These machines were ready just in time for doing significant early fission experiments (20b).

An important category of reactions generated by accelerators is the production of artificially radioactive materials (17f). These substances are of capital importance for biological studies. Accordingly Bohr directed parts of his institute's efforts toward biology.

Once again a confluence of circumstances helped Bohr in these new endeavors. First, the Rockefeller philanthropic support for science had redirected its emphasis to biology (17c), so that Bohr, on excellent terms with the Rockefeller foundation, had access to appropriate funding. Secondly, in 1934 he was able to attach Georg von Hevesy to his institute (17e). The two men had been friends since Bohr's Manchester days (7b). In the early 1920s Hevesy had spent some years at Bohr's institute, during which he had made the first applications of isotope tracer techniques to the life sciences (17h). The radioactive materials then available for such purposes were small in quantity and, even worse, highly toxic. The availability of the new artificially radioactive substances eliminated both drawbacks. The work of Hevesy in the 1930s at Bohr's institute made isotope tracer methods flourish. And so Bohr became the godfather, and Hevesy the father, of nuclear medicine (17h).

I turn now to Bohr's experiences during World War II.

On 9 April 1940 German military forces occupied Denmark after only token resistance. It was the first time foreign armies had set foot on Danish soil since the 1864 war with Prussia (Chapter 3). Before relating what befell Bohr personally I once again outline the Danish setting, this time by sketching the relations between Denmark and Germany from 1864 until the end of World War II in May 1945 (21b).

Bohr spent the early war years in Copenhagen, managing somehow to keep his institute going (21c). Among the memorable events of that period are a visit by Heisenberg in the autumn of 1941, not a pleasant encounter (21c), and the arrival in early 1943 of a letter from England inviting Bohr, in guarded terms, to join the Allied war effort, a proposal which Bohr declined (21c).

In September 1943, after being informed that he ran grave risks of imprisonment by the Germans, Bohr and his family fled to Sweden. He spent about a week there, an interlude filled with cloak-and-dagger events (21c). From Stockholm Bohr was flown to London, where his son Aage joined him soon afterward. Shortly after his arrival in England his Copenhagen institute was briefly occupied by German military police (21c).

Right after arrival in London Bohr was informed that a joint Anglo-American project for producing atomic bombs was underway, though no definitive results had as yet been obtained (21d). The news astonished him greatly, since up till that time he had been quite dubious about practical applications of the fission process (20c). He was asked to join the project as consultant, and accepted. From then until August 1945 we follow him on numerous trips back and forth between London and his US headquarters in Washington, and between Washington and Los Alamos, always accompanied by Aage (21d,e).

Bohr played only a minor role in the actual weapons program (21d). From late 1943 onwards his major concern was less with the war effort than with the radical changes in the post-war political climate that could be anticipated because of the new weapons. These, he became convinced, might actually hold out a promise for improved international relations precisely because of their unmanageable threats to the security of nations. He further believed it necessary for the Western leaders to consult the Russians* at once on this issue, because, he reasoned, if one deferred such contact until after the war, serious distrust would disrupt relations between wartime Allies, with potentially grave consequences.

Being a man of action Bohr started attempts at bringing his ideas personally to the attention of Churchill and Roosevelt. These efforts of his date back to a time when the first atomic device had not even been tested. Surely, then, Bohr must be considered as the pioneer of 'glasnost'.

In (21e) I give a detailed account of the steps which led to Bohr's personal meetings with Churchill on 16 May 1944 and with Roosevelt on the following 26 August. I describe the negative outcome of those encounters and indicate why that result was inevitable.

After his return to Denmark in August 1945 (21e) Bohr continued his efforts at promoting an open world. In the spring of 1948 he tried in vain to convince US Secretary of State George Marshall of the importance of an initiative by his government. Whereupon Bohr decided to bring his appeal to the general public in the form of an open letter to the United Nations. That document was delivered on 9 June 1950, two weeks before the outbreak of the Korean war – which suffices to explain why it produced very little reaction. Bohr still persisted. In November 1956 he addressed a second letter to the UN, again without much response.

Times have changed only very recently, when Mikhail Sergeyevitch Gorbachev made glasnost a reality. In 1985 and 1989 conferences were organized centering on Bohr's theme of an open world. See (22c) for all these post-war developments.

After the war Bohr's research formed only a minor part of his activities (22b). His furthest reach toward the ever moving frontiers of physics dates

---

* It is now known that ever since the spring of 1942 Stalin received personal briefings from Soviet scientists about the possibilities of atomic weapons.[43]

back to the 1930s and deals with the foundations of quantum electrodynamics (16b). He took no part in the development of elementary particle physics which began to flourish in the 1950s.*

Bohr published copiously in his later years, however, on complementarity in and beyond physics. More than 20 addresses he delivered have appeared in print. Furthermore he has written on occasions of the passing of friends and colleagues. See (22b) for his post-war writings.

Most of Bohr's energy in that period was devoted to the glasnost issue, and to help in establishing various new institutions such as CERN (22d), Nordita, a joint Scandinavian venture in theoretical physics (22e), Risø National Laboratory, and a new branch of his institute also located at Risø (22f). In the 1950s he also traveled a good deal: several trips to the US, two to Israel, to Iceland, Greenland, India, and, one last time, to the USSR.

In June 1962 Bohr suffered a minor cerebral hemorrhage from which he appeared to recover. The following November he died at his home, from heart failure. He was 77 years old (22h).

In an epilog (Chapter 23) I tell of the reactions of sorrow and sympathy which reached Niels' wife Margrethe, including a letter from President Kennedy, and of her later life. She survived her husband by 22 years.

To conclude I return to the question raised at the beginning of this section: Why is it that many members of my generation barely know that Bohr was such a significant figure? Note first that physics is an ahistoric discipline: progress achieved in earlier times is often served up in undergraduate courses almost as matters of course, without reference to the struggles it took major figures to make new steps. In the case of Bohr his prime scientific contributions lay in guiding physics through the complex years of the old quantum theory, which was superseded by quantum mechanics. He created a new institute which in its day was the world's leading center for theoretical physics. Today there are many such centers rather than a single one that stands out in excellence. Bohr's philosophical contributions are less familiar to those many physicists who are more pragmatically minded. His noble efforts to promote an open world have largely fallen through the cracks in the ice of the cold war. Perhaps most important of all, only those who knew him personally could experience the immense inspiration exuding from his intuitive grasp of physics and his humane personality.

---

* On 31 January 1958 Pauli gave a lecture at Columbia University about recent work by him and Heisenberg on elementary particles. Bohr and I were in the audience. Afterward we talked with Pauli. Pauli turned to Bohr and said, 'You probably think these ideas are crazy.' Bohr replied, 'I do, but unfortunately they are not crazy enough.'

References

1. *New York Times*, 18 October 1957.
2. J. R. Killian, *Sputnik, scientists and Eisenhower*, p. 119, MIT Press 1977.
3. Ref. 2, p. 24.
4. See the photograph in Ref. 2, p. 18.
5. *New York Times*, 25 October 1957.
6. All mentioned speeches have been reproduced in a pamphlet printed for the Awards Committee, copy in NBA.
7. R. S. Westfall, *Never at rest*, Cambridge University Press 1980.
8. J. Franck, interview by T. S. Kuhn, M. Mayer, and H. Sponer, 10 July 1962, NBA.
9. A. Pais, NBR, p. 215.
10. Translation by P. E. Pinkerton of Heinrich Düntzer's *Poetical works, life of Schiller*, Dana Estes, Boston 1902.
11. L. Rosenfeld, *Quantum theory in 1929*, Rhodos, Copenhagen 1971.
12. N. Bohr, in *La théorie quantique des champs*, Ed. R. Stoops, Interscience, New York 1962.
13. This letter is reproduced in an article by W. Schröder, *Nachr. Akad. der Wiss. Göttingen, math.-phys. Klasse*, 1985, p. 85.
14. P. Bridgman, letter to the father of J. C. Slater, 4 February 1924, copy in the Library of the American Philosophical Society, Philadelphia.
15. W. Heisenberg, *Jahrb. der Bayer. Akad. der Wiss.* 1963, p. 204; repr. in *Werner Heisenberg, Gesammelte Werke*, Vol. 4C, p. 144, Eds. W. Blum *et al.*, Piper, Munich 1986.
16. P. A. M. Dirac, *Principles of quantum mechanics*, 1st edn 1930 to 4th edn 1958, Oxford University Press.
17. S. Tomonoga, *Quantum mechanics*, Interscience, New York 1962.
18. R. P. Feynman, *Lectures in Physics*, Vol. 3, Addison-Wesley, Reading, Mass. 1965.
19. List of visitors from abroad who worked for longer periods at the Institute for Theoretical Physics, unpublished document, NBA.
20. N. Mott, letter to his mother, December 1928, repr. in *A life in science*, p. 28, Taylor and Francis, Philadelphia 1986.
21. M. Dresden, *H. A. Kramers*, p. 481, Springer, New York 1987.
22. S. Rozental, *Erindringer om Niels Bohr*, p. 31, Gyldendal, Copenhagen 1985.
23. *L. Rosenfeld, selected papers*, p. 302, Eds. R. Cohen and J. Stachel, Reidel, Boston 1979.
24. Reprinted in 1985 at the Niels Bohr Institute.
25. N. Bohr, letter to the minister of education, 29 March 1932, NBA.
26. *Politiken*, 7 November 1933.
27. H. A. Kramers, quoted in A. S. Eve, *Rutherford*, p. 304, Cambridge University Press 1939.
28. A. Einstein, letter to P. Ehrenfest, 23 March 1922.
29. Cf. SL, Chap. 22.
30. Here I use a quotation from Kant selected by W. Heisenberg, *Ann. der Philos.* **2**, 172, 1931; repr. in *Werke* (Ref. 15), part C, Vol. 1, p. 29.

31. H. Hendriksen, letter to N. Bohr, 31 December 1947, NBA.
32. Ref. 22, p. 34.
33. Private communication by Professor Ge Ge.
34. M. Bohr, interview by T. S. Kuhn, 23 January 1963, NBA.
35. See also H. Bohr, NBR, p. 325, and N. Blaedel, *Harmoni og Enhed*, p. 188 ff., Rhodos, Copenhagen 1985.
36. *Niels' Saga*, private printing, copy in NBA.
37. In particular about vivisection, see *Blixeniana 1985*, p. 311 ff., Blixen Selskabet, Copenhagen 1985.
38. Cf. N. Bohr, letter to H. Wildenvey, 7 March 1947, NBA.
39. J. Kalckar, *Det inkommensurable*, Rhodos, Copenhagen 1985.
40. Th. Mann, *Tagebücher 1937–1939*, entries for 5 and 7 February 1939, Ed. P. Mendelssohn, S. Fischer, Frankfurt 1980.
41. M. Andersen, NBR, p. 321.
42. Cf. N. Blaedel, Ref. 35, p. 119.
43. See *Moscow News Weekly*, No. 16, 1989, No. 41, 1989; also A. Vucinich, *Empire of knowledge*, p. 200 ff., University of California Press, Berkeley 1984.

2

'In Denmark I was born ...'

At Ved Stranden No. 14, facing Christiansborg Castle, the seat of the Danish Parliament, there stands one of Copenhagen's handsomest mansions.[1] As one enters the front door of the neoclassical building, one sees an archway leading into a courtyard. A plaque inside the archway records its residents since the first buildings were erected there in the middle of the sixteenth century. In the seventeenth century several mayors of Copenhagen made their homes on these grounds. After those early residences were all destroyed in the great Copenhagen fire of 1795 (which laid waste nearly a quarter of the city, about a thousand houses), the present building was constructed during 1796–7. In 1873 the wealthy Danish Jewish banker David Baruch Adler and his family moved in. After his death in 1878 his widow Jenny continued to live there until she died, in 1902. From 1903 to 1913 the house was one of the residences of King George I of Greece; in those years the building was known as King George's Palace. From 1914 onward it has been occupied by business firms, presently by McKinsey & Co., a branch of an American consultant management company, which has restored the interior in late nineteenth century style. On a visit in 1986 I was shown the ceiling paintings of what once was the music room, and several relief sculptures by the Danish artist Thorvaldsen, remnants of the interior as it looked, when, on Wednesday 7 October 1885, Niels Bohr was born there, as is recorded on a plaque on the building's façade unveiled on his 75th birthday. In that same year another Dane was born who would also achieve world renown and would die in the same year as Bohr: Karen Blixen, perhaps better known under her pen name, Isak Dinesen.

Niels belongs to the fifth generation of the Danish Bohr dynasty.

In about 1741, when there were Germans but not yet a German nation, a boy by the name of Christian Baar was born in Mecklenburg, a grand duchy bordering on Schlesvig-Holstein, which then still was Danish territory. He became a soldier, a fusilier in a battalion commanded by a German prince. After his discharge in 1770 he settled in the Danish city of Helsingør (Elsinore), where he worked as gardener. The city records show that on 20 September 1776, he became *Borger* (burgher) of Helsingør. Burghership, which could be acquired by anyone living in a community who was judged to be skilled, whether foreign or Danish born, is not identical with Danish citizenship, a concept formalized only on 15 January of that year by the 'law of right to citizenship', signed by the ruling absolute monarch, Christian VII. We further know that in 1789 Christian Baar became a janitor at the Øresund Customs House, a state post that could only be held by Danish citizens. Thus he must have been citizen by then.

Meanwhile Christian had married, three times in fact, and had become a father. In 1771 his first wife bore him a son, Christian Friderich Baar; she died two months later. Within a year Christian remarried; his second wife died three months thereafter (from pregnancy complications, one might guess). In 1773 he married once more, to Johanne Engelke Bomholt fromNorway. Half a year later their first son was born. His father registered him under the name Christian Fredrik Gottfred *Bohr*. There can be little doubt as to what caused the change in surname. In Danish the double *a* is pronounced *oh*.

In all, Christian and Johanne had three sons and two daughters. Shortly after Johanne died, in 1789, Christian, apparently a vigorous sort of fellow, married once more and had another three children. With the last of these, Niels Erdmann Bohr – who became a tailor – the name Niels enters for the first time in the Bohr family tree.

Seven of Christian's nine children did not lead particularly memorable lives. However, it was otherwise with the other two. There was Christian Fredrik,the first Bohr to attend university, in Copenhagen, where he also got quite involved in the study of the organ and of the violin. Difficult financial conditions led him to leave the university for one year and move to Norway, then joined in a double monarchy with Denmark, where he spent the rest of his life. Soon he became a teacher of music and science, developing a taste for mathematics and physics. He published a dozen books and pamphlets on the teaching of arithmetic, geometry, and the singing of psalms, and also produced research papers on geographical, meteorological, and lunar eclipse observations, which kept him in contact with scientists in Berlin, London, Paris, Stockholm, and Copenhagen. In 1816 he was appointed *Astronomisk Observator* in Bergen. On 29 March 1819 he was elected[2] member of the Royal Norwegian Academy of Sciences and Letters, and on 24 February 1824 also of the Royal Swedish Academy of Sciences in Stockholm.

With Christian Fredrik there begins what may by now fairly be called the major Bohr tradition: devotion both to learning and to teaching. It was said of him that he had rare pedagogical talents. He was particularly concerned about the fact that most artisan apprentices began their training without knowledge of arithmetic and writing, and were barely able to read. In order to ameliorate this situation, he and a few others founded a Sunday school in

Bergen – not so much for religious education as for training in reading, writing, and arithmetic. He alone took on the teaching duties, devoting in addition several weekday evenings to training further the most gifted pupils, so that these might become assistants at the Sunday school. He also founded a school for poor girls, so that they might 'learn the most necessary female occupations, and thus develop to useful maid servants'. On top of all these activities he became organist and cantor in Bergen's Cathedral, the *Domkirke*. He was a much beloved man. On the day of his funeral many vied for the honor of carrying his coffin to the grave.[3]

Then there was Christian Fredrik's next youngest brother Peter Georg, great grandfather of Niels, who studied theology and then held various teaching positions, some in Denmark, some in Norway. In 1818 he became rector of the *lærde Skole** in Rønne, the main town on the island of Bornholm (the school is now called *Bornholm's Amtsgymnasium i Rønne*). He wrote several articles of a pedagogical character and, in 1836, an essay about 'the situation in Denmark three hundred years ago'.[4] The occasion was the 300th anniversary of the founding of the Lutheran church as Denmark's state church. The essay ends with an invitation to the readers to attend a lecture by P. G. Bohr, to be given at the lærde Skole, to which is invited 'anyone who derives joy from the victory of light over darkness, from the progress of science, and from the shaping of youth'.

Peter Georg had four sons and two daughters with his second wife, Brigitte Steenberg Sandal, a minister's daughter. (His first marriage had remained childless and had ended in divorce.) All sons studied theology, two became ministers, the other two teachers. The oldest of the four, Henrik Georg Christian Bohr, a teacher, was Niels' grandfather.

Henrik studied theology and taught Latin, history, and geography at the von Westenske Institut (another *lærde Skole*) in Copenhagen of which he later became rector. In 1860 he was granted the right to use the title of professor, in recognition of his contributions. He has been described as a strong, brilliant, cultured person whose educational methods combined sensibility with old-fashioned discipline, including an occasional caning.[5] One of his students, who remembered him as 'an able school master and a cheerful gentleman', has left us samples of Henrik's style, one of which goes like this.[6] Some days after having handed in a Danish essay, this pupil was sternly asked in class whether he had written that piece himself. Yes, he had. Had someone helped him? No, no one had. 'Are you sure?' asked Henrik and picked up a cane. Yes, he was sure. Whereupon the teacher's severe expression changed into a broad smile as he gave the boy some coins, telling him to go buy some pastry, then come back and eat it while his essay was being discussed in class.

* Upon matriculation a pupil from a *lærde Skole* was qualified for entering the University of Copenhagen.

Henrik Bohr published several high school textbooks on history and a biography of Tordenskjold, the Norwegian/Danish naval hero, all of which went through numerous editions. He also wrote an essay[7] with the following elaborate title (in translation): 'The ABC of good fortune or newest dream table according to which, as is shown by the example of the tailor's apprentice, one can never lose in playing lottery. Written as consolation, solace, and hope for those who lost their fortune in lottery, as well as for the pleasure and use of others'. The subject is intriguing. Could Niels' grandfather have believed that one can beat the system in games of chance? What is a dream table? Who was the tailor's apprentice? Reading this witty essay, one finds that the dream table establishes a correspondence between a specific type of dream and the lottery number to be picked: A dream about porridge – add the first digit of your house number to your age; a woman dreaming of her suitor – pick 8; a man dreaming of his courtship – pick 74; a dream about brandy – 1(!); and so on. The way one never loses at lottery is by not playing at all. The tailor's apprentice was a man who could not dream. So he told his wife to use *her* dreams and then to play the lucky number, giving her every week some money for the purpose. After several months the wife returned much more money than the husband had laid out. When asked about her experiences, she replied that she had not played at all but used the money for buying yarn for knitting and that she had sold her product at a profit.

In 1840 Henrik married Augusta Rimestad, a judge's daughter. They had seven children. The eldest fought with distinction in the bloody battle of Dybbøl (in 1864) between Denmark and Prussia/Austria, and also as a volunteer on the French side in the 1870–1 Franco-Prussian war. He later became an engineer and director of the telegraph administration of China. The next son succeeded his father as school rector. The third son and seventh child, Christian, born in 1855, was Niels' father.

Christian was the first among Niels' lineal ancestors to be born in Copenhagen, the first to obtain a Ph.D., in medicine, in 1880 (on a study of suspended fat droplets in natural milk), and the first to pursue a university career, in Copenhagen. He became privat docent* in 1881, lektor (associate professor) in 1886, and professor in 1890. During 1905–6 he was rector of the university. His specialty was physiology. 'He was an excellent physicist with a good mathematical knowledge . . . The most characteristic trait in Bohr's personality was his marked originality.'[8] In 1885 he was awarded a

---

* In Denmark someone who obtains the doctor's degree automatically acquires the *jus docendi*, the right to lecture at the university where the degree is obtained. The university must provide a heated lecture room and is further required to announce the lectures in the semiannual catalogue. The right was used by scholars not employed by the university to advance their academic careers. The privat docent is neither a member of the faculty nor paid by the university. The rules governing privat docentship are not the same in all countries.

silver medal by the Royal Danish Academy of Sciences for a paper on the deviation from Boyle–Mariotte's law of oxygen at low pressures.[9]

As a scientist Christian Bohr is principally remembered for his discovery of the influence of carbon dioxide on the release of oxygen by hemoglobin. To this day these findings are known as the 'Bohr effect'.[10] As a consequence of this work and also of his theoretical ideas on the physiology of respiration, he was proposed for the Nobel Prize in physiology or medicine, in 1907 and 1908 by Johan Erik Johansson, professor of physiology at the Karolinska Institute in Stockholm, in 1908 also by Leopold Meyer, professor of gynecology in Copenhagen. In his 1908 report to the Nobel Committee, Karl Mörner, professor of biochemistry at the Karolinska, concluded that one should not make this award 'until there shall be more certainty regarding the significance of Bohr's work'. His main reservation, concerning the respiration theory, turned out later to be justified.[11]

Among Bohr's considerable number of publications,[12] several are in collaboration with junior colleagues and students. 'He knew how to get pupils going, following their progress, instilled in them his own energy, and made them persevere till late at night[13] . . . The number of his pupils' publications was extremely large.'[8] Among his other characteristics, Bohr was 'sensitive, friendly and helpful, simple and modest, on occasion almost shy. He was not really eloquent.'[13] He had a keen interest in sport, and was a connoisseur of Icelandic sagas, of Goethe, and of Holberg, whose founding of native Danish theatre in the early eighteenth century did much to help bring to an end the era in which, it was said, a Danish gentleman would write in Latin to his friends, talk French to the ladies, call his dogs in German, and only use Danish to swear at the servants.[14]

By a decree of 1875, Danish women were allowed for the first time to pursue studies at the university. Those interested needed additional coaching to prepare them for admission. Christian Bohr was one of those who took on this task. He and one of the young ladies he met in this way fell in love. Her name was Ellen Adler.

In the late eighteenth century Ellen's great-grandfather Isaac David Adler, a merchant, became the first of his clan to settle in Copenhagen. He hailed from Altona (close to Hamburg), then still a city under Danish rule. Isaac David begat Baruch Isak, stockbroker; Baruch Isak begat David Baruch.[15]

At the age of 16, David Adler set out on a business apprenticeship, first in Hamburg, then in London. He may well have come into some money in 1843 when his father died. At any rate, in 1848 he established his own firm in London: Martin Levin & Adler.

On 11 December 1849 David was married in the New Synagogue in London to Jenny Raphael, born in Hamburg in 1831. The ancestry of his bride, one of the eleven children of the Anglo-Jewish banker John Raphael, can be traced to Amsterdam. Her great-grandfather Nathan, a merchant, was known as 'Nathan from Amsterdam and Harwich'. Tradition has it that his father had been personal physician to members of the House of Orange. Descendants of Nathan were connected with many well-known and highly respected Anglo-Jewish families; one of his daughters married the son of the Rabbi of London's Great Synagogue. Jenny's grandfather Raphael Raphael had been co-founder of a London brokerage firm.

The ancestry of Jenny's mother, Emma Schiff, can be traced back eight generations, from London via Altona to Frankfurt am Main. Throughout her family there was a pattern of scholarship and culture. It is perhaps of passing interest that her great-grandfather had been married to a widow whose son by her previous marriage was the father of Heinrich Heine.

Let us return to David and Jenny Adler. In 1850 they moved to Denmark. Once settled in Copenhagen, David opened a branch of the London firm (which continued to operate until 1907). He became a central figure in the Danish financial world as one of the co-founders of Privatbanken (1856), where for the first time in Denmark one could cash checks, and also of Handelsbanken (1873), both major banks to this day. In the early years there was financial trouble to cope with, but eventually he could be counted among the wealthiest men in Denmark.

David felt himself foremost to be a Dane but never forgot that he was a Jew. Throughout his life he remained a member of the Jewish Congregation (for a number of years he was on its Board of Representatives) though he did not observe religious precepts. One of his favourite books was Lessing's *Nathan der Weise*, a plea for religious tolerance. He, his wife, and their daughter Hanna are buried in the old Jewish cemetery on the street called Møllegade, in Copenhagen. The chief rabbi spoke at David's grave. The inscription on the well-kept tombstone contains no Hebrew. My visit to Møllegade was the most colorful event in the preparation of this book. It took some effort to find the cemetery guardian. When I finally located him in a pub, he turned out to be a kind and quite inebriated gentleman, who I had to support while he staggered back to the graveyard.

Jews had been permitted communal worship in Copenhagen since 1684.[16] Until the nineteenth century they were generally tolerated in Denmark but had, shall we say, their disagreeable experiences, such as the big anti-Jewish riots of 1819. They were accorded civil rights by a rescript of 1814, but were not accepted as fully equal before the law until the 'June constitution' of 1849. The next few decades saw a great flowering of Jewish participation in Danish science, literature, the press, and also in politics.

David Adler, too, was drawn into Denmark's political life. From 1864 to 1869 he was a member of Parliament in the *Folketing* (Lower House), and from 1869 to his death in 1878 in the *Landsting* (Upper House). In these capacities he was able to speak for his two ideals: human rights and liberal economic policies. He was a representative of the bourgeoisie, which he considered the backbone of society. As a political speaker he was not a success. He did prepare himself well, but had difficulty controlling his strong temperament when taking the floor. Among other public offices, he was nine years on the town council of Copenhagen; was co-founder and member of *Grosserer-Societetet*, the Danish Chamber of Commerce; and was active on the committees for the decoration of the National Theatre in Copenhagen and for Denmark's participation in the Paris Exposition of 1878.

The Adler marriage was a very happy one. Jenny is remembered as a gentle loving woman, understanding in dealing with her husband's temperament, the central figure in the home, loved by family and friends, worshipped by the servants. She learned to speak Danish fluently. Nor would one ever guess from her letters that she was foreign born. They had three sons and three daughters. Ellen was the youngest of the six. On 26 March 1876 she made her *Trosbekjendelsen*,[17] the profession of faith.* (Presumably the other children did likewise at the appropriate times.) Bertel David, the oldest son, succeeded his father in the banking business.

Hanna, the next to youngest, went to the university. In 1892 she became one of the first two women to obtain a master's degree in physics.** She became Denmark's pioneering figure in co-education, making an early trip to the United States to study conditions in American schools. 'She was so deeply impressed with the Negro problem in America that she writes that she almost decided to stay in America to work for the Negroes.'[19] She founded a private school, 'Hanna Adler's Fællesskole' (co-educational school), which she later transferred to the city of Copenhagen. She insisted on small classes and short hours as the best way for education to work. At the age of 84, during World War II, she was interned by the Germans and should have been sent to Theresienstadt, but was soon released as a result of a petition to the German occupation authorities signed by high officials in the Department of Education, the mayor of Copenhagen, the rector of the university, and 400 of her former pupils.[20]

In 1874 David Adler bought the mansion at Ved Stranden 14 and moved in with his wife, six children, and servants. Their living quarters, nineteen rooms, occupied the top two floors. Below he had his banking offices. He had only four years left to enjoy his beautiful home. Weakened already in 1872 by a long illness, he died in 1878 at the young age of 53. An obituary in a Danish paper said of him: 'Nowhere in our country and beyond its borders

---

* This equivalent of a Christian confirmation, required by the rescript of 1814, took place during a ceremony in a synagogue.

** The other was Kirstine Meyer, née Bjerrum, the first Danish woman to obtain a doctorate in physics. She became a distinguished educator and historian of science. Niels Bohr thought highly of her.[18] An oil portrait of her is in the possession of the Bohr family.

was his death talked of without sincere testimony to his abilities, his zeal for all good causes, his patriotism and liberalism, his warm heart, and his open and honest character. [20a] David's widow and two unmarried daughters continued to live at Ved Stranden till Jenny's death in 1902.

On 14 December 1881, Ellen Adler and Christian Bohr were married at a civil ceremony in Copenhagen's City Hall. The record of this event states that Christian was baptized and confirmed and also contains a 'declaration by the applicants that children, if any, born from the marriage are intended to be brought up in the Mosaic faith.' [17] On 9 March 1883 their first child arrived, a girl who was named Jenny. The birth registration shows[21] that she was born at Ved Stranden 14. At the census of 1 February 1885 she was registered[22] as Jenny Bohr, unmarried, religious affiliation: none.

On her 25th birthday Ellen gave birth, also at Ved Stranden 14, to the first of her two sons, Niels Henrik David Bohr.[23]

Soon after the occupation of Denmark by the Germans in 1940, plans were made to record for posterity the status of Danish culture at that time. The result was an eight-volume collection[24] of essays. It was natural that Niels Bohr would be chosen to write a general introduction; it was typical that he would go through twelve proofs before being satisfied.[25] In these opening remarks, which must be counted among his clearest writings, he speaks of 'the little country which always lay far removed from the highways of culture', but also notes that 'we can permit ourselves to be proud of the way in which we have used our situation to foster our own development and our participation in the collaboration toward the progress of human culture.' He writes of renowned Danes who contributed to science, literature, and religious leadership, Hans Christian Andersen among them. He cites from one of Andersen's poems:

> I Danmark er jeg født, der har jeg Hjemme,
> der har jeg Rod, derfra min Verden gaar,

which I freely translate as

> In Denmark I was born, there is my home,
> there are my roots, from there my world unfolds.

These lines he would also often quote in conversation, with special emphasis on the word *derfra* (from there).

Bohr was of course aware how well these words applied to himself. Born and bred a Dane, yet citizen of the world. Securely rooted in his native culture, yet forever thinking internationally. The Bohr family is listed in the handbook of Danish patrician families.[26] Patrician, Niels was, and he knew it full well. In fact he did use the power and influence that derive therefrom, not to his personal advantage, however (though there were some who did not always see it that way), but, as we shall have occasion to note several times later on, in assuming responsibilities for advancing science and its institutions, in helping others, in attempting to influence political events, and in trying to promote a better understanding of science in the world at large.

As I have seen myself, social class never affected Bohr's relations with his fellow men. He was in the best sense a simple man.

Notes on sources concerning personal data

All over Denmark one finds excellently kept records of principal biographical data. The main sources are the following.

1. The *Kirkebog*, the church record, kept and preserved by every Lutheran parish church. A parent must see to the registration of a child, right after birth, in the *Kirkebog* corresponding to his parish of residence. He or she does so regardless of his or her religious affiliation, since the Lutheran Church, being the State Church, keeps birth records as a matter of civil government assignment. (The non-separation of Church and State causes the Danes no pain.) The sex, but not necessarily the name, along with the parents' names and legal residence are recorded at that time. Ved Stranden belongs to the parish of the Holmens Kirke, the church where for generations royal marriages have taken place. Accordingly Jenny Bohr is registered in Holmens *Kirkebog*.[21] Niels, however, is registered[23] in *Garnisonskirken*, the Garrison Church, for reasons I shall come back to in the next chapter.

2. The *Borgerlig Vielsesbog*, a record of civil marriages along with biographical data of the newly-weds. This is kept in City or Town Hall Archives.

3. *Københavns Politis Mandtaller*, a police record of every person's residence. Up till 1924 the police delivered twice a year a sheet to every *house*, on which all residents were obliged to be registered.

4. *Krack's* (or *Krak's*) *Vejviser*, a directory of Copenhagen, which includes the names and residences of all inhabitants. It was begun in 1770, and in 1862 Thorvald Krack (or Krak) acquired exclusive publication rights. At one time, it was printed twice a year.

References

1. H. E. Langkilde, *Mellem byen og Bremerholm*, Arkitektens Forlag, Copenhagen 1984. Describes the history of the site, the building, and its early inhabitants.

2. O. Schmidt, *Det Kongelige Norske Videnskabernes Selskab, Matrikkel* 1760–1960, Sentrum Trykkeri, Trondheim 1960.

3. All these and other details are found in *Christian Fredrik Gottfred Bohr, et Mindeskrift*, by Dr I. Neumann, bishop of Bergen's diocese, Chr. Dahl, Bergen 1833.

4. P. G. Bohr, *Historisk Udsigt over Tilstanden i Danmark for 300 Aar siden*, published by Rønne's Lærde Skole 1836.

5. See the recollections of his pupil the later literary critic George Brandes, *Levned*, Vol. 1, p. 53, Gyldendal, Copenhagen 1905.

6. V. Bergsøe, *De forbistrede Drenge*, Gyldendal, Copenhagen 1898.

7. H. G. C. Bohr, *Lykkens ABC, eller allernyeste Drømmetavle, hvorefter, som Skræddersvendens Exempel viser, aldrig kan tabes i Lotteriet. Skreven til Trost, Husvalelse og Haab for Dem, der havde sat deres Formue overstyr ved Lotterispil, saa og til Fornøjelse og Nytte for Andre*, published by Selskabet for Trykkefrihedens rette Brug, Copenhagen 1838.

8. J. Bock, *Ugeskrift for Læger*, No. 6, 1911.

9. C. Bohr, *Ann. der. Phys. und Chem.* **27**, 459, 1886.

10. This is the reaction $HbO_2^- + H_2O + CO_2 \rightarrow HbH + HCO_3^- + O_2$. See K. E. Rotschuh, *Geschichte der Physiologie*, p. 209, Springer, Berlin 1953; also articles in *Nature*, **220**, 1122, 1968; **222**, 1227, 1240, 1969. For the role of August Krogh in this discovery, see J. T. Edsall, *J. Hist. Biol.* **5**, 205, 1972.

11. Documents in the Archives of the Nobel Committee, Karolinska Institute, Stockholm.

12. C. Bohr's scientific oeuvre was reviewed by R. Tigerstedt, *Skand. Arch. f. Physiol.* **25**, V, 1911.

13. *Illustreret Tidende* 1911, No. 20.

14. Cf. T. Vogel-Jørgensen, *Bevingede Ord*, p. 306, Gads, Copenhagen 1963.

15. My best source about the Adler family is the collection of essays *Hanna Adler og Hendes Skole*, Gads Forlag, Copenhagen 1959.

16. P. Katz, *Jøderne i Danmark i det 17. Århundrede*, Reitzel, Copenhagen 1981.

17. *Borgerlig Vielse* 1871–81, p. 240, City Hall Archives, Copenhagen.

18. N. Bohr, *Fysisk Tidsskr.* **39**, 113, 1941. See also CW, Vol. 5, p. 140, footnote.

19. Margrethe and Aage Bohr, interview with S. Kuhn, 23 January 1963, NBA.

20. L. Yahil, *Et Demokrati paa Prøve*, p. 442, Gyldendal, Copenhagen 1967.

20a. *Illustrirte Tidende*, 15 December 1878.

21. *Holmens Kirkebog* 21–68, p. 13, No. 123.

22. Census Records, Landsarkiv for Eastern Denmark, Copenhagen.

23. Garnisons Kirkebog, No. 42, p. 127, No. 118.

24. *Danmarks Kultur ved Aar 1940*, Det Danske Forlag, Copenhagen, 1941–3. Bohr's essay opens Vol 1.

25. J. Rud Nielsen, *Physics Today*, October 1963, p. 22.

26. Th. Hauch-Fausbøll and S. Nygaard, *Patriciske Slægter*, Vol. 5, Vilhelm Trydes Forlag, Copenhagen 1930.

3

Boyhood

Denmark, Europe's oldest kingdom, is a small country. Its territory (not counting Greenland) is about one-third that of New York State. It had been much larger in earlier times. As late as the beginning of the seventeenth century, it had reigned over large areas, now part of Sweden, covering about one and a half times Denmark's present size. Those lands were lost to Sweden in the wars of 1645 and 1658 that brought Denmark on the verge of ruin. It still had Norway as a union partner, but had to cede that too, in 1814, after the Napoleonic wars. In the 1860s a third catastrophe took place.

It happened in the early days of the reign of Christian IX, which began when Niels' father was a young boy and ended while Niels was a university student. There may never have been a king with closer ties to Europe's other rulers; in fact he came to be known as the father-in-law of all Europe. His son Frederik became King Frederik VIII of Denmark. Son Vilhelm became King George I of Greece (and bought Ved Stranden 14). Daughter Alexandra married Edward VII and thus became Queen of England. Daughter Dagmar married Alexander III to become Tsarina Maria Feodorovna of all Russians. In 1906 grandson Carl was crowned King Haakon VII of Norway. Another grandson married the sister of German emperor Wilhelm II. All this took place in the decades of waning royal prerogative, or, in the words of Dinesen, in the eleventh hour of Danish aristocracy.[1]

In 1862 Bismarck had become prime minister of Prussia and at once began the unification and enlargement, under Prussian aegis, of all German lands. His first targets were Slesvig, a Danish duchy, and Holstein, of which the Danish king was duke but which belonged to the Roman–German empire. The history of that region is quite complex. Some time earlier, the Viscount Palmerston, prime minister of England, had written to Queen Victoria: 'The former history of Denmark and the two Duchies seems to be so confused and to be so full of irregular transactions, that some events may be quoted in support of almost any pretensions.'[2] Bismarck, keenly interested in the duchies' seaboards, so essential to Prussia's future as a maritime power, had put it bluntly in his low German: *'Dat mött wi hebben'* (that we must have).[3]

On 1 February 1864, combined Prussian and Austrian armies crossed the border. Denmark was defeated after heroic resistance, the last major battles fought on Danish soil. The resulting loss of about one-third of its territory together with one-third of its population was devastating. In the space of a few months it sealed the decline of Denmark (which had begun with the 1807–14 war with England) from an influential to a secondary European power. These losses were incomparably graver to Denmark than those of Alsace and Lorraine were to the French in the war of 1870–1. (After World War I the treaty of Versailles led to the return of parts of North Slesvig to Denmark.) It may be noted that right after the war David Adler, Niels Bohr's grandfather, contracted for the Danish public loan through Raphael & Son in London.

The official handbook[4] of Denmark, published by the Danish Foreign Office records:

After the war [of 1864] there was a period of paralysis, a common sense of being left behind in a small weak kingdom without any prospects . . . In many ways the shattering defeat underlay political developments right down to the Second World War . . . 1864 . . . was a stunning blow but it led eventually to a drastic settlement with the past, not only as regards foreign and domestic policies but also socially and culturally.

From those days dates Hans Peter Holst's expression[5] of a new Danish fortitude:

> For hvert et Tab der kan Erstatning findes
> Hvad udad tabes, det maa indad vindes.

(For every loss replacement can be found / what is outwardly lost must be inwardly gained.) These lines were reproduced on the commemorative medal of the 1872 industrial exhibition in Copenhagen. Referring to Denmark in the earliest years of the twentieth century, Maurice Egan, United States minister to Denmark, wrote: 'It is uplifting to see a little nation, struggling with obstacles that would have disheartened a less energetic people, remembering that art, literature, and music are as much a part of their natural life as the material interests.'[6] The little nation was clearly ready for a cultural hero.

That was the Denmark in which Niels Bohr grew up.

All those who have reminisced about Christian and Ellen Bohr's home have recalled a close-knit, harmonious, and stimulating family.

Margrethe Bohr, Niels' wife, has said: 'The children had such a very happy home life with this combination of a very intelligent and wise father and a very lovable mother. She was a wonderful woman. She wasn't merely lovable. She was also very clear in thought . . . The mother read very much to [the children]. When [Niels] was older he discussed scientific and other topics with his father. The father knew from the time when he was a small boy what was in him. I know my mother-in-law used to tell me that his father saw this when Niels was only a boy because he could answer so well little questions about volume and such things. This was as a little boy of five or six or something like that. I remember my mother-in-law told me his father always said, "People will listen to him; people will come to Niels and listen to him." And then he also said of himself, but this is only after a while. "Yes," he said, "I'm silver but Niels is gold."'[7] Niels himself has recalled: 'My father was a physiologist and he . . . understood that something was expected of me.'[8]

'[The Bohr family] were what we call good Danish citizens; the quite exceptional human qualities, in any case, came more from the Adler family, I think. The goodness, the interest in all people, that I think is a characteristic of the Adler family.'[7]

Paula Strelitz, Niels' second cousin, remembered: 'Christian Bohr was a man who instilled respect but was always friendly. His smile at a child came from his clear blue eyes which seemed to penetrate deeply into those he was talking to. The young felt his warm interest for their problems, his joy in discussing with them . . . He was the soul of his home where he found understanding and love.'[9]

Ole Chievitz, a friend of Niels' from their school days, said[9] after Ellen's death: Ellen Bohr cast her warm glow over everything, to such an extent that I could imagine that people who met her for the first time may have thought that it was an affectation, but after being together with her a few times one would find out that it was true and strong, like everything else in her personality. She was incomparably unselfish, not just as a mother who sacrifices everything for her children or other dear ones – no, she sacrificed most where the need was greatest, regardless how far people were from her own circle . . . she could wax enthusiastic about great personalities . . . she had quite determined opinions about crucial issues, and was good at taking initiatives and at acting forcefully.'

Niels' sister Jenny, who was two years older than he, studied history at the University of Copenhagen and also took courses in English at Oxford. Thereafter she gave private lessons for some years and, in 1916, passed an examination in pedagogy. She taught history and Danish at Hanna Adler's school and at a school in Helsingør.[10] Otherwise I know rather little about her. 'When she grew up she was always a nervous child. She was not as healthy as the [other children] in that way; [her mother] had a very difficult birth with her. In any case, she was nervous and caused, in that way, a lot of anxiety. However, she went through school and was very able. She had a very nice personality also, but her nerves gave her difficulty later in life in dealing with other people . . . She never married . . . she was very interested in teaching – that was all she did. She didn't do much work because she didn't feel so well always.'[7] (See further (18a).)

A central figure in Niels' life was his brother Harald, younger by a year and a half, who became an outstanding mathematician. He died in 1951, aged 63. According to a school friend of both, 'The relationship between the two brothers was the most beautiful imaginable. Niels had other good friends during his boyhood but Harald was his only real friend and confidant. (I believe this was mutual.) They admired each other, Niels counted himself for nothing and Harald for everything – and vice versa.'[11] They had their private games. 'As a boy Harald had hit upon the idea that he and Niels should take turns teasing each other. "Now I begin," said Harald. It did not last long before Niels begged, "Oh Harald, stop it, stop it." "All right, then it is your turn." But Niels' imagination in this respect (limited by his complete lack of malice) could at most lead him to accuse Harald of having a dirty spot on his pants, or something like that.'[9] This recollection conforms to my own impression that teasing was not part of Niels' nature.

The close brotherly ties remained as they grew up. 'When Harald became engaged, he decided that the best topic of conversation with his fiancée was Niels; he spoke of his genius, his lack of shortcomings, his thoughtfulness toward him, etc. When the young lady met Niels, he took her into another room after a few minutes and confided in her how wise, helpful, and unique Harald was, what his brother meant to him.'[9] In matters of science, '[Niels] always wanted to discuss things with Harald; he always liked to hear Harald's reaction to everything.[7]

Any impression that Niels was the more passive of the two may be dispelled by the story from Niels' childhood which Oskar Klein, later one of his earliest scientific collaborators, heard told. '[One day the brothers'] mother heard some very violent sounds from the boys' room and saw that Niels was on top of Harald, saying "You won't believe!" And they were discussing some theoretical question. And he was a little like that all through his life.'[12] Harald never ceased to tease Niels, and later 'was very open about criticizing and even laughing at his brother and his naïveté in political affairs.[13]

When I saw the brothers together, it struck me more than once that one could see in Harald's face – but not in Niels' – some traits of his Jewish ancestry. I have been fortunate enough to witness their affectionate ways, both in Copenhagen and in Princeton when they both spent the spring term of 1948 at the Institute for Advanced Study. By then Harald was a leading mathematician,[14] highly influential both in Denmark's academic world and in international mathematics. 'Once Harald was asked why he was one of the greatest mathematical lecturers in the world while Niels was such an unsuccessful public speaker. He answered, "Simply because at each place in my lecture I speak only about those things which I have explained before, but Niels usually talks about things he means to explain later."'[15]

In April 1947 the mathematics students at the University of Copenhagen arranged a special meeting to celebrate Harald Bohr's 60th birthday. In the course of a speech he gave on that occasion, Harald said of Niels: 'I cannot help saying – this, by the way, cannot be a surprise to anyone who has known me – that I feel a greater debt of gratitude to him than to anyone else for all that he has meant right from earliest youth for my whole outlook both as a scientist and a person.' [16]

In November 1962, the month of his death, Niels said of Harald: 'He was in all respects more clever than I. He was a great mathematician, you know.'[8]

At the time Christian Bohr married Ellen Adler he was assistant to Professor Peter Panum, the founder of modern physiology in Denmark, and lived[17] in the assistant quarters of the *Kirurgisk Akademi* (Adademy of Surgery) on Bredgade, at that time 'the city's most fashionable street . . . with mansions on both sides.'[18] The building, No. 62, dates from 1787 when it became the seat of *Det Kongelige Kirurgiske Akademi.* From then until 1842 it was a separate institution for the education and training of surgeons. Thereafter, it was taken over by the university and until 1942 served as its anatomical institute. Since 1946 it has housed *Københavns Universitetets medicinsk historisk Museum.*

After their marriage the young couple settled at Rosendalsvej (now Slagelsegade) number 3 (according to the police records[17] of May and December 1882). In 1883 Christian went (for the second time) to Leipzig to work in Carl Ludwig's laboratory of physiology. Until December of that year no record of residence is found in the standard sources, indicating that Ellen had gone with him to Leipzig and that daughter Jenny was born (at Ved Stranden 14, in March) during a relatively brief visit by Ellen to her mother's home.

There now followed a two year period in which the Bohr family moved to and fro. Records[17] show that in December 1883 and May 1884 they resided at Ved Stranden 14. In November 1884 and May 1885 we find them located at the apartment house Bredgade 58. That is also their legal address given in the *Kirkebog* of *Garnisonskirken* (Bredgade lies in its parish) at the time (October) Niels was born, indicating that once more Ellen had gone to her mother's home (registered, as noted earlier, as Niels' place of birth) to give birth in comfort. The records of 1 November show[17] that the whole family lived at Ved Stranden again. Thus Niels spent the first months of his life there, but not much longer than that.

On 2 May 1885 Panum died. Christian was one of three who applied for the vacant post. On 23 February 1886 his election as Panum's successor was announced; his rank was to be lektor. After considerable discussion he was also given the right to occupy Panum's professorial apartment at Bredgade 62.[19] That was the home where Harald was born and where he and Niels would live until after they had received their doctorates. That was the registered address on 20 June 1887, the day on which both Niels, 20 months old, and Harald, 2 months old, were *navngivet*, given a name, that is, the day on which their christian names were inscribed in a *Kirkebog*.[20]

A boyhood friend remembered: 'It was wonderful to be invited to the professor's home. The beautiful well-proportioned rooms with the comfortable furniture and the many books were pleasing, and many gay – and wild – games took place on the academy's broad stairs or in the court or yard.'[8] Margrethe Bohr has said: 'They had three maids . . . and they had an old nurse who was also so sweet . . . And Niels and Harald were so sweet to her, and Niels helped her to sew buttons on, and Harald played the violin while they did it.'[5] My friend K. M. Møller knew an old *Akademi* janitor who could recall the boys playing ball in the yard and occasionally beating each other up.

There was yet another home that played an important role in Niels' younger days: Nærumgaard, an estate ten miles north of Copenhagen and two miles west of the Øresund, already acquired in 1867 by his grandfather David Adler (whom Niels never knew). Of the beautiful house dating from 1781 it has been written: '[David Adler's] house was hospitable in patriarchal style.'[21] In Niels' day it was widowed grandmother Jenny who opened the house to her grandchildren and other family. It was there that for many years the Bohr family spent their summer vacations. At meals Jenny would sit at the head of the table in the large dining room, the grandchildren close to her, the rest of the family further away. One day a guest came with a bicycle that had broken down on the way. Niels, eleven or twelve at that time, at once began to take the bicycle apart, enlisting the other children as helpers. Repairs took time, the aunts were getting nervous and suggested taking the bicycle to a shop. But Christian said: 'Leave the boy alone. He knows what he is doing.' After three hours the work was done.[7]

It was stipulated in David Adler's will that after Jenny's death Nærumgaard should be donated to the community of Copenhagen as a home for underprivileged children. That is how the estate is used to this day. Walking toward the house one will see a tablet above its main entrance with the inscription: D. B. Adler og hustru Jenny Adler*/Børnehjem NÆRUMGAARD/Københavns Kommunes fra 1908.

Stately surroundings formed the setting for most of Bohr's life: Ved Stranden 14, the Kirurgisk Akademi, Nærumgaard, and later the Residence of Honor on the grounds of the Carlsberg Breweries. In his father's house were many mansions.

It is a ten minute walk from Bredgade 62 to Toldbodgade 10, now an office building, but until 1909 the site of Gammelholms Latin- og Realskole, where

Niels and Harald began their formal education all the way to their Studenterexamen, which, if passed, entitles pupils to enter the University. On 1 October 1891 Niels started[23] school in Gammelholm's new quarters. (The school had existed elsewhere since 1872, but in the preceding May it had been festively opened on Toldbodgade.) One week later Niels was baptized.

'Neither of his parents were religious. I don't think they went to church,' Margrethe Bohr has said.[7] And recalling a childhood recollection of Niels: 'He said, "I think of a little boy whose father took him by the hand and took him to the church to listen on Christmas eve." And then he said also, "I think his father took the little boy to the church so that he shouldn't feel different from all other boys. And his father never said anything about religion to him – not anything!"'

The idea of baptism came from Niels' mother. Margrethe again: 'Then they got christened later. My mother-in-law was a little weak in health, and she got suddenly worried that they should have troubles. It's no problem now, but it was then. It could be then a little problem if perhaps you were the only one in the class who hadn't been christened, and so on.'[7] So it came to pass that on 6 October 1891, all three children, Jenny, aged $8\frac{1}{2}$, Niels, aged 6, and Harald, aged $4\frac{1}{2}$, were baptized in *Garnisonskirken*.[24]

Reminiscences* of two classmates give us a picture of Niels' school days.

'In those years Niels was tall, rather coarse of limb, and strong like a bear. He was not particularly handsome. He was called *Tykke*, the fat one, even though he was not any fatter than other boys. Even then, however, he had strong, slightly hanging, jowls; that must have been the reason for the nickname. From those days I also remember Niels' beautiful eyes which on occasion could have a "distant" look.

'In those years he was definitely not afraid to use his strength when it came to blows during the break between classes. I do not remember what we fought about, but Niels acquired the reputation of a strong boy, a violent boy, one might say, for during all of his adolescence he had difficulty in gauging the consequences of his activities. He would mete out uncontrolled "black eyes", things like that. He has beaten me up innumerable times. He regretted those actions after he had calmed down.'

'Niels' impulsiveness also became manifest when one told him that this or that was not allowed. I remember the time that this challenge led to a carefully torn up psalm book being scattered over the playground from the

* These were written half a century later, in 1952[25] and 1963[11] respectively, and therefore are mellowed remembrances. I present next a composite selection of these two recollections (which on the whole are compatible), interspersed with a few comments by others.

second floor; and another time when an enormous bag filled with orange peel and other delicacies was kicked around the class room.

'Niels may have been wild those years but he also was a conscientious pupil. He did well at school. I do not remember whether he was ever number one in class, but there were a couple of other boys who used to battle for first and second place. I would put him somewhere among numbers 3–4–5 in a class of 20. I have the impression that he was not ambitious, and was not driven to his achievements by this quality (or burden). I seem to remember to have heard that he was a bit slow in his earliest development, with regard to speaking and reading. In any event, that was before my time. I can only remember him as capable, and that in all areas. He undoubtedly had special gifts for mathematics and physics, but he also had interests in and a feeling for subjects such as history and natural history. It was otherwise with languages. It was the general practice that in the break before the French hour the assignment was translated by a pupil with a talent for languages. In that respect I remember Niels as an attentive listener, and I do not think that his Latin was particularly error free either. He had absolutely no gift for singing, but our singing teacher stressed that, even if he could not sing, he was very good at marking time.

'I do not recall what Niels read in his spare time. I only remember that in his very young years he lent me his treasure, the complete Indian Stories by Cooper. From a little later I remember his deep knowledge of Icelandic Sagas.

'His handwriting was poor – even as a boy.' Also, 'spelling was not his strong suit' and he often wrote incorrectly.'[7] But 'he thought very quickly and I remember several occasions when his ideas came faster than his ability to apply the sponge to the blackboard. This resulted in the erasing with his fingers or his arms when his thoughts demanded new figures or numbers. Neither he nor the blackboard looked good afterwards.'

'In our time . . . pupils had to recite poems which they had to learn by heart. Niels had special gifts for this art, just as his choice of poetry was unusual and good . . . I was impressed when during the Danish hour he recited by heart a long poem by Ibsen . . . There is no doubt that Niels had a lyrical and rhythmical sense and I would think that those who would know how to unravel the thread might find a connection between the imagination which lay behind his ways of reciting poetry and the imagination which in later years played a great role in his scientific achievements . . . He could be dreamy or absent-minded when he felt so inclined, but this was not a dominant trait.

'Niels had good skills with his hands, even though, because of a certain clumsiness, this did not always end without pain or injury. In school we had classes in wood and metal work. In addition Niels and Harald had good equipment at home, including a lathe for metal work. Pretty fine things were produced with the help of those tools.

'In physical exercise he was one of the best . . . his strength helped him there . . . he was considered a good soccer player which did not prevent him from falling incessantly over his own legs . . . he was considered clumsy . . . did not have control over his legs when going down the stairs, but almost fell down the stairs.' An anecdote: Physical exercise teacher Swendsen, ex-sergeant, was sick at one time; Sergeant Pedersen was to substitute for him. In the first hour Pedersen took one of the students aside and asked whether Swendsen beat his pupils a lot – because he would like to educate in Swendsen's spirit.

'Niels was no "lion" at school balls . . . he had not much interest in the weak [sic] sex . . . I do not recall that he was ever given a part in school plays.

'During his school years Niels did not have especially close friends, with the exception of Ole Chievitz; for six years they shared a desk.' When Christian and his family moved to Bredgade 62, Johann Chievitz, lektor (later professor) of anatomy was already living there. His son Ole entered Gammelholm Skole in 1907, in the sixth grade.[23] He later became a surgeon and professor of medicine. He will be remembered in Danish history as one of the leaders of the Danish Resistance during World War II (21b). At his funeral, in 1946, Niels Bohr spoke movingly of his old friend.[26]

'In the course of time more and more boys left school and in the last two years only eight pupils were left. Niels and five others chose the mathematical branch. He always did very well even with the most difficult problems. The mathematics teacher was quite impressed with and almost afraid of him – perhaps his own grasp was not that firm.' Perhaps even then Niels understood the virtues of weak teachers; he certainly did so later. His son Aage recalled: 'Always when we complained, with regard to our children, that the teachers were not good enough he would say, "Well, one of the biggest impressions on children can be when they suddenly realize that the teacher doesn't understand the subject." '[7]

'Niels was equally good at physics. There he was ahead of the textbook and, to my great astonishment, told me that this or that in the book was nonsense. "What will you do if such a point comes up in the final examination?" I asked. "Explain of course that this is all bosh, that the phenomena need to be interpreted quite differently. I was almost horror struck by such audacity, but fortunately his examination questions dealt with something about which Niels agreed with the book.

'Then came the final examination, in those days taken in white tie and tails. We had twelve oral and four written exams. Niels passed with honors (udmærkelse).

'In his school days Niels Bohr was a quite ordinary gifted boy, without smugness. In his very young years he could be quite shy; but that passed. When he left school he was a promising young honours student, for the rest a young man like the rest of us.'[27]

References

1. I. Dinesen, Copenhagen season, in *Last tales*, Random House, New York 1975.
2. Lord Palmerston, letter to Queen Victoria, 23 October 1850, quoted in H. C. F. Bell, *Lord Palmerston*, Vol. 2, p. 7, Longmans, Green, London 1936.
3. M. F. Egan, *Ten years near the German frontier*, p. 233, Doran, New York, 1919.
4. *Denmark, an official handbook*, Press and Cultural Relations Department, Ministry of Foreign Affairs, Ed. B. Rying, English transl. R. Spink. 15th edn, Copenhagen 1974.
5. T. Vogel-Jørgensen, *Bevingede Ord,* Gads Forlag, Copenhagen 1963.
6. Ref. 3, p. 145.
7. Aage and Margrethe Bohr, interview with T. S. Kuhn, 23 January 1963, NBA.
8. N. Bohr, interviewed by T. S. Kuhn, L. Rosenfeld, A. Petersen, and E. Rüdinger, 1 November 1962, NBA.
9. Paula Strelitz, untitled and undated typed MS, NBA.
10. A. S. Bering Liisberg, *Studenterne 1903*, Berlingske Bogtrykkeri, Copenhagen 1928.
11. A. V. Jørgensen, *Naturens Verden*, 1963, p. 225.
12. O. Klein, interviewed by J. L. Heilbron and L. Rosenfeld, 15 July 1963, NBA.
13. L. Rosenfeld, interviewed by T. S. Kuhn and J. L. Heilbron, 22 July 1963, NBA.
14. For his oeuvre see, *H. Bohr, collected mathematical works*, 3 vols. Dansk Matematisk Forening, Copenhagen 1952.
15. R. Courant, NBR, p. 303.
16. Ref. 14, Vol. 1, p. XXXIII.
17. *Københavns Politis Mandtaller*, City Hall Archives, Copenhagen.
18. *København, Før og Nu*, Vol. 3, Ed. S. Aakjær, Hassings Forlag, Copenhagen 1947.
19. *Aarbog for Kjøbenhavns Universitet 1881–1882*, pp. 102–5, 109–112, Schultz, Copenhagen 1883.
20. *Garnisonskirkebog*, No. 42. Niels: p. 127, No. 118: Harald: p. 159. No. 47.
21. *Hanna Adler og hendes Skole*, Gads Forlag, Copenhagen 1959.
22. *Husmoderens Blad*, 9 August 1909.
23 See *Gammelholms Examenprotokol* for 1903.
24. For Niels and Harald see Ref. 20; for Jenny see *Holmens Kirkebog* 21–68, p. 13, No. 123.
25. A. Berlème, Små erindringer om Niels Bohr, typed MS, dated January 1952, NBA.
26. N. Bohr, *Ord och Bild*, **55**, 49, 1946; repr. in *Ole Chievitz*, Nordisk Boghandel, Copenhagen 1956.
27. For more on Bohr's boyhood see NBR, pp. 11–37.

4

Toward the twentieth century: from ancient optics to relativity theory

(a) 1903

The year was 1903. The Wright brothers had launched the first successful manned airplane flight. Henry Ford had founded his motor company. The first Tour de France had been run and the first World Series in baseball had been played (Boston beat Pittsburgh). Paul Gauguin and Camille Pissarro had died, and Pablo Picasso was in his blue period. Copenhagen had its first Social Democratic mayor and its first motorized taxicab. Niels Ryberg Finsen had become the first Dane to win a Nobel Prize, in medicine.

As to the world of physics in 1903, Joseph John Thomson had published his *Conduction of Electricity through Gases*, a book based on his discovery, a few years earlier, of the first subatomic particle, the electron. The Nobel Prize in physics for that year had been shared by Henri Becquerel 'in recognition of the extraordinary services he has rendered by his discovery of spontaneous radioactivity' and Pierre and Marie Curie 'in recognition of the extraordinary services they have rendered by their joint researches on the radiation phenomenon discovered by Professor Henri Becquerel'. Ernest Rutherford, the MacDonald professor of physics at McGill University in Montreal, was wondering[1] how one gram of radium could give out sufficient energy during its life to raise five hundred tons a mile high. Together with Frederick Soddy he had introduced the term 'atomic energy' for the first time.[2] One hydrogen atom was believed to contain about a thousand electrons.[3] Josiah Willard Gibbs, the sage of Yale, had died that spring. Ludwig Boltzmann had succeeded the ailing Ernst Mach as professor of the history and theory of inductive sciences at the University of Vienna. Einstein, working on a trial basis as technical expert third class at the Patent Office in Bern, had married and written a not very memorable paper on statistical physics. Heisenberg, Dirac, and Pauli were toddlers, Schrödinger was attending the Gymnasium in Vienna, and Niels Bohr had entered the University of Copenhagen to commence his studies in physics.

It was an ideal moment for an aspiring young man to enter the field. Half a century of laboratory research had generated an unparalleled backlog of data that demanded understanding. Very recent experiments had brought to light entirely new kinds of physical phenomena. The great twentieth century upheavals that were to rock physics to its foundations had barely begun. The era of classical physics had just come to an end.

All these novelties were to leave their mark on Bohr's scientific career. It is therefore appropriate to sketch briefly the status of physics at the beginning of the twentieth century.

With the advantage of almost a century's hindsight, it is not all that difficult to recognize the period at issue as one clearly rich not only in major advances but also in unresolved questions and budding paradoxes. Yet in 1871 James Clerk Maxwell from Cambridge, one of the leading physicists of that time, had found it necessary to sound these words of caution: 'The opinion seems to have got abroad that in a few years all the great physical constants will have been approximately estimated, and that the only occupation which will then be left to men of science will be to carry on these measurements to another place of decimals ... But we have no right to think thus of the unsearchable riches of creation, or the untried fertility of those fresh minds into which these riches will continue to be poured.'[4] As had happened before and as will happen again, it was far less obvious to most of those in the midst of events how acute the state of their science was. Perhaps the main cause for this recurrent phenomenon is the physicists' inclination to protect the corpus of knowledge as it exists at any given time, to extend rather than modify the areas where order appears to reign.

I shall not endeavor to catalog in their fullness every problem in physics that had accumulated around the turn of the century, but to focus on two main areas that have a more direct bearing on what is to follow: the roads to the theory of relativity, the subject of this chapter, and to the quantum theory, the subject of the next chapter. I shall leave a third area, the structure of matter, for Chapters 7 and 8. Spectacular progress on all these topics had been made during Bohr's high school and student years. It will add to the perspective, however, to start this cursory sketch much earlier.

(b) The nature of light; beginnings

Light, long believed to have been created on the first day, now is known to have been present since the first split microsecond after creation. The study of light originated from inquiry and speculation about the nature of vision. One of the oldest scientific questions asked by man must surely be: How do we see? We cannot know how far back that question goes. It is certain, however, that as long ago as two and a half millennia the problem was addressed by Greek thinkers. From that period date the beginnings of geometrical optics and perspective: the properties of light to reflect; to refract, that is, to be deflected when passing from one medium to another; and to propagate in a straight line from the light emitter to the eye. That description of the linkage between observed and observer was not clear in antiquity, however. Until after the Middle Ages it remained a point of debate whether vision comes about because something is traveling from the object to the eye or from the eye to the object, much like the manner in which a blind man finds his way by reaching out with a stick.[5] The ancient Greeks also considered the oldest known spectrum of colors – the rainbow, the sign of the covenant, the phenomenon which Aristotle had attempted, unsuccessfully, to interpret.[6]

After this brief reminder of the venerable age of optics, I jump about two thousand years and land in the seventeenth century, an era of 'change . . . so radical that classical optics was destroyed and disappeared for good. Today a book on optics written earlier than the seventeenth century would be incomprehensible to the majority of people.' [7] It befits a biography of Bohr to introduce that period with contributions by two Danish men of science.

The first of these, Rasmus Bartholin, a member of the powerful Bartholin family which played a dominant role in the University of Copenhagen for about a hundred and fifty years, was a professor of mathematics and medicine there.[8] In 1669 he published his observation of a new phenomenon, the first major piece of experimental physics research done in Denmark. Studying the transition of a beam from air into a crystal of Icelandic spar, he discovered double refraction: upon entering that crystal, light suffers not one deflection but two at once, the beam splits into two parts. 'I believe [that this phenomenon] can serve lovers of nature and other interested persons for instruction or at least for pleasure,' he commented.[9] It would take another 150 years before it would become clear how profoundly instructive double refraction actually is, as we shall find out a few pages on.

The other Dane, Ole Rømer, was Bartholin's amanuensis, later his son-in-law. Working at the recently established Royal Observatory in Paris he measured for the first time the velocity of light. Whether this velocity is finite or infinite had been much debated through the centuries, Aristotle, Kepler, and Descartes opting for infinity. Training a telescope on Io, Jupiter's innermost moon, Rømer found, in 1676, that this satellite shows a peculiar variation in its motion around Jupiter,[10] from which the value[11] 214300 kilometers per second for the light velocity could be deduced – about two-thirds the modern value. Rømer, a remarkably versatile man, became the Danish king's mathematician (mathematicus regius), professor of astronomy at the University of Copenhagen, and eventually chief of police of that city.

Rømer's work provides but one example of the marvels revealed by the new seventeenth century instrument, the telescope, a culmination of the development of lenses that had begun[12] in the late thirteenth century. 'So great was the upheaval caused by the triumph of the telescope that everything was new and changed.'[7]

There was inevitable resistance (of short duration) to that novelty. A new question had appeared that could not have occurred in antiquity: What do we mean when we say that we see? From those times onward the science of seeing would move ever further beyond the mere application of the naked eye.

At about the same time there occurred another major experimental development, this one due to Newton, unmatched in all of history for his combined achievements as instrument builder, experimentalist, and theorist. In 1666, at the age of 23, he began his experiments with sunlight falling on triangular glass prisms and showed for the first time that 'Colours are not *Qualifications of Light*, derived from Refractions, or Reflections of natural Bodies (as 'tis generally believed) but *Original and connate properties* . . . [white light] is not similar or homogenial but consists of Difform Rays, some of which are more Refrangible than others . . . [it is] a confused aggregate of rays indued with all sorts of colours, as they were promiscuously darted from the various parts of luminous bodies.'[13] By refraction, white light, up till then believed to be a pure substance, had been unfolded into the solar spectrum 'from the least refracted scarlet to the most refracted violet'.

Newton recorded all these findings in his profound and lucidly written *Opticks*,[14] a book which is also full of provocative qualitative ideas dealing with such subjects as the origins of the rainbow, of double refraction, and the meaning of Rømer's observations. Perhaps most interesting of all are his conjectures on the constitution of light, summarized[14] in his 29th Query: 'Are not the Rays of Light very small Bodies emitted from shining substances? . . . Nothing more is requisite for producing all the variety of Colours, and degrees of Refrangibility, than that the Rays of Light be Bodies of different Sizes, the least of which may make violet, the weakest and darkest of the Colours, and be more easily diverted by refracting Surfaces from the right Course; and the rest as they are bigger and bigger, may make the stronger and more lucid Colours, blue, green, yellow and red, and be more and more difficultly diverted.' Thus, Newton conjectured, light consists of material bodies, moving in straight lines through a homogeneous medium, with velocities independent of colour (since otherwise an aging beam of white light would change color), but with sizes (weights) that are different for different colors. From this hypothesis he was able to account quantitatively for a variety of optical phenomena including the laws of light refraction.

Not until the nineteenth century did flaws in Newton's picture become manifest. Two examples: In 1665 Grimaldi had stated that 'light is propagated or diffused not only directly, by refraction, or by reflection, but also in still a fourth way – by diffraction,' [15] a process in which light bends a bit when it passes through a hole in a barrier, so that the transition between light and shadow on a screen behind the barrier is slightly fuzzy. Newton's interpretation of this effect is not right. Nor was his prediction correct that the velocity of light is smaller in air than in liquids or solids.

(c) Particles or waves?

Meanwhile, almost simultaneously with Newton's suggestion of light as small bullets, a quite distinct proposal about the nature of light had been put forward. In 1690 Christian Huyghens had published his *Traité de la Lumière*,[16] intending to translate this work later from French to Latin, 'so doing in order to obtain greater attention to the thing'.[17] Huyghens, aware of the work by the 'eminent geometrician' [18] Newton, proposed that light 'spreads, as Sound does, by spherical surfaces and waves: for I call them waves from their resemblance to those which are seen to be found in water when a stone is thrown into it'.[19]

These plausible analogies raise a crucial new question. A stone creates waves in water. Sound reaches us because some body in vibration propagates its disturbance by a sequence of collisions of air molecules that results in pressure waves traveling to our ears. What is the corresponding transmission for light waves? It cannot be a disturbance of air since light goes right through a vacuum. Instead, Huyghens postulated that it must be another form of matter, 'Ethereal matter',[19] that is, 'a material substance of a more subtle kind than visible bodies, supposed to exist in those parts of space which are apparently empty'.[20]

The notion of an all-pervasive ether (or aether) is old, going back at least to Plato. 'Nature's abhorrence of a vacuum was a sufficient reason for imagining an all surrounding aether ... aethers were invented for the planets to swim in, to constitute electric atmospheres and magnetic effluvia ...' [20] All these aethers faded away quietly. As Maxwell wrote in 1869: 'The only aether which has survived is that which was invented by Huyghens to explain the propagation of light.' [20] So it remained until 1905 when Einstein took matters in hand and dispensed with this last aether as well,[21] as we shall see in (g).

Let us return to the closing years of the seventeenth century when two views about the nature of light had just emerged: the corpuscular theory and the wave theory. It would become clear after the birth of quantum mechanics, in 1925, that both these theories contain elements of truth, though the particles would not resemble those of Newton nor the waves those of Huyghens. In 1700, however, these two theories had to be considered incompatible. A particle is at a given place at a given time (or at least its center is), while a wave is spread out in space at one time (think of a wave in water). In technical terms, particles are localized, waves are not. Hence, the two theories were mutually exclusive: they could not both be right. There were natural philosophers of the highest distinction, Hooke, Leibnitz, Euler, and, of course, Huyghens among them, who were strongly critical of the corpuscular picture. Newton's authority was so immense, however, that, all told, his views held the upper hand all through the eighteenth century.

So it remained until the beginning of the nineteenth century, when 'real progress was brought about by two young men of genius, neither of whom belonged to the academic world. One was an English physician, Thomas Young, and the other a French government civil engineer, Augustin Fresnel. Thanks to the extraordinary ideas of these two intruders, the corpuscular theory had become, within a few decades, of historical interest only, and the wave theory acquired fundamental importance in the physics of the nineteenth century.'[22]

The decisive turn began with Thomas Young's interpretation (1801)[23] of light interference, a phenomenon that had been known (though not by that name) to Newton[24] as well as Huyghens, but not understood by them. To illustrate what is at issue, consider what happens when we drop (not too far apart) *two* stones into a pond of water, each creating waves. Now, Young says,[25] 'Neither series of waves will destroy the other, but their effects will be combined: if . . . the elevations of one series coincide with those of the other, they must together produce a series of greater joint elevations [we say, the waves are in phase]; but if the elevations of one series are so situated as to correspond to the depression of the other, they must exactly fill up those depressions, and the surface of the water must remain smooth [we say, the waves are out of phase] . . . Now I maintain that similar effects take place whenever two portions of light are thus mixed; and this I call the general law of the interference of light.' When, at a given point, two light waves are out of phase they produce no light at all at that point: light superposed on light can yield darkness, a behavior evidently at variance with a corpuscular picture.

Such properties of light may not be familiar to the general reader. I therefore thought it might help to illustrate them with a few pictures. This also gives me the opportunity to introduce some simple concepts relevant not only to light but also to other topics that will come later.

Consider a violin string vibrating in a special way in which a 'pure' tone is generated. This corresponds to the 'pure' motion (known as a sine wave), shown in Fig. 1, in which the string moves between the positions OABCDE and OFBGDH. Only part of the string is drawn. The sequence of hills and troughs continues from O to the other fixed end point Z of the string. The distance OD is called the wavelength of the motion, denoted by the symbol

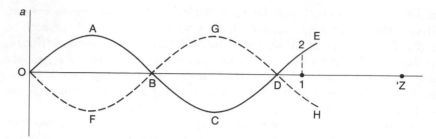

Fig. 1. A string OZ vibrating in a 'pure' mode between the positions marked by the continuous and the dashed curves (a denotes the amplitude).

λ. The quantity a, the wave amplitude, plotted in the vertical direction, is the displacement from the string's rest position, the straight line OZ, for example from point 1 to point 2. The amplitude varies from point to point along the string.

In Fig. 2(a) we see two pure waves of the preceding kind move in phase along the string (thin lines, one dashed). In this figure only one position of

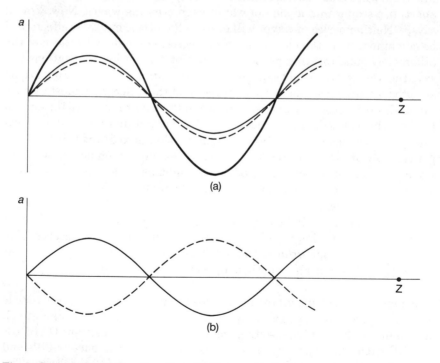

Fig. 2. Superposition of two 'pure' wave modes, one the continuous curve, one the dashed curve: (a) in phase; (b) out of phase. The thicker curve is the resulting total amplitude.

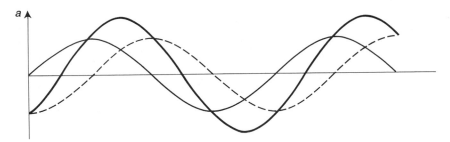

Fig. 3. Two wave modes intermediate between in and out of phase.

each wave is shown (corresponding to OABCDE in Fig. 1). The total amplitude at each point equals the sum of the 'thin' and the 'dashed' amplitude. The result is the 'thicker' amplitude in Fig. 2(a), still a pure wave. In Fig. 2(b) two waves move out of phase. As a result the string does not move at all; it stays at rest along OZ.

There exists, of course, a continuum of possibilities between 'in phase' and 'out of phase', an example being given in Fig. 3, where two waves enhance each other in some regions, partially cancel each other elsewhere, resulting in a non-pure wave. One can have more complicated situations in which two (or more) waves with different wavelengths interfere, again yielding non-pure waves.

What has the motion of a violin string to do with light? Not much, except that they are both vibrations and that the string actually illustrates some properties of light. For example, the case of the string at rest in Fig. 2(b) is the analog of two light waves out of phase producing darkness, zero net vibration.

I now return to the historical narrative.

Since Young had not expressed his correct interpretation of interference in rigorous mathematical terms, he left room for ridicule by the proponents of the corpuscular theory. It was the experimentalist and theorist Fresnel who in a series of memoirs (1815–17) formulated these ideas in a precise mathematical way,[26] and so was able for the first time to account quantitatively for such a wealth of available experimental data that the defenders of the particle picture were silenced. One problem he could treat – it is known as the Young experiment – is shown in Fig. 4. Light from a source passes through a slit that generates a beam moving in various directions, then hits a screen with two sufficiently narrow slits. The waves emerging from each slit hit a photographic plate on which they produce an interference pattern: lines of strongest intensity (waves in phase), the dark regions, surrounded by regions of weaker illumination (partially out of phase), no light in between (totally out of phase). Note that the light

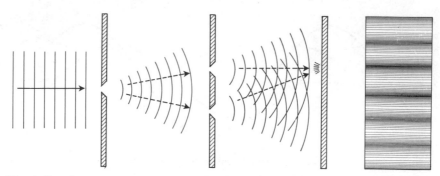

Fig. 4. Interference of light waves. A light beam passes through a slit, spreads in various directions, passes through two slits, then hits a screen, where it produces an interference pattern, seen frontally to the right.

intensity is proportional to the square of the net amplitude. Fresnel's theoretical considerations reproduced a quantitative description of such patterns, and also of Grimaldi's diffraction processes.

We also owe to Young and Fresnel the explanation of Bartholin's double refraction. In order to see their point, let us note that Huyghens' two analogies mentioned above, water waves and sound waves, have an important distinguishing characteristic. In the case of the stone hitting the water, or of the vibrating string, the wave propagates along the water (or the string), whereas the amplitude is perpendicular to that direction. Such waves are called transverse. A sound wave, on the other hand, propagating in a certain direction, is the result of a sequence of air compressions and dilations in that same direction: the amplitude and the propagation are parallel. Such waves are called longitudinal. What about light? Huyghens thought it was longitudinal. In 1817 Young suggested, however, that light waves are at least in part transverse.[27] Shortly thereafter, Fresnel showed (I omit all details) that transverse waves are necessary to account for double refraction. In actual fact light is purely transverse, but that took much longer to appreciate. For example, in the late 1890s the eminent theoretician Boltzmann still believed that light consisted of both transverse and longitudinal vibrations.[28]

(d) Color, visible and invisible

Until into the seventeenth century the belief was widespread that light was something distinct from color, that light itself was colorless. Rather it was believed that a separate emanation, guided by luminous rays, traveled from the object to the viewer's eye. The white light from the sun acquired color when it illuminated bodies, one thought.[29]

There were some, however, who argued that color was an intrinsic property of light, Grimaldi for example, in the seventeenth century. (Huyghens in his *Traité*[15] did not deal with color.) Matters were set straight in Newton's conclusions[30] derived from his experiments with prisms: 'All homogeneal light has its proper colour answering to its degree of refrangibility . . . colour cannot be changed by reflections and refractions.' Here we have an operational definition of homogeneal, now called monochromatic, light: it is a mode of light that cannot be decomposed further by prisms. Monochromatic light of one kind or another is defined by the amount it bends when passing through some fixed kind of prism. Distinct kinds of monochromatic light correspond to distinct colors. 'The homogeneal light and rays which appear red, or rather make objects appear so, I call rubrific or red-making, those which make objects appear yellow . . . I call yellow-making . . . and so of the rest.' It was clear to Newton that color is to light what pitch is to sound. Objects exposed to sunlight, a mixture of colors, appear to have a specific color because of selective action: a flower 'is red' because it absorbs all but red light and reflects the rest; an object is white because it reflects everything, black because it absorbs nearly all colors; and so on.

Newton's list of colors had seven entries: red, orange, yellow, green, blue, indigo, and violet. As was mentioned earlier, light corpuscles corresponding to distinct colors were, he said, of distinct sizes, a supposition never documented by experimental fact. Along with the rapid nineteenth century development of the wave theory, it became evident that the distinguishing parameter of monochromatic light actually is its wavelength, and that white light is a superposition of a range of wavelengths. Also from that century dates the beginning of spectroscopy as a quantitative experimental science. That is to say, the wavelength λ corresponding to some specific color was actually measured. It was found that these lengths range from about 0.35×10^{-4} cm (centimeters) for violet to twice that much for red – values of the order of a million times smaller than those for sound wavelengths in the median range.

Another quantity that characterizes a monochromatic wave is its frequency, defined as the number of wavelengths, or cycles, that it travels per second, and denoted by the symbol ν. Evidently the product of λ and ν equals the velocity v with which the wave moves. For light, $v = 3 \times 10^{10}$ cm s^{-1} (centimeters per second). Thus for violet light ν is about 4×10^{14} cps (cycles per second), etc. I shall come back in (8d) to more details on the structure of the visible spectrum.

Now it came to pass, once again for the first time in the nineteenth century, that new kinds of light were discovered, with wavelengths much larger than red and much smaller than violet.

It had, of course, been known since time immemorial that sunlight heats up bodies. In 1800 William Herschel asked: How does this property depend on color? To find out he first generated a solar color spectrum, then exposed a thermometer successively to various small spectral portions. Moving from violet to red he found an increase in heating. When placing his thermometer beyond the red he found an even higher reading, however! 'The full red falls still short of the maximum of heat; which perhaps lies even a little beyond visible refraction . . . radiant heat will at least partly, if not chiefly, consist, if I may be permitted the expression, of invisible light; that is to say, of rays coming from the sun that have such a momentum as to be unfit for vision.'[31] Herschel had discovered infrared light.

While terms like invisible or (also used in those days) black light may seem self-contradictory, they actually are not. As with the telescope, the meaning of 'seeing' was extended; you see infrared with a thermometer. If, however, infrared radiation truly deserves to be called light, one should demand that it reflect, refract, interfere, etc., in a way qualitatively similar to – though possibly quantitatively different from – visible light. In other words, extensions of the good old spectrum of light should be consolidated by application of a general rule of physics, the horse principle: If it looks like a horse, feels like a horse, and smells like a horse, then it is a horse. The first to confirm experimentally the reflective and refractive properties with the help of prisms, mirrors, and, of course, thermometers, was Herschel himself. He reported on 219 experiments (all done in 1800), some with sunlight, some with 'red hot iron cooled till it can no longer be seen in the dark', some with 'culinary heat' (stoves), others with chimney fires. Herschel nevertheless remained curiously reluctant to accept his rays as an extension of the visible spectrum, but others rapidly took the point.[32]

One of these, Johann Ritter from Jena, repeated and confirmed Herschel's discovery and next raised a new question: If there is radiation beyond the red, why should the same not also be true beyond the violet? Thermometry would be of no help there, but there was another criterion. It had been known since the days of the alchemists that sunlight blackens certain silver salts. As can be seen from his writing, Ritter also knew from others that violet is the most effective blackener among the visible rays. Accordingly he exposed to the solar spectrum a strip of white paper covered with silver chloride and found (1801)[33] that the blackening was even more pronounced *beyond* the violet. He had 'seen' ultraviolet radiation by means of what is, essentially, a photographic plate. As time went by, others applied the horse principle to show that these rays too are light.

In terms of frequencies, ultraviolet brings us to the region of 10^{16} cps, infrared down to 10^{13} cps. There the story still does not end. Niels Bohr was a young boy when the infrared region was extended to much lower frequencies.[33a] He was in high school when Röntgen discovered X-rays (1895, range around 10^{18} cps) and Villard found γ-rays (1900, 10^{20} cps). He was a Ph.D. when it was finally settled (by the same criteria mentioned above) that both these radiations are 'ultra ultraviolet light'.[34]

Still later even higher frequencies (up to 10^{32} cps, a billion times a billion higher than visible light) were found in cosmic radiation. In the other direction, beyond the infrared, lie microwaves (10^{12} cps), radar (10^{10} cps) and radio waves, from UHF (10^9 cps) to extreme long-range radio waves (10^2 cps, a million times a million lower than visible light).

I should explain next why it is much more sensible to refer to X-rays and γ-rays, and also to radar and radio waves, as electromagnetic waves rather than as light.

(e) Of Maxwell's theory, Hertz's experiment, and the definition of classical physics

In 1864 Maxwell published a memoir[35] entitled *A Dynamical Theory of the Electromagnetic Field*. Its aim: 'To explain the [electromagnetic] action between distant bodies without assuming the existence of forces capable of acting directly at sensible distances. The theory I propose may therefore be called a theory of the Electromagnetic Field.' This description of forces in terms of fields was new. Earlier it had generally been assumed that forces such as those between two electrically charged particles exerted themselves instantaneously between them. Maxwell, on the other hand, considered this action to be transported by an electric field that is present at all points in space and time. The strength of the field and the direction in which it acts can be measured by placing a test body, a tiny charged particle, at the place and time of one's choice. Likewise a magnetic field is measured by its action on a tiny magnet. A familiar example is a compass, which measures the direction of the earth's magnetic field at some point in space and time. (It does not measure the field's strength. In order to do that, one would need an (almost) free test body, suspended on a long thin wire, for example.)

Einstein later wrote about this novel way of dealing with forces: 'Since Maxwell's time, Physical Reality has been thought of as represented by continuous fields . . . not capable of any mechanical interpretation. This change in the concept of Reality is the most profound and the most fruitful that physics has experienced since the time of Newton.'[36]

Maxwell's memoir represents the synthesis and culmination of contributions dating back to the eighteenth century, of men like Coulomb, Volta, Ørsted, Ampère, and above all Faraday, the greatest of the nineteenth century experimentalists.[37] Even a brief systematic account of their work lies beyond the scope of this book.[38] I shall single out only two instances. In 1820 Ørsted, Denmark's leading physicist in the first half of the nineteenth century, discovered that an electric current – a charge in motion – generates magnetic action, as is seen from the experimental fact that a compass needle changes direction when an electric current is made to pass through a nearby wire. (He published this result in Latin.[39]) He also coined the term electromagnetism to express that electric and magnetic phenomena are inseparably intertwined. This became even more evident when, in 1831, Faraday found the converse: a moving magnet generates electric action, inducing electric currents to flow in a nearby metallic wire.[40] Electric and magnetic phenomena are only separable when charges and/or magnets are at rest. Motion mixes them.

All these and many more experimental results from those earlier days can be seen, Maxwell showed, as consequences of 'field equations', his Maxwell equations, that describe the evolution in space and time of electric and magnetic fields generated by charges and magnets, at rest or in motion. In his language the Ørsted–Faraday findings can simply be phrased like this: An electric field changing with time generates a magnetic field, and vice versa.

Had Maxwell's memoir ended at this stage it would still be remembered as one of the greatest nineteenth century documents in theoretical physics. Maxwell went much further, however, most notably by showing that his electromagnetic equations also form the theoretical basis for optical phenomena. His argument proceeds in three steps.

Step 1. It had been shown by Ampère that Ørsted's results can be put (in modern terminology) in the following quantitative form, Ampère's law. A moving electric charge e creates a magnetic field with strength B. The resulting magnetic force acting on a nearby compass needle equals evB/c. Here v is the component of the charge's velocity which is perpendicular to B, and c is some other velocity, a quantity expressible, like v, in so many centimeters per second (cm s^{-1}). Also, c is a *universal constant*, that is, it is always the same velocity regardless how big e or v or B, or anything else, is. The magnitude and universality of c can be determined by experiments that measure the magnetic force for various choices of e, v, and B.

Maxwell's equations incorporate Ampère's law. The value of the constant c, *which necessarily appears in these equations*, remained (and still is) a piece of experimental input. In his memoir Maxwell quoted[41] the best experimental value known at that time: c equals 3×10^{10} cm s^{-1}.

Step 2. Measurements of the velocity of light had considerably improved since Rømer's time. Maxwell quoted[41] two experimental answers: 3.14 and 2.98×10^{10} cm s^{-1} (present best value: $2.99792458 \times 10^{10}$ cm s^{-1}). The obvious and tantalizing question arose: Why should the velocity of light be (practically) the same as Ampère's c?

Step 3. Maxwell was ready for this challenge. Consider, he said in essence, a region of space very far removed from charges or magnets. In that region there either are (practically) no electric and magnetic fields, or else there may be superpositions of pure electromagnetic waves propagating with the velocity c that, as said, appear in his equations:

[This] seems to show that light and magnetism are affections of the same substance and that light is an electromagnetic disturbance propagated through the field according to electromagnetic laws.[41]

These lines may well be the crowning statement in nineteenth century physics. They record the unification of electricity, magnetism, and light, and define light the way it is done to this day. Moreover light and its invisible extensions are predicted to be electromagnetic waves, propagating as shown in Fig. 5. The arrow marked c denotes the direction of propagation of the light wave. These waves are electromagnetic because they carry an electric field vibrating in the plane marked E and a magnetic field vibrating in H. Two years after Maxwell, the Danish physicist Ludwig Lorenz independently realized that light should be interpreted as electromagnetic waves.[42]

As is indicated in Fig. 5, the electric and magnetic fields are oriented perpendicular to the direction of the light ray and vibrate in planes perpendicular to each other. The same is true for a bundle of light rays moving parallel to each other. In general the electric and magnetic fields for different rays in the bundle *need* not be parallel to each other, however, though for each ray they are perpendicular to each other and to the ray direction. When these fields *are* parallel, we say that the bundle is (linearly) polarized.

Maxwell's picture of light was a prediction: the existence of electromagnetically created vibrations with the requisite properties had yet to be demonstrated experimentally. That was done in 1887, after Maxwell's death, by Heinrich Hertz. By means of oscillatory electric spark discharges, he managed to generate electromagnetic waves with frequencies of about 10^8 cps (wavelength 3 meters), a typical VHF frequency now used for

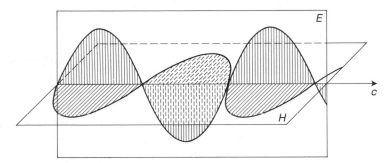

Fig. 5. A pencil of light moves in the direction c. The associated electric (magnetic) field vibrates in the plane marked E (H).

television. In a series of papers he showed that, like visible light, these waves reflect, diffract, interfere, are transverse, and propagate with the velocity c:

The described experiments appear, at least to me, to a high degree suited to remove doubt in the identity of light and waves.[43]

We are now ready to define what is meant by classical physics. It is a picture of the inanimate world ruled by Newton's mechanical and Maxwell's electromagnetic laws. It is a good picture. It enables us to build bridges and to calculate to very high precision the orbits of planets, spacecrafts, and moonshots. It also makes possible the design for electric lighting and heating, and of circuitry for radio, television, and computers. It is in fact a sufficiently adequate picture for comprehending very many physical phenomena encountered in daily life.

Yet closer inspection shows that classical physics has gross inadequacies. To pick but very few random examples, it does not explain why the sun shines, why a red flower selects for reflection only red light, why some substances are good conductors of electricity while others are insulators, how a photocell stops elevator doors from closing, how a transistor works. All such and countless other phenomena demand natural laws newer and richer than those that rule the classical world. These new laws should, however, not contravene those classical descriptions which, after centuries of struggle, were so successfully established. Much of what will follow is devoted to the new physics as it evolved during the twentieth century, most particularly to Niels Bohr's leading role in those developments.

Even before the twentieth century had begun there were indications that Maxwell's theory was flawed – not his electromagnetic field equations, but his accompanying picture for the mechanism of wave transmission.

(f) Trouble with the aether: the Michelson–Morley experiment

In 1864 Maxwell had written: 'We have some reason to believe, from the phenomena of light . . . that there is an aetherial medium filling space and permeating bodies, capable of being set in motion and of transmitting that motion from one part to another.'[44] Following distinguished predecessors, Maxwell assumed that an aether was necessary for understanding the propagation of electromagnetic waves through space. This aether transmits vibrations, just as the matter of which (in our previous example) the violin string is made: 'There can be no doubt that the interplanetary and interstellar spaces are not empty but are occupied by a material substance or body, which is certainly the largest, and probably the most uniform, body of which we have any knowledge.'[45] Lecturing on the aether in 1873, Maxwell said:

Interstellar regions will no longer be regarded as waste places in the universe, which the Creator has not seen fit to fill with the symbols of the manifold order of His kingdom. We shall find them to be already full of this wonderful medium; so full that no human power can remove it from the smallest portion of space, or produce the slightest flaw in its infinite continuity. It extends unbroken from star to star . . .'[46]

This panegyric may serve to underscore the contrast with the modern era in which the aether is completely abandoned.

There came a time when the existence of the omnipresent and elusive aether at last became a subject of experimental inquiry. The year was 1887, the same in which Hertz had confirmed Maxwell's electromagnetic theory of light. The place was Cleveland, Ohio. The scientists involved were Albert Michelson and Edward Morley (MM).

The experiment they performed was delicate and difficult. In order to appreciate their strategy, it is necessary to state in more detail what Maxwell meant by aether and to define more precisely than I have done so far the meaning he attached to the velocity of light c. The aether through which light was assumed to be propagated is an all-pervasive medium in a state of absolute rest. Maxwell's universal velocity c is the speed of light relative to this resting aether. Stars, not planets, were believed to be at rest relative to this resting aether. Thus the velocity c is the speed of light as measured by a hypothetical observer standing on a fixed star. The need for specifying a velocity relative to an observer is familiar from daily experience. Example: two men sit in a train. One of them gets up and walks forward with a velocity of 3 mph, as seen by the other man. A third man standing on a platform sees the train go by with a speed of 60 mph. To him the same walker moves forward with a speed of $60 + 3$ mph.

Back to light as seen by Maxwell. As said, the velocity c is the one registered by an observer on a fixed star ('on the platform'). An earthling actually measures the light produced by some fixed source at rest relative to the earth ('the other man on the train'). But the earth moves relative to the fixed stars, just as the train rushes past the platform. Hence our earthling will expect to observe a light velocity different from c; in fact he will anticipate that the light velocity is different for different directions of a light beam relative to the direction of the earth's motion. Why is the detection of such differences so delicate and difficult? because the earth velocity v is something like ten thousand times smaller than c. Moreover, as it happens, in the MM experiment an effect is looked for proportional to the square of the ratio v to c, that is, one needs an accuracy of one part in a hundred million, quite a difference compared to our example of $60 + 3$.

I shall forego all details of the actual experiments which can be found in numerous simple accounts.[47] As to the results obtained: as early as 1881 Michelson had attempted to measure the light velocity differences mentioned above, and found none! From this surprising negative result he concluded that there had to be something wrong with the underlying assumption of the aether:

The result of the hypothesis of a stationary aether is . . . shown to be incorrect, and the necessary conclusion follows that the hypothesis is erroneous.[48]

His subsequent experiment jointly with Morley,[49] performed with much improved precision, led to the same result: *the velocity of light is independent of the speed with which the light source moves relative to observer.*

It was an unexpected, bizarre, and disquieting turn of events. Why should the velocity of light on the moving earth follow rules different from that of a man on a moving train? In a lecture before the Royal Institution on 27 April 1900, Lord Kelvin referred to the MM experiment as 'carried out with most searching care to secure a trustworthy result' and characterized its outcome as 'a nineteenth century cloud over the dynamic theory of light'.[50] Some time later he wrote: 'Michelson and Morley have by their great experimental work on the motion of the aether relatively to the earth raised the one and only serious objection against our dynamical explanations.'[51]

Those lines were written in 1904, one year before Einstein's relativity theory restored sanity.

(g) In which classical physics comes to an end and Einstein makes his first appearance

The MM result defied logic – classical logic, that is. Something had to be wrong with the extrapolation of the 60 + 3 example to light. Some have tried to save the situation by what may be called conventional means, mainly by hanging on to the aether but defining its properties differently. All such attempts have been to no avail. The correct answer, given by Einstein, is that classical logic itself needs modification in terms of a radically new doctrine, now called the special theory of relativity.

As Einstein thus makes his first appearance in this story, the time is June 1905. He is twenty-six, six and a half years older than Niels Bohr who has just completed the second year of his university studies. He is German born but a Swiss citizen by now, employed as a technical expert third class in Bern. He is married and has a one year old son, Hans Albert, who is to end his life as a respected professor of hydraulic engineering in Berkeley, California. In the preceding four years he has published five scientific papers, some of which prepare him, but not the world, for his scientific outburst during the year 1905, large in quantity (six papers), spectacular in quality. His first publication of that year, completed in March, lays the foundations for the quantum theory of light, a contribution to which I shall turn shortly (5h). With his June paper on special relativity, Einstein becomes the first to strike the grandest broad theme of twentieth century physics: the need for reanalysis of the interpretation of measurements, in this particular case principally of distances in space, intervals in time, and addition of velocities.

I have written elsewhere[52] of the historical evolution leading to special relativity and shall not repeat myself here, bearing in mind also that relativity theory will not be a central theme in the present book. In particular I must abstain from discussing the role of Einstein's two most distinguished precursors, the Dutch physicist Lorentz and the French mathematician Poincaré. Nor shall I scrutinize once again the influence of the MM result on Einstein's thinking. I shall rather confine myself mainly to indicating the new interpretation of that experiment and the ultimate fate of the aether in the context of the new theory. To that end we should consider the two basic postulates of special relativity.

Postulate 1. All laws of physics take the same form for all observers in uniform motion (that is, with velocities constant in size and direction) relative to each other.

(Remark. The theory at hand is called *special* because of its specific reference to *uniform* relative motion. The extension of postulate 1 to the case of general relative motion is called general relativity. That theory, Einstein's greatest accomplishment and one of the highest achievements in all of science, will play no role in this book.[53])

Postulate 1 was nothing new for mechanics. Consider the basic Newtonian law of mechanics: a force acting on a particle equals the particle's mass times its acceleration. Acceleration means change of velocity with time. Acceleration therefore remains unaltered if we add a constant velocity to the observer's motion. In other words, since velocity does not enter in Newton's law, we can change the observer's velocity by a constant amount without changing the law.

The situation is utterly different for Maxwell's equations. As I have noted these imply Ampère's law according to which magnetic forces do depend on velocity. More generally, in these equations the light velocity c appears. The MM experiment implies that Maxwell's definition of c in terms of motion relative to the fixed stars will not do. Einstein's first postulate asserts that we should in fact refrain from giving a preferred status to the one type of observer who rests relative to the fixed stars. In his own words: 'The unsuccessful attempts to discover any motion of the earth relative to the "light medium" [the aether] lead to the conjecture that to the concept of absolute rest there correspond no properties of the phenomena.'[54] He does not so much say that there is no aether as that the aether concept is useless.

In his theory, 'the introduction of a "luminiferous aether" will prove to be superfluous.'[54] All that is good and well, but what about the MM experiment?

Postulate 2. The velocity of light in a vacuum is the same whether the light be emitted by a body at rest or by a body in uniform motion: we may say (though Einstein himself did not put it that way) that in special relativity the negative outcome of the MM experiment is elevated to the status of a postulate which, evidently, violates everyday intuition; it is in conflict with classical physics. The classical era had come to an end.

The second postulate implies that the formula for the 'classical sum' of two velocities $(60+3=63)$ cannot be generally valid. Closer analysis shows that in relativity theory the 'classical sum' formula for adding velocities needs to be replaced by a more general 'relativistic sum' formula, displayed in Ref. 55 of this chapter. From this new formula the following consequences can be drawn. First, the 'relativistic sum' of c and any other velocity equals c. Secondly, *the universal velocity* c *is the maximum velocity attainable.* More precisely, an object moving with a velocity less than c can never be accelerated to a velocity larger than c. Does that mean that I cannot speak of a velocity $c+17$ mph? Of course I can speak thereof, but, and this is the point, relativity theory predicts that no velocity measurement can ever yield the experimental answer $c+17$.

Results such as these came as a profound surprise, and, especially initially, were resisted by some of the classically minded.[56] On the other hand, it was soothing to realize that relativity does not upset classical intuition, because everyday experience deals with velocities that are small compared to the velocity of light. Consider once more the example of the man on the platform who sees the man on the train move with a velocity of $60+3=63$ mph. The relativistic sum rule[55] is universal, it applies to any two velocities. It predicts in fact that '63' is not right, the correct answer is actually one ten-thousandth of a billionth of a per cent less. Moral: in principle relativity changes everything; in practice you may ignore it at the level of everyday, classical experience, when objects move at low velocities. The same is true for other uncommon consequences of relativity not mentioned heretofore. Examples: a yardstick in motion relative to an observer appears shortened compared to what is measured by an observer moving with (is at rest relative to) the rod. A clock moving relative to an observer appears to run slower than a clock moving along with him. Again, these unfamiliar effects play no role in practice for small velocities.

Let us summarize. Einstein's abolition of the aether marked the end of the mechanical analogies initiated by Huyghens according to which aether is needed in order for light to propagate, just as sound propagation needs (for example) air. By dispensing with the aether, Einstein purified the meaning of the Maxwell equations, themselves unchanged, to the modern level of perfection. The aether in absolute rest is abandoned in favor of an absolute velocity, c. Classical physics forms a harmonious, though approximate, part of the fundamentally new world picture created by relativity theory.

Perhaps the most extraordinary aspect of Einstein's two relativity papers, the one from June and a brief sequel from September[57] is their level of perfection. They contain the full axiomatic basis of the theory. In particular they make clear from the outset the new position of classical theory: it is not an exact theory, to be sure, but unchanged for all practical purposes. All later contributions to special relativity may be considered elaborations of Einstein's two basic postulates.

Even before relativity appeared on the scene, developments in a quite different direction had taken place which, in their own distinct way, had signaled other limitations of the classical world picture: the earliest papers on the quantum theory had appeared. As we shall see next, the quantum theory, unlike relativity, caused monumental confusion in its early stages.

References

1. E. Rutherford, *Proc. Phys. Soc. London* **18**, 595, 1903.
2. E. Rutherford and F. Soddy, *Phil. Mag.* **5**, 576, 1903; see further IB, p. 115.
3. IB, p. 178.
4. *The scientific papers of James Clerk Maxwell*, Vol. 2, p. 241, Ed. W. D. Niven, Dover, New York.
5. See V. Ronchi, *The nature of light*, Harvard University Press, Cambridge, Mass. 1970.
6. R. C. Dales, *The scientific achievement of the middle ages*, Chapt. 5, University of Pennsylvania Press, Philadelphia 1978.
7. Ref. 5, p. 97.
8. *Prominent Danish scientists through the ages*, Ed. V. Meisen, p. 25, Levin and Munksgaard, Copenhagen 1932.
9. W. F. Magie, *A source book in physics*, p. 280, Harvard University Press, Cambridge, Mass. 1965.
10. Ref. 9, p. 335.
11. E. Bergstrand, *Handbuch der Physik*, Vol. 24, p. 6, Springer, Berlin 1956.
12. Ref. 5, p. 69.
13. I. Newton, letter to the Royal Society, 19 February 1671, *Phil. Trans. Roy. Soc.* **7**, 3075, 1672, repr. as I. Newton, *New theory about lights and colours*, Werner Fritsch, Munich 1965.
14. I. Newton, *Opticks*, 4th edn, repr. by McGraw Hill, New York 1931; also repr. in Ref. 9, p. 298 ff; the query on Light as small Bodies first appeared in the Latin edition of 1706. See also *The optical papers of Isaac Newton*, Vol. 1, *The optical lectures*, Ed. A. E. Shapiro, Cambridge University Press 1984.
15. Ref. 9, p. 294.
16. English transl. S. P. Thompson: *Treatise on light*, University of Chicago Press 1955; quotations are from this edition.

17. Ref. 16, p. vi.
18. Ref. 16, p. 4.
19. Ref. 16, p. 11.
20. Ref. 4, Vol. 2, p. 763.
21. For a detailed history of the aether up to 1905 see E. T. Whittaker, *A history of aether and electricity*, Vol. 1, Nelson & Sons, London 1951.
22. Ref. 5, p. 235.
23. See *Miscellaneous works of the late Thomas Young*, Ed. G. Peacock, Vol. 1, p. 179, Murray, London 1855, repr. by Johnson Reprint Corp., New York 1972.
24. Ref. 5, p. 182.
25. Ref. 23, p. 202.
26. Ref. 5, pp. 241–57.
27. Ref. 23, p. 383.
28. L. Boltzmann, *Populäre Schriften*, p. 196, Barth, Leipzig 1896. See also IB, Chap. 2.
29. See Ref. 5, pp. 114, 141, 142, 224.
30. Ref. 14, Book I, part 2, proposition II; cf. also Ref. 5, p. 170.
31. W. Herschel, *Phil. Trans. Roy. Soc.* 1800, p. 255. This and several subsequent papers on infrared, all dating from 1800, are reprinted in Vol. 2 of *The scientific papers of Sir William Herschel*, Ed. J. L. E. Dreyer, published by the Royal Society and the Royal Astronomical Society, London 1912.
32. For a discussion of Herschel's work and of his and others' reactions see E. S. Cornell, *Ann. Sci.* **3**, 119, 402, 1938; D. J. Lovell, *Isis* **59**, 46, 1968.
33. Ritter's paper is reprinted in *Die Begründung der Elektrochemie und die Entdeckung der Ultravioletten Strahlen*, p. 57ff., Ed. A. Hermann, Academisches Verlagsgesellschaft, Frankfurt am Main 1968.
33a. See SL, Chap. 19, section (a).
34. For X-rays see IB, Chap. 2. For γ-rays see IB, Chap. 3, section (b).
35. Ref. 4, Vol. 1, p. 526.
36. A. Einstein, in *James Clerk Maxwell*, p. 66, Cambridge University Press 1931.
37. For a guide to Maxwell's precursors see W. T. Scott, *Am. J. Phys.* **31**, 819, 1963.
38. For a detailed history see Ref. 21.
39. For an English version see Ref. 9, p. 437.
40. See Ref. 9, p. 473.
41. Ref. 35, p. 580.
42. L. V. Lorenz, *Det Dan. Vid. Selsk. Oversigt*, 1867, p. 26.
43. H. Hertz, *Ann. der Phys.* **31**, 421, 1887. This and other papers by Hertz are collected in *H. Hertz, Über sehr schnelle elektrische Schwingungen*, Ed. G. Hertz, Akad. Verlagsgesellschaft, Leipzig 1971; also in *Electric waves*, transl. D. E. Jones, Dover, New York 1962.
44. Ref. 35, p. 528.
45. J. C. Maxwell, *Encyclopaedia Britannica*, 9th edn, Vol. 8, 1878, repr. in Ref. 4, Vol. 2, p. 763.
46. Ref. 4, Vol. 2, p. 322.
47. See e.g. K. W. Ford, *Basic physics*, Chap. 19, Blaisdell, Waltham, Mass. 1968.
48. A. A. Michelson, *Am. J. Sci.* **22**, 110, 1881.

49. A. A. Michelson and E. W. Morley, *Am. J. Sci.* **34**, 333, 1887; *Phil. Mag.* **24**, 449, 1887; *J. de Physique* **1**, 444, 1888.
50. Lord Kelvin, *Baltimore lectures*, Appendix B, Clay, London 1904.
51. Ref. 50, p. vi; see further SL, Chap. 6, section (a).
52. SL, Chaps 6–8.
53. Its history and implications are discussed in SL, Chaps 9–15.
54. A. Einstein, *Ann. der Phys.* **17**, 891, 1905. I follow the English translation by A. I. Miller in *Albert Einstein's special theory of relativity*, Addison-Wesley, Reading, Mass. 1981. This book contains a step-by-step analysis of Einstein's paper.
55. The 'relativistic sum' of two parallel velocities v_1 and v_2 is equal to $(v_1 + v_2)/(1 + (v_1 v_2/c^2))$.
56. For a detailed discussion of the reception of special relativity theory see S. Goldberg, *Understanding relativity*, Birkhäuser, Boston 1984.
57. A. Einstein, *Ann. der Phys.* **18**, 639, 1905.

5

Natura facit saltum: the roots of quantum physics

(a) The age of continuity

Discrete features in the description of some natural phenomena date back to Greek atomists' speculations on the existence of smallest parts of matter. The concept of continuity first entered science about a century later, with Aristotle's definition: 'Things are said to be continuous whenever there is one and the same limit of both wherein they overlap and which they possess in common.'[1] As examples of things continuous he mentioned lines, surfaces, solids, motions, time, and place.[2] The most significant use to which he put his principle of continuity was in the area of biology, however.

'Nature proceeds little by little from things lifeless to animal life in such a way that it is impossible to determine the exact line of demarcation nor on which side thereof an intermediate form should lie. Thus after lifeless things in the upward scale comes the plant, and of plants one will differ from another as to its amount of apparent vitality; and in a word the whole genus of plants, whilst it is devoid of life as compared with an animal, is endowed with life as compared with other corporeal entities. Indeed ... there is observed in plants a continuous scale of ascent [the zoophytes] towards the animal.'[3]

'For nature passes from lifeless objects to animals in such an unbroken sequence, interposing between them beings which live and yet are not animals, that scarcely any difference seems to exist between two neighbouring groups owing to their close proximity.'[4]

For more than two thousand years these two passages from Aristotle's writings would continue to exert momentous influence on Western thought. Thus in the fifteenth century Nicolas Cusanus wrote: 'There is in the genera of things such a connection between the higher and the lower that they meet in a common point; such an order obtains among the species that the highest species of one genus coincides with the lowest of the next higher genus, in order that the universe may be one, perfect, continuous.'[5] Leibnitz in the seventeenth century: 'All the different classes of beings which taken together make up the universe are, in the ideas of God who knows distinctly their essential gradations, only so many ordinates of a single curve so closely united that it would be impossible to place others between any two of them, since that would imply disorder and imperfection ... The *law of continuity* [my italics] requires that ... it is necessary that all the orders of natural beings form but a single chain.'[6] John Locke in 1690: 'The animal and vegetable kingdoms are so nearly joined, that if you will take the lowest of one and the highest of the other, there will scarce be perceived any great difference between them.'[7] In the eighteenth century Kant wrote of 'the famous law of the continuous scale of created beings'.[8] Another author of that period remarked that in natural history the classification in terms of species is as arbitrary as are the circles drawn by astronomers on the earth's globe.[9]

Speculations such as these, without direct observational support, mostly regarding natural history but also other areas, led to the widespread belief among scholars that continuity would be a trait of the ultimate world picture. This view found its recurrent and trenchant expression in the dictum *Natura non facit saltum* (Nature does not make a leap), which, I am told,[10] goes at least as far back as the writings of the medieval Aristotelian philosopher Meister Eckhart.

As to the age of quantitative science, Newton's equations of mechanics, Maxwell's equations of electrodynamics, and Einstein's special relativity, are all compatible with the continuous world picture. Discrete features make their notable appearance in the nineteenth century with the birth of chemistry, however. Nowhere have I read conjectures to the effect that the chemical elements observed form but part of a continuum of forms of matter.

It was not until the twentieth century that science made one of its greatest leaps ever, when it was found that nature does leap. It began in physics, from there spread to chemistry, and ultimately to biology as well. This development is known as the quantum theory. Much of what follows is devoted to the explanation of what that theory is about.

The quantum theory was discovered in 1900 as the result of forty years of tortuous efforts at understanding a physical law first stated in 1860. Let us begin by recalling what that law was.

(b) Kirchhoff's law

In the good old cold days, the kitchen stove was a main center of family life. One could see the color of heat by looking into the stove's eye, a small aperture. As the temperature increases the color changes from dull to bright red, then to orange and yellow and perhaps even to white. One does not, therefore, need to be a physicist to know that there exists a connection between color, temperature, and heat, the latter being of course a form of energy.

The discovery of the quantitative expression for this connection led to the quantum theory.

There was a time when it was not rare for prominent physicists to leave their mark both on experiment and on theory, Newton being the most shining example. The modern dichotomy, experimental and theoretical physics as two distinct activities – yet forever in lively contact – first became noticeable in the later nineteenth century. Maxwell, Boltzmann,[11] Einstein,[12] and Bohr did (published) experimental work. Lorentz left the Leiden chair in theoretical physics for the Teyler Institute in Haarlem hoping to find opportunities there to do experimental work as well. All these men are above all else remembered, however, for their theoretical contributions. Physicists whose activities were seminal both in theory and in experiment have become ever more rare, Rutherford (d. 1937) and Fermi (d. 1954) being the last examples to date of this endangered species. The complexities of modern experimental as well as theoretical manipulations have grown so immensely that most probably this species is in fact extinct.

Gustav Robert Kirchhoff was one of the few nineteenth century physicists to do basic experimental as well as theoretical work, most of it in Heidelberg. On the experimental side,[13] during 1859–61 he discovered two new elements, cesium and rubidium. As a theorist he contributed significantly to the mechanics of fluid motion and to the theories of electric currents. He will be best remembered, however, for what has become known as Kirchhoff's law of blackbody radiation. Which brings us back to the kitchen stove.

In more abstract terms, our stove is an example of an isolated impenetrable cavity filled with various sorts of electromagnetic radiation, visible light, infrared, ultraviolet, the whole system being held at some fixed temperature or other. The radiation is constantly being 'mixed' as it is reflected or absorbed and reemitted by the walls. This mixing guarantees that after a sufficiently long time possible temperature differences within the cavity even out, so that we can speak of 'the' temperature of the whole system. Generally this state of affairs is called thermal equilibrium, but in our particular case it is called blackbody radiation, characterized by the so-called *spectral density*, the amount of energy per unit volume residing in the various radiation frequencies at some given temperature.

The stove's eye emits blackbody radiation. One gets only a rough idea of the spectral density simply by looking, since seeing red, for example, does not mean that all radiation we observe is red but only that the dominant frequency lies in the red. The precise determination of the spectral density distribution was still in its infancy when, in 1860, Kirchhoff announced his law.

For our purposes it suffices[14] to state his result as follows: The spectral density depends of course on the frequency v, but, apart from that, only on the temperature. That is to say, the spectral density is a universal function of the radiation only and does not depend on the volume or shape of the cavity, nor on the material of which it is made. This law had been conjectured earlier,[15] but it was Kirchhoff who for the first time gave its general derivation, with only the help of the then young science of thermodynamics.

Having discovered *that* the spectral density depends only on frequency and temperature, the next question any physicist will ask is: *How* does it depend on these two variables? It was the answer to this question that led to the quantum theory. Kirchhoff himself had nothing to do with that extraordinary denouement, even though he had at once realized that 'it is a highly important task to find this universal function. Great difficulties stand in the way of its experimental determination. Nevertheless there appear grounds for the hope that it has a simple form, as do all functions which do not depend on the properties of individual bodies.'[16] The experimental difficulties he had in mind were twofold: to construct blackbodies[17] suitable for careful experimentation as well as sufficiently sensitive detectors of radiation intensity.[18] Thus Kirchhoff's result posed not only great theoretical but also great experimental challenges.

The hunt for his law was on.

(c) 1860–1896

'It would be edifying if we could weigh the brain substance which has been sacrificed on the altar of [Kirchhoff's law],' Einstein wrote[19] in 1913. Forty years would pass between Kirchhoff's discovery that there exists a universal function and the determination of what that function is. For present purposes there is no reason for discussing all the intervening efforts in detail.[20] A few highlights should suffice.

The Stefan–Boltzmann law. The question of how the total energy emitted by a heated body varies with temperature has a venerable and confused history going back all the way to Newton.[21] The first step in the right direction was not made until 1879, when Stefan conjectured[22] from an analysis of experimental data that this energy should be proportional to the fourth power of the temperature – a definite advance, but still not quite precise. The true significance of Stefan's guess was not appreciated until in 1884 Boltzmann demonstrated[23] theorctically that Stefan's guess holds strictly only for the energy emitted by a blackbody. (In that case this energy equals the spectral density summed (integrated) over all frequencies times the volume of the blackbody.)

Boltzmann's reasoning was based on two disciplines, both modern for that time, thermodynamics and the Maxwell theory, specifically on the notion that electromagnetic waves contained in a cavity exert pressure on the walls. His proof, which can now easily be reproduced in a good undergraduate course, was a great novelty for its time. Remember in particular that Boltzmann did this work three years before Hertz demonstrated the existence of electromagnetic waves (4e)! Lorentz called[24] Boltzmann's contribution 'a true pearl of theoretical physics'. Planck later wrote: 'Maxwell's theory received powerful support through the short but now famous contribution of Boltzmann on the temperature variation of the heat radiation of a blackbody.'[25]

Wien's displacement law (1893).[26] The next step was again based on an interplay of thermodynamics and the Maxwell theory. It was Wien's proof that the blackbody spectral density must be of the following form: the third power of frequency times a function that depends only on the ratio of frequency to temperature. That function was still unknown in 1893, yet clearly Wien's law importantly restricted its possible form.

By 1893 the stage had been reached which later was characterized by Lorentz[24] in these words:

The derivation of Stefan's law [by Boltzmann] was the first great advance in radiation theory since Kirchhoff. When W. Wien discovered his displacement law nine years later, one had come as far as was at all possible with the help of the laws of thermodynamics and of the general electromagnetic theory, and the point had been reached where the special radiation theories had to set in which are based on definite ideas about the mechanism of the phenomena.

The point reached was in fact as far as one would come in understanding a few properties of blackbody radiation by means of classical physics only. As has been mentioned, Kirchhoff's spectral function (5b), the big prize, could only be found by making the major step from classical physics to quantum physics. I am almost ready to describe that transition. What remains to be sketched is the confusion immediately preceding the discovery of the quantum theory. Let us have a glimpse of that next.

(d) 1896: physics takes a bizarre turn

The 'definite ideas' to which Lorentz referred, aiming at finding the explicit form for the spectral function, go back[20] to the 1860s and 1870s. All these ideas, guesswork rather than pieces of theoretical analysis, are eminently forgettable with one notable exception, another contribution by Wien.[27] His was a guess too, but a brilliant one. His proposal is often called 'Wien's law', though we shall see in section (g) that actually it is not a law in the strict general sense of the word.

In an effort to keep the present text as accessible as possible, I have put a number of important formulae relevant to this chapter among the references, Wien's law being the first such instance.[28]

Unbeknownst to Wien, his law marked the end of the universal validity of classical physics and the onset of a bizarre turn in science. Consider the situation in 1896, the year in which Wien made his guess. On the one hand Wien's law fitted very well with all experimental data known at that time, as was also confirmed later. Therefore this law had something to do with reality. On the other hand, it would have been possible at that time to calculate rather than guess at an explicit form for the spectral density $\rho(v, T)$ (v = frequency, T = temperature) on the basis of certain general principles of classical physics, more specifically of statistical mechanics, a discipline defined below in section (f). Had Wien made that elementary calculation he would have found that the spectral density is proportional to T, a behavior violently different from his experimental law and therefore in violent disagreement with experiment! (Nevertheless this classical result is by no means irrelevant, as we shall see in section (g).)

This story has two morals. First, at the turn of the century good theoreticians were not yet familiar with statistical mechanics, a branch of theoretical physics that was indeed less than twenty years old. Secondly, the success of Wien's law indicates, to us, not to Wien, that already in 1896 it should have been clear that there was something seriously amiss with classical physics. This failure of classical concepts will be the subject of several chapters to follow.

Kirchhoff did not live to learn the outcome of the challenges he had posed. When his failing health began to hamper his experimental work, he finally accepted a professorship in theoretical physics in Berlin that had been offered him several times earlier. Upon his death in 1887 his chair was offered to Boltzmann, who declined, then to Hertz, who also declined, then to Planck who accepted.

It was there, in Berlin, that Planck found the correct answer to Kirchhoff's query concerning the spectral density.

(e) Introducing Max Planck

When Planck was born in Kiel, in Holstein, his native city was still in Danish territory. '[He] would remember, even in his old age, the sight of Prussian and Austrian troops marching into his native town [in 1864 (Chapter 2) when he was six years old].' [29] Throughout his life, war would cause him deep personal sorrow. He lost his eldest son during World War I. In World War II, his house in Berlin burned down during an air raid. In 1945 his other son was executed when declared guilty of complicity in a plot to kill Hitler.

Planck's ancestry was German. His father had moved to the University of Kiel as professor of jurisprudence. Both his grandfather and great-grandfather had been theology professors in Göttingen. In 1867 the family moved from Kiel to Munich where Planck went to high school. He was a good but not sparkling student, ranking between third and eighth.[30] 'He accepted the authority of the school as later he would the authority of the established corpus of physics.' [31] He was not only gifted in science but also in music. Also in later years, he played the piano and the organ. While a student at the University of Munich, he was a member of its singing club, and also composed an operetta. When it was performed the audience delighted in its 'gay and lovely melodies'.[31]

Planck himself has described[29] how he came to choose physics as his life's vocation: 'The outside world is something independent from man, something absolute, and the quest for the laws which apply to this absolute appeared to me as the most sublime scientific pursuit in life.' He received the first impetus in this direction when a high school teacher acquainted him with the law of the conservation of energy. 'My mind absorbed avidly, like a revelation, the first law I knew to possess absolute, universal validity, independently of all human agency: The principle of the conservation of energy.' Planck's preoccupation with the absolute and its independence of man's folly is a persistent theme in his writings, never more poignantly expressed than at his moments of discovery. It is also a reflection of Planck's deep religiosity, to which he did admit, though he allowed that he did not believe in a personal God, let alone a Christian God.[31] Such beliefs and sentiments rather than an urge for making revolutionary discoveries ('I am ... disinclined to questionable adventures' [32]) drove Planck in his private search for the absolute, of which he caught more than a glimpse in 1900.

Planck began his university studies in Munich and continued them at the Friedrich Wilhelm University in Berlin, the leading German university of its day. 'I studied experimental physics and mathematics; there were no classes in theoretical physics as yet.' [29] One of his Berlin professors was Kirchhoff, whom he admired even though he found him dry and monotonous as a teacher. His main stimulus in that period came from his independent reading of Clausius' papers on thermodynamics which caused him to immerse himself in entropy questions. The second law of thermodynamics became the topic of his thesis, presented in 1879. That was two years after the appearance of Boltzmann's fundamental paper on the second law in which its statistical nature was emphasized.

At this point I must digress to explain, ever so briefly, the meaning of entropy and the second law, and of their probabilistic interpretation, which, as I shall explain, was so crucial to Planck's discovery of the quantum theory.

(f) A brief digression on statistical mechanics

Consider a chamber filled with air, a large collection of molecules in a state of chaotic motion resulting from molecular collisions. Could it happen that at some moment all these molecules will find themselves in only one half of the chamber? Yes it can, but the probability is exceedingly small, about one in a billion billion billion for a chamber about the size of a room. Such a tiny probability results of course from the large number of molecules in the chamber; had that number been one, the odds would have been 50 per cent.

For the overwhelming majority of physically interesting questions, it is not necessary to know the *exact* configuration of large assemblies of particles: averages will do. Thus the temperature of a body is proportional to the *average* kinetic energy of its constituent molecules; the pressure of a gas is proportional to the *average* force which the molecules exert on the walls of their container. The concept 'temperature of one particle' is in fact meaningless. Such concepts as temperature, pressure, along with energy, and what came to be called entropy, are all macroscopic. The branch of science dealing with the interrelations of these quantities is called thermodynamics. It is not an easy subject. The connection between these macroscopic concepts and the underlying microscopic, molecular properties is called statistical mechanics. It is a difficult subject.

Let us return to the chamber, supposed to be airtight. Divide it into two halves by putting a partition in the middle, then evacuate one of the halves. We now have a 'half-ordered' system: no molecules in one part, many molecules moving chaotically in the other. Remove the partition. In practically no time the molecules will spread throughout the whole chamber, 'half order' has again become disorder. This is a special application of the second law of thermodynamics according to which any system (gaseous, liquid, or solid) left to itself, an isolated system, will tend spontaneously to a state of maximum possible disorder, that is, the state of thermal equilibrium. It is reasonable to introduce a measure for the degree of disorder in a system. That measure is called entropy.

There was, however, no mention of disorder nor of entropy when the German physicist Clausius first propounded the second law in 1850. For an understanding of Planck's later tribulations, it is important to look back for a moment at these beginnings. The principle introduced[33] by Clausius, in essence the second law, said that heat cannot flow from a colder to a warmer body without some other accompanying change (such as, for example, the accompanying cooling down of a refrigerator standing in a warmer kitchen). The term entropy also stems from Clausius, who in 1865 stated: the energy of the universe is constant (first law); the entropy of the universe tends to a maximum (second law).[34] *

The discovery of the molecular basis of the second law, the link between

---

* At that time Clausius also gave the first quantitative definition of entropy change. Let a system in thermal equilibrium at temperature T be brought to another state of equilibrium by supplying or extracting a very small smount of heat Q. Then the entropy change equals Q divided by T. It is important to note that this relation is purely thermodynamic, there is no reference to the molecular constitution of bodies.

the macroscopic concept of entropy and the molecular concept of degree of order, dates from the 1870s, when Planck was in high school. This development, one of the great advances in nineteenth century physical theory, is principally due to Boltzmann.[35] In 1872 he believed he had found a molecular proof for the fact that entropy can only increase when an isolated system is on its way toward equilibrium. This implies an element of irreversibility in the evolution of mechanical systems in the course of time. This drew the serious criticism that such behavior violates the reversibility inherent in the laws of Newtonian mechanics to which the molecules are subject. Our example of the air-filled chamber (used by Boltzmann himself) suggests that entropy cannot *always* increase: we saw there that it is highly improbable though not impossible for an isolated system to go from lower to higher order.

Boltzmann took the criticism to heart and in 1877 arrived at the modern view: in the approach to equilibrium, entropy increases *almost* always. Increase is not the actual but the most probable course of events. How almost is almost? That is a very tough question, about which even today not all has been said. In any event, Boltzmann was the first to establish a link between entropy and probability: 'If we apply this [reasoning] to the second law we can identify the quantity which we commonly designate as entropy with the probability of the actual state.'[36] The explicit relation between entropy and probability, known as the Boltzmann principle, is given in Ref. 37.

In statistical mechanics the notion of probability made its first entry at a basic level, without, however, altering in any way the fundamental laws of physics which were at that time Newtonian mechanics and Maxwellian electrodynamics. Boltzmann's introduction of probabilistic features was an extremely useful technique, indispensable for dealing in a practical manner with very complex systems. 'The entropy of a particle' is as meaningless a notion as the temperature of a particle; entropy and temperature do not enter in the fundamental dynamical equations. Entropy is a useful concept only in situations where only the good Lord can predict in detail the positions and velocities of a large number of particles at a later time from their values at an earlier time. That predictability, known as *classical causality*, also remained in full force after statistical mechanics had made its appearance.

(g) In which Planck stumbles on a new law that ushered in the physics of the twentieth century

After receiving his Ph.D., Planck wrote about forty papers, mainly on thermodynamics. Then, in 1900, he discovered the quantum theory.

In 1889 Planck had moved to Berlin as the successor to Kirchhoff, first as associate professor, then (1892) as full professor. While there, 'measurements made in the German Physico-Technical Institute ... directed my attention to Kirchhoff's law'.[29] The universality of that law exerted a strong fascination on him. 'Since I had always regarded the search for the absolute as the loftiest goal of all scientific activity, I eagerly set to work.'[29]

Planck's road toward meeting the challenge posed by Kirchhoff (to find the spectral function of blackbody radiation) provides one of the most striking examples of progress in science resulting from the interplay of theory and experiment, and by the theorist's trial and error. It has in fact been said of Planck that he made so many mistakes that eventually he *had* to find the right answer.[38]

Planck later wrote about how in 1895 he began his wobbly road: 'At that time I regarded the principle of the increase of entropy as ... immutably valid ... whereas Boltzmann treated [it] merely as a law of probabilities – in other words as a principle that could admit of exceptions.'[29] In 1897 he wrote to a colleague that he considered it 'easier and offering better prospects to adopt the second law of thermodynamics as a strictly valid law [in the sense of Clausius]'.[39] Accordingly he attempted to base his early arguments (1895–8) on the dynamics of Newton/Maxwell. Boltzmann rapidly noted, however, that his reasoning contained serious flaws. There followed a confrontation (in print,[40] 1897–8), which ended by Planck frankly admitting that he had been in error.[41]

So Planck started all over again, choosing next the middle ground between dynamics and statistical mechanics: thermodynamics, 'my own home territory where I felt myself to be on safe ground'.[29] He now bestirred himself to prove the universal validity of Wien's exponential law – still, at that time, a viable solution for the Kirchhoff function – from first thermodynamic principles, and in 1899 thought[42] he had done so: 'I believe to be forced to conclude that Wien's law [is a] necessary consequence of the application of the entropy increase principle to the theory of electromagnetic radiation and that therefore the limits of validity of this law, if they exist at all, coincide with those of the second law of thermodynamics.'

Wrong again.

It is now 7 November 1899. Planck concluded the nineteenth century part of his career with an invocation of the absolute. He had found that the constants a and b in Wien's exponential law (see Ref. 28) together with the velocity of light and the Newtonian constant of gravitation suffice to find a system of 'natural units': 'With the help of a and b it is possible to give units for length [now called the Planck length], mass, time, and temperature which, independently of special bodies and substances, retain their meaning for all times and for all cultures, including extraterrestrial and extrahuman ones.'[42]

As noted above, Planck's allegation about Wien's law was incorrect. This time it was not a theoretician who found an error. Rather, experimental evidence had been presented, in a paper from Berlin, submitted on 2 February 1900, according to which Wien's conjecture did not agree with all the facts: 'it has . . . been demonstrated that the Wien–Planck spectral equation does not represent the blackbody radiation measured by us . . .'[43] Not that the data on which Wien had based his conjecture were flawed. Rather these data had been extended to a hitherto unexplored region, the far infrared. It was there that Wien's law failed signally.

Interest in this new frequency region had been much stimulated by Hertz's discovery in 1887 of electrically generated waves. There was a clear need for filling the large gap still existing between the Hertzian wavelengths and the infrared domain then known. That gap was not fully closed until the 1920s.[44] Yet the Berlin data continuing to be amassed in 1900 were sufficient to set the stage, finally, for the discovery of the Kirchhoff function. Planck or no Planck, the correct expression for the spectral function could not possibly have been discovered until 1900. What is so truly astonishing is that Planck found this expression in that very same year. It helped him mightily that he was there at the right time and at the right place; and that in the course of his previous efforts he had obtained several important lasting results that now stood him in good stead.

It is indeed fitting at this point to note that so far I have stressed Planck's failures rather than his progress. That was done because his role is by no means fully revealed by the statement that in 1900 he discovered the quantum. Planck is a transitional figure *par excellence* not just because of what he discovered but also, perhaps equally importantly, because of the way he made the discovery for which he is so justly revered, never losing sight of his goal in spite of many setbacks. By 1900 he had written six papers on his favourite subject, filling 162 printed pages, which contain several lasting contributions[45] that are vital to what happened next.

Planck most probably first wrote down his law on the evening of Sunday 7 October 1900,[46] as the result of new experimental information he had received earlier that day. During the preceding months two groups at the Physico-Technical Institute had continued their spectral function measurements which were of excellent quality, as later data confirmed. On the afternoon of that Sunday a colleague had told Planck that in the far infrared this function is proportional to the temperature T rather than to Wien's exponential. So there, in the infrared, appeared the temperature dependence of $\rho(\nu, T)$ predicted by the classical theory (as already noted in section (d))!

This classical result is now known as the Rayleigh–Einstein–Jeans (REJ) law, after the three men who contributed to its formulation. That law, finally correctly stated[47] in 1905*, was as little known to Planck in 1900 as it had been to Wien in 1896. It is a curious twist of history that Planck could only discover the first *quantum* law after the *classical* data on infrared radiation had been obtained.

Shortly after 7 October Planck was informed that his new formula for the spectral density fitted the entire experimental spectrum very well. He publicly stated[49] this result for the first time in a discussion on 19 October. On 14 December he submitted a paper[50] that includes his famous law. That date marks the birth of quantum physics. His search for the absolute had finally been rewarded.

Planck's paper of 14 December is based partly on solid physical theory, partly on 'a fortunate guess', to use his own words.[29] As a piece of improvisation it ranks among the most fundamental works of the twentieth century. Planck's law is written out in Ref. 56. It contains a new fundamental constant h, which Planck called the quantum of action (since h has the dimensions of an action, energy × time), and which now is most often called the constant of Planck. His law also makes clear how Wien's 'law' (5d) and the REJ law fit into the description: they are limiting cases. Wien holds only for high frequencies, REJ only for low frequencies.

(In this paragraph, which readers not interested in technical details can skip, I indicate what Planck did and what he found. (For more details, see Ref. 51.) He imagined a cavity containing radiation and also a set of electrically charged material resonators (linear oscillators), the latter serving to induce thermal equilibrium by mixing. In 1899 he had derived an important proportionality[52] between the spectral density $\rho(v,T)$ and the average resonator energy $U(v,T)$ such that from U one can find ρ. He had also noted a simple relation between U and the resonator entropy S for the case that Wien's law holds true.[53] In 1900 he found that this relation took another form, also simple,[54] when ρ is proportional to T. Now comes Planck's guess: interpolate between these two $S–U$ relations.[55] His interpolation formula combined with a few standard thermodynamical steps led him to his law.)

It is to Planck's greatest credit and highest glory that, not content with a result based only on a 'fortunate guess', he went on to search for a deeper meaning of his law. He later called the resulting labor the most strenuous of his life.[57] First of all, he finally abjured the heresy of an absolute second law of thermodynamics and embraced Boltzmann's interpretation of equilibrium as the most probable state.[58] In fact Boltzmann's relation[37] between entropy and probability W now became central to his thinking. That

* For the history of the REJ law see Ref. 48.

transition to the statistical interpretation 'was bought at an immense sacrifice that even decades later remained painful to him'.[59]

In this paragraph, which can again be skipped, I indicate Planck's strategy for introducing his new constant h, which was 'completely indispensable for obtaining the correct expression for entropy'.[57] Experiment had given him every reason to believe that he had the correct spectral density ρ. From ρ he could read off[52] the average resonator energy U. Simple thermodynamics had led him[55] from U to the resonator entropy S. In turn S is related to probability W by Boltzmann's principle.[37] Problem: To find and interpret the expression for the fundamental probability W which, by arguing backward, yields the known ρ: from W to S to U to ρ.

Planck later called his quest for W 'an act of desperation ... I had to obtain a positive result, under any circumstance and at whatever cost'.[32] The form for W with which he ended up is correct, but his method was invention rather than derivation from first principles. The converse is in fact true: his paper marked the first step toward *establishing* new first principles. I need not state here all the *ad hoc* assumptions that Planck made except for the most important one, the *quantum postulate*:

In order to find the correct resonator entropy S it must be assumed that the energy U of a resonator with frequency v can only take on *discrete* energy values, to wit, *integer* multiples of h times v, in contrast to classical theory where U can be *any* multiple, integer or not, of v. We now say that U is quantized.

Thus was the quantum theory born as an offshoot from statistical mechanics.

In times of transition such as the one Planck went through, one needs to distinguish the act of making discovery from the act of understanding discovery. It is evident that Planck did not at once understand that the appearance of h meant an end to classical physics:

I tried immediately to weld the elementary quantum of action somehow in the framework of classical theory. But in the face of all such attempts this constant showed itself to be obdurate.... My futile attempts to put the elementary quantum of action into the classical theory continued for a number of years and they cost me a great deal of effort.[29]

That comment by Planck shows how unaware he was at that time of the possibility of deriving a blackbody radiation law from classical theory. Had he known this he would have hit upon the REJ law – and history would have been quite different! As Einstein later wrote about this odd situation: 'The imperfections of [Planck's derivation] ... remained at first hidden which latter fact was most fortunate for the development of physics.'[60] But he also wrote: 'His derivation was of unmatched boldness.'[61]

Later judgements of Einstein and Bohr may serve as prolog for much that is to follow in this book. Einstein:

This discovery [i.e. the quantum theory] set science a fresh task: that of finding a new conceptual basis for all of physics.[62]

And Bohr:

A new epoch was inaugurated in physical science by Planck's discovery of the quantum of action.[63]

(h) Particles or waves?

Planck's radiation law was rapidly accepted as correct, simply because further experiments in the years immediately after 1900 confirmed his result to ever better accuracy. His derivation caused no stir, however. Five years passed, in fact, before the quantum made its second appearance in the literature.

That next step, in 1905, was due to Einstein.[64] His starting point was the experimental validity of Wien's 'law' (5d) for high frequencies. His tools were classical statistical mechanics. His finding was the *light-quantum hypothesis*: within the domain of validity of the Wien formula, monochromatic light with frequency v behaves as if it consists of mutually independent quanta with energy hv. So far this statement, referring to free radiation only,* is in the nature of a theorem. Einstein went much further, however, by adding the speculation that the same behavior of light also holds true for the emission and absorption of light by matter, and by giving several experimental tests for this assumption. Later he showed that light-quanta can also be assigned a definite momentum (hv/c). They therefore behave like particles, eventually called photons.[65]

Einstein's new proposal that under certain specific circumstances light behaves like particles hit upon very strong resistance. One reason was that, unlike Planck, he could not at once claim experimental support for his predictions; experiment had not yet progressed far enough. Even when later data did confirm his light-quantum predictions, it still took time, well into the 1920s, until the photon was finally accepted as inevitable.[66] What finally settled the issue was the Compton effect (1923): in the process of scattering a light beam by tiny electrically charged particles, light behaves like a stream of particles, photons, in the sense that the collisions between light and particles obey the same laws of energy and momentum conservation as in the collision between billiard balls.

The primary reason for the nearly two-decades-long opposition to the light-quantum is obvious. We have seen (4c) how in the early 1800s the work of Young and Fresnel had led to the verdict: Huyghens' wave description of light is in, Newton's particle description is out. Along comes young

* Note a basic difference: Planck had introduced quanta for *material* resonators, Einstein next did so for *light*.

Einstein and says that, at least under certain circumstances, light nevertheless behaves as particles. Then what about the interference of light and all other successes of the wave picture? The situation was incomparably more grave than the Newton–Huyghens controversy, where one set of concepts simply had to yield to another. Here, on the other hand, it became clear, as time went by, that *not only could the wave picture lay claim to success, for some phenomena, that excluded the particle picture but also that the particle picture could make similar claims, for other phenomena, that excluded the wave picture.* What was going on?

From the outset Einstein was well aware of these apparent paradoxes, which became ever more strident as time went by. In 1924 he put it like this:

There are ... now two theories of light, both indispensable and – as one must admit despite twenty years of tremendous effort on the part of theoretical physicists – without any logical connection.[67]

The resolution came in 1925 when quantum mechanics made clear that Huyghens and Einstein both were right – but that comes later.

During the intervening years, from 1900 to 1925, quantum phenomena were dark and mysterious, and became increasingly important. Planck remarked on this in 1910: '[The theoreticians] now work with an audacity unheard of in earlier times, at present no physical law is considered assured beyond doubt, each and every physical truth is open to dispute. It often looks as if the time of chaos again is drawing near in theoretical physics.'[68]

That very well describes the state of affairs when Niels Bohr's work of 1913 produced further grand successes and added further mysteries to quantum physics.

References

1. Aristotle, *Metaphysica* XI, 1069a5.
2. Aristotle, *De categoriis* 4b20, 5a1–4; also *Physica* VI, 231a24.
3. Aristotle, *Historia animalium* VIII, 1, 588, B4–12.
4. Aristotle, *De partibus animalium*, IV5, 681a12–15.
5. Quoted in A. O. Lovejoy, *The great chain of being*, p. 80, Harvard University Press 1953.
6. Ref. 5, p. 144.
7. J. Locke, *Essay concerning human understanding*, III, Chap. vi, par. 12.
8. Ref. 5, p. 241.
9. Ref. 5, p. 231.
10. This information came to me from Res Jost who learned it from Professor Gerhard Huber in Zürich.
11. Walther Thirring has told me that a magnet can be seen in the Vienna Physics Institute which to this day is known as 'the Boltzmann magnet'.
12. See e.g. SL, Chap. 29.

13. See IB, Chap. 9, section (b).

14. The more general formulation is discussed in SL, Chap. 19, section (a).

15. In 1858 the Scottish physicist Balfour Stewart had given a less precise and less universal formulation. The priority arguments which arose have a protracted and uncommonly interesting history accentuated by nationalist sentiments, see D. M. Siegel, *Isis* **67**, 565, 1976.

16. G. Kirchhoff, *Ann. der Phys. und Chem.* **109**, 275, 1860.

17. For the history of the construction of blackbodies up to 1900 see O. Lummer in *Rapports du Congrès International de Physique*, Vol. 2, p. 41, Gauthier-Villars, Paris 1900. For developments up to the late 1960s see R. A. Smith, F. E. Jones, and P. Chasmar, *The detection and measurement of infrared radiation*, Oxford University Press 1968.

18. For details on the history and development of radiation detectors see R. A. Smith *et al.* (Ref. 17, 1968) and E. S. Barr, *Am. J. Phys.* **28**, 42, 1960; *Infrared Phys.* **3**, 195, 1963.

19. A. Einstein, *Naturw.* **1**, 1077, 1913.

20. For many particulars about this period see H. Kangro, *History of Planck's radiation law*, Taylor and Francis, London 1976.

21. I. Newton, *Opuscula* II, 423, 1744.

22. J. Stefan, *Sitzungsber. Ak. Wiss. Wien, Math. Naturw. Kl. 2 Abt.* **79**, 391, 1879.

23. See *Wissenschaftliche Abhandlungen von L. Boltzmann*, Ed. F. Hasenöhrl. Vol. 3, pp. 110, 118, Chelsea, New York 1968.

24. H. A. Lorentz, *Verh. Deutsch. Phys. Ges.* **9**, 206, 1907.

25. M. Planck, in *J. C. Maxwell*, Macmillan, New York 1931.

26. W. Wien, *Ber. Preuss. Ak. der Wiss.* 1893, p. 55; also *Ann. der Phys.* **52**, 132, 1894.

27. W. Wien, *Ann. der Phys.* **58**, 662, 1896.

28. Wien's exponential law is $\rho(v,T) = av^3 e^{-bv/T}$, where ρ is the spectral function, and a and b are parameters.

29. M. Planck, *Scientific autobiography and other papers*, p. 7, transl. F. Gaynor, William and Norgate, London 1950.

30. J. L. Heilbron, *The dilemma of an upright man*, University of California Press, Berkeley 1986.

31. A. Hermann, *Planck*, Rowohlt, Reinbek 1973.

32. M. Planck, letter to R. W. Wood, 7 October 1931, American Institute of Physics Archives, New York.

33. R. Clausius, *Ann. der Phys. und Chem.* **79**, 368, 500, 1850, transl. in W. F. Magie, *A source book in physics*, p. 228, Harvard University Press 1965.

34. R. Clausius, *ibid.* **125**, 353, 1865, esp. p. 400; transl. in Magie (Ref. 33), p. 234.

35. For references and some more details see SL, Chap. 4, section (b).

36. For this English translation see Magie (Ref. 33), p. 262.

37. The entropy S is related to the probability W by $S = k \ln W$, where k is a constant called the Boltzmann constant. As W rises or falls so does S.

38. For many details and references to the remainder of this section see especially M. Klein in *History of twentieth century physics*, Academic Press, New York 1977; also SL, Chap. 19, section (a); Refs 20 and 31; and A. Hermann, *Frühgeschichte der Quantentheorie*, Mosbach, Baden 1969.

39. Ref. 20, p. 131.
40. Ref. 23, pp. 615, 618, 622.
41. The best account of the Boltzmann–Planck controversy is by R. Jost, in *Lecture notes in physics*, Vol. 100, p. 128, Springer, New York 1979.
42. M. Planck, *Ann. der Phys.* **1**, 69, 1900, esp. p. 118.
43. O. Lummer and E. Pringsheim, *Verh. Deutsch. Phys. Ges.* **2**, 163, 1900.
44. See Barr (Ref. 18).
45. See e.g. SL, pp. 369, 370.
46. SL, p. 368.
47. The REJ law is

$$\rho(v,\ T) = \frac{8\pi v^2}{c^3}\, kT.$$

The appearance of the Boltzmann constant (Ref. 37) shows the statistical mechanical origin of this relation.
48. SL, Chap. 19, section (b).
49. M. Planck, *Verh. Deutsch. Phys. Ges.* **2**, 207, 1900.
50. M. Planck, *ibid.* **2**, 237, 1900.
51. SL, pp. 368–70.
52. The proportionality is

$$\rho(v,\ T) = \frac{8\pi v^2}{c^3}\, U(v,\ T),$$

where c is the velocity of light.
53. The relation is

$$\frac{\mathrm{d}^2 S}{\mathrm{d} U^2} = \frac{\text{constant}}{U}.$$

54. The relation is

$$\frac{\mathrm{d}^2 S}{\mathrm{d} U^2} = \frac{\text{constant}}{U^2}.$$

55. The interpolation is

$$\frac{\mathrm{d}^2 S}{\mathrm{d} U^2} = \frac{\alpha}{U(\beta + U)}.$$

56. Planck's law is

$$\rho(v,T) = \frac{8\pi h v^3}{c^3}\frac{1}{e^{hv/kT}-1}.$$

57. M. Planck, in *Nobel lectures in physics 1901–1921*, p. 407, Elsevier, New York 1967.
58. As is evident from the appearance of the Boltzmann constant (Ref. 37) in his law.
59. M. von Laue, *Naturw.* **45**, 221, 1958.
60. A. Einstein autobiographical notes, in *Albert Einstein, philosopher-scientist*, p. 39, Ed. P. A. Schilpp, Tudor, New York 1949.
61. A. Einstein, *Verh. Deutsch. Phys. Ges.* **18**, 318, 1916.
62. A. Einstein, in *Out of my later years*, p. 229, Philosophical Library, New York 1950.
63. N. Bohr, in *Philosophy in mid century*, p. 308, La Nuova Italia Editrice,

Florence 1958; also in *Max Planck Festschrift 1958*, p. 169; *Naturw. Rundschau*, July 1960, p. 252.

64. A. Einstein, *Ann. der Phys.* **17**, 132, 1905; English transl. A. B. Arons and M. B. Peppard, *Am. J. Phys.* **33**, 367, 1967. For a more detailed discussion than given here see SL, Chap. 19, section (c).

65. For the evolution of the photon concept see SL, Chap. 21.

66. See SL, Chap. 19, section (f) and Chap. 21, section (f).

67. A. Einstein, *Berliner Tageblatt,* 20 April 1924.

68. M. Planck, *Phys. Zeitschr.* **11**, 922, 1910.

6

Student days

(a) Physics in Denmark, from a college of the clergy to the epoch of Ørsted

The preceding two chapters were meant to be a sketch of the status of physics at about the time Bohr began his university studies. To set the stage for his activities from then on, we must consider in addition how teaching of and research in physics had developed in Denmark up to the beginning of the twentieth century. An appreciation of those local conditions, to be given in this section, is quite important not just in regard to Bohr's student days but, even more so, in order to understand how very much Bohr changed the state of affairs within the decade following the completion of his university studies.

Pope Sixtus IV, patron of letters and the arts, will be remembered for the construction under his aegis of the Sistine chapel, the initiation of the Sistine choir, and the founding of the University of Copenhagen. It is believed[1] that this last issue was settled in the course of the pilgrimage to Rome of His Catholic Majesty Christian I, king of Denmark and Norway. At any rate, the necessary authorization for establishing this school was formalized by the papal bull of 19 June 1475. On Tuesday 1 June 1479, the University was inaugurated as a Catholic institution with a solemn mass de spiritu sancto in Copenhagen's *Vor Frue Kirke* (Church of Our Lady), in the king's presence. Western European exact science was in its infancy then; Copernicus was only a boy of six.

In that period universities were essentially religious institutions, meant to prepare future men of the clergy, other church officials, and teachers in Latin schools for their coming tasks. Times were no longer favorable for Catholic institutions when Copenhagen University was founded, however. The struggle against papal power, culminating in the Reformation, had begun. The university languished; by 1531 all its academic activities, limited to start with, had come to an end.[2] A new beginning was made after the Reformation had transformed Denmark into a Lutheran state (1536). A new charter, the *Fundatio et Ordinatio universalis Scholae Hafniensis*, signed in 1539 by King Christian III would remain in force for the next two hundred years.

Also from 1539 date the first two faculty appointments in the philosophical sciences. One, in mathematics, for teaching theoretical and practical arithmetics, the main topic, and also astronomy, cosmography, Euclid's geometry, and theoretical and practical music. The other, in physics, for teaching four hours a week Aristotle's writings on physics and ethics, using a text 'in Greek or in Latin translation if [the professor] were not sufficiently familiar with the Greek language'.[3] In the words of the charter: 'We maintain all sciences at this university regardless of the fact that they teach us many things that cannot be grasped by the common people [but rather] in order to spread God's works so that others may participate in God's glorious gifts.'[4] The professor's oath of office may serve as a last example of the continued religious basis of the university: 'I swear that with God's grace I shall faithfully and diligently perform my duties so as to strengthen Christ's church and honor this University.'[5]

These few backward glimpses are meant to illustrate that, in Copenhagen as elsewhere, universities then and now had only their name in common. Teaching focused largely on the Scriptures and major texts from antiquity. Learning took precedence over explanation and critical insight, form dominated content. The syllabus was still much like that handed down from the schools of the Roman Empire: the trivium, the lighter sciences, comprising grammar, rhetoric and logic (whence our 'trivial'); and the quadrivium, arithmetic, music, geometry, and astronomy. What in post-Reformation and post-Renaissance passed for science was dominated by Aristotelian doctrine, reconciled with theology by men like Thomas Aquinas. At Oxford, 'in 1586 questions "disagreeing with the ancient and true philosophy" were not even allowed to be discussed'.[6]

The development of European higher learning from the middle ages into the eighteenth century is a complex and probably not fully digested topic[7] that does not lend itself to a description in terms of a linear evolution. The subject is certainly not sufficiently illuminated by merely recalling the great figures of the period, many of whom in fact made their major contributions outside university context. To quote but one example, in 1559 Tyge (Tycho) Brahe, the University of Copenhagen's most illustrious alumnus during the first century of its existence, was sent there by his guardian to study rhetorics and philosophy in preparation for a diplomatic career, but fortunately struck out to become the founder of modern observational astronomy.

In Chapter 4 I mentioned the inclination of physicists to protect knowledge acquired by past generations, having specifically in mind at that point the transition from classical physics to the era of relativity and the quantum. By sharpest contrast, such protectiveness had of course no place in the transition from imposed belief on past authority and censorship by church and/or state to the times when man turned to a critical examination of the world around him, guided by his own observations. That transition began to take firm, though by no means generally accepted, shape in the course of the seventeenth century.

These new convictions had their major precursors, who often had to pay heavily for their new audacity. In the thirteenth century Roger Bacon's advocacy of the experimental basis of all science cost him twenty-four years in prison. In the sixteenth century the opposition by Petrus Ramus, the great teacher at the University of Paris, to Aristotelianism and scholastic logic cost him his life, in the massacre of Bartholomew's Eve. In 1600 Giordano Bruno was burned at the stake, one reason being his preference of the Copernican over the Aristotelian system, and in the seventeenth century Galilei in his old age was cruelly treated by the Church for his experimental confirmation of the Copernican world system. These men and a few others were the first scientists, a term which, incidentally, is of much more recent vintage. In the early nineteenth century William Whewell, professor of mineralogy and of moral theology and casuistical divinity at Cambridge University, wrote: 'We need very much a name to describe a cultivator of science in general. I should incline to call him a Scientist.'[8]*

Back to Denmark. By the end of the seventeenth century it had produced a number of eminent scientists. We have already encountered Brahe, Bartholin, and Rømer (4b). In addition Niels Steensen (Steno) must be mentioned. This brilliant polymath made fundamental discoveries in anatomy, such as 'Steno's duct', the excretory duct of the salivary glands, and in mineralogy ('Steno's law'**). He was one of the founders of the science of geology. Steno devoted the last twenty years of his life to serving the Catholic Church, first as a priest, then as bishop, leading all the while a severely ascetic life. He is the only prominent scientist I know of who has been beatified (in October 1988). His most famous pronouncement will touch the scientist as well as the devout:

> Pulchra sunt quae videntur,
> Pulchroria quare scientur,
> Longe pulcherrima quae ignorantur.

(Beautiful are the things we see/More beautiful those we understand/Much the most beautiful those we do not comprehend.)

---

* Meanwhile my friend Robert Merton has taught me more fine points about the origin of that term (to be published).

** According to which the angles between crystal surfaces of a given species of mineral are characteristic constants independent of the crystal's size.

In spite of the appearance of such renowned figures, science at the university had remained weak, however. Its emended charter of 1732, written shortly after the complete destruction of the university by the great fire of 1728, no longer provided for a chair in physics: 'Philosophia Nauralis shall be taught by one of the professors in medicine or in mathematics such that one day a week he shall teach physics but the other days, at his preference, mathematics or medicine.' Perhaps that was just as well since whatever physics was then taught continued to be Aristotelian.[9]

The great change began in the middle of the eighteenth century. In 1742 *Det Kongelige danske Videnskabernes Selskab* (the Royal Danish Academy of Sciences and Letters) was founded. The trend of its publications was soon directed toward the natural sciences.[10] In 1753 Christian Kratzenstein[11] was appointed *professor physices experimentalis designatus medicinae*, that is, he became a professor in the faculty of medicine but was charged with teaching experimental physics.[12] In 1796 his successor was appointed professor of physics, still in the medical faculty. In 1800 the next professor of physics was assigned to the philosophical faculty.

So it remained until Hans Christian Ørsted changed physics in Denmark from an appendage to other subjects into a fully fledged independent field of study.

Ørsted's interest in science was aroused when at the age of 11 he became a helper in his father's pharmacy. 'In those days there were no chemical laboratories in Denmark except for pharmacies, and the physical instruments which a few rich men had acquired were collections of curios rather than generally available tools for experimental research.'[13] Ørsted prepared himself largely by self-education for entrance in Copenhagen University where he studied chemistry, physics, and mathematics, and also developed a lasting interest in philosophy. He received a doctor's degree in 1799, and in 1806 became professor of physics and chemistry at the university, and also member of the *Videnskabernes Selskab*. (The next year the calamitous bombardment of Copenhagen by the British once again destroyed most of the university.) In 1815 he was elected secretary of that Society, a post he kept until his death. 'For thirty-six years the factual leadership of the Society, under various presidents, lay in Ørsted's hands.'[14]

I have already mentioned Ørsted's major contribution in 1820, the discovery of electromagnetism (4e). He also discovered a new chemical element, argylium, now better known as aluminum, and did important research on the compressibility of gases and liquids.

Ørsted's work on electromagnetism at once created a great sensation. His original paper of 1820 was written in Latin (4e), but in that same year translations appeared in Danish, Dutch, English, French, German, and Italian. Faraday and Ampère wrote in high praise of him. In 1821 volume 31 of the prestigious *Journal für Chemie und Physik* opened with an editorial announcing a change in format 'in part because a new epoch in chemistry and physics appears to have begun with Ørsted's important discoveries on the connection between magnetism and electricity'. A contributor wrote: 'Ørsted's experiments regarding magnetism are the most interesting ones performed in more than a thousand years.'[15]

As a result of his growing international prestige, Ørsted became an increasingly influential figure on the national scene. This he put to use in fulfilling his long-standing ambition of broadening Danish science at the base. A visit to London during which he attended lectures at the Royal Institution gave him the inspiration for founding, in 1824, *Selskabet for Naturlærens Udbredelse*, the society for the dissemination of science. He was its president from its beginnings until his death, and himself gave twenty-six of the popular lectures which the Society offered to the general public, both in Copenhagen and in the provinces.[16] The Society still exists and is now housed in the H. C. Ørsted Institute on the Nørre Alle in Copenhagen. Among its later presidents we find Niels Bohr.

Ørsted was also the driving force behind the founding (1829) of the *Polytekniske Læreanstalt* (now called the Technical University of Denmark), an institution for education on a scientific basis in engineering and other technical subjects, modeled after the *École Polytechnique* in Paris, which Ørsted had visited. He assumed its directorship, which he held for the rest of his life. As concurrent professor at the university, he promoted close ties between the institutions, including joint courses on various subjects.

Finally, by the Royal Decree of 1 September 1850, a separate faculty of mathematics and natural sciences was established at the university.[17] Ørsted who had suggested this move nearly forty years earlier became its first professor of physics.[18] By and large, physics was housed at the *Læreanstalt*, however. In the first thirty years of the new faculty's existence, the average number of its students has been estimated at about 20. In 1982 it was[19] 5000.

While Ørsted's role in experimental physics and in the evolution of scientific institutions in his native country deserves great respect, the same cannot be said of his impact on the teaching of theoretical physics, a subject for which he lacked taste and insight. For example, it is clear from his writings that he never even digested Newton's laws of mechanics and of gravitation. His textbooks on physics held back the evolution of theoretical physics in Denmark and, late in his life, came under deserved criticism.[20]

The first Danish theoretical physicist of prominence was Ludwig Lorenz whose independent contributions to electromagnetism in the 1860s mark him out as a distinguished contemporary of Maxwell.[21] That work was done after Ørsted's epoch had come to an end, with his death in 1851. By that time the industrial revolution brought about by steam power technology and machine tool engineering was at its peak. Ørsted did not live to witness another revolution which his work had helped shape: 'The "electrical revolution" [which] changed the whole way of life of Western Europe and North America by universalizing a science-based technology.'[22] The role of science in all these practical developments was evident. So was its impact on universities: 'During the closing years of the nineteenth and the opening years of the twentieth centuries there was a revolution not merely in the subjects but in the method of study. Whereas in the past reliance had been placed on authority and exact scholarship, greater attention was now given to intelligent understanding and to creative and original thought ... everywhere new courses were being devised.'[23] Universities had become centers for scientific research.

That was academia when Niels Bohr became a student.

In what used to be Bohr's private office in the Institute for Theoretical Physics on Blegdamsvej, there still hangs in the same prominent position a copy of a painting of Ørsted addressing a meeting of Scandinavian scientists. (The original can be seen in the Great Hall of Copenhagen University.) I never asked Bohr why he had chosen that particular print for decorating his office. I could imagine, however, that in spite of different attitudes toward theoretical physics he may have felt an affinity to Ørsted. Both men made seminal contributions to science. Both created new Danish institutions for promoting science. Both played leading roles in the *Videnskabernes Selskab*. Both traveled extensively and knew leading personalities of their time; Ørsted personally met prominent figures from Goethe to Faraday. Both were devoted husbands and fathers. There was something boyish in both their looks. Each of them had close ties to a brother who himself was highly eminent; Ørsted's brother Anders, jurist and statesman, laid the basis for all later Danish jurisprudence. Both enjoyed high esteem and deep affection not only in but also outside scientific circles. Hans Christian Andersen said of Ørsted: 'He was the man I loved best,' and in his charming tale 'The clock' portrayed Ørsted as a prince, himself as a poor boy. And Kierkegaard: 'He has always appeared to me as a musical chord[24] that Nature has struck in just the right way.'[25]

Finally, Bohr's own words, spoken at the commemoration of the hundredth anniversary of Ørsted's death apply equally to himself: 'He readily assumed heavy burdens when it concerned society's needs and the common good. Resolving such problems gave him the means for using his talents in a way that agreed harmoniously with his personality.'[13]

(b) In which Bohr begins his university studies and starts mobilizing help in writing

On 10 December 1922 Bohr received the Nobel prize in physics. For that occasion he prepared a brief autobiographical sketch,[26] in which he tells us:

'My interest in the study of physics was awakened while I was still in school, largely owing to the influence of my father.' Christian Bohr has poignantly recorded[27] the role of science in his own life: 'When I speak of that period of my earliest childhood which I can clearly recollect myself, then, like the whole of my later life, it was characterized to the highest degree by one single gift, if I may call it such, which goes back as far as I can remember, and which was never out of my mind for a single week, I dare say hardly a single day ... the love of natural science ... it still dominates my life.'

In the autumn of 1903 Bohr became one of Copenhagen University's approximately 1500 students (there were another 500 at the *Læreanstalt*), a comfortably small number by present standards (in 1984 there were 26000) but on a par with contemporary levels. In that year Columbia, Princeton, and Yale had 4500, 1400, and 2800 students respectively (in round numbers).[28]

Bohr had chosen physics as his major subject, and astronomy, chemistry, and mathematics as his minor subjects. His principal teacher, Christian Christiansen, was the first Danish physicist of stature after Ørsted and Lorenz. He had been professor at the university and the *Læreanstalt* since 1886. Among his contributions, two stand out. His discovery of the anomalous dispersion of light in liquids* came to wide attention especially because of its rapid interpretation by Sellmeyer[30] and by Helmholtz.[31] Also, he was the first to note[32] that under suitable circumstances blackbody radiation emanates from a hole in a cavity (see (5b)), an idea at once taken up by Boltzmann.[33] In addition he worked on optical properties of crystals, heat conduction, air currents, and frictional electricity.

In 1903 Christiansen was the one and only professor, not in experimental or in theoretical physics, but in physics *tout court*. In fact, along with his experimental researches just mentioned, he also founded the study of theoretical physics at the university. His textbook on the elements of theoretical physics[34] was widely praised and was translated into German,[35] English,[36] and Russian.[37] There were two other physicists who held faculty appointments in Copenhagen: Martin Knudsen, docent (roughly equivalent to a reader in Britain), who taught physics to medical students, and who later became well known for his work on highly dilute gases (now called Knudsen gases);[38] and Peter Prytz, professor of experimental physics at the *Læreanstalt*.[39] These two men played no particular role in Bohr's education, unlike Christiansen, about whom Bohr later wrote: 'I was fortunate enough to come under the guidance of Professor Christiansen, a profoundly original and highly endowed physicist.'[40] The appreciation was

---

* Anomalous dispersion means that the prismatic colors generated by white light appear in reversed order compared with the usual Newtonian sequence. (Violet, which normally refracts most, here refracts least, etc.). Christiansen first found this effect by using a thin-walled glass prism filled with a solution of the organic compound fuchsine.[29]

mutual. Christiansen to Bohr in 1916: 'I have never met anybody like you who went to the bottom of everything and also had the energy to pursue it to completion, and who in addition was so interested in life as a whole.' [41] Among other teachers Bohr has recalled[42] Thorvald Thiele in mathematics, and Harald Høffding, the best known Danish philosopher of his day, a versatile liberal humanist, with whom Bohr took the compulsory freshman course in philosophy.

Bohr had known Christiansen and Høffding long before becoming a university student. Christian Bohr, Christiansen, Høffding,[43] and the famous linguist Vilhelm Thomsen would gather at the home of one or the other for further discussion after the conclusion of the *Videnskabernes Selskab*'s evening meetings. 'From the time that we were old enough to benefit from listening to the conversations and until the gatherings were interrupted on our part by the early death of my father, we brothers [Niels and Harald] were allowed to be present when the meetings were held at our home, and from there we have some of our earliest and deepest impressions.'[44] Høffding evidently appreciated young Niels, for at one time during the latter's student years he sent him some sheets of a new edition of his book on logic[45] with a request for his 'customary criticism'.[46] Two months later he wrote to Bohr thanking him for 'the good collaboration'.[47] In later years Bohr spoke with great respect of Høffding ('he introduced us to philosophy's beauties which lie both so far and so near'[48]), admiring his ever searching open mind, in particular his efforts at understanding the principles of quantum mechanics.[49] He once took Heisenberg along to listen to a 'beautiful lecture on Socrates' by the 85 year old Høffding.[50] When Bohr visited Høffding during his final illness, he read poetry to him.

There has been some discussion in philosophical circles as to whether Høffding's ideas influenced Bohr in his later formulation of the complementarity concept. Some assert,[51] others deny,[52] that this is the case. I shall reserve my own view until a later chapter (19a), where I intend to argue that, in any technical sense, no philosopher ever influenced Bohr. That, however, is not meant to imply that young Bohr lacked interest in philosophical issues. He was in fact one of a circle of twelve students from a variety of disciplines who would regularly meet to discuss philosophical topics. Their group, called *Ekliptika*, later became an old boys' network. Members, along with their later professions, included Harald, who had become a student in 1904; Viggo Brøndal, professor of romance philology; Einar Cohn, distinguished economist; Kai Henriksen, section director of the Zoology Museum; Poul Nørlund, director of the National Museum, and Niels Erik Nørlund director of the Institute for Geodesy, future brothers-in-law of Niels; Edgar Rubin, professor and founder of modern psychology in Denmark; Peter Skov, ambassador to various countries, including the Soviet Union; and Vilhelm Slomann, director of the Museum of Industrial

Arts. Slomann has left us a vivid picture of their activities: 'Niels and Harald were active members and listened attentively to the various communications. When the discussions were at a low ebb it would often happen that one of them would say a few generous words about the lecture and then would continue in a soft voice, at a furious pace and with vehement intensity, but often interrupted by the other. Their ways of thinking seemed to be coordinated, one corrected either the other or his own expressions, battling heatedly and cheerfully for the last word. Ideas changed color and were refined. It was not a defense of preconceived ideas; rather, something new emerged. This mode of thinking *à deux* was such team work that no one else could play along. The chairman ... let them carry on. Only when everybody moved in closer he might say, to no effect: "Louder Niels!" ' [53]

Along with their verbal games the brother students also enjoyed sports, particularly soccer, at which they had been proficient since their high school days, playing first on the top team of *Københavns Boldklub*, later on that of *Akademisk Boldklub*. Harald, halfback, nicknamed *lille* Bohr (little B.), was on the Danish national team in four international matches. He reached the height of his soccer career during the London Olympic games of 1908 (the year before he got his Master's degree), where the Danish team won a silver medal, beating France by the score of 17–1 in the semi-finals, then bowing to England 0–2.[54] He was a national figure, as a story told[55] by Niels illustrates: 'He really was a famous man – all that nonsense that I was a great soccer player is very dubious. One day he was riding the streetcar together with my mother and got off before her, and the conductor had not seen that he had said goodbye to her. So the conductor went up to her and said I am very sorry to disturb you, but I should like madam to know that madam was sitting next to a great soccer player.'

Niels himself played goalie. Among his more memorable exploits on the field was a game against a German club during which most of the action took place on the German side of the field. Suddenly, however, 'the ball came rolling toward the Danish goal and everyone was waiting for Niels Bohr to run out and grab it. But astonishingly he kept standing in the goal, totally uninterested in the game, devoting his attention rather to the goal post. The ball would certainly have gone in if the shouts of a resolute spectator had not awakened Bohr. After the match he gave the embarrassed excuse that a mathematical problem had suddenly occurred to him that absorbed him so strongly that he had carried out some calculations on the goal post.' [56]

In concluding this part about fun and games, I should like to comment once more about the closeness of the two brothers during their student years. In 1904 a fellow student wrote:[57] 'Niels Bohr ... is the kindest, most modest person you can imagine. He has a brother ... The two are inseparable. I have never known people to be as close as they are.'

Let us now turn to Bohr's earliest contributions to physics.

'I was not set for a career in theoretical physics – that was just due to [chance],' Bohr said toward the end of his life.[42] Remember that at the beginning of this century the separation between purely experimental and purely theoretical engagement had just barely begun. Among Bohr's secondary courses was one in experimental inorganic chemistry. His teacher has recalled that Bohr was second to none in breaking glassware.[58] 'Oh, that must be Bohr,' he is said[59] to have remarked when one day the laboratory was rocked by explosions.

However that may be, Bohr's first scientific paper contains some lovely physics experiments he had performed. The *a propos* was the prize investigation proposed in 1905 by the *Videnskabernes Selskab* concerning a method proposed in 1879 by Lord Rayleigh for determining the surface tension of liquids. His idea was this. When a liquid jet with a non-circular cross-section emerges from a cylindrical tube, its surface vibrates. Rayleigh showed that from the velocity and cross-section of the jet and the wavelengths of its surface vibrations one can determine the surface tension of the liquid. He had not, however, performed quantitative experiments to implement this method. The problem posed by the Academy[60] was to do just that.

The question was purely experimental. Bohr, however, included in his work essential improvements on Rayleigh's theory by taking into account the influence of the liquid's viscosity and of the ambient air, and by extending the earlier theory from infinitesimal to arbitrarily large vibration amplitudes. In order to execute his experiments he had first of all to cope with one complication. The university had no physics laboratory.

In 1899 Christiansen had asked the university authorities for an Institute of Physics, noting that 'Copenhagen University hardly owned a single piece of physical apparatus.'[61] His request was denied; the facilities of the *Læreanstalt* had to suffice. These, however, also left much to be desired. Bohr himself has recalled[42] that he could not be accommodated at the necessary time because of other work in progress. In 1906 Prytz made another request: 'The position of the physical sciences . . . in this country . . . is marked by neglect to a high degree . . . For a hundred years there has existed a physical instrument collection . . . at the *Læreanstalt* for joint use with the university. There is, however, a lack of space and equipment for the execution of scientific work. One cannot, in this country, perform modern experiments, one cannot undertake precision measurements of weights or lengths . . . extremely important recent research elsewhere cannot be taken up here . . . It will presumably be clear from the foregoing that physics occupies a position unworthy of our country . . . there is a lack of necessary

collaboration between science and technology . . .'[62] Again there was no
substantial response. As we shall see later, it remained so for another
decade, when Bohr himself took matters in hand.

The prize problem had been announced in February 1905. The deadline for
submission was 30 October 1906. Bohr spent most of the intervening time
working intensely on the problem, doing the experimental part in his
father's laboratory. 'I did the experiments completely alone in the
physiological laboratory . . . it was a great amount of work,'[42] which was
technically demanding. Just a few details. He was his own glass blower,
preparing long tubes with elliptical cross-section so as to produce an
elliptical jet with mean radius less than a millimeter. He examined every
tube under a microscope and accepted only those with uniform elliptical
cross-section. The jet had to be maintained under stable conditions over
long periods (it should not rapidly break up into drops) and at constant
temperature. The jet velocity was accurately determined by cutting the jet
at a given position at two different times, measuring the time interval and,
photographically, the length of the segment cut out. Bohr analyzed the
vibration amplitudes of the liquid used, tapwater, by photographic
observation in nearly monochromatic light.[63] In order to avoid perturbing
vibrations due to passing traffic, many observations he made were at night.

As the deadline grew near, Christian Bohr put pressure on Niels to stop
refining his results and sent him to Nærumgaard to finish the writing. The
manuscript was submitted on the very deadline, anonymously of course,
under the motto 'βγδ'. Two days later Bohr submitted an addendum.[64] On 23
February 1907 the Academy notified him that he had won its gold medal. In
1908 he submitted a modified version to the Royal Society in London.[65] It
was his first and last paper on experiments he himself performed. His second
publication[66] was his last to deal with surface tension of liquids; it was
purely theoretical. Both papers were favorably referred to in later
literature.[67]

The manuscript of the prize essay, never published in its original form, is
preserved in the Bohr Archives. It is handwritten, by Harald Bohr.[68] In the
manuscript of the addendum, which also survived, one recognizes parts
written by Niels, others by Harald, still others by Ellen, their mother.

These are the earliest known examples of Niels' lifelong practice, to do
the work himself but find others to do the writing. I do not know whether in
the examples just mentioned he dictated or whether his family only
prepared a fair copy. In any event, dictating became his routine.

One can think of two reasons for these habits. Bohr's own handwriting
was poorly legible as witness a joke circulating in Los Alamos Laboratory
during World War II. In those years Bohr traveled under the assumed name

Nicholas Baker and accordingly was called Uncle Nick by his friends. When one day a letter from him arrived at the laboratory an argument arose whether it was signed Niels Bohr or Uncle Nick.

A much more important reason for Bohr's mobilizing others to do the writing was, I think, his intensely felt need for continued improvisations and refinement even as results were being committed to paper. His favorite definition of a manuscript was: a document in which to make corrections. I have spent some happy and entertaining hours helping him do just that.

Much later Margrethe Bohr has recalled: 'In his younger days he had so much in his head that just had to be put down, and he could concentrate while he dictated . . . . He dictated whole papers, not notes. I think he had it fairly well prepared in his head.'[69]

In order to give the proper setting to Bohr's next paper, his master's thesis, it is necessary first to take another look backward, this time into what was known about the nature of matter.

(c) The atom: status in 1909

All matter in our world, your nose, my shirt, the moon, is built up of basic chemical substances. The smallest portion of each of these is called a molecule. Noses, shirts, moons are aggregates of various species of molecules. The number of molecular species is uncountably large. All molecules are composites of even more fundamental units. These are the atoms. The word atom means: that which cannot be cut. The number of atomic species, or chemical elements, is just over a hundred. Order the elements in a linear array of increasing atomic weight. With some anomalies, this sequence exhibits periodicities in chemical properties. Splice the array such that elements with similar chemical properties are written one underneath the other, and the resulting scheme is the periodic table of elements.[70]

All this (with the exception of some thirty elements) was known to Maxwell when in 1873 he gave an evening discourse entitled 'Molecules' that began[71] as follows: 'An atom is a body that cannot be cut in two. A molecule is the smallest portion of a particular substance . . . Do atoms exist or is matter infinitely divisible? The discussion of questions of this kind had been going on ever since man began to reason, and to each of us, as soon as we obtain the use of our faculties, the same old questions arise as fresh as ever. They form as essential a part of the science of the nineteenth century of our own era as that of the fifth century before it.'

Maxwell himself was a confirmed atomist, a believer in the reality of atoms. It is clear from his words, however, that atomism was still under debate in his days; and that this problem was more than two millennia old, predating the century of Aristotle.* Thus in the fifth century BC Anaxagoras argued in favor of infinitely divisible matter, while Democritus was an atomist, though not quite in our sense, believing that atoms exist in an infinite variety of sizes and shapes, any one variety being forever incapable of transforming itself into any other. Numerous are the treatises devoted to the atomic debates from that time on.[72] I shall confine myself to just one example from the dawn of the scientific era, Descartes' pronouncement[73] in the early seventeenth century:

There cannot exist any atoms or parts of matter that are of their own nature indivisible. For however small we suppose these parts to be, yet because they are necessarily extended, we are always able in thought to divide any one of them into two or more smaller parts, and may accordingly admit their divisibility. For there is nothing we can divide in thought which we do not thereby recognize to be divisible; and, therefore, were we to judge it indivisible our judgement would not be in harmony with the knowledge we have of the thing; and although we should even suppose that God had reduced any particle of matter to a smallness so extreme that it did not admit of being further divided, it would nevertheless be improperly styled indivisible, for though God had rendered the particle so small that it was not in the power of any creature to divide it, he could not however deprive himself of the ability to do so, since it is absolutely impossible for him to lessen his own omnipotence.

I return to the days of Maxwell. Chemistry had developed into a systematic science in which the coding of information in terms of the language of atoms had become pervasive. Nevertheless many chemists retained an ambivalent position toward atomic reality. Thus in 1869 the president of the London Chemical Society said[74] in an address to the membership: 'It sometimes happens that chemists of high authority refer publicly to the atomic theory as something they would be glad to dispense with, and which they are ashamed of using. . . . All chemists use the atomic theory [yet] a considerable number view it with mistrust, some with positive dislike.'

Regarding the attitude of physicists, one finds men of distinction on both sides of the issue, expressing themselves with varying degrees of emphasis. Confining myself to people mentioned earlier I can count Newton, Young, Clausius, Boltzmann, and (as said) Maxwell in the atomist's camp. Later in life Planck, originally among the opposition, wrote[75] about his attitude during the 1890s: 'I had been inclined to reject atomism,' this being the main reason for his resistance to Boltzmann's interpretation of the second law of thermodynamics (5d).

Physicists were able, well before chemists, to calculate properties of

---

* The issue of divisibility of matter bears some relation to, but is not identical with, the problem of continuity discussed in (5a).

molecules. Already in 1816 Young gave[76] an estimate of the size of water molecules. In 1873 Maxwell reported[77] a value for the diameter of a hydrogen molecule. By the 1880s such calculations had produced quite sensible results for molecular radii[78] as well as for the number of molecules per unit volume for given pressure and temperature.[72]

The denouement came in the early years of the twentieth century, mainly as a result of Einstein's work on the long-known phenomenon of Brownian motion, the motions of microscopically visible particles suspended in a liquid. Einstein was able to account quantitatively for these highly irregular motions as being due to collisions between those particles and the molecules of the liquid.[79] In 1914 the impact of his work was summarized like this: 'The atomic theory has triumphed. Until recently still numerous, its adversaries, at last overcome, now renounce one after the other their misgivings which were for so long both legitimate and useful.'[80]

Meanwhile the understanding of the atom had changed drastically.

'An atom is a body that cannot be cut,' Maxwell had said. In the 1890s it came as a great surprise, if not as a shock, that this statement was not correct. An atom of gold is and remains the smallest particle associated with the chemical element gold, and likewise for all other atomic species. Every atom is cuttable, however.

The first observations of subatomic fragments, electrons, dates from the 1890s. The story of their discovery is quite complex.[81] I must content myself here with giving only some highlights.

The tool with which electrons were discovered was a partially evacuated glass tube with two metal terminals sealed inside, and with a high voltage applied between the terminals. When the gas pressure inside the tube is sufficiently low the gas glows – as in a neon tube used for lighting – and, it turns out, electricity flows from the lower voltage terminal, the cathode, to the other one, the anode. When the gas pressure is lowered still further, the glow ceases but electricity still keeps flowing. What is the constitution of this invisible stream, called cathode rays?

In April 1897 Joseph John Thomson, professor of physics and director of the Cavendish Laboratory in Cambridge, England, announced[82] the answer, in a lecture given in London: 'On the hypothesis that the cathode rays are charged particles moving with high velocities [it follows] that the size of the carriers must be small compared with the dimensions of ordinary atoms or molecules. The assumption of a state of matter more finely subdivided than the atom is a somewhat startling one . . .' Thomson later recalled[83] that 'I was told long afterwards by a distinguished colleague who had been present at my lecture that he thought I had been "pulling their legs".' Nevertheless he was right. His charged particles, the electrons, have a mass about one two-thousandth that of the lightest atom, the hydrogen atom, and a negative electric charge. Our everyday electric current or TV tube function because a directed stream of electrons is knocked out of atoms. In Thomson's words (1899):[84] 'Electrification essentially involves the splitting up of the atom, a part of the mass of the atom getting free and becoming detached from the original atom,' the part of the mass being one or more electrons. An atom minus one, two, . . . electrons is said to be singly, doubly, . . . ionized.

Electrons are the first known universal constituent of matter, they are contained within atoms of whatever species. Their discovery shaped the answer to a rather long-standing question: the Maxwell equations inform us that electric and magnetic fields are produced by given electric charges and currents but do not tell us from what these charges and currents are made. The new developments made clear that at the microscopic level the constituents are principally electrons. This led to a refinement of the electromagnetic theory due most especially to Lorentz. The resulting picture is known as the Maxwell–Lorentz theory. It was developed in the 1890s, a period which therefore brought great advances in experiment as well as theory.

This, however, was still not all that happened during that decade.

In 1905 Rutherford began a lecture at Yale with these words: 'The last decade has been a very fruitful period in physical science, and discoveries of the most striking interest and importance have followed one another in rapid succession . . . The rapidity of this advance has seldom, if ever, been equalled in the history of science.' [85] It is evident from the way he continued that he was neither referring to the beginnings of quantum physics nor to the discovery of relativity theory. Instead he had in mind the electron and the earliest observations of several new kinds of radiation that ushered in yet another new chapter, entitled radioactivity, in the story of the structure of matter.

Between 1896, the year radioactivity was first detected, and 1900 the following discoveries about these radiations were made. They consist of three species, called α-, β-, and γ-rays, emanating from individual atoms. It was a complete mystery at that time from which part of the atom they came, what caused their production, and why some but not all atomic species are radioactive. It was further known by 1900 that β-rays are electrons. It took longer to realize that γ-rays are very energetic photons, and that α-rays are doubly ionized helium atoms.[86]

All this stirring activity took place while Bohr was a bright and eager high school student. In the Niels Bohr Archives one finds notes partly written by him, partly by his mother, of a carefully prepared talk on the status of radioactivity which he gave at a colloquium or seminar conducted by Christiansen.

I now continue the account of Bohr's own activities as a university student. The year is 1909. By then the reality of atoms was generally accepted, except by a few who tenaciously held out. Atoms were not, however, what Democritus or Maxwell had thought them to be. They could break up: they therefore had internal structure. But nobody knew as yet what that structure was, even though an experiment had been performed in that very year, 1909, that contained a clue to the answer (7(b)).

(d) Niels Bohr, M.Sc., Ph.D.

During the decade 1901–10 five students at the University of Copenhagen obtained the degree magister scientiarum in mathematics, and seven in physics. In April 1909, Harald became the first of the brothers to get his master's degree, in mathematics, even though he had become a student the year after Niels entered the university. Niels passed nine months later. Presumably the work on the prize essay had protracted his university studies.

Evidently the number of those who obtained a master's degree was small. Indeed, from 1848, the year of inception of this degree, until 1916 the average number per annum of those who passed[87] in the faculty of mathematics and natural sciences was three to four. Taking the examination for the master's degree was pretty serious business in those years, as is reflected in the publication in the official university yearbook of all problems set for each individual candidate. Thus we know[88] what Niels' tasks were: three days, eight hours each of laboratory work, one in chemistry, two in physics, all in September 1909; three October days of supervised written closed-book examinations, one problem per day, two in mathematics, one in physics. (How can one measure the width of a spectral line with greatest possible precision?) Prior to all that, Bohr had, by late June, to hand in a paper, the *store Opgave* (big problem), essentially a master's thesis, to which a six-week period was allotted. His topic, assigned by Christiansen, was: 'Give an account of the application of the electron theory to the explanation of the physical properties of metals.' Bohr met all requirements satisfactorily and on 2 December 1909 received his degree. The manuscript of his master's thesis, handwritten by his mother, is in the Bohr Archives; an English translation has been available[89] since 1972.

Since Bohr's doctor's thesis, entitled 'Studies on the electron theory of metals', is a vastly elaborated version of his master's thesis – it is four times as long – it is simplest to turn next to the events leading up to his Ph.D., and thereafter comment on both theses. Before doing so, I should note that already in 1910, the year in which Niels started to work for his doctorate, Harald defended *his* doctor's thesis. As was customary, it was a public event, the defendant appearing in white tie and tails. As was also customary, in those times and later, the event was reported in Danish newspapers, one of which noted that the majority of those attending were soccer players, and that Harald, 'the well-known soccer player' had become 'a rising comet in the heavens of mathematics'.[90]

I return to Niels' doctoral work. 'I had most of it in the examination paper but then it was, a few months later, made into a dissertation[91] . . . With the dissertation I had no discussion with anybody. And Christiansen didn't care, you know. He was not interested. He was afraid of influencing people . . . On the essential things I was quite alone.'[92]

Bohr spent much of his time of preparation in a quiet place in the countryside, as he had done before when working for his master's degree. As was to be his mode of operation throughout his later life, he went through many preliminary outlines before reaching the final version. Niels to Harald, June 1910: '[I] have succeeded in writing fourteen more or less divergent rough drafts.'[93] It is equally typical for him that, after he had obtained his degree, he had a personal copy of his thesis bound with blank sheets between the pages on which he marked corrections, addenda, and deletions.

Early in 1911 Bohr was ready. On 12 April the thesis, written in Danish, was accepted by the faculty to be defended for the doctor's degree.[94] The defense took place on 13 May. The ceremony began with Bohr intoning the traditional 'Honourable and learned (*højtærede og højlærde*) professors and doctors, ladies and gentlemen'. The occasion was reported the next day in Danish newspapers.[95] 'Dr Bohr, a pale and modest young man did not take much part in the proceedings, whose short duration [an hour and a half] was a record. The small auditorium was filled to overflowing, and people were standing far out in the corridor . . . Professor Christiansen, [the principal opponent, expressed] regret that the book had not been published in a foreign language. Here in Denmark there is hardly anyone well enough informed about the theory of metals to be able to judge a dissertation on the subject.' Christiansen reminded the audience that not since the days of Ørsted and Lorenz had anyone in Denmark been active on the subject dealt with in the thesis and concluded by expressing his happiness 'that this lack had now been remedied by Niels Bohr'.

The archives contain the names of foreign scientists to whom the young doctor sent a copy of his work. The fairly extensive list[96] includes Lorentz, Planck, Poincaré, and Rayleigh, all of whom are referred to in the thesis. It appears that none of these responded, presumably because they had trouble reading Danish. Among others who did reply,[97] several confessed to have had language difficulties. In 1911 Bohr, helped by a friend who did not know physics, made an attempt at an English translation. The result left much to be desired.[98] Subsequent efforts, up till 1920, to get the thesis published in

England and the United States all failed.[99] Only after Bohr's death did a good English translation become available.[100]

Through most of his life Bohr learned new science from discussions with others; reading was secondary. Such was not yet the case while he was working for his degrees. As noted earlier, he himself had said that he had no discussions in those times, and Christiansen had said that no one in Denmark knew much about the thesis subject. Harald, his confidant, was a postdoc in Göttingen through most of this period.

Reading was therefore Bohr's main source of information, as witness the scholarly nature of this thesis, which contains a careful study and critical analysis of papers by others. This earlier literature, limited in volume, contained several points in need of correction, he found ('I have the bad habit of believing I can find mistakes by others.'[101]) He noted errors in the work of men no less than Thomson[102] and Poincaré.[103] From the quoted literature we see that he was familiar with Planck's work on blackbody radiation. ('It seems impossible to explain the law of heat radiation if one insists upon retaining the fundamental assumptions underlying the electromagnetic theory.'[104]) Most important of all, he had read two fundamental papers by Einstein, dating from 1909, which contain the germs of the concept of complementarity.[105] I shall come back to these articles later (11c).

Having consulted all available sources, Bohr correctly concluded that the best approach to the electron theory of metals was the one initiated by Drude[106] and further elaborated by Lorentz.[107] Its basic idea is to consider a metal as consisting of positively charged essentially immobile ions and of electrons that move almost freely between these ions. In the absence of external electromagnetic forces, the electron motions are random in all directions, so that there is no net flow of electric current. When an electric field is applied, the motions become directed, resulting in a current. The motions are inhibited by a sort of friction caused by ion–electron collisions. The forces between electrons are small compared to the ion–electron forces and are neglected. The resulting picture is that of a gas of free electrons moving through an array of obstacles, the ions. It was thought that Boltzmann's treatment of molecular gases would apply to the electron gas as well.

This model of a metal gives a picture not only of its electrical but also of its thermal conductivity. Compare a metal bar with a column of gas, both held at different temperatures at their respective ends. Just as heat diffuses through the gas from the higher to the lower temperature end by collisions between molecules, so heat will diffuse through the metal by ion–electron collisions. Drude noted that, at the same temperature, these collision effects were the same for the conduction of heat as for electricity. Thus their ratio – always at the same temperature – should be the same for all metals. That was just what had been observed half a century earlier, for some range of temperatures, a phenomenon known as the Wiedemann–Franz law (1853).

This agreement with experiment was considered the main success of the theory. The quantitative interpretation of other related effects caused difficulties, however, among them the Thomson effect (hold a metal bar at temperatures that increase from one end to the other and pass an electric current in that direction, then heat is absorbed) and the Peltier effect (join two different metals at two points to make a closed circuit and pass a current around, then heat is emitted at one junction and absorbed at the other). The situation was not ameliorated by Lorentz's more rigorous treatment of ion–electron collisions in which he treated both ions and electrons as perfectly elastic hard spheres, so that electrons would be deflected only upon bodily contact with ions.

It became Bohr's main program to extend Lorentz's theory by generalizing the ion–electron forces to an arbitrary dependence on their relative distance. While his is the most advanced of the classical treatments,[108] he too was unable to resolve all the mentioned difficulties. In fact he noted new paradoxes related to the so-called Hall effect. If we send a current through a metal bar placed in a magnetic field perpendicular to the current, then an electric field is generated perpendicular to both the current and the magnetic field. For a number of metals the theory appeared to give a decent quantitative account of the strength of the induced electric field. It could not explain, however, why this field is abnormally strong for other metals (e.g. bismuth), even less why it points in a direction opposite from what was predicted (as for iron, zinc, lead). Bohr had already noted these difficulties in his master's thesis, but stated them more emphatically[109] in his doctor's thesis:

It does not seem possible at the present stage of the development of the electron theory to explain the magnetic properties of bodies from this theory.

So it remained for another fifteen years. Sommerfeld wrote[110] in 1927: 'During the last twenty years the idea of the electron gas has been more and more discredited.' And shortly afterward: 'One may say that the confidence in the electron theory of metals was . . . completely shattered . . . until the quantum theory created a new situation.'[111]

By that time it had become clear that the idea of an electron gas kicking around inside a metal was a good one – but the gas is not a classical gas in the sense of Boltzmann. It is a quantum gas. I shall defer explaining what is meant by that until we reach quantum mechanics (13a). Suffice it to say here that the classical electron theory of metals has receded into history without later traces. It has turned out that the right answer obtained classically for the Wiedemann–Franz law was accidental.

As to Bohr, his doctor's thesis had pushed him to the outer frontier of classical physics. In 1912 he wrote an additional brief note on the subject,[112] then left it alone. It could just be that these experiences encouraged him to push into areas beyond, into the mysteries of quantum physics, as he was soon to do.

(e) Death of father. Bohr becomes engaged

Bohr's thesis opens with the prefatory inscription: 'Dedicated with deepest gratitude to the memory of my father.'

When on the evening of 2 February 1911, Margrethe Nørlund, Niels' financée, came for dinner at the Christian Bohrs, all was well.[112a] After dinner Christian went back to work in his laboratory. He came home toward midnight, complaining of chest pains. His assistant was called in. Shortly afterward the pain had passed, however. Christian talked about what had happened, saying that he now had to stop smoking for a while. A few moments later he collapsed and died.[113] On 14 February he would have been 56 years old.

On 4 February Christian was cremated at the crematorium of Bispebjerg's hospital – an unusual procedure for that time. Between 4 and 12 February a plot was bought in Assistens Kirkegaard, one of Copenhagen's old cemeteries (it dates from 1760). There, on 12 February, his remains were buried, not far from the graves of Ørsted and H. C. Andersen. No priest was present at the funeral.*

Some time later the artist Jens Ferdinand Willumsen proposed to Christian's widow Ellen that he execute a monument for Christian's grave.[114] The suggestion was accepted and the monument was put in place in 1912.[115] In a recent report[116] on the conservation of tombstones in the cemetery, it is described in these words: 'Sculptors of recent times are abundantly represented in this section. Most notable is J. F. Willumsen's monument for the Bohr family, which belongs to the most mastodontic domineering monuments not just of this section but of the entire cemetery. Its placement near the poplar avenue with its high trees tempers the monument's impression of immensity, however.' My own impression upon seeing this enormity (a pillar with a laurel wreath and an owl on top) was that it probably reflects more on the character of the artist than on that of his subject. More importantly, however, Ellen Bohr found it worthy of both men.[117]

1911, the year of his father's death and of his doctor's degree can be said to mark the end of the first phase of Bohr's life. Meanwhile the second phase had begun. In 1909 he first met his future wife, Margrethe Nørlund,

---

* I owe the information in this paragraph to K. M. Møller.

daughter of Alfred Nørlund, pharmacist from the town of Slagelse, and of Emma Holm. She was the sister of Niels Erik and Poul Nørlund, friends of Niels from the Ekliptika circle. She was a student at *Frøken Branners Pigeskole* in Slagelse, a type of institution founded in Denmark in the late nineteenth century, where women studied home economics, hygiene, physiology, nursing, and practical things about the house, and where they could train for teaching at such schools. From Margrethe's recollections[118] half a century later: '[Niels] studied together with my brother at the university, and my brother told me first about him. Yes, let me think, where did I meet him for the first time. I think it was at a dinner party. He was sitting on one side of me. I think I met him for the first time there . . . but I don't think I talked with him that evening. Then I was invited to their home. I lived in the country together with my brother. There I then got to know him. That must have been in 1909 . . . Then he came with my brother to see us. He came to the country and spent an Easter, I think, with us. Then I was also invited to [Harald's] doctoral dissertation. I remember we had a party. So I met him a few times; I met him sometimes during the spring. Then he came down to my home. That summer [of 1910] we were engaged.'

The finest comment on the meeting of Niels and Margrethe was made[119] shortly after Niels' death by Richard Courant, friend of the Bohrs for many decades:

Some people have speculated about the lucky circumstances which combined to make Niels so successful. I think the ingredients of his life were by no means matters of chance but deeply ingrained in the structure of his personality . . . It was not luck, rather deep insight, which led him to find in young years his wife, who, as we all know, had such a decisive role in making his whole scientific and personal activity possible and harmonious.

Margrethe's role began, as best I know, at the time of Niels' Ph.D. examination. The manuscript of the text of his introductory remarks at his thesis defense, *'Højtærede og højlærde . . .'*, is in her handwriting.[96]

References

1. C. Paludan-Müller, *Historisk Tidsskr.* **2**, 241, 1880.
2. H. F. Rørdam, *Kjøbenhavns Universitetets Historie*, Vol. 1, Bianco Lunos, Copenhagen 1869.
3. Ref. 2, pp. 59, 84, 314.
4. Ref. 2, p. 110.
5. Ref. 2, p. 111.
6. V. H. H. Green, *The Universities*, p. 193, Penguin Books, London 1969.
7. Cf. A. R. Hall, *The scientific revolution 1500–1800*, Beacon Press, Boston 1966.
8. W. Whewell, *History of the inductive sciences*, Wm. Parker & Son, London 1834. See also R. Yeo, *Ann. Sci.* **36**, 493, 1979.

9. O. Bostrup, *Fysisk Tidsskr.* **69**, 11, 1971, esp. pp. 16, 22.
10. *Det Kongelige danske Videnskabernes Selskab 1742–1942*, Vol. 2, p. 12, Munksgaard, Copenhagen 1950.
11. For a biography see E. Snorrason, *C. G. Kratzenstein*, Odense University Press, 1974.
12. For the history of that period see especially *Københavns Universitetet 1479–1979*, Vol. 12, Gads, Copenhagen 1983.
13. N. Bohr, *Fysisk Tidsskr.* **49**, 6, 1951.
14. Ref. 10, Vol. 1, p. 541.
15. I. S. C. Schweigger, *J. für Chem. und Phys.* **31**, 1, 1821.
16. For more details see M. C. Harding, *Selskabet for Naturlaerens Udbredelse*, Gjellerup Forlag, Copenhagen 1924.
17. The time of this faculty's appearance is not unusual. The establishment of similar faculties in France dates from 1808. In 1891 they existed at only three of the German universities. Uppsala made the step in 1956; see Ref. 12, p. 73.
18. For a biography of Ørsted see O. Bang, *Store Hans Christian*, Rhodos, Copenhagen 1986.
19. Ref. 12, p. 85.
20. See O. Pedersen in *Hans Christian Ørsted*, p. 142, Isefjordvaerket 1987.
21. See M. Pihl, *Der Physiker L. V. Lorenz*, Munksgaard, Copenhagen 1939.
22. G. L.'E. Turner, *Nineteenth century scientific instruments*, Sotheby Publication, University of California Press, Berkeley 1983.
23. Ref. 6, p. 211.
24. Here I have taken the liberty of translating Kierkegaard's 'Klangfigur' (Chladni figure) by 'musical chord'.
25. F. Bulle, *Fysisk Tidsskr.* **49**, 20, 1951.
26. *Les prix Nobel en 1921–1922*, p. 126, Norstedt, Stockholm 1923.
27. C. Bohr, handwritten note, NBA; repr. in CW, Vol. 6, p. XIX.
28. *Minerva Jahrbuch der gelehrten Welt, 1903–4*, pp. 508, 1196, 1197, Teubner Strassburg 1904.
29. C. Christiansen, *Ann. der Phys.* **141**, 479, 1870; **143**, 250, 1871.
30. W. Sellmeyer, *Ann. der Phys.* **143**, 272, 1871.
31. H. Helmholtz, *Ann. der Phys.* **154**, 582, 1875, esp. pp. 591, 595.
32. C. Christiansen, *Ann. der Phys.* **21**, 364, 1884.
33. L. Boltzmann, *Ann. der Phys.* **22**, 31, 1884.
34. C. Christiansen, *Inledning til den matematiske Fysik*, 2 vols, Gyldendal, Copenhagen 1887–90.
35. *Elements der theoretischen Physik*, transl. Johs. Müller, Bart, Leipzig 1894.
36. *Elements of theoretical physics*, transl. superv. by W. F. Magie, Macmillan, London 1897.
37. For biographical sketches of Christiansen see E. Wedemann, Ref. 35, 4th edn, 1921, p. XI; also K. Prytz, *Fysisk Tidsskr.* **16**, 81, 1917.
38. For biographical sketches see J. C. Jacobsen, *Overs. dan. Vidensk. Selsk. Virks. 1949–1950*, p. 1; N. Bohr, *ibid.*, p. 7.
39. For a biographical sketch see H. M. Hansen, *Fysisk Tidsskr.* **29**, 1, 1929.
40. Ref. 26. See, however, N. Bohr letter to H. Bohr, 27 March 1909, NBA; repr. in CW, Vol. 1, p. 499.

41. C. Christiansen, letter to N. Bohr, 12 May 1916, NBA; repr. in CW, Vol. 2, p. 496.
42. N. Bohr, interview with T. S. Kuhn, L. Rosenfeld, A. Petersen, and E. Rüdinger, 1 November 1962, NBA.
43. H. Høffding, *Erindringer*, p. 171 ff., Gyldendal, Copenhagen 1928.
44. N. Bohr, *Overs. dan. Vidensk. Selsk. Virks. 1931–1932*, p. 131.
45. H. Høffding, *Formel Logik*, 5th edn, Gyldendal, Copenhagen 1907.
46. H. Høffding, letter to N. Bohr, 22 November 1906, NBA.
47. H. Høffding, letter to N. Bohr, 25 January 1907. See also the preface in Ref. 45 where the author thanks 'one of my earlier listeners'.
48. N. Bohr, *Berlingske Tidende*, 10 March 1928.
49. Ref. 42, interview 17 November 1962; also unpublished MS of a talk on Høffding's attitudes toward relativity and quantum theory, August 1932, NBA.
50. CW, Vol. 6, p. 24.
51. M. Jammer, *The conceptual development of quantum mechanics*, pp. 172–3, McGraw-Hill, New York 1966; G. Holton, *Thematic origins of scientific thought*, pp. 142–4, Harvard University Press 1973; J. Faye, *Stud. Hist. Philos. Sci.* **19**, 321, 1988.
52. D. Favrholdt, *Danish Yearb. Philos.* **13**, 206, 1976; see also J. Witt-Hansen, *ibid.* **17**, 31, 1980.
53. V. Slomann, *Politiken*, 7 October 1955, transl. in CW, Vol. 6, p. xxiv.
54. N. Middelboe, *KB-Chelsea og hjem igen*, Thaning & Appels, Copenhagen 1944.
55. Niels Bohr, taped conversation in Tisvilde with Aage Bohr and L. Rosenfeld, 12 July 1961, NBA.
56. *Akademisk Boldklub gennem 50 Aar, 1889–1939*, Saabye & Christensen, Copenhagen 1939.
57. NBR, p. 32.
58. N. Bjerrum, unpublished MS, NBA.
59. NBR, p. 31.
60. See CW, Vol. 1, p. 4. The question clearly originated from Christian who had been engaged on surface tension experiments (*Ann. der Phys.* 1905). Bohr had helped him in analyzing that work.
61. *Aarbog for Kjøbenhavns Universitetet, den polytekniske Læreanstalt og Kommunitetet, 1898–1901*, p. 778, Schultz, Copenhagen 1902.
62. *Aarbog* (Ref. 61) for 1906–7, p. 1003, Schultz, Copenhagen 1911; also Ref. 16, p. 366.
63. The jets turned out to vibrate in an almost pure harmonic mode.
64. CW, Vol. 1, p. 67.
65. N. Bohr, *Trans. Roy. Soc.* **209**, 281, 1909, repr. in CW, Vol. 1, p. 29. Another gold medal was awarded for the same prize problem, see P. O. Pedersen, *ibid.* **207**, 341, 1907.
66. N. Bohr, *Proc. Roy. Soc.* A **84**, 395, 1910, repr. in CW, Vol. 1, p. 79.
67. Cf. CW, Vol. 1, p. 11.
68. Sample pages are found in CW, Vol. 1, p. 21.

69. Interview of Margrethe Bohr, Aage Bohr, and L. Rosenfeld by T. S. Kuhn, 30 January 1963, NBA.
70. See further IB, Chap. 11, section (a).
71. J. C. Maxwell, *Collected works*, Vol. 2, p. 376, Dover, New York.
72. For additional comments and a few references, see SL, Chap. 5, section (a); IB, Chap. 4, section (b).
73. R. Descartes, *Principles of Philosophy*, Part 2, principle 20; see e.g. *The philosophical works of Descartes*, transl. E. Haldane and G. Ross, Dover, New York 1955.
74. A. W. Williamson, *J. Chem. Soc. (London)* **22**, 328, 1869.
75. M. Planck, *Naturw.* **28**, 778, 1940.
76. T. Young, *Miscellaneous works*, Murray, London 1855. Repr. by Johnson Reprint, New York 1972, Vol. 1, p. 461.
77. Ref. 71, Vol. 2, p. 361.
78. A. W. Rücker, *J. Chem. Soc. (London)* **53**, 222, 1888.
79. See SL, Chap. 5, section (d).
80. J. Perrin, *Les Atomes*, 4th edn, Librairie Alcan, Paris 1914.
81. See IB, Chap. 4.
82. J. J. Thomson, *The Royal Institution library of science*, Vol. 5, p. 36, Eds. W. Bragg and G. Porter, Elsevier, Amsterdam 1970.
83. J. J. Thomson, *Recollections and reflections*, p. 341, Bell and Sons, London 1936.
84. J. J. Thomson, *Phil. Mag.* **48**, 547, 1899, esp. p. 565.
85. E. Rutherford, *Radioactive transformations*, pp. 1 and 16, Constable, London 1906.
86. A detailed account is found in IB, Chaps. 2, 3, and 6.
87. Ref. 12, p. 95.
88. *Aarbog* (Ref. 61) for 1909–10, p. 1214, Schultz, Copenhagen 1914.
89. CW, Vol. 1, p. 131.
90. *Politiken*, 1 February 1910.
91. Ref. 42, interview on 31 October 1962.
92. Ref. 42. At one point a fellow student helped him locate a mathematical error. N. Bohr, letter to H. Bohr, 28 July 1910, CW, Vol. 1, p. 515.
93. N. Bohr, letter to H. Bohr, 26 June 1910, CW, Vol. 1, p. 511.
94. CW, Vol. 1, p. 294.
95. CW, Vol. 1, pp. 98, 99.
96. NBA, microfilms of manuscripts, roll 2.
97. CW, Vol. 1, pp. 101, 102, 397–409.
98. CW, Vol. 1, p. 103.
99. CW, Vol. 1, pp. 103–10, 114–15, 117–19.
100. CW, Vol. 1, p. 291.
101. N. Bohr, letter to H. Bohr, 1 July 1909; CW, Vol. 1, p. 507.
102. CW, Vol. 1, p. 352, footnote 1; also p. 155.
103. CW, Vol. 1, p. 353, footnote 3.
104. CW, Vol. 1, p. 378.
105. CW, Vol. 1, p. 378, footnote 4.

106. P. K. L. Drude, *Ann. der Phys.* **1**, 566, 1900; **3**, 369, 1900; **7**, 687, 1902.
107. See e.g. H. A. Lorentz, *The theory of electrons*, pp. 9, 63, 281, Teubner, Leipzig 1909.
108. E. Grüneisen, *Handb. der Phys.* **13**, 64, Springer, Berlin 1928.
109. CW, Vol. 1, p. 395.
110. A. Sommerfeld, *Naturw.* **15**, 825, 1927.
111. H. A. Bethe and A. Sommerfeld, *Handb. der Phys.* **24**, part 2, p. 334, Springer, Berlin 1933.
112. N. Bohr, *Phil. Mag.* **23**, 984, 1912; CW, Vol. 1, p. 439.
112a. As told by Margrethe Bohr to the late Christian Crone.
113. *Politiken*, 4 February 1911.
114. See E. Bohr, letter to J. F. Willumsen, 9 June 1911, Archive of the Willumsen Museum, Frederikssund.
115. *Extrabladet*, 4 April 1912.
116. Report of 1985–1987 listing monuments in the Assistens Kirkegaard selected for consideration during the cemetery's reorganization, section Q, overall appraisal, p. 216; 2nd revised edn 1987.
117. E. Bohr, letter to J. F. Willumsen, 1 April 1912, Willumsen Archive.
118. Ref. 69, interview of 23 January 1963.
119. R. Courant, NBR, p. 304.

7

In which Bohr goes to England for postdoctoral research

(a) Cambridge: Thomson, father of the electron

One day in late September 1911, as Bohr was crossing the Great Belt by ferry, he wrote[1] to his fiancée: 'I am taking off with all my silly fierce spirit' (*Jeg rejser ud med alt mit dumme vilde Mod*). Financed by a stipend from the Carlsberg Foundation (a Danish institution) for a year's study abroad,[1a] he was on his way to Cambridge to start postdoctoral research under J. J. Thomson, the director of the Cavendish. In his baggage he carried the poor translation of his Ph.D. thesis, which he had helped prepare a little earlier[2] (6d).

At the time of Bohr's arrival at the Cavendish, it was, along with the Physico-Technical Institute in Berlin, one of the world's two leading centers in experimental physics research. Thomson, its third illustrious director, successor to Maxwell and Rayleigh, had added to its distinction by his discovery of the electron, work for which he had received the Nobel Prize in 1906. (To date the Cavendish has produced 22 Nobel laureates.) In those days, 'students from all over the world looked to work with him . . . Though the master's suggestions were, of course, most anxiously sought and respected, it is no exaggeration to add that we were all rather afraid he might touch some of our apparatus.'[3] Thomson himself was well aware that his interaction with experimental equipment was not always felicitous: 'I believe all the glass in the place is bewitched.'[4] (In his student days he once nearly lost his eyesight by causing a laboratory explosion.[5]) Nevertheless his role in the experimental program was crucial, as is made particularly clear in an obituary of Thomson written by another Nobel laureate who had worked under him at the Cavendish: 'When results were coming out well his boundless, indeed childlike, enthusiasm was contagious and occasionally embarrassing. Negatives just developed had actually to be hidden away for fear he would handle them while they were still wet. Yet when hitches occurred, and the exasperating vagaries of an apparatus had reduced the man who had designed, built, and worked with it to baffled despair, along

would shuffle this remarkable being, who, after cogitating in a characteristic attitude over his funny old desk in the corner, and jotting down a few
figures and formulae in his tidy handwriting, on the back of somebody's
Fellowship thesis, or on an old envelope, or even the laboratory check-book,
would produce a luminous suggestion, like a rabbit out of a hat, not only
revealing the cause of trouble, but also the means of cure. This intuitive
ability to comprehend the inner working of intricate apparatus without the
trouble of handling it appeared to me then, and still appears to me now, as
something verging on the miraculous, the hallmark of a great genius.'[6]

These comments point to theoretical physics as Thomson's main
strength. There too lay his ambition. 'J.J. spent a good part of most days in
the arm chair of Maxwell, doing mathematics . . . In the period with which
we are now concerned, two major fields . . . occupied J.J.'s attention. One
was virtually to rewrite physics . . . in terms of the newly discovered
electron . . . The other was to get beyond Maxwell.'[7]

It was natural therefore that, having discovered the electron, Thomson
would become deeply involved in the problem of atomic structure. The
question was not new to him. In 1882 he had won the Adams prize for an
essay[8] on fluid vortices, essentially doughnut-shaped tubes of fluid in which
the liquid describes a vortex motion, that is, it rotates in the direction of the
doughnut's central circle. Such motions show a remarkable indestructibi-
lity. In a section of this paper entitled 'Sketch of a chemical theory'
Thomson had considered the possibility (as had others before him) of
associating a specific vortex structure with each atomic species.[9] Speculations of this and other kinds had gently faded away when the electron
appeared on the scene and Thomson at once betook himself to construct
atomic models out of electrons. It should be stressed that at the beginning of
the twentieth century only very few physicists had the inclination and the
courage to explore the structure of the atom: 'It is perhaps not unfair to say
that for the average physicists of the time, speculations about atomic
structure were like speculations about life on Mars – very interesting for
those who like that sort of thing, but without much hope of support from
convincing scientific evidence and without much bearing on scientific
thought and development.'[10]

Any model of an atom should evidently account for its two most
important qualities: an atom is electrically neutral; and it has a
characteristic weight. Thomson, the first model builder to play with
electrons, initially took the view that the negative charge of the electrons
present in an atom is compensated by a positive charge uniformly smeared
out over a sphere of fixed radius. He further supposed that this positive
medium, whatever it might consist of, does not contribute to the atom's
mass which therefore is exclusively due to electrons. Hence these particles
should be present by the thousands in each atom.[11] He expounded this model

in 1903, when he became the first of a continuing series of distinguished scientists to give the Silliman lectures at Yale.[12]

Thomson's model raised the central difficulty on which all attempts at an understanding of atoms within the framework of classical physics would ultimately come to grief: the atom's stability. Thomson showed in considerable detail that, given his picture of the positive charge distribution, there do exist electron configurations that are stable – as long as these particles are at rest. He preferred, however, to assume that his electrons move in some sort of closed orbits, his reason being that such motions might explain the magnetic properties of substances.[12a] Long before, Ampère, in his pioneering work on magnetism (4e), had proposed that magnetism was caused by electric charges in motion: '...The way I conceive the phenomena presented by magnets, by considering them as if they were assemblages of electric currents in very small circuits about their particles...'[12b] Could these circuits not simply be electrons moving inside atoms? By a general classical theorem (post-dating Ampère) such orbits are unstable, however, since now the electrons will necessarily lose energy by emission of electromagnetic radiation. I shall not discuss here the ways in which Thomson and others attempted, unsuccessfully, to cope with this extremely troublesome instability.[13] Suffice it to say for now that quantum mechanics is necessary for the resolution of this fundamental problem.

Nevertheless there was some progress. It was Thomson himself who in 1906 made the discovery, perhaps his greatest as a theoretician, that his early atomic model was fallacious, that in fact 'the number of corpuscles [his name for electrons] in an atom ... is of the same order as the atomic weight of the substance'.[14] The most famous of his several theoretical reasons for this revision was his theory of the scattering of X-rays by gases. In his primitive though qualitatively correct treatment he assumed that this effect is due exclusively to the scattering by X-rays off the interatomic electrons which are treated as free particles. To this day the scattering of low-energy photons by electrons is known as Thomson scattering. From a comparison of his formulae with experimental data Thomson concluded, correctly, that the number of electrons per atom lies somewhere between 0.2 and 2 times the atomic number. What, then, causes the atom to have the mass it has? On that question Thomson remained silent.

Bohr knew of Thomson's ideas on atomic structure, since these are mentioned in one of the latter's books[15] which Bohr had quoted several times[16] in his thesis. This problem was not yet uppermost in his mind, however, when he arrived in Cambridge. When asked later why he had gone there for postdoctoral research he replied: 'First of all I had made this great study of the electron theory. I considered ... Cambridge as the center of physics and Thomson as a most wonderful man.'[17] In other words, Bohr looked forward above all to discuss with Thomson matters related to his thesis.

Several physicists have given me an account of Bohr's first meeting with Thomson.[18] It went about as follows. Bohr entered Thomson's office carrying one of the latter's books, opened it on a certain page, and politely said: 'This is wrong.' In order to appreciate this encounter it should be noted, first, that Bohr was forever a courteous man and, secondly, that his English was poor at that time. His mastery of English improved considerably in later years, though he always kept his own charming accent. Margrethe: 'The pronunciation was not always so good but the vocabulary was good. Even to the last he would not always pronounce it so well.'[19] My own favorite is the way he used to refer to a certain deadly weapon as 'the atomic bum'. With regard to writing in a foreign language Bohr once said: 'It is more difficult to write in one's own language; for there one knows precisely what the words mean. In a foreign language one doesn't know it quite so well and so one can let the words mean just what one wants them to mean.'[19a]

This first encounter with Thomson did not lay the basis for the relationship Bohr had hoped for. In October 1911 he wrote to Harald: 'Thomson has so far not been as easy to deal with as I thought the first day. He is an excellent man, incredibly clever and full of imagination ... extremely friendly, but ... it is very difficult to talk to him. He has not yet had time to read my paper [the thesis] and I do not know if he will accept my criticism.'[20] Margrethe remembered: 'Thomson was always very nice – he was a very charming and a very spiritual man but he just was not so great as my husband because he didn't like criticism.'[19]

Meanwhile Bohr kept himself occupied by attending lectures by Larmor and Jeans on various topics in the theory of electromagnetism. Also he 'together with 15 young people'[20] did experimental research. Thomson had suggested to him a problem related to cathode ray production.[20] 'I worked on it but there was nothing to get out of it.'[17] He had his troubles in the laboratory. 'You had to blow glass and you had to do all such things. And the glass broke for him.'[19] His inadequate English caused him problems too. 'A poor foreigner who doesn't even know the names of things he cannot find is very badly off; [things may improve] when I take a dictionary along tomorrow.' He began to read English books to improve his knowledge of the language. 'In Cambridge I read ... *The Pickwick Papers* and I looked up every word [in the dictionary]. I thought that was a way to get into English.'[17]

There were other diversions. In October he joined a soccer club.[20] Harald came for a two week visit at Christmas time.[17] In January 1912 he thanked his mother for a Christmas gift, a pair of skates, which he had meanwhile used with pleasure.[21]

As for physics, however, Cambridge was of no real help. Early in 1912 Niels wrote to Margrethe: 'In this [spring] term I shall not go to the laboratory but only follow lectures and read, read, read (and perhaps also calculate a little and think).' [22] Late in life Bohr reminisced: 'It was a disappointment that Thomson was not interested to learn that his calculations were not correct. That was also my fault. I had no great knowledge of English and therefore I did not know how to express myself. And I could say only that this is incorrect. And he was not interested in the accusation that it was not correct ... Thomson was a genius who actually showed the way to everybody. *Then* some young man could make things a little better ... The whole thing was very interesting in Cambridge but it was absolutely useless.' [23]

Then, while still attached to Cambridge, Bohr met Rutherford and his whole life changed.

(b) Manchester: Rutherford, father of the nucleus

Ernest Rutherford was the second son and the fourth of the twelve children of James Rutherford, a small business man, and Martha née Thompson who had been a schoolteacher before her marriage. His parents, both British born, had emigrated to New Zealand, where Rutherford was born on a farm in the province of Nelson on the South Island. After a spectacular scientific career he died as Lord Rutherford of Nelson. His ashes were laid to rest in Westminster Abbey – as were J. J. Thomson's – in the presence of representatives of king and government. After his death one of his closest co-workers described him as having been a man of volcanic energy, intense enthusiasms, with an immense capacity for work and a robust common sense, a man who 'had no cleverness – just greatness'.[24] Another wrote: 'He was always a charming blend of boy, man, and genius.' [25]

Rutherford received his early education in New Zealand. In high school he won a prize in English literature and a French scholarship and kept order with a cricket stump after becoming school librarian. In college he won prizes in science and mathematics and played on the rugby team.[26] His earliest physics research dates back to those college days, when he was already aware of current developments from reading the *Proceedings of the Royal Society.*[27] Most notable among his earliest work, published in New Zealand, is a report on his detection with a magnetometer of radio waves travelling a distance through space, work that predates Marconi's announcement in 1896 of wireless transmission of telegraph signals.

At the beginning of October 1895 Rutherford arrived in Cambridge, on a research fellowship, to work in the Cavendish. He has recalled with gratitude the kindness shown by Thomson and his wife to a young man from the colonies. Nor did it take long for Thomson to recognize the exceptional abilities of his new research student.

It was a marvelous time for an aspiring experimentalist to start his career. Three months after his arrival Röntgen published his discovery of X-rays; another three months later came Becquerel's first paper on radioactivity; a year thereafter, Thomson's announcement of the electron.

After having settled down at the Cavendish, Rutherford began by continuing his experiments with radio waves. 'It was so successful that the [Cavendish] laboratory held for a time the record for long distance telegraphy, communications being established between the laboratory and the observatory two miles away.'[28] It was only natural, however, that he did not pursue this work for long but rather threw himself energetically upon the study of X-rays, a subject that interested Thomson greatly. In 1896 the two men published an impressive joint paper[29] on ionization induced by X-rays. In 1897 Rutherford turned to radioactivity, the central subject of his future oeuvre. In 1898 he announced the discovery of two distinct kinds of radioactive rays, α-rays and β-rays. It cannot be stressed enough that the equipment used in these various discoveries had to be refined, if not invented, as experiment progressed. Those early tools were primitive compared with what is now available for a good undergraduate laboratory course. But how well they worked and what insights they yielded!

Both Rutherford's scientific productivity and his rise in the academic world proceeded uncommonly rapidly. In 1898 he moved to Canada to become professor of physics at McGill University in Montreal. 'It is not too much to say that at McGill [Rutherford] laid down the fundamental principles of radioactivity.'[30] Young people traveled there to work with him, among them Soddy who collaborated with Rutherford in formulating the radioactive transformation theory according to which radioactive bodies contain unstable atoms of which a fixed fraction decays per unit time; and Hahn who later would be one of the discoverers of nuclear fission.

In 1903 Rutherford was elected to the Royal Society; in 1905 he received its Rumford medal; in 1908, at the age of 37, he was awarded the Nobel Prize for chemistry 'for his investigations of radioactive elements and the chemistry of radioactive substances'. Meanwhile, in 1907, he had left Montreal to take up a professorship at the University of Manchester. There, he achieved a feat which I believe to be unique: to make the greatest discovery of his career after having won a Nobel Prize.

'In Manchester [Rutherford's] research students were mostly senior men who had already won a reputation.'[24] In 1908 one of these, Geiger, had published a paper[31] on the scattering of α-particles by thin foils of gold and aluminum in which he reported that 'some of the α-particles ... were deflected by quite an appreciable angle'. Early in 1909 Rutherford suggested to Marsden, a twenty year old New Zealand born undergraduate, that he pursue this matter further. In Marsden's words: 'One day Rutherford came into the room where [Geiger and I] were counting α-particles . . . turned to me and said, "See if you can get some effect of α-particles directly reflected from a metal surface." . . . I do not think he expected any such result . . . To my surprise, I was able to observe the effect looked for . . . I remember well reporting the result to Rutherford a week after, when I met him on the stairs.'[32] In May 1909 Geiger and Marsden submitted a paper[33] in which they reported that about 1 in 8000 α-particles were deflected by more than 90°.

On several occasions Rutherford has told that this finding was the most incredible result in his life.[34] Even allowing for his exuberant language this is no exaggeration. An α-particle, weighing about 8000 times more than an electron, traveling at a speed of something like 10000 miles per second, hits a bunch of electrons and – we are still in the Thomson period – some nondescript smeared out jelly of positive charge. That under those circumstances an α-particle would rebound at a large angle is as incredible as that a loaded Mack truck would veer back upon hitting a Volkswagen.

A year and a half later, in December 1910, Rutherford knew the answer to this puzzle. He wrote to a colleague: 'I think I can devise an atom much superior to J.J.'s.'[35] How much of the intervening time Rutherford had spent brooding on this problem I do not know. It should be remembered, however, that Rutherford had neither much expertise in nor much taste for theoretical physics. It is perhaps more interesting to note that no other theorist had responded to this challenge, nor that this seminal experiment had been repeated anywhere else . . .

Rutherford's atom (of some specific element) consists of a number Z of electrons, each with charge $-e$, and a small-sized central body with charge Ze in which practically all the mass of the atom is concentrated. This body is many thousands of times heavier than the electron. Not until October 1912 did Rutherford refer to it as the nucleus. ('The atom must contain a highly charged nucleus.'[36]) He further assumed that the role of the Z electrons in α-particle scattering can be neglected (actually a good approximation) so that this process is entirely due to the electrostatic (Coulomb) interaction between the α-particle and the nucleus. The theoretical exercise is then to calculate the path of an α-particle as it first approaches, then moves away from the nucleus. These orbits are hyperbolae, just like those of non-returning comets that pass by the sun. Rutherford produced a formula that describes the dependence of the orbits on the angle of scattering, on the α-particle velocity, and on Z. In particular, the probability for α-particle scattering is proportional to Z^2. At that time the data were not yet sufficient to verify these predictions in all detail, but it did not take long before it was found that his answers worked extremely well.

On 7 March 1911, Rutherford presented his results publicly for the first time. An eyewitness has recalled: 'I remember well the occasion on which the idea was first put forward. It was at a meeting of the Manchester Literary and Philosophical Society to which all workers in the laboratory were invited. Rutherford's account of his theory, backed by Geiger with some new experimental evidence, created a profound impression.'[24]

The definitive paper on the subject appeared in the May 1911 issue of *Philosophical Magazine*.[37] Here Rutherford records a first (decent) estimate of the radius of a nucleus: about a hundred thousand times smaller than that of an atom. Thus if one imagines an atom blown up to the size of a football field, then the nucleus would be the size of a marble placed at the kick-off point. Nuclei are not only heavy. They are also exceedingly small, even by atomic standards. Matter consists largely of emptiness.

In the autumn of 1911, only months after the birth of the nuclear atom, Bohr met Rutherford for the first time.

It happened in Manchester, in early November,[38] in the course of a visit by Bohr to a friend of his late father. Bohr's recollection of that occasion: 'He invited Rutherford and I talked with Rutherford . . . but we didn't talk about Rutherford's own discovery [of the nucleus] . . . I told Rutherford that I would like to come up and work and also to get to know something about radioactivity. And he said I should be welcome, but I had to settle with Thomson. So I said I would when I came back to Cambridge.'[17]*

The next meeting between the two men took place on the following 8 December, during the Cavendish Research Students' Annual Dinner. Those were fancy occasions. On that day a ten course dinner was served, the menu including turbot, shrimp, plover, mutton, turkey, pheasant, and, of course, plum pudding. There followed toasts, to the king, to 'our guests', including J. J. Thomson, and to the 'old students', including Rutherford, who had come down from Manchester in order to give an after dinner speech. He was introduced as the one who 'of all young physicists who through the years had worked at the famous laboratory . . . could swear at his apparatus most forcefully'.[39] Afterward the assembly burst into songs such as 'Oh my darlings! Oh my darlings! Oh my darlings ions mine! You are lost and gone forever/When just once you recombine!' and 'My name is J. J. Thomson and my lab's in Free School Lane/There's no professor like J. J. my students all maintain' and 'For an alpha ray/Is a thing to pay/And a

---

* Here Bohr added: 'I am not sure whether this occurred toward the end of 1911 or the beginning of the next year. But I think it was toward the end of 1911.'[17] I am rather convinced that here Bohr's own recollections of the order of two events is not precise: those of his first meeting with Rutherford in November 1911 (dated by his letter to his mother[38]) and of his second meeting during the Cavendish dinner (see what follows next) in December, of which he said elsewhere[39] that it was the first time he saw Rutherford. The dates of the earliest Bohr–Rutherford letters[40] actually make it most plausible that the plans for Bohr's coming to Manchester were not made before that December occasion. See also Ref. 40a.

Nobel Prize/One cannot despise/And Rutherford/Has greatly scored/As all the world now recognize'.*

On that evening or shortly thereafter arrangements were made for Bohr's transfer to Manchester. These were confirmed in an exchange of letters in January 1912. In March Bohr wrote to Thomson: 'I leave Cambridge with the deepest impression of your work and inspiring personality.'[40b] Much later he commented: 'I just said to Thomson that I only had a year now in England and should be glad to know something about radioactivity . . . I said it had been a very nice time . . . So that is really all there is to be said about Cambridge.'[17]

Manchester in 1912 was the world's foremost center of experimental studies in radioactivity. The discovery of the nucleus is in fact a by-product of such explorations. When Bohr arrived in Manchester in March of that year, radioactivity was his foremost interest. Bohr: 'When I came to Manchester I thought how wonderful it would be to get into the technique of radioactivity . . . And I went for a few weeks to the course they had.'[41] Rutherford: 'Bohr, a Dane, has pulled out of Cambridge to get some experience in radioactive work.'[42] Even while at Cambridge Bohr already knew of Rutherford's nuclear model ('Thomson didn't believe it . . . he was simply very difficult to Rutherford'[17]), but even upon arrival in Manchester it was not, not yet, his main concern. That was not unusual. At that time 'the Rutherford model was not taken seriously. We cannot understand today, but it was not taken seriously at all. There was no mention of it in any place.'[43] Rutherford's own reticence must have been an important contributing factor. He remained silent about his model during a major international conference (the first Solvay conference) held in the fall of 1911. In his 670 page book,[36] completed a year later, only three pages are devoted to α-particle scattering. 'Rutherford does not appear to have considered his discovery as the epoch making event it turned out to be.'[10]

Bohr's notes of his laboratory course begin on 16 March and end on 3 May.[44] Thereafter Rutherford set him the problem of studying the absorption of α-particles in aluminum. 'I am at the laboratory all day, which is absolutely necessary . . . Rutherford comes regularly to hear how things are going . . . [he] takes a real interest in the work of all the people working with him.'[45] That period did not last long. He was dubious how much would come out of his problem[45] and eager to do theory. 'A few weeks later I said to Rutherford that it would not work to go on making experiments and that I would better like to concentrate on the theoretical things[17] . . . So that is what I did, you see. And then, from then on, I worked at home . . . And then I actually didn't see the others too much because I just worked there . . . You

* I am grateful to Professor Sir Sam Edwards for providing me with a copy of the proceedings of that evening.

see, there was not so much to talk about. I knew how Rutherford looked at the atom, you see, and there was really not very much to talk about[41] . . . Most people knew very little in Manchester.'[17] Most, perhaps, but certainly not all. There were in fact two who would steer Bohr in important new directions: Hevesy and Darwin.

Georg von Hevesy, a few months older than Bohr, and another research student with a Ph.D., was a physical chemist who would make a brilliant career in novel applications of radioactivity. He was fond of telling an early instance of this. In his boarding house in Manchester 'the landlady always served the same food all week, and when I suggested as much she said it was not possible – "Every day fresh food is served." So one day when she wasn't looking I added a dose of radioactive material. And the next day the hash was radioactive!'[46]

Hevesy and Bohr were to become lifelong friends. We shall meet him again in several later chapters. 'He was a Hungarian nobleman [see (17d)], you see, who had great experience in treating people, and so on. And he just showed some interest in me, you see. He had such very fine manners. He knew how to be helpful to a foreigner, you see . . . Hevesy told me that there are more radioactive substances than there is room for them in the periodic table. And that I didn't know.'[17]

By 1910 it was known for a fact that there exist several groups of chemically identical substances with distinct atomic number A, defined as the atomic weight of a substance characterized by the nearest integer multiple of the atomic weight of hydrogen. In 1913 Soddy introduced the term isotopes for the members of any such group.[47] For example, the five substances at one time called thorium, radiothorium, radioactinium, ionium, and uranium-X are isotopes of thorium with $A = 232, 228, 227, 230$, and 234, respectively. Bohr has recalled how after listening to Hevesy the idea immediately struck him that isotopes have a different A but the same Z, and that 'the immediate conclusion was that by radioactive decay the element . . . would shift its place in the periodic table by two steps down or one step up, corresponding to the decrease or increase in the nuclear charge [Z] accompanying the emission of α- or β-rays respectively'.[48] (It was known by then that for an α-particle $Z = 2$; for an electron, of course, $Z = -1$.) These shifts are now known as the radioactive displacement law.

'When I turned to Rutherford to learn his reactions to such ideas, he expressed, as always, alert interest in any promising simplicity but warned with characteristic caution against overstating the bearing of the atomic model and extrapolating from comparatively meagre experimental evidence[48] . . . And I said to him that it would be the final proof of his atom . . . I wanted to publish these things but then I got into other things[17] . . . I said to him "I feel that this will, in a few years, be considered as the basis for the Rutherford atom, because it is clear that it is a far more extensive and definite thing that you have elements where all the properties are the same and which change in this regular way" ... He was a bit impatient, and he had so much to do and he did not want to go into it, and so on ... I could have published it just as a suggestion. And I went five times to Rutherford and so on about it.'[41]

Thus did Bohr remember until the end of his life how Rutherford dissuaded him from making his first entry into the physics of the atom and the nucleus.

Rutherford must either not have listened or not have understood or not have believed what Bohr was trying to tell him. Bohr's idea of the radioactive displacements clearly implied that both α- and β-rays originate in the nucleus. Yet in his book completed in 1912 Rutherford wrote that radioactivity has two distinct causes: '... the instability of the central mass and the instability of the electronic distribution. The former type of instability leads to the expulsion of an α-particle, the latter to the appearance of β- and γ-rays.'[49]

I have discussed elsewhere[50] the evolution of the isotope concept and the displacement law. Suffice it to say here that the initial presentations in print of this law were either incomplete or (including one by Hevesy!) incorrect.

Charles Galton Darwin, grandson of the great Charles Robert, was Bohr's other source of inspiration. He had come to Manchester with an applied mathematics degree from Cambridge, so Rutherford set him to work on a theoretical problem, the energy loss of α-particles when traversing matter. While waiting for some radium he needed for his experiment,[51] Bohr came across a paper Darwin had written on this subject.[52] Its starting point was the Rutherford atom. Darwin noted correctly that the energy loss will be almost entirely due to collisions between the α-particle and the interatomic electrons; the nucleus plays a negligible role. Hence the process is in a sense complementary to α-particle scattering which, as just stated, is almost entirely due to the nucleus. In more detail, the α-particle loses velocity by setting in motion a swarm of electrons, possibly knocking one (or more) of them out of the atom. Darwin did not speculate on precisely how the electrons move inside the atom but explored two alternative assumptions: they are distributed homogeneously over either the atom's volume or its surface. He further assumed that electrons are free when they collide with an α-particle. His results depend on only two parameters: Z and the atomic radius r. Using available data Darwin found that his values for r were greatly at variance with earlier estimates made with the help of Boltzmann's gas theory. In particular, 'in the case of hydrogen it seems possible that the formula for r does not hold on account of there being only few electrons in the atom. If it is regarded as holding then [their number equals] one almost exactly.'[52] Thus as late as the spring of 1911 it was not yet absolutely clear that the hydrogen atom contains one and only one electron!

Bohr realized that Darwin's difficulties were caused by his assumption that electrons are free while colliding with α-particles. In his own version he treated the electrons surrounding the nucleus as 'atomic vibrators', that is, as elastically bound to the nucleus. As he himself would show before long, that is not the actual state of affairs either. Nevertheless his results were a distinct improvement over Darwin's (he also considered β-rays). Far more important for the evolution of his ideas, however, is the fact that he subjected his vibrators to quantum constraints: 'According to Planck's theory of radiation ... the smallest quantity of energy which can be radiated out from an atomic vibrator is equal to v [times] k,'[53] where v is the number of vibrations per second and k (we now call it h) is Planck's constant. *Thus did the quantum theory enter the interior of the atom for the first time in Bohr's writings.*

Bohr finished his paper[53] on this subject only after he had left Manchester; it appeared in 1913. The problem of the stopping of electrically charged particles remained one of his lifelong interests. In 1915 he completed another paper[54] on that subject, which includes the influence of effects due to relativity and to straggling (that is, the fluctuations in energy and in range of individual particles). In 1940–1 he published three papers[54a] on the stopping of fission fragments in matter. A review and update of the subject appeared[55] in 1948. His last purely scientific paper, published[55a] in 1954 together with Jens Lindhard, deals with the passage of highly charged ions through matter. Furthermore, Volume 8 of his collected works contains the texts of twenty-two unpublished papers on the same general topic.

Bohr's 1913 paper on α-particles, which he had begun in Manchester, and which had led him to the question of atomic structure, marks the transition to his great work, also of 1913, on that same problem. While still in Manchester, he had already begun an early sketch of these entirely new ideas. The first intimation of this comes from a letter, from Manchester, to Harald: 'Perhaps I have found out a little about the structure of atoms. Don't talk about it to anybody ... It has grown out of a little information I got from the absorption of α-rays.'[56] I leave the discussion of these beginnings to the next chapter.

On 24 July 1912 Bohr left Manchester for his beloved Denmark. His postdoctoral period had come to an end.

Bohr's stay in Manchester had lasted three months. During that time Rutherford had expressed interest in his activities but had been reserved about his ideas on isotopes. In that period Rutherford had been preoccupied with writing a book;[36] his own research interests had shifted from α- to β- and γ-radioactivity.[57] The new physics Bohr had learned had come from Hevesy and Darwin rather than from him. Why, then, was Rutherford to be the most inspiring scientific figure in Bohr's life? It was because Rutherford's discovery of the nucleus led to the most important discovery by Bohr of the structure of the atom as a whole. Why did Bohr later say of him: 'To me he had almost been like a second father.'[38]? It was because of his exposure to Rutherford's independent ways of making scientific judgements, his style of leadership, guiding others while vigorously continuing his own researches, and his concern for his younger collaborators. In 1926, looking back to the Manchester days and the discovery of the nucleus, Bohr wrote:

This effect [the large angle scattering of α-particles], though to all appearances insignificant, was disturbing to Rutherford, as he felt it difficult to reconcile it with the general idea of atomic structure then favoured by the physicists. Indeed it was not the first, nor has it been the last, time that Rutherford's critical judgement and intuitive power have called forth a revolution in science by inducing him to throw himself with his unique energy into the study of a phenomenon, the importance of which would probably escape other investigators on account of the smallness and apparently spurious character of the effect. This confidence in his judgement and our admiration for his powerful personality was the basis for the inspiration felt by all in his laboratory, and made us all try our best to deserve the kind and untiring interest he took in the work of everyone. However modest the result might be, an approving word from him was the greatest encouragement for which any of us could wish.[58]

Nor would those who later worked in Bohr's institute fail to recognize his own style in what another collaborator has written about Rutherford: 'Although there was no doubt as to who was the boss, everybody said what he liked without constraint ... He was always full of fire and infectious enthusiasm when describing work into which he had put his heart and always generous in his acknowledgement of the work of others.'[59]

References

1 Quoted in N. Blaedel, 'Harmony and unity', p. 34, Springer, New York 1988.
1a. N. Bohr, letter to the Carlsberg Foundation, 20 June 1911, Archives of the Carlsberg Foundation.
2. Chapter 6, section (d).
3. G. Jaffe, J. Chem. Educ. 29, 230, 1952.
4. Lord Rayleigh, The life of Sir J. J. Thomson, p. 25, Cambridge University Press 1942.
5. Lord Rayleigh, Obit. Not. FRS 3, 587, 1940.
6. F. W. Aston, The Times, London, 4 September 1940, p. 9.

7. G. P. Thomson, *J. J. Thomson and the Cavendish Laboratory in his day,* p. 115, Nelson, London 1964.

8. J. J. Thomson, *A treatise on the motion of vortex rings,* Macmillan, London 1883; repr. by Dawsons of Pall Mall, London 1968.

9. For more on the vortex models see IB, Chap. 9, section (b), part 3.

10. E. N. da C. Andrade, *Proc. Roy. Soc.* A **244**, 437, 1958.

11. See further IB, Chap. 9, section (c), part 1.

12. J. J. Thomson, *Electricity and matter,* Scribner, New York 1904.

12a. J. J. Thomson, *Phil. Mag.* **6**, 673, 1903.

12b. A. M. Ampère, transl. in W. F. Magie, *A source book in physics,* p. 457, McGraw-Hill, New York 1935.

13. See further IB, Chap. 9, section (c), part 3.

14. J. J. Thomson, *Phil. Mag.* **11**, 769, 1906.

15. J. J. Thomson, *The corpuscular theory of matter,* Constable, London 1907.

16. CW, Vol. 1, pp. 300, 305, 352, 355.

17. N. Bohr, interview with T. S. Kuhn, L. Rosenfeld, A. Petersen, and E. Rüdinger, 1 November 1962, NBA.

18. IB, pp. 194, 195.

19. M. Bohr, A. Bohr, and L. Rosenfeld, interview with T. S. Kuhn, 30 January 1963, NBA.

19a. J. Rud Nielsen, *Physics Today,* October 1963, p. 22.

20. N. Bohr, letter to H. Bohr, 23 October 1911, CW, Vol. 1, p. 527.

21. N. Bohr, letter to Ellen Bohr, 4 October 1911, CW, Vol. 1, p. 523.

22. Quoted in Ref. 1, p. 50.

23. Ref. 17, and interview on 7 November 1962, NBA.

24. J. Chadwick, *Nature* **140**, 749, 1937.

25. A. S. Eve, *Nature* **140**, 746, 1937.

26. For reminiscences of some who knew him in New Zealand see *The Times,* London, 25 October 1937.

27. D. Wilson, *Rutherford, simple genius,* Chap. 2, MIT Press, Cambridge, Mass. 1983.

28. J. J. Thomson, *Nature* **118** (Suppl.), 43, 1926.

29. J. J. Thomson and E. Rutherford, *Phil. Mag.* **42**, 392, 1896.

30. A. S. Eve, *Rutherford,* p. 433, Cambridge University Press 1939.

31. H. Geiger, *Proc. Roy. Soc.* A **81**, 174, 1908.

32. E. Marsden, in *Rutherford at Manchester,* p. 8, Ed. J. B. Birks, Benjamin, New York 1963.

33. H. Geiger and E. Marsden, *Proc. Roy. Soc.* A **82**, 495, 1909.

34. Cf. E. N. da C. Andrade, *Rutherford and the nature of the atom,* p. 111, Doubleday, New York 1964.

35. E. Rutherford, letter to B. Boltwood, 14 December 1910; repr. in L. Badash, *Rutherford and Boltwood,* p. 235, Yale University Press 1969.

36. E. Rutherford, *Radioactive substances and their radiations,* p. 184, Cambridge University Press 1913.

37. E. Rutherford, *Phil. Mag.* **21**, 669, 1911.

38. Cf. CW, Vol. 1, p. 106, and N. Bohr, letter to Ellen Bohr, 31 October 1911, CW, Vol. 1, p. 533.

39. N. Bohr, *Proc. Phys. Soc. London* **78**, 1083, 1961.
40. N. Bohr, letter to E. Rutherford, 18 January 1912; E. Rutherford, letter to N. Bohr, 27 January 1912; CW, Vol. 2, p. 3.
40a. J. Heilbron and T. S. Kuhn, *Hist. Stud. Phys. Sci.* **1**, 233, 1969, footnote 57.
40b. N. Bohr, letter to J. J. Thomson, 13 March 1912, NBA.
41. Ref. 17, interview on 7 November 1962.
42. E. Rutherford, letter to B. Boltwood, 18 March 1911, quoted in A. S. Eve, *Rutherford*, p. 218, Cambridge University Press 1939.
43. Ref. 17, interview on 31 October 1962.
44. CW, Vol. 2, pp. 4, 11.
45. N. Bohr, letter to H. Bohr, 27 May 1912, repr. in CW, Vol. 1, p. 549.
46. G. von Hevesy, Radiation physics in the early days, speech at a physics department meeting in Berkeley, 23 May 1962, NBA.
47. F. Soddy, *Nature* **92**, 400,1913.
48. Ref. 39, p. 1085.
49. Ref. 36, p. 622.
50. IB, Chap. 11, section (c), esp. second footnote on p. 225.
51. CW, Vol. 2, p. 4.
52. C. G. Darwin, *Phil. Mag.* **23**, 901, 1912.
53. N. Bohr, *Phil. Mag.* **25**, 10, 1913, repr. in CW, Vol. 2, p. 18.
54. N. Bohr, *Phil. Mag.* **30**, 581, 1915, repr. in CW, Vol. 2, p. 57.
54a. N.Bohr, *Phys. Rev.* **58**, 654, 1940; **58**, 839, 1940 (with J. K. Bøggild, K. J. Brostrøm, and T. Lauritsen); **59**, 270, 1941; CW, Vol. 8, pp. 319, 323, 327 respectively.
55. N.Bohr, *Danske Vid. Selsk. Mat.-Fys. Medd.* **18**, No. 8, 1948, CW, Vol. 8, p. 425.
55a. N. Bohr and J. Lindhard, *ibid.* **28**, No. 7, 1954, CW, Vol. 8, p. 593.
56. N. Bohr, letter to H. Bohr, 19 June 1912, CW, Vol. 1, p. 559.
56a. N. Bohr, letter to E. Rutherford, 24 July 1912.
57. Cf. E. Rutherford, *Phil. Mag.* **24**, 453, 1912.
58. N. Bohr, *Nature* **118** (Suppl.), 51, 1926.
59. E. N. da C. Andrade, in *The collected papers of Rutherford*, Vol. 2, p. 299, Interscience, New York 1963.

8

Bohr, father of the atom

(a) Young man in a hurry

One of the sessions at the spring 1963 meeting of the American Physical Society was devoted to memories of Niels Bohr. Jens Rud Nielsen, a long-time friend, spoke of his early recollections. 'When I think of Bohr as he appeared nearly fifty years ago, the speed with which he moved comes to mind. He would come into the yard, pushing his bicycle, faster than anybody else. He was an incessant worker and seemed always to be in a hurry. Serenity and pipe smoking came much later.'[1]

Young Bohr certainly did not waste much time in trying to secure an academic position at the University of Copenhagen. Less than a month after he had obtained his doctorate, the faculty in mathematics and natural sciences received[2] his request for a docentship in physics – a position to be newly established. In September the faculty decided[3] not to proceed with this application. Two weeks later Bohr left for his postdoctoral year in England. He made his next move even before returning to Denmark.

It was stated at the faculty meeting of 23 February 1912 that as of 31 August Christiansen would resign from his physics professorship. He had reached the mandatory age and was in delicate health. On 20 March formal announcement was made of the resulting vacancy and the period for application for this post was set to end on 10 April.[4] We know of Bohr's reaction to these events from a letter[5] by Harald to Carl Oseen, professor of mechanics and mathematical physics in Uppsala, probably the first scientist from abroad to develop a lasting esteem for Niels ever since the summer of 1911 when he had met the brothers at a mathematics congress in Copenhagen. ('I have learned much from you and have still much to learn.'[6])

Harald told Oseen that he had discussed the vacancy with his brother during Niels' recent brief visit home from Manchester. 'It is hard to doubt that the faculty will propose Knudsen who is an outstanding physicist and who has quite considerable seniority. Therefore my brother had initially thought not to apply because he and all of us considered it obvious that he would get the docentship which would be vacant after Martin Knudsen.' But, Harald continued, he had been informed by a confidential source that the faculty might bypass Niels both for the professorship and the docentship. 'As conditions are in this country, it would, if this should happen, in fact mean that it would for many years, maybe forever, be impossible for my brother to get a scientific post at the university.' (Note that there existed only one Danish university at that time. The second one, in Aarhus, was founded in 1928.) Thus, with perhaps questionable logic, Niels was gong to apply for Christiansen's position anyway.

Accordingly Bohr, mentioning Manchester 'where I am working at this time', made his *allerunderdanigste* (most obedient) application, addressed *Til Kongen* (to the king), the standard formal procedure.[7] Knudsen had of course also applied. In April the faculty unanimously decided to propose Knudsen.[8] In May they announced their decision which was accompanied with praise for Bohr. 'If a teaching position in mathematical physics would have been at issue – a position which our university unfortunately lacks – then there could hardly have been any doubt that Dr Bohr would have been the right choice. As things stand, however, the faculty can only choose docent Knudsen.'[9] Knudsen's appointment came through in June, effective 1 September. In August Knudsen proposed one of his close co-workers as best qualified for the succession to the docentship.[10]

Knudsen was to hold his professorship until 1941. After his death in 1949 Bohr gave a eulogy in the *Videnskabernes Selskab* in which he recalled that Knudsen's scientific oeuvre had commanded the highest regard and admiration, as had his tireless work for the well-being of the Danish scientific community.[11] The personal relations between the two men had been rather cool, however.[12] Knudsen's attitude toward the quantum theory may well have been a contributing factor. Some time in 1914, after Bohr had done his major work (to which we shall turn shortly), someone asked Knudsen what Bohr's theory was all about. He replied: 'I don't know, I haven't read his papers.'[1] Rud Nielsen has recalled: '[In about 1920] I was helping [Knudsen] write a textbook. When I tried to bring it in accord with modern physics he would grumble, "If we have to use quantum theory to explain this we may as well not explain it".'[1]

Nevertheless it was Knudsen who got Bohr his first academic job. A few days after his return from Manchester, Bohr received a letter[13] from Knudsen asking him if he would be interested in taking over the post of teaching assistant at the *Læreanstalt* and informing him that he intended to propose someone other than Bohr for his successor as docent. On 31 July 1912 Bohr replied[14] that he was planning to apply for a docentship but would meanwhile be happy to accept Knudsen's offer.

(b) In which Bohr leaves the church and gets married

The next day Niels and Margrethe were married in Slagelse's Town Hall.

It was a civil marriage, as Niels' parents' had been. Niels must have been against a religious ceremony, since only on the preceding 16 April he had resigned his membership in the Lutheran Church. Any idea of accidental near coincidence of resignation and wedding dates would be far fetched, the more so since the same scenario was repeated by Harald, who resigned[14a] on 12 November 1919 and got married the following 17 December at Copenhagen's Town Hall.

Margrethe has left us[15] her recollections of Niels' responses to religion during his youth: 'There was a period of about a year . . . [he was] 14 or 15 or something like that . . . where he took it very seriously; he got taken by it. Then it suddenly went all over. It was nothing for him. Then he went to his father, who had left him quite alone in this regard, and said to him, "I cannot understand how I could be so taken by all this; it means nothing whatsoever to me." And then his father didn't say anything; he just smiled. And then Niels says, "And this smile has taught me so much which I never forgot." So they never exerted any influence but let him do what he liked . . . And since then it had no interest for him.' Margrethe's own feelings were similar: 'You know, it was often at that age – and I have experienced it myself – that one got very religious and would listen to the minister about confirmation. Then it all dissolved. And for me it was exactly the same; it disappeared completely.'[15] (At the time of her marriage she was still a member of the Lutheran church, however.)

On the wedding day, 1 August 1912, the town of Slagelse was hung with flags. The ceremony, which took barely two minutes, was conducted by the chief of police (the mayor was on vacation) in the presence of the immediate family only. Harald was the groom's best man. The wedding banquet was held in the assembly hall of the *Industriforening* (industrial association).[15a]

Margrethe remembered: 'My mother liked a wedding and she liked to do it in the proper way and so on, and therefore she wanted to know the date and how long [Niels] would be home and so on. "Oh, is it really necessary to know all this," he said. And what was it he said about the wedding dinner – "We should think about what train to take and get away from it all." He wanted to see if we couldn't make the dinner earlier in the day, and my mother didn't like to have so many people early in the day. My mother calculated three hours for the dinner. And then he said, "How is it really possible to take three hours for a dinner? Can't we take the ferry at 7:00?"'[15]

The ferry was the one across the Great Belt. The Bohrs were on their way to England for their honeymoon. First they stopped a week in Cambridge, where Bohr completed his paper on the absorption of α-particles (see the previous chapter). Then they went on to Manchester, where on 12 August Bohr handed his manuscript to Rutherford for publication in *Philosophical Magazine*. (Actually Bohr held up his manuscript for another few months in order to await forthcoming experimental data from the Manchester laboratory.) 'Both Rutherford and his wife received us with a cordiality that laid the foundation of the intimate friendship that through many years connected the families.'[16] From Manchester the young couple traveled to Scotland and returned to Copenhagen around 1 September.[15]

Bohr now took up his duties as assistant to Knudsen. In addition he had become privatdocent.[17] As such, he lectured[18] on the mechanical foundations of thermodynamics, from 16 October to 18 December. In January 1913 he applied[19] for a leave of absence for the fall semester of that year.

It was Knudsen again who took the initiative for obtaining Bohr's first faculty position. In March 1913 he proposed Bohr for a docentship.[20] In April the faculty endorsed the proposal,[21] which was approved by the Royal Decree of 16 July 1913.[22]

Bohr was now docent, charged with instructing medical students. Meanwhile he had made the most important scientific discovery of his entire life. We shall therefore leave for a while the further account of his academic career in order to catch up with his scientific progress. Before doing so, one more impression of Bohr at that time, this one by Courant:

My friendship with Niels goes back to the year 1912 . . . I vividly remember him at that time as a somewhat introvert, saintly, extremely friendly yet shy young man . . . Harald was . . . the center of an admiring circle of mathematicians and physicists [in Göttingen]. Against all symptoms of admiration Harald vigorously remonstrated; he protested that he was merely an ordinary person while his slightly older brother, then still quite unknown, was made of pure gold and most certainly would soon be recognized as one of the great scientists of our time.'[23]

I knew Bohr only during the years of serenity and pipe smoking. Nevertheless the picture that I have sketched in the foregoing – the result of reading – of Bohr as a young man strikes familiar chords. I would not characterize the Bohr I knew as modest, much less as immodest, but rather as a man with supreme confidence and a strong sense of destiny, not quite in a hurry but always intensely, perhaps compulsively, engaged in one project or another. I now realize that these traits had been manifest from very early on.

(c) The Rutherford memorandum

We are now coming close to Bohr's most important contribution, his work of 1913 on the constitution of atoms. As was mentioned toward the end of the previous chapter, his earliest ideas concerning this problem go back to the later part of his stay in Manchester. An outline of his thoughts at that time has been preserved in a draft entitled 'On the constitution of atoms and molecules' – the same title he was to use for his three definitive papers of 1913 – written in June/July 1912, which he had prepared for Rutherford's perusal and which he sent to him on 6 July 1912.[24] This draft, commonly referred to as the Rutherford memorandum, was not published until after Bohr's death.[25]

In order to place this document in proper context, I should recapitulate briefly what was known about atomic structure at the time Bohr wrote this outline. First, electrons had been discovered and it had been realized that these are universal constituents of matter. Secondly, it was known that the atom's mass is concentrated in a tiny central body, the nucleus. Recall (Chapter 7) that Rutherford, in deducing the existence of the nucleus from a theoretical analysis of large-angle α-particle scattering data, had justifiably ignored the role of electrons in this scattering process. He had, one might say, treated the atom as 'naked', as a nucleus without surrounding electrons. Thirdly, Darwin had equally justifiably ignored the influence of the nucleus in his treatment of α-particle absorption. Thus up to that time, June 1912, the nucleus and the atomic electrons had been considered *separately*. The central question of what the structure of an atom was like, given that it contains a nucleus surrounded by electrons, had not yet been systematically addressed.

Bohr, in refining Darwin's work (see again Chapter 7), had taken into account 'the forces by which the electrons are kept in their positions in the atoms', and had vaguely remarked: 'Under the influence of these forces the electrons will have a sort of vibratory motion if they are disturbed by an impulse from outside.'[26] Now, in the Rutherford memorandum, he faced head on the problem of the structure of atoms and molecules undisturbed by outside influences. This paper has been carefully analyzed by others.[27] I confine myself to its principal points. The key theme is *stability*.[28]

It was noted in the previous chapter that Thomson had run foul of stability in his discussion of orbiting electrons because these particles emit radiation. Let us call this phenomenon radiative instability. It was pointed out there that in Thomson's model one can find stable configurations for the case that all electrons are at rest. In three respects the situation is different for the Bohr–Rutherford model, to use at once the name by which it has been known since 1913, in which electrons surround an almost pointlike nucleus, and electrostatic forces between all these various particles vary as the inverse square of their respective relative distances.

First difference. By an early nineteenth century theorem such a system is necessarily unstable when all particles are at rest, whence the opening statement in Bohr's memorandum: 'In such an atom there can be no equilibrium figuration without motion of the electrons.'

Second difference. Consider a ring of n equidistant electrons rotating around the nucleus. Bohr: 'It can be shown simply that a ring like the one in question possesses no stability in the ordinary mechanical sense,'[25] for n larger than one. He had found that, quite apart from radiative instability, there is (as there is not in Thomson's case) another, mechanical, instability that occurs even before radiation is taken into account.

Unbeknownst to Bohr, this observation was not new. In 1904, before the discovery of the nucleus, the Japanese physicist Nagaoka had already discussed[29] an atom model of just the kind Bohr was considering. In that same year it was noted that 'such a system is essentially unstable and breaks up with extreme rapidity.'[30]

Third difference. The Thomson atom has a characteristic radius, the radius of his sphere of positive electricity, the size of which is chosen by fiat. There is no such length in the new model with its pointlike nucleus. Bohr: 'There seems to be nothing to allow us from mechanical considerations to discriminate between different radii and times of vibration [of electron rings].'[25] Thus the nuclear model offered nothing but paradoxes: lack of stability, lack of definite size.

Bohr's further calculations showed a peculiarity if the number of electrons is larger than seven: in that case an electron 'is capable of leaving the atom'. This number seven being close to the period (eight) in the periodic table of elements led him to speculate that the chemical properties of elements might result from the fact that the electrons do not in general arrange themselves in one ring but rather in multiple concentric rings. This result is most interesting for two reasons. On the one hand, these calculations are not right.[31] On the other, they gave him the smell of an idea which is in fact correct: 'The chemical properties is [sic] assumed to depend on the stability of the outermost ring, the "valency electrons".'[25] That idea was to become the essence of quantum chemistry.

Let us return to the paradoxes of the nuclear model. These did not cause Bohr to despair. On the contrary, he proposed to resolve them by means of introducing a new 'hypothesis for which there will be given no attempt at a mechanical foundation (*as it seems hopeless*) [my italics] . . .'[25] Appended to this statement is the following footnote: 'This seems to be nothing else than what was to be expected as it seems rigorously proved that the mechanics cannot explain the facts in problems dealing with single atoms.'[25]

Before turning to the content of the hypothesis, let us pause a moment and briefly look back. Bohr was, I think, not dismayed by the difficulties he had run into because he was prepared for them. Already in the introduction to his doctor's thesis, he had opined that mechanics, that is, classical physics, does not work inside atoms:

The assumption [of mechanical forces] is not a priori self-evident, for one must assume that there are forces in nature of a kind completely different from the usual mechanical sort; for while on the one hand the kinetic theory of gases has produced extraordinary results by assuming the forces between individual molecules to be mechanical, there are on the other hand many properties of bodies *impossible to explain if one assumes that the forces which act within the individual molecules ... are mechanical also* [my italics]. Several examples of this, for instance calculations of heat capacity and of the radiation law for high frequencies, are well known; we shall encounter another one later, in our discussion of magnetism.' [32]

Bohr knew very well that his two quoted examples had called for the introduction of a new and as yet mysterious kind of physics, quantum physics. (It would become clear later that some oddities found in magnetic phenomena are also due to quantum effects.) Not for nothing had he written in the Rutherford memorandum that his new hypothesis 'is chosen as the only one which seems to offer a possibility of an explanation of the whole group of experimental results, which gather about and seems to confirm conceptions of the mechanismus [*sic*] of the radiation as the ones proposed by Planck and Einstein'. His reference in his thesis to the radiation law concerns of course Planck's law (5d). I have not yet mentioned the 'calculations of heat capacity' made by Einstein[33] in 1906, the first occasion on which the quantum was brought to bear on matter rather than radiation. The heat capacity of a specific substance is (put a little loosely) the amount of heat it takes to increase the temperature of one gram of that substance by one degree Celsius. It had been known since the 1870s that at low temperatures the heat capacity of some materials (diamond for instance) is far lower than was expected on (classical) theoretical grounds. In showing that this effect was a new manifestation of Planck's quantum in action, Einstein had pioneered a new discipline, the quantum theory of the solid state.

Now then, what *is* Bohr's hypothesis? It is that there exists a relation between the kinetic energy W ($W=\frac{1}{2}mv^2$, m=mass, v=velocity) of an electron running around in a circle within the atom and its frequency v (the number of times per second the electron makes a full turn), given by $W=Kv$. This relation smacks of Planck's relation $E=hv$ between the total energy of an oscillator and its frequency (5g), and of Einstein's relation $E=hv$ between the energy and the frequency of a photon (5h).

Bohr knew of course that K had to be related to Planck's constant h, but the memorandum does not state what that connection is. Perhaps his paper was too hurriedly written, perhaps some of its pages are missing. At that time he certainly did not yet know the exact relation between K and h. (Some have tried to reconstruct how Bohr might have estimated K. Such attempts remind me too much of the 'If/Then' parlor game. (If my aunt had a moustache, then she might have been commander of the fire brigade.)) Nor does Bohr prove explicitly that his hypothesis actually stabilizes the atom and gives definition to its radius. The memorandum is nevertheless a crucially important document because of its general message: it is hopeless to try to understand atomic structure on a classical basis; one needs the quantum to stabilize the atom.

The simplest system Bohr considered in the memorandum is a hydrogen molecule, a two-nuclei/two-electron system. I shall not discuss here his comments on this and other issues about which Bohr said later: 'You see, I'm sorry because most of that was wrong.'[34]

One most important point could have been mentioned, but does not appear at all in Bohr's draft paper. He had noted that his nuclear model, unlike Thomson's, is mechanically unstable, but does not point out that his model, like Thomson's, is radiatively unstable. Seven months later that difficulty was to become *the* central issue to him. By then he had realized that the message of atomic structure can be read in atomic spectra.

Before I turn to this development, I must move backward once again in order to make clear what was known about spectra when Bohr made a major stride toward their unraveling.

(d) 'The language of spectra . . . a true atomic music of the spheres'[35]

When Newton let sunlight pass through a prism he had observed 'a confused aggregate of rays indued with all sorts of colors' (4b). This spectrum of colors appeared to him to be continuous. The resolving power of his experimental arrangement was not sufficient to show that the solar spectrum actually consists of a huge number of discrete lines interspersed with darkness. The first observation of discrete spectra is apparently due to the Scotsman Thomas Melvill who was born the year before Newton died. He found that the yellow light produced by holding kitchen salt in a flame shows unique refraction, that is, the light is monochromatic. Actually, no single atomic or molecular spectrum is monochromatic, but in the case of kitchen salt the yellow so-called D-line is much more intense than all other lines. Moreover, it was found subsequently that the D-line is in fact a doublet, a pair of close-lying lines. It would also be clear later that the D-line stems from the heated sodium atoms contained in the salt molecules.

As to the solar spectrum, the discovery of some of its discrete features dates from the early nineteenth century, when first Wollaston, then Fraunhofer, observed dark lines in this spectrum. The latter noted, moreover, that one of these lines has precisely the same frequency as the D-line seen when heating kitchen salt. This coincidence comes about because, essentially, the radiating power of any substance as seen in its 'emission spectrum' equals its absorbing power as seen in its dark line 'absorption spectrum'. Thus Fraunhofer's dark D-line could eventually be explained by the fact that the outer layers of the sun contain sodium, which picks out for absorption the D-line frequency generated in the sun's interior.

The precise quantitative statement of this relation between emission and absorption was first made in a paper by Kirchhoff, published in 1859. Six weeks later he had readied a sequel in which he showed that from this relation one can derive what we now call Kirchhoff's law, the law which in turn led Planck to the quantum theory (5b, g). Thus the origins of quantum physics ultimately go back to experimental studies of sunlight and kitchen salt.

The preceding remarks give a first intimation of how rich and fruitful nineteenth century studies of spectra were. It will not serve the present purpose to follow this evolution step by step.[36] Confining myself then to topics necessary for what will follow I turn to the early stages of *analytical* spectroscopy.

As happens so frequently in the development of new domains in experimental physics, these origins can be traced to the invention of a new experimental tool, in this case the Bunsen burner, now so familiar from elementary laboratory exercises in chemistry. Why was this simple gadget so important to spectroscopy? In order to generate the emission spectrum of a substance, one has in general to heat it. If the heating flame has colors of its own, as with candlelight, then the observation of the spectrum of the substance gets badly disturbed. The virtue of the Bunsen burner is that its flame is non-luminous! And so it came about that analytical spectroscopy started with a collaboration between Kirchhoff and Bunsen, then both professors in Heidelberg. Their tools were simple: a Bunsen burner, a platinum wire with a ringlet at its end for holding the substance to be examined, a prism, and a few small telescopes and scales.

Their results were of the greatest importance.[37] They observed (as others had conjectured earlier) that there is a unique relation between a chemical element and its atomic spectrum. Spectra may therefore serve as visiting cards for new elements: 'Spectrum analysis might be no less important for the discovery of elements that have not yet been found.'[37] They themselves were the first to apply this insight by discovering the elements cesium and rubidium. Ten more new elements had been identified spectroscopically before the century was over: thallium, indium, gallium, scandium, germanium, and the noble gases helium, neon, argon, krypton, and xenon.

The discovery in 1869 of helium by means of a mysterious yellow line found in the spectrum of the sun (whence its name) that had no counterpart in terrestrial spectra beautifully illustrated what Kirchhoff and Bunsen had foreseen: '[Spectrum analysis] opens . . . the chemical exploration of a domain which up till now has been completely closed . . . It is plausible that [this technique] is also applicable to the solar atmosphere and the brighter fixed stars.'[37] The fact that a number of nebulae are luminous gas clouds was another discovery by astronomical means. The spectra of these clouds revealed another substance never seen on earth, accordingly named nebulium, assumed to be a new element. It took sixty years before it was realized that this substance actually is a mixture of metastable oxygen and nitrogen.[38] Another hypothesized stellar element, coronium, turned out to be very highly ionized iron.

Perhaps the most important insight we owe to Kirchhoff and Bunsen is that very minute amounts of material suffice for chemical identification:

The positions occupied [by the lines] in the spectrum determine a chemical property of a similar unchangeable and fundamental nature as the atomic weight . . . and they can be determined with almost astronomical accuracy. What gives the spectrum-analytic method a quite special significance is the circumstance that it extends in an almost unlimited way the limits imposed up till now on the chemical characterization of matter.[37]

Many more advances in experimental spectroscopy date back to the nineteenth century, such as the discovery that molecules exhibit characteristic 'band spectra', bunches of tightly spaced lines. In fact, by the time Bohr entered the field, the first six volumes of Kayser's excellent handbook of spectroscopy[39] had appeared, counting in all 5000 pages. I shall conclude this sketch of experimental spectroscopy with just one remark, however, concerning the spectrum of atomic hydrogen, so essential for what is to follow.

It appears that at least parts of this spectrum were first detected by Ångström: 'To my knowledge I was the first who, in 1853, observed the spectrum of hydrogen.'[40] Soon thereafter four (and only four) lines of this spectrum were identified and their frequencies measured, by Plücker (1859)[41] and by Ångström (1860).[42] The latter achieved an accuracy impressive for those days: about one part in ten thousand.

The question of what makes a hot body shine must have come to a man's mind long long ago, even long before Newton's conjecture about the mechanism for light emission, found in that utterly remarkable set of open questions, appended to his *Opticks*, which he left for later generations to ponder. Query 8 reads: 'Do not all fix'd Bodies, when heated beyond a certain degree, emit Light and shine; and is not this Emission perform'd by the vibrating motions of its parts?'

The more specific suggestion that these 'parts' are actually parts of atoms or molecules came later, in the nineteenth century. In 1852 Stokes suggested: 'In all probability . . . the molecular vibrations by which . . . light is produced are not vibrations in which the molecules move among one another, but vibrations among the constituent parts of the molecules themselves, performed by virtue of the internal forces which hold the parts of the molecules together.'[43] Maxwell's contribution 'Atom' to the 1875 edition of the Encyclopedia Britannica contains the following 'conditions which must be satisfied by an atom . . . permanence in magnitude, capability of internal motions or vibration, and a sufficient amount of possible characteristics to account for the difference between atoms of different kinds'.[44]

After the discovery of electrons it became extremely plausible that spectra are associated with the motions of these particles inside atoms. One finds several conjectures to this effect in the early years of the twentieth century. Thomson thought (1906), however, that line spectra would be due 'not to the vibrations of corpuscles [i.e. electrons] inside the atom, but of corpuscles vibrating in the field of force outside the atom'.[45] Johannes Stark believed that band spectra stem from electron excitations of neutral bodies, line spectra from ionized bodies.[46] I mention these incorrect ideas of serious and competent physicists only to illustrate how confused the status of spectra was right up to Bohr's clarifications of 1913.

One evening in the 1950s when Bohr and I were at a party in Princeton, I asked him what he remembered about the thinking on spectra prior to his own work on the subject. He pointed to an open piano in the room and replied that it was like that, many keys, some white, some black, very complicated. Later he put it like this:

One thought [spectra are] marvelous, but it is not possible to make progress there. Just as if you have the wing of a butterfly then certainly it is very regular with the colors and so on, but nobody thought that one could get the basis of biology from the coloring of the wing of a butterfly.[34]

In the 1860s, shortly after the first quantitative measurements of spectral frequencies, a new game came to town, less ambitious than trying to find mechanisms for the origin of spectra: spectral numerology, the search for simple mathematical relations between observed frequencies.[47] A textbook published[48] in 1913, at practically the same time that Bohr interpreted the hydrogen spectrum, contains no less than twelve proposed spectral formulae. All these have long been forgotten except for one that will live forever: the Balmer formula for the spectrum of atomic hydrogen.

After receiving a Ph.D. in mathematics, Balmer became a teacher at a girl's school in Basel, and later also privatdocent at the university there. He was 'neither an inspired mathematician nor a subtle experimentalist, [but rather] an architect . . . [To him] the whole world, nature and art, was a grand unified harmony, and it was his aim in life to grasp these harmonic relations numerically.'[49] In all he published three physics papers. The first two, completed at age 60, made him immortal; the third, written when he was 72, is uninteresting.

What Balmer did is slightly incredible. Having at his disposal only the four frequencies measured by Ångström, he fitted them with a mathematical expression that predicts an infinity of lines – and his formula is in fact correct! It reads in modernized notation

$$v_{ab} = R\left(\frac{1}{b^2} - \frac{1}{a^2}\right),$$

where the symbols have the following meaning. As usual, v stands for frequency. Each distinct pair of values for a and b denotes a distinct frequency. The index b takes on the values 1, 2, 3, . . . to infinity; a also runs through the integers but is always larger than b, thus if $b = 2$ then $a = 3, 4, ...$ R is a constant. Balmer found[50] that he could fit the four Ångström lines very well if these are made to correspond to $b = 2$ and $a = 3, 4, 5, 6$, respectively, and if R (itself a frequency, a number of oscillations per second) is given the value $R = 3.29163 \times 10^{15}$ per second. Now, a century later, it is known that[51] $R = 3.28984186 \times 10^{15}$ per second, which shows that Balmer's R value was correct to better than one part in a thousand.

Having come that far, Balmer told the professor of physics at Basel University what he had found. This friend told him that actually another 12 lines were known from astronomical observations. Balmer quickly checked that these also fitted his formula, for $a = 2$, and $b = 5$ to 16. Whereupon, he wrote his second physics paper,[52] in which he stated that 'this agreement must be considered surprising to the highest degree'.

Balmer's formula has stood the test of time as more hydrogen lines kept being discovered. Soon his results became widely known;[53] they were quoted in the 1912 edition of the Encyclopedia Britannica.[54] For nearly thirty years no one knew, however, what the formula was trying to say.

Then Bohr came along.

(e) In which Bohr hears about the Balmer formula

Bohr had not mentioned spectra at all in the Rutherford memorandum, nor did he at once turn to them in September 1912, upon his return to Copenhagen from his honeymoon. He was fascinated by the atom, however, so much so that shortly afterward he felt that his work as Knudsen's assistant was too demanding. He remained in a hurry. 'I had very much to do because I became then for a short time the assistant of Knudsen . . . and worked the whole day with experiments on friction of gases at very low pressures . . . And that took all the time, you see. So I went to Knudsen and said I would rather not, you see . . . I went into the country with my wife and we wrote a very long paper on these various things,'[55] a touching use of the plural 'we'. The long paper must have been an attempt to complete a promised sequel[56] to his work on α-particles, dealing with 'the relation between the frequencies and the dimensions of the orbits of the electrons in the interior of the atoms'. That paper was never published because, as Bohr wrote to Rutherford: 'I have met . . . with some serious trouble arising from . . . instability . . . which has not allowed the execution of the calculation.' [57] Rutherford tried to calm him down. 'I do not think you need feel pressed to publish in a hurry your second paper on the constitution of the atom, for I do not think anyone is likely to be working on that subject.' [58]

The year 1913 came and still Bohr's mind was not on spectra. Bohr to Rutherford in January: 'I do not at all deal with the question of calculation of frequencies corresponding to the lines in the visible spectrum.' [59] On 7 February he sent to Hevesy a list of 'the ideas I have used as the foundation of my calculations', [60] in which spectra do not appear either.

Shortly after 7 February Bohr heard of the Balmer formula. By 6 March he had completed a paper containing its interpretation. That event marks the beginning of the quantum theory of atomic structure.

On a number of occasions Bohr has told others (including me[61]) that he had not been aware of the Balmer formula until shortly before his own work on the hydrogen atom and that everything fell into place for him as soon as he heard about it. The man who told him was H. M. Hansen, one year younger than Bohr, who had done experimental research on spectra in Göttingen. One week before he died Bohr recalled: 'I think I discussed [the long paper written in the country] with someone . . . that was Professor Hansen . . . I just told him what I had, and he said "But how does it do with the spectral formulae?" And I said I would look it up, and so on. That is probably the way it went. I didn't know anything about the spectral formulae. Then I looked it up in the book of Stark [Ref. 62] . . . other people knew about it but I discovered it for myself. And I found then that there was this very simple thing about the hydrogen spectrum . . . and at that moment I felt now we'll just see how the hydrogen spectrum comes.' [63] Since in those days Bohr was well read in the scientific literature and since the Balmer formula was quoted rather often, notably in one of the textbooks[64] by Bohr's teacher Christiansen, it could well be that he had actually seen it earlier but without noticing its relevance to his own thinking and then, as is common, had forgotten all about it.

In the course of reminiscing about what he did next, Bohr once remarked: 'It was in the air to try to use Planck's ideas in connection with such things.' [34] Let us see what ideas there were about the atom at that time.

First there was the Viennese physicist Arthur Haas who in 1910 discussed a model for the hydrogen atom consisting of one electron moving on the surface of a positively charged sphere with radius r – not the Rutherford model. He introduced a quantum postulate which, transcribed in terms of Bohr's quantity K (see the preceding section (c)), reads: $K = \frac{1}{2}h$. He obtained the correct expression for r, now called the Bohr radius (see further below). There is no mention of spectra in his work.[65] Sommerfeld, commenting on Haas's work during the Solvay Conference of October 1911, thought it plausible 'to consider the existence of molecules as a consequence of the existence of [Planck's constant]'.[66] Bohr said later that he was unaware of Haas's results when he did his own work on hydrogen. His paper on that subject[67] does contain reference to Haas, however.

Then there was Nicholson from Cambridge, who in 1911 associated spectral lines with various modes of vibration of electrons around their equilibrium orbits in the field of a central charge. He argued that a one-electron atom cannot exist and that the simplest and lightest atoms are, in this order, coronium, with atomic weight about half that of hydrogen, hydrogen, and nebulium, with 2, 3, 4 electrons respectively; helium was considered to be a composite.[68] It was a bizarre collection. Helium is an element, coronium and nebulium are not (as mentioned earlier), and there is no element lighter than hydrogen. For a further insight into the understanding of atoms at that time, it is most significant to note his statement that hydrogen should have three electrons instead of one, in fact that there could be no one-electron atom. Hydrogen was therefore still poorly understood. In fact, in his α-particle paper Bohr had declared 'that the experiments on absorption of α-rays *very strongly suggest* [my italics] that a hydrogen atom contains only one electron',[69] an indication of near conviction but not of absolute certainty.

So far Nicholson's views on atoms are merely passing curiosities, but in a subsequent paper[70] he made a very important comment on angular momentum, a quantity to be called L from here on. L is defined (not in full generality) as follows. Consider a particle with mass m moving with velocity v along a circle with radius r. Then L relative to the circle's center equals the product mvr. Now, Nicholson noted that this product just equals the ratio of the particle's energy to its frequency. This ratio, Planck had proposed in another context, should equal h. 'If therefore the constant h of Planck has ... an atomic significance, it may mean that the angular momentum of a particle can only rise or fall by discrete amounts when electrons leave or return.'[70] In modern terms, Nicholson had quantized angular momentum. He went on to calculate L for hydrogen, finding an integral multiple of $h/2\pi$ (correct) equal to 18 (weird).

Bohr was not impressed by Nicholson when he met him in Cambridge in 1911[71] and much later said that most of Nicholson's work was not very good.[72] Be that as it may, Bohr had taken note of his ideas on angular momentum, at a crucial moment for him, as is seen in his letter to Rutherford of 31 January 1912.[59] He also quoted him in his own paper on hydrogen.[67] It is quite probable that Nicholson's work influenced him at that time.[73]

Finally, there was the work of Niels Bjerrum dealing with molecules rather than atoms. Bjerrum had been Bohr's chemistry teacher at the University of Copenhagen; later they became good friends. 'I remember vividly a walk here in [Copenhagen] in 1912 when [Bohr] told me of his new ideas.'[74] In that year Bjerrum published a paper,[75] one section of which is entitled: 'Applications of the quantum hypothesis to molecular spectra.' Those spectra arise as the result not only of electronic but also of nuclear motions. In a diatomic molecule, for example, the vibrations of the two nuclei along the axis joining them generate 'vibrational spectra'. Furthermore this axis can rotate in space, producing 'rotational spectra'. In 1911 Walther Nernst had pointed out[76] that it is a necessary consequence of the quantum theory that the associated vibrational and rotational energies of molecules must vary discontinuously. Bjerrum was the first to give the explicit expression for the discrete rotational spectral frequencies. That contribution, which does not directly link with what Bohr did next, will be remembered as the first instance of a correct quantum theoretical formula in spectroscopy.

(f) Triumph over logic: the hydrogen atom(*)

On 6 March 1913 Bohr sent a letter[77] to Rutherford in which he enclosed 'the first chapter on the constitution of atoms', asking him to forward that manuscript to *Philosophical Magazine* for publication. Up to that point Bohr had three published papers to his name: two resulting from his prize essay, his doctor's thesis and a short sequel thereto,[78] and his paper on α-particle absorption. These had earned him respect within a small group of physicists. His new paper[67] was to make him a world figure in science and, eventually, beyond.

Two factors decisively influenced Bohr's next advance. First, his insight that 'it seems hopeless'[24] to understand the atom in terms of classical physics, an area of science for which he nevertheless, and with good reason, had the greatest respect, then and later. Secondly, his recent awareness of the Balmer formula. He was convinced (as we have seen) that his answers had to come from the quantum theory. Planck and Einstein had made the first bold sallies into this new territory. The problems they had addressed concerned systems consisting of very many particles. By contrast Bohr wanted to understand hydrogen, a system containing two particles only. Planck and Einstein had applied quantum concepts to statistical mechanics; Bohr was the first to do so in the domain of dynamics. In this he was on his own, far more so than he had been before, or would later be.

To my knowledge, there are no letters nor later interviews describing in detail what Bohr went through in those intense few weeks. Probably he would have been unable to reconstruct later a day by day account of his thoughts during that period. He would, I think, ceaselessly have gone back and forth between trying out, one after the other, new postulates outside classical dynamics and matching those with the guidance provided by the Balmer formula. One finds a residue of these vacillations in the printed paper[67] which contains not one but two derivations of Balmer's expression. The first[79] is based on a hypothesis about which, five pages later, Bohr writes: 'This assumption . . . may be regarded as improbable', after which it is replaced by another one.[80] Later in 1913 Bohr again treated the Balmer formula differently.[81] Every subsequent version is a distinct improvement over its predecessor; connoisseurs will enjoy detailed comparisons.[82] I shall confine myself to a summary of the principal points.

All three treatments have in common the postulate that an electron inside a hydrogen atom can move only on one or another of a discrete set of orbits (of which there are infinitely many), in violation of the tenets of classical physics, which allows a continuum of possible orbits. Bohr called his orbits 'stationary states'. Their respective energies, taken in order of increase, will be denoted by E_a, where $a = 1, 2, 3$, and so on. We shall refer to $a = 1$ as the 'ground state', the lowest orbit, closest to the nucleus, which has the lowest energy E_1.

Now, for the first time, I believe, Bohr refers to radiative instability. As a result of the energy lost by radiation, 'the electron will no longer describe stationary orbits'. In particular, according to classical law, an electron in the ground state will not stay there but will spiral into the nucleus.

Bohr circumvented this disaster by introducing one of the most audacious postulates ever seen in physics. He simply declared that the ground state *is* stable, thereby contravening all knowledge about radiation available up till then!

So much for the ground state. What about the higher stationary states? These are unstable, the electron will drop from a higher to some lower state. Consider two states with energies E_a larger than E_b (thus a larger than b). Then, Bohr assumes, transitions $a \rightarrow b$ are accompanied by the emission of one light quantum with frequency v_{ab}, given by

$$E_a - E_b = h v_{ab}.$$

(In the first (abandoned) version it was assumed that more light-quanta than one could be emitted.) Thus the discreteness of spectra is a consequence of the discreteness of atomic states. Transitions between these states are the *only* way in which an atom emits (or absorbs) radiation.

Next, Bohr returned to his earlier hypothesis (see section (c)) $W = Kv$, which links the kinetic energy W of an atomic state to its frequency v. In terms of his new language, W and v refer specifically to the ground state and should thus be renamed W_1 and v_1. Likewise one can assign W_a and v_a to a stationary state a. (Please keep track of the distinction between v_a and v_{ab}.

The former is a 'mechanical frequency' of an electron in orbit, the latter an 'optical frequency' of light emitted in a transition.) Bohr now makes an explicit proposal for K:

$$W_a = \tfrac{1}{2}ah\nu_a .$$

(If $a=1$, then $W_1 = \tfrac{1}{2}h\nu_1$, which is what Haas had used.) This equation associates an integer a to each state. It is the first example of a *quantum number*.

It is a straightforward calculation, given in many elementary texts,[83] to derive the Balmer formula from the last two equations written down and a third one which expresses that the electron is kept in orbit by the balance between the centripetal force which pulls the electron away from and the attractive electric force which pulls it toward the nucleus. One finds that

$$E_a = -\frac{hR}{a^2},$$

from which the Balmer formula follows at once.

At this point the frog jumps into the water, as an old saying goes. Bohr was able to predict the value of R!! Let m and $-e$ denote the mass and charge of the electron and Ze the charge of the nucleus ($Z=1$ for hydrogen of course). Bohr found

$$R_Z = \frac{2\pi^2 m Z^2 e^4}{h^3},$$

where R_1 is our old R. Using the best known experimental values for m, e, and h, and putting $Z=1$, Bohr obtained $R = 3.1 \times 10^{15}$, 'inside the uncertainty due to experimental errors' with the best value of R obtained from spectral measurements.

This expression for R_Z is the most important equation that Bohr derived in his life. It represented a triumph over logic. Never mind that discrete orbits and a stable ground state violated laws of physics which up till then were held basic. Nature had told Bohr that he was right anyway, which, of course, was not to say that logic should now be abandoned, but rather that a new logic was called for. That new logic, quantum mechanics, will make its appearance later on in this book.

Bohr was also able to derive an expression for r_a, the radius of the ath orbit:[84]

$$r_a = \frac{a^2 h^2}{4\pi^2 Z m e^2}.$$

This yields the 'Bohr radius' $r_1 = 0.55 \times 10^{-8}$ cm for stable hydrogen, in agreement with what was then known about atomic size. Bohr noted further that the bigger radii of higher states explain why so many more spectral lines had been seen in starlight than in the laboratory. 'For $a=33$, the (radius) is equal to 0.6×10^{-5} cm corresponding to the mean distance of the molecules at a pressure of about 0.2 mm mercury ... the necessary condition for the appearance of a great number of lines is therefore a very small density of a gas,' more readily available in the atmosphere of stars than on the surface of the earth.

The capstone of Bohr's work on the Balmer formula is the story of the Pickering lines. In 1896 Charles Pickering from Harvard had found a series of lines in starlight which he attributed to hydrogen even though this did not fit Balmer. In 1912 these same lines were also found in the laboratory, by Alfred Fowler in London. Bohr pointed out that 'we can account naturally for these lines if we ascribe them to helium',[67] singly ionized helium, that is, a one-electron system with $Z=2$. According to the formula for R_Z this would give a Balmer formula with R replaced by $R_2 = 4R$. Fowler objected: in order to fit the data the 4 ought to be replaced by 4.0016, a difference which lay well outside experimental error.[85] Whereupon Bohr remarked in October 1913 that the formulation in his paper rested on the approximation in which the nucleus is treated as infinitely heavy compared to the electron; and that an elementary calculation shows that, if the true masses for the hydrogen and helium nuclei are used, then the 4 is replaced by 4.00163, 'in exact agreement with the experimental value.'[86] Up to that time no one had ever produced anything like it in the realm of spectroscopy, agreement between theory and experiment to five significant figures. (This high precision could be attained because the hydrogen/helium ratio R_1/R_2 is independent of the values of e and h).

Bohr's paper on hydrogen appeared in July 1913. Two sequels followed, one (September)[87] on the structure of atoms heavier than hydrogen and on the periodic table, the other (November)[88] on the structure of molecules. The plethora of experimental data on their spectra available at that time could not then and cannot now be represented as compactly and simply as for hydrogen. One useful formula had been discovered, however, in its most general form by the Swiss physicist Ritz.[89] It says that the frequencies of a spectrum can be grouped in series, represented by the difference of two functions, each of which depends on a running integer. This, Bohr suggested, indicates an origin of spectra similar to that for hydrogen: 'The lines correspond to a radiation emitted during the passing of the system between two stationary states,'[67] a notion that underlies all of spectroscopy to this day.

Following an idea first stated in classical context by J. J. Thomson, Bohr also correctly identified the origins of X-ray spectra: an electron in an inner ring is knocked out of an atom, after which an electron from an outer ring makes a quantum jump into the unoccupied slot, emitting an energetic light-quantum in the process.[87]

For the rest Bohr wisely left spectra alone and, in parts 2 and 3, concentrated on the ground states of atoms and molecules. These parts are elaborations of the Rutherford memorandum. Electrons are arranged in one or more coaxial and coplanar rings; mechanical stability is analyzed in further detail. At this stage Bohr was able to use another discovery dating from 1913: the number of electrons per atom of a given element equals its place (hydrogen, 1; helium, 2; etc.) in the periodic table[90] (see further (10b)).

Unlike his treatment of hydrogen, Bohr had to borrow here and there further experimental information as additional input. Accordingly this part of his work is of a much more improvised nature than his discussion of hydrogen. The same can be said of his quantum postulate for a general atom or molecule. It is based on an alternative form of his hydrogen condition $W_a = \frac{1}{2}ahv_a$: if (and only if) the orbit in question is circular then, he showed (probably inspired by Nicholson), this condition is equivalent to

$$L_a = a\,\frac{h}{2\pi},$$

where L_a is the angular momentum in state a, equal to $h/2\pi$ in the ground state. This reformulation led him to a conjecture for an extended quantum postulate for the ground state of an arbitrary atom or molecule: if in these systems all electrons move in circular orbits, then in the ground state the angular momentum of each individual electron shall equal $h/2\pi$, regardless of the number of rings over which the electrons are distributed.[91]

There existed no equivalent of a Balmer formula in this general case, so Bohr had no way to move back and forth between a spectral formula and his extended postulate. No wonder then that this conjecture is incorrect. So are many of his tentative conclusions about the relation between the occupation of rings of electrons and the periodic table. For example, he suggested that neon has an inner and an outer ring (correct) filled with eight and two electrons respectively – the reverse of the true numbers. Clearly, it was too soon to tackle these issues. It would take another decade until the beginnings of their clarification, the result of efforts (to which I shall turn later) by Bohr and by others (see further (10e)).

The most important novelty in the later parts of Bohr's trilogy concerns the origin of β-radioactivity. Recall (7b) that as late as the autumn of 1912 Rutherford had suggested that this process consists of an expulsion of an electron orbiting around the nucleus. Bohr gave the correct answer: 'On the present theory it seems ... necessary that the nucleus is the seat of the expulsion of the high speed β-particles.'[92] He argued as follows. The chemical properties of elements are dictated by the configuration of their electronic orbits. Isotopes have identical chemical properties, hence identical electron configurations. There are numerous instances in which one isotope emits β-rays with velocities different from another. Thus they are non-identical with regard to β-radioactivity. Hence by exclusion this process must be of nuclear origin.

Another topic which occupied Bohr during all this work was his old love, magnetism. In July 1913 he wrote to Harald: 'At the moment I am working again on magnetism...I really think that this time I have got hold of a little of the truth.'[93] He had indeed. His idea was to confront quantum theory with Ampère's suggestion (7a) that magnetism is caused by charged particles moving in small closed orbits inside matter. He found that an electron circling with angular momentum $L_a = ah/2\pi$ generates a little magnet with strength (magnetic moment) M_a given by

$$M_a = a\mu, \quad \mu = \frac{eh}{4\pi mc}.$$

This important result was originally meant to be included in part 2 of the trilogy, but was eventually omitted. Drafts of a section on magnetism have survived, however.[94] In 1920 Pauli gave the quantity μ the name by which it has been known ever since: the Bohr magneton.[95]

Bohr's final paper[81] in the eventful year 1913 was presented to the *Fysisk Forening* (Danish Physical Society) on 20 December. Not only does it summarize the main points of the trilogy with greater balance and clarity than before, but it also contains a new and vastly superior way of looking at the Balmer formula, which, this time, Bohr did not *derive* from a quantum postulate but rather *postulated*. ('I have tried to make my considerations somewhat clearer by interchanging the order of my arguments.'[96]) From there on he reasoned as follows.

Step 1. According to classical theory an electron with mechanical frequency v_n and energy E_n circling a central charge Ze emits light with that same frequency v_n,

$$v_n^2 = \frac{2(-E_n)^3}{\pi^2 m Z^2 e^4}.$$

Step 2. It follows from the condition $E_a - E_b = hv_{ab}$ and the Balmer formula that $E_n = -hR_Z/n^2$. Insert this in the expression for v_n.

Step 3. Use the Balmer formula again for a transition n to $n-1$, where n is very large. One finds approximately

$$v_{n,n-1} = \frac{2R_Z}{n^3}.$$

This optical frequency is small because n is large.

Step 4: the critical new idea. 'On one point...we may expect a connection with the ordinary conceptions; namely that it will be possible to calculate [low optical frequencies] on the basis of classical electrodynamics.'[81] As support for this idea Bohr recalled the fact that for low frequencies Planck's radiation law coincides with classical predictions (the Rayleigh–Einstein–Jeans law (5d)). In the present instance, this low frequency connection[97] between classical and quantum theory amounts to equating, for large n, the mechanical frequency v_n with the optical frequency $v_{n,n-1}$. This results in Bohr's earlier expression for R_Z! This style of reasoning, which Bohr later called 'the correspondence principle' will recur several times later on.

Let us summarize Bohr's achievements in 1913.

The very existence of line (and band) spectra suggests, he noted, that electrons move in discrete stationary orbits inside atoms and molecules. Spectra (including X-ray spectra) arise because of quantum jumps between these states. (It would take until the 1980s before such individual jumps were directly observed.[98]) The quantitative confirmation of these ideas by his treatment of hydrogen and ionized helium mark a turning point in the physics of the twentieth century and the high point in Bohr's creative career. The insistence on the role of the outermost ring of electrons as the seat of most chemical properties of the elements, in particular their valencies, constitutes the first step toward quantum chemistry. The sharp distinction between atomic/molecular and nuclear physics begins with his realization that β-rays emanate from the nucleus.

Atoms had been postulated in ancient times. As the year 1913 began, almost unanimous consensus had been reached, after much struggle, that atoms are real. Even before that year it had become evident that atoms have substructure, but no one yet knew by what rules their parts moved. During that year, Bohr, fully conscious that these motions could not possibly be described in terms of classical physics, but that it nevertheless was essential to establish a link between classical and quantum physics, gave the first firm and lasting direction toward an understanding of atomic structure and atomic dynamics. In that sense he may be considered the father of the atom.

(g) Reactions, including Bohr's own

> Your theory is having a splendid effect on Physics, and I believe when we really know what an atom is, as we must within a few years, your theory even if wrong in detail will deserve much of the credit.
>
> H. MOSELEY *in November 1913*[99]

The first response to Bohr's new ideas reached him even before the first paper of his trilogy had appeared in print. After Rutherford had read that article in manuscript form he had written to Bohr, in March: 'There appears to me one grave difficulty in your hypothesis, which I have no doubt you fully realize, namely how does an electron decide what frequency it is going to vibrate at when it passes from one stationary state to the other? It seems to me that you have to assume that the electron knows beforehand where it is going to stop.'[100] In typical Rutherford style he had gone right to the heart of the matter by raising the issue of cause and effect, of causality: Bohr's theory leaves unanswered not only the question why there are discrete states but also why an individual electron in a higher state chooses one particular lower state to jump into. In 1917 Einstein would add a related question: How does an individual light-quantum, emitted in an atomic transition, know in which direction to move?[101] These questions were to remain unresolved until, as we shall see later, quantum mechanics gave the surprising answer: they are meaningless.

Back to March 1913, Bohr did not answer Rutherford's question in his return letter, probably because 'I am now working on the next chapters'.[102] Presumably the two men discussed the issue when Bohr, worried about Rutherford's objections to the length of his paper, made a quick trip to Manchester (around 1 April). Arthur Eve, later Rutherford's principal biographer, saw them together: 'In 1913, when I was staying with the Rutherfords, there came into the room a slight-looking boy whom Rutherford at once took into his study. Mrs Rutherford explained to me . . . that her husband thought very highly of his work . . . it was Niels Bohr.'[103]

Margrethe Bohr remembered: 'We were eagerly awaiting after the papers went off to Rutherford – oh, we were waiting for the answer. I remember how exciting it was. And Rutherford was delighted with the first paper he sent over; with the second one he was not so pleased as with the first one. And Niels was a little disappointed.'[104] More generally, Rutherford's position remained cautious for some time. March 1914: 'While it is too early to say whether the theories of Bohr are valid, his contributions . . . are of great importance and interest.'[105] August 1914: 'N. Bohr has faced the difficulties by bringing in the idea of the quantum. At all events there is something going on which is inexplicable by the older mechanics.'[106]

The older generation did not go along, as was to be expected. When Lord Rayleigh, then past seventy, was asked what he thought about Bohr's theory he replied: 'I have looked at it, but I saw it was no use to me. I do not say that discoveries may not be made in that sort of way. I think it is very likely they may be. But it does not suit me.'[107]

J. J. Thomson's reactions were unusual. Lecturing on atomic structure in 1914[108] and in 1923[109] he did not mention the quantum theory at all. Only in 1936, at age eighty, did he write about Bohr's papers of 1913: '[They] have in some departments of spectroscopy changed chaos into order, and . . . were, I think, the most valuable contributions which quantum theory has ever made to physical science.'[110]

On 12 September 1913, Bohr spoke for the first time about his work before an international audience, at a meeting in Birmingham. The journal *Nature* quoted a comment by Jeans at that conference: 'Dr Bohr . . . arrived at a convincing and brilliant explanation of the laws of spectral series.' [111] On 13 September *The Times* of London mentioned Dr Bohr and his theory – the first press report ever (outside Denmark) of his scientific activities.

As a final entry from the British side I note the one at the head of this section, written by Henry Moseley, the brilliant young experimentalist whose work on X-ray spectra during 1913–14 did so much to clarify the meaning of the periodic table. (He was killed at the Front in 1915.) His comment is, I think, the finest and most succinct of all.

Reactions elsewhere – they also came rapidly – were a mixture, differing in proportion from case to case, of perfectly understandable and in fact reasonable incredulity on the one hand and great interest on the other. [112] In the fall of 1913 Harald wrote to Niels that people in Göttingen 'were exceedingly interested in your paper' and had asked him for reprints, but that some, with the exception of the great mathematician Hilbert, 'do not dare to believe that they can be objectively right; they find the assumptions too "bold" and "fantastic" '. [113] At about the same time Sommerfeld, professor of theoretical physics in Munich, wrote to Bohr: 'Although I am for the present still a bit skeptical about atomic models, your calculation of the constant [in the Balmer formula] is nevertheless a great achievement.' [114] Paschen, the distinguished experimental spectroscopist from Tübingen believed Bohr at once upon hearing of the helium result. [115]

Robert Pohl remembered the reaction in Berlin. 'Shortly after the publication of Bohr's first paper something unusual happened in the *Physikalische Gesellschaft* [Physical Society] in Berlin.' Normally, communications at its meetings were original papers, but that time Professor Emil Warburg, a brilliant physicist and teacher, announced a report 'on a very important paper, that was Bohr's paper, . . . He explained in his dry but clear way . . . that this was a real advance, and I believe that the few hundred listeners at once understood: "There Bohr has had a stroke of genius [*einen ganz grossen Wurf*], Planck's *h* proves to be the key for understanding the atom." ' [116]

Einstein reacted very positively. In September 1913 Hevesy had met him in Vienna and had asked him for his opinion. Einstein replied that Bohr's work was very interesting, and important if right – faint praise, as I know from having heard him make that comment on other occasions. Then, however, Hevesy told him of the helium results, whereupon Einstein said: 'This is an enormous achievement. The theory of Bohr must then be right.' [117]

In the early summer of 1914 Bohr gave seminars on his work in Göttingen and Munich. 'I had never met any German physicists before and had much pleasure in talking with them.' [118] Fifty years later Alfred Landé reminisced about the Göttingen talk, at which he was present. 'He spoke rather poor German with his usual very soft voice, and in the front row were all the bigwigs. They shook their heads and said, "If it's not nonsense, at least it doesn't make sense." I spoke with Max Born after the lecture, and he said to me, "All this is absolutely queer and incredible, but this Danish physicist looks so like an original genius that I cannot deny that there must be something to it . . ." The older people, as always, simply couldn't follow the times. It was too complicated and upsetting . . . There were people who from the beginning said, "This is all nonsense, it is just a cheap excuse for not knowing what is going on." Then others said that there must be something to it, and others after a rather short time just took it for the only truth, took it for granted.'[119]

Not so Bohr himself.

On balance these various responses by others must have given him much satisfaction, but never obscured for him the uncertain basis on which his work was founded. Already in his December 1913 talk he had said: 'You understand, of course, that I am by no means trying to give what might ordinarily be described as an explanation . . . I hope I have expressed myself sufficiently clearly so that you have appreciated the extent to which these considerations conflict with the admirably coherent group of conceptions which have been rightly termed the classical theory of electrodynamics.'[81]

Landé recalled that Bohr 'was very dissatisfied with this model . . . It was makeshift. I think he always had the idea that it was makeshift and something provisional.'[119] Max Born: 'Bohr had, I remember, a more pessimistic view, contrary to Sommerfeld.'[120] James Franck: 'He was not at all convinced, as we were, that that was the end and that's all. He said, "No you can't believe that. This is a rough approach. It has too much of approximation in it and it is philosophically not right."'[121]

Finally, Niels to Harald in 1915: 'Apart from such mathematical disciplines as potential theory, hydrodynamics, etc., . . . there is literally nothing so well founded that one can say anything definite about it . . . It is still worse with the things I am working with at the moment, for which the fundamental basis isn't even generally known, but for which everything depends on new experimental results . . . everything depends on intuition and experience.'[122]

Interpreting experiments, intuition, experience – Bohr could not have put together more succinctly the three qualities that would continue to be his own main strengths as a physicist.

References

1. J. Rud Nielsen, *Physics Today*, October 1963, p. 22.

2. Diarium af det matematisk-naturvidenskabelige Fakultet, deposited at the Rigsarkiv (National Archives), 7 June 1911.
3. Diarium, 12 September 1911.
4. *Aarbog for Københavns Universitet*, 1910–1913, pp. 472, 492, Schultz, Copenhagen 1915.
5. H. Bohr, letter to C. W. Oseen, 7 March 1912, NBA.
6. C. W. Oseen, letter to N. Bohr, 3 September 1911, NBA.
7. N. Bohr, letter addressed to the king of Denmark, undated, but certainly written in March or April 1912, NBA.
8. Diarium, 26 April 1912.
9. *Aarbog* 1910–1913, p. 492, faculty meeting on 18 May 1912.
10. Diarium, 27 August, 1912.
11. N. Bohr, address in the *Videnskabernes Selskab*, 9 December 1949; also *Berlingske Aftenavis*, 14 February 1941.
12. Summary of interview by C. Weiner with M. Bohr and J. Pedersen, 11 August 1971.
13. M. Knudsen, letter to N. Bohr, 30 July 1912, NBA.
14. N. Bohr, letter to M. Knudsen, 31 July 1912, NBA.
14a. For Niels, see *Garnisonskirkebog*, No. 42, p. 127; for Harald, *ibid.* p. 159.
15. M. Bohr, A. Bohr, and L. Rosenfeld interviewed by T. Kuhn, 30 January 1963, NBA.
15a. *Slagelse Posten*, 1 August 1912.
16. N. Bohr, *Proc. Phys. Soc. London*, **78**, 1083, 1961.
17. See N. Bohr, letter to the Department of Religious and Educational Affairs, 14 March 1914, NBA.
18. Lecture notes are found in NBA.
19. Diarium, 10 January 1913.
20. Diarium, 17 March 1913.
21. Diarium, 1 April 1913.
22. *Aarbog* 1910–1913, pp. 1029, 1030.
23. R. Courant, NBR, p. 301.
24. N. Bohr, letter to E. Rutherford, 6 July 1912, CW, Vol. 2, p. 577.
25. CW, Vol. 2, p. 136.
26. N. Bohr, *Phil. Mag.* **25**, 10, 1913, esp. p. 12; CW Vol. 2, p. 20.
27. See most especially J. L. Heilbron and T. S. Kuhn, *Hist. Stud. Phys. Sci.* **1**, 211, 1969, repr. in J. Heilbron, *Historical studies in the theory of atomic structure*, Arno Press, New York 1981.
28. The role of stability in Bohr's theory is discussed in detail by U. Hoyer, *Arch. Hist. Exact Sci.* **10**, 177, 1973.
29. H. Nagaoka, *Nature* **69**, 392, 1904; *Phil. Mag.* **7**, 445, 1904.
30. G. A. Schott, *Phil. Mag.* **8**, 384, 1904.
31. Cf. Ref. 27, p. 246, footnote 88.
32. CW, Vol. 1, p. 175. For incomprehensible reasons this important passage is not included in the English translation, CW, Vol. 1, p. 300.
33. A. Einstein, *Ann. der Phys.* **22**, 180, 1907; for further details see SL, Chap. 20.
34. Interview of N. Bohr by T. S. Kuhn, L. Rosenfeld, E. Rüdinger, and A. Petersen, 7 November 1962.

35. A. Sommerfeld, *Atombau und Spektrallinien*, preface to the 1st edn, Vieweg, Braunschweig 1919.

36. For many more details see W. McGucken, *Nineteenth century spectroscopy*, Johns Hopkins Press, Baltimore 1969.

37. G. Kirchhoff and R. Bunsen, *Ann. der Phys. und Chem.* **110**, 160, 1860; also *ibid.* **113**, 337, 1861; transl. in *Phil. Mag.* **20**, 89, 1860; **22**, 329, 448, 1861 respectively.

38. See further IB, pp. 168–70.

39. H. G. J. Kayser, *Handbuch der Spectroscopie*, 6 vols., Hirzel, Leipzig 1900–1912 (more volumes appeared later).

40. A. Ångström, *Ann. der Phys. und Chem.* **144**, 300, 1872.

41. J. Plücker, *ibid.* **107**, 497, 638, 1859.

42. A. Ångström, *Recherches sur le spectre solaire*, Uppsala University Press 1868.

43. G. G. Stokes, *Mathematical and physical papers*, Vol. 3, p. 267, Cambridge University Press 1901.

44. J. C. Maxwell, *Encyclopaedia Britannica*, 9th edn, 1875; repr. in *Collected works*, Vol. 2, p. 445, Dover, New York.

45. J. J. Thomson, *Phil. Mag.* **11**, 769, 1906.

46. J. Stark, *Prinzipien der Atomdynamik*, Vol. 2, sections 19, 25, Hirzel, Leipzig 1911; see also F. Horton, *Phil. Mag.* **22**, 214, 1911.

47. For details see Ref. 35, Chap. 3; Ref. 39, Vol. 1, pp. 123–7; IB, pp. 171–4.

48. H. Konen, *Das Leuchten der Gase und Dämpfe*, p. 71 ff., Vieweg, Braunschweig 1913.

49. A. Hagenbach, *Naturw.* **9**, 451, 1921.

50. J. Balmer, *Verh. Naturf. Ges. Basel*, **7**, 548, 1885.

51. P. Zhao, W. Lichten, H. Layer, and J. Bergquist, *Phys. Rev. Lett.* **58**, 1293, 1987. The value quoted actually refers to infinite nuclear mass.

52. J. Balmer, *Verh. Naturf. Ges. Basel.* **7**, 750, 1885.

53. See IB, p. 164.

54. Article 'Spectroscopy', by A. Schuster, in *Encyclopaedia Britannica*.

55. Ref. 34, interviews on 1 and 7 November 1962.

56. Ref. 26, p. 27; CW, Vol. 2, p. 35.

57. N. Bohr, letter to E. Rutherford, 4 November 1912, CW, Vol. 2, p. 577.

58. E. Rutherford, letter to N. Bohr, 11 November 1912, CW, Vol. 2, p. 578.

59. N. Bohr, letter to E. Rutherford, 31 January 1913, CW, Vol. 2, p. 579.

60. N. Bohr, letter to G. von Hevesy, 7 February 1913, CW, Vol. 2, p. 529.

61. IB, p. 164.

62. Ref. 46, Vol. 2, p. 44.

63. Ref. 34, interviews on 31 October and 7 November 1962.

64. C. Christiansen, *Lærebog i Fysik*, Chap. 23, Nordisk Forlag, Copenhagen 1903.

65. A. Haas, *Wiener Ber.* IIa, **119**, 119, 1910; *Jahrb. der Rad. und Elektr.* **7**, 261, 1910; Phys. Zeitschr. **11**, 537, 1910.

66. A Sommerfeld, in *Théorie de rayonnement et les quanta*, p. 362, Gauthier-Villars, Paris 1912.

67. N. Bohr, *Phil. Mag.* **26**, 1, 1913; CW, Vol. 2, p. 159.

68. J. W. Nicholson, *Phil. Mag.* **22**, 864, 1911.

69. Ref. 26, p. 24, CW, Vol. 2, p. 32.
70. J. W. Nicholson, *Mon. Not. Roy. Astr. Soc.* **72**, 677, 1912.
71. N. Bohr, letter to C. W. Oseen, 1 December 1911, CW, Vol. 1, p. 426.
72. Ref. 34, interview 7 November 1962.
73. See R. McCormmach, *Arch. Hist. Exact Sci.* **3**, 160, 1966.
74. N. Bjerrum, unpublished manuscript written in 1955, NBA.
75. N. Bjerrum, *Nernst Festschrift*, p. 90, von Knapp, Halle 1912; Engl. transl. in *Niels Bjerrum, selected papers*, p. 34, Munksgaard, Copenhagen 1949.
76. W. Nernst, *Zeitschr. Electrochem.* **17**, 265, 1911.
77. N. Bohr, letter to E. Rutherford, 6 March 1913, CW, Vol. 2, p. 581.
78. N. Bohr, *Phil. Mag.* **23**, 440, 1912, CW, Vol. 1, p. 439.
79. Ref. 67, section 2.
80. Ref. 67, section 3.
81. N. Bohr, *Fysisk Tidsskr.* **12**, 97, 1914. English transl. in CW, Vol. 2, p. 303.
82. These are found in Ref. 27.
83. See e.g. K. W. Ford, *Basic physics*, Chap. 24, Blaisdell, Waltham, Mass. 1968.
84. In Bohr's paper it is almost everywhere assumed that the orbits are circular rather than elliptic.
85. A. Fowler, *Nature* **92**, 95, 1913.
86. N. Bohr, *Nature* **92**, 231, 1913.
87. N. Bohr, *Phil. Mag.* **26**, 476, 1913, CW, Vol. 2, p. 187.
88. N. Bohr, *Phil. Mag.* **26**, 857, 1913, CW, Vol. 2, p. 215.
89. W. Ritz, *Phys. Zeitschr.* **9**, 521, 1908.
90. For details see IB, Chap. 11, section (d).
91. Ref. 67, section 5.
92. Ref. 87, section 6.
93. N. Bohr, letter to H. Bohr, July 30, 1913, CW, Vol. 1, p. 563.
94. CW, Vol. 2, pp. 254, 256.
95. W. Pauli, *Phys. Zeitschr.* **21**, 615, 1920.
96. N. Bohr, letter to C. W. Oseen, 3 March 1914, CW, Vol. 1, p. 128.
97. Bohr was already aware of this connection when writing his first paper on hydrogen, see Ref. 67, p. 14, CW, Vol. 2, p. 174.
98. Cf. A. L. Robinson, *Science* **234**, 24, 1986.
99. H. G. Moseley, letter to N. Bohr, 16 November 1913, CW, Vol. 2, p. 544.
100. E. Rutherford, letter to N. Bohr, 20 March 1913, CW, Vol. 2, p. 583.
101. A. Einstein, *Phys. Zeitschr.* **18**, 121, 1917; see also SL, Chap. 21, section (d).
102. N. Bohr, letter to E. Rutherford, 21 March 1913, CW, Vol. 2, p. 584.
103. A. S. Eve, *Rutherford*, p. 218, Cambridge University Press 1939.
104. M. Bohr, A. Bohr, and L. Rosenfeld, interview by T. S. Kuhn, 30 January 1963, NBA.
105. E. Rutherford, *Proc. Roy. Soc.* A **90**, 1914, insert after p. 462.
106. E. Rutherford, *Nature* **94**, 350, 1914.
107. R. J. Strutt, *Life of John William Strutt, third baron Rayleigh*, p. 357, University of Wisconsin Press, Madison, Wisc. 1968.
108. J. J. Thomson, *Atomic theory*, Clarendon Press, Oxford 1914.
109. J. J. Thomson, *The electron in chemistry*, Lippincott, Philadelphia 1923.
110. J. J. Thomson, *Recollections and reflections*, p. 425, Bell, London 1936.

111. *Nature*, **92**, 304, 1913.

112. See also IB, Chap. 10.

113. H. Bohr, letter to N. Bohr, fall 1913, CW, Vol. 1, p. 567.

114. A. Sommerfeld, letter to N. Bohr, 4 September 1913, CW, Vol. 2, p. 603.

115. W. Gerlach, interview with T. S. Kuhn, 18 February 1963, NBA.

116. R. W. Pohl, interview with T. S. Kuhn and F. Hund, 25 June 1963, NBA.

117. G. von Hevesy, letter to N. Bohr, 23 September 1913, CW, Vol. 2, p. 532.

118. N. Bohr, letter to C. W. Oseen, 28 September 1914, CW, Vol. 2, p. 560.

119. A. Landé, interview by T. S. Kuhn and J. L. Heilbron, 5 March 1962, NBA.

120. M. Born, interview by T. S. Kuhn, 17 October 1962, NBA.

121. J. Franck, interview by T. S. Kuhn and M. Mayer, 10 July 1962, NBA.

122. N. Bohr, letter to H. Bohr, 2 March 1915, CW, Vol. 1, p. 575.

9

How Bohr secured his permanent base of operations

(a) The early schools in quantum physics

The contributions which mark out Planck, Einstein, and Bohr as the founders of the quantum theory are now in place. Planck's on blackbody radiation (5g) and Einstein's on the light-quantum and on heat capacities ((5h) and (8c)) have been sketched only lightly; Bohr's on atomic structure has been dealt with in much more detail, as befits this book.

Planck had started it all, of course, with the introduction into physics of his new constant, which in turn had been an inspiration to Einstein and Bohr. Yet the directions in which these last two men took off, armed with this constant, differed so much from Planck's and from that of each other that all three deserve to be remembered as founders of the quantum theory. They had, one might say, established four strongholds in new territory which were not as yet linked by roads that pass from one to the other. That roadnet was to be part of a new design, quantum mechanics, which made its first appearance in 1925. The period from 1900 until that year, 1925, is now known as the era of the old quantum theory. Its most striking characteristic was – as has been stressed repeatedly in the foregoing – a large measure of success based on inadequate rhyme and reason. In addition, as we shall begin to see in the next chapter, stimulating success was matched by frustrating failure.

Bohr's trilogy of 1913 appeared at just about midway in the old quantum theory era. During the first half of that period, no more than a handful of papers on quantum theory saw the light of day – but what papers! Very few realized at that time that physics was no longer what it used to be. It has already been recalled that Planck himself initially looked for a classical justification of his radiation law. Debye has remembered reactions to a seminar on Planck's papers, held in 1902: 'We did not know whether quanta were fundamentally new or not.'[1] It was also a rarity in those years for theorists to join the founders in the pursuit of quantum physics. On the experimental side we should note ongoing studies of spectra, and improved measurements of the blackbody spectral distributions, of heat capacities at low temperatures, and of the photoelectric effect.

All that changed after the appearance of Bohr's papers. (Bohr to Rutherford in 1916: 'The whole field of work has indeed from a very lonely state suddenly got into a desperately crowded one where almost everybody seems hard at work.'[2]) It is not hard, I think, to guess why. Bohr's spectacular successes with the spectra of hydrogen and ionized helium held out promise for an understanding of other spectra as well. Remember (8d) that a huge backlog of spectral data amassed in the previous half century was awaiting interpretation. Moreover, at just about the time of Bohr's papers, newly discovered spectral phenomena (to be discussed later) posed fresh challenges. As a result we now observe for the first time that research in quantum physics begins to spread, not only in Europe but also in the United States.[3] In particular we witness the emergence of three schools where the old quantum theory was seriously pursued, in order of appearance in Munich, Copenhagen, and Göttingen. In all three instances Bohr's influence, directly or indirectly, was manifest. Let us see next how these schools came into being, leaving their scientific activities until Chapter 10.

In Munich the central figure was Arnold Sommerfeld, a physician's son, professor of theoretical physics there from 1906 until his retirement in 1938. (In 1927 he was offered but declined a professorship in Berlin as successor to Planck.) During the first third of this century he was arguably the best theoretical physics teacher.[4] His textbooks are among the finest to this day. His *Atomic Structure and Spectral Lines* was known in its early years as the bible of spectroscopists. Its first German edition[5] appeared in 1919, its eighth in 1960; the first English edition[6] came out in 1923. Sommerfeld was justly proud of having been the first teacher to give a course (1908–9) in relativity theory and may also have been the first to do so for the Bohr theory (1914–15).[7] His familiarity with both subjects enabled him to be the first to apply relativity and quantum theory jointly, in his theory of fine structure (see the next chapter).

Sommerfeld himself has left us the best vignettes about his style of teaching: 'I used to organize my lectures in such a way that they were too easy for advanced students and too difficult for beginners'[8] and 'Once when I wanted to announce a course on a problematic subject, my . . . assistant asked if I knew something about it. I replied: "If I did I would not give a course on it." '[9] The most impressive list[10] of his doctoral students includes four Nobel laureates, Bethe, Debye, Heisenberg, and Pauli.

Sommerfeld's active interest in quantum physics dates back to 1911 when he presented two papers[11] on the significance of Planck's constant for molecular physics. He was one of the first to congratulate Bohr on his derivation of the Balmer formula (8g). In 1914 his student Walther Kossel was among the first to build further[12] on the Bohr papers (specifically on Bohr's ideas regarding X-rays), work which Bohr considered 'very important'.[13] From then on, frequent papers on quantum theory originated from the Munich school, not least those by the master himself.

Max Born, grandson and son of distinguished physicians, gave direction to theoretical physics in Göttingen, where earlier he had been a student, then a Privatdozent.[14] Born himself had already worked on quantum problems earlier, however. In two important papers[15] dating from 1912 he and von Kármán had refined Einstein's quantum theory of heat capacities. In 1918 he and Landé had applied[16] Bohr's ideas to the structure of crystal lattices.

Sommerfeld was a mathematical physicist concerned mostly with calculations that bear on experiment. Born was primarily a physical mathematician, less interested in the search for novel physical ideas than in treating known physical issues with improved mathematical rigor, in accordance with the spirit of Göttingen which at that time was *the* Mecca for mathematical research. With respect to the old quantum theory Born came particularly into his own as its mathematical methods grew in complexity. Among his many good books his *Lectures on Atomic Mechanics* (1925) is the best of its kind.[17] He was among the first (perhaps the first) to realize that quantum physics required a new kind of mathematical underpinning. In the spring of 1924 he baptized this as yet unborn theory: *Quantenmechanik*.[18]

Born, too, had students who were to become physicists of the first rank. His first assistant in Göttingen was Pauli, his second Heisenberg. Many Americans would come to Göttingen as well as Munich to complete their education in modern physics. Karl Compton has remembered: 'In the winter of 1926 I found more than twenty Americans in Göttingen at this fount of quantum wisdom.'[19]

Research in Göttingen on quantum problems received a major impetus as a consequence of the series of seven lectures that Bohr gave there in June 1922, a happening that came to be known as the Bohr *Festspiele* (festival). A young physicist in the audience recalled forty years later:

'[This] great event . . . has led many to theoretical physics who otherwise might have turned elsewhere . . . the glamour surrounding this event can no longer be put in words . . .'[20] In attendance were not only the local physicists and mathematicians but also many from elsewhere, including Sommerfeld who came from Munich accompanied by his student Heisenberg, and Pauli who came from Hamburg. On that occasion debates on the meaning of the quantum theory revealed differences in style. During the discussions in which Sommerfeld took an active part, the differences between Munich and Copenhagen with respect to the assessment of quantum concepts became manifest. In Munich the formulations were more concrete and thus more comprehensible ... In Copenhagen one believed that the appropriate language for the new [physics] was not yet available ... one was more reticent in regard to concrete formulations, one expressed oneself very cautiously and in general terms which were more difficult to grasp ... I must confess that the sympathies of us beginners tended more toward Copenhagen.[20] As Heisenberg later put it: 'I learned optimism from Sommerfeld, mathematics in Göttingen, and physics from Bohr.'[21]

By the time of these *Festspiele* Bohr's fame had spread far and wide. Let us catch up with him.

(b) In which Bohr returns to Manchester and then becomes Denmark's first professor of theoretical physics

In the previous chapter we followed Bohr's academic career up to July 1913, when he was appointed docent, charged with the teaching of physics to medical students. He and Knudsen, the university professor of physics since 1912, had their offices in the *Polytekniske Læreanstalt* – there was as yet no university physics institute.

Bohr was far from content. His duties did not provide him with sufficient opportunities for pursuing his own kind of physics. On 3 March 1914, he wrote[22] to Oseen: 'Together with Dr Hansen I have started some experiments ... but so far we have made no progress since we have both very little time and only a small amount of money and no assistance whatsoever. No laboratory is attached to my position ... I have the sole job of teaching physics to the medical students ... I have no possibility of obtaining pupils or assistance. That is why I am working toward the establishment of a teaching position in theoretical physics ... but there is not much hope that I shall succeed ... In a few days I start to lecture on the electron theory of metals.'[23]

In spite of his misgivings Bohr, still in a hurry, went ahead anyway. On 10 March he wrote again to Oseen ('the matter is expected to cause trouble'[24]) and also to Rutherford[25] asking for testimonials. On 13 March he made his pitch to the Government Department of Religious and Educational Affairs. 'The undersigned takes the liberty of petitioning the department to bring about the founding of a professorship in theoretical physics at the university as well as to possibly entrust me with that post,'[26] appending an account of his qualifications. In motivating his proposal he stressed that the rapid growth of physics during the past 20–30 years had led other universities to establish separate chairs for experimental and for theoretical physics. As was noted earlier (5b) the division between experimental and theoretical physics was of recent vintage at that time. Thus around 1900 there were only two professors officially designated as theoretical physicists in the United States, only one in Holland, and none in the British Empire.[27]

Bohr's application received strong support. Rutherford wrote:[28] 'I have had the best of opportunities of forming a definite opinion of his abilities . . . I personally feel strongly that his theories show great originality and merit . . . In my opinion Dr Bohr is one of the most promising and able of the young Mathematical Physicists in Europe today.' In addition seven members of the mathematics–physics faculty gave their endorsement: 'It will be of the greatest interest for students and physics researchers to be kept à jour with this [theoretical] side of the developments of physics which in recent years has been extraordinarily vigorous . . . Dr N. Bohr has . . . shown himself fully qualified for this task.'[29] On 21 April the faculty as a whole recommended Bohr for a full professorship in theoretical physics,[30] but the Department shelved that proposal. In Bohr's words: 'In these times its final confirmation by the authorities may suffer a long delay, if it ever comes. Even in ordinary times such a matter always take a long time here.'[31]

Temporary solace was on its way, however. In May, Rutherford wrote to Bohr that he was looking for a successor to Darwin whose tenure as reader had expired. 'I should like to get some young fellow with some originality in him.'[32] In that letter Rutherford did not offer the position to Bohr, presumably because of his awareness of Bohr's ongoing efforts toward securing a position in Denmark. Some correspondence (not preserved) must have followed, for on 19 June Bohr wrote[33] to Rutherford: 'I cannot say how glad I am for your offering me the vacant readership for next year and with how great a pleasure I accept it . . . the post which I applied for at all events cannot be expected before September 1915.' He arranged for a leave of absence; H. M. Hansen was to substitute for him in lecturing to the medical students. Bohr intended to take up his duties in Manchester in September.[34]

First, however, he and Harald took a holiday trip to the Tyrol. On the way they stopped in Göttingen and Munich, where Niels talked in seminars and also met Sommerfeld for the first time.[31] That was in July – just before the outbreak of World War I. We have Bohr's recollections[35] of what happened next.

From Munich we traveled on to Tyrol . . . where we met aunt Hanna [Adler] . . . then we came to the high mountains . . . then we saw in the newspapers that everybody was traveling home, and then we thought, yes, that is perhaps the wisest thing to do . . . and then we crossed the border [back] into Germany by train, I believe less than half an hour before Germany declared war on Russia . . . the others came too late and were delayed in Tyrol for a month . . . That was a big catastrophe that [aunt Hanna] had to miss school . . . Then we came to Munich and took the Berlin train which was so tremendously full that one had to stand in the corridors almost the whole night . . . When we arrived in Berlin there was this unbounded enthusiasm, there was a screaming and yelling that now one would have war again . . . It is always extremely difficult to say what people really meant by that . . . In any case it is the custom in Germany to find such enthusiasms as soon as something military is concerned . . . Then we took the train to Warnemünde, the last which had a ferry connection with Denmark . . . and so we came home.

The coming of war did, of course, complicate travels to Manchester, but in October 1914 Niels and Margrethe managed to reach England 'after a stormy voyage around Scotland'.[36]

Bohr originally intended to stay in Manchester for only one academic year, hoping for his professorship to come through meanwhile. Since there was still no official word after that period, he actually stayed on till July 1916, even though 'I frequently long to be home again and I am looking forward so much really to start working at home with the others'.[37] The war, of course, strongly affected activities in the Manchester laboratory. In February 1916 Bohr wrote[38] to a colleague: 'Here things have changed very much on account of the war . . . Professor Rutherford is giving all his time to work in connection with the war.'[39]

Rutherford had joined the Board of Invention and Research (as had J. J. Thomson), created in July 1915, which oversaw the British scientific war effort. His own contributions dealt primarily with anti-submarine warfare. 'To use a favorite expression of his, the work he did for the Navy in the war was "colossal".'[40] Initially the methods were slightly primitive. Thus one day Rutherford set out in a small boat on the Firth of Forth, together with a colleague who had absolute pitch, in order to detect the noise of a British submarine lying underwater, engines running. This colleague stuck his head underwater while Rutherford held him by the heels. When he emerged he could name the pitch. 'Rutherford used to tell this story with gusto and add, "I'm not sure now whether I shouldn't have let go!"'[41] Part of the Manchester laboratory was set aside for research on more reliable acoustical devices. After the United States had entered the war Rutherford traveled to America to confer with his counterparts over there. In spite of all these activities he continued to find time for participation in physics research in his laboratory.

For the Bohrs this Manchester period was carefree. 'We are both very happy to be here. We have met so much kindness and feel so much at ease . . . The work at the laboratory is going on nearly as usual although there are much fewer young people than usual, and especially no foreigners except me.'[37] Among social events Bohr remembered with pleasure the monthly discussions among a group of Rutherford's friends which included Chaim Weizmann, later the first president of Israel, 'for whose distinctive personality Rutherford had great esteem'.[36]

As citizen of a neutral country, Bohr could not participate in war activities. Fulfilling his principal task, to teach, he gave courses on thermodynamics,[42] on electrodynamics and electron theory,[43] and on the kinetic theory of matter.[44] 'I succeeded quite well in giving these lectures in English, but it has required a fair amount of work.'[13] Once again he made an attempt at doing some experimental work,[36] but other activities forced him to 'give up doing experiments which I had made a small start on'.[13] I shall come back in the next chapter to his theoretical activities during the Manchester years which were only marginally hampered by the fact that 'here I see no foreign journals'.[45]

Then, in the very beginning of 1916, Bohr received the first intimation that, as the result of a newly enacted civil servants law, his appointment to the desired professorship appeared to be imminent.[46] He was surprised. 'I never really expected the professorship to come this year.'[47] As a result he declined an invitation to lecture at the University of California at Berkeley.[47]

News of Bohr's professorship was announced[48] in Danish newspapers as early as 21 March 1916, but it was not until 5 May 1916, that the Department formally appointed him as of the preceding 1 April, with the further stipulations that Bohr's docent post would be abolished and that he would continue to be responsible for the elementary physics course for medical students.[49]

In the early summer of 1916 the Bohrs returned to Denmark. Four years earlier Bohr had left Manchester full of exciting but undigested ideas about the atom. Now he departed as the master of that field, professor in Copenhagen, his wife who was expecting their first child at his side.

(c) In which Bohr acquires his own institute

The Royal Danish Court and State Calendar, published annually[50] under the joint auspices of the king's or queen's cabinet and the prime minister's office, contains a section in which dignitaries and functionaries are ranked in five classes. Included in the third class are professors at the University of Copenhagen. Thus Bohr's appointment to professor was tantamount to his being inducted into the Danish establishment. Thirty years later he would become a Knight of the Order of the Elephant, thereby ranking high in first class, right after the members of the Royal House, the prime minister, and the chief justice of the Supreme Court.

Let us return to the more humble beginnings in 1916. It is the custom that a professor presents himself at a public audience to the king or queen shortly after being appointed. Dress: morning coat and white gloves, the latter not to be removed when shaking hands with the monarch. Accordingly Bohr called on Christian X, a rather stiff military type. I have it on good authority that this event went about as follows. After the introduction the King said he was pleased to meet the famous soccer player Bohr, whereupon Niels replied something like, I am sorry but Your Majesty must be thinking of my brother. The king was taken aback since according to the rules of the game one does not contradict the monarch during a public audience. So Christian started all over again, saying how pleased he was, etc. Bohr now became very uncomfortable and replied that indeed he was a soccer player, but that he had a brother who was the *famous* soccer player. Whereupon the King said, '*Audiensen er forbi*' (the audience is over), and Bohr took his leave, walking backwards, as custom demands.

The next step in Bohr's joining the establishment came in 1917 when, on 1 March, he was proposed for membership in the *Videnskabernes Selskab*. His election followed on 27 April.[51]

Let us turn to Bohr's activities at the university. For the four years following assumption of his new duties Bohr continued to be in the *Læreanstalt* having at his disposal nothing but one small office of less than 150 square feet. Every working day he would bicycle back and forth between his home in Hellerup, a Copenhagen suburb, and his place of work. In regard to teaching medical students the faculty soon recommended that H. M. Hansen, Bohr's earlier substitute, be appointed as docent, a proposal that the Department of Education did not at once agree to. Hansen nevertheless gave the course, financially supported by outside sources and teaching one term without pay. In the spring of 1918 the Department gave in.[52]

Meanwhile Bohr had started teaching advanced courses on topics including mechanics,[53] recent developments in atomic theory,[54] and electromagnetic theory.[55] In the spring of 1917 he also conducted a series of eleven students' colloquia on subjects such as spectra, heat capacities, and radioactivity.[56] The audience consisted of a small number of advanced students and of staff members of the physics and chemistry departments.[52] As to his educational style, 'I have been trying in several ways to introduce the English methods in my University work here.'[57] In May 1917 he wrote to a colleague[58] of his hopes to experiment on spectra even though conditions for doing so were highly unfavorable.

Two important events bring us back to 1916. In August of that year Bohr received a letter[59] mailed from Copenhagen by a young Dutchman he had never heard of, who introduced himself as a student in physics and mathematics from Leiden, in possession of a 'doctorandus' degree (the equivalent of a high grade masters), who wanted to study for the Ph.D. and who asked if he might call on Bohr. The writer was Hendrik Antonie Kramers, son of a medical doctor, Hans to his family and friends (of whom I was one). After the two had met over a cup of coffee[60] Bohr decided to give Kramers a chance, a splendid decision as it turned out. In the fall of 1916 the two began a collaboration which, with minor interruptions, was to last until 1926, when Kramers left to become a professor at the University of Utrecht. (The content of their research will be discussed in the next chapter.)

Initially Kramers shared Bohr's small office, financially supported from a grant at Bohr's disposal. Already in 1917 Bohr could write: 'I have been very pleased in my collaboration with Dr [sic] Kramers who I think is extremely able and about whom I have the greatest expectations.'[61] Bohr was in attendance[62] when Kramers defended his doctoral thesis (on quantum physics) in Leiden, in May 1919. Also in that month Kramers was appointed scientific assistant in Copenhagen.[63] In 1923 he became lecturer. 'The Copenhagen years from about 1916 to 1925 witnessed [Kramers'] meteoric rise from an apprentice in atomic physics to heir apparent to Bohr. [In the days of the old quantum theory] he was the dominant figure next to Bohr in Copenhagen.'[64]

Kramers also started a new tradition. He was the first of the many physicists from abroad who would find a Danish spouse. Bohr was one of the official witnesses at their marriage.[65]

The second main event during 1916 was the birth on 25 November of Christian Alfred, the Bohr's first son. Rutherford sent congratulations: 'This will always be a remembrance of your stay in Manchester.'[66] From those days on Margrethe's help in taking dictation waned of course – but now there was Kramers.

Bohr was quite understandably not content with his cramped working quarters. With a speed which we have seen to be characteristic, he decided to take action. On 18 April 1917 he sent a long letter[67] to his faculty that begins as follows:

I hereby request the Faculty to work for the establishment of an institute for theoretical physics, where the necessary conditions can be created for the growth and development of this subject here in Denmark. Such an institute would have the dual task of being the centre for education in theoretical physics and of giving the opportunity for carrying out numerical computations and experimental investigations in connection with the scientific work in this subject.

Note that from the start Bohr used the later adopted name *Institut for teoretisk Fysik*, even though the proposed institution was supposed to (and in the event did) house activities not just in theoretical but also in experimental physics. Bohr later explained[68] that choice of name: 'There was in Göttingen an institute . . . called the institute for theoretical physics . . . they called the new things theoretical physics and we kept the name. It may not be practical you see; we could perhaps much better have called it an institute for atomic physics.'

In his letter to the faculty, Bohr gave cost estimates, 120000 Kr (Kroner) for the building, 60000 Kr for furniture, books, and instruments, 9500 Kr for annual maintenance. Funds should also be provided for a permanent assistant and a mechanic. The most interesting part of this document is Bohr's motivation:

While previously one supposed for apparently good reasons that we possessed with the so-called classical mechanics and electrodynamics a secure basis for our scientific conceptions . . . it has [since] been shown that [this] earlier theoretical basis completely fails in fundamental aspects. Theoretical physics therefore now faces a task which can be justly characterized as the opposite of that which one had thought until a short time ago, namely to infer from the [experimental] information gained on the internal structure of matter the general laws . . . Therefore it is . . . necessary that the practitioners . . . carry out and guide scientific experiments in direct connection with the theoretical investigations.

These lines illustrate a point I have made several times before: during the early years of this century the separation between experiment and theory had begun to evolve but was not yet generally established, as is further exemplified in Bohr's own hopes, repeatedly noted, to engage in experimental work. He expressed such desires again in August 1918: 'I look forward immensely to start experiments again.'[69] Thereafter he concentrated uniquely on theory – and on directing and administering his institute.

Back to the prehistory of the institute,* in May 1917 the faculty forwarded Bohr's letter to the Konsistorium (the university's executive committee consisting of academics and administrators and, these days, students, God help us all) accompanied by a strong endorsement of their own,[70] stressing that Bohr lacked 'a laboratory in which he and his pupils can do experiments'. At that time Bohr wrote to a friend: 'We shall see what . . . Parliament will say.'[58] In June the Konsistorium appointed a committee that included Bohr to work out further plans and assigned a distinguished architect to work with Bohr. In December this committee suggested to the minister of education the acquisition from the *Kommune* (Municipality) of grounds for the institute along *Blegdamsvej*, a main road (not paved[52] until 1911) named after the *blegemaend*, the bleachers, who would use grass land in the area to process linens washed in the Sortedamssø, a nearby lake. That land, now a handsome park, *Fælledparken* (its first trees were planted[52] in 1909) lies right behind the present institute. After some hassles the grounds were bought in August 1918.

Meanwhile Aage Berlème, an ex-schoolmate of Bohr from *Gammelholm Skolen*, now a wealthy businessman, had taken an initiative to garner outside financial support for Bohr's plans. In November 1917 he circulated a printed appeal for funds towards Bohr's institute, signed by himself, the

---

* The reader is urged to consult ref. 52 for more details about that period.

rector of the university, Professor Emeritus Høffding, and others from the academic and business world,[71] stressing the importance of the project for the industrial and cultural future of the country, and emphasizing that Bohr's name was familiar by now in scientific circles the world over. By 15 December he was able[72] to report to the university that he had achieved his stated aim, to collect 80000 Kr, just the sum, as it happened, needed to buy the desired plot of land. Contributions had come from industry and private sources, including several members of the Jewish community. This was a piece of news considered sufficiently interesting to be reported in the Danish press.[73]

In October 1918 the proposal for the institute was tabled in parliament; the next month, just before the end of World War I, permission was granted[74] by the minister of education for work to begin. A week after the Armistice, Bohr received a letter from Rutherford asking him whether he might be interested in a professorship in Manchester. 'Between us we could try and make physics boom.'[75] Bohr, of course, could not now contemplate this: 'I have morally pledged myself to do what I can to help in the development of scientific physical research here in Denmark.'[76]

It was and would remain typical of Bohr to involve himself in the construction (later in the extension) of his institute in regard not just to broad outlines but also to minute detail. Thus on 10 January 1919 he writes[74] to the minister of education requesting an extra 8500 Kr for a modification of the basement floor. On 17 January he writes again,[74] submitting a detailed proposal for equipment, from blackboards to vacuum pumps and chemicals.

More serious were Bohr's requests[77] of 14 October and 5 November 1919 for increased funding, especially in view of the intense unrest in Denmark at that time. The high post-war inflation rate of the Krone caused grave apprehension, labor unrest was rampant. 'Denmark came closer to a revolution than it had been for nearly four hundred years, even though not quite resembling the revolutions that had occurred to the south and east.'[78] Strikes by masons and carpenters contributed to a two-year delay in the institute's completion. Cost overruns were considerable. The final government costs for construction and equipment were 400000 and 175000 Kr respectively, three times Bohr's initial estimates. Additional smaller amounts came from other sources.

In the midst of all this turmoil more young physicists wishing to work with the young master began to arrive. Oskar Klein came from Sweden in 1918, Rubinowicz, the Pole, Hevesy, the Hungarian, and Rosseland, the Norwegian, came in 1920. Hevesy was temporarily housed in the physical chemistry laboratory, the others in the library which adjoined Bohr's office. Bohr had also invited Rutherford to be guest of honor at the opening of his institute. Rutherford came in 1920 – too early for the occasion.

In 1919 Bohr began to look for a secretary and was fortunate to find Betty Schultz, who remembered: 'I went out to his home . . . I took shorthand and knew a little English and such things, but when I came there he didn't ask for anything except whether I had been interested in science. And I said, "No, I do not know what it is," and then I was engaged.'[79] She first reported for work on 2 January 1919 and was housed in Bohr's office. 'And there was professor Bohr and Kramers and I sitting in one room . . . When he should work with Kramers I could go home and Kramers went away when we worked.'[79] She took dictation, typed manuscripts, made order in the reprints, and 'I did the bookkeeping in a very little book; we had not much money at that time.'[79] Miss Schultz – we later called her *Fru* (Mrs) – stayed with Bohr for the rest of his life and became a formidable personality at the institute.

In November 1920 the first paper (by Klein and Rosseland[80]) was submitted which carried as a by-line the new institute even though it was not ready until 1921. It consisted then only of what now is the central building of the complex. The exterior with its plaster-covered brick surfaces is simple in appearance and clean in line. Only the main door reflects the neo-classical style then prevalent in Denmark. (See the Freemason Lodge next door, built in 1923!) In January 1921 Bohr and Kramers could transfer their books and papers to Blegdamsvej. Bohr's first letter[81] sent from his new office was to Rutherford – who else?

The official inauguration took place on 3 March 1921 (though on the building the starting year is marked as 1920). The prime minister was supposed to attend but did not show up. After short speeches by the rector and the minister of education, Bohr delivered an address[82] which concluded with what would become the institute's main theme, that is:

The task of having to introduce a constantly renewed number of young people into the results and methods of science . . . Through the contributions of the young people themselves new blood and new ideas are constantly introduced into the work.

Thereafter the rector declared *Universitetets Insistut for teoretisk Fysik* formally opened. In 1965, the year in which Bohr would have been 80, it was renamed *Niels Bohr Institutet*.

Between 1917 and 1921 the planning and construction of the institute took much of Bohr's energies. It would be very wrong to suppose that nothing else was on his mind, however. He continued his lecture courses, in the spring of 1918 on electron theory[83] and on thermodynamics,[84] in the fall of 1918 and winter of 1919 on general theoretical physics and mechanics.[85] The terrible Spanish flu pandemic caused the university to close in the autumn of 1919. Thereafter (as far as I know) Bohr never again gave courses for students.

It is not uncommon for a professor in his mature years to combine teaching with a goodly amount of administrative duties. Bohr, however, 35 years old when his institute opened its doors, managed to do something which I believe to be unique: to combine all these activities with an intense and most important research program of his own at the frontiers of physics (to be detailed in the next chapter). He worked under strains which stretched his formidable physical strength to the limit – and beyond. In September 1917 he informed the faculty that he had to take a few weeks' holiday because of overexertion.[86] In December 1917 he wrote to Rutherford: 'I have not been quite well these last terms.'[87] In August 1918: 'I feel a little overworked.'[88] In the autumn of 1918, colleagues wrote[89] to express the hope that Bohr had recovered from illness. In October 1919 Bohr wrote that he had gone to the country to rest.[90] In October 1920 a friend wrote[91] that he had heard about Bohr being 'extraordinarily tired and harassed'. A few weeks after the opening of the institute, Bohr wrote: 'I have for a long time been overworked and I now feel rather unwell; the doctor has therefore advised me most urgently to take a few weeks perfect rest.'[92] He had to postpone for a year a series of lectures in Göttingen originally planned for the summer of 1921 (these became the *Festspiele* of 1922) and to cancel his attendance at the Solvay conference of October 1921.

By September 1921 Bohr felt better but in need above all for quiet, so that he could finish his latest scientific paper.[93] Once again he was off and running, his base of operations now secure.

References

1. U. Benz, *Arnold Sommerfeld*, p. 74, Wissenschaftliche Verlagsgesellschaft, Stuttgart 1975.
2. N. Bohr, letter to E. Rutherford, 6 September 1916, NBA.
3. For the United States see especially K. R. Sopka, *Quantum physics in America 1920–1935*, Arno Press, New York 1980.
4. For a biography of Sommerfeld see Ref. 1.
5. A. Sommerfeld, *Atombau und Spektrallinien*, Vieweg, Braunschweig, 1919, who also published all later German editions.
6. Atomic structure and spectral lines, transl. H. L. Brose, Methuen, London 1923.
7. Ref. 1, pp. 71, 82.
8. A. Sommerfeld, *Am. J. Phys.* **17**, 315, 1949.
9. A. Sommerfeld, *Scientia*, Nov./Dec. 1942, p. 123.
10. For a detailed list of Sommerfeld students see *Geheimrat Sommerfeld*, Deutsches Museum, Munich 1984.
11. A. Sommerfeld, *Phys. Zeitschr.* **12**, 1057, 1911; and his contribution to the first Solvay conference, see *La théorie du rayonnement et les quanta*, p. 313, Gauthier-Villars, Paris 1912.

12. W. Kossel, *Verh. Deutsch. Phys. Ges.* **16**, 898, 953, 1914; **17**, 339, 1915.
13. N. Bohr, letter to H. M. Hansen, 12 May 1915, CW, Vol. 2, p. 517.
14. For biographical details see M. Born, *My life*, Scribner's, New York 1975; N. Kemmer and R. Schlapp, *Biogr. Mem. FRS*, **17**, 17, 1971.
15. M. Born and Th. von Kármán, *Phys. Zeitschr.* **13**, 297, 1912; **14**, 15, 1913. See also M. Born, *Naturw.* **1**, 499, 1913.
16. M. Born and A. Landé, *Sitz. Ber. Preuss. Akad. Wiss.* 1918, p. 1048, *Verh. Deutsch. Phys. Ges.* **20**, 202, 1918.
17. M. Born, *Vorlesungen über Atommechanik*, Vol. I, Springer, Berlin 1925.
18. M. Born, *Zeitschr. Phys.* **26**, 379, 1924; Engl. transl. in B. L. van der Waerden, *Sources of quantum mechanics*, p. 181, Dover, New York 1968.
19. K. T. Compton, *Nature*, **139**, 238, 1937.
20. F. Hund, in *Werner Heisenberg und die Physik unserer Zeit*, Ed. F. Bopp, Vieweg, Braunschweig 1961.
21. W. Heisenberg, *Gesammelte Werke*, Part C, Vol. 1, p. 4, Piper, Munich 1984.
22. N. Bohr, letter to C. W. Oseen, 3 March 1914, CW, Vol. 2, p. 555.
23. Lecture notes 6 March–20 May 1914, NBA.
24. N. Bohr, letter to C. W. Oseen, 10 March 1914, CW, Vol. 2, p. 557.
25. N. Bohr, letter to E. Rutherford, 10 March 1914, CW, Vol. 2, p. 591.
26. Printed in *Københavens Universitetet Aarbog 1915–1920*, part IV, p. 283, Schultz, Copenhagen 1922.
27. *Minerva Jahrbuch der gelehrten Welt*, Vol. 10, 1900–1901, Teubner, Strassburg 1901.
28. E. Rutherford, letter dated 16 March 1914, no addressee, NBA. This letter was sent directly to Bohr, see N. Bohr, letter to E. Rutherford, 21 March 1914, CW, Vol. 2, p. 592.
29. Letter to the Department of Religious and Educational Affairs, April 1914, printed in Ref. 26, part IV, p. 285.
30. Diarium af det matematisk-naturvidenskabelige Fakultet, deposited at the Rigsarkiv (National Archives), 21 April 1914.
31. N. Bohr, letter to C. W. Oseen, 28 September 1914, CW, Vol. 2, p. 560.
32. E. Rutherford, letter to N. Bohr, 20 May 1914, NBA.
33. N. Bohr, letter to E. Rutherford, 19 June 1914, CW, Vol. 2, p. 594.
34. His official letter of appointment was sent by the Manchester University Registrar on 29 September 1914, NBA.
35. N. Bohr, recollections, taped in Tisvilde, 12 July 1961.
36. N. Bohr, *Proc. Phys. Soc. London*, **78**, 1083, 1961.
37. N. Bohr, letter to C. Christiansen, 1 June 1915, CW, Vol. 2, p. 494.
38. N. Bohr, letter to A. D. Fokker, 14 February 1916, CW, Vol. 2, p. 499.
39. For the role and fate of physicists during World War I see further IB, Chap. 11, section (g).
40. *E. Rutherford's collected papers*, Vol. 2, p. 310, Allen and Unwin, London 1963.
41. For these and other details see A. S. Eve, *Rutherford*, Chap. 9, Cambridge University Press 1939.
42. Lecture notes 15 January–21 May 1915, NBA.
43. Lecture notes 23 April–20 May 1915, 21 March–23 April 1916, NBA.
44. Lecture notes 15 October–8 December 1915, 25 January–18 February 1916, NBA; also CW, Vol. 1, p. 581.

45. N. Bohr, letter to H. Bohr, 10 October 1915; CW, Vol. 1, p. 579.
46. V. Henriques, letter to N. Bohr, 23 December 1915; N. Bohr, letter to V. Henriques, 16 January 1916, CW, Vol. 2, pp. 521, 523.
47. N. Bohr, letter to H. Bohr, 14 March 1916, CW, Vol. 1, p. 585.
48. A. Berlème, letter to N. Bohr, 21 March 1916, NBA.
49. *Aarbog* (Ref. 26), part IV–V, p. 283.
50. *Kongelig Dansk Hof- og Statskalender*, Schultz, Copenhagen.
51. *Kong. Dansk, Vid. Selsk. Protokoll*, Nos 374 and 383, 1917.
52. P. Robertson, *The early years*, Akademisk Forlag, Copenhagen 1979.
53. Lecture notes starting 8 September 1916, NBA.
54. Lecture notes 6 October–15 December 1916, NBA.
55. Lecture notes, spring term until 22 May 1917, NBA.
56. List of colloquia 22 February–25 May 1917, NBA.
57. N. Bohr, letter to E. Rutherford, 27 December 1917, CW, Vol. 3, p. 682.
58. N. Bohr, letter to S. H. Weber, 31 May 1917, CW, Vol. 2, p. 610.
59. H. A. Kramers, letter to N. Bohr, 25 August 1916, CW, Vol. 2, p. 537.
60. See the excellent biography by M. Dresden, *H. A. Kramers*, Springer, New York 1987.
61. N. Bohr, letter to C. W. Oseen, 28 February 1917, CW, Vol. 2, p. 574.
62. Ref. 60, p. 113.
63. *Aarbog* (Ref. 26) p. 328.
64. Ref. 60, p. 463.
65. Ref. 60, p. 117.
66. E. Rutherford, letter to N. Bohr, 18 December 1916, NBA.
67. *Aarbog* (ref. 26) p. 316; Engl. transl. in full in Ref. 52, p. 20.
68. N. Bohr, interviewed by T. S. Kuhn, L. Rosenfeld, A. Petersen, and E. Rüdinger, 1 November 1962, NBA.
69. N. Bohr, letter to O. W. Richardson, 15 August 1918, CW, Vol. 3, p. 14.
70. *Aarbog* (Ref. 26) p. 318.
71. Berlème appeal, November 1917, NBA.
72. Berlème, printed report to contributors, November 1918, NBA.
73. *Nationaltidende* and *Berlingske Tidende*, 3 January 1918.
74. *Aarbog* (Ref. 26), p. 320.
75. E. Rutherford, letter to N. Bohr, 17 November 1918, NBA.
76. N. Bohr, letter to E. Rutherford, 15 December 1918, NBA.
77. *Aarbog* (Ref. 26), p. 322.
78. E. Rasmussen, in Vol. 13 of *Danmarks Historie*, Politikens Forlag, Copenhagen 1978.
79. B. Schultz, interviewed by A. Petersen and P. Forman, 17 May 1963, NBA.
80. O. Klein and S. Rosseland, *Zeitschr. Phys.* 4, 46, 1921.
81. N. Bohr, letter to E. Rutherford, 18 January 1921, NBA.
82. For the full text see CW, Vol. 3, p. 293.
83. Lecture notes 7 February–6 March 1918, NBA.
84. Lecture notes 18 April–23 May 1918, NBA.
85. Lecture notes 17 September 1918–15 March 1919, NBA.
86. Diarium af det matematisk-naturvidenskabelige Fakultet, deposited at the Rigsarkiv (National Archives), 1 September 1917.

87. N. Bohr, letter to E. Rutherford, 27 December 1917, CW, Vol. 2, p. 344.
88. N. Bohr, letter to O. W. Richardson, 15 August 1918, CW, Vol. 3, p. 314.
89. T. S. Epstein letter to N. Bohr, 2 October 1918; O. Klein, letter to N. Bohr, 29 November 1918, NBA; E. A. Owen, letter to N. Bohr, 23 December 1918, NBA.
90. N. Bohr, letter to E. Rutherford, 20 October 1919, NBA.
91. P. Ehrenfest, letter to N. Bohr, 17 October 1920, CW, Vol. 3, p. 29.
92. N. Bohr, letter to P. Ehrenfest, 23 March 1921, CW, Vol. 3, p. 30.
93. N. Bohr, letter to P. Ehrenfest, 1 September 1921, CW, Vol. 3, p. 626.

10

'It was the spring of hope, it was the winter of despair'[1]

(a) Mathematics in physics

Mathematics plays a many-splendored role in physics, from the coding of experimental results in terms of numbers to the formulation of physical laws in terms of equations. We do not know why the language of mathematics has been so effective in formulating those laws in their most succinct form. Nor can we foretell whether this will forever continue to be true. 'The miracle of the appropriateness of the language of mathematics for the formulation of the laws of physics is a wonderful gift which we neither understand nor deserve. We should be grateful for it and hope that it will remain valid in future research.'[1]

The struggles of physicists with mathematics in physics can, very crudely, be collected under two headings: they calculate and they reflect. They calculate the consequences of the equations as they stand. They reflect on the possible needs for refinements of their concepts, to be expressed by modified equations, guided most often (but not always) by novel experimental information. Far more rarely are they preoccupied with the need not just for refinement but, more drastically, for revision. The major twentieth century example are Einstein's almost solitary search for a revised world geometry that led him to his relativity theories; and the transformation of the old quantum theory into quantum mechanics. The main concern of the present chapter is the final preparatory phase of this last transition, the quantum physics of the years 1913 until about 1924.

That period is exceptionally complex. The equations used in those years were those of classical physics, supplemented by 'quantization rules' such as the one (Chapter 8) that the angular momentum of an electron orbiting around a nucleus can take on only integer multiple values of $h/2\pi$. But rules such as these violate the principles of classical mechanics which these very equations express. In other words the procedure is mathematically inconsistent. In the period to be considered, the quantum theory of the atom would claim several more successes (to be discussed below) in addition to the initial ones by Bohr. There were also spectacular failures, however (also to be discussed), which made increasingly clear that the procedure used, pasting quantum rules on to the classical equations, was but a poor palliative for a systematic, consistent framework.

What to do in this confused situation in which striking, if only partial, successes showed that the quantum theory, at least some of the quantum theory, was here to stay in spite of its failures? In which it was also clear that the classical theory, for more than two hundred years man's most reliable guide to the understanding of the inanimate world, could not just be thrown out in spite of its shortcomings? During the dozen years under consideration these questions became ever more pressing. A crisis in physics was developing.

As in any crisis, reactions varied quite considerably. Many preferred to sit this one out until it would go away. Those who had the courage (I cannot find a better word) to persist tried, in a variety of ways depending on personal temperament, to move ahead in this muddled territory, largely by analyzing data in search of further quantum rules, and by superimposing those on a more refined mathematical treatment of the classical equations. It was not ideal but there was nothing better – yet.

Of course, there was not a well-defined moment at which physicists said: Yesterday all was well, today we have a crisis. These insights developed at different times and with different intensities from one physicist to the next. Heisenberg, who led the way out of these quandaries, has left us his recollections[2] of those troubled years:

> I remember that in being together with young mathematicians and listening to Hilbert's lectures and so on, I heard about the difficulties of the mathematicians.* There it came up for the first time that one could have axioms for a logic that was different from classical logic and still was consistent . . . . That was new to many people. Of course it came also by means of relativity. One had learned that you could use the words 'space' and 'time' differently from their usual sense and still get something reasonable and consistent out . . . . I could not say that there was a definite moment at which I realized that one needed a consistent scheme which, however, might be different from the axiomatics of Newtonian physics. It was not as simple as that. Only gradually, I think, in the minds of many physicists developed the idea that we can scarcely describe nature without having something consistent, but we may be forced to describe nature by means of an axiomatic system which was thoroughly different from the old classical physics and even a logical system which was different from the old one.

How did the founders respond?

As early as in 1910 Planck had written: '[Theoreticians] now work with an audacity unheard of in earlier times, at present no physical law is considered assured beyond doubt, each and every physical truth is open to

* That must have been between October 1923 and September 1924.

dispute. It often looks as if the time of chaos again is drawing near in theoretical physics.'[3] And in 1923: 'In view of these events [quantum effects] doubts may arise as to whether physics may continue to claim to be the best founded among the natural sciences.'[4] He remained actively interested in the quantum theory but could, in those years, no longer be considered one of its guiding figures.

Einstein was otherwise engaged, first in the formulation of general relativity, the greatest of his great contributions, then in working out some of its consequences, then in cosmology, then in the first attempts at a unified field theory. Nevertheless he also found time to do some very important work on quantum physics, to which I shall return below.

Bohr, the youngest of the trio, emerged as the leading figure of this period in quantum physics. As I have mentioned earlier (8g) Bohr was convinced from the outset of the inadequacies of the old quantum theory. As Heisenberg put it: 'Bohr realized that an inconsistency . . . means that you just talk nonsense – that you do not know what you are talking about.'[2] Bohr's friend Paul Ehrenfest wrote in 1923: 'We should be reminded time and again by *Bohr* himself what the *real* problem is with which he struggles: the unveiling of the *principles* of the theory which one day will take the place of the classical theory.'[5]

In those years Bohr relied heavily on the proposition that all classical predictions apply whenever quantum effects can be ignored. This led him to formulate and put to good use the so-called correspondence principle which we have already briefly encountered in (8f), and which will be discussed in greater detail in section (c). In the quantum domain Bohr had of course no choice but to use the available mathematics – the classical equations with quantum rules superimposed. There are in fact hundreds of pages of unpublished notes in the Bohr Archives which show that a considerable amount of calculations often preceded his published work which itself is light on equations, reflecting Bohr's deep conviction that all of quantum physics should for the time being be considered provisional. This lends a tentative style to his scientific writing which remained a characteristic from then on. As, late in life, Einstein said so well of Bohr: 'He utters his opinions like one perpetually groping and never like one who believes he is in possession of definite truth.'[6] As Bohr himself often used to say: Never express yourself more clearly than you think.

Bohr's reservations in regard to overreliance on mathematics goes a long way toward explaining his opinions about some of his more mathematically oriented confrères. 'He thought that in every *fine point* that came up Sommerfeld was wrong.'[7] James Franck has recalled: 'As far as Born was concerned . . . Born was to him too much of a mathematician . . . I remember also that Bohr made a remark once when Wigner spoke in one of the meetings. He told me that he did not understand a word of it, and said, "You know, I am really an amateur. And if they go really into high mathematics I can't follow."'[8]

In some respects one may say that Bohr and Kramers, his closest co-worker during those years, complemented each other. Kramers had a strong bent and great gifts for mathematics. Bohr, on the other hand, had an unparalleled talent for discerning, one might even say divining, how progress could be made by judicious use of experimental data. That is what Heisenberg had in mind when he said: 'Bohr was not a mathematically minded man. He was, I would say, Faraday but not Maxwell.'[2] That is also what Einstein had in mind when he wrote, more elegantly: 'That this insecure and contradictory foundation [of quantum physics in those years] was sufficient to enable a man of Bohr's unique instinct and tact to discover the major laws of the spectral lines and of the electron shells of the atoms together with their significance for chemistry appeared to me like a miracle – and appears to me as a miracle even today [1949]. This is the highest form of musicality in the sphere of thought.'[9]

(b) The old quantum theory 1913–1916: sketches(*)

1. *Introductory*. Let us now see what kinds of atomic problems kept theorists busy during the second half of the old quantum theory period. In broad terms, the main lasting advances during those years were these. First, it became clear that atomic states are characterized by more quantum numbers than the single one introduced by Bohr for hydrogen. Secondly, it came to be seen that Bohr's rule: a higher atomic state jumps to a lower one under emission of a light-quantum, needed refinement. Not all such high→low transitions are in general admissible; the first restrictive rules governing what transitions are actually allowed, the so-called selection rules, were derived. Thirdly, a spectral line is characterized not only by its frequency but also by its intensity; the first calculations of the latter were made. Finally, the quantum theoretical foundations were laid for the explanation of the periodic table of elements.

Never mind that today we can derive these results in better ways. This was progress, in which Bohr took part. This period can no longer be appreciated by merely reciting what he himself contributed, however. Rather, it is of the essence to surround him with other actors and their roles. Yet it is neither desirable nor in fact possible to make this part of the story into a fully fledged history of the old quantum theory. It is not desirable because the reader would lose sight of our main character. It is impossible because that fascinating subject alone can easily fill a book larger than the present one. Fortunately it is not necessary either. Those interested will be

able to find elsewhere excellent treatments of this subject in its entirety.* In
addition there exist essays on the specific topics which I sketch next, one by
one.

2. *How order was brought in the periodic table of elements.* We are now back
in 1913. In November the last part of Bohr's trilogy had appeared (8f). It
seems that Bohr was in need of catching his breath. In that month he wrote
to Moseley: 'For the present I have stopped speculating on atoms. I feel that
it is necessary to wait for experimental results.'[14]

He did not have to wait long. A week earlier Moseley had in fact informed
Bohr of his very interesting though as yet preliminary experimental results
concerning X-ray spectra. ('The paper is not yet written.'[15]) In order to see
what Moseley was after we must briefly go back to the discovery of the
nucleus.

It was recalled in (7b) how Rutherford came to understand that an atom of
a specific element consists of a definite number Z of electrons surrounding a
nucleus with charge Ze (the electron's charge equals $-e$), and that he had
found the probability of α-particle scattering to be proportional to Z^2. At
that time he did not yet know the value of Z for a given species of atom. By
February 1914 he was able to conclude[16] from more detailed measurements
that Z is approximately equal to $\frac{1}{2}A$, where A is the atomic weight in units of
the weight of atomic hydrogen. That is indeed a good approximation, but
not yet the whole story. It was Moseley who in 1913–14 found the correct Z
values, and more than that. He brought order in the periodic table.

Originally[17] that table had served to systematize the elements by means of
the rule that elements arranged according to increasing A exhibit a
periodicity in their chemical valencies. There were several exceptions,
however. Thus, by weight nickel should precede cobalt, but by valency
cobalt should precede nickel. Nor did the rule provide for sufficient
guidance to the search of new elements. For example $A = 1$ for hydrogen, 4
for helium. It used to be a favorite pastime to search for intermediate
elements with $A = 2$ or 3.

In January 1913 van den Broek[18] made the next step: 'The serial number of
every element in the sequence ordered by atomic weights equals half the
atomic weight and therefore the intraatomic charge.'[19] That new rule,
quoted[20] by Bohr in the second paper of his trilogy, gives hydrogen and
helium serial numbers 1 and 2 respectively – there is no gap between them.
The rule is still imperfect, however, since it implies that Z equals $\frac{1}{2}A$. In
November 1913 van den Broek made the final step: his rule is good 'but the
nuclear charge [Z] is not equal to half the atomic weight'.[21] Thus did Z and A

---

* See especially the book by Born[10] and fine reviews by Pauli[11] and Van Vleck,[12] as well as
the early editions of Sommerfeld's *Atombau und Spektrallinien* and the detailed account by
Mehra and Rechenberg.[13]

become *independent* nuclear parameters, with Z identified with the serial or atomic number marking the position in the periodic table.

Rutherford liked that idea.[22] Moseley discussed it with Bohr, in 1913, as the latter has recalled: 'I got to know Moseley really partly in this discussion about whether the nickel and cobalt should be in the order of their atomic weights. Moseley ... asked what I thought about that. And I said: "There can be no doubt about it. It has to go according to the atomic number." And then he said, "We will try and see." And that was the begining of his experiments ... And then he did it with tremendous speed[23] ... working day and night with a very characteristic excess of energy.'[24]

Moseley's experiments, 'undertaken for the express purpose of testing van den Broek's hypothesis, which Bohr has incorporated as a fundamental part of his theory',[25] dealt with secondary X-rays. For ease of understanding it will help to explain what these are in language not yet developed when he set to work. Suppose an X-ray knocks an electron from an inner ring of electrons out of an atom. The vacated spot will be reoccupied by an electron from a ring farther out, dropping into the inner one by emitting a 'secondary' X-ray. It was suggested by Kossel[26] that secondary X-rays with shortest wave lengths, the so-called K radiations, correspond to transitions into the innermost ring, and that the spectral line with longest wave length of this set, called the K_α-line, corresponds to an electron dropping down from the next innermost ring.

Moseley was able[27] to determine accurately the frequencies of K and other secondary X-rays. It will suffice to state his answer for $f(Z)$, the frequency of the K_α-line as function of the nuclear charge Z of the atomic species at hand, a result he had already mentioned[15] in his November 1913 letter to Bohr,

$$f(Z) = R(Z-1)^2 \left(\frac{1}{1^2} - \frac{1}{2^2} \right),$$

that is, $f(Z)$ follows a Balmer-type formula!

Before discussing what this formula means, let us see what it does. Using this relation as a diagnostic, Moseley could assign a Z value, hence also a definite number of electrons, to all known elements. Furthermore he could state firmly that seven elements were missing between hydrogen ($Z=1$) and uranium ($Z=92$). All of these have been found since. No wonder that Rutherford put Moseley's work on a par with the very discovery of the periodic table.[28]

As we now know, the meaning of the $f(Z)$ formula is this. First, in transitions between inner rings the jumping electron is exposed (for sufficiently large Z) to an electric field of the nucleus so much stronger than that of the outer electrons present that the latter can approximately be neglected. Secondly, the inner ring of *all* elements heavier than hydrogen contains only two electrons. To generate K_α one of these is first ejected. Hence the electron jumping from ring '2' to ring '1' (which produces K_α) is exposed to the nuclear charge Z *minus* the charge of the other electron still in ring '1'. The result is a Balmer formula for *effective* charge $Z-1$. (Evidently Moseley's formula is not quite rigorous, but it served its purpose.)

In late 1913 this simple picture was clear neither to Moseley nor to Bohr. Moseley speculated[15] that the lines might be caused by several electrons jumping simultaneously. That much Bohr could refute.[29] He could not yet help with the $(Z-1)^2$ factor, however, since at that time he still believed[20] that the number of electrons in the innermost ring was not always equal to 2, but varied with Z (2 for $Z=2-6$; 4 for $Z=7-9$; 8 for $Z=10-24$; . . .).

It was of course clear to Bohr (and to all others concerned) that Moseley's results put the whole question of atomic structure on a much more concrete basis. One finds numerous references to this work in Bohr's later papers. Bohr has written of him: '[This work] has secured [Moseley] a place among the foremost workers in science of his time, although he was not able to devote more than four short years to scientific investigation.'[30]

On 10 August 1915, Moseley, second lieutenant Royal Engineers, was mortally wounded during the battle of Suvla Bay . . .

3. *The Stark effect.* Once again we must go back to November 1913. On the 20th of that month Stark announced[31] to the Prussian Academy of Sciences an important new discovery: when atomic hydrogen is exposed to a static electric field its spectral lines split, the amount of splitting being proportional to the field strength (the *linear* Stark effect). After Rutherford read this news in *Nature*, he at once wrote to Bohr: 'I think it is rather up to you at the present time to write something on . . . electric effects.'[32]

We now encounter for the first time the widening interest in quantum theory mentioned in the preceding chapter. Even before Bohr sat down to work on the Stark effect, Warburg from Berlin published an article[33] in which the Bohr theory is applied to this new phenomenon. Bohr's own paper[34] on the subject appeared in March 1914. The next year he returned[35] to the same topic.

None of these early papers hit the mark. In particular, according to Bohr each hydrogen line should split into a doublet; experiments soon showed that the actual situation is more complex.[36]

There the matter more or less rested until 1916 when Paul Epstein, a Sommerfeld Ph.D., and Karl Schwarzschild, the astrophysicist from Göttingen best known for his derivation of the 'Schwarzschild radius' in general relativity, independently showed[37] that the linear Stark effect in hydrogen is one of the rare instances of an exactly soluble problem by means of the old quantum theory. The energy values of the split levels depend on more than one quantum number. The excellent agreement with experiment of their formula for these levels ranks next to the Balmer formula as the greatest quantitative success of the old quantum theory. Some years later Bohr[38] and especially Kramers[39] extended these results to include discussions of polarization and line intensities (see below).

A few additional comments. (a) The Epstein–Schwarzschild results remain valid in quantum mechanics. (b) The fact that hydrogen and only hydrogen shows a *linear* Stark effect could only be fully understood after the introduction of parity in quantum mechanics. (c) Hydrogen and all other atoms exhibit quadratic (and higher) Stark effects, proportional to the square (and higher powers) of the electric field strength. Their proper treatment can only be given in terms of quantum mechanics.

4. *The Franck–Hertz experiment.* The contributions by Bohr, Moseley, and Stark mark 1913 as a vintage year in atomic physics. Also in 1913 James Franck and Gustav Hertz in Berlin published two papers,[40] entitled 'On collisions between gas molecules and slow electrons'. In 1914 this research led to a spectacular confirmation of Bohr's basic ideas.

Their third paper[41] deals with collisions between electrons and mercury vapor, a particularly simple substance since its molecules consist of only one atom. This is what they found. If the electron kinetic energy is less than 4.9 eV, the collisions are elastic, that is, the electron can change direction but not velocity. When the energy reaches 4.9 eV many collisions become completely inelastic, the electron gives up its entire kinetic energy to the atom. A bit above 4.9 eV many electrons still give 4.9 eV to the atom, then continue with an energy less by that amount.

That was just the kind of behavior Bohr had predicted.

In my earlier discussion of the Bohr trilogy (Chapter 8) I did not yet mention that these papers also contain several interesting suggestions concerning the scattering, absorption, and energy loss of particles (photons, electrons) that impinge on an atom from the outside. In particular Bohr had suggested[42] that 'an electron of great velocity in passing through an atom and colliding with the electrons bound will loose [*sic*] energy in distinct finite quanta.' That is precisely what we see in the Franck–Hertz experiment. The energy 4.9 eV corresponds to minus the difference in energy of the most loosely bound electron in the mercury atom (E_1) and the energy of that electron when, due to collision, its energy is raised to the first available discrete excited state (E_2). When the kinetic energy of the impacting electron is less than $E_2 - E_1$, then the bound electron cannot be excited (elastic collisions), when it is a bit more, then all the bound electron can do is to pick up an energy amount $E_2 - E_1$.

According to the Bohr theory the excited electron should eventually drop back to its original orbit under emission of a light–quantum with frequency v fixed by the Bohr relation

$$hv = E_2 - E_1.$$

Now the beauty of Franck and Hertz's work lies not only in the measurement of the energy loss $E_2 - E_1$ of the impinging electron, but they also observed that, when the energy of that electron exceeds 4.9 eV, mercury began to emit ultraviolet light of a definite frequency equal to v as defined in the above formula. Thereby they gave the first direct experimental proof of the Bohr relation!

This, however, was not at once clear to the authors. In their 1914 paper[41] they expressed the belief that their 4.9 eV energy was the ionization limit for mercury, the minimum energy that needs to be transferred to a bound electron to free it from the atom. In 1915 Bohr proved[29] that this interpretation is incorrect. Only some years later did Franck and Hertz agree in print, in a paper entitled 'The confirmation of Bohr's atom theory of the optical spectrum from an investigation of the inelastic collisions of slow electrons with gas molecules'.[43]

5. *New quantum numbers; the fine structure of the hydrogen spectrum.* Bohr wrote several papers during his 1914–16 stay in Manchester. The first[44] concerned corrections to the Balmer formula due to relativity effects. The second[45] was a reply to criticisms of his theory by Nicholson. Then followed [45]a sequel to his earlier work on the stopping of α- and β-particles and an elaboration[46] of his ideas on atomic constitution, including comments on the findings of Moseley, Stark, and Franck and Hertz. Finally he prepared a long article on refinements of theoretical methods in the quantum theory. In March 1916 Bohr wrote[47] fromManchester to Oseen about what happened next: 'I had already had a proof of my paper[48] . . . when Sommerfeld's new and exceedingly interesting and important paper on the structure of spectral lines appeared. This paper has quite changed the present state of the Quantum theory, and I have therefore postponed the publication of my paper for the present.' Sommerfeld's two papers[49] to which Bohr alluded indeed changed the course of the old quantum theory both because of their much improved general methodology and because of their application to specific new problems in atomic theory.

Foremost among the latter was Sommerfeld's attempt at treating a long-known phenomenon, the fine structure of the hydrogen spectral lines. In 1887 Michelson and Morley had already observed that one of the Balmer lines is actually a 'double line'.[50] In 1892 Michelson found the same 'fine structure' for another line. 'The visibility curve is practically the same as for a double source.'[51]

I believe it is plausible that Bohr knew of this effect at the time he wrote his 1913 paper on hydrogen. It is certain that he was aware of it later that year. Right after Stark's discovery, discussed above, he wrote[52] to Rutherford that this effect 'offer[s] also a plausible explanation of ordinary double spectral lines ... these are due to the effect of electric fields'. He again stated as much in a paper which appeared in March 1914: 'It seems probable that the lines are not true doublets, but are due to an effect of the electric field in the discharge [in a vacuum tube filled with hydrogen gas].'[34] A month or so later he concluded[53] 'that my suggestion was wrong,' however,* but that rather the existence of doublets 'seems to me strongly to indicate a complex structure of the nucleus which acts upon the outer electron with forces which do not vary exactly as the inverse square of the distance apart, though very nearly so'.[53] This was not the true explanation either.

In September 1914 new fine structure experiments had led to the conclusion: 'Balmer's formula has been found inexact.'[54] Bohr, aroused, continued to ponder the question and then came forth[44] with an idea (which he had mentioned already nine months earlier in a letter[55]) that went in the right direction. 'Assuming that the orbit is circular ... but replacing the expressions for the energy and momentum of the electron by those deduced on the theory of relativity,' he could report small deviations from Balmer's formula.

Then, in the same paper, Bohr made the right conjecture about fine structure: '*It might ... be supposed that we would obtain a doubling of the lines if the orbits are not circular ... In [those] cases the orbit will rotate round an axis through the nucleus* [my italics].' Let us see what he meant.

In the hydrogen atom the electron is attracted to the nucleus by a force that varies as the inverse square of their distance – the same distance dependence as in the gravitational attraction between the sun and a planet. Just as the closed orbit of a planet, the Kepler motion, is in general elliptic, so the orbit of the electron in hydrogen is also in general an ellipse, with the nucleus at one focus. In his trilogy Bohr had, with great profit, restricted himself to circular motion. Now he raised the issue of elliptic orbits.

Bohr went even further than that. The elliptic shape of closed orbits is a unique consequence of the inverse square law in Newtonian mechanics. Newton himself already knew[56] that for *small* deviations of that law the orbit can still be considered as an *approximate* ellipse, but now its major axis itself will slowly rotate, precess, in the plane of the orbit. Bohr's related remark, 'the orbit will rotate around an axis', had another reason than an altered force law, however. According to relativity theory, the electron's

* In the earlier discussion of the Stark effect it was tacitly assumed that the external electric field is strong enough to cause a Stark splitting large compared to the fine structure splitting. The more complex case where these splittings are comparable was treated by Kramers in his thesis.[39]

mass is not constant but will depend on the electron's velocity, which varies from place to place along the ellipse. This velocity dependence, too, leads to precession. Bohr could estimate that this relativistic effect is small, since the electron goes around the nucleus more than 10000 times in the time the major axis turns around once.

Pursuing Bohr's idea, Sommerfeld became the first to show that relativity theory gives a quantitative account of the hydrogen fine structure.[57]

Sommerfeld's two papers mentioned earlier and a more elaborate version[58] published later in 1916 surely deserve a lengthy chapter in the history of the old quantum theory, but in a biography of Bohr only a brief sketch of Sommerfeld's major results must suffice.

(a) General formulation of quantum rules. During the first half of the quantum theory period, quantum rules had been guessed at, by Planck and by Einstein for linear oscillators and by Bohr for atomic orbits. In all these instances a single quantum number had sufficed. Questions such as What do these rules have in common? How does one treat more general systems? had been raised already during the Solvay conference in 1911. Not until 1915 was a systematic answer given, independently (and in this order) by William Wilson[59] from King's College, London, Jun Ishiwara[60] from Tokyo (quantum theory was spreading!), Planck,[61] and Sommerfeld.[49] Remarkably, their methods (the use of so-called phase integrals) were in essence identical. I shall not describe their mathematically elegant and rather involved procedures* but note only, first, that this advance *organizes better* rather than *explains* the rules of the quantum game; secondly, that it was only Sommerfeld who applied this rather general reasoning to specific new problems in atomic physics.

(b) The hydrogen atom, neglecting relativity effects. That was the problem Bohr had tackled, but only for circular orbits. It was Sommerfeld who first raised and answered the question: How does one handle ellipses? For circles the only spatial variable (or, as we say, the only degree of freedom) is its radius. Bohr's restriction of the classical continuum of possible radii to a discrete set had quantized the atom's size. In the elliptic case the atom not only has size but also (loosely speaking) shape, expressed for example by the ratio of the minor axis (length 2*b*) to the major axis (length 2*a*) (two degrees of freedom). Sommerfeld showed that the classically possible continuum in regard to *both* size and shape is restricted to a discrete set of elliptic (including circular) orbits, characterized by two quantum numbers, *n* and *k*:

$$\frac{b}{a} = \frac{k}{n}.$$

* For details see Refs. 10, 11, and 38, section 3.

Here n is the quantum number, now called principal quantum number, introduced by Bohr for circular orbits. The quantity k, which used to be called auxiliary or also azimuthal quantum number, is a *new* quantum number, also taking on integral values only. Since b at most equals a, it follows that k is restricted to the values $0, 1, 2, \ldots, n$. Circular orbits correspond to $k = n$.

I should note a flaw in this result. It became clear on experimental grounds that the case $k = 0$ had to be excluded. All attempts at justifying this additional restriction in terms of the old quantum theory have turned out to be fallacious.[62] Later, quantum mechanics showed that $k = l + 1$, where $l = 0, 1, 2, \ldots$ is the angular momentum quantum number encountered earlier (8f) for the special case of circular orbits; hence $k = 0$ is inadmissible.

The inclusion of elliptic orbits – and there is no logical reason to exclude them – shows that Bohr's circular orbits are but a puny subset of all allowed quantum orbits. Then what remains of Bohr's successes regarding hydrogen? The amazing answer is: everything. As Sommerfeld showed, all n states corresponding to fixed n but varying k are 'degenerate', that is, they have the same energy. It follows that Bohr, who, of course, knew nothing about this degeneracy, was lucky. His restriction to $k = n$ gave all the representative energy values of the hydrogen levels. Furthermore, again for fixed n and varying k, half the major axes of the corresponding ellipses are all equal, hence equal to the radius of the circular orbit, $k = n$. Also Bohr's results for the *sizes* of orbits therefore remained essentially unchanged.

Sommerfeld stressed that the degeneracy he had discovered is unique for the inverse square two-body law in the hydrogen atom and that this degeneracy no longer exists in more complex atoms, multibody systems in which each of the several electrons is acted on by more complicated forces, due not only to the nucleus but also to the other electrons. This fact is clearly of capital importance for the interpretation of spectra other than that of hydrogen.

(c) The hydrogen atom, including relativity effects. As already noted, Bohr knew that relativity leads to precession of the orbits. Sommerfeld duly acknowledged Bohr's point and then went much further by noting that this precession removes the degeneracy of orbits with fixed n, varying k. That fact, he asserted, explains the fine structure. He then proceeded to calculate explicitly the revised formula for the energy levels of hydrogen. The biggest contribution, depending on n only, is the one originally found by Bohr. A much smaller term, depending on both n and k accounts for the fine structure. Sommerfeld's formula, not given here, is found in any good textbook.

I shall defer until later in this chapter a brief discussion of the agreement between theory and experiment regarding fine structure.[63] Suffice it for now to say this agreement, which on the whole was extremely good, was considered a triumph both for quantum and for relativity theory.* It is fitting that from 1916 on the quantum rules in atomic physics were called the Bohr–Sommerfeld rules.

To conclude this sketch of Sommerfeld's contributions in 1916, I mention his introduction of a third quantum number, which, however, has nothing to do with fine structure. Having quantized the 'shape' of an orbit he was the first to ask next: 'The question arises whether the *position* of the orbit can also be quantized. For that purpose it is necessary, to be sure that at least a preferred direction of reference in space should exist.' [65] That is, the orbital position, given, say, by the direction of the normal to the orbital plane, is only well defined relative to some other fixed direction, such as that of an external electric or magnetic field. For these examples, discussed by Sommerfeld[66] later in 1916, the quantum theory allows only a discrete set of relative directions labeled by a new quantum number generically called m.

Thus the orbits of the electron in hydrogen are now characterized by three quantum numbers, n, k, and m. In the presence of an external field, the states with fixed n and k, but varying m, split up. This is the explanation of the Stark effect treated in detail by Epstein and Schwarzschild[37] (as mentioned).** What is the range of m-values? That question caused confusion, just as had been the case for $k = l + 1$. Eventually it became clear that m ranges over the $2l + 1$ values $-l$, $-l+1$, ..., $+l$.

In February 1916 Einstein wrote[67] to Sommerfeld that he considered his new work 'a revelation'. In March 1916 Bohr wrote[68] to Sommerfeld: 'I do not believe ever to have read anything with more joy than your beautiful work.' It would become clear some ten years later that Sommerfeld's fine structure formula is quite correct (though with an important reinterpretation of the meaning of k), while his derivation is wide of the mark. With good reason, I think, this derivation has been called 'perhaps the most remarkable numerical coincidence in the history of physics'.[69] I shall come back to the true explanation later.

In 1926, after quantum mechanics had arrived, Bohr wrote[70] the fitting epitaph to this episode, having in mind his own as well as Sommerfeld's work:

It is hard to say whether it was good or bad luck that the properties of the Kepler motion could be brought into such a simple connection with the hydrogen spectrum as was believed at one time ...

---

* No wonder then that the small but vocal band of opponents to relativity theory now turned their venom also against the quantum theory of fine structure.[64]

** The mathematical analysis in terms of the third quantum number differs for an electric as compared with a magnetic external field.

(c) In pursuit of principles: Ehrenfest, Einstein, and Bohr

As I have already stated, the new logic called for by quantum phenomena did not arrive until the mid-1920s. The search for general principles underlying quantum physics began earlier, however, producing three general ideas which later could be incorporated in the new quantum mechanics.

1. *Ehrenfest*[71] *on adiabatics.* Paul Ehrenfest studied physics in his native Vienna, where his contact with Boltzmann (under whose guidance he obtained the Ph.D.) was decisive in directing him to his principal scientific devotion, statistical physics. As was noted earlier (5d, e) that was the branch of physics which had served Planck and Einstein as their prime tool in their earliest work on quantum theory. Ehrenfest studied their papers carefully. As a result he became probably the first after the founders to publish on quantum problems, beginning in 1905.[72] These early papers already showed what Einstein later called 'his unusually well developed faculty to grasp the essence of a theoretical notion, to strip a theory of its mathematical accoutrements until the simple basic idea emerged with clarity. This capacity made him . . . the best teacher in our profession whom I have ever known.'[73] He was respected by all who knew his work except by himself.

Ehrenfest's intitial reactions to Bohr's work were decidedly negative. In 1913 he wrote[74] to Lorentz: 'Bohr's work on the quantum theory of the Balmer formula . . . has driven me to despair. If this is the way to reach the goal I must give up doing physics.' After Sommerfeld had come out with his work on fine structure, Ehrenfest wrote[75] to him: 'Even though I consider it horrible that this success will help the preliminary but still completely monstrous Bohr model on to new triumphs, I nevertheless wish physics at Munich further success along this path.'

Ehrenfest's contribution of interest to us here, his 'adiabatic principle', was inspired by his critical analysis of the contributions by Planck and Einstein, not by those of Bohr, even though, as it turned out, the main applications of his principle were to issues in atomic physics. He published[76] this work in ever more systematic detail in the course of the years 1911–16, most of it from Leiden where, since late 1912, he had been installed as successor to Lorentz.

The gist of the adiabatic principle can be stated as follows. If you give me the quantum rules for a particular system, then I can tell you the rules for a whole class of other systems. The proof is based on the hypothesis that Newtonian mechanics continues to apply as long as systems are in a stationary state, while the quantum theory only comes in to account for jumps from one such state to another. As Bohr had stressed from the beginning,[29] this assumption also applied to his own work. Here I shall only indicate Ehrenfest's reasoning in terms of a special case: the general argument is too technical for the style adopted in this book.*

Consider a system in periodic motion characterized by a single quantum number, call it n, and by specific values of parameters such as the nuclear charge, the intensity of some external field of force, etc. Now let these parameters be subjected to extremely slow and smooth changes, called adiabatic transformations (a term borrowed from thermodynamics). What happens to the number n? The adiabatic principle says: n does not change, it remains invariant. In his unpublished paper of 1916, Bohr put it like this: 'The great importance in the Quantum theory of this invariant character has been pointed out by P. Ehrenfest; it allows us by varying the external conditions to obtain a continuous transformation through possible states from a stationary state of any periodic system to the state corresponding with the same value of n of any other such system containing the same number of moving particles.'[77] The 'other' system may be quite different from the starting system. For example, one can connect in this way the rule for quantizing a (one-dimensional) oscillator with the one for the (non-relativistic) Bohr atom. This clearly brings much improved coherence to the old quantum theory: one still did not know why any system is quantized but now one could at least link the quantization of vastly distinct systems.

Ehrenfest knew that already in 1914 Einstein had recognized[78] the importance of his work but was not aware of Bohr's unpublished paper of 1916. When in 1918 Bohr incorporated this manuscript in a major paper he stressed 'the great progress . . . recently obtained by Ehrenfest'.[79] When in that year Kramers returned to Copenhagen from a visit to Leiden, with regards from Ehrenfest, Bohr sent him a letter, the beginning of a long correspondence, in which he wrote: 'I hope very much to meet you when the war is over.'[80] In 1922 Ehrenfest wrote[81] to Bohr about the adiabatic principle: 'I have never discovered anything – and quite surely never will discover anything – that I can love so fervently.'

The two men first met in 1919 when Bohr gave a lecture in Leiden on 'Problems of the atom and the molecule'[82] and attended Kramers' thesis defense. In December 1921 Ehrenfest lectured in Copenhagen.[83] He had come to venerate and love Bohr. In 1919, right after Bohr's visit to Leiden, he wrote to him: 'You had gone, the music had faded away.'[84] When in 1929 he took along his gifted young student Hendrik Casimir to a physics meeting in Copenhagen he said to him along the way: 'Now you are going to meet Niels Bohr and that is the most important thing to happen in the life of a young physicist.'[85]

2. *Einstein on probability.* In November 1916 Einstein wrote[86] to a friend: 'A

---

* See Refs. 10 and 11 for more details.

splendid light has dawned on me about the emission and absorption of radiation.' He had found a new and improved way of understanding Planck's blackbody radiation law, which, moreover, linked this law to Bohr's concept of quantum jumps. In 1917 Bohr, of course greatly interested in this development, lectured[87] on Einstein's new contribution before the *Fysisk Forening* (Danish Physical Society) of which – as if he did not have enough to do – he was president.*

Einstein's work is contained in three overlapping papers.[89,90] It deals with a system in thermal equilibrium consisting of a gas of particles 'which will be called molecules'[89] and of electromagnetic radiation with spectral density ρ (defined in Chapter 5). Let E_m and E_n, smaller than E_m, denote the energies of two levels of the molecule. Einstein introduced the following new hypothesis. The probability per unit time that the molecule absorbs radiation in making the transition $n \rightarrow m$ is proportional to ρ; the probability for emission, $m \rightarrow n$, consists of the sum of two terms, one proportional to ρ, another, corresponding to 'spontaneous emission', independent of ρ. Combining this hypothesis with some experimental facts about the behavior of ρ at very high and very low frequencies he found that he could obtain Planck's law if, and only if, the transitions $m \rightleftarrows n$ are accompanied by a *single monochromatic* energy quantum with frequency v given by $E_m - E_n = hv$ – Bohr's quantum hypothesis!

The central novelty and lasting feature of this work is *the introduction of probabilities in quantum dynamics*. I mention two further points Einstein raised[91] in this connection.

Einstein remarked that his mechanism of spontaneous emission of radiation and Rutherford's description,[92] dating back to 1900, of the spontaneous decay of radioactive matter are generically identical: 'It speaks in favor of the theory that the statistical law assumed for [spontaneous] emission is nothing but the Rutherford law of radioactive decay.'[89] Ever since 1900 the spontaneous nature of radioactive processes had been a source of bafflement.[93] While Einstein could not explain this phenomenon either, he was the first to note that it could only be understood in a quantum theoretical context.

Einstein rightly considered that (as said) his contribution shed 'splendid light', but he was by no means content with all he had done. He stressed that his theory which was statistical in nature (it deals only with probabilities) could not predict the direction in which a light-quantum moves after spontaneous emission. Hence his work did not satisfy the causality demand of classical physics: a unique cause leads to a unique effect. That bothered him greatly. In 1920 he wrote[94] to Born:

That business about causality causes me a great deal of trouble . . . Can the

---

* At that time the Society, founded in 1908, had about seventy members.[88]

quantum absorption and emission of light ever be understood in the sense of the complete causality requirement, or would a statistical residue remain? I must admit that there I lack the courage of conviction. However, I would be very unhappy to renounce complete causality.

Quantum mechanics would demand such renunciation. Einstein would never make peace with that.

3. *Bohr on correspondence.* Barring the period of World War II, the longest gap in time during which Bohr did not publish was between 1915 and 1918. A letter he wrote[95] in the summer of 1918 explains why. 'I know that you understand . . . how my life from the scientific point of view passes off in periods of overhappiness and despair, of feeling vigorous and overworked, of starting papers and not getting them published, because all the time I am gradually changing my views about this terrible riddle which the quantum theory is.' Bohr had so very much to cope with at that time. He had begun his demanding efforts to establish an institute of his own. Quantum physics, in Copenhagen and elsewhere, was in a state of rapid flux. Its logical foundations, Bohr's overriding concern, were as obscure as ever. 'I suffer from an unfortunate inclination to make results appear in systematic order,' he wrote[96] in 1919. The subject was hardly ripe for doing so.

As mentioned, in 1916 Bohr withdrew a general review. He needed more time for reflection. The result of these ruminations was a lengthy memoir 'On the quantum theory of line spectra'. Part I appeared[38] in April 1918, part II in the following December,[97] part III in 1922.[98] 'Already at the appearance of part I a manuscript of the whole treatise existed . . . [The] delay of the later parts was due in the first place to the nature of the subject.'[99] Quantum physics kept evolving before Bohr's eyes, even as he was attempting to commit his thoughts to paper.

In his later years Bohr used to say that he had perhaps never worked harder than in the course of preparing this work. His papers came out during the confusing years of war and immediate post-war and were published in a rather out of the way journal. All this, as well as their difficult style, may have limited their initial impact. 'In the last few years I have often felt myself scientifically very lonesome, under the impression that my efforts to develop the principles of the quantum theory systematically to the best of my ability have been received with very little understanding.'[100]

The topics covered in the memoir are these. In part I, a general introduction, Bohr recapitulated the developments sketched in the preceding parts of this section, acknowledged his indebtedness to Einstein and Ehrenfest for what was to follow, and announced the main new topics and results he intended to describe. Part II, the most important one, deals with the hydrogen atom including its fine structure and its behavior in external electric and magnetic fields. Here he also gave his own treatment of the phase integral method, including his 'perturbation theory,' (inspired by Ehrenfest's adiabatic principle) which describes what happens if the forces inside the atom are modified by small external forces. Part III treats of the spectra of higher elements. It contains an appendix in which Bohr recapitulated developments since 1918 and retracted some earlier conclusions. A planned part IV, to deal with molecules was never published but has survived in fragmentary draft form.[101] So has the draft of another paper (1921), meant to replace[102] parts III and IV, in which Bohr states with great precision the kind of interplay between theory and experiment so typical for the days of the old quantum theory.

The question is not only the development of the interpretation of experimental facts, but just [as] much by means of these to develop our deficient theoretical conceptions.[103]

In the three-part paper the main tool, of Bohr's making, is the correspondence principle, perhaps better called correspondence postulate, not so named by him until 1920, in a lecture given in Berlin.[104] (Prior to that he had called it the analogy principle.) We have already briefly met this principle in (8f) when discussing Bohr's last and best discussion in 1913 of the hydrogen spectrum. To repeat, in that case he had argued that for large values of the principal quantum number n the hydrogen levels lie so close together that they form 'almost a continuum'; and that therefore the *classical* continuum description of the emission of radiation should be very nearly valid for transitions between two very close-lying states both with very large n. Now, in 1918, he produced a quite similar kind of reasoning applied to other atomic properties.

Comments by Kramers, closest to Bohr in those years, may help to recreate the climate of those times. In 1923 he wrote: 'It is difficult to explain in what [the correspondence principle] consists, because it cannot be expressed in exact quantitative laws, and it is, on this account, also difficult to apply. [However,] in Bohr's hands it has been extraordinarily fruitful in the most varied fields.'[105] Also in 1923, in the issue of *Naturwissenschaften*[106] commemorating the first ten years of the Bohr theory: 'In this night of difficulties and uncertainty Bohr['s] ... principle is a bright spot.' And in 1935, on the occasion of Bohr's 50th birthday: 'In the beginning the correspondence principle appeared to the world of physicists as a rather mystic wand that did not work outside Copenhagen,'[107] not unlike Sommerfeld who earlier had called the principle 'a magic wand ... which allows us to apply the results of the classical wave theory to the quantum theory'.[108] In later years Oskar Klein, also close to Bohr around 1920, remarked[109] that Bohr had made great progress at that time 'in spite of the abyss, whose depth he never ceased to emphasize, between the quantum theoretical mode of description and that of classical physics'.

Bohr's new applications of the correspondence principle* resulted from an important change in outlook since 1913. At that earlier time his prime concern had been to understand the discreteness of the hydrogen spectrum and, more specifically, the particular frequency values of its spectral lines. Meanwhile, new developments had forced him to reconsider his basic postulate according to which an electron in a state, any state, with energy E_1 can jump to a state with lower energy E_2 accompanied by the emission of a photon with frequency v: $E_1 - E_2 = hv$. In 1913 he had not yet considered the fine structure which splits E_1 and E_2 into various energy levels. Can any of the split E_1-levels go to any of the split E_2's? Can any of the split E_1's (or E_2's) go into a lower split E_1 (or E_2)? The Stark effect also leads to splitting; accordingly the same questions arise there too. It was known already in 1916 that not all possible transitions occur. An example was the experimentally studied[111] fine structure of singly ionized helium in transitions $n = 4 \rightarrow n = 3$. If all accompanying changes in the auxiliary quantum number k were permitted, then one should find $4 \times 3 = 12$ spectral lines. The number actually seen was considerably smaller. Speculations arose:[58] Are some transitions forbidden? Or allowed but producing lines with too low an intensity to be detectable?

Bohr's memoir of 1918–22 centered on the now paramountly important question of line intensities. In general terms, he continued to adopt the strategy followed in 1913 (8f): in the low-frequency limit, equate optical frequencies (corresponding to transitions between neighboring stationary states with high n) with the (classical) mechanical frequencies of an electron circling a center of charge, which in turn equal the light frequencies emitted according to the classical theory. Now, however, he had to extend his earlier reasoning to the case that more than one quantum number appears. His main results can be summarized as follows.

(i) Consider classically an ensemble of orbiting electrons emitting very low frequency radiation. Let some a priori conceivable frequency actually be missing as a consequence of the detailed classical theory. Invoking the correspondence principle, Bohr argued that this same frequency should as well be forbidden in the quantum theory. From this he could deduce** a selection rule for Δk, the change in k in low-frequency quantum jumps: $\Delta k = \pm 1$ for one-electron systems (hydrogen, ionized helium), $\Delta k = 0, \pm 1$ for more complicated systems. The same result was also obtained[112] independently by Sommerfeld's student Adalbert Rubinowicz. In the example $n = 4 \rightarrow n = 3$, this rule reduces the number of fine structure lines from 12 to 5 – an almost correct result. I shall come back in (11f) to a last needed refinement.

---

* For a discussion of this work in much more detail than given here, see Refs. 11 and 110.
** Bohr realized that this answer holds only for radiation of the electric dipole type.

(ii) Applying the same reasoning to emission in some fixed direction, Bohr obtained another selection rule valid for an atom in an external field: $\Delta m = 0, \pm 1$.

(iii) In more detail, emission with $\Delta m = 0$ corresponds to light polarized* parallel to the field direction. For $\Delta m = \pm 1$ light is polarized perpendicular to that direction.

(iv) Bohr correctly guessed[113] the range of admissible m values.

(v) All previous statements referred to what happens at low frequencies. Bohr made the daring and, it turned out, correct extrapolation that *the selection and polarization rules stated above hold for all frequencies.*

Bohr also outlined the way one could estimate intensities of allowed spectral lines by correspondence arguments. Inspired by Einstein's notion of spontaneous emission (actually so named first by Bohr[114]) he produced a classical formula for the probability per unit time for emission of light of a given frequency by an ensemble of atoms. He did not himself work out the consequences of that equation. Kramers, who was given this task, did so brilliantly, first working out the general theory in much more detail, then via correspondence arguments calculating spectral intensities for fine structure and the Stark effect. Finally, his comparison of the results with experiment turned out to work very well. Kramers' resulting paper, his thesis,[39] contains the principal confirmations of Bohr's ideas.

During 1921–4 Bohr continued to elaborate and improve his presentation of the principles of the quantum theory.

1921. A review of the situation in the preface[115] to a book[116] containing the German translation of his collected papers of the years 1913–16, including the one[48] he had withdrawn in 1916; an amplification[117] of his results on polarization; his report to the Solvay conference of October 1921. Because of Bohr's forced absence due to illness this report was presented by Ehrenfest, along with comments of his own.[118]

1922. A simplified presentation of the correspondence principle and its applications, in the Guthrie lecture[119] before the Physical Society of London; further elaborations[120] of selection principles; publication[121] in German, English, and French of a selection of Bohr's papers from the years 1914–21; unpublished notes[122] of his Göttingen lectures.

1923. Appearance in book form[123] of a German translation of the three-part memoir; a lecture[124] in Liverpool on the correspondence

* Polarization direction was defined in (4e).

principle, given before the British Association for the Advancement of Science; a general review[125] on line spectra and atomic structure; publication of the first part[126] of a planned new comprehensive treatise on atomic structure in which Bohr announced[127] that this was 'the first of a series of essays ... [on] atomic structure'. Bohr did not publish the manuscript[128] of the second part, nor did he complete fragments[129] of manuscripts from 1923–4, presumably meant to be incorporated in later parts.

The correspondence principle is, I think, Bohr's greatest contribution to physics after his derivation of the Balmer formula. It is the first manifestation of what would remain the leading theme in his work: *classical physics, though limited in scope, is indispensable for the understanding of quantum physics*. In his own words:

Every description of natural processes must be based on ideas which have been introduced and defined by the classical theory.[130]

At first glance cognoscenti might well think that Bohr wrote this after 1927, when he began developing complementarity concepts. However, these lines date from 1923!

(d) The crisis

Epstein's paper[37] of 1916 on the Stark effect concludes as follows: 'It seems that the efficiency of the quantum theory borders on the miraculous and that it is by no means exhausted.'

In a letter[131] to Rutherford with good wishes for the year 1918 Bohr wrote: 'At present I am myself most optimistic as regards the future of the theory.'

These upbeat assessments of the years 1913–18 are quite natural. The Franck–Hertz experiment had confirmed Bohr's hypothesis of quantum jumps. The Stark effect and (it seemed) the fine structure of hydrogen had been successfully interpreted. Quantization rules had been systematized by the phase integral method of Sommerfeld and others. Ehrenfest, Einstein, and Bohr's new principles had proved fruitful, even though they were evidently not yet new *first* principles. Thus hope prevailed over despair, even though failures had already begun to manifest themselves. It was only during the final years of the old quantum theory that these latter took central stage and that a sense of crisis developed, resulting principally from two particular causes.

1. *Helium.* In July 1926 Heisenberg, then in Copenhagen, submitted a paper[132] in which for the first time the correct quantitative explanation is given of the helium spectrum. It also contains good, though approximate,

results for the spectral frequencies; helium is a three-body system for which to this day no rigorous treatment exists. The tools Heisenberg used were: wave mechanics, discovered earlier in 1926, electron spin (1925), and the Pauli exclusion principle (also 1925). I shall come back to all these concepts later and note for now only that none of them belonged to the arsenal of the old quantum theory, which, in a word, was a mess insofar as the helium problem was concerned.

All during those not so good old days, the understanding of the helium spectrum was inadequate not only theoretically but also experimentally. It had been known since the late 1890s that this spectrum consists of two distinct kinds of lines: parahelium, a set of singlets (unsplit lines), and orthohelium, believed to be doublets. Attempts to resolve the doublets further remained unsuccessful until January 1927 when it was found at Cal Tech[133] and in Berlin[134] that the doublets actually are triplets. 'Within the last few months interest has been revived in these [doublets] by the theoretical work of Heisenberg which predicts a triplet structure ... It is now possible to show that the helium lines really have a structure similar to that predicted by Heisenberg.' [133]

I shall deal only briefly with the helium spectrum in the old quantum-theory, a subject which can fill a monograph (as indeed it has[135]), and emphasize mainly the activities in Copenhagen.

Bohr's first comment on this problem I know of dates from 1915 when he suggested[29] that the two distinct kinds of helium lines might be associated with two distinct shapes of orbits. He did not get involved in earnest until 1916 when after Kramers' arrival he proposed almost at once a collaboration on helium. In November Bohr wrote[136] to Rutherford: 'I have used all my spare time in the last months to make a serious attempt to solve the problem of the ordinary [i.e. non-ionized] helium spectrum ... working together with ... Kramers ... I think really that at last I have a clue to the problem.'

Initially Bohr was optimistic. He wrote to colleagues that the theory 'was worked out in the fall of 1916',[96] and of having obtained a 'partial agreement with the measurements'.[137] Some 200 pages of Bohr's calculations, never published, remain in the Niels Bohr Archives.[138]

Bohr's faith waned, however, as time went by. More and more he left the problem to Kramers, who continued to tackle it with his considerable mathematical ingenuity.[139] Bohr himself came back several times to helium, in most detail in an unpublished part of his Solvay report (1921)[140] and in the fourth of his Göttingen lectures.[141] Eventually Kramers published the helium results in a paper[142] submitted in December 1922. Six years of hard work had gone into these efforts. An interesting feature of his final helium model is that it was no longer plane, the two electrons move in different planes. Perhaps the most important of his negative results concerns Bohr's and Ehrenfest's idea that classical mechanics should apply to electrons while moving in stationary orbits: 'We must draw the conclusion that already in this simple case mechanics is not valid.'[142]

Meanwhile Born and Heisenberg in Göttingen had also independently been working on helium. Their conclusions[143] were in the same vein as those of Kramers who had published five months before they did. Born to Bohr, March 1923: 'Our result is quite negative.'[144] Bohr on Born and Heisenberg, in a paper submitted that same month (in which parahelium is still considered to have a doublet spectrum): 'This investigation may ... be particularly well suited to provide evidence of the fundamental failure of the laws of mechanics to describe the finer [sic] details of the motion of systems with several electrons.'[145] In that same year Sommerfeld summarized the situation more succinctly: 'All attempts made hitherto to solve the problem of the neutral helium atom have proved to be unsuccessful.'[146]

2. *The Zeeman effect.* The influence of an external electric field on spectral lines, the Stark effect, had been a great success for the old quantum theory. It was quite the opposite with the longer-known influence of an external magnetic field, the Zeeman effect.

Zeeman was a young *privaatdocent* in Leiden when in 1897 he discovered[147] that spectral lines split when atoms are placed in a magnetic field. Lorentz at once provided an interpretation[148] in terms of a simple model for an electron moving in an atom. Considering only effects proportional to the first power of the field (the linear Zeeman effect), he showed that a spectral line should split into a doublet or triplet depending on whether the emitted light is parallel or perpendicular to the field direction. For this discovery, Zeeman and Lorentz shared the physics Nobel Prize for 1902.

I have often wondered why Lorentz was cited for this particular contribution because it was well known by 1902 that his explanation was incomplete, to say the least. In Lorentz's words (1921): 'Unfortunately, however, theory could not keep pace with experiment and the joy aroused by [this] first success was but short-lived. In 1898 Cornu discovered – it was hardly credible at first! – that [a sodium line] is decomposed into a quartet ... Theory was unable to account ... for the regularities observed ... to accompany the anomalous splitting of the lines.'[149] It did not take long to find out that this 'anomalous Zeeman effect' is the rule, the 'normal' effect (Lorentz's prediction) the exception.[150]

These anomalous splittings constituted the second main debacle of the old quantum theory. The situation here was not so unlike that for helium. Theoretical understanding was out of the question without spin. Experimentally, disarray was caused by the apparent experimental evidence that the linear effect in hydrogen was normal, as was stated in handbooks[151] as late as 1925. It turned out later that even for this simplest of systems the splitting is actually anomalous. This experimental confusion largely explains, I think, why during 1913–16 Bohr, focused as he was on hydrogen, referred only to the normal Zeeman effect. His comments[152] on that subject remained rather qualitative; he himself called them 'of preliminary nature'.[153]

The year 1916 produced good results when Sommerfeld[66] and independently Debye[154] showed that the normal Zeeman effect fitted nicely in the old quantum theory. The necessary new ingredient was Sommerfeld's 'third quantum number' m mentioned at the end of section (b). In 1918 Bohr noted[155] that his selection and polarization rules related to m also agree well for the normal effect. In 1922 he commented as follows[156] on the inexplicable anomalous effect: 'The difficulty consists . . . in the fact that the ordinary electrodynamic laws can no longer be applied to the motion of the atom in a magnetic field in the same way as seemed to be the case in the theory of hydrogen,' still believed to be normal. In those years Bohr repeatedly conjectured[157] that the anomaly might be due to an as yet unclear influence of inner on outer atomic electrons.

All through the years of the old quantum theory the anomalous Zeeman effect remained a mystery.* Sommerfeld in 1919: 'A genuine theory of the Zeeman effect . . . cannot be given until the reason for the multiplicities can be clarified.'[159] Pauli in early 1925: 'How deep seated the failure of the theoretical principles known till now is can be seen most clearly in the multiplet structure of spectra and their anomalous Zeeman effect.'[160]

3. *The fourth quantum number.* Pauli also struck[160] a more positive note, however, mentioning 'empirical regularities of outstanding simplicity and beauty established in this domain during recent years'. These were in first instance due to Sommerfeld who in 1920 had introduced[161] a fourth quantum number, denoted by j and called the 'inner quantum number'. In doing so he had adopted a reasoning utterly different from the one that had led to the first three quantum numbers, n, k (or l), and m. Recall that these had originated from geometrical considerations, the quantization of size, shape, and spatial orientation of orbits. Sommerfeld's new style of reasoning went something like this. The three old quantum numbers are inadequate for the description of the anomalous Zeeman effect. This effect does not appear (he thought) for hydrogen but only for atoms containing more electrons, which move about in some complicated way. Assume, purely *ad hoc*, that these complex motions are characterized by an additional angular momentum corresponding to 'a hidden rotation'.[161] Associate a new quantum number j with the quantization of this new variable and a new selection rule,

---

* To which in 1922 Stern and Gerlach added observations of inexplicable splitting patterns of atomic beams passing through a magnetic field.[158]

$\Delta j = 0, \pm 1$. This, Sommerfeld asserted, leads to 'a harmony of integer ratios which will surprise even those who have been spoiled by the modern quantum theory'.[161] Pauli characterized the new style like this: 'Sommerfeld tried to overcome the difficulties . . . by following, as Kepler once did in his investigation of the planetary system, an inner feeling of harmony.'[162]

There now followed several years during which theoretical physicists experimented with extra quantum numbers and quantum rules. In 1921, Landé, particularly adept at these games, made[163] another radical proposal: j and m shall take *half*-integer values for certain groups of elements such as, for example, the alkalis, the atoms of which consist of one valence electron orbiting around a 'core' of inner electrons. In 1923 Landé proposed, more specifically, that this core performed a 'hidden rotation' with angular momentum $\frac{1}{2}$, in units $h/2\pi$. Moving back and forth between experimental facts and improvised rules, he managed to put together a scheme which in a review of 1925 was described as 'completely incomprehensible [but with which] one masters completely the extensive and complicated material of the anomalous Zeeman effect'.[164]

The first step toward closing this gap between progress and understanding was made in 1924, by Pauli.

4. *Enter Pauli.* Wolfgang Pauli, son of a medical doctor who later became a university professor, godson of Ernst Mach, began his schooling in his native Vienna. He had already in his high school years delved deeply into mathematics and physics. When in the autumn of 1918 he enrolled in the University of Munich he brought with him a paper (published shortly afterward) on general relativity. At the instigation of Sommerfeld, who had, of course not failed to recognize the brilliance, erudition, and ventripotence of his young student, Pauli began in 1920 the preparation of a review article on relativity. After its appearance,[165] Einstein (whom Pauli met for the first time that year) wrote: 'Whoever studies this mature and grandly conceived work might not believe that its author is a twenty-one year old man.'[166] This article appeared in English translation[167] in 1958, the year of Pauli's death. It is still one of the best presentations of the subject.

On 10 December 1945 Pauli was honored[162] for his Nobel Prize at a dinner at the Institute for Advanced Study in Princeton (he did not go to Stockholm for the occasion). His late wife told me that Pauli was deeply moved when during an after dinner toast Einstein said in essence that he considered him as his successor. (I have not seen this in writing.)

In this book I shall, of course, only be concerned with Pauli's contributions to the quantum theory, old and new, but I would be remiss if I did not intimate as well the depth of his knowledge of relativity. During the years I knew him personally (from 1946 on) he would ask me every once in a while something like: 'Pais, I don't know what to work on next. What shall I do?' I would reply: 'Pauli, don't worry, something will come. Meanwhile, however, why don't you start thinking about writing a book on the history of physics in the first half of the century?' Whereupon Pauli would commence his characteristic rocking to and fro, then say, well, perhaps that was not a completely stupid idea. It is our loss that he never followed this up.

Pauli has recalled[162] that during his student days 'I was not spared the shock which every physicist accustomed to the classical way of thinking experienced when he came to know Bohr's "basic postulate of quantum theory" for the first time'. His first paper on atomic physics dates from 1920. In 1921 he received his Ph.D. summa cum laude on a thesis dealing with the quantum theory of ionized molecular hydrogen, whereafter he was for half a year assistant to Born in Göttingen. In 1922 he went to Hamburg, first as assistant, then as *privatdozent*. From that period date the first occurrences of the Pauli effect of which he was very proud: something would go wrong whenever he entered a laboratory. He would tell with glee how his friend Otto Stern, experimentalist at Hamburg, would consult him only through the closed door leading to his working space. In 1928 Pauli was appointed professor at the ETH in Zürich, the post he held for the rest of his life.

When in 1922 Pauli went to Göttingen to attend Bohr's lecture series there, 'a new phase of my scientific life began when I met Niels Bohr personally for the first time . . . During these meetings . . . Bohr . . . asked me whether I could come to Copenhagen for a year'.[162] Pauli accepted and went to Bohr's institute from fall 1922 to fall 1923. 'He at once became, with his acutely critical and untiringly searching mind, a great source of stimulation to our group.'[168] During that year he wrote two papers[169] on the Zeeman effect, dealing mainly with improvements on Landé's scheme. This work did not satisfy him. 'A colleague who met me strolling rather aimlessly in the beautiful streets of Copenhagen said to me, "You look very unhappy"; whereupon I answered fiercely, "How can one look happy when he is thinking about the anomalous Zeeman effect?"'[162]

Then, in late 1924 after his return to Hamburg, Pauli made his first major discovery. By an ingenious argument he could demonstrate that Landé's model of alkali atoms, a valence electron orbiting around a core with angular momentum $\frac{1}{2}$, was untenable. Yet Landé's results worked well! Pauli found a way out. There *is* a 'hidden rotation', which, however, is not due to the core but to the valence electron itself! The anomalous Zeeman effect 'according to this point of view is due to a peculiar non-classically describable two-valuedness [*Zweideutigkeit*] of the quantum theoretical properties of the valence electron'.[170] (The two-valuedness refers to the values $\pm\frac{1}{2}$ of the m quantum number associated with $j=\frac{1}{2}$.)

What does this two-valuedness signify in physical terms? Stay tuned.

(e) Bohr and the periodic table of the elements

1. *From electron rings to electron shells.* At the end of the previous chapter I alluded to Bohr's engagement in important research at the very time he was practically worn out from his labors to get his institute started. These scientific efforts, to which I now turn, dealt with a subject that had been dear to his heart ever since the days of the Rutherford memorandum (8c): atomic structures more complex than those of hydrogen. The style he was to adopt in this work was forecast in his speech of appreciation to Sommerfeld on the occasion of the latter's lecture in Copenhagen in September 1919. At that time Bohr spoke[171] of future projects, among them

One of the problems for which one might expect less from a mathematical-deductive method than from a physical-inductive approach, the problem of the structure of the atoms and molecules of the elements.

Three months later, in a lecture before the Chemical Society of Copenhagen, Bohr expressed 'my hope and conviction that it will not take many years before it will become necessary for fruitful work on most problems, as well within the so-called physics as in the so-called chemistry, to pay the closest regard to results obtained in the other field'.[172] In February 1920 he broached this same theme more firmly: 'Through the recent development in physics . . . a connection between physics and chemistry has been created which does not correspond to anything conceived of before.'[173]

Much had changed since 1913 when Bohr had discussed complex atoms in his trilogy. In particular his pancake picture according to which electrons move in a set of concentric plane orbits had run into numerous troubles. Neither improved X-ray data[174] nor molecular spectra (band spectra) could be incorporated in a planar model. Flat atoms led[175] to a far too large compressibility of crystals. Among other difficulties there was Kramers' inability to account for helium as a plane structure (see the preceding section). By 1919 Bohr had had enough of his earlier picture. 'I am quite prepared or rather more than prepared to give up all ideas of electronic arrangements in "rings".'[176] In his view the main difficulties concerned 'the properties of crystals, band spectra, ionization potentials [in particular for helium], etc.'[177] From about that time one moved away from two-dimensional rings to three-dimensional shells of electrons.*

Meanwhile, in 1916, the first successful links, based on physico-chemical reasoning, between the Bohr theory and the periodic table of the elements had been established by Kossel.[179] His starting point was the striking stability of atoms of the noble gases, manifested by the facts that they are relatively hard to ionize and their inability to form compounds with other

---

* Also from that time date a variety of picturesque and forgettable models built out of one or more cubes.[178]

atoms. He interpreted these properties to mean that the electron configurations in such atoms consist of 'closed shells', that is, they strongly resist turning into positive (negative) ions by giving off (adding on) an electron. These closed shells occur for $Z = 2$, 10, 18, 36, 54, 86, (helium, neon, argon, krypton, xenon, radon; Kossel only considered elements with Z up to 25).

Consider next elements with Z one less than this sequence, 1 (hydrogen), 9, 17, 35, ... (fluorine, chlorine, bromine, ..., the halogens) which are known to turn easily into negative ions by picking up an electron. That is so (Kossel said) because these ions acquire once again noble gas configurations. For the same reason the alkalis, $Z = 3$, 11, 19, ... (lithium, sodium, potassium, ...) easily turn into positive ions. Arguments like these led Kossel to propose that electrons occupy 'concentric rings or shells on each of which only a certain number of electrons should be arranged', these numbers being (see the Z values of noble gases) 2, 8, 8, 18 ..., counting from inner to outer shells. Further evidence for this behavior could be read off from other experimental data, among them those concerning optical spectra.[180]

These good beginnings of a descriptive picture could not simply be extended to all the elements, however.

2. *The mystery of the rare earths.* By the 1920s areas in the table of elements had been located which did not at all fit the simple periodicities originally postulated by Mendeleev in 1869, when, incidentally, none of the noble gases were yet known. The most striking deviations were a group of scarce elements closely resembling each other in chemical and spectroscopic properties, the rare earth metals or lanthanides, that name being derived from a Greek verb meaning 'to lie hidden'. Since in 1869 only two of these were known, cerium and erbium, they did not at once draw any particular attention. At the beginning of the twentieth century their number had risen to thirteen: the fourteenth and last one, prometheum ($Z = 59$) was not found until 1947. The Z values in this group range from 58 through 71.

Efforts to fit these elements into the Mendelecvian scheme only caused trouble, leading some to think that the whole idea of the periodic table might be wrong, others that they should separately be placed in a third dimension relative to the periodic table. In any event it was clear that the rare earths as a group had to occupy an exceptional position in the scheme of things.*

3. *Bohr's quantum number assignments.* Thus, when in 1920 Bohr turned his full attention to the issue of the periodic table, he had available a mixed bag of some promising results and a fair amount of confusion. He developed his own ideas in a sequence of papers beginning with a lecture before the *Fysisk*

---

* See Ref. 181 for the complicated history of the rare earths.

Forening in December 1920 (unpublished)[182] in which he acknowledged the benefits of earlier work by Kossel, Kramers (on helium), Landé, and Sommerfeld. Plans for a long follow-up paper were dropped because of overwork. Instead Bohr submitted in February 1921 a letter to *Nature*.[183] Then followed[184] a short article addressed to general audiences; a communication 'On the constitution of atoms' to the Solvay conference of April 1921 (unpublished);[185] a second letter to *Nature* (September 1921);[186] another lecture before the *Fysisk Forening* (October 1921);[187] the last four of the Göttingen lectures (June 1922, unpublished),[122] the most detailed exposé of Bohr's ideas on atomic constitution; and a lecture in Uppsala (August 1922).[188] Later articles contain refinements in formulation.* In comparing these various papers, one will note occasional modifications from one to the next. For example, Bohr's proposal for the electron distribution in noble gas atoms is incorrect in his first, correct in his second, letter to *Nature*. In what follows I shall confine myself to the answers on which Bohr ultimately settled. These deal only with the ground states of atoms, even though he made ample use of spectral data in the visible and the Röntgen domain which of course involve excited states.

In Bohr's new work** he forsook all his earlier speculations of 1913 on the structure of complex atoms. At that earlier time he had conjectured (8f) that if all electrons in these systems move in circular orbits then each of them shall have angular momentum $h/2\pi$ in the ground state. That idea, still found in his December 1918 note[190] on a hypothetical triatomic hydrogen molecule, was abandoned in his December 1920 lecture[182] (if not earlier): 'It seems impossible to explain satisfactorily [the] periodic variation of the properties of the elements by starting with the simple assumption that the electrons in the normal [ground] states move in circular orbits.' No more restrictions to circular orbits, nor preferences for a special angular momentum value. In summary, his new picture, the central field model, was the following. Every electron in a complex atom is assigned its own principal quantum number n and auxiliary quantum number k, corresponding to its motion in a central field of force. In the ground state, electrons reside in quantum levels with the lowest available energy. An electron in a given orbit is specified further by a value of k, and is given† the overall designation n_k, the range of k being $k = 1, 2, \ldots, n$ (see (10b)). An atomic species is fully characterized by a specific set of occupation numbers, the set being called a configuration, which informs us how many electrons are in the n_k orbits $1_1, 2_1, 2_2, 3_1, 3_2, 3_3, \ldots$. The bulk of the gospel according to Bohr consists in the determination of the configuration for each element.

---

* The lectures marked unpublished did not appear shortly after they were delivered. Since 1977 they are all available in Volume 4 of the Collected Works.

** A paper by Helge Kragh on Bohr's work during 1920–3[189] has been particularly helpful to me in preparing the rest of this section.

† Note to the perplexed expert: $k = 1, 2, 3, \ldots$ corresponds to $s, p, d, \ldots$ states.

The impact of Bohr's new ideas was immediate and strong, as can be seen from an exchange of letters following Bohr's first *Nature* article.[183] Landé to Bohr: 'Until your full and detailed exposition [promised in the *Nature* paper] appears, there is no sense in doing any more work in atomic theory.'[191] Sommerfeld to Landé: 'We must relearn completely.'[192] Sommerfeld to Bohr: '. . . The greatest advance in atomic structure since 1913[193]. . . If, as it appears, you can reconstruct mathematically the numbers 2, 8, 18, . . . of the elements in the periods, that is in fact the fulfillment of the boldest hopes in physics.'[194]

Sommerfeld did not know Bohr's mathematical reasoning because none was given in his first *Nature* letter. Nor did the second letter[186] give any such details, prompting Rutherford to complain: 'It is very difficult to form an idea of how you arrive at your conclusions. Everybody is eager to know whether you can fix the "rings of electrons" by the correspondence principle or whether you have recourse to the chemical facts to do so.'[195] After the text of Bohr's second lecture before the *Fysisk Forening*[187] had become known in Göttingen, Franck wrote to Bohr: 'The curiosity of the local physicists to get to know your methods mathematically as well is tremendous.'[196]

Neither then nor later would their and our curiosity be satisfied, since *none* of the list of papers mentioned above contains any technical derivations, nor do there appear to be any unpublished calculations in the Bohr Archives that bear on this work. Heisenberg, who attended Bohr's Göttingen lectures, has characterized[197] them like this. 'Each one of his carefully formulated sentences revealed a long chain of underlying thoughts, of philosophical reflections, hinted at but never fully expressed. I found this approach highly exciting; what he said seemed both new and not quite new at the same time . . . We could clearly sense that he had reached his results not so much by calculations and demonstrations as by intuition and inspiration and that he found it difficult to justify his findings before Göttingen's famous school of mathematics.' Kramers, the closest witness in Copenhagen, later recalled: 'It is interesting to remember that many physicists abroad believed . . . that [the theory] was based to a large part on unpublished calculations . . . while the truth was that Bohr, with divine vision, had created and deepened a synthesis between spectroscopic and chemical results.'[107]

It is conceivable though not certain that Bohr might have demurred since in his papers he repeatedly mentioned a variety of principles that had guided him, stressing, however, that 'it is a matter of taste . . . whether to put the main emphasis on the general considerations or on the bare experimental facts'.[198] Four general principles appear in his work on atomic constitution.

The building up principle (Aufbauprinzip), first stated[199] in his October 1921 lecture. 'We attack the problem . . . by asking the question: How may an atom be formed by the successive capture and binding of the electrons one by one in the field of force surrounding the nucleus?' The pertinence of this question has already been seen above when it was noted that a neutral alkali atom minus one electron can be related to a neutral noble gas atom. Extending this kind of argument Bohr gathered valuable insight on neutral atoms by imagining them to be built up step by step from multiply ionized states. Not until 1923 did he make fully explicit the crucial postulate that the quantum numbers of the electrons already present are not disturbed by adding a further electron, calling this 'the postulate of invariance and permanence of quantum numbers'.[200] The building up principle has remained a good though approximate tool also in later improved theories of atomic constitution.

The correspondence principle, mentioned in every one on the list of papers given above. It becomes nowhere clear, however, in what technical sense it applies to atomic constitution.*

Symmetry arguments. Used only infrequently. Sample: 'I believe,' said Bohr, that the four 2_1-orbits in carbon form a tetrahedron and that hence the occurrence of a fifth 2_1-electron 'is inconceivable'.[202] This argument leaves much to be desired if only because, as transpired later, the four electron orbits in question are actually inequivalent.

The penetrating orbit (Tauchbahn) effect, which describes the strong distortion from simple circular or elliptic orbits of an outer electron due to the presence of a core of inner electrons. Take for example an alkali atom, where one valence electron orbits partly outside but also partly inside the core, as a geometric consequence of the fact that the outside part of its orbit is a stretched ellipse while the core is nearly spherical. Once inside the core the valence electron experiences a stronger (less screened) influence of the nuclear field. Its inside motion can approximately be pieced together from segments of ellipses, which, however, have lower n values corresponding to tighter binding. Bohr first stated this effect in qualitative terms in his unpublished first Copenhagen lecture[182] in December 1920. Shortly thereafter the idea appeared first in print in a paper[203] by Schrödinger (submitted January 1921). In the Göttingen lectures one does find some numerical discussions of this effect, described by Bohr like this: 'In the interior of the atomic core the electron moves in a loop that is very nearly of the same shape [but] for different principal quantum numbers.'[204] With the help of this argument Bohr was able to show correctly that the valence electron in sodium carries $n = 3$.

In his Göttingen lectures Bohr took his audience on a guided tour of the configuration of all elements, noting several times on the way how

---

* A subsequent attempt in this direction[201] was not very enlightening either.

preliminary his reasoning was. Already for the relatively simple case of lithium ($Z=3$) he called his arguments 'quite uncertain'.[205] He concluded his tour on notes of optimism: 'We might proceed further . . . and construct hundreds or thousands of elements,' but also of caution: 'I hardly need emphasize how incomplete and uncertain everything still is.'[206] Those who care to read these lectures in their entirety will be rewarded with much insight into Bohr's style of doing physics. Here, however, I shall select only one item, his successful treatment of the rare earths. (The gist of this reasoning was already stated in his first letter to *Nature*.[183])

Let us first look at a few features of the building up principle. Up till $Z=18$, argon, the electrons fill in an orderly way the sequence of states $1_1, 2_1, 2_2, 3_1, 3_2$, reflecting the fact that in this region an electron is bound the tighter the smaller n and, for given n, the smaller k are. Thereafter 'irregularities' begin because the competition between n and k for lowest energy changes character. Thus the filling of 3_3 is deferred a few steps; in $Z=19$, 20, 4_1-electrons are added, etc. As we reach lanthanum ($Z=57$) the outermost electrons are three: two 6_1 and one 5_3. At that stage the 4_4-orbits are still empty. These latter are now added, one by one, Bohr said, as we move through the rare earth region, from $Z=58$ to 71. But the 4_4-orbits are smaller than those of the ever present two 6_1, one 5_3. Thus the peculiarity of the rare earths is that the building up takes place *inward, not outward*, all these elements having in common the same three outer (valence) electrons. This, according to Bohr, explains the great chemical similarities of the rare earths. Bohr noted further that another such irregular phenomenon occurs starting right after $Z=89$, actinium. Beginning with $Z=90$, thorium, electrons are again added far *inside* the atom (in states 5_4), resulting in a second group of rare earths, the actinides, which is now known to extend into the transuranic region, including neptunium, plutonium, etc. – but that is a later story. Bohr's interpretation of the rare earths is the one we use today.

It is, to repeat Einstein's words, a miracle that Bohr was able to produce some good physics with methods that were primitive if not wrong, and that at the very time when the helium and Zeeman crises were beginning to peak. Nor is it surprising that, even apart from details, his results were incomplete and in part incorrect. Incomplete because his implicit assumption, at least 'in the first approximation',[183] of the uniqueness of ground state configurations does not hold as well as he had anticipated,* and, more important, because he could not produce a criterion for the famous maximum occupation numbers 2, 8, 18, . . . of closed shells. Incorrect,

---

* Ambiguities arise owing to the quantum mechanical effects of overlapping and configuration mixing.

because he supposed that for given n the maximum occupation number is the same for all k, that is, equal to 4 for $n = 2$ and $k =$ either 1 or 2, adding up to 8 for all $n = 2$ states; equal to 6 for $n = 3$ and $k =$ either 1 or 2 or 3, adding up to 18, etc. ('It is not right how many electrons we put in the various things. We did that just by symmetry and then it was not right.'[23]) One still finds these numbers in the 1923 survey[207] of X-ray data (clearly important for an understanding of inner shells) by Bohr and the Dutch experimentalist Dirk Coster, who was spending that year in Copenhagen. By the way, this is Bohr's first paper with joint authorship.

Nevertheless Bohr's new general strategy of labeling atoms by n_k-configurations continues to be fruitful and important. What Sommerfeld put so well in October 1924 still holds true today: 'It will be inevitable that improved spectroscopic data will produce conflicts with Bohr's atomic models. I am nevertheless convinced that in broad outline they are conceptually correct since they so beautifully account for general chemical and spectroscopic traits.'[208]

4. *The exclusion principle.* Two months after Sommerfeld had written these lines, Pauli made a spectacular discovery which put Bohr's models on their modern footing. This work should occupy a central position in any history of quantum physics. In the present context it is treated only briefly, the main purpose here being to stress that it was a direct outgrowth of Bohr's preoccupation with atomic constitution.[209] Pauli to Sommerfeld in December 1924: 'I have made headway with a few points . . . [regarding] . . . the question of the closure of electron groups in the atom.'[210] This, in summary, is what he had found.

At the end of section (b), part 5, it was noted that the electron states in a hydrogen atom are labeled by three quantum numbers, n, k, and m, and that m ranges over the $2k - 1$ values $-(k-1), \ldots, (k-1)$. Let us count the total number of states N associated with a given n. For $n = 1$: $k = 1$, $m = 0$, hence $N = 1$. For $n = 2$: $k = 1$, so $m = 0$; or $k = 2$, so $m = -1, 0, 1$; hence $N = 1 + 3 = 4$, etc. For general n, $N = n^2$. Starting from this counting, Pauli introduced three further postulates.

(i) In the spirit of Bohr's central field model, he assigned not only an n and a k but also an m to each electron in a complex atom.

(ii) In his discussion of the anomalous Zeeman effect (section (d), part 2) he had introduced the new hypothesis that the valence electron in alkali atoms exhibits a two-valuedness. Now he assumed the same to be true for all electrons in all atoms, so that each electron is characterized by four quantum numbers, n, k, m, and a fourth one capable of two values. It follows that the number of states for given n is not N but $2N$, hence 2 for $n = 1$, 8 for $n = 2$, 18 for $n = 3$: the mystical numbers 2, 8, 18 ruling the periodic table emerge!!

(iii) That is all well and good, but why could there not be seventeen electrons occupying a state with some fixed value for the four quantum numbers? Pauli decreed: 'In the atom there can never be two or more equivalent electrons for which . . . the values of all [four] quantum numbers coincide. If there is an electron in the atom for which these quantum numbers have definite values then the state is "occupied",' full, no more electrons allowed in. Pauli added a further comment: 'On the grounds of these results there seems to be no basis for a connection, suspected by Bohr, between the problem of the closure of electron groups in the atom and the correspondence principle.' [211]

Pauli's decree, called the exclusion principle, is indispensable* not just for the understanding of the periodic table but for ever so much more in modern quantum physics.

5. *The discovery of hafnium.*[212] According to the exclusion principle the maximum number of 4_4-states equals two times $(2 \times 3 + 1) = 14$, the number of rare earths. Had Bohr known this in 1922, he might not have had brief doubts whether that number is 14 or 15. At issue was the nature of the element $Z = 72$. In his Göttingen lecture Bohr had proclaimed: 'Contrary to the customary assumption . . . the family of rare earths is completed with lutetium [$Z = 71$, now called cassiopeium] . . . if our ideas are correct the not yet discovered element with atomic number 72 must have chemical properties similar to those of Zirconium and not those of the rare earths.' [213] On chemical grounds that idea had been suggested as early as 1895 by Bohr's distinguished teacher Julius Thomsen from the *Læreanstalt*. In Bohr's language, $Z = 72$ should have four valence electrons, as does zirconium, not three, as do the rare earths.

That conjecture conflicted with a result of the French chemist Georges Urbain who after years of strenuous chemical analysis had claimed that $Z = 72$ was a rare earth, which he had named Celtium. On 21 June 1922, the day of the quoted Göttingen lecture, Bohr was apparently not convinced (nor were many others) by Urbain. Yet at about that same time X-ray analyses of the Moseley type, performed in Paris, seemed to confirm Urbain's answer. This conclusion was mentioned in a report by Rutherford which appeared in June, in *Nature*, ('Now that the missing element of number 72 has been identified . . .' [214]), which Bohr read shortly after his return from Göttingen. Bohr, taken aback, wrote to Franck: 'The only thing I still know for sure about my lectures in Göttingen is that several of the

---

* But of course by no means sufficient. I would in fact mislead the reader if I did not mention just one more point. The first two closed shells, occupied by 2, 8 electrons, fill all states with $n = 1, 2$, respectively. The third closed shell also has 8 electrons, corresponding to $n = 3$, $k = 1, 2$. The fourth period, the first of the 'long periods' has 18 electrons, built out of $n = 3$, $k = 3$, and $n = 4$, $k = 1, 2$. These important details can only be understood from the energy properties of atomic states.

results communicated are already wrong. A first point is the constitution of element 72 . . .'[215] Bohr then consulted Coster,[216] who replied[217] that he did not believe the Paris X-ray findings. Meanwhile Bohr himself had come to the same conclusion.[218]

At this juncture Hevesy persuaded Coster – both men were then in Copenhagen – to do an X-ray experiment of their own, right then and right there, using X-ray equipment acquired by Bohr for his institute and installed in its basement. At first Coster did not feel like it, expecting $Z = 72$ to be rare even for a rare earth. No, said Hevesy, we are not going to look for a rare earth but for an analog of Zirconium. So they borrowed a number of Zirconium-rich mineral samples from the Mineralogy Museum in Copenhagen and set to work, Hevesy chemically purifying the minerals, Coster starting the X-ray exposures in late November. By December they were sure: they had identified $Z = 72$ in all their borrowed Zirconium samples. Nor was the new element rare, but in fact as common as tin and a thousand times more plentiful than gold.[219] In their first announcement in print, which appeared[220] on 10 January 1923 they baptized $Z = 72$: 'For the new element we propose the name Hafnium (Hafniae = Copenhagen).'

The story of the name for $Z = 72$ would be pure entertainment, were it not that it carries nationalistic undertones.[221] In Copenhagen, Hafnium had been suggested by Coster and Kramers. Hevesy and Bohr preferred Danium, which eventually was agreed upon by all. Accordingly Hevesy sent off a correction to the *Nature* letter,[220] which, however, was not inserted. On the publication date of that letter Hevesy talked to the press in Copenhagen – about Danium. This explains why shortly afterward Bohr received a letter of inquiry[222] from the editor of a learned British journal who had 'read in the English papers that you have discovered two new elements called Danium and Hafnium.' On 2 February 1923 *The Times* of London reported (not true) that Hafnium had been isolated by the scientific director of the British Museum. Meanwhile Urbain kept insisting on the name Celtium. From Canada came the suggestion to abandon all those names in favor of Jargonium.[223] But Hafnium it remained.

Bohr himself was absent from Copenhagen on the December day when Coster and Hevesy became convinced of their discovery. He first learned the good news in the following way. 'While Coster telephoned these results through to Bohr, Hevesy took the train to Stockholm to be in time for Bohr's announcement at [his] Nobel lecture.'[221]

(f) The Nobel Prize

1. *The Prize and the press.* Nobel Committees are tight-lipped about their deliberations prior to the announcement of the winning candidate. Yet

already in October 1922 the news appeared in Danish papers[224] that Bohr was to receive the Nobel Prize for physics. The rumors were correct; on 9 November the Royal Swedish Academy of Sciences awarded him the prize for 1922, 130000 Swedish Kronor. He was the sixth Dane and the first Danish physicist to be so honored.

These days, announcements of Nobel awards make front page news in the world press. It was not always like that. To find the first communication of Bohr's prize in the *New York Times*, turn to page 4, the middle of column 2, of its 10 November 1922 edition, to find, in its entirety, the following item:

Nobel prize for Einstein
The Nobel Committee has awarded the physics prize for 1921 to Albert Einstein, identified with the theory of relativity, and that for 1922 to Professor Neils [*sic*] Bohr of Copenhagen.

Thus, without the flourishes so familiar from modern coverage, did the good citizens of New York and elsewhere hear of the honors bestowed on two great men. This news item is more telling, I think, about the public perception of the Nobel Prize than about that of Einstein and Bohr. In 1922 Einstein had in fact already been the subject of extensive press reports, in the *New York Times* and other papers.[225] While the same was not at all true for Bohr, that was to change within the year thereafter, as we shall see in Chapter 12.

I should explain how Einstein and Bohr each could receive an unshared prize at the same time. A prize award may be postponed for one year and one year only. (Thereafter it is added to the main fund, as was the case for the 1916, 1931, and 1934 physics prizes.) That happened to the prize for 1921, awarded to Einstein in 1922. This holding over procedure helped the indomitable Rutherford set a still unbroken world record for most junior collaborators awarded the Nobel Prize at the same time: Bohr, Frederick Soddy, chemistry 1921, and Frances Aston, chemistry 1922.

2. *Who nominated Bohr?* The award procedure begins with an analysis by the five member Nobel Committee for physics, appointed by the Swedish Academy from its membership, of all valid nominations that have come in. After studying reports by Committee members of the most promising candidates' work, the Committee makes a recommendation to the physics section (*Klass*) of the Academy whose membership may or may not agree with the Committee's findings. The final decision, made by vote of the Academy *in pleno*, need not follow the *Klass* recommendation.

Before turning to the case of Bohr, I should first comment more broadly on the role of the burgeoning quantum theory in the deliberations of the Committee. It will indeed be obvious that motivations for nominating Bohr cannot be put in perspective without some indication of what befell the other two founding fathers, Planck and Einstein. It is a pleasure to note first of all that the first nomination[226] ever made by Einstein was for Planck, in 1918: '[Planck has] laid the foundations of the quantum theory, the fertility of which for all physics has become manifest in recent years'; that Bohr's first nomination ever (1920) was for Einstein, for his work on Brownian motion, the photoelectric effect, the quantum theory of heat capacities, but 'first and foremost' relativity;[227] and that Planck nominated Bohr in 1922.*

The Nobel Committees in the hard sciences, physics, chemistry, and physiology or medicine, tend to be conservative in outlook. (It is quite a different story for the Committees for literature and for peace.) The confrontation with the quantum theory, so successful yet so confusing in those days, therefore posed many a dilemma. Consider the case of Planck (discussed in detail by Nagel[229]), nominated every single year from 1907 to 1919, when he won the deferred 1918 prize. His nomination for 1907 received only passing mention, but in 1908 he was the choice of the *Klass* by an 8–1 vote. The final Academy vote was for someone else, however, largely as the result[230] of machinations by Mittag-Leffler, a brilliant mathematician and distinctly unappealing character.[231] After the defeat of 1908, the Committee had gotten 'cold feet as far as Planck was concerned. Also, of course, the importance but also the contradictions of quantum theory came more into focus from 1910 on, so the award to Planck was postponed in the hope that the difficulties of the quantum theory could be sorted out.'[232] That had still not happened in 1919, but by then 'the Committee does not hesitate to declare that the time is ripe to reward the work of Planck . . . sufficient evidence for the importance of his discovery . . . a final formulation [of the quantum theory] exceed[s] the present range of vision',[233] a judgement accepted both by the *Klass* and the full Academy.

I have related elsewhere[234] the story of Einstein's nomination. Suffice it to say here that his award also was for his work on quantum theory (not remarkable) but not for relativity (most remarkable). In any event the order of awards for quantum physics was perfect: first Planck, then Einstein, then Bohr.

Now to the nominations for Bohr.

My information, to follow next, on how Bohr was chosen is derived from letters of recommendation and Committee reports made available to me from the physics Committee files. I wish to express my gratitude to the Nobel Committee, most especially to its Secretary Bengt Nagel, for generous help.

In 1914 Wien referred to the application of the quantum theory to spectra,

* See Ref. 228 for complete lists of nominees and nominators in physics and chemistry for 1901–37.

in his nomination for Planck, without, however, referring to Bohr.[235] The atomic model of Rutherford and Bohr was mentioned[236] for the first time in 1915, in a report for the eyes of the chemistry Committee concerning the nomination of a prize for Moseley (who was killed that same year). Bohr received his first personal nomination in 1917 when Orest Chwolson from Petrograd (Leningrad) proposed him for a shared prize with his teacher Knudsen. Nominations in subsequent years follow.

1918. Stefan Meyer from Vienna makes three proposals because the prizes for 1916 (never awarded) and 1917 (awarded in 1918) 'have not yet been announced' : first, Planck; second, Einstein; third: a prize shared by Bohr and Sommerfeld.

1919. Max von Laue from Würzburg and Rutherford, who also cites the work on stopping power, each propose Bohr. Heinrich Rubens from Berlin and Wien from Würzburg each propose a shared prize for Bohr and Planck.

1920. Von Laue and Wien repeat their proposals. Friedrich Neesen from Berlin nominates Bohr and Planck.

1921. Von Laue repeats his proposal.

1922. Bohr is nominated by William Lawrence Bragg, Robert Millikan ('for having made atomic spectroscopy the most potent instrument man now possesses for solving the secrets of the sub-atomic world'), Planck ('the first successful penetration in the domain of inner-atomic phenomena'), Wilhelm Conrad Röntgen ('with deepest conviction and with great pleasure'), and Rutherford. Von Laue proposes one prize for Einstein, one for Bohr (recall that 1921 had been deferred). Meyer nominates Einstein, Bohr, Sommerfeld. August Schmauss from Munich suggests either Bohr or a shared prize between Bohr and Sommerfeld. Julius Lilienfeld from Leipzig proposes a shared prize for Bohr and Debye. Hjalmar Tallqvist and Karl Lindman, two Finnish professors, jointly propose a shared prize for Bohr and Sommerfeld.

I now turn to the responses to the Bohr nominations found in Committee reports.

1917. The nomination is recorded without comment.

1918. The successes for hydrogen and ionized helium are noted, as are the further consequences of Bohr's picture worked out by Sommerfeld, Schwarzschild, and Epstein. Since, however, the theory neither explains the spectra of other elements nor the Zeeman effect, 'an award is for the present out of the question'.

1919. Bohr's atom model 'has made possible a large amount of research'. The Committee requests a detailed account of its member Vilhelm Carlheim-Gyllensköld, professor of physics in Stockholm. This report, 15 typed pages long, is presented to the Committee in September. It contains an analysis of Bohr's work and the conclusion that 'the significance of Bohr's contributions for spectral analysis is manifest'. The Committee notes that

Bohr's ideas are 'in conflict with physical laws that have so long been considered indispensable' and that they 'therefore cannot be considered to contain the real solution to the problem'. The Committee therefore wishes to await further developments and is not yet prepared to propose Bohr.

1920. The Committee again stresses the conflict with physical laws. 'One must wait for further developments.'

1921. The same.

1922. The Committee, impressed by the list of distinguished nominators and also by Bohr's recent work on the periodic system, asks its member Oseen for a detailed evaluation. In August, Oseen presents the Committee with a report, 32 typed pages long, containing sections on historical antecedents, the results of 1913, the Stark and Zeeman effects, the periodic system, and on the limitations of the theory. 'Bohr himself has very strongly emphasized the logical difficulties.' The report concludes as follows. 'If finally one asks whether Bohr's atomic theory deserves a Nobel Prize, then, it seems to me, there cannot be more than one answer. I believe that [it] is fully worthy of a Nobel Prize both because of the assured results and because of the powerful stimulus which this theory has given to experimental as well as theoretical physics.' Whereupon the Committee recommended Bohr for the 1922 prize, a proposal with which the *Klass* and the full Academy concurred.

A few additional comments. The Committee reports strike me as reasonable throughout. Oseen not only wrote a thoughtful and brilliant report on Bohr's work but almost simultaneously did likewise on Einstein. He must be considered as the pivotal figure in two of the most important and difficult decisions the Academy ever had to make.

Bohr was also nominated, twice, for the Nobel Prize in chemistry: in 1920, to share with Nernst, and again in 1929, to share with Coster and Hevesy.

Many have wondered why Einstein never received a second Nobel Prize, for relativity. A small contribution: after 1923 he was never again nominated.

I belong to those who regret (even more after recent studies) that Sommerfeld's work was never sufficiently recognized by the Nobel Committee. He was nominated every year but one from 1917 until (at least) 1937.

3. *The ceremonies.* On 10 November 1922 Bohr must have received a telegram signed by Christopher Aurivillius, secretary of the Swedish Academy, informing him that he had won the Nobel Prize. Also on that day Aurivillius must have written Bohr a letter with more details. I have neither seen the cable nor the letter but am convinced that these communications were sent since I did see the corresponding documents received by Einstein.

The Nobel ceremonies[237] held at the Great Hall of the Academy of Music, on

10 December as always, began at five in the afternoon with the arrival of King Gustav V and members of his family. The orchestra of the Royal Opera first played the Royal Hymn, also sung by the standing audience, then the overture to the Magic Flute. Next the president of the Nobel Foundation spoke, followed by the scherzo from Mendelssohn's Midsummer Night's Dream.

Then Svante Arrhenius, director of the Nobel Institute for Physical Chemistry in Stockholm and president of the physics Committee, rose to make the presentation of the physics prizes. First Einstein, cited 'for his services to theoretical physics, and especially for his discovery of the law of the photoelectric effect'. ('There is probably no living physicist whose name has become known in such wide circles . . .'). Einstein himself, by then a professor in Berlin, could not be present because he and his wife were in Japan at that time. Rudolf Nadolny, German ambassador to Sweden, acted as Einstein's representative (whereby hangs a tale[238]). Next, Bohr, cited 'for his investigations of the structure of atoms, and of the radiation emanating from them. In this presentation Arrhenius recalled names (Kirchhoff, Bunsen, Balmer, Ritz, Sommerfeld) and achievements (the quantum postulate, the hydrogen atom, the correspondence principle, complex atoms) encountered in the preceding pages. 'Your great success has shown that you have found the right roads to fundamental truths, and in so doing you have laid down principles which have led to the most splendid advances and promise abundant fruit for the work of the future.' Then Bohr received his medal and diploma from the hands of the king. The presentations of the chemistry and literature prizes followed, there was more music, and the ceremonies were over.

The traditional banquet, held in those days in Stockholm's elegant Grand Hotel, began at seven o'clock. The after dinner proceedings began as usual with a speech and toast to the laureates. Next followed toasts proposed by the laureates themselves. Nadolny, who spoke first, expressed the sentiments of his government rather than those of Einstein when mentioning 'the joy of my people that once again one of them has been able to achieve something for all of mankind'. The records show[237] that his toast was received with 'long applause'. Bohr spoke next, proposing 'the toast to the vigorous growth of the international work on the advancement of science which is one of the high points of human existence in these, in many respects, sorrowful times'.[239] His words were followed by 'particularly warm applause'. There were more toasts, then there was a ball, then everybody retired. A good time was presumably had by all.

When the next day Bohr gave the obligatory Nobel lecture, this one on 'The structure of the atom',[240] he had at first to improvise until his notes and slides, which he had forgotten at his hotel, had been fetched.[241] His talk, a broad survey, culminated in his views on the periodic table and the announcement of the discovery of element 72 by Coster and Hevesy. His final words were typically sobering: 'The theory is yet in a very preliminary stage and many fundamental questions will await solution.'

Whom did Bohr nominate? In 1974 a revision of the Nobel Foundation statutes permitted for the first time access to nominating letters and their evaluation, but only for prizes given fifty or more years ago. This has enabled me to see who Bohr nominated between 1920 and 1939.

1920. Einstein, as mentioned previously.

1923. Franck, for the Franck–Hertz experiment and its stimulus for further experimentation, by him and others.

1925. Repeat of same proposal. Franck and Hertz win the prize that year.

1926. Owen Willans Richardson from London, mainly for the 'Richardson effect', the emission of electrons by heated metals.

1928. Richardson again, or else a shared prize for him and Irving Langmuir who also was active in the same area. In 1929 Richardson wins the deferred 1928 prize. In 1932 Langmuir wins the chemistry prize.

1929. Same proposal for the deferred 1928 prize. For 1929: Robert Williams Wood of Baltimore, either alone or shared with Chandrasekhara Venkata Raman of Calcutta, both for important discoveries in resonance radiation.

1930. Wood and Raman again. Raman wins the prize for 1930. Wood never made it.

1931. Heisenberg, for 'having developed the quantum theory into a rational atomic mechanics'. Bohr also points out 'Professor Schrödinger's great merits, which, however, should in my judgement be considered separately so that these two outstanding physicists' merits shall not be rewarded simultaneously'. The physics prize for 1931 was never awarded.

1932. Proposes Heisenberg and Schrödinger for the 1931 and 1932 prize respectively. The 1932 prize is deferred.

1933. Proposes Heisenberg for the deferred 1932 prize, Schrödinger for the 1933 prize. Heisenberg wins the 1932 prize, Schrödinger shares the 1933 prize with Dirac.

1934. (Prize never awarded.) Proposes Stern for his development of molecular beam techniques and the 'surprising and for our attitude to nuclear physics decisive result' – indeed – that the proton has a magnetic moment of unexpected size (more about that later).

1935. Again proposes Stern for the 'deferred' 1934 prize, and Frédéric and Irène Joliot-Curie for their discovery of 'induced radioactivity which has opened a quite new and already extraordinarily fruitful epoch' (see (17f)). That year the Joliot-Curies win the chemistry prize. In 1944 Stern receives the deferred 1943 physics award.

1939. Proposes Ernest Lawrence 'for his extraordinarily great contributions to the study of nuclear reactions,' the result of his invention of the cyclotron (17b). Lawrence receives the award that same year.

The main interest in this recitation of choices is to catch glimpses of Bohr's views on science and scientists – and to note his high batting average.

References

1. E. Wigner, *Comm. Pure Appl. Math.* **13**, 1, 1960.
2. W, Heisenberg, interviewed by T. S. Kuhn, 25 February 1963, NBA.
3. M. Planck, *Phys. Zeitschr.* **11**, 922, 1910.
4. M. Planck, *Naturw.* **11**, 535, 1923.
5. P. Ehrenfest, *Naturw.* **11**, 543, 1923.
6. A. Einstein, letter to B. Becker, 20 March 1954.
7. F. C. Hoyt, interviewed by T. S. Kuhn, 28 April 1964, NBA.
8. J. Franck, interviewed by T. S. Kuhn, 14 July 1962, NBA.
9. A. Einstein, in *Albert Einstein: philosopher-scientist*, Ed. P. A. Schilpp, Tudor, New York, 1949.
10. M. Born, *Vorlesungen über Atommechanik*, Vol. I, Springer, Berlin 1925.
11. W. Pauli, *Handbuch der Physik*, Vol. 23, p. 1, Springer, Berlin 1924; repr. in W. Pauli, *Collected scientific papers*, Vol. 1, p. 269, Interscience, New York 1964; Müller-Pouillet's *Lehrbuch der Physik*, 11th edn, Vol. 2, part 2, p. 1709; repr. in *Collected papers*, Vol. 1, p. 636.
12. J. H. Van Vleck, *Bull. Nat. Res. Council*, **10**, part 4, 1926.
13. J. Mehra and H. Rechenberg, *The historical development of the quantum theory*, Vol. 1, Springer, New York 1982.
14. N. Bohr, letter to H. G. J. Moseley, 21 November 1913, CW, Vol. 2, p. 546.
15. H. G. J. Moseley, letter to N. Bohr, 16 November 1913, CW, Vol. 2, p. 544.
16. E. Rutherford, *Phil. Mag.* **27**, 488, 1914.
17. See, e.g., IB, Chap. 11, section (a).
18. For more on van den Broek see IB, Chap. 11, section (d).
19. A. J. van den Broek, *Phys. Zeitschr.* **14**, 32, 1913.
20. N. Bohr, *Phil. Mag.* **26**, 476, 1913, repr. in CW, Vol. 2, p. 188.
21. A. J. van den Broek, *Nature* **92**, 372, 1913.
22. E. Rutherford, *Nature* **92**, 423, 1913.
23. N. Bohr, interview by T. Kuhn, L. Rosenfeld, E. Rüdinger, and A. Petersen, 1 November 1962, NBA.
24. C. G. Darwin in *Niels Bohr and the development of physics*, Ed. W. Pauli, McGraw-Hill, New York 1955.
25. H. G. J. Moseley, *Nature* **92**, 554, 1913.
26. W. Kossel, *Verh. Deutsch. Phys. Ges.* **16**, 953, 1914.
27. H. G. J. Moseley, *Phil. Mag.* **26**, 1024, 1913; **27**, 703, 1914.
28. E. Rutherford, *Proc. Roy. Soc.* A **93**, xxii, 1917.
29. Ref. 14 and N. Bohr, *Phil. Mag.* **30**, 394, 1915, CW, Vol. 2, p. 391.
30. N. Bohr, *Phil. Mag.* **31**, 174, 1916.
31. J. Stark, *Sitz. Ber. Preuss. Ak. Wiss.* 1913, p. 932; also *Nature* **92**, 401, 1913; *Ann. der Phys.* **43**, 965, 983, 991, 1017, 1914. For details see also Ref. 13, p. 202.
32. E. Rutherford, letter to N. Bohr, 11 December 1913, CW, Vol. 2, p. 589.
33. E. Warburg, *Verh. Deutsch. Phys. Ges.* **15**, 1259, 1913.

34. N. Bohr, *Phil. Mag.* **27**, 506, 1914, CW, Vol. 2, p. 347.
35. N. Bohr, *Phil. Mag.* **29**, 332, 1915, CW, Vol. 2, p. 375.
36. For Bohr's own reservations see an unpublished manuscript repr. in CW, Vol 2, p. 370.
37. P. S. Epstein, *Phys. Zeitschr.* **17**, 148, 1916; *Ann. der Phys.* **50**, 489, 1916; K. Schwarzschild, *Sitz. Ber. Preuss. Akad. Wiss.* 1916, p. 548.
38. N. Bohr, *Kong. Dansk. Vid. Selsk. Skrifter*, 1918, p. 1, esp. section 4, CW, Vol. 3, p. 67.
39. H. A. Kramers, same *Skrifter*, 1919, p. 287 (his Ph.D. Thesis); repr. in H. A. Kramers, *Collected scientific papers*, p. 3, North-Holland, Amsterdam 1956.
40. J. Franck and G. Hertz, *Verh. Deutsch. Phys. Ges.* **15**, 373, 613, 1913.
41. J. Franck and G. Hertz, *ibid.* **16**, 457, 1914.
42. N. Bohr, *Phil. Mag.* **26**, 1, 1913, CW, Vol. 2, p. 161, esp. section 4.
43. J. Franck and G. Hertz, *Phys. Zeitschr.* **20**, 132, 1919.
44. N. Bohr, *Phil. Mag.* **29**, 332, 1915, CW, Vol. 2, p. 377.
45. N. Bohr, *Nature* **95**, 6, 1915, CW, Vol. 2, p. 385.
46. N. Bohr, *Phil. Mag.* **30**, 581, 1915, CW, Vol. 2, p. 259.
47. N. Bohr, letter to C. W. Oseen, 17 March 1916, CW, Vol. 2, p. 571.
48. The proof of this paper is reprinted in CW, Vol. 2, p. 431.
49. A. Sommerfeld, *Sitz. Ber. Bayer. Ak. Wiss.* 1916, pp. 425, 459.
50. A. A. Michelson and E. W. Morley, *Phil. Mag.* **24**, 463, 1887.
51. A. A. Michelson, *Phil. Mag.* **34**, 280, 1892.
52. N. Bohr, letter to E. Rutherford, 31 December, 1913, CW, Vol. 2, p. 591.
53. N. Bohr, letters to A. Fowler, 28 April 1914, and to E. Rutherford, 20 May 1914, CW, Vol. 2, pp. 506 and 592, respectively.
54. W. E. Curtis, *Proc. Roy. Soc.* A **90**, 605, 1914, esp. pp. 614, 620.
55. N. Bohr, letter to A. Fowler, 15 April 1914, CW, Vol 2, p. 504.
56. I. Newton, *Principia*, liber 1, sectio 9. Best accessible in the University of California Press edition, Berkeley 1966 (Ed. F. Cajori).
57. For an essay on the history of fine structure see H. Kragh, *Hist. Stud. Phys. Sci.* **15**, 67, 1985.
58. A. Sommerfeld, *Ann. der Phys.* **51**, 1, 125, 1916.
59. W. Wilson, *Phil. Mag.* **29**, 795, 1915; **31**, 156, 1916.
60. J. Ishiwara, *Proc. Tokyo Math. Phys. Soc.* **8**, 106, 1915.
61. M. Planck. *Verh. Deutsch. Phys. Ges.* **17**, 407, 438, 1915.
62. See Ref. 11, p. 393.
63. For a detailed discussion see Ref. 57.
64. For this episode see especially Ref. 57 and Ref. 13, p. 657 ff.
65. Ref. 58, section 7.
66. A. Sommerfeld, *Phys. Zeitschr.* **17**, 491, 1916.
67. Einstein/Sommerfeld Briefwechsel, Ed. A. Hermann, Schwabe, Stuttgart 1968.
68. N. Bohr, letter to A. Sommerfeld, 19 March 1916, CW, Vol. 2, p. 603.
69. R. Kronig in *Theoretical physics in the twentieth century*, Eds. M. Fierz and V. Weisskopf, p. 50, Interscience, New York 1960.
70. N. Bohr, letter to C. W. Oseen, 29 January 1926, CW, Vol. 5, p. 238.

71. For an account of Ehrenfest's early life and work see M. Klein, *Paul Ehrenfest*, North-Holland, Amsterdam 1970.
72. Ref. 71, Chap. 10.
73. A. Einstein, *Out of my later years*, p. 236, Philosophical Library, New York 1950.
74. P. Ehrenfest, letter to H. A. Lorentz, 25 August 1913, quoted in Ref. 71, p. 278.
75. P. Ehrenfest, letter to A. Sommerfeld, May 1916, quoted in Ref. 71, p. 286.
76. Complete references are found in P. Ehrenfest's review article, *Naturw.* **11**, 543, 1923.
77. Ref. 48, p. 436.
78. A. Einstein, *Verh. Deutsch. Phys. Ges.* **16**, 820, 1914.
79. Ref. 38, Introduction.
80. N. Bohr, letter to P. Ehrenfest, May 1918, CW, Vol. 3, p. 12.
81. P. Ehrenfest, letter to N. Bohr, 8 May 1922, NBA.
82. This lecture is reproduced in CW, Vol. 3, p. 201.
83. CW, Vol. 3, p. 36.
84. P. Ehrenfest, letter to N. Bohr, 4 June 1919, CW, Vol. 3. p. 16.
85. H. B. G. Casimir in NBR, p. 109.
86. A. Einstein, letter to M. Besso, 18 November 1916, repr. in *Albert Einstein–Michele Besso correspondance*, p. 78, Ed. P. Speziali, Hermann, Paris 1972.
87. Lecture on 26 April 1917, notes in NBA.
88. *Fysisk Tidsskr.* **17**, 67, 1918–19.
89. A. Einstein, *Verh. Deutsch. Phys. Ges.* **18**, 318, 1916.
90. A. Einstein, *Mitt. Phys. Ges. Zürich* **16**, 47, 1916; *Phys. Zeitschr.* **18**, 121, 1917.
91. For more details see SL, Chap. 21, sections (b), (c), and (d).
92. E. Rutherford, *Phil Mag.* **49**, 1, 1900.
93. IB, Chap. 6, section (e).
94. A. Einstein, letter to M. Born, 27 January 1920, repr. in *The Born–Einstein letters*, p. 23, Walker, New York, 1971.
95. N. Bohr, letter to O. W. Richardson, 15 August 1918, CW, Vol. 3, p. 14.
96. N. Bohr, letter to A. Sommerfeld, 27 July 1919, CW, Vol. 3, p. 17.
97. N. Bohr, *Kong. Dansk. Vid. Selsk. Skrifter*, 1918, p. 37, CW, Vol. 3, p. 103.
98. N. Bohr, *ibid.* p. 101, CW, Vol. 3, p. 167.
99. CW, Vol. 3, p. 178.
100. N. Bohr, letter to A. Sommerfeld, 30 April 1922, CW, Vol. 3, pp. 39, 691. Cf. also N. Bohr, letter to A. Haas, 11 April 1922, CW, Vol. 3, p. 647.
101. CW, Vol. 3, p. 185.
102. CW, Vol. 3, p. 36.
103. CW, Vol. 3, p. 397.
104. CW, Vol. 3, p. 241.
105. H. A. Kramers and H. Holst, *The atom and the Bohr theory of its structure*, p. 139, Knopf, New York 1923.
106. H. A. Kramers, *Naturw.* **4**, 550, 1923.
107. H. A. Kramers, *Fysisk Tidsskr.* **33**, 82, 1935.
108. A. Sommerfeld, *Atombau und Spektrallinien*, 3rd edn, p. 338, Vieweg, Braunschweig 1922.

109. O. Klein, NBR, p. 77.
110. P. Kristensen, *Fysisk Tidsskr.* **84**, 124, 145, 1986.
111. F. Paschen, *Ann. der Phys.* **50**, 901, 1916.
112. A. Rubinowicz, *Naturw.* **19**, 441, 465, 1918.
113. N. Bohr, CW, Vol. 3, p. 142, footnote.
114. CW, Vol. 3, p. 73.
115. CW, Vol. 3, p. 303; English transl. in CW, Vol. 3, p. 325.
116. N. Bohr, *Abhandlungen über Atombau*, Vieweg, Braunschweig 1921.
117. N. Bohr, *Zeitschr. Phys.* **6**, 1, 1921; English transl. in CW, Vol. 3, p. 350.
118. CW, Vol. 3, p. 357.
119. N. Bohr, *Proc. Phys. Soc. London* **35**, 275, 1923; CW, Vol. 3, p. 417.
120. N. Bohr, *Phil. Mag.* **43**, 1112, 1922; CW, Vol. 3, p. 447.
121. N. Bohr, *Drei Aufsätze über Spektren und Atombau*, Vieweg, Braunschweig 1922; *The theory of spectra and atomic constitution*, Cambridge University Press 1922; *Les spectres et la structure de l'atome*, Hermann, Paris 1922.
122. Repr. in CW, Vol. 4, p. 341.
123. N. Bohr, *Über die Quantentheorie der Linienspektren*, Vieweg, Braunschweig 1923.
124. CW, Vol. 3, p. 576.
125. N. Bohr, *Ann. der Phys.* **71**, 228, 1923, English transl. in CW, Vol. 4, p. 611.
126. N. Bohr, *Zeitschr. Phys.* **13**, 117, 1923; English transl. in CW, Vol. 3, p. 457.
127. CW, Vol. 3, p. 458, footnote.
128. Found in CW, Vol. 3, p. 501; English transl. in CW, Vol. 3, p. 532.
129. CW, Vol. 3, pp. 559–74.
130. CW, Vol. 3, p. 458.
131. N. Bohr, letter to E. Rutherford, 27 December 1917, CW, Vol. 3, p. 682.
132. W. Heisenberg, *Zeitschr. Phys.* **39**, 499, 1926.
133. W. V. Houston, *Proc. Nat. Acad. Sci.* **13**, 91, 1927.
134. G. Hansen, *Nature* **119**, 237, 1927.
135. H. G. Small, The helium atom in the old quantum theory, Ph.D. thesis, University of Wisconsin, 1971. See also Ref. 13, p. 348ff.
136. N. Bohr, letter to E. Rutherford, 29 November 1916, CW, Vol. 2, p. 545.
137. N. Bohr, letter to C. W. Oseen, 28 February 1917, CW, Vol. 2, p. 573.
138. CW, Vol. 4, p. 341.
139. M. Dresden, *H. A. Kramers*, pp. 119–22, Springer, New York 1987.
140. CW, Vol. 4, p. 122.
141. CW, Vol. 4, p. 379.
142. H. A. Kramers, *Zeitschr. Phys.* **13**, 312, 1923.
143. M. Born and W. Heisenberg, *Zeitschr. Phys.* **16**, 229, 1923.
144. M. Born, letter to N. Bohr, 4 March 1923; CW, Vol. 4, p. 669.
145. Ref. 125, see esp. CW, Vol. 4, p. 643, footnote.
146. A. Sommerfeld, *Rev. Sci. Instr.* **7**, 509, 1923.
147. P. Zeeman, *Phil. Mag.* **43**, 226; **44**, 55, 255, 1897.
148. H. A. Lorentz, *Ann. der Phys.* **63**, 279, 1897; *Phys. Zeitschr.* **1**, 39, 1899.
149. H. A. Lorentz, *Physica* **1**, 228, 1921.
150. For more historical details see IB, Chap. 4, section (c); Ref. 13, p. 445.

151. See e.g. Ref. 11, *Collected works*, p. 417; see further C. Jensen, *Hist. Stud. Phys. Sci.* **15**, 81, 1984.
152. See Refs. 29, 35, 36.
153. CW, Vol. 2, p. 370.
154. P. Debye, *Phys. Zeitschr.* **17**, 507, 1916.
155. Ref. 97, section 5.
156. Ref. 98, Appendix.
157. Refs. 101, 104, 128, 156.
158. O. Stern, *Phys. Zeitschr.* **23**, 476, 1922.
159. A. Sommerfeld, *Atombau und Spektrallinien*, 1st edn, p. 439, Vieweg, Braunschweig 1919.
160. W. Pauli, *Collected works* (Ref. 11), p. 437.
161. A. Sommerfeld, *Ann. der Phys.* **63**, 221, 1920, Section II.
162. W. Pauli, *Collected works* (Ref. 11), p. 1073.
163. A. Landé, *Zeitschr. Phys.* **5**, 231, 1921.
164. S. Goudsmit, *Physica* **5**, 281, 1925.
165. It is reproduced in *Collected works* (Ref. 11), Vol. 1, p. 1.
166. A. Einstein, *Naturw.* **10**, 184, 1922.
167. W. Pauli, *Relativity theory*, transl. G. Field, Pergamon, London 1958.
168. N. Bohr, in *Theoretical physics in the twentieth century*, Eds. M Fierz and V. Weisskopf, p. 1, Interscience, New York 1960.
169. W. Pauli, *Zeitschr. Phys.* **16**, 155, 1923; **20**, 371, 1924.
170. W. Pauli, *Zeitschr. Phys.* **31**, 373, 1925.
171. CW, Vol. 3, p. 19.
172. CW, Vol. 3, p. 221.
173. N. Bohr, lecture before the *Videnskabernes Selskab*, 13 February 1920, CW, Vol. 3, p. 227.
174. See J. L. Heilbron, *Isis* **58**, 462, 1967.
175. M. Born and A. Landé, *Verh. Deutsch. Phys. Ges.* **20**, 210, 1918.
176. N. Bohr, letter to O. W. Richardson, 25 December 1919, quoted in Ref. 174, p. 478.
177. N. Bohr, letter to R. Ladenburg, 16 July 1920, CW, Vol. 4, p. 711.
178. See e.g. J. L. Heilbron in *Lectures on the history of atomic physics 1900–1920*, p. 40, Academic Press, New York 1977.
179. W. Kossel, *Ann. der Phys.* **49**, 229, 1916.
180. W. Kossel and A. Sommerfeld, *Verh. Deutsch. Phys. Ges.* **20**, 240, 1919.
181. J. W. van Spronsen, *The periodic table of chemical elements*, Elsevier, New York 1969.
182. Repr. in CW, Vol. 4, p. 43.
183. N. Bohr, *Nature* **107**, 104, 1921, repr. in CW, Vol. 4, p. 71.
184. N. Bohr, *Die Umschau* **25**, 229, 1921, English transl. in CW, Vol. 4, p. 83.
185. CW, Vol 4, pp. 91, 99.
186. N. Bohr, *Nature* **108**, 208, 1921, repr. in CW, Vol. 4, p. 175.
187. N. Bohr, *Fysisk Tidsskr.* **19**, 153, 1921; *Zeitschr. Phys.* **9**, 1, 1922; English transl. in CW, Vol. 4, p. 263. This lecture was included as the third essay in Ref. 121.

188. N. Bohr, *Fysisk Tidsskr.* **20**, 112, 1922; English transl. in CW, Vol. 4, p. 421.
189. H. Kragh, *Hist. Stud. Phys. Sci.* **10**, 123, 1979.
190. N. Bohr, *Medd. Kgl. Vetenskaps Ak.* **5**, No. 28, 1918, CW, Vol. 2, p. 473.
191. A. Landé, letter to N. Bohr, 21 February 1921, CW, Vol. 4, p. 722.
192. A. Sommerfeld, letter to A. Landé, 3 March 1921, quoted in P. Forman, *Isis* **64**, 151, 1973.
193. A. Sommerfeld, postcard to N. Bohr, 7 March 1921, CW, Vol. 4, p. 740.
194. A. Sommerfeld, letter to N. Bohr, 25 April 1921, CW, Vol. 4, p. 740.
195. E. Rutherford, letter to N. Bohr, 26 September 1921, NBA.
196. J. Franck, letter to N. Bohr, 21 February 1922, NBA.
197. W. Heisenberg, *Physics and beyond*, p. 38, Harper and Row, New York 1971.
198. CW, Vol. 4, p. 397.
199. Ref. 187, CW, Vol. 4, p. 277.
200. Ref. 125, esp. CW, Vol. 4, p. 632.
201. F. C. Hoyt, *Phys. Rev.* **25**, 174, 1925.
202. CW, Vol. 4, p. 392.
203. E. Schrödinger, *Zeitschr. Phys.* **4**, 347, 1921.
204. CW, Vol. 4, p. 397.
205. CW, Vol. 4, p. 391.
206. CW, Vol. 4, p. 406.
207. N. Bohr and D. Coster, *Zeitschr. Phys.* **12**, 342, 1923, Engl. transl. in CW, Vol. 4, p. 519; see also D. Coster, *Naturw.* **11**, 567, 1923.
208. A. Sommerfeld, *Atombau und Spektrallinien*, 4th edn p. VI, Vieweg, Braunschweig 1924.
209. For more on the history of the exclusion principle see IB, Chap. 13, section (b).
210. W. Pauli, letter to A. Sommerfeld, 6 December 1924, repr. in *W. Pauli, scientific correspondence*, Vol. 1, p. 182, Springer, New York 1979; see also W. Pauli, letter to N. Bohr, 12 December 1924, *ibid.*, p. 186.
211. W. Pauli, *Zeitschr. Phys.* **31**, 765, 1925.
212. For more on the hafnium story see Refs. 13, p. 364; 178, section V, part 3; 189, section 5.
213. CW, Vol.4, p. 405.
214. E. Rutherford, *Nature* **109**, 781, 1922.
215. N. Bohr, letter to J. Franck, 15 July 1922, CW, Vol. 4, p. 694.
216. N. Bohr, letter to D. Coster, 3 July 1922, CW, Vol. 4, p. 675.
217. D. Coster, letter to N. Bohr, 16 July 1922, CW, Vol. 4, p. 677.
218. N. Bohr, letter to D. Coster, 5 August 1922, CW, Vol. 4, p. 678.
219. D. Coster, *Physica* **5**, 133, 1923; G. von Hevesy, *Arch. Kemi*, **3**, 543, 1951.
220. D. Coster and G. von Hevesy, *Nature* **111**, 79, 1923; see also *ibid.* pp. 182, 252, 322, 462.
221. See P. Robertson, *The early years*, Akademisk Forlag, Copenhagen, 1979; H. Kragh and P. Robertson, *Centaurus* **23**, 275, 1980.
222. Letter by Editor of *Raw Materials Review* to N. Bohr, 20 February 1923, NBA.
223. T. L. Walker, *Nature* **112**, 831, 1923.
224. See *Social Demokraten*, 26 October 1922.

225. See SL, Chap. 16.
226. SL, p. 513.
227. SL, p. 508.
228. E. Crawford, J. L. Heilbron, and R. Ullrich, *The Nobel population 1901–1937*, Office of the History of Science and Technology, University of California, Berkeley, 1987.
229. B. Nagel, in *Science, technology, and society in the time of Alfred Nobel*, p. 352, Pergamon, New York 1982.
230. Ref. 229, p. 363.
231. E. Crawford, *The beginnings of the Nobel institution*, Cambridge University Press, New York 1984.
232. B. Nagel, letter to A. Pais, 7 May 1981, SL, p. 502.
233. Ref. 229, p. 373.
234. SL, Chap. 30.
235. Ref. 229, p. 370.
236. Ref. 231, p. 136.
237. See *Les Prix Nobel 1921–1922*, Norstedt & Sons, Stockholm 1923.
238. SL, pp. 503, 504.
239. CW, Vol. 4, p. 26.
240. Original Danish version: CW, Vol. 4, p. 429; German transl.: *Naturw.* 11, 606, 1923; English transl.: *Nature* 112, 29, 1923, also CW, Vol. 4, p. 467.
241. O. Klein, NBR, p. 84.

11

Bohr and Einstein

(a) Comparisons

Bohr and Einstein were in their early and late sixties respectively when I first met them. Since I am one (perhaps the last) of those who knew both men rather well personally in their later years it is hardly surprising that I have been asked off and on how, in my view, they compared. That question used to make me mildly uncomfortable and in the past I have tended to respond evasively, simply because the better one believes one understands people the more superficial and hopeless comparisons tend to become. That remains true today, but by now I am at least in a position to reply to my questioners: read this book and my earlier Einstein biography, note not only facts but also nuances contained therein, and you will have the best answer I am capable of giving.

It must be admitted that a comparison between Bohr and Einstein is far more interesting than similar, more frivolous, ones of the kind often indulged in by us physicists, a competitive breed. After all we are dealing here with men who were arguably the two leading figures in science in this century. I therefore decided, for what it is worth, to insert a brief précis in which I enlarge on a few preliminary remarks found in Chapter 1. My choice for doing so at this point was dictated by the fact that in the next section Einstein makes his first personal appearance in this book. I shall defer some juxtapositions until later, most notably how one appreciated the other, and what their positions and roles were in regard to atomic weapons; Einstein will make further appearances later on.

As I collect my thoughts I miss Pauli, who, better than any other physicist, knew both men during the heights of their scientific activities and who had such a firm grasp of their respective oeuvres.

First, physics, by which both Bohr and Einstein were possessed if not obsessed. Both would speak with intense enthusiasm and optimism about work they were engaged in. Both had enormous powers of concentration. Both realized quite early not only the importance but also the paradoxes resulting from Planck's discovery of his radiation law. In his younger days

Einstein's spectrum of scientific activities was broader than Bohr's. Also in their younger days both had an urge for doing experiments, at which Bohr did better (his prize essay). Bohr published 200 papers in scientific journals, Einstein 270 (both in approximate numbers). All their respective most important papers appeared under their own name only. Both men were indefatigable workers, driving themselves on occasion to states of exhaustion which would lead to illness, more serious in the case of Einstein.[1] Both taught courses in their younger but not their later years, neither had his own Ph.D. students. Neither experienced difficulty or pain in admitting to himself, if not to others, that occasionally he had been on a wrong scientific track. (Einstein to Ehrenfest in 1915: 'That fellow Einstein suits his convenience. Every year he retracts what he wrote the year before.'[2]) Neither was in the least overwhelmed by medals, prizes, honorary degrees, and other distinctions showered upon them; their prime concern was always with what they did not understand rather than with past achievements.

Their life spans were almost identical: Bohr lived to be 77, Einstein 76. The same is true for their fathers who died at a relatively young age: Bohr's was 56, Einstein's 55. Einstein remained scientifically active until, literally, the day he died.[3] From the point of view of pure science, Bohr was more spectator than actor in his later years.

I have already noted Bohr's areligious attitudes. Neither did Einstein believe 'in a God who concerns himself with fates and actions of human beings'.[4] Einstein would often invoke God in his spoken and written words ('God does not play dice'). When, in the 1930s, the celebrated actress Elisabeth Bergner asked Einstein whether he believed in God, he replied: 'One may not ask that of someone who with growing amazement attempts to explore and understand the authoritative order in the universe.' When she asked why not, he answered: 'Because he would probably break down when faced with such a question.'[5] Imagery like that would never occur to Bohr's mind.

Neither Bohr nor Einstein had overt emotional problems. Einstein's handwriting was clear, Bohr's was poor. Music was a profound necessity in Einstein's life, not in Bohr's. Both men had remarkably gentle voices. Both felt strongly attracted to the visual arts. Both were well read outside the sciences. Both mastered foreign languages passably but not really well. Each spoke English with a distinct and lovable accent. Each had a great wit and sense of humor and occasionally liked to tell jokes.

Bohr greatly enjoyed sports, soccer in his youth, tennis later, skiing through most of his life. Einstein did not care for any such diversions. Both loved to sail. Einstein never owned or drove a car; Bohr did. As I know from experience, his driving could on occasion be a bit scary. Both traveled extensively (Einstein only when in his forties). Both were pipe smokers (in his younger days Bohr also smoked cigarettes[6]), though Einstein was forbidden to do so in later years.

In regard to family, both men grew up in closely knit warm parental homes. In Bohr's case the father dominated; in Einstein's the mother. Bohr's father was an eminent scientist, Einstein's a small businessman who had to cope with a series of failures. ('The misfortune of my poor parents, who for so many years have not had a happy moment, weighs heavily on me.'[7]) Bohr came from a distinctly upper class milieu; Einstein's was middle class. Bohr's younger brother was (after his wife) the person most close to him. There may never have been anyone to whom Einstein felt closer than his younger sister (his only sibling). Niels' marriage to Margrethe (she survived him) was to both a source of great harmony, strength, and singlemindedness. Einstein was married twice (he survived both spouses), undertakings at which, in his words, 'I twice failed rather disgracefully'.[8] He had several extramarital affairs.

The Bohrs had six sons. Einstein and his first wife had one daughter (whose later fate is unknown[9]) before and two sons during their marriage. He also had two stepdaughters as a result of his second marriage. Bohr was a family man, a wonderful, devoted father. About Einstein I am less clear in that respect; later letters indicate that relations sometimes left something to be desired. The children brought joy but also tragedy to their parents. At the time of writing, three of the Bohr sons continue distinguished careers; the same was true for Einstein's older son. But the Bohrs lost their oldest son in a sailing accident (to which I will return later) while their youngest, his name was Harald, was incapacitated by disease* and died aged about ten. Einstein's younger son was schizophrenic and died (at age 55) in a mental hospital.

The Bohrs have eight grandsons and nine granddaughters, Einstein had two grandsons (one died at age six) and, by adoption, one granddaughter. It belongs to my happy memories to have seen Niels sitting on the floor, playing with his grandchildren.

In other personal relations or encounters neither man was swayed by class or rank. Both were quite accessible to men and women from all walks of life, when not busy otherwise. Both were shrewd observers of human nature, always friendly and courteous, but could be sharply critical of people in more private discussions. On general social issues both men spoke up and took action on behalf of the downtrodden. Both personally met numerous leading statesmen of their time, including Winston Churchill and Franklin Roosevelt.

Beginning in 1914, but most especially after World War II, Einstein signed or co-signed numerous politically oriented declarations. Bohr did so

---

* I believe it was meningitis. The boy had to be institutionalized for the rest of his life.

only once, in 1950 (I shall come back to this later (22c)). Both were highly sympathetic, though not uncritically so, to the cause of Israel.

In the foregoing, similarity by and large outweighed disparity. In two respects Bohr and Einstein were extreme opposites, however. To Bohr one and only one place was home: Denmark. Einstein never fully identified with any one country or nation; he would call himself a gypsy, or a bird of passage. He lived in – rather than visited – many places, Germany (Ulm, Munich, Berlin), Switzerland (Aarau, Bern, Zürich), Milan, Prague, and Princeton.

The most striking of all their differences – related in part, perhaps, to their distinct attachments to what constitutes home – was Einstein's apartness, Bohr's conjointness. (The *Oxford English Dictionary* defines: '*Apart*. Away from others in action or function; separately, independently, individually; *Conjoint*. United, combined, associated as a colleague.') Einstein was not a lonely figure. He did have collaborators. Elsewhere[10] I have in fact counted more than thirty of them. Nevertheless it was his deepest need to think separately, to be by himself. Bohr, on the other hand, craved togetherness, in life and in thought. Bohr created a major school; Einstein did not.

All these comments may perhaps be helpful to get some idea of the two personalities. I conclude with similarities which could well be more illuminating than anything written above. Both had a deep need for simplicity, in thought and in behavior. Each had a lifelong boyish – not juvenile, boyish – curiosity, and pleasure in play. They took science very seriously, but to them it was ultimately a game.

(b) First encounters

Bohr had never yet met Einstein when on 26 January 1920 he wrote to the *Videnskabernes Selskab* to propose Einstein as foreign member. On 20 April Einstein replied that he accepted with pleasure.* In that April Bohr went to Berlin. Margrethe stayed home; she was expecting their third child. On the twenty-seventh Bohr gave a lecture on the series spectra of elements.[11] On that visit Bohr met Planck for the first time. Later he recalled: 'I stayed with Planck – he was quite a curious person . . . I was very well prepared [for my lecture] since I had fine slides with spectral lines in color . . . There was a dinner afterward and I sat between Rubens and Sommerfeld. Suddenly Rubens said, "That was an odd experience to be present at such a lecture, because it seemed like a lottery whether the speaker will say *der*, *die*, or

* *Vidensk, Selsk. Protokoll*, Nos. 8451, 8671, 1920.

das,* whereupon Sommerfeld immediately replied, "No, that is quite wrong, there was a distinct preference for the *das*." '[12]

During the year before, Einstein had written to Planck that Ehrenfest was keeping him informed about Bohr's thinking: 'His must be a first-rate mind, extremely critical and far-seeing, which never loses track of the grand design.'[13] Now Planck could see for himself. He was much impressed. Right after Bohr had returned he wrote a 'friendly letter' to Planck which is lost, but of which we know from the reply in which Planck wrote, among other things: 'I can assure you of one thing, and I am quite sincere: the firm conviction which, as I know well, is shared by many of my colleagues, that what we received from you in many respects far exceeds what we could offer you. About myself I know quite accurately that I do not exaggerate. For while it is not given to me to respond with rapidity to intellectual stimuli, I make up for that by intensity. Believe me that many of your remarks continue to give me food for thought.'[14]

From that same visit also dates the first personal encounter between Bohr and Einstein. The latter's fame had reached its zenith by then (as the result of the experimental discovery in 1919 of the bending of light[15]), while Bohr's was still in the ascendant. Einstein was enchanted. Shortly afterward he thanked Bohr by letter[16] for 'the magnificent gift from Neutralia [Denmark] where milk and honey still flow', and continued: 'Not often in life has a person, by his mere presence, given me such joy as you did. I now understand why Ehrenfest loves you so. I am now studying your great papers and in doing so – especially when I get stuck somewhere – I have the pleasure of seeing your youthful face before me, smiling and explaining. I have learned much from you, especially also about your attitude regarding scientific matters.' Bohr replied: 'To me it was one of the greatest experiences ever to meet you and talk with you and I cannot express how grateful I am for all the friendliness with which you met me on my visit to Berlin. You cannot know how great a stimulus it was for me to have the long hoped for opportunity to hear of your views on the questions that have occupied me. I shall never forget our talks on the way from Dahlem [a Berlin suburb] to your home.'[17] In the next section I shall mention Bohr's recollections of the substance of these talks.

Bohr and Einstein met again in August 1920, when Einstein stopped in Copenhagen on his way back from a trip to Norway. Einstein to Lorentz: 'The trip to Kristiania [Oslo] was really beautiful, the most beautiful were the hours I spent with Bohr in Copenhagen. He is a highly gifted and excellent man. It is a good omen for physics that prominent physicists are mostly also splendid people.'[17a] I have not found any comment by Bohr on this visit.

* The German definite article preceding a masculine, feminine, or neuter noun respectively.

The next contact occurred when Bohr wrote[18] to Einstein on the day each had been informed of his Nobel Prize: '. . . The external recognition cannot mean anything to you . . . For me it was the greatest honor and joy . . . that I should be considered for the award at the same time as you. I know how little I have deserved it, but I should like to say that I consider it a good fortune that your fundamental contribution in the special area in which I work [i.e. the quantum theory of radiation, see the next section] as well as contributions by Rutherford and Planck should be recognized before I was considered for such an honor.' As mentioned, Einstein was in Japan at that time. On his way back he answered Bohr's letter from aboard ship somewhere near Singapore: 'I can say without exaggeration that [your letter] pleased me as much as the Nobel Prize. I find especially charming your fear that you might have received the award before me – that is typically Bohr-like [*bohrisch*]. Your new investigations on the atom have accompanied me on the trip, and they have made my fondness for your mind even greater.'[19]

As noted earlier (10f) Einstein was unable to be in Stockholm to receive his prize in person. To make up for that he went to Sweden in 1923, where in July he addressed an audience of about 2000 on 'Basic ideas and problems of the theory of relativity',[20] and afterward had a pleasant chat with King Gustav.[21] These events took place in the city of Göteborg which was celebrating its 300th anniversary. On the way back Einstein visited Bohr in nearby Copenhagen.

Bohr remembered: 'Sommerfeld was not impractical, not quite impractical; but Einstein was not more practical than I and, when he came to Copenhagen, I naturally fetched him from the railway station. Just at that time Margrethe and I lived with my mother because we were counting on moving to the institute and therefore had moved from [our home in] Hellerup. The point was that we took the street car from the station and talked so animatedly about things that we went much too far past our destination. So we got off and went back. Thereafter we again went too far, I can't remember how many stops, but we rode back and forth in the street car because Einstein was really interested at that time; we don't know whether his interest was more or was less skeptical – but in any case we went back and forth many times in the street car and what people thought of us, that is something else.'[12]

So much for starters. In later years Bohr and Einstein did not meet often nor can their correspondence be called extensive. Yet Einstein was to play a singularly important role in Bohr's life, as we shall see later. They were destined to become intellectual antagonists, but that in no way diminished their mutual respect and affection. When Einstein was gone and Bohr had only one more year to live he once said: 'Einstein was so incredibly sweet. I want also to say that now, several years after Einstein's death, I can still see Einstein's smile before me, a very special smile, both knowing, humane, and friendly.'[12]

(c) More on Einstein and the light-quantum

The first time Bohr and Einstein found themselves in scientific opposition goes back to 1924, the final year of the old quantum theory. As will be discussed in the next section, at issue was their difference of opinion concerning the reality of light-quanta. By way of introducing this subject I first briefly recapitulate and extend my earlier remarks on Einstein's thoughts about light-quanta in the days of the old quantum theory.

In 1905 Einstein had proposed[22] (5h) that under certain circumstances monochromatic light with frequency v behaves as if it consists of light-quanta, photons, particle-like objects, with energy E given by $E = hv$. The most widely remembered application of his hypothesis which Einstein made in that paper is to the photoelectric effect, the emission of electrons from a metal surface irradiated by light with (sufficiently high) frequency v. Einstein suggested that this effect arises because a photon transfers all its energy to an electron, thereby knocking it out of an atom inside the metal. The electron will in general suffer an energy loss, call it P, before it reaches the metal's surface. He therefore proposed that upon ejection the electron's energy W is given by the 'photoelectric equation'

$$W = hv - P.$$

Ten years went by before Millikan verified the correctness of this equation. His reaction (1916) to his own result is worthy of note: 'Einstein's photoelectric equation ... appears in every case to predict exactly the observed results ... Yet the semicorpuscular theory by which Einstein arrived at his equation seems at present wholly untenable,'[23] a statement that vividly illustrates the strong opposition (already remarked on in (5h)) at that time to the photon concept. The wave picture of light was still holding sway over the particle picture.

Einstein himself needed no convincing that his light-quanta simply had no place in the wave theory which had been generally adopted since the early nineteenth century. Even before Planck did so himself, he had realized that Planck's radiation law meant that a new kind of physics was called for. 'All my attempts, however, to adapt the theoretical foundations of physics to this [new kind of] knowledge failed completely. It was as if the ground had been pulled out from under one, with no firm foundation to be seen anywhere, upon which one could have built.'[24] Not for nothing did he refer to the light-quantum hypothesis as a 'heuristic point of view' in the very title of his 1905 paper. (*Webster's Dictionary* defines *heuristic* as 'providing aid and direction in the solution of a problem but otherwise unjustified or incapable of justification'.)

In 1909 Einstein made his next comment on the paradoxes posed by light-quanta in a very important paper:*

I already attempted earlier to show that our current foundations of the radiation theory have to be abandoned ... It is my opinion that the next phase in the development of theoretical physics will bring us a theory of light that can be interpreted as a kind of fusion of the wave and the [particle] theory ... [The] wave structure and [the] quantum structure ... are not to be considered as mutually incompatible.[26]

This profound statement foreshadows the fusion achieved in quantum mechanics – the new mechanics so offensive to Einstein's later views.

In 1916 Einstein contributed once again to the quantum theory of radiation, giving his new derivation of Planck's law mentioned in (10c). This work is introduced with encomiums to Planck: 'His derivation is of matchless audacity,' and to Bohr: 'Since the Bohr theory of spectra has achieved its great successes, it seems no longer doubtful that the basic idea of the quantum theory must be maintained.'[27] I have mentioned earlier that these investigations caused Einstein to be troubled by the lack of causality, in particular because his theory (correctly) could not predict the direction in which an individual photon is emitted in an atomic transition. That state of affairs caused him to remark: 'These features of the elementary processes would seem to make the formulation of a proper quantum treatment of radiation almost unavoidable. The weakness of the [present] theory lies in the fact that, on the one hand, no closer connection with the wave concepts is obtainable and that, on the other hand, it leaves to chance [Zufall] the time and the direction of the elementary processes; nevertheless, I have full confidence in the reliability of the road entered upon.'[28]

Bohr, too, quoted these lines, in his 1949 memoir[29] on his discussions with Einstein, adding: 'When I had the great experience of meeting Einstein for the first time during a visit to Berlin in 1920, these fundamental questions formed the theme of our conversations. The discussion, to which I have often reverted in my thoughts, added to all my admiration for Einstein a deep impression of his detached attitudes.'[29]

Years later Bohr enlarged, in informal setting: 'I have reported on [these Berlin] discussions [but] ... that had to be put a little bit courteously. But, with Einstein's sense of humor, one could easily say everything possible to him and I believe I said it like this: I cannot quite understand what it really is he hopes to prove about the quantum theory. Of course it is in a way quite difficult to say something like that in a fair manner since on the one hand it

* This paper deals with energy fluctuations in a subvolume of a cavity filled with thermal radiation. For a discussion of this work, see Ref. 25.

could not have been analyzed more subtly than was done in his famous paper[s] of [1916–17]. On the other hand he himself adds comments in [those papers] which show that he was distressed by it, and that he must have believed that it was too crazy with that [direction of] radiation, even though it was one of the most brilliant strokes of genius, it was almost the decisive point. I believe that I said to him that I did not understand what he was after, because if he were really able to prove that radiation was [i.e. consisted of] particles more or less in the commonly accepted sense, did he then really believe that one could imagine, that he himself could imagine, to see a law passed in Germany which would make it illegal to use diffraction gratings [apparatus to verify the wave nature of light]? Or conversely if he could prove that [light] was wavelike did he then think that one could get the police to stop people from using photocells [apparatus that demonstrates the particle nature of light]? All that was in a way just pleasantry, but the meaning was that I myself felt that one could not decide such an elementary question, a choice between such different pictures, one could imagine that we had really come upon something new, that one must feel one's way further.'[12]

Thus did Bohr reminisce about discussions he had had more than forty years earlier. I can well believe that ideas like these were expressed by Bohr to Einstein, in fact I have witnessed discussions between them that were much in that vein. Yet I find it difficult to accept that in 1920 Bohr would speak about light in the way just reported.

Because in 1920 Bohr did not believe in light-quanta.

(d) 'The culmination of the crisis': the BKS proposal

In his April 1920 Berlin lecture, with Einstein in the audience, Bohr had the following to say[30] about light-quanta: 'I shall not here discuss the familiar difficulties to which the "hypothesis of light-quanta" leads ... *Above all I shall not consider the problem of the nature of radiation* [my italics].' If Bohr had put the particle and the wave picture of light on more or less equal footing in private discussions with Einstein, he was evidently not prepared to do so publicly. In fact he had already begun to look for ways of dispensing with light-quanta altogether.

In a 1921 manuscript[31] Bohr intimated how he intended to proceed: 'Einstein's light-quantum seems to offer the only simple possibility of accounting for ... photoelectric action, if we adhere to an unrestricted application of the notions of conservation of energy and momentum ... [however] the interesting arguments ... by Einstein ... rather than supporting the theory of light-quanta will seem to bring the legitimacy of conservation of energy and momentum to the radiation processes into doubt.' In his 1922 Nobel lecture[32] he said: 'The hypothesis of light-quanta . . . is not able to throw light on the nature of radiation.' In 1923 he was more explicit: 'A general description of phenomena, in which the laws of the conservation of energy and momentum retain in detail their validity in their classical formulation, cannot be carried through . . . the conservation of energy, as defined by means of classical conceptions, seems at once to be excluded.'[33]

Several questions arise.

First, why was Bohr opposed to the photon? Note to begin with that in his earlier work on atomic structure he had discussed emission and absorption of light in atomic transitions without, however, examining the mechanisms for these processes, nor the nature of light itself. Note further that Bohr was but one among numerous leading theoreticians (not to mention experimentalists, such as Millikan) to take a stand against the photon.[34] Their principal common reason was that Maxwell's theory of wave propagation of electromagnetic fields had been thoroughly confirmed by experiment and was considered both as one of the most simple and one of the most solid parts of physical theory. Quantum phenomena had cast doubts on classical theory but, it was widely believed, these had only to do with interactions between matter and radiation – an obscure region of theory in any event – not with radiation itself. Planck in 1907: 'I am not seeking the meaning of the quantum of action in the vacuum, but rather in places where emission and absorption occur, and [I] assume that what happens in the vacuum is rigorously described by Maxwell's equations.'[35] Bohr echoed this view in 1919: 'As regards the wave theory of light I feel inclined to take the often proposed view that the fields in free space . . . are governed by the classical electrodynamical laws and that all difficulties are concentrated on the interaction between electromagnetic forces and matter.'[36]

Secondly, what was the status of the energy conservation principle in 1923, when Bohr put it in doubt? In the domain of macroscopic physics this principle had occupied the status of a fundamental law ever since the mid-nineteenth century.[37] For what follows it is essential to realize, however, that in 1923 this had never yet been experimentally tested at the level of *individual* microscopic processes such as atomic transitions, collisions of electrons with electrons or atoms, etc. As we shall presently see, the first verifications that energy and momentum conservation do hold at the microscopic level date from 1925. To this day these laws are believed to hold strictly.

Thirdly, what good could it possibly do for the theory of light and matter to abandon energy conservation? The answer is that energy non-conservation is inevitable if one were to accept the odd, in fact false, dichotomy held by the anti-photon camp that in emission or absorption of light the energy of material, atomic, systems changes discontinuously, in the quantum way, while the (electromagnetic) energy of light changes continuously, in the classical way.

Bohr was not the first to contemplate energy non-conservation as a means for avoiding light-quanta. Already in 1910 Einstein had briefly toyed with that idea but had rejected it.[38] In 1916 Nernst published an article 'On an attempt to revert from quantum mechanical considerations to the assumption of continuous energy changes',[39] in which he proposed that energy is conserved only statistically, that is, when averaged over an assembly of individual processes of a specific kind. That paper influenced Bohr, as is seen from his unpublished manuscript written in 1917 or 1918: 'It would seem that any theory capable of an explanation of the photoelectric effect as well as interference phenomena must involve a departure from the ordinary theorem of conservation of energy as regards the interaction between radiation and matter. This view has been expressed by several authors and an interesting attempt to build a theory on this basis has been made by Nernst.'[40]

In 1919, Darwin, friend of the Manchester days, wrote[41] to Bohr: 'At present I consider the case against conservation quite overwhelming,' and enclosed a draft manuscript that contains the phrase: 'The proofs of the necessity for contradictions in [classical versus quantum] physics all rest on the exact conservation of energy; some experiments are most simply explained by denying that the conservation is anything more than statistical.'[42] In 1922 Darwin went in print: 'The speculations connected with [the quantum theory] have as their basis the law of conservation of energy ... [however] there seems no reason to maintain the exact conservation of energy.'[43] Also in that year Sommerfeld remarked[44] that the 'mildest cure' for reconciling the wave with the particle picture would be to abandon energy conservation.

The situation changed drastically in 1923, when a crucial high-quality experiment by Arthur Compton[45] 'created a sensation among physicists of that time'.[46] He had observed the 'Compton effect': when light is scattered by electrons, its frequency diminishes by an amount that depends on the angle of scattering. Compton found this change to be in agreement with the predictions (made by himself and independently by Debye[47]) that follow from the assumptions, first, that a light beam behaves as a bundle of light-quanta, secondly, that energy and momentum are conserved in light-quantum–electron scattering.[48] In 1924 Sommerfeld called this result 'probably the most important discovery that could have been made in the current state of physics'.[49] It seemed that the issue of possible non-conservation of energy had been laid to rest.

Bohr, Kramers, and Slater (BKS) thought otherwise, however.

In 1917 Edwin Kemble received a Harvard Ph.D. on what was probably the first doctor's thesis in the United States devoted to quantum theory (spectra of diatomic molecules).[50] He is the only American physicist quoted[51] by Bohr in his 1918 memoir on line spectra. In 1919 he joined the Harvard faculty and at once started teaching quantum theory, at that time 'the most mature and sophisticated course in quantum theory given in the United States'.[52] In 1920 he introduced two fresh graduate students to the new lore, John Slater and John Van Vleck, who both would go far in quantum physics.

In the fall of 1923, after receiving his Harvard Ph.D., Slater went to Europe for further studies. He first spent a few months in Cambridge, where, probably because of Compton's recent discovery, he started thinking about radiation. In November he wrote home: 'You know those difficulties about not knowing whether light is old-fashioned waves or Mr Einstein's light particles . . . I had a really hopeful idea . . . I have both the waves and the particles, and the particles are sort of carried along by the waves, so that the particles go where the waves take them, instead of just shooting in straight lines, as other people assume.' [53] Thus Slater held on both to particles and to waves, the latter being a 'sort of' pilot field that monitors the motion of photons. 'It is . . . the function of the field to determine the paths of quanta, and to specify the probability that they will travel along these paths.' [54] His vision blends continuity, the radiation field, with discontinuity, atomic transitions.[55,56]

Shortly before Christmas, Slater moved on to Copenhagen, filled with his ideas on radiation, which, a few days later, he began to explain to Bohr and Kramers. 'It has gotten them decidedly excited, I think . . . they don't agree with it all . . . but . . . with a good deal . . . Prof. Bohr wanted me to write down [my ideas] and he told Dr Kramers not to talk to me until that was done, and then went and spent all the time talking to me himself.' [57] Disagreement had arisen, obviously because Slater liked light-quanta, and Bohr did not.

Weeks of feverish activity followed. Slater on 6 January 1924: '[I] have come to the conclusion that the part they believe is the only part that really leads to any results anyway . . . So I am willing to let them have their way.' [58] Bohr started to draft a paper. Slater on 13 January: 'The paper he [B.] has written will presumably be published; I haven't seen it yet but will tomorrow.' [59] On 18 January: 'I have finally become convinced that the way they [BK] want things, without the little lump carried along on the waves . . . is better . . . I am going to have a chance at least to suggest changes.' [60] On 22 January: 'That paper is just about done. Prof. Bohr has done all the writing, but it suits me all right.' [61] On 28 January: 'The paper is finally finished and off to the publisher.' [62] I do not know of any other paper carrying Bohr's name that was prepared in such a rush.

Thus did the BKS proposal[63] make its appearance, stimulated by, in Bohr's words, 'the essentially new idea . . . suggested by Slater, a young and very promising American physicist'.[64]

I like to call the BKS paper a proposal rather than a theory because it suggests rather than works out a research program. The paper is obscure in style and contains no mathematical details whatsoever.[65] Since this soon turned out not to be the right direction, I shall only briefly indicate below its main points.* While this work had no lasting influence, it nevertheless deserves its place in history, since, as Heisenberg put it a few years later, 'this investigation represents the actual culmination of the crisis in the [old] quantum theory'.[69] Better than any other contribution it illustrates the tensions and confusions experienced by the best of physicists and adds perspective to the liberation caused by the events of 1925, to be described later.

BKS begin by recalling that 'the exchange of energy and momentum between matter and radiation claims essentially discontinuous features. These have even [!!] led to the introduction of light-quanta . . .' They abandon light-quanta in their own paper, replacing this concept by a new one 'due to Slater . . . the atom, even before the process of transition between stationary states takes place is capable of communicating with distant atoms through a virtual radiation field', a field distinct from the conventional, real, radiation field. This virtual field, carried by the atom in a given stationary state, was supposed to know and carry all the possible transition frequencies to lower states, waiting, one might say, to release one of these frequencies. Emission of light in an atomic transition is, BKS posited, not spontaneous but rather induced by the virtual fields 'by probability laws analogous to those which in Einstein's theory hold for induced transitions'. Accordingly, 'the atom is under no necessity of knowing what transitions it is going to make ahead of time'.[70]

Does communication with a distant atom, the receipt of a light signal emitted by another atom 'even before transition takes place' not violate causality? It does. 'We abandon any attempt at a causal connexion between the transition in distant atoms, and especially a direct application of the principles of conservation of energy and momentum, so characteristic of classical theories . . . Not only conservation of energy . . . but also conservation of momentum [reduce to] a statistical law.' Regarding Compton's results, BKS noted, correctly, that so far his experiments had only confirmed energy–momentum conservation *averaged* over many

---

* Elsewhere I have given a few more details.[66] Klaus Stolzenburg has given the most complete historical account.[67] See also Refs. 56 and 68. These various papers contain additional references.

individual processes, which was not in conflict with their statistical viewpoint.

Let us see how colleagues reacted to these extremely radical steps, relinquishing both causality and energy–momentum conservation. Einstein did not like it at all. 'Abandonment of causality as a matter of principle should be permitted only in the most extreme emergency.' [71] After 1923 he and Bohr did not meet personally until late 1925, when the storm had blown over, nor did they correspond in the meantime;[72] all communication was indirect. A friend wrote to Einstein: 'I was in Copenhagen and talked with Mr Bohr . . . How strange it is that the two of you, in the field where all weaker imaginations and powers of judgement have long ago withered, alone have remained and now stand against each other in deep opposition.' [73] Einstein to Born on abandoning causality: 'In that case I would rather be a cobbler, or even an employee in a gaming house, than a physicist.' [74] To Ehrenfest on abolishing light-quanta: 'They can't be done without.' [75]

Bohr had asked Pauli to find out Einstein's response.[76] Pauli replied by sending a list of counter-arguments Einstein had mentioned to him, and by adding his own attitude: '. . . Completely negative. I was much strengthened in this opinion also because many other physicists, perhaps even most, reject this point of view . . . One cannot prove anything logically and also the available data are not sufficient to decide for or against your view . . . Even if it were psychologically possible for me to form a scientific opinion on the grounds of some sort of belief in authority (which is not the case, however, as you know), this would be logically impossible (at least in this case) since here the opinions of two authorities are so very contradictory.' [76] Born, Klein, and Schrödinger were among those who reacted positively.[77]

In the early months of 1925 two important experiments showed conclusively that BKS had been on the wrong track. Walther Bothe and Hans Geiger developed counter coincidence techniques for the purpose of checking whether in the Compton effect the secondary photon and electron are produced simultaneously, as causality demands. They found[78] that these two particles are both created within a time interval less than 10^{-3} seconds. (Later experiments[79] have cut down this interval to less than 10^{-11} seconds.) Causality had been established and the randomness of the relative moments of creation demanded by BKS disproved.

Compton's and Alfred Simon's studies of the Compton effect in a cloud chamber enabled them to check energy–momentum conservation in *individual* events. They found[80] these laws to be in good order. If BKS had served one good purpose it was to stimulate the *first* experiments in which causality as well as conservation were verified in elementary particle processes.

The experimental news came as a relief to many. 'Einstein was triumphant.'[81] In July 1925 Pauli wrote[82] to Kramers: 'I regard it as a magnificent stroke of luck that the interpretation of [BKS] was so rapidly refuted by [these] beautiful experiments . . . every unprejudiced physicist . . . can now [regard] light-quanta just as much (and just as little) physically real as electrons,' and added, 'It is of course true that Bohr himself, even if these experiments had not been done, would no longer have adhered to this interpretation.' Which brings us to the reactions by B, K, and S.

In April 1925, within days of hearing of the Bothe–Geiger results, Bohr wrote[83] to Darwin: 'It seems . . . that there is nothing else to do than to give our revolutionary efforts as honourable a funeral as possible.' This lighthearted comment should not obscure the fact that the period just past had been difficult for him. In January 1926 he wrote: 'The recent years have been very confusing, and we have at times been close to despair, especially when the hope of describing the radiation phenomena with simple pictures had to be given up after Compton's and Geiger's [experiments]. However it was at the same time very comforting that there is now no longer any reason to doubt the energy principle.'[84]

Kramers' role in the whole episode was most unusual, as we learn from Dresden's biography.[85] From interviews with Kramers' family, friends, and students, Dresden has pieced together strong evidence – which I find convincing – that in the summer of 1921, before Compton's discovery, Kramers had obtained the theory of the Compton effect which, to repeat, is based on light-quanta and conservation principles.* Kramers' wife has recalled that at that time her husband was 'insanely excited . . . Bohr and Kramers immediately started a series of daily no holds barred arguments . . . After these discussions which left Kramers exhausted, depressed, and let down, [he] got sick and spent some time in hospital.' Dresden adds that thereafter 'Kramers did not merely acquiesce to Bohr's views; he made Bohr's views his own . . . [afterward] Kramers and Bohr were scientifically closer, more in tune with each other, than before'. Kramers' writings of 1923 unequivocally show his conversion: 'The theory of light-quanta may . . . be compared with medicine which will cause the disease to vanish but kill the patient . . . The fact must be emphasized that this theory in no way has sprung from the Bohr theory, to say nothing of its being a necessary consequence of it.'[86]

Slater's first response (July 1925) was to publish a letter[87] in which he remarked that 'under their [BK] suggestion I became persuaded' to give up light-quanta and that now 'the simplest solution of the radiation problem then seems to be to return to the view of the virtual field to guide corpuscular quanta'. In January 1926 Bohr wrote to Slater: 'I have a bad

* Dresden is careful to note that he has no documentary evidence. The matter never came up during the many discussions I had with Kramers in the 1940s and 1950s.

conscience in persuading you to our views.'[88] In May Slater replied: 'You need not have a bad conscience.'[89]

Almost forty years went by before Slater openly expressed his towering resentment about his Copenhagen days. 'I was in favor of exact conservation . . . I agreed that we didn't have any good evidence on the existence of photons, I was willing to knock the photons, I didn't care too much . . . I liked Kramers quite well . . . but in this respect he was being Bohr's man . . . Kramers was always Bohr's yes-man and wanted to do exactly the same thing . . . The changes they made I didn't like, but I didn't see that I could fight against them . . . I completely failed to make connection with Bohr . . . I've never had any respect for Mr Bohr since . . . I had a horrible time in Copenhagen.'[90] Similar remarks are found in Slater's later autobiography.[91] One might better understand this rancor if it had turned out to be true – it did not – that virtual fields indeed guide photons, and if Slater had not gone on to make a distinguished career of his own in quantum mechanics.

Kramers' and Slater's responses underline that it was not always easy for younger people to cope with the immense power of Bohr's personality. Once Bohr and I talked about a similar but distinct event when a senior theoretical physicist had talked a younger colleague out of publishing a result that later turned out to be correct and important. When I remarked that this was a sad story, Bohr literally rose and said: 'No, the young man was a fool.' (That is verbatim.) He explained that one should simply never be talked out of anything that one is convinced of. That, of course, is sometimes easier said than done. But I shall never forget Bohr's comment which I have tried to live by in later years, as well as I could.

(e) The new era dawns: de Broglie

Early in 1925, when Bohr still believed in BKS, it occurred to him that the new view on the interaction between light and atoms might perhaps also apply to collisions between atoms. Barely a few weeks before he heard of the Bothe–Geiger results he submitted a paper on that subject: 'On the behavior of atoms in collisions'.[92] The article did appear, but after experiments had put an end to BKS. Bohr had time, however, to insert an addendum (July 1925)[93] in which he was able to comment on the changed situation: 'In this state of affairs one must be prepared to find that the generalization of the classical electrodynamic theory that we are striving for will require a fundamental revolution in the concepts upon which the description of nature has been based until now.' Toward the end of the addendum he noted: 'The renunciation of space-time pictures is characteristic of the formal treatment of problems of the radiation theory and of the mechanical theory of heat attempted in recent papers by de Broglie and Einstein.'

The fundamental revolution had begun.

On 10 September 1923 Louis de Broglie from Paris submitted a paper[94] the thrust of which went in a direction diametrically opposite to BKS. Where Bohr wanted to exclude light-quanta as particles and stick to waves, de Broglie, inspired by Einstein's particle–wave duality for light (see the preceding section (c)), proposed that matter too, specifically electrons, should under suitable circumstances, not behave like the familiar particles but like never yet suggested waves. 'After long reflection in solitude and meditation, I suddenly had the idea, during the year 1923, that the discovery made by Einstein in 1905 should be generalized by extending it to all material particles and notably to electrons.'[95]

In his 10 September paper de Broglie assigned to an electron a 'fictitious associated wave' with frequency v and wavelength λ (the 'de Broglie wavelength') given by $E = hv$ and $p = h/\lambda$, where E and p are the electron's energy and momentum respectively. He further assumed that, when an electron moves around in an atom, its associated wave is stationary, just like a wave moving along a frictionless violin string held fixed at its end points. As is familiar from acoustics such a string can only produce certain specific frequencies, that is, notes: the fundamental tone, the lowest possible frequency, and the overtones, with higher frequencies, in all *a discrete set of frequencies*. Likewise, de Broglie asserted, the frequencies of the associated waves in the atom should take on discrete frequencies only. Hence, from $E = hv$, the electron's energy is quantized!!

Two weeks later de Broglie published another paper,[96] in which he indicated how one 'should seek experimental confirmation of our ideas': a bundle of electrons traversing an aperture whose dimensions are small compared with the de Broglie wavelength 'should show diffraction phenomena'.

In this second paper de Broglie also made an analogy often used since. There are two versions of *classical* optics: the ancient, still useful, Newtonian geometrical optics where one overlooks interference and diffraction phenomena and approximates light paths by straight lines altered only by reflection and refraction; and the more fully fledged wave optics which includes all light phenomena. de Broglie suggested that

The new [de Br.] *dynamics of the free material point (including Einstein's) stands to the old* [classical] *dynamics as wave optics to geometrical optics* [his italics].

de Broglie extended his two articles to form his doctoral thesis,[95] which he defended in November. After Einstein had received and read an advance copy of this thesis[97] he wrote[98] to Lorentz: 'I believe it is a first feeble ray of light on this worst of our physics enigmas.'

It took longer for de Broglie's ideas to be noticed in Denmark. Slater has recalled: 'None of us in Copenhagen in the spring of 1924 had known of the work of Louis de Broglie in Paris ... His main publications did not reach general attention until early 1925 . . . Even in 1925 they were not common knowledge.' [99]

Two final comments. In his addendum Bohr mentioned not only de Broglie but also Einstein. The reason was this. In 1924 Einstein had turned his attention to a quantum version of statistical physics. I have discussed elsewhere[100] the important new conclusions to which that work led him. Here I recall only the point he made that bears on de Broglie. As indicated in the preceding section (c), in 1909 Einstein had expressed the opinion that the future of radiation theory lay in a fusion of the particle with the wave theory. Now, early in 1925, he was led[101] by similar reasonings to anticipate the very same kind of fusion for the theory of matter. In his paper[102] he acknowledged 'a very notable contribution' by de Broglie. His and de Broglie's roads to duality for the case of matter were quite distinct, however.

It is perhaps most proper to consider de Broglie as the forerunner rather than the creator of the new 'wave mechanics', a subject with which we shall deal before long. As de Broglie wrote in 1970: 'I did not have any doubts at that time [1923] about the physical reality of the wave and the localization of the particle in the wave.' [103] This statement evokes a picture of the wave piloting the particle on its course – just like Slater had imagined the relation between the radiation field and the photon to be. All through his life de Broglie would continue, unsuccessfully, to try and make sense of his wave as an *onde pilote* (to use his own term). That, however, is not the right way of looking at things, as we shall see.

(f) Spin

On 20 November 1925 there appeared[104] a one-page letter to the Editor of *Naturwissenschaften* signed by two young Dutchmen from Leiden, George Uhlenbeck, who had a master's degree in physics, and Samuel Goudsmit, a graduate student. It contains the correct interpretation of Sommerfeld's 'hidden rotation' (10d), which, earlier that year, had been traced by Pauli to an intrinsic two-valuedness of the electron (same section). After Goudsmit, already an expert in atomic spectroscopy, had explained these developments to Uhlenbeck, the latter had a great idea: 'It was then that it occurred to me that since (as I had learned) each quantum number corresponds to a degree of freedom of the electron, the fourth quantum number must mean that the electron had an additional degree of freedom – in other words, the electron must be rotating.' [105]

I have discussed this discovery elsewhere in detail.[106] If I repeat here just a few of these earlier remarks it is to recall Bohr's role in these events. If I do so at this point it is because the work of Uhlenbeck and Goudsmit is entirely

in the spirit of the old quantum theory, even though the new quantum
mechanics had already arrived a few months earlier.

Our two Dutchmen pictured the electron classically as a small sphere
that rotates around an intrinsic axis while orbiting the nucleus, similar to
the earth–sun system. Furthermore the electron should carry an intrinsic
magnetic moment. They imposed two quantum restrictions on the electron's rotation: the corresponding angular momentum, the spin, shall have
the unique value $\frac{1}{2} h/2\pi$; and this spin can have only two orientations in an
external magnetic field, either parallel or antiparallel. Spin, they showed,
explains the anomalous Zeeman effect, provided that the ratio of the
electron's magnetic moment to its spin shall be twice as large as the same
ratio of the magnetic moment and the angular momentum due to the
electron's orbital motion. That curious extra factor two would remain
unexplained until 1926.

Uhlenbeck and Goudsmit concluded their Letter by conjecturing that the
two possible spin orientations might explain the fine structure of hydrogen
and alkali spectra. This guess needs clarification since, as mentioned before
(10b), as early as 1916 Sommerfeld had given a good explanation of fine
structure in terms of the precession of electron orbits. We have seen that
this relativistic effect caused the hydrogen levels to depend both on the
principal quantum number n and the auxiliary quantum number k; and that
in atomic transitions k was allowed to change by ± 1 only (10c).

What had looked so good in 1916 did no longer look quite right in 1925,
however, as Sommerfeld himself meanwhile had acknowledged.[107] Two
examples: the doublet splitting of a hydrogen line in the red so-called
H_{α}-line was found to be smaller than predicted; and there occurred a fine
structure line (called the 4686 line) in the spectrum of ionized helium that
violated the selection rule for k.[108]

To give the punch line right away: half a year later the conjecture that
spin provides the needed remedies turned out to be correct. Two puzzles
needed resolution, however, before the right answers could be obtained.

First, the spin can couple to a magnetic field. This yields an additional
precession of electron orbits. But, so it seemed, in a free atom there is only
an electrostatic field so the spin has nothing to couple to. As we shall see in a
moment, this caused Bohr initially to doubt the spin idea. Secondly, after
that question was resolved, it appeared, initially and incorrectly, that the
angular velocity of precession (due to spin) of the hydrogen orbit was too
large by a factor 2 to account for the experimental data.[109]

These matters were still unresolved when in December 1925 Bohr arrived
in Leiden to attend the festivities for the golden jubilee of Lorentz's
doctorate. One evening in 1946, the hour was late, Bohr told me in his home
in Gamle Carlsberg what happened to him on that trip.*

---

* The next two paragraphs are taken from Ref. 110.

Bohr's train to Leiden made a stop in Hamburg, where he was met by Pauli and Stern who had come to the station to ask him what he thought about spin. Bohr must have said that it was very very interesting (his favorite way of expressing his belief that something was wrong), but he could not see how an electron moving in the electric field of the nucleus could experience the magnetic field necessary for producing fine structure. (As Uhlenbeck said later: 'I must say in retrospect that Sem and I in our euphoria had not really appreciated [this] basic difficulty.' [105]) On his arrival in Leiden, Bohr was met at the train by Ehrenfest and Einstein who asked him what he thought about spin. Bohr must have said that it was very very interesting but what about the magnetic field? Ehrenfest replied that Einstein had resolved that. The electron in its rest frame sees a rotating electric field; hence by elementary relativity it also sees a magnetic field. Bohr was at once convinced. (Bohr, later, to Kronig: 'This remark acted as a complete revelation to me, and I have never since faltered in my conviction that we at last were at the end of our sorrows.' [111]) When told of the factor 2 he expressed confidence that this problem would find a natural resolution. He urged Goudsmit and Uhlenbeck to write a more detailed note on their work. They did.[112] Bohr added an approving comment.[113]

After Leiden Bohr traveled to Göttingen. There he was met at the station by Heisenberg and Jordan who asked what he thought about spin. Bohr replied that it was a great advance and explained about the magnetic field. Heisenberg remarked that he had heard this comment before but that he could not remember who made it and when. On his way home the train stopped at Berlin where Bohr was met at the station by Pauli, who had made the trip from Hamburg for the sole purpose of asking Bohr what he now thought about spin. Bohr said it was a great advance, to which Pauli replied: 'eine neue Kopenhagener Irrlehre' (a new Copenhagen heresy). After his return home Bohr wrote to Ehrenfest that he had become 'a prophet of the electron magnet gospel'.[114]

Finally, on 20 February 1926 Bohr wrote[115] almost identical letters to Heisenberg and to Pauli: 'We have felt it as a minor triumph . . . that at least the difficulties with the much discussed factor two seem to be only apparent . . . Thomas, a young Englishman who has been here the last six months . . . has discovered that the calculations made so far probably contain an error.' Llewellyn Thomas had noted[116] that earlier calculations of the precession of the electron spin had been performed in the rest frame of the electron, without taking into account the precession of the electron orbit around its normal. Inclusion of this relativistic effect reduces the angular velocity of the electron by the needed factor $\frac{1}{2}$.

Now, still within the framework of the old quantum theory, all the pieces could be put together. Combine the Sommerfeld precession (of 1916) with the Thomas precession (of 1926). The result: *Still* Sommerfeld's old fine structure formula *but* with k replaced by $j+\frac{1}{2}$ where j is the total (orbital plus spin) angular momentum. Moreover, the selection rule $\Delta k = \pm 1$ is to be replaced by $\Delta j = 0, \pm 1$.

Now hear this. With these changes, all good results of the old Sommerfeld formula are retained and all earlier difficulties disappear. In the case of the H_α-line, a transition forbidden in the old scheme is now allowed, resulting in a fine structure line lying between two others. This explains the too-small doublet splitting alleged earlier. The mysterious 4686 line in helium, forbidden in the old scheme, is now allowed. Amazing.

In March 1926 Kramers received a letter from America written[117] by Ralph Kronig, a young Columbia University Ph.D. who had spent two years studying in Europe, including a stay in Copenhagen from January to November 1925. Kronig reminded Kramers that, prior to Goudsmit and Uhlenbeck, he, Kronig, already had the idea of spin, though he too was missing the factor 2 in the fine structure; and that he and Kramers had discussed these matters in Copenhagen. Heisenberg's hazy recollection, mentioned a few lines earlier, of having heard part of the spin story before must refer to a discussion with Kronig. Returning to Kronig's letter, he told Kramers that he had not published because 'Pauli ridiculed the idea, saying "that is indeed very clever but of course has nothing to do with reality".' And added: 'In the future I shall trust my own judgement more and that of others less.'

After Kramers had told this story to Bohr, the latter wrote to Kronig, expressing his 'consternation and deep regret'.[111] Kronig replied: 'I should not have mentioned the matter at all [to Kramers] if it were not to take a fling at the physicists of the preaching variety, who are always so damned sure of, and inflated with, the correctness of their own opinion.'[118] He asked Bohr to refrain from public reference to the affair since 'Goudsmit and Uhlenbeck would hardly be very happy about it'. Kronig is an eminent physicist and a gentleman. So is Uhlenbeck who has written: 'There is no doubt that Ralph Kronig anticipated what certainly was the main part of our ideas.'[105]

References

1. See SL, Chap. 16, section (a).
2. A. Einstein, letter to P. Ehrenfest, 26 December 1915.
3. See SL, p. 477.
4. A. Einstein, quoted in the *New York Times*, 25 April 1929.
5. Elisabeth Bergner, *Bewundert und viel gescholten*, p. 212, C. Bertelsmann, Munich 1978.
6. F. C. Hoyt, interviewed by T. S. Kuhn, 28 April 1964, NBA.
7. SL, p. 41.

8. See *Albert Einstein–Michele Besso correspondance 1903–1955*, p. 537, Ed. P. Speziali, Hermann, Paris 1972.

9. See *The collected papers of Albert Einstein*, Vol. 1, Ed. J. Stachel, Princeton University Press 1987.

10. SL, Chap. 29.

11. English transl. CW, Vol. 3, p. 241.

12. N. Bohr interviewed in Tisvilde by A. Bohr and L. Rosenfeld, 12 July 1961, NBA.

13. A. Einstein, postcard to M. Planck, 23 October 1919, SL, p. 416.

14. M. Planck, letter to N. Bohr, 7 May 1920, CW, Vol. 3, p. 677.

15. SL. Chap. 16, section (b).

16. A. Einstein, letter to N. Bohr, 2 May 1920, CW, Vol. 3, 22, 634.

17. N. Bohr, letter to A. Einstein, 2 May 1920, CW, Vol. 3, 22, 634.

17a. A. Einstein, letter to H. A. Lorentz, 4 August 1920, Lorentz Archive Leiden, copy in NBA; see also *Albert Einstein in Berlin 1913–1933*, Vol. 1, p. 226, Eds. C. Kristen and H. J. Treder, Akad. Verl., Berlin 1979.

18. N. Bohr, letter to A. Einstein, 11 November 1922, CW, Vol. 4, 28, 685.

19. A. Einstein, letter to N. Bohr, 11 January 1923, CW, Vol. 4, 28, 686.

20. A. Einstein, *Grundgedanken und Probleme der Relativitätstheorie*, Imprimerie Royale, Stockholm 1923.

21. SL, p. 504.

22. A. Einstein, *Ann. der Phys.* **17**, 132, 1905. This paper is analyzed in detail in SL, Chap. 19, sections (c) and (e), the responses by others are discussed *ibid.*, section (f).

23. R. A. Millikan, *Phys. Rev.* **7**, 18, 1916.

24. A. Einstein, autobiographical sketch, in *Albert Einstein: philosopher-scientist*, Ed. P. Schilpp, Tudor, New York 1949.

25. SL, Chap. 21, section (a).

26. A. Einstein, *Phys. Zeitschr.* **10**, 817, 1909; see also *ibid.* **10**, 185, 1909.

27. A. Einstein, *Verh. Deutsch. Phys. Ges.* **18**, 318, 1916.

28. A. Einstein, *Phys. Zeitschr.* **18**, 121, 1917.

29. N. Bohr, in Ref. 24, p. 205.

30. N. Bohr, *Zeitschr. Phys.* **2**, 423, 1920, English transl. in CW, Vol. 3, p. 242; see esp. p. 244.

31. N. Bohr, unpublished MS, 1921, CW, Vol. 3, p. 397, esp. pp. 412, 413. The same idea, but stated less explicitly, is found in his Solvay report, CW, Vol. 3, p. 374.

32. N. Bohr, *Nature* **112**, 29, 1923, CW, Vol. 4, p. 467.

33. N. Bohr, *Zeitschr. Phys.* **13**, 117, 1923, English transl. in CW, Vol. 3, p. 457; esp. Chap. III.

34. Cf. SL, Chap. 19, section (f).

35. M. Planck, letter to A. Einstein, 6 July 1907, Einstein Archives.

36. N. Bohr, draft of a letter to C. G. Darwin, July 1919, CW, Vol. 5, p. 15.

37. Cf. IB, Chap. 6, section (b).

38. SL, p. 418.

39. W. Nernst, *Verh. Deutsch. Phys. Ges.* **18**, 83, 1916.

40. N. Bohr, Principles of the quantum theory, unpublished MS, CW, Vol. 5, p. 15.
41. C. G. Darwin, letter to N. Bohr, 20 July 1919, CW, Vol. 5, p. 314.
42. CW, Vol. 5, p. 14.
43. C. G. Darwin, *Nature* **110**, 841, 1922.
44. A. Sommerfeld, *Atombau und Spektrallinien*, 3rd edn, p. 311, Vieweg, Braunschweig 1922.
45. A. H. Compton, *Phys. Rev.* **21**, 483, 1923.
46. S. K. Allison, *Biogr. Mem. Nat. Acad. Sci.* **38**, 81, 1965.
47. P. Debye, *Phys. Zeitschr.* **24**, 161, 1923.
48. SL, Chap. 21, section (f). For a detailed history see R. H. Stuewer, *The Compton effect*, Science History, New York 1975.
49. Ref. 44, 4th edn, p. VIII.
50. For more on Kemble see K. Sopka, *Quantum physics in America 1920–1935*, Arno Press, New York 1980.
51. CW, Vol. 3, p. 82.
52. J. H. Van Vleck, quoted by Ph. Morse in *Biogr. Mem. Nat. Acad. Sci.* **53**, 297, 1982.
53. J. C. Slater, letter to his family, 8 November 1923. This and further letters are found in 'Excerpts from personal letters and records on visit to Copenhagen in spring of 1924,' deposited in the Library of the American Philosophical Society, Philadelphia. In Refs. 54 and 57–62 this source will be quoted as 'Excerpts'.
54. Excerpts.
55. Cf. J. C. Slater, *Nature* **113**, 307, 1924.
56. Slater's ideas are described in much more detail by H. Konno, *J. Hist. Sci. Soc. Japan*, **25**, 39, 1983.
57. J. C. Slater, letter to his family, 2 January 1924, Excerpts.
58. J. C. Slater, letter to his family, 6 January 1924, Excerpts.
59. J. C. Slater, letter to his family, 13 January 1924, Excerpts.
60. J. C. Slater, letter to his family, 18 January 1924, Excerpts.
61. J. C. Slater, letter to his family, 22 January 1924, Excerpts.
62. J. C. Slater, letter to his family, 28 January 1924, Excerpts.
63. N. Bohr, H. A. Kramers, and J. C. Slater, *Phil. Mag.* **47**, 785, 1924, repr. in CW, Vol. 5, p. 99. German transl.: *Zeitschr. Phys.* **34**, 69, 1924.
64. N. Bohr, letter to A. A. Michelson, 7 February 1924, CW, Vol. 5, p. 10.
65. A later paper by Slater completed in December 1924, *Phys. Rev.* **25**, 395, 1925, is clearer. See also R. Becker, *Zeitschr. Phys.* **27**, 173, 1924.
66. SL, Chap. 22; IB, Chap. 14, section (a).
67. CW, Vol. 5, pp. 3–96, see also N. H. Wasserman, Ph.D. thesis, Harvard University, June 1981.
68. M. Klein, *Hist. Stud. Phys. Sci.* **2**, 1, 1970.
69. W. Heisenberg, *Naturw.* **17**, 490, 1929.
70. J. C. Slater, Ref. 65.
71. Undated document in the Einstein Archives, obviously written in 1924.
72. A. Einstein, letter to K. Joel, 3 November 1924, Einstein Archives.
73. F. Haber, letter to A. Einstein in 1924, undated, repr. in CW, Vol. 5, p. 26.

74. A. Einstein, letter to M. Born, 29 April 1924, repr. in *A. Einstein–M. Born Briefwechsel,* p. 118, Nymphenburger Verlag, Munich 1969.
75. A. Einstein, letter to P. Ehrenfest, 12 July 1924.
76. W. Pauli, letter to N. Bohr, 2 October 1924, CW, Vol. 5, p. 418.
77. CW, Vol. 5, pp. 24, 29, 30.
78. W. Bothe and H. Geiger, *Naturw.* **13**, 440, 1925; *Zeitschr. Phys.* **32**, 639, 1925.
79. A. Bay, V. P. Henri, and F. McLennon, *Phys. Rev.* **97**, 1710, 1950.
80. A. H. Compton and A. W. Simon, *Phys. Rev.* **26**, 289, 1925.
81. M. Born, letter to N. Bohr, 15 January 1925, CW, Vol. 5, p. 302.
82. W. Pauli, letter to H. A. Kramers, 27 July 1925, CW, Vol. 5, p. 442.
83. N. Bohr, letter to C. G. Darwin, 21 April 1925, CW, Vol. 5, p. 81.
84. N. Bohr, letter to S. Rosseland, 6 January 1926, CW, Vol. 5, p. 484.
85. M. Dresden, *H. A. Kramers*, esp. Chap. 14, Springer, New York 1987.
86. H. A. Kramers and H. Holst, *The atom and the Bohr theory of its structure,* p. 175, Gyldendal, Copenhagen 1923.
87. J. C. Slater, *Nature* **116**, 278, 1925.
88. N. Bohr, letter to J. C. Slater, 28 January 1926, CW, Vol. 5, p. 497.
89. J. C. Slater, letter to N. Bohr, 27 May 1926, CW, Vol. 5, p. 499.
90. J. C. Slater, interviewed by T. S. Kuhn and J. H. Van Vleck, 3 October 1963, NBA.
91. J. C. Slater, *Solid state and molecular theory: A scientific biography*, Wiley, New York 1975.
92. N. Bohr, *Zeitschr. Phys.* **34**, 142, 1925, English transl. in CW, Vol. 5, p. 194.
93. CW, Vol. 5, p. 204.
94. L. de Broglie, *C. R. Acad Sci. Paris* **177**, 507, 1923.
95. L. de Broglie, preface to his reedited Ph.D. thesis, *Recherches sur la théorie des quanta*, Masson, Paris 1963.
96. L. de Broglie, *C. R. Acad. Sci. Paris* **177**, 548, 1923.
97. For the role of Einstein in the acceptance of de Broglie's thesis see SL, Chap. 24.
98. A. Einstein, letter to H. A. Lorentz, 16 December 1924.
99. Ref. 91, pp. 12, 13.
100. SL, Chap. 23.
101. SL, Chap. 24.
102. A. Einstein, *Sitz. Ber. Preuss Ak. der Wiss.* 1925, p. 3.
103. L. de Broglie, *Found. Phys.* **1**, 5, 1970.
104. G. E. Uhlenbeck and S. A. Goudsmit, *Naturw.* **13**, 953, 1925.
105. G. E. Uhlenbeck, *Physics Today* **29**, June 1976, pp. 43, 45.
106. IB, Chap. 13, section (c).
107. A. Sommerfeld, *Zeitschr. Physik* **5**, 1, 1921.
108. Cf. the review by L. Janicki and E. Lau, *Zeitschr. Phys.* **35**, 1, 1925; also W. Houston, *Nature* **117**, 590, 1926.
109. This calculation is reproduced in L. Pauling and S. Goudsmit, *The structure of line spectra*, p. 58, McGraw Hill, New York 1930. In November 1925 the factor 2 was already known to Heisenberg, see his letter to S. Goudsmit of 21 November 1925, repr. in S. Goudsmit, *Delta* **15**, p. 77, summer 1972.
110. IB, pp. 278, 279.

111. N. Bohr, letter to R. de L. Kronig, 26 March 1926, CW, Vol. 5, p. 234.

112. G. E. Uhlenbeck and S. Goudsmit, *Nature* **117**, 264, 1926, repr. in CW, Vol. 5, p. 288.

113. N. Bohr, *Nature* **117**, 265, 1926, CW, Vol. 5, p. 289.

114. N. Bohr, letter to P. Ehrenfest, 22 December 1925, CW, Vol. 5, p. 329.

115. N. Bohr, letters of 20 February 1926, to Heisenberg: CW, Vol. 5, p. 372, to Pauli: CW, Vol. 5, p. 462.

116. L. H. Thomas, *Nature* **117**, 514, 1926; *Phil. Mag.* **3**, 1, 1927.

117. R. de L. Kronig, letter to H. A. Kramers, 6 March 1926, CW, Vol. 5, p. 233.

118. R. de L. Kronig, letter to N. Bohr, 8 April 1926, CW, Vol. 5, p. 236.

12

'A modern Viking who comes on a great errand'

(a) Bohr & Sons

Having traced the growth of Niels Bohr's physics up to 1925, roughly the midpoint of his life, I write next of the growths of his family, of his stature in the international world of science, and of his institute up to that time.

I have already mentioned the arrival of the Bohr's first son, Christian, in 1916. Five more sons followed, Hans Henrik (born in 1918), Erik (1920), Aage Niels (1922), Ernest David (1924, named after both Rutherford and Niels' maternal grandfather), and Harald (1928).

As of the early 1920s the family occupied the residential quarters in the top two floors of the institute's one and only building. In 1924 Bohr acquired a property (still owned by the family) in Tisvilde on Sjaelland, forty miles northwest of Copenhagen, close to the seashore. It was an old gamekeeper's home, a thatched one story house named *Lynghuset*, the heather house. It stands in a forest grove of scattered high pines on heather-covered hilly grounds. It was an untouched landscape then (no more so, alas) that attracted artists, among them the painters Julius Paulsen and William Scharff, the poet Hans Hartvig Seedorff, and the pianists Victor and Dagmar Bendix, all of whom became good and stimulating friends of the Bohr family.[1]

Close to but separate from the Bohr house there stands a small one-room cottage, *Pavillonen*, the pavillion, ideal for undisturbed work. In the beginning there were only paraffin lamps. Electric light came later, telephone connections later still. Here the family spent summer vacations and shorter stays. 'In this beautiful area that he loved so much [Bohr] found rest and recreation'[2] – and time to do more work. 'Many young scientists . . . also came out to Tisvilde with us in the summer, and in their intervals of their work [with Bohr] they took part in [the sons'] games and sport.'[2] Bohr himself also found time 'for a bicycle ride in the woods, bathing from the beach, and ball games, at which he was very skilled up to late in life.'[2] I was fortunate to be one of those young scientists, spending several months in the country with the Bohr family at one time. During that period I was witness to the strong and happy ties between parents and children.

That was in 1946, when the boys had grown to men in their twenties. Conversations with the sons have given me a picture of family life in earlier years. I found further details in three sketches written by Hans, respectively on the occasion of his father's seventieth birthday,[3] for a memorial volume published shortly after Niels' death,[2] and for the 1985 centenary of his birth.[4]

'Father always took an interest in us and from the beginning tried to teach us something about the things he himself liked best and thought important . . . The dinner table was generally a meeting place at which my father was eager to hear what each of us had done, and to tell us what he had done . . . He was no doubt not a teacher in the accepted sense of the word . . . but if you were patient and listened, a wide and rich perspective opened up . . . he was nearly always preoccupied with one problem or another . . . he always wanted to include us and every time he put forward the problem he elaborated his ideas . . . When our friends came to see us, my father was eager to get to know them and to hear their opinions . . . My mother was the natural and indispensable center. Father knew how much mother meant to him and never missed an opportunity to show his gratitude and love[2] . . . Her opinions were his guideline in daily affairs.'[3] Margrethe was the stricter and more disciplining of the two.

'There were memorable evenings when we, together with neighbors, played poker for fun. My father had a good talent at bluffing[4] . . . Among our best memories are the evenings when father read aloud. [He] had a profound sense of poetry . . . although it was humor and subtlety that appealed most to him.'[2] Bohr liked to illustrate subtlety by a story about his great-grandfather, the schoolteacher Peter Georg Bohr, who once explained to his class the text 'He that seteth his hand to the plough and looketh back'. That means, he said, that you must be guided by ancient wisdom. A student raised his hand and objected; the text said: '. . . and looketh not back'. 'Of course,' replied Peter Bohr, 'it means that you must move on without being constrained by the past.' To which Niels used to add that this was an example of deep truth, a statement just as true as its opposite, in contradistinction to a triviality, the opposite of which is false; and that it was the task of science to reduce deep truths to trivialities.

Bohr was fond of posing little puzzles, to the children or to others. One (I have seen him do this) went like this. Take a fork, hold it vertically, teeth up. Pinch the outer teeth tightly between two fingers. Let go with the fingers, hold those tight together, and move them to a nearby glass. Open the fingers inside the glass and you will hear the sound carried by the fingers from the fork into the glass. How come? (The answer is found in Ref. 5; try it.)

Bohr always liked to do things with his hands. 'When anything broke he could almost always repair it in such an effective way that it lasted.'[1] Other favorite manual activities included felling trees in Tisvilde. 'Each one [of the children] had his allotted task to perform, with axe or saw or pulling, and my father preferably took part in everything from the felling itself to stacking the logs.'[2]

The children got to know the visiting scientists. 'Memories of our childhood are linked with many "uncles", among them Uncle Kramers, Uncle Klein, Uncle Hevesy, and Uncle Heisenberg.'[2]

Teasing belonged to the style of the family. When Niels was the target he would say: 'You never can make me a bigger fool than I am in my own eyes.'[4] When frictions arose Bohr would only rarely hand out a smack. More often he would quote a dictum he was fond of: 'It is not enough to be wrong, one must also be polite.'

To conclude, on the occasion of Niels' seventieth birthday, Hans wrote: 'Father's horizons are wide and his sky is high and not closed off but always open for broad views and for harmony.'[3] Shortly after his death: 'We miss his counsel and support. However great he was as a scientist and however profound his insight into life itself, for us it was as a human being that he was the greatest.'[2] And in 1985: 'He was always an optimist who never lost his faith in the future of mankind.'[4]

(b) International recognition

Bohr was in his mid-thirties when he began to receive a veritable stream of international honors, demands from abroad for lectures, and offers of professorships outside Denmark.

Among his awards up to 1930 were the Goldberg medal of the University of Kristiania (Oslo) (1918), the Hughes medal of the Royal Society, London (1921), the Nobel Prize (1922), the Barnard medal of Columbia University (1925), the Matteucci medal of the Italian Society of Science, the Franklin medal (1926), the Planck medal, and the Faraday medal (1930). At home Bohr received the Ørsted medal in 1924, with the explanation[6] that one had waited giving him this award until a special occasion, the centenary meeting of the Selskab for Naturlærens Udbredelse which (as mentioned earlier) Ørsted had founded.

Also in that period Bohr was elected foreign member in the National Academies of Finland, Holland, Norway, Sweden (1923), the Lincei in Rome (1924), the US, the USSR, Austria, England (the Royal Society) (1925); and received honorary degrees from Cambridge and Liverpool (1923), Manchester (1925), Oxford (1926), Edinburgh, and Kiel (1929).

In that period the first offer of a foreign professorship came from Berlin.

The year after his first visit there Planck wrote[7] to him: 'Among us colleagues the idea has arisen whether it might not be possible, one way or another, to have you here for longer periods ... We are thinking that you might be elected member of the *Akademie der Wissenschaften* and obtain a salaried position of the kind Einstein has, who is entirely free to pursue his scientific work and ideas, with the right (but not the obligation) to lecture at the University and to make use of the scientific institutes.[8] As far as we can see such a plan can be realized ... We would consider it a privilege and a gain of the very first rank for our science.' Bohr replied: 'I cannot find the words to express what it would mean to me to be together on a daily basis with you and Einstein and other prominent colleagues.'[9] A Berlin position would have had numerous advantages for him, closer contact with other leading men of science, much improved financial conditions, freedom from administrative and teaching duties. Nevertheless he declined, citing his deep sense of obligation to his own Danish enterprise.

Next, in 1923, Bohr heard from Jeans: 'A Royal Society Committee has been appointed with the duty to recommend to Council names for appointment to our newly created Professorships ... It is the intention of the Royal Society to pick out only the very ablest men and to give them every possible freedom which is reasonably possible.'[10] The offer included a salary three times Bohr's present one, grants for apparatus and assistance, and a free choice of laboratory in England to be attached to. 'Rutherford explained that he would very gladly do his best for you at Cambridge.'[10] Rutherford, who in 1919 had moved from Manchester to Cambridge to succeed J. J. Thomson as Director of the Cavendish Laboratory, himself also wrote[11] to Bohr: 'You will have heard from Jeans that the Royal Society offers you the first of the Yarrow Professorships ... everybody who counts ... would be delighted to have you come to Cambridge, and would rally around you ... I am quite sure there will be room for both of us and more work than we can hope to accomplish ... You need not, unless you wish so, be worried by administrative matters ... Of course the Yarrow Professors are supposed to be entirely free from the routine of teaching but may give a few lectures when they are inclined.'

From letters[12] both to Jeans and to Rutherford we see how Bohr was torn between his commitments to Denmark and his desire to work near Rutherford, his hero. A few weeks later he raised the possibility of giving up his Copenhagen professorship, retaining his directorship there, and spending part of the year in England.[13] Jeans replied: 'Speaking quite frankly, I do not think there is the slightest chance that the Committee would be agreeable to the plan you speak of.'[14] Whereupon Bohr declined: 'I feel ... great obligations towards the institute which with so great generosity to myself has been created in Copenhagen.'[15]

Two more offers came the year thereafter, from the United States.

(c) First trip to America

In February 1923 Bohr wrote[16] to Ehrenfest: 'I am thinking a little about making a trip to America from where I have received invitations from several places . . . I have acquired a bit of an inclination to get to know the state of affairs in America.' During the following half year his travel plans took shape; a heavy schedule of lectures was worked out. In September Bohr took off. Kramers accompanied him as far as England where on 17 September Bohr lectured[17] on the correspondence principle before the British Association for the Advancement of Science meeting in Leeds. Two days later he sailed from England.

From 1 to 3 October Bohr gave three lectures in Toronto. On 12 October he started the Simpson lectures (five of them) at Amherst College.[18] Later in October he lectured twice at Harvard, where, among others, he met Percy Bridgman who wrote shortly afterward: 'The impression he made on everyone who met him was a singularly pleasant one personally. I have seldom met a man with such evident singleness of purpose and so apparently free from guile . . . I know from many sources that Bohr makes the same impression on others that he does on me, and besides this, he is now idolized as a scientific god through most of Europe.'[19]

On 19 November Bohr gave a lecture at Columbia University. He also visited Schenectady, Baltimore, Washington DC, and Princeton, and went as far west as Chicago, 'where I attended the meeting of the American Physical Society [and where] I met Michelson [of the Michelson–Morley experiment] who I believe found in me a more conservative scientist than he had expected.'[20] From the proceedings[21] of that meeting: 'Professor Niels Bohr was elected an honorary member at the meeting of the Council held on Friday, November 30. On Saturday morning Professor Bohr addressed the Society on "The Quantum Theory of Atoms with Several Electrons". This address was attended by about 350 persons.'

Meanwhile, from 6 to 15 November, Bohr had given the most distinguished series of lectures of his first American trip, the six Silliman lectures at Yale, established by a bequest from Augustus Ely Silliman, and designed to illustrate the presence and the providence, the wisdom and goodness of God, as manifested in the natural and moral world. In announcing[22] these talks, the *New York Times* had called Bohr 'a modern Viking who comes on a great errand'. In introducing Bohr at his first lecture the president of Yale called him 'the winner of the blue ribbon in science'.[23]

Bohr's notes of the Silliman lectures have been preserved.[24] Far more important than these are the lengthy and detailed reports of Bohr's talks, which, every single day following one of his lectures, appeared in the *New York Times*. These newspaper articles are of a far higher quality than most of those which today pass for science reporting. They played a central role in bringing twentieth century conceptions about the structure of matter *for the first time to the attention of a wide audience.* On 6 and 20 January 1924 the Sunday editions of the *New York Times* carried long articles on Bohr and the atom in their special features section. On 3 February the *Times* wrote:

> The atom is getting to be a leading topic of conversation nowadays, even in circles where it had never been discussed before except in relation to persons or things having been blown to atoms. Dr Niels Bohr is responsible largely for this addition to popular conversation. Since he came to this country last fall to lecture on his theory of the structure of the atom at Yale University and elsewhere, there has been a remarkable display of interest in his discoveries of the remarkable convolutions within this infinitesimal particle of matter . . .

After Bohr had returned to Copenhagen, shortly before Christmas, he gave[20] Rutherford some of his general impressions of America: 'Although a strenuous time, my visit to America was a very refreshing experience which gave me many thoughts not only about scientific problems but also about various other aspects of life. Although one cannot avoid feeling how great the possibilities for the future are, I do not think I should like to live there all my life and to miss the traditions which, although so disastrous for a peaceful evolution, give the color to the life in the old countries.' These sentiments along with his obligations made him decline two offers from the United States.

In January 1924 Bohr received[25] a telegram offering him the Bartol Research Professorship* of the Franklin Institute. It was, in the words of its director, 'What I believe the most desirable research opportunity in this country . . . unparalleled facilities for research . . . freedom of action . . . generous support . . . reasonable freedom from personal financial care and those onerous duties relating to administration'.[26] In February Michelson wrote to Bohr: 'Is there any chance that you might be willing to move to the United States permanently and join our physics department at Ryerson Laboratory [Chicago]?'[27]

All in all Bohr's voyage to the New World had been a great success. He had made new personal contacts. He had been offered two positions, both of which he declined. He had brought the atom to the attention of the public at large. Most important in the long run, however, was his first encounter with American philanthropy, a contact in which, as we shall see next, he played a pioneering role insofar as physics is concerned. In order to give some feeling for the way philanthropy had evolved up till the 1920s, I shall begin by taking a look back at ways of giving in earlier times, a subject about which I ought to perhaps know more than I actually do.

---

* The Bartol Research foundation was established with funds left to the Franklin Institute by one of its members.

(d) Bohr as fund raiser

Philanthropy in its original form, material help for the poor and the weak, is at least as old as the writings of the Bible, where such support is urged, as also in the Koran, as a moral precept. Giving could therefore be motivated by a blend of religious command and compassion. The seventeenth century English medical doctor and philosopher Sir Thomas Browne took an extreme position: 'I give no alms to satisfie the hunger of my Brother, but to fulfill and accomplish the Will and Command of my God,'[28] an opinion which, I like to think, was a minority view.

Giving was at one time the prerogative of the wealthy. That is no longer so. In the United States, for example, people in the lowest income brackets generally give a larger proportion of their take-home pay than most of those earning more. Incidentally, individuals rather than foundations and other organizations dominate giving. In 1978, in the US, they (including their bequests) accounted for 90 per cent, $180 per capita, which was seven per cent of the national budget. Religious organizations received about half this amount.*

The other half did not go to needy individuals but to causes, among them support for the advancement of knowledge. That form of philanthropy, sustenance of the spirit rather than of the body, is ancient as well. Plato bequeathed his Academy (which survived nearly 900 years) to his successors with an endowment of productive land. The Ptolemies endowed antiquity's most famous library, the extraordinary collection at Alexandria. In the first century AD Pliny the Younger endowed a school in his native Como.[30]

During the next 1500 years, 'the idea of permanent provisions for worthy purposes fitted admirably into the ideals and practices of the Christian Church, and from the fourth century until the Reformation, practically all endowments were Church endowments'.[31] Among the early post-Reformation developments one should recall the great Elizabethan Charitable Uses Act of 1601. Its enumeration of charitable purposes included 'schooles of learning, free schooles, and schollers in universities'.

From the eighteenth century on one finds instances of bequests that lead us into the present. Benjamin Franklin gave a thousand pounds each to the cities of Boston and Philadelphia, for loans to 'young married artificers of good character'. In 1908 Philadelphia used this gift (which had grown to over $400000) to establish the Franklin Institute. In 1796 Benjamin Thompson (Count Rumford) funded the largest prize for scientific research up to that time; he also left part of his estate to Harvard for the endowment of a professorship. The Rumford medal is still awarded, the Rumford chair

---

* For these figures see Ref. 29. I have restricted myself to the US because only for that country could I find detailed information.

still exists. In 1846 the Smithsonian Institution in Washington DC, was founded from an earlier bequest of half a million dollars by the Englishman James Smithson 'for the increase and diffusion of knowledge among men'. Among those who gave large sums for founding universities and research institutions one may recall Andrew Carnegie, Ezra Cornell, Johns Hopkins, Leland Stanford, and John Davison Rockefeller, founder of the Rockefeller dynasty, who gave the funds for the establishment of the University of Chicago (with the stipulation that it not be named after him).

Rockefeller exemplifies the transition of a giver out of religious duty to one who gave out of social obligation. 'When he secured his first job as a clerk . . . which paid him six dollars a month . . . he gave away 6 per cent of his total wage to the Sunday school and various missions related to his [Baptist] church interests.'[32] The scope of his philanthropy grew apace with his eventually immense fortune. In 1901 he founded The Rockefeller Institute for Medical Research (now The Rockefeller University) aimed at improving the deplorable conditions of American medical training. In 1903 he established the General Education Board for the promotion of education within the United States 'without distinction of sex, race, or creed'. In 1913 followed the Rockefeller foundation which in its first ten years disbursed $76 million, mainly on public health, medical education, and war relief.[33] 'During the course of his lifetime Rockefeller gave away $531 million, more than any other man in history.'[34] He was the most prominent figure among a small group of men who 'acquired their fortunes under conditions unique in the history of the [US] and not infrequently by methods which, if permissible at the time, no longer accord with social conscience or the requirements of law. They enriched the intellectual and cultural life . . . with a stream of universities, foundations, institutes, libraries, and endowments without parallel in any other age . . .'[35]

Bohr, or rather his institute, was among the earliest European recipients of this largesse. Before we come to that some remarks are in order on European foundations, less well endowed than their main American counterparts, but no less important for their influence on the cultural scene.

Among the oldest European foundations that support higher learning are the Carlsberg foundation in Copenhagen, established in 1876, the Carl Zeiss foundation (Jena, 1889) for aid to the natural sciences and mathematics, the Nobel foundation (1900), the Cecil Rhodes fund (1902), and the Koppel foundation in Berlin (1905).

The Carlsberg foundation,[36] of particular interest here, was established by Jacob Christian Jacobsen, owner of Denmark's largest beer brewery, with an initial gift of one million kroner (more followed soon), the interest of which was at the disposal of the foundation, partially to begin with, fully after his own and his wife's death. Jacobsen considered this gift in part as a repayment for the inspiration he felt he owed to H. C. Ørsted, whose lectures he had followed as a young man (though not as a regular student), in part because 'he wanted his country's voice to be heard in the international concert. He had lived through 1864'[37] (Chapter 3). The formal recipient of the grant was the *Videnskabernes Selskab* which was charged with selecting from among its membership a board of five foundation directors. The Carlsberg laboratories, founded by Jacobsen in 1875, and devoted to biochemical research, were incorporated as a section of the foundation. Jacobsen's only son Carl (after whom the breweries were named) later became Denmark's major benefactor in the arts.

Eventually Jacobsen left his interests in the breweries entirely to the foundation (after provisions for next of kin). Moreover he declared in his will that, after the death of his wife and son, his beautiful spacious residence, situated on the brewery grounds, should be offered free for life to the Danish man or woman most prominent for his (her) activities on behalf of science, literature, the arts, or other meritorious activity on behalf of society, that person to be proposed by the membership of the *Videnskabernes Selskab* for approval by the foundation's board. In 1919 Høffding, Bohr's teacher, became the first occupant of the *Æresbolig* (Residence of Honor).

Bohr himself was among the many stipendiaries supported by the foundation for studies abroad (in 1911, see (7a)). In 1912–13 he received further grants for his work on atomic structure. From 1922 on he was awarded numerous Carlsberg subsidies for the support of collaborators,* acquisition of laboratory equipment, and extensions of his institute, well over a hundred grants in all during his lifetime.[39]

The deterioration in education and the intellectual life brought about by World War I caused a new trend to develop in science, of a kind that was precisely in Bohr's style: an emphasis on its international character. In 1919 the International Research Council was established with headquarters in Brussels, for the purpose of coordinating international efforts in different branches of science. The International Union for Pure and Applied Physics (IUPAP), dating from 1931, was one of its outgrowths. Also from the immediate post-war years dates the founding of the Committee on Intellectual Cooperation under the auspices of the League of Nations; it counted Einstein and Marie Curie among its early members.[40] In harmony with these developments a new mode of philanthropy emerged, centered on international support.

As far as I know, the first foundation with that specific aim in mind was

* Up until 1930 these included Heisenberg, Klein, Kramers, and Rosseland.[38]

founded by Danish law no. 555 of 4 October 1919 'for the support of Danish science in connection with international research', with a capital of 5 million kroner. This was the Rask–Ørsted foundation (which in 1972 was absorbed in another Danish organization), named after Ørsted and the renowned early nineteenth century Danish linguist Rasmus Rask.[41] The purposes of this foundation and those of Bohr evidently matched each other perfectly. Up till 1930 it provided thirteen Rask–Ørsted fellowships to visitors of the Bohr institute, including Coster from Holland, Hevesy from Hungary, Yoshio Nishina from Japan, Pauli from Austria, and Rubinowicz from Poland.[38] (I belong to a younger generation that later received such a fellowship.) Fellowship support from this source was only exceeded by similar grants from the International Education Board (IEB).

The IEB was founded[42] by John D. Rockefeller, Jr, in January 1923 for 'the promotion and advance of education throughout the world'. The idea for this board had originated with Wickliffe Rose, long active already then in foundation work, who in 1922 had become the president of the General Education Board, having made his acceptance conditional on the creation of an international effort; in 1923 he became president of the IEB as well. As areas of support he initially selected the natural sciences and agriculture; the humanities were included later. 'At no time was any consideration given to the idea of weighing the claims of one country against another and dividing the assistance on a basis of geographical balance. Always, the criterion was ability: which man, which institution, which locality offered the greatest opportunity for the advancement of knowledge?'[43]

In an early memorandum[44] Rose proposed: 'Begin with physics, chemistry, and biology. Locate the inspiring, productive men in each of these fields. Ascertain of each whether he would be willing to train students from other countries.' He might as well have written: select Bohr and others like him.

Bohr could not have been aware of the existence of the IEB at the time he began to make plans for his American trip. It is known, however, that at that time he was 'very interested in the possibility of obtaining economic support for [his] institute',[45] presumably from the Rockefeller foundation (which in 1922 had awarded 62 fellowships in physical chemistry and medicine[46]). Bohr was fortunate enough to have an advance man in New York in Christen Lundsgaard, a Dane who was associated at that time with The Rockefeller Institute for Medical Research (and who later became professor of medicine in Copenhagen). In April Lundsgaard wrote[47] to the General Education Board about Bohr's aspirations. His letter was forwarded to Rose.[48] In May, Berlème, an old friend of Bohr (see Chapter 9), appeared on the New York scene, from where he informed Bohr: 'The institution that has the money is not the Rockefeller Foundation – which

certainly also has a lot of money. But in 1923 something was founded . . .
named the International Education Board . . .'[49] He proposed that Bohr
apply to the IEB, sending his application to Lundsgaard who would forward
it, and leaving the amount to be requested to Lundsgaard's discretion.

In June Bohr sent off[50] his application, a document that gives a clear
picture of the size of his operation in 1923:

An extension such as that contemplated is absolutely necessary if the institute
shall accomplish the task for which it was established. The necessary enlargement
of the building and purchase of equipment will take about 20000 dollars. This sum
is too large to be raised in this country, even taking into account the possibility of
support from private individuals, since the economic depression in Denmark
makes it difficult to procure considerable sums from private sources . . .

It is the intention to enlarge the institute's building by some ten rooms, of which
about half would be arranged for experimental work and the rest as smaller rooms
for theoretical workers . . .

The fixed personnel consists, besides the director, of one associate professor, a
secretary, a mechanician, a janitor (half time) and a boy . . .

In the two years since the founding of the institute the following numbers of
foreign physicists have worked there . . . (only a stay of at least one semester has
been counted): from the United States 4, Norway 1, Sweden 1, Holland 1, Poland 1,
Hungary 1, Japan 2 . . .

After changing the $20000 to $40000 Lundsgaard forwarded this letter to
the IEB. In November 1923, following his Silliman lectures, Bohr had an
interview concerning his request at the IEB offices in New York. His
proposal was discussed[51] at the IEB meeting of 19 November, after which
Rose wrote to Bohr[52] that the Board was contemplating awarding him
$40000 for expansion and equipment, with the understanding that the
necessary land and increased maintenance would be provided by others.

Early in December 1923 Rose sailed for Europe on a five months' trip that
would lead him to nineteen countries for visits to some fifty universities and
other institutions. His first stop was England. In his diary we find this entry:
'13 December 1923. Talk with Rutherford: He was delighted to learn what
the Board proposed to do for Bohr; Bohr was his student; he is greatly
concerned about him; Bohr too ready to give his time and energy to anybody
demanding it; has been working on salary altogether inadequate for proper
maintenance of his family; . . . his family has been under considerable
financial stress.'[53] On 17 March 1924 Rose visited Bohr at his institute. Two
days later they met again at the Hotel Angleterre, at which time Bohr asked
if he could write to him later informally about the needs of the institute. 'He
would not like to be insistent on matters of this kind but should like
opportunity to call attention; it was agreed this should be done.'[53]

In April Bohr certified to the IEB that the city of Copenhagen had
purchased suitable land as a gift to the institute (after Bohr's old teacher

Høffding had intervened with the mayor[54]) and that the university had pledged an increase in maintenance costs.[55] In May the IEB committed itself 'to the University of Copenhagen' for a sum not exceeding $40000.[55] In June Bohr had the money in the bank.[56] It was the IEB's very first institutional grant to the field of physics.*

The institute's expansion cost more than had been foreseen, so Bohr went after supplemental funds. First he got 60000 Kr out of the Carlsberg funds,[58] then $5000 from the IEB, then another 40000 Kr from the Carlsberg foundation.** Moreover the IEB, during its existence (it was integrated into the Rockefeller foundation in 1938) became the main provider of fellowships for young physicists, fifteen in all, Heisenberg among them.[39]

The importance of Bohr's role in providing guidance to others' research had soon become widely recognized, as can be seen, for example, by the following lines found[59] in the *New York Times*, in 1924: 'Working with Dr Bohr is regarded by scientists as working with the foremost of the exponents of the new atomic physics, which is revolutionizing science.' To that role we must now add a different though related one, his raising of funds for the purpose of providing facilities so that others could be close to him not only in mind but also in body. Those efforts did not just benefit the evolution of the Copenhagen institute to a world center of theoretical physics. Rather, it is essential to realize that Bohr must be seen above all as a trailblazer who led the way towards new modes of support for physics worldwide, as can be seen by reading once again the *New York Times*:

The appropriation [of $40000] was regarded by scientists . . . as a striking example of the growing recognition accorded to scientific research . . . It is the hope of many American men of Science that the recognition of the importance of research, shown in the Rockefeller grant to Dr Bohr, will spur the movement to develop more research laboratories in this country and more American colleges and universities specializing in research.[60]

(e) The institute up till mid-1925. Introducing Heisenberg

Bohr's insistence on more space for his institute was no idle whim. In January 1924, 'five to six people sit at one table and compute'.[61] There were nine visitors from abroad that year who stayed for one month or longer.[62] Cramped quarters did not visibly affect productivity, however. The number of papers published under the institute by-line was 9 (in 1921), 14 (1922), 44 (1923), 25 (1924), 35 (1925).[63]

---

* Later in 1924 August Krogh (Nobel Laureate in physiology 1920) received $300000 from the Rockefeller foundation plus $100000 from the IEB for a new building that would integrate five existing physiological laboratories. In 1927 Johannes Nicolaus Brønsted received $100000 from the IEB for physical chemistry.[57] (Both men were Danish professors.)

** For comparison, at that time the dollar was worth about 6 Kr.

All visitors would, of course, consult Bohr on their scientific activities. Furthermore, 'for most of them accommodation had to be found, financial assistance arranged, and the usual host of small problems had to be seen to that arise for a visitor arriving in a new country. In addition there was the day-to-day maintenance of the institute to supervise, doctoral theses to be refereed for the faculty, and correspondence to be answered . . . It was part of Bohr's nature to carry out these various duties with a great deal of thoroughness . . . Occasions where a single day could be devoted exclusively to research were becoming less and less frequent.'[64] Nevertheless, among the numbers of papers noted above, eighteen were by Bohr himself (including three in collaboration).[63]

From 1924 onward Bohr was formally and permanently relieved from one other obligation: teaching students. That was the result of a special action by the Carlsberg foundation. Article IXc of its statutes authorizes the board to pay 'salaries for life or for certain years to highly gifted men, so that they can work comfortably as *frie Videnskabsmaend*' [free scholars], independent of a public position'. Bohr was one of the happy few to receive this support, as a general mark of respect, from 1 April 1924 until his death. Accordingly, in 1924 the faculty recommended that 'until further notice Professor Bohr be released from obligatory teaching and from the administration of courses leading to the Magister examination.'[65]

All these activities by Bohr, his own research, the supervision of others, administrative duties, a large correspondence, were clearly enough to keep him fully occupied. The academic year 1923–4 was even much more strenuous. On top of all else he lectured in America, negotiated with foundations, and began preparations for the actual extension of the institute. By the summer of 1924 Bohr was once again worn out. Bohr to Michelson: 'Since I wrote to you last time [in February 1924[66]] I have not been quite well and have been forced for a time to abstain from scientific research. Although I am much better now I must be careful.'[67] Bohr to Rutherford: 'I was forced to take a complete rest and went to Switzerland for a walking tour with a friend. It was a very refreshing journey and after my return I felt much better; in order, however, to gain my full working power after the very strenuous time I have had this year I am for once taking a real summer holiday with my family in the north of Sjaelland.'[68] Rutherford to Bohr: 'You know that it is my opinion that you work far too hard for your health, and you would do just as much good work if you took matters easily. This is the advice of a grandfather, but nevertheless good, as I have found in my own experience.'[69]

In his original proposal to the IEB Bohr had suggested (as we have seen) an extension of the existing building. It was finally decided, however, to construct two new buildings. One, to the right and rear of the original building, was to house new experimental equipment, a 200000 volt X-ray generator, precision instruments for spectroscopy in the visible and the infrared regions, and various large workshop items. The other, to the right and in front, was to be a three-story residence for the Bohrs. Long after they had moved elsewhere it remained known as 'the villa' – but no more. At present it houses administrative offices.

Construction began in 1924. Margrethe Bohr has recalled how Bohr remained forever fond of taking part in such activities: 'The institute was always building. As soon as they had finished one thing they were starting another. Oh, I hoped I should never see an architect again . . . But he liked it; he liked architects, and he liked handwork to occupy himself with, and he liked to see it. He certainly took part in every little detail; it amused him . . . It must have taken a good part of his time, some of his time. But it was a relaxation for him.'[70] The new buildings were supposed to be finished in one year. As almost always happens, complications arose, however, in particular because of a major strike in early 1925 about wage claims. Plans for an official opening were dropped. Occupation of new space began in the summer of 1926; the buildings were formally certified complete the following October.[71]

The Bohrs' old living quarters in the main building had been converted to office space, while part of the top floor had been turned into a three-room visitor's flat. The first to occupy that guest space was Werner Heisenberg.

Heisenberg has appeared before in these pages, but only in passing. Now, as he is about to take center stage in the evolution of quantum physics, he should be introduced more properly.[72]

Heisenberg grew up in Munich, where his father was the professor in Greek philology at the university. Already in his high school years he immersed himself in independent physics studies. Also as a young boy he started to play the piano, at which he excelled throughout his life. In the autumn of 1920, immediately after he had enrolled in the University of Munich to study physics with Sommerfeld, he met Pauli. That was the beginning of a lifelong friendship.

Heisenberg was twenty, still working toward his Ph.D., when he first met Bohr during the Göttingen *Festspiele* of June 1922 (9a). After one of Bohr's lectures Heisenberg rose to make an objection. '[Bohr] replied hesitantly . . . and at the end of the discussion he came over to me and asked me to join him that afternoon for a walk over the Hain mountain . . . This walk was to have profound repercussions on my scientific career, or perhaps it is more correct to say that my real scientific career only started that afternoon[73] . . . We had a talk of, I would say, about three hours . . . It was my first conversation with Bohr, and I was at once impressed by the difference in his way of seeing quantum theory from Sommerfeld's way. For the first time I saw that one of the founders of quantum theory was deeply worried by its difficulties . . . He never looked at the problems from the mathematical point of view, but from the physics point of view. I should say that I have learned more from Bohr than from anybody else about that new type of theoretical physics which was . . . more experimental than mathematical . . . Later on, of course, I have tried to learn that way of thinking from him, so that was a very exciting experience.' [74] 'After returning from this walk on the Hainberg, Bohr told friends: "He understands everything." ' [75]

During that walk Bohr invited Heisenberg to spend some time in Copenhagen. A year and a half would go by before that came to pass. In the meantime Heisenberg finished his doctor's thesis with Sommerfeld, on the stability of laminar flow in liquids, and spent time in Göttingen, in part as Born's assistant. Then he came to Copenhagen for a two weeks' visit. 'During the Easter vacation of 1924 I finally boarded the Warnemünde ferry for Denmark . . . When I eventually disembarked I had some troubles with customs – I knew no Danish and could not account for myself properly. However, as soon as it became clear that I was about to work in Professor Bohr's institute, all difficulties were swept out of the way and all doors were opened for me.' [76]

'I saw very little of Bohr; he had his hands full with administrative tasks . . . But after a few days he came into my room and asked me to join him in a few days' walking tour through Sjaelland. In the institute there was little chance for lengthy talks, and he wanted to get to know me better. And so the two of us set out with our rucksacks.' [77] They took the trolley to the northern end of the city, then walked north to Elsinore where they visited Kronborg castle, connected with the legend of the Danish prince Hamlet. Then west, to Tisvilde, then back via Hillerød and a visit to Frederiksborg castle, in all a hike of over 100 miles.

During that first brief visit plans were laid for longer stays. Heisenberg spent from September 1924 to April 1925 at Bohr's institute, supported by IEB and Carlsberg moneys. When, early in 1926, Kramers received appointment as professor of theoretical physics in Utrecht, Bohr made application for him to be replaced as lektor by Heisenberg, effective 1 May. [78] As a result Heisenberg was lektor in Copenhagen from May 1926 to June 1927. (On 15 June 1927 Bohr requested a one year extension of Heisenberg's appointment. [79] Heisenberg went to Leipzig, however, as full professor, effective 1 October.) During Heisenberg's second stay 'every few days Bohr and I take riding lessons together so as not to go to rack and ruin in physics'. [80] I shall return later to Heisenberg's physics activities during those two periods.

Evidently Bohr had quickly recognized Heisenberg as a young physicist of exceptional quality. Frank Hoyt, then a young physics Ph.D. from the University of Wisconsin, who was at the institute from October 1922 to September 1924, has recalled that during that period Bohr once said to him: 'Now everything is in Heisenberg's hands – to find a way out of the difficulties [of the quantum theory].'[81] That showed Bohr's remarkable insight and foresight.

Because that is exactly what happened.

References

1. About Bohr in Tisvilde see also W. Scharff, NBR, p. 315; M. Andersen, NBR, p. 321; N. Blaedel, 'Harmony and unity', Springer, New York 1988.
2. Hans Bohr, NBR, p. 325.
3. Hans Bohr, Om Far, unpublished MS from 1955, NBA.
4. Hans Bohr, Erindringer om min Far, Berlingske Søndag, 22 September 1985.
5. Hold the fork close to the table and make it touch the table at the moment you open your fingers.
6. Fysisk Tidsskr. 23, 1, 1925.
7. M. Planck, letter to N. Bohr, 23 October 1921, NBA.
8. For more on Einstein's Berlin position see SL, Chap. 14, section (a).
9. N. Bohr, letter to M. Planck, undated, NBA.
10. J. Jeans, letter to N. Bohr, 17 July 1923, NBA.
11. E. Rutherford, letter to N. Bohr, undated, clearly written in late July 1923, NBA.
12. N. Bohr, letters to J. Jeans and E. Rutherford, 3 August 1923, NBA.
13. N. Bohr, letter to J. Jeans, 22 August 1923, NBA.
14. J. Jeans, letter to N. Bohr, 29 August 1923, NBA.
15. N. Bohr, letter to J. Jeans, 9 September 1923, NBA.
16. N. Bohr, letter to P. Ehrenfest, 23 February 1923, NBA.
17. CW, Vol. 3, p. 576.
18. Science 58, 302, 1923.
19. P. Bridgman, letter to the father of J. C. Slater, 4 February 1924, copy in the Library of the American Philosophical Society, Philadelphia.
20. N. Bohr, letter to E. Rutherford, 9 January 1924, CW, Vol. 5, p. 486.
21. Phys. Rev. 23, 104, 1924.
22. New York Times, 5 November 1923.
23. New York Times, 7 November 1923.
24. CW, Vol. 3, p. 581.
25. R. B. Owens, telegram to N. Bohr, 17 January 1924, NBA.
26. R. B. Owens, letter to N. Bohr, 6 February 1924, NBA.
27. A. A. Michelson, letter to N. Bohr, 26 February 1924, NBA.
28. I found this quotation in an interesting article on philanthropy by M. Feingold, Daedalus, Winter 1987 issue, p. 164.
29. C. Bakal, Charity U.S.A., p. 10, Times Books, New York 1979.
30. Encyclopedia of the Social Sciences, Vol. 5, p. 531, Macmillan, New York 1937.

31. F. P. Keppel, *The Foundation*, p. 15, Macmillan, New York 1930.
32. R. B. Fosdick, *The story of the Rockefeller foundation*, p. 4, Harper, New York 1952.
33. *Science* **57**, 578, 1923.
34. Ref. 29, p. 27.
35. Ref. 32, p. 5.
36. For its history see K. Glamann, *Carlsbergfondet*, Rhodos, Copenhagen 1976.
37. Ref. 36, p. 15. For the reference to 1864 see Chap. 3.
38. P. Robertson, *The early years*, Universitetsforlag, Copenhagen 1979.
39. For an account of Bohr's grants by this and other foundations see especially F. Aaserud, *Redirecting science*, Cambridge University Press, 1990.
40. SL, p. 316.
41. For details about this foundation see *Danmarks Kultur ved Aar 1940*, Vol. 7, p. 69, Det Danske Forlag, Copenhagen 1943.
42. For a history of the IEB see G. W. Gray, *Education on an international scale*, Harcourt Brace, New York 1941.
43. Ref. 32, p. 150.
44. Ref. 42, p. 16.
45. C. Lundsgaard, letter to N. Bohr, 26 March 1923, NBA.
46. *Science* **57**, 549, 1923.
47. C. Lundsgaard, letter to A. Flexner, 6 April 1923, Rockefeller Archive Center, Tarrytown, N.Y.
48. A. Flexner, letter to C. Lundsgaard, 17 April 1923, Rockefeller Archive Center.
49. A. Berlème, letter to N. Bohr, 8 May 1923, NBA.
50. N. Bohr, letter to the IEB, 27 June 1923, Rockefeller Archive Center.
51. Minutes of the IEB meeting, 19 November 1923, Rockefeller Archive Center.
52. W. Rose, letter to N. Bohr, 21 November 1923, NBA.
53. W. Rose, Log of journey, Rockefeller Archive Center.
54. Ref. 38, p. 92.
55. N. Bohr, letter to the IEB, 16 April 1924, minutes of the IEB meeting 26 May 1924, Rockefeller Archive Center.
56. Københavns Handelsbank to N. Bohr, 12 June 1924, NBA.
57. Ref. 42, p. 25.
58. N. Bohr, letter to W. Rose, 8 January 1925, NBA.
59. *The New York Times*, 27 January 1924.
60. *The New York Times*, 28 January 1924.
61. *Berlingske Tidende*, 23 January 1924.
62. Ref. 38, p. 156.
63. H. M. Hansen, *Fysisk Tidsskr.* **29**, 59, 1931.
64. Ref. 38, p. 78.
65. Diarium af matematiske-naturvidenskabelige Fakultet, 12 April 1924, deposited at the Rigsarkiv (National Archives).
66. N. Bohr, letter to A. A. Michelson, 7 February 1924, NBA.
67. N. Bohr, letter to A. A. Michelson, 5 July 1924, NBA.
68. N. Bohr, letter to E. Rutherford, 12 July 1924, NBA.

69. E. Rutherford, letter to N. Bohr, 18 July 1924, NBA.
70. M. and A. Bohr, interviewed by L. Rosenfeld and T. S. Kuhn, 30 January 1963, NBA.
71. Ref. 38, p. 106.
72. For good short biographies of Heisenberg, in English, see A. Hermann, *Werner Heisenberg*, Internationes, Bonn, 1976; D. Cassidy and H. Rechenberg in *Werner Heisenberg, Collected Works*, Series A, part I, p. 1, Springer, New York 1985.
73. W. Heisenberg, *Physics and beyond*, p. 38, Harper and Row, New York 1971.
74. W. Heisenberg, interviewed by T. S. Kuhn, 30 November 1962, NBA.
75. Hermann (Ref. 72), p. 19.
76. Ref. 73, p. 45.
77. Ref. 73, p. 46.
78. N. Bohr, letter to Konsistorium, 14 April 1926, *København Universitetets Aarbog 1925–1926*, p. 145, Schultz, Copenhagen 1926.
79. Ref. 65, 15 June 1927.
80. W. Heisenberg, letter to M. Born, 26 May 1926, repr. in Hermann (Ref. 72), p. 35.
81. F. C. Hoyt, interviewed by T. S. Kuhn, 28 April 1964, NBA.

13

'Then the whole picture changes completely': the discovery of quantum mechanics

(a) A last look back: Bohr as 'director of atomic theory'

The thirteenth edition of the *Encyclopaedia Britannica*, published in 1926, contains three supplementary volumes 'covering recent years'. These include[1] an entry 'Atom' written by Bohr, dealing largely with the theory of the periodic system, actually a rather primitive version that did not yet include spin. Bohr also mentioned briefly a new theory dating from July 1925, Heisenberg's quantum mechanics, 'which constitutes a bold departure from the classical way of describing natural phenomena ... It has in particular allowed the Balmer formula to be derived.' In his contribution Bohr continued to treat atoms with more than one electron in terms of the old quantum theory, however, since 'the methods of quantum mechanics have not yet been applied to [this] problem'.[1] Another entry, by Charles Barkla, also refers[2] to quantum mechanics: 'A new theory ... has been formulated by Heisenberg which, whether fruitful or not, promises to put quantum mechanics in much more logical form. Its physical significance, however, is not apparent.'

Quantum mechanics, which bids fair as the most profound novel set of scientific ideas of the twentieth century, was – as will be explained below – not once but twice born, first in 1925, then again in 1926. This chapter is devoted to the development of the theory in those two years, when – as Barkla indicated – it was clear that a great advance had been made but not yet what that advance meant. Before plunging into this brand new subject I shall take one last look back, with particular emphasis on Bohr's role, to what had happened to the quantum theory of the atom from 1913 to where we are now, at the end of the old quantum theory. The time is early 1925.

Bohr had started it all with his simplest description of the states of the hydrogen atom in terms of one quantum number only, the principal quantum number n. In the course of a few years it had become clear that those states labeled by n only are actually highly degenerate (a term explained in (10b)). To each n belong in general several states with distinct values of the orbital quantum number l, all of them degenerate. To each n and l belong in general several states with distinct magnetic quantum number m, all of them degenerate. To each n, l, and m belong two states labeled by s, the spin, again degenerate. Relativistic effects lift the degeneracies in l and s, whereby the fine structure of the hydrogen spectrum is explained. An external magnetic field lifts the degeneracies in m and s, whereby the Zeeman effect, including its anomalies, is explained. Thus all the four quantum numbers of modern atomic spectroscopy had been emplaced in the context of the old quantum theory. So had all their respective selection rules as we know them today.

The theory of the hydrogen spectrum, including its fine structure, is perhaps the finest showpiece of the old quantum theory. Today that subject is most often taught with the help of the streamlined methods of relativistic quantum mechanics, and that is as it should be. Students might further be edified, however, by also learning the oldtimer's derivation in terms of the Sommerfeld and the Thomas precessions, that do lead to the right answers as well (up to important refinements that post-date World War II).

The discovery of selection rules, in which Bohr played a dominant role, is one of the concrete applications of his second major contribution to quantum theory, his correspondence principle. These selection rules illustrate so well that insistence on the validity of classical physics as a limit of quantum phjysics is ever so much more than an obeisance to the wisdom of our ancestors. Rather, this link between the old and the new has predictive power of its own. It is my impression that Bohr may have overestimated that power, however, as in the case of his work on the structure of complex atoms. I also believe that Bohr's reticence in accepting the photon may in part be due to the fact that the wave–particle duality of light, and also the photoelectric equation, lie beyond the domain of applicability of the correspondence principle.

Bohr's work on the ground states of complex atoms laid the foundation of quantum chemistry. His efforts in that direction were the direct inspiration for another major achievement of the old quantum theory, Pauli's formulation of the exclusion principle. Bohr's assignments of quantum numbers to individual electrons inside atoms remain basic to the modern quantum chemical approach (see, for example, Slater's book on that subject[3]).

Finally, the birth of quantum statistics must be mentioned among the important advances that belong to the old quantum theory. I content myself with the briefest mention of that subject, since it was one to which Bohr did not contribute and since I have discussed its history elsewhere.[4]

In the second half of 1924 and early 1925 it was noted by Satyendra Nath Bose[5] and by Einstein[6] that classical statistical mechanics, referred to in (5f), has a quantum theoretical counterpart, now called Bose–Einstein statistics, with new and exciting consequences. In February 1926, Enrico Fermi pointed out[7] the existence of yet another kind of quantum statistics which (unlike the Bose–Einstein case) applies to particles (like electrons) that obey the exclusion principle. At that relatively late date Fermi's work was still entirely in the spirit of the old quantum theory: he treated the exclusion principle as 'an additional rule to the Sommerfeld quantization conditions'. In August 1926 Dirac gave both these new statistics their proper quantum mechanical underpinnings[8] – whence also the name Fermi–Dirac statistics.

All in all, the old quantum theory had produced a rich harvest: quantum numbers, selection rules, the exclusion principle, the first steps toward quantum chemistry and quantum statistics. As has been discussed earlier, while all that went on it had become increasingly obvious that all was far from well with quantum physics, however. To repeat: the Bohr–Sommerfeld quantum rules appeared quite often to be highly successful, yet, in a deep sense, they were paradoxical, as Bohr well knew. The spectrum of helium – not to mention heavier elements – was impenetrable, and remained so all through 1925, as witness Bohr's remark mentioned above. (Clarity came in July 1926, as we shall see in the next chapter.) The duality of the particle and wave pictures, necessary for light, as experiment had shown, conjectured for matter by de Broglie, was a mystery that did not fit into anything known before, including the correspondence principle.

In retrospect the numerous successes of the old quantum theory of the atom are all the more fabulous and astounding because they are based on analogies – orbits similar to the motions of planets around the sun, spin similar to planets that rotate while they are orbiting – which the new quantum mechanics was to show are in fact false. It is fitting that Bohr himself shall be given the last word on this most curious state of affairs. In 1943 he wrote[9] to Sommerfeld:

I have often reflected how this accident [the degeneracies of states in the hydrogen atom] on the one hand facilitated the first groping attempts at tackling the problem of spectra, while on the other hand it was probably the reason why, in spite of all paradoxes, the picture of atomic orbits in stationary states was clung to for so long.

As I have stressed before, the development of the old quantum theory was due to joint efforts by many. Among them, Bohr had emerged, as Sommerfeld put it[10] in 1921, as 'director of atomic theory' – in the sense of the man who gave direction, not just by his own researches but also by inspiring others. Also during 1925–6 Bohr continued to guide younger physicists. During those two years he did not, however, generate any of the ideas, in which he was passionately interested, that laid the foundations for a new era.

One can think of several reasons for this. During the year preceding the dramatic turn of events initiated by Heisenberg, Bohr's own ideas had been centered on the BKS theory. The experimental proof that this was not the right direction had been produced only a few months before Heisenberg completed his first paper on quantum mechanics. Secondly, in 1925 Bohr was quite preoccupied with the extension of his institute. A third reason, perhaps the most important one, I think, was that the new mechanics, based of course on physical intuition, demanded new mathematical techniques, not the mode of progress that – as we have seen – best fitted Bohr's style.

Even though it is not the purpose of this book to present a history of quantum mechanics, and even though Bohr did not play a major role in advancing theory during 1925–6, it is nevertheless imperative to give a sketch of what happened in those two years. For an understanding of Bohr the scientist it is indeed crucial to know his responses to the new developments, most particularly because from 1927 on the interpretation of quantum mechanics became and thereafter remained the scientific issue most dear to him, as we shall begin to see in the next chapter.

(b) Kramers in 1924

From the very beginnings of the quantum theory of the atom in 1913 it had been clear, especially to Bohr (see (8g)), that the new quantum rules were in conflict with classical theory. During the following years the classical theory was nevertheless held on to, with quantum rules superimposed, in the hope that this procedure might eventually find its logical justification. It was only in the early 1920s that, mainly as a result of failures, the much more radical insight began to emerge that actually classical models might have to be abandoned in the atomic domain, in particular that the concept of atomic orbits was highly suspect. For example, in February 1924 Pauli wrote[11] to Bohr: 'The most important question seems to me to be this: *to what extent may definite orbits of electrons in the stationary states be spoken of at all* [his italics]. I believe that this can in no way be assumed as self-evident ... Heisenberg has in my view precisely hit the mark on this point, in that he doubts the possibility of speaking of definite orbits.'

To be critical of atomic orbits was one (good) thing, to do atomic physics without them was something else. The first successful effort in that direction, due to Kramers, dates from 1924. Born has said[12] of that contribution: 'It was the first step from the bright realm of classical mechanics into the still dark and unexplored world of the new quantum mechanics.'

Kramers' work deals with the dispersion of light, that is, the emission of secondary light by an atom exposed to and excited by a light beam. Its results were announced in two letters to *Nature*, one[13] submitted in March 1924, one[14] the following July, both after the BKS proposal had been submitted (in January 1924). Kramers had his first results on dispersion prior to the time he was sidetracked into BKS, however.[15] Unlike that ill-fated adventure, his work on dispersion has survived and must be counted among his best contributions.

According to the classical theory of dispersion, which made its beginnings in the 1870s,[16] the intensity of the light emitted by an irradiated atom depends on the irradiation frequency and on the classical frequencies of orbital motions of electrons inside the atom. Quantum theory obviously demands that the role of these classical frequencies should somehow be taken over by Bohr's transition frequencies between stationary states. This was the problem that Kramers addressed. As a link with the classical answers he, of course, used the correspondence principle, which in this instance demands that the scattered radiation should continue to depend on the classical frequencies of electron motions in the limit of large quantum numbers. As a quantum theoretical tool he used Einstein's concepts of spontaneous emission. As a *mathematical* trick he replaced the atom by a set of oscillators vibrating with the Bohr frequencies – not unlike what was done in the BKS theory but without the introduction of statistical energy conservation. Combining those ingredients with very clever guesses he arrived at his so-called dispersion relation which expresses the probability for the emission of the secondary light in terms of the irradiation and Bohr frequencies.

The technical details of Kramers' two letters[13,14] need not concern us here. Most interesting, on the other hand, are his comments on the results:

[The dispersion relation] contains only such quantities [to wit, transition quantities referring to two stationary states] as allow of a direct physical interpretation on the basis of the quantum theory of spectra and atomic constitution, and exhibits no further reminiscence of the mathematical theory of multiple periodic systems [that is, of orbits].

The impact of Kramers' work was immediate. In June 1924 Born submitted a paper[17] in which he (unsuccessfully) attempted to apply Kramers' methods to the interaction between electrons. There he wrote: 'It is not to be expected . . . that the interaction between the electrons of one and the same atom should comply with the laws of classical mechanics; this disposes of any attempts to calculate the stationary orbits . . .'

As 1924 wore on one finds more expressions critical of classical orbits, notably by Pauli who in December wrote[18] to Sommerfeld: 'The model concepts [that is, the use of orbits] are now in a severe fundamental crisis which, I believe, will finally end with a further radical sharpening of the contrast between classical and quantum theory.' And, some days later,[19] to Bohr: 'Not only the dynamical concept of force but also the kinematical concept of motion in the classical theory must undergo profound modifications. Therefore I have also avoided the term "orbit" altogether in my paper [of December 1924 on the Zeeman effect[20]].' Bohr, too, may have had similar thoughts in mind when a few weeks thereafter he used the term 'atomic swindle' in a letter[21] to Pauli.

In later times Kramers' dispersion relations have proved ever more successful. Their first extension dates from 1925, as we shall see in a moment. Next came applications to X-ray data by Kronig[22] and Kramers.[23] I have described elsewhere how these relations, now often called Kramers–Kronig relations, could be derived from progressively more general assumptions, and how they have found important applications in the physics of elementary particles.[16]

(c) Heisenberg in 1924

When in September 1924 Heisenberg settled down for a half year's stay in Copenhagen he was not quite 23 years old, yet even before that time he had already authored (or co-authored, with Sommerfeld and with Born) twelve papers on the quantum theory (and two on turbulence), largely on the vexing problems of helium and the anomalous Zeeman effect.[24] After his arrival Heisenberg decided at once to learn Danish. 'At the same time, being at the institute, I had to learn English.'[25] Bohr's institute with its international population must have been among the first to introduce English as the *lingua franca*. With the help of the landlady at his boarding house Heisenberg began with Danish. 'After about ten or twelve weeks in Copenhagen, Bohr asked me to give a talk at the Colloquium, and I expected that this talk should be in Danish, so I prepared my talk in Danish. I was quite proud that I had now prepared a good talk, as I thought. Just half an hour before the Colloquium started, Bohr told me, "Well, it's obvious that we talk in English." That was, of course, very bad. Well, I tried the best I could, but I think it was extremely poor.'[25] Later, as lektor in Copenhagen, he did give his courses in Danish.[26]

When Heisenberg arrived in Denmark the BKS paper had appeared but not yet its experimental refutation. Of that period he has recalled: 'I remember that already before the Bothe–Geiger experiment was really carried out that Bohr felt that it should come out the way it later did come out, that this statistical conservation was not the real point.'[27] Also, Kramers' two notes[13,14] on dispersion had appeared. 'I felt, now the idea of using the harmonic oscillators somehow in connection with the atomic model appeals to me.'[27]

Heisenberg was eager to get on with his researches in quantum physics. 'To get into the spirit of the quantum theory was, I would say, only possible in Copenhagen at that time.'[26] During his first long stay it was not always easy for him to spend time with Bohr. 'One always had the impression that Bohr was under some stress to fit all the duties he had in connection with the institute.'[26] Once it took Bohr days to make peace between two of his mechanics who did not get along.[26] As a result, 'everybody first talked to Kramers before they talked to Bohr .... Kramers was, besides Bohr, the man who made the strongest impression on me.'[26]

At the time of Heisenberg's arrival Bohr was engaged in a study of the polarization of fluorescent light. In early October he had readied[28] a preliminary draft of a paper on this subject; the final version[29] was sent in on 1 November. In typical Bohr style it does not contain a single formula. As his first research project in Copenhagen, Heisenberg undertook detailed calculations of this effect. 'I was very happy to see that in this case of the polarization of the fluorescence one could give a strict rule ... The fact that the numbers came out was, of course, a confirmation that I was on the right track.'[27] I shall pass over the contents of this work by Bohr and by Heisenberg since it is of no particular concern for present purposes. The discussions between the two that preceded the publication of Heisenberg's paper[30] are quite revealing, however.

After Heisenberg had completed his calculations he went to tell Bohr who thought it looked all right. He then asked Bohr if he would mind that he (H.) would publish his results. A day or so later Heisenberg was called to the presence of Bohr and Kramers who now tried to explain to him that his ideas did not work. 'And I was completely shocked. I got quite furious ... So we had quite a heated discussion ... [Then] they said, "Well, we must think about it again" ... We all were quite happy at the end of the thing ... I was quite glad about it, and I think everybody was quite happy.'[27] Bohr praised Heisenberg's paper in letters[31] written during November and December.

Heisenberg went home for the Christmas vacation and from there sent the proofs of the paper to Bohr, who wrote back to him[32] suggesting some changes. Heisenberg replied:[33] 'I am really very angry [*sehr böse*] at you for this proposal.' Much later Heisenberg said: 'I have really, in this whole period, been in real disagreement with Bohr .... I [could get] really very angry about Bohr ... and the most serious disagreement was at the time of the uncertainty relations ... Bohr, of course, when he had really seen the argument, would always agree on it; there was never any difficulty of this kind.'[27] I shall discuss the issue of the uncertainty relations in the next chapter.

Heisenberg always got along well with Kramers. He admired his knowledge of physics and of languages and also his musical talents. 'Well, how can a man know so much?'[26] They used to play music together, Heisenberg at the piano, Kramers on the cello, and also produced a joint paper,[34] completed in December 1924, Heisenberg's last contribution in that year. Its redaction was entirely due to Kramers.[35]*

In this paper we find for the first time a detailed derivation of Kramers' dispersion relation which the latter had barely sketched in his earlier writing.[13,14] As mentioned before, Kramers had based those two papers on Einstein's concepts (see (10c)) of the probabilities for light emission and absorption, quantities that are quadratic functions of the transition amplitudes. In Kramers and Heisenberg expressions are given for the first time in terms of the amplitudes themselves.** This step from quadratic to linear was absolutely crucial for Heisenberg's first paper on quantum mechanics the next year.

In addition to this methodological point the paper also contains new physics. Kramers had dealt only with elastic processes, that is, the frequency of the incident and secondary light are identical but the latter may be emitted in any arbitrary direction. The new paper also contains inelastic processes of the type†

$$hv + E_a = hv' + E_b,$$

where E_a (E_b) is the energy of the initial (final) atomic state and v (v') is the frequency of the incident (secondary) light. The states a and b may or may not be the same. The frequency v' is smaller (larger) than v if the atom jumps from a lower to a higher (higher to lower) state. These inelastic transitions, already suggested in 1923 by Adolf Smekal,[36] were not observed until 1928. They are now called Raman scattering, after their discoverer.[37]

Later Heisenberg remarked about this collaboration: 'One felt one had now come a step further in getting into the spirit of the new mechanics. Everybody knew there must be some new kind of mechanics behind it and nobody had a clear idea of it, but still, one felt this was a new step in the right direction . . . Almost one had matrix mechanics at this point without knowing it[27] . . . This new scheme [matrix mechanics] was a continuation of what I had done with Kramers . . . a more systematic continuation of which

* This may explain references to BKS, again of no relevance to this paper, both in the abstract and the conclusion.

** It cannot be deduced from the two *Nature* letters[13,14] whether or not Kramers knew these expressions earlier.

† Here, as in Kramers' earlier two papers, small velocity changes of the atom as a whole are neglected.

one could hope, but not know, that it would be a consistent scheme[38]. . . I always regretted that Kramers never got the Nobel Prize.'[26]

Matrix mechanics arrived in July 1925. A comment by Pauli[39] in the preceding May may serve as a fitting final farewell to the old quantum theory: 'Physics is . . . much too difficult for me and I wished I were a film comedian or something like that and that I never had heard anything about physics! Now I do hope that Bohr will save us all with a new idea. I urgently request that he do so.'

(d) 1925: how quantum mechanics emerged 'quite vaguely from the fog'(*)

In April 1925 Heisenberg completed yet another unsuccessful paper[40] on the anomalous Zeeman effect. (Recall: at that time spin had not yet arrived.) Then he left Copenhagen for Göttingen where already in July 1924 (aged 22!) he had become *privatdozent*. From Germany he wrote to Bohr[41] to thank him for the most wonderful half year of studies he had experienced to date.

His next project was 'fabricating quantum mechanics'.[42] First, he tried for a few weeks (following ideas gleaned from his paper with Kramers) to guess how to treat the intensities of the hydrogen spectral lines.[43] 'Then I realized that I couldn't; it was too complicated stuff.'[44] Next he turned to simpler mechanical systems. A letter[45] dated 5 June gives the first glimpses of what he was up to. By that time he had become unwell, however. 'I had this . . . very bad attack of hay fever. I couldn't see from my eyes, I just was in a terrible state.'[44] So he decided to seek better air and on 7 June left[46] for the North Sea island of Helgoland. 'I took a night train to Cuxhaven . . . I was extremely tired and my whole face was swollen. So I tried to get breakfast in a small inn there and the landlady said, "Well, you must have had a pretty bad night. You must have been beaten by somebody."'[44] In Helgoland he hardly slept, dividing his time between inventing quantum mechanics, climbing around on rocks and learning by heart poems from Goethe's *West-Östicher Divan*.[47] It was in Helgoland that Heisenberg made his breakthrough (to which I turn in a moment). 'It was about three o'clock at night when the final result of the calculation lay before me . . . At first I was deeply shaken . . . I was so excited that I could not think of sleep. So I left the house . . . and awaited the sunrise on top of a rock.'[48] That was 'the night of Helgoland'.[49]

On 19 June Heisenberg returned to Göttingen.[46] On 24 June he sent an outline of his results to Pauli, noting that 'everything is still unclear to me.'[50] On 9 July Heisenberg writes[51] to Pauli that his views are getting more radical by the day and that his efforts are directed towards killing the concept of orbits. Pauli's response is very positive.[52] On 25 July his paper announcing the discovery of quantum mechanics[53] is received by the *Zeitschrift für Physik*.

Heisenberg has compared[54] his discovery with what occasionally happens in the course of mountain climbing:

When you do some mountaineering . . . you sometimes . . . want to climb some peak but there is fog everywhere . . . you have your map or some other indication where you probably have to go and still you are completely lost in the fog. Then . . . all of a sudden you see, quite vaguely in the fog, just a few minute things from which you say, "Oh, this is the rock I want." In the very moment that you have seen that, then the whole picture changes completely, because although you still don't know whether you will make the rock, nevertheless for a moment you say, ". . . Now I know where I am; I have to go closer to that and then I will certainly find the way to go . . ." So long as I only see details, as one does on any part of mountaineering, then of course I can say all right, I can go ahead for the next 15 yards, or 100 yards, or perhaps one kilometer, but still I don't know whether this is right or may be completely off the real track.'

That perfectly characterizes Heisenberg's most important contribution,[53] one of the great jumps – perhaps the greatest – in the development of twentieth century physics. His paper combines brilliant vision with firm assertion. Its abstract at once sets the correct tone for a new future: 'The present paper seeks to establish a basis for theoretical quantum mechanics founded exclusively upon relationships between quantities which are in principle observable' – which atomic orbits are not. It bids farewell to the old quantum theory: 'We should concede that the partial agreement of the quantum rules with experience is more or less fortuitous.' And it starts a frontal attack on the classical picture of orbits: 'Even for the simplest quantum theoretical problems the validity of classical mechanics cannot be maintained.' Yet Heisenberg is not by any means clear about what he is doing. He is still groping. He (quite properly) concluded his paper by stressing the need for 'a more intensive mathematical investigation of the method which has been quite superficially employed here.'

I proceed to summarize Heisenberg's main points but at once replace his notation by an improved one that would come in use a few months later. This, to the best of my ability in following him through the fog, is what he did.

What, in one dimension, is a classical orbit? It is described by one coordinate x that varies continuously as a function of the time t, an orbit is given symbolically as $x(t)$. Now Heisenberg seeks inspiration from his previous work with Kramers. There the issue had been to find amplitudes $A(v)$ for the scattering of light with frequency v by an atom. $A(v)$ should depend on the transitions from atomic states n to states m, as indicated by the symbol (*not* used by Kramers–Heisenberg) $A_{mn}(v)$. Now Heisenberg reasoned (I think), let us try to do something similar for $x(t)$, represent it by the 'quantum symbol' $x_{mn}(t)$, where, to fix ideas, m and n refer to quantum states of a harmonic oscillator, the simplest example he discussed in his paper.* There are two possibilities. Either m equals n: $x_{nn}(t)$, which shall represent the coordinate at time t insofar as the system is in state n. Or m does not equal n, when $x_{mn}(t)$ shall represent what one might call a coordinate in transition. Likewise the classical velocity $v(t)$ in the orbit shall be represented by $v_{mn}(t)$. All these quantities satisfy Heisenberg's criterion of being 'in principle observable'.**

Classically the continuous orbit $x(t)$ satisfies an equation of motion which tells us how the particle moves from one position and velocity to another. Heisenberg assumes that each of the quantities $x_{mn}(t)$ satisfies that same equation. Next he asks: what is the energy of the particle in the state n? Again he takes over the classical expression for the energy, a function of $x(t)$ and $v(t)$. Classically one proceeds by finding solutions of the equations of motion, substituting those in the energy expression and so obtaining the corresponding energy values. Heisenberg proceeded likewise in trying to find the quantized energies E_n. But now he had to make a crucial decision. The energy of the oscillator (our example) depends on the squares of $x(t)$ and $v(t)$. If one represents $x(t)$ by $x_{mn}(t)$, then how should one represent $x^2(t)$?

'It seems that the simplest and most natural assumption would be'

$$x_{mn}^2(t) = \sum_k (x_{mk}(t) \times x_{kn}(t)),$$

where $\sum_k$ means: sum over all possible values of k. Ever since 1925 that assumption has proved to be perfect.

Before proceeding further, Heisenberg noted that 'a significant difficulty arises, however, if we consider two quantities $x(t)$, $y(t)$ and ask for their product $x(t)y(t)$'. In view of what he had done for $x^2(t)$, he was forced to assume more generally that

$$[x(t)y(t)]_{mn} = \sum_k (x_{mk}(t) \times y_{kn}(t)).$$

What was the difficulty? '*Whereas in classical theory $x(t)y(t)$ is always equal to $y(t)x(t)$, this is not necessarily the case in quantum theory* [my italics].' Initially Heisenberg was much troubled by this unfamiliar multiplication property. He later recalled: 'There was a very disagreeable situation about it that xy is not equal to yx ... [I] was very dissatisfied with this situation ... it worried me terribly that xy was not equal to yx.'[44] The reader who is puzzled by this peculiar behavior of products, all-pervasive in quantum

---

* He also treated an anharmonic oscillator and a rotator.
** Thus x_{mn} can be simply related to the intensity of light emitted in the transition $n \rightarrow m$.

mechanics, is therefore in the good company of the man who first noticed this. As a help to the non-initiate I append to this chapter some simple do-it-yourself examples where $x \times y$ does not equal $y \times x$ (see section (h)).

Returning to the energy issue Heisenberg raised the question: Does the energy conservation law work in my new scheme? The classical energy H now becomes represented by an assembly H_{mn}. He needed to show that $H_{nn} = E_n$, the energy in the state n, should not depend on time; that H_{mn} should be zero for m unequal to n – the energy should not jump; and that E_n should be quantized – discrete. While in Helgoland, he was able to prove all these properties for his examples, results he later called 'a gift from heaven'.[44]

On 19 June Heisenberg returned to Göttingen. On 9 July he finished writing up his results.[46] He brought his paper to Born, asking him to submit it for publication if he approved. Then he took off for Leiden and Cambridge and a vacation. He remembered that he was not back in Göttingen until late August.[44] Shortly afterward he wrote[55] to Pauli about 'decisive progress, mainly by Born and Jordan'.

When Heisenberg had given his paper to Born he had said (Born remembered[56]) 'that he had written a crazy paper and did not dare send it in for publication; I should read it [Heisenberg said], and, if I liked it, send it to the *Zeitschrift für Physik*. I read it and became enthusiastic . . . and began to think about it, day and night . . . this multiplication law must have a meaning.' Then 'one morning about 10 July 1925 I suddenly saw light: Heisenberg's symbolic multiplication was nothing but the matrix calculus, well known to me since my student days.'[57] Whereupon Born started a collaboration with his student Pascual Jordan in which they transcribed and extended Heisenberg's result in systematic matrix language.[58] When Heisenberg, still on vacation, received a copy of their manuscript he was 'very happy that Born and Jordan could have done so much about it.'[44]

Assemblies like x_{mn} or v_{mn} are called square matrices. They are conveniently written in a square array such that x_{23}, for example, occupies the intersection of the second row and third column (see section (h)). A specific entry like x_{23} is called a matrix element. A matrix with zero elements only for $m = n$ is called a diagonal matrix.

Born and Jordan showed that Heisenberg's requirements for the energy matrix, that it be diagonal with time-independent diagonal elements, can generally be satisfied for all one-dimensional systems. The most important relation of their paper deals with the momentum (mass times velocity) matrix p_{mn} and the coordinate matrix q_{mn} for any one dimensional system:

$$\sum_k (p_{nk} \times q_{km} - q_{nk} \times p_{km}) = \begin{cases} h/2\pi i & \text{if } n \text{ and } m \text{ are equal,} \\ 0 & \text{if } n \text{ and } m \text{ are not equal.} \end{cases}$$

Shortly after the completion of this article Born received a reprint of a paper by the British physicist Paul Dirac[59] which contained many of the results he and Jordan had just found. 'This was – I remember well – one of the greatest surprises of my scientific life. For the name Dirac was completely unknown to me, the author appeared to be a youngster [Dirac was eight months younger than Heisenberg], yet everything was perfect in its way and admirable.'[60] Dirac had obtained the same 'commutation relations' between p_{mn} and q_{mn} and had written them in the more symbolic form

$$pq - qp = \frac{h}{2\pi i}\, 1,$$

where 1 is the unit matrix, all diagonal elements equal 1, all others are zero.

In those days Dirac invented several notations that are now part of the physics language.[61] Numbers a, b, c, ... that commute with anything $(ax = xa)$ he called c-numbers, where 'c stands for classical or maybe commuting'. Sets of numbers that do not commute he termed q-numbers, where 'q stands for quantum or maybe queer'.[62] Dirac was the first, I believe, to receive his Ph.D. thesis on quantum mechanics.[61]

Heisenberg had not known about matrices when he wrote his first paper on quantum mechanics. 'I think I then read some textbooks about matrices and then tried out myself how matrices worked.'[54] He caught up rapidly and soon was collaborating with Born and Jordan. The resulting paper[63] completes the first phase in laying the mathematical foundations of matrix mechanics, a name (not much used anymore) that infuriated Heisenberg[64] because he found it too mathematical.

Quantum mechanics is now taught in good undergraduate courses where students are rapidly made familiar with matrix manipulations. Even now Pauli's contribution[65] in the fall of 1925, the derivation of the Balmer formula, belongs to the more difficult uses of matrix methods. It was also the first instance of what one may call an application of the new techniques to a realistic atomic problem – just as Bohr's treatment of the hydrogen atom had been in the old quantum theory of the atom. In early November Heisenberg expressed his admiration for Pauli's feat.[66]

(c) Bohr's earliest reactions

It was noted that already in June 1925 Heisenberg had begun writing to Pauli about his new work. It is interesting to observe that between early June and late August he did not at all communicate with Bohr! During that period Bohr was busy preparing lectures that contain his final pronouncements on the old quantum theory, which 'is in a most provisional and unsatisfactory stage'.[67] In the outline (all that is preserved[68]) of his talk in Oslo on 24 August, on recent developments in atomic theory, there is no mention of the new quantum mechanics. The first time Heisenberg wrote[69] to Bohr on his work was in fact on 31 August, and then only cryptically: 'As Kramers [who in June had visited Göttingen] perhaps has told you ... I committed the crime of writing a paper on quantum mechanics ... It will probably appear in the next issue of the *Zeitschrift* [*für Physik*].' On that same 31 August Bohr delivered a lecture on 'Atomic theory and mechanics' at a mathematics congress in Copenhagen. A draft of the manuscript prepared (I would think) after the lecture mentions that 'very recently Heisenberg ... has taken a step probably of extraordinary scope'.[70] A definitive and clearly reworked text of this talk, which appeared in December,[71] contains a concluding section on Heisenberg's theory and a note added in proof[72] on Pauli's calculation of the Balmer formula.* Meanwhile Bohr had been briefed in detail by Heisenberg who in mid-September had come to Copenhagen for a one month visit.

Letters by Bohr from the fall of 1925 show his delight in the new developments. To Ehrenfest: 'I am full of enthusiasm [about Heisenberg's work] and generally about the prospects for further developments.'[74] To Heisenberg, after hearing about Pauli's derivation of the Balmer formula: 'I do not know whether to congratulate him [P.] or you the most.'[75] To Fowler in Cambridge, the same day: 'I have just heard that Dirac has made some important contributions.'[76] Quantum mechanics must also have been a topic when in December Bohr met Einstein in Leiden during the celebration of the golden jubilee of Lorentz's doctorate.[77] Unfortunately the substance of their discussion is not known.[78]

Finally, Bohr to Rutherford on 27 January 1926: 'Due to the last work of Heisenberg prospects have at a stroke been realized which although only vague[ly] grasped have for a long time been the centre of our wishes.'[79]

On the same day Schrödinger's first paper on wave mechanics was received by the *Annalen der Physik*.

(f) Early 1926: the second coming of quantum mechanics

Erwin Schrödinger, only two years younger than Bohr, was born and raised in Vienna. His father was a successful businessman who encouraged the academic interests of his only child. Young Erwin received private tuition until age 11. Then he went to the *Gymnasium*, where he was a first-rate student both in sciences and in languages, with great interests in literature and painting, but not in music. In 1906 he started studies in mathematics

---

* In an editorial [73]preceding this paper, it is noted that 'the mathematics required will be severe'.

and physics at the University of Vienna, showing himself again to be an outstanding student. Already in 1910 he received the Ph.D., on a topic in experimental physics. In 1914 he became *privatdozent*. During World War I he served as artillery officer but managed to remain scientifically active. His academic career led him via a number of brief appointments at German universities to Zürich, where he spent the most productive years of his life and produced his fundamental papers on wave mechanics. (In 1927 he succeeded Planck in Berlin, later spent many years at the Institute for Advanced Studies in Dublin, and eventually returned to his beloved Austria, where he died.)*

Schrödinger had already been actively interested in the quantum theory of the atom before he discovered wave mechanics. In 1921 he had conceived, independently of Bohr, the idea of interpenetrating orbits[81] (see (10e)). In 1924 he had written[82] about the BKS theory. In the fall of 1925 he had begun preparing notes for a lecture course[83] on atomic physics, including the hydrogen spectrum and the Stark and Zeeman effects. Schrödinger's wave mechanics was not an offspring of the work on atomic constitution by Bohr and his school, however, as had been true for Heisenberg's matrix mechanics. Nor had that discovery by Heisenberg guided him. His direct inspiration had rather come from de Broglie and Einstein. In April 1926 he had this to say[84] about the roots of his ideas: 'My theory was stimulated by de Broglie and brief but infinitely far-seeing remarks by Einstein. I am not aware of a generic connection with Heisenberg. I, of course, knew of his theory but was scared away, if not repulsed, by its transcendental algebraic methods which seemed very difficult to me.'**

It was recalled in (11e) that Einstein had referred to de Broglie in one of his contributions to statistical mechanics, a discussion of energy fluctuations in a gas; and that in turn de Broglie had been inspired by Einstein to attribute wave properties to material particles. It is not surprising that Schrödinger had taken note of these papers[90] since statistical mechanics was a prominent topic in his earlier work. In fact, only weeks before his discovery of wave mechanics he had completed a paper[91] devoted to Einstein's theory of quantum gases, which the latter had presented in early January 1926 to the Prussian Academy of Sciences.

---

* See Mehra and Rechenberg[80] for many details of Schrödinger's life and scientific evolution.
** In November 1925 Schrödinger wrote to Einstein that he was absorbed by de Broglie's work.[85] In April 1926 he wrote to him: 'The whole business would not have been produced now, and perhaps never (I mean, not by me), if [one of your papers] had not impressed me with the importance of de Broglie's ideas.'[86]
Already in July 1925 Walther Elsasser had likewise become intrigued by de Broglie's waves and had correctly identified their first experimental intimations.[87] Even before discovering matrix mechanics Heisenberg had written approvingly of Elsasser's work.[88] In the autumn of 1925 some of Einstein's ideas were also discussed by the Göttingen group.[89]

Odd as it may seem, it was Schrödinger's aspiration from the very beginning and forever thereafter to incorporate, one might say, quantum theory into classical theory. Thus, in April 1926, he quoted Born and Jordan:[58] 'The new [matrix] mechanics presents itself as an essentially discontinuous theory.' And then continued: 'Conversely wave mechanics, based on classical theory, represents *a step towards a continuum theory*' [his italics].[84] Already in the opening paragraph of his January 1926 paper[92] he had explained what classical pictures had inspired him: 'The appearance of integers [quantum numbers] comes about [in wave mechanics] in the same natural way as for example the integer quality of the *number of nodes* [his italics] of a [classical] vibrating string.' Let us see what he had in mind.

Consider an elastic string held fixed at its end points A and B (Fig. 6) and which when at rest spans the straight line segment AB. Make the string vibrate in the 'ground tone', the specific mode where it moves back and forth between the shapes ACB and ADB. The shape ADB is the reflection of ACB relative to the rest position AB. The string can also be made to vibrate in the 'first harmonic' mode, where it moves between the shapes ACDEB (Fig. 7) and the reflection thereof. Point D which does not move up and down is called a node. The string can further vibrate as in Fig. 8, the 'second harmonic', which has two nodes, D and E. Likewise there are vibration patterns with 3, 4, ... nodes. Clearly, the more nodes, the shorter the wavelength and the higher the frequency.

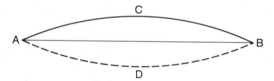

Fig. 6 A string vibrating in the ground tone.

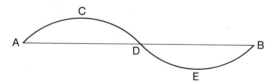

Fig. 7 The same string vibrating in the first harmonic mode.

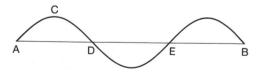

Fig. 8 The same string vibrating in the second harmonic mode.

The ground tone and the harmonics are not the only vibration modes of the string. Any superposition of those nodes is also a possible motion. The important fact is that *any* string motion can always be represented as such a superposition. We say that the set of special motions with 0, 1, 2, . . . modes is a complete set. This is expressd by the general equation

$$\psi(x, t) = \sum_n c_n \psi_n(x, t).$$

Here $\psi(x, t)$, a function of the position x and the time t, is the general amplitude at a given point x, and a given time t. The function ψ is called a wavefunction or also a state, and $\psi_n(x, t)$ is the special amplitude for an n-node motion. The number c_n indicates the amount which the mode ψ_n contributes to ψ. The modes ψ_n are often called eigenstates ('*eigen*' is German for 'proper').

The actual way the string vibrates is determined by an equation for ψ, called the wave equation, and by some additional conditions such as that ψ shall vanish at A and B. Similar classical wave equations occur for two-dimensional problems such as the vibrations of a circular drum. Instead of nodal points one here deals with nodal lines; eigenstates are labeled by two integers. Also three-dimensional cases are familiar in classical physics, for example the vibrations of a spherically symmetric ball, where one encounters two-dimensional nodal surfaces and eigenstates with three labels. In all these cases eigenstates are characterized by specific values, called energy eigenvalues, of the vibrational energy. If some eigenvalues coincide, one speaks of energy degeneracy.

The idea that quantum numbers for atomic states bear some resemblance to the integers that characterize vibrations in terms of numbers of nodes is already found in de Broglie's work of 1923, but only qualitatively. The major quantitative discovery of Schrödinger, announced in his first paper[92] on wave mechanics, was to find the wave equation, the 'Schrödinger equation' for the hydrogen atom (neglecting relativity effects), solve it, observe that the three integers for this three-dimensional problem precisely correspond to the three quantum numbers n, l, m encountered in previous chapters on the old quantum theory, reproduce all the degeneracies known since that earlier period, and derive the Balmer formula. In one phrase, he had found that the respective energies of the Bohr levels are in one-to-one correspondence with the energies of a set of eigenstates. (Spin came later, as we shall see.)

So now there were two distinct derivations of the Balmer formula, one by Pauli via matrix mechanics, one by Schrödinger via wave mechanics. (Pauli's paper[65] had been received by the editors on 17 January 1926, Schrödinger's[92] only ten days later. This explains the latter's absence of reference to Pauli.) Schrödinger went one step further than Pauli, however.

The often mentioned Balmer formula refers to the set of discrete energy levels of an electron bound in hydrogen. The levels get denser the higher the energy region until one reaches a limit, the ionization limit, beyond which the levels fill a continuum corresponding, in classical terms, to energies of *unbound* electrons in hyperbolic orbits in which an electron comes from far away, bends around the nucleus, and moves off far away again. I have not mentioned these unbound states before, simply because there was not much to say about them. Among the advances produced by Schrödinger's wave equation one must certainly include the account, for the first time, of not only the discrete but also the continuous hydrogen levels.

During the next half year Schrödinger's paper of January 1926, 'Quantization as eigenvalue problem', was followed by three others[93] with the same title. These contain elaborations of the mathematical technology and applications to other problems, the Stark effect, intensities and polarizations of spectral lines, and a relativistic version of the Schrödinger equation. During those months it rapidly became evident that the matrix and wave methods gave identical results also in instances other than hydrogen. The obvious question arose: What have these so different looking formalisms to do with each other? The answer: they are in all generality equivalent expressions of the same state of affairs, was given independently by several physicists, Schrödinger,[84] Pauli,[94] and Carl Eckart[95] from Cal Tech. Leaving aside all (very important!) technicalities I only note the main point: for m not equal to n Heisenberg's 'mn matrix elements' correspond to transitions between Schrödinger's eigenstates n and m. The 'nn-matrix elements' correspond to the probability of finding the system in the state n. Once that is understood, the transcription of one language into another, including whatever one desires, such as commutation relations, becomes a relatively simple matter. Ever since that was clear, the term quantum mechanics has been understood to refer both to matrix and to wave mechanics.

The answer to the much more profound question of what do Schrödinger's electron waves have to do with the good old picture of electrons as particles would take longer to become clear – in fact there are some, not many, who believe that the dust has still not settled on that issue. Let us see next what was thought about this problem during 1926.

(g) The summer of 1926: Born on probability, causality, and determinism*

Most physicists active in 1925–6 were familiar with large parts of the mathematical techniques used in wave mechanics because of many

* This section is an abbreviated version of my essay 'Max Born and the statistical interpretation of quantum mechanics'.[96]

similarities with such classical subjects as acoustics. The methods of matrix mechanics were much harder to assimilate. George Uhlenbeck has told me: 'The Schrödinger theory came as a great relief, now we did not any longer have to learn the strange mathematics of matrices.' Isidor Rabi has told me how he looked through books on classical mechanics for a nice problem to solve by Schrödinger's method, found the symmetric top, went to Kronig, and said: 'Let's do it.' They did.[97] Eugene Wigner has told me: 'People began making calculations but it was rather foggy.' Indeed, until the summer of 1926, quantum mechanics, whether in its matrix or its wave formulation, was high mathematical technology, manifestly important because of the answers it produced, but without clearly stated underlying physical principles. No wonder that Planck would write to Schrödinger at that time that he was reading his papers like a child reads a puzzle.[98]

Schrödinger was the first, I believe, to propose such principles in the context of quantum mechanics, in a note completed not later than May 1926 which appeared[99] on 9 July. He suggested that waves are the basic reality, particles are only derivative things. In support of this monistic view he considered a wave packet made up out of linear harmonic oscillator wavefunctions.

What is a wave packet? It is a superposition of eigenfunctions so chosen that at a given time the packet looks like a blob localized in a more or less small region. You saw a wave packet when as a child you played with a jump rope held at one end by you, at the other by a friend. Let the rope hang loosely, then give it a single jerk. You see a single localized bump propagate from your to your friend's hand. That bump is a wave packet.

Back to Schrödinger. He examined what happened to his wave packet in the course of time and found (his italics): 'Our wave packet holds *permanently together*, does *not* expand over an ever greater domain in the course of time.' [99] This result led him to anticipate that a particle is nothing more nor less than a very confined packet of waves, and that, therefore, wave mechanics would turn out to be a branch of classical physics, a new branch, to be sure, yet as classical as the theory of vibrating strings or drums or balls.

Schrödinger's calculation was correct; his anticipation was not. The case of the oscillator is very special: wave packets almost never hold permanently together in the course of time. A more profound break with the past was called for. This was made by Born in June 1926.

On 2 November 1925 Born had left Göttingen for a tour of the United States. Later that month he lectured on quantum mechanics at MIT, out of which grew the first book ever[100] dealing with the new theory. Also at MIT he, together with Norbert Wiener, published the first paper[101] on quantum mechanics to be written in the United States. After further lectures, in

Chicago, Madison, Berkeley, and at Cal Tech and Columbia University he returned to Göttingen.

On 25 June 1926 Born's first paper[102] on wave mechanics was received. It is entitled 'Quantum mechanics of collision phenomena' and deals with the scattering by a center of force of a steady beam of particles coming in with the same velocity and from the same direction. *It is the first paper to contain the quantum mechanical probability concept.** In order to make this decisive new step, 'it is necessary [Born wrote half a year later[103]] to drop completely the physical pictures of Schrödinger which aim at a revitalization of the classical continuum theory, to retain only the formalism and to fill that with new physical content'.

In his June paper Born described the scattering by a wavefunction ψ_{mn}, where the label n symbolizes the initial beam direction, while m denotes some particular direction of observation of the scattered particles.** At that point Born introduced quantum mechanical probability: 'ψ_{mn} determines the probability for the scattering of the electron . . . into the direction [m].'

At best this statement is vague. Born added a footnote in proof to his evidently hastily written paper: 'A more precise consideration shows that the probability is proportional to the square of ψ_{mn}.' This is still not right: he should have written 'absolute square' (a term explained in section (h)). But he clearly had got the point. And so the correct expression for the quantum mechanical probability entered physics via a footnote!

If Born's paper lacked formal precision, causality and determinism were brought sharply into focus as the central issue:

One obtains the answer to the question, *not* 'what is the state after the collision' but 'how probable is a given effect of the collision' . . . Here the whole problem of determinism arises. From the point of view of our quantum mechanics there exists no quantity which in an individual case causally determines the effect of a collision . . . I myself tend to give up determinism in the atomic world.[102]

Born was not yet quite clear, however, about the distinction between the new probability in the quantum mechanical sense and the old probability as it appears in classical statistical mechanics: 'It does not seem out of the question that the intimate connection which here appears between mechanics and statistics may demand a revision of the thermodynamic-statistical principles.'[102]

---

* Even earlier Schrödinger had gathered all the necessary mathematical tools for introducing probability but had not given the correct physical interpretation of those results; see the third paper in Ref. 93.

** Technically, Born wrote the wavefunction at large distances from the force center as $\exp ikz + \psi_{mn}(\exp ikr)/r$, where z and r respectively denote the distance of the incoming plane wave and the scattered beam from the center, and $k = 2\pi mv/h$, where m is the mass and v the velocity of the incoming particles.

One month after the June paper, Born completed a sequel with the same title.[104] His formalism is firm now and he makes a major new point. He considers a wavefunction ψ referring to a system with discrete, non-degenerate eigenstates ψ_n and notes that, in the expansion $\psi = \sum c_n \psi_n$, $|c_n|^2$ is the probability for the system to be in the state n.* In June he had discussed *probabilities of transition*, a concept which, at least phenomenologically, had been part of physics since 1916 when Einstein had introduced his A and B coefficients in the theory of radiative transitions – and at once had begun to worry about causality (see (10c)). Now Born introduced the *probability of a state*. That had never been done before. He also expressed beautifully the essence of wave mechanics:

The motion of particles follows probability laws but the probability itself propagates according to the law of causality.

During the summer of 1926 Born's insights into the physical principles of quantum mechanics developed rapidly. On 10 August he read a paper[105] before the meeting of the British Association at Oxford, in which he clearly distinguished between the 'new' and the 'old' probabilities in physics: 'The classical theory introduces the microscopic coordinates which determine the individual processes only to eliminate them because of ignorance by averaging over their values; whereas the new theory gets the same results without introducing them at all . . . We free forces of their classical duty of determining directly the motion [that is, the orbits] of particles and allow them instead to determine the probability of states.'

What stimulated Born's radical new ideas? As I see it, his inspiration came from Einstein, not, however, the latter's statistical papers bearing on light, but his never published speculations during the early 1920s on the dynamics of light-quanta and wave fields. Born states so explicitly in his second paper:[104] 'I start from a remark by Einstein on the relation between [a] wave field and light-quanta; he [E.] said approximately that the waves are only there to show the way to the corpuscular light-quanta, and talked in this sense of a 'ghost field' [*Gespensterfeld*] [which] determines the *probability* [my italics] for a light-quantum . . . to take a definite path . . .'

It is hardly surprising that Einstein was concerned that early with these issues. In 1909 he had been the first to write about particle–wave duality. In 1916 he had been the first to relate the existence of transition probabilities (for spontaneous emission of light) to quantum theoretical origins – though how this relation was to be formally established he did of course not know as yet. Little concrete is known about his ideas of a ghost field or guiding field ('*Führungsfeld*'). The best description we have is from Wigner,[106] who knew

---

* Those familiar with the elements of quantum mechanics will note that this statement is sloppy. It needs to be added that ψ is normalized and that the set ψ_n is orthonormal. Those in need of further explanations are urged to consult a simple textbook on quantum mechanics.

Einstein personally in the 1920s: '[Einstein's] picture has a great similarity with the present picture of quantum mechanics. Yet Einstein, though in a way he was fond of it, never published it. He realized that it is in conflict with the conservation principles . . . This, Einstein never could accept and hence never took his idea of the guiding field quite seriously . . . The problem was solved, as we know, by Schrödinger's theory.' [107]

Born was even more explicit about his source of inspiration in a letter to Einstein[108] written in November 1926 (for reasons not clear to me, this letter is not found in the published Born–Einstein correspondence): 'About me it can be told that physicswise I am entirely satisfied since my idea to look upon Schrödinger's wave field as a *'Gespensterfeld'* in your sense proves better all the time. Pauli and Jordan have made beautiful advances in this direction . . . Schrödinger's achievement reduces itself to something purely mathematical; his physics is quite wretched [*recht kümmerlich*].'

Thus it seems to me that Born's thinking was conditioned by the following circumstances. He knew and accepted the fertility of Schrödinger's formalism but not Schrödinger's attempt at interpretation: 'He [Schr.] believed . . . that he had accomplished a return to classical thinking; he regarded the electron not as a particle but as a density distribution given by the square of his wavefunction $|\psi|^2$. He argued that the idea of particles and of quantum jumps be given up altogether; he never faltered in this conviction . . . I, however, was witnessing the fertility of the particle concept every day in [James] Franck's brilliant experiments on atomic and molecular collisions and was convinced that particles could not simply be abolished. [Franck was professor of experimental physics in Göttingen.] A way had to be found for reconciling particles and waves.' [109] His quest for this way led him to reflect on Einstein's idea of a ghost field. His next step, from ψ to $|\psi|^2$, was entirely his own. We owe to Born the beginning insight that ψ itself, *unlike* the electromagnetic field, has no direct physical reality.

It is a bit strange – and caused Born some chagrin – that in the early days his papers on the probability concept were not always adequately acknowledged. Heisenberg's own version[110] of the probability interpretation, written in Copenhagen in November 1926, does not mention Born. One finds no reference to Born's work in the two editions of Mott and Massey's book[111] on atomic collisions, nor in Kramers' book[112] on quantum mechanics. In his authoritative *Handbuch der Physik* article of 1933, Pauli refers to this contribution by Born only in passing, in a footnote.[113] Jörgen Kalckar has written to me about his recollections of discussions with Bohr on this issue. 'Bohr said that as soon as Schrödinger had demonstrated the equivalence between his wave mechanics and Heisenberg's matrix mechanics, the "interpretation" of the wavefunction was obvious . . . For this reason, Born's paper was received without surprise in Copenhagen. "We had never dreamt that it could be otherwise," Bohr said.' A similar comment was made by Mott: 'Perhaps the probability interpretation was the most important of all [of Born's contributions to quantum mechanics], but given Schrödinger, de Broglie, and the experimental results, this must have been very quickly apparent to everyone, and in fact when I worked in Copenhagen in 1928 it was already called the "Copenhagen interpretation" – I do not think I ever realized that Born was the first to put it forward.'[114] In response to a query, Casimir, who started his university studies in 1926, wrote to me: 'I learned the Schrödinger equation simultaneously with the interpretation. It is curious that I do not recall that Born was especially referred to. He was of course mentioned as co-creator of matrix mechanics.' The very same comments apply to my own university education which started a decade later.

Born may not at once have realized the profundity of his work in the summer of 1926. In a later interview[115] he said:

We were so accustomed to making statistical considerations, and to shift it one layer deeper seemed to us not so very important.

Nevertheless his contributions mark the first important steps towards the physical interpretation of quantum mechanics, even though they are not by any means the last word on that subject, as we shall see in the next chapter, where Bohr rejoins the fray.

(h) Appendix: *c- and q-numbers for pedestrians*

The most familiar kinds of numbers are the integers, the rational numbers, those that can be written as the quotient of integers, like 57/23, and the irrational numbers like the square root of 2, not a ratio of integers. These and their negatives belong to the class of real numbers. They can be marked on a line that runs from minus to plus infinity.

Complex numbers cannot be marked on that line. They contain the square root of minus one, always denoted by i, so $i^2 = -1$. A real number times i is called an imaginary number. The sum of a real and an imaginary number, like $4 + 5i$, is called a complex number. Complex numbers are conveniently depicted in the 'complex plane', where their real part is marked off on one straight line, the imaginary part on another straight line perpendicular to the first.

Complex numbers can be subjected to addition: $(4+5i)+(1+2i)=5+7i$; subtraction: $(4+5i)-(1+2i)=3+3i$; multiplication: $(4+5i)\times(1+2i)=-6+13i$; and division:

$$\frac{(4+5i)}{(1+2i)}=\frac{(4+5i)\times(1-2i)}{(1+2i)\times(1-2i)}=\frac{14-3i}{5}.$$

The complex conjugate of a complex number is another complex number in which i is replaced by $-$i. Thus $4-5i$ is the complex conjugate of $4+5i$. The absolute square of a complex number is its product with its complex conjugate. It is always real and never negative, thus $(4+5i) \times (4-5i) = 41$.

Both real and complex numbers satisfy the commutative law of multiplication: for any pair a and b, $a \times b = b \times a$. Numbers that satisfy this law are called c-numbers.

A wavefunction is in practice nearly always a complex function, that is, a real function $+$ i times another real function. Its absolute square is always real and never negative, a necessary property of a probability density.

A q-number is another name for a matrix. As was noted in section (d), matrices are square arrays with matrix elements that are c-numbers. Simple examples are

$$A = \begin{bmatrix} 1+2i & 3+4i \\ 5+6i & 7+8i \end{bmatrix}, \qquad B = \begin{bmatrix} 9+10i & 11+12i \\ 13+14i & 15+16i \end{bmatrix}.$$

The notation A_{mn} refers to the element of A that stands in row number m, column number n, thus $A_{12} = 3 + 4i$. Two matrices are said to be equal (unequal) if all (not all) their respective matrix elements are equal. It has no meaning, however, to say that one matrix is smaller or larger than another.

Let C denote the product matrix $A \times B$. According to the rule given in section (d), the elements of C are given by

$$C_{11} = A_{11} \times B_{11} + A_{12} \times B_{21}; \qquad C_{12} = A_{11} \times B_{12} + A_{12} \times B_{22};$$
$$C_{21} = A_{21} \times B_{11} + A_{22} \times B_{21}; \qquad C_{22} = A_{21} \times B_{12} + A_{22} \times B_{22}.$$

Thus $C_{11} = -28 + 122i$, $C_{12} = -32 + 142i$, $C_{21} = -36 + 316i$, $C_{22} = -40 + 358i$.

Let D denote the product $B \times A$. Then $D_{11} = -28 + 154i$, $D_{12} = -32 + 238i$, $D_{21} = -36 + 210i$, $D_{22} = -40 + 326i$. Thus A and B do not commute, $A \times B$ does not equal $B \times A$.

What has been exemplified with the help of matrices having two rows and columns can be applied for matrices of any size – even for matrices with infinitely many rows and columns. The latter are by no means a rarity. It can be shown, for example, that the commutation relation for p and q found in section (d) can only be satisfied with infinite matrices!

References

1. N. Bohr, *Encyclopaedia Britannica* 13th edn., Vol. 29, p. 262, CW, Vol. 4, p. 657.
2. C. G. Barkla, *ibid.*, Vol. 31, p. 269.
3. J. C. Slater, *Quantum theory of atomic structure*, McGraw-Hill, New York 1960.

4. SL, Chap. 25; IB, Chap. 13, section (d).
5. S. N. Bose, *Zeitschr. Phys.* **26**, 178, 1924.
6. A. Einstein, *Verh. Preuss. Ak. der Wiss.* 1924, p. 261; 1925, pp 3, 18.
7. E. Fermi, *Rend. Acc. Lincei* **3**, 145, 1926; *Zeitschr. Phys.* **36**, 902, 1926, repr. in *Enrico Fermi, collected works*, Vol. 1, pp. 181, 186, University of Chicago Press 1962.
8. P. A. M. Dirac, *Proc. Roy. Soc.* A **112**, 661, 1926.
9. N. Bohr, letter to A. Sommerfeld, 15 April 1943, NBA.
10. A. Sommerfeld, letter to N. Bohr, 25 April 1921, NBA.
11. W. Pauli, letter to N. Bohr, 21 February 1924, CW, Vol. 5, p. 412.
12. M. Born, *My life*, p. 216, Taylor and Francis, London 1976.
13. H. A. Kramers, *Nature* **113**, 673, 1924, repr. in CW, Vol. 5, p. 44.
14. H. A. Kramers, *Nature* **114**, 310, 1924, repr. in CW, Vol. 5, p. 45.
15. M. Dresden, *H. A. Kramers*, pp. 145, 157–8, Springer, New York 1987.
16. Cf. IB, p. 499ff.
17. M. Born, *Zeitschr. Phys.* **26**, 379, 1925, English transl. in B. L. van der Waerden, *Sources of quantum mechanics*, p. 181, Dover, New York 1968.
18. W. Pauli, letter to A. Sommerfeld, 6 December 1924, CW, Vol. 5, p. 37.
19. W. Pauli, letter to N. Bohr, 12 December 1924, CW, Vol. 5, p. 426.
20. W. Pauli, *Zeitschr. Phys.* **31**, 373, 1925.
21. N. Bohr, letter to W. Pauli, 10 January 1925, CW, Vol. 5, p. 438.
22. R. de L. Kronig, *J. Am. Optical Soc.* **12**, 547, 1926.
23. H. A. Kramers, *Atti del Congr. di Como* **2**, 545, 1927; *Phys. Zeitschr.* **30**, 522, 1929; repr. in H. A. Kramers, *Collected scientific papers*, pp. 333, 347, North-Holland, Amsterdam 1956.
24. For a complete list of references to these papers see *Werner Heisenberg's collected works*, Series A, part I, p. 631, Springer, New York 1985.
25. W. Heisenberg, interview by T. S. Kuhn, 11 February, 1963, NBA.
26. Ref. 25, interview on 19 February 1963.
27. Ref. 25, interview on 13 February 1963.
28. CW, Vol. 5, p. 54.
29. N. Bohr, *Naturw.* **12**, 1115, 1924, English transl. in CW, Vol. 5, p. 148.
30. W. Heisenberg, *Zeitschr. Phys.* **31**, 617, 1925.
31. N. Bohr, letters to J. Franck, 1 November 1924, to R. H. Fowler, 5 December 1924, CW, Vol. 5, pp. 344 and 334.
32. N. Bohr, letter to W. Heisenberg, 2 January 1925, CW, Vol. 5, p. 62.
33. W. Heisenberg, letter to N. Bohr, 8 January 1925, CW, Vol. 5, p. 357 (in German), p. 359 (in English).
34. H. A. Kramers and W. Heisenberg, *Zeitschr. Phys.* **31**, 681, 1925, English transl. in van der Waerden (Ref. 17), p. 223.
35. Van der Waerden (Ref. 17), p. 16.
36. A. Smekal, *Naturw.* **11**, 873, 1923.
37. Cf. C. V. Raman and K. S. Krishnan, *Nature* **121**, 501, 1928; see also G. Landsberg and L. Mandelstam, *Naturw.* **16**, 557, 1928.
38. Ref. 25, interview on 5 July 1963.
39. W. Pauli, letter to R. de L. Kronig, then in Copenhagen, 21 May 1925, repr. in *W. Pauli, scientific correspondence*, Vol. 1, p. 214, Springer, New York 1979.

40. W. Heisenberg, *Zeitschr. Phys.* **32**, 841, 1925.
41. W. Heisenberg, letter to N. Bohr, 21 April 1925, NBA.
42. W. Heisenberg, letter to W. Pauli, 21 June 1925, repr. in Ref. 39, Vol. 1, p. 219.
43. W. Heisenberg, letter to N. Bohr, 16 May 1925, CW, Vol. 5, p. 363.
44. Ref. 25, interview on 22 February 1963.
45. W. Heisenberg, letter to R. de L. Kronig, 5 June 1925, repr. in *Theoretical physics in the twentieth century*, p. 23, Eds. M. Fierz and V. Weisskopf, Interscience, New York, 1960.
46. Ref. 24, p. 4.
47. A. Hermann, *Werner Heisenberg*, p. 32 (communication by C. F. von Weizsäcker), Rowohlt, Hamburg 1976.
48. W. Heisenberg, *Der Teil und das Ganze*, p. 879, Piper, Munich 1969.
49. Ref. 48, p. 80.
50. W. Heisenberg, letter to W. Pauli, 24 June 1925, repr. in Ref. 39, Vol. 1, p. 225.
51. W. Heisenberg, letter to W. Pauli, 9 July 1925, repr. in Ref. 39, Vol. 1, p. 231.
52. W. Pauli, letter to H. A. Kramers, 27 July 1925, repr. in Ref. 39, Vol. 1, p. 232.
53. W. Heisenberg, *Zeitschr. Phys.* **33**, 879, 1925, English transl. in van der Waerden (Ref. 17), p. 261.
54. Ref. 25, interview on 25 February 1963.
55. W. Heisenberg, letter to W. Pauli, 18 September 1925, repr. in ref. 39, Vol. 1, p. 236.
56. M. Born, interview by P. P. Ewald, June 1960, NBA.
57. Ref. 12, p. 217.
58. M. Born and P. Jordan, *Zeitschr. Phys.* **34**, 858, 1925, English transl. in van der Waerden (Ref. 17), p. 277.
59. P. A. M. Dirac, *Proc. Roy. Soc.* A **109**, 642, 1925, repr. in van der Waerden (Ref. 17), p. 307.
60. Ref. 12, p. 226.
61. For a sketch of Dirac's scientific contributions see e.g. A. Pais, in *Paul Adrien Maurice Dirac,* p. 93, Eds. B. Kursunoglu and E. P. Wigner, Cambridge University Press 1987.
62. P. A. M. Dirac, in *History of twentieth century physics*, p. 86, Academic Press, New York 1977.
63. M. Born, W. Heisenberg, and P. Jordan, *Zeitschr. Phys.* **35**, 557, 1926; English transl. in van der Waerden (Ref. 17) p. 321.
64. W. Heisenberg, letter to W. Pauli, 16 November 1925, repr. in Ref. 39, Vol. 1, p. 255.
65. W. Pauli, *Zeitschr. Phys.* **36**, 336, 1926, cf. also P. A. M. Dirac, *Proc. Roy. Soc.* A **110**, 561, 1926.
66. W. Heisenberg, letter to W. Pauli, 3 November 1925, repr. in Ref. 39, Vol. 1, p. 252.
67. N. Bohr, letter to W. Heisenberg, 10 June 1925, CW, Vol. 5, p. 364.
68. N. Bohr, CW, Vol. 5, p. 252; also *ibid.*, p. 281.
69. W. Heisenberg, letter to N. Bohr, 31 August 1925, CW, Vol. 5, p. 366.
70. CW, Vol. 5, p. 261.
71. N. Bohr, *Nature* **116** (Suppl.), 845, 1925, CW, Vol. 5, p. 269.
72. Ref. 70, footnote 17.

73. CW, Vol. 5, p. 272.
74. N. Bohr, letter to P. Ehrenfest, 14 October, 1925, NBA.
75. N. Bohr, letter to W. Heisenberg, 26 November 1925, CW, Vol. 5, p. 224.
76. N. Bohr, letter to R. H. Fowler, 26 November 1925, CW, Vol. 5, p. 337.
77. N. Bohr, letter to P. Ehrenfest, 22 December 1925, CW, Vol. 5, p. 329.
78. See, however, N. Bohr, letter to J. C. Slater, 28 January 1926, CW, Vol. 5, p. 497.
79. N. Bohr, letter to E. Rutherford, 27 January 1926, CW, Vol. 5, p. 457.
80. J. Mehra and H. Rechenberg, *The historical development of quantum theory*, Vol. 5, Springer, New York 1987.
81. E. Schrödinger, *Zeitschr. Phys.* **4**, 347, 1921.
82. E. Schrödinger, *Naturw.* **12**, 720, 1924.
83. Ref. 80, pp. 410, 467.
84. E. Schrödinger, *Ann. der Phys.* **79**, 734, 1926, esp. footnote on p. 735.
85. Ref. 80, p. 420.
86. E. Schrödinger, letter to A. Einstein, 23 April 1926, repr. in *Briefe über Wellenmechanik*, p. 24, Ed. K. Przibram, Springer, Vienna, 1963.
87. W. Elsasser, *Naturw.* **13**, 711, 1925.
88. W. Heisenberg, letter to W. Pauli, 29 June 1925, Ref. 39, Vol. 1, p. 229.
89. See Ref. 58, Chap. 4, and Ref. 63, Chap. 4, section 3.
90. For more on the relations between the work of de Broglie, Einstein, and Schrödinger see SL, Chap. 24.
91. E. Schrödinger, *Sitz. Ber. Preuss. Ak. Wiss.* 1926, p. 23.
92. E. Schrödinger, *Ann. der Phys.* **79**, 361, 1926.
93. E. Schrödinger, *Ann. der Phys.* **79**, 489; **80**, 437; **81**, 109, all in 1926.
94. W. Pauli, letter to P. Jordan, 12 April 1926, repr. in Ref. 39, Vol. 1, p. 315.
95. C. Eckart, *Phys. Rev.* **28**, 711, 1926.
96. A. Pais, *Science* **218**, 1193, 1982.
97. R. de L. Kronig and I. I. Rabi, *Phys. Rev.* **29**, 262, 1927.
98. Mrs E. Schrödinger, interview by T. S. Kuhn, 5 April 1963, NBA.
99. E. Schrödinger, *Naturw.* **14**, 644, 1926.
100. M. Born, *Probleme der Atomdynamik*, Springer, Berlin, 1926; in English: *Problems of atomic dynamics*, MIT Press, 1926; repr. by Ungar, New York 1960.
101. M. Born and N. Wiener, *J.Math. Phys. MIT* **5**, 84, 1926 (February issue); *Zeitschr. Phys.* **36**, 174, 1926.
102. M. Born, *Zeitschr. Phys.* **37**, 863, 1926.
103. M. Born, *Gött. Nachr.* 1926, p. 146.
104. M. Born, *Zeitschr. Phys.* **38**, 803, 1926.
105. M. Born, *Nature* **119**, 354, 1927.
106. E. Wigner, in *Some strangeness in the proportion*, p. 463, Ed. H. Woolf, Addison-Wesley, Reading, Mass. 1980.
107. The conflict with the conservation laws arose because Einstein had in mind that every single particle should have its own guide field – unlike what is the case in the Schrödinger theory of many particle systems.
108. M. Born, letter to A. Einstein, 30 November 1926, Einstein Archives.
109. M. Born, *My life and my views*, p. 55, Scribner's, New York 1968.

110. W. Heisenberg, *Zeitschr. Phys.* **40**, 501, 1926.
111. N. F. Mott and H. S. W. Massey, *The theory of atomic collisions*, 1st edn 1933, 2nd edn 1949, Oxford University Press.
112. H. A. Kramers, *Grundlagen der Quantentheorie*, Akademie Verlag, Leipzig 1938.
113. *Handbuch der Physik*, Vol. 24/1, p. 106, Springer, Berlin 1933.
114. N. F. Mott, in Ref. 109, pp. x–xi.
115. M. Born, interview by T. S. Kuhn, 17 October 1962, NBA.

14

The Spirit of Copenhagen

> This problem of getting the interpretation proved to be rather
> more difficult than just working out the equations.
>
> P. A. M. DIRAC [1]

(a) The Copenhagen team in 1926. Heisenberg resolves the helium puzzle

In his letter with New Year's wishes for 1926, Bohr wrote to Rutherford: 'We have had a very busy time all the autumn with the enlargement of the institute, but now I hope that we shall have more quiet working conditions for some time.' [2] The renovation took longer than he had expected, however. In May he wrote: 'The work on the reconstruction is now almost completed.' [3] That project may again have taxed his strength. In any event, during June and July Bohr was out with a serious influenza followed by some weeks of complete rest. [4] He did publish, during 1926, a comment on Goudsmit and Uhlenbeck's paper on spin (see (11f)), a contribution 'Atom' to the *Encyclopaedia Britannica* (13a), a note on a lecture in the *Videnskabernes Selskab* on wave mechanics, [5] and notes of appreciation for J. J. Thomson [6] and Rutherford [7] – but no new scientific contributions of his own.

Bohr's institute continued to be as lively as always, however. In 1926, 32 papers, either experimental or theoretical, were published. Among the theorists present for large parts of that year were Kramers, who left in May, as did Thomas. Oskar Klein arrived that same month for a stay that was to last five years; in January 1928 he succeeded Heisenberg as lektor. David Dennison from the United States was there, doing fine work on the quantum mechanics of molecules.

In September 1926 Dirac came for a half year's stay. He had first met Bohr in May 1925 when the latter gave a talk in Cambridge on the fundamental problems and difficulties of the quantum theory. Of that occasion Dirac said later: 'People were pretty well spellbound by what Bohr said .... While I was very much impressed by [him], his arguments were mainly of a qualitative nature, and I was not able to really pinpoint the facts behind them. What I wanted was statements which could be expressed in terms of equations, and Bohr's work very seldom provided such statements. I am really not sure how much my later work was influenced by these lectures of Bohr's . . . . He certainly did not have a direct influence, because he did not stimulate one to think of new equations.'[8]

Of his Copenhagen days Dirac has recalled: 'I admired Bohr very much. We had long talks together, very long talks, in which Bohr did practically all the talking.'[9] Bohr was fond of Dirac from the very beginning. 'Apart from his outstanding talents . . . he is a very special likable man . . . just now he is writing a beautiful paper on radiation and collisions in quantum mechanics.'[10] That paper[11] has become famous for laying the foundations of quantum electrodynamics, the application of quantum mechanics to electromagnetic radiation and its interaction with matter. Another major contribution[12] by Dirac, also written in Copenhagen, is his so-called transformation theory, an improved general treatment of the basic quantum mechanical equations.

Dirac was one of the great masters of the early development of quantum mechanics. If his work is not much dealt with in this book it is because (to repeat) this is not a history of quantum mechanics, and also because his contacts with Bohr, always most cordial, were limited. This was largely due, I am sure, to the differences between Bohr's intuitive and Dirac's sparse mathematical style. I am reminded of the occasion when Bohr came into my office in Princeton one day, shaking his head while telling me of a discussion he had just had with Dirac. It was in the early 1950s, during the time of the cold war. Bohr had expressed his dislike of the abusive language the American press was using in reference to the Russians. Dirac had replied that all this would come to an end in a few weeks' time. Bohr had asked why. Well, Dirac had remarked, by then the reporters will have used up all the invective in the English language, so therefore they will have to stop.

Bohr's most significant contacts in 1926 with institute visitors were those with Heisenberg. 'Heisenberg is now here and we are all very much occupied with discussions about the new development of the quantum theory and the great prospects it holds out.'[3] In January 1926 Bohr wrote[13] to Oseen about Heisenberg: 'He is as congenial as he is talented.' In August he wrote to Heisenberg's father: 'In spite of his youth he has succeeded to realize hopes of which earlier we hardly dared dream . . . In addition his vigorous and harmonious personality makes it a daily joy to work together with him toward common goals.'[14]

As was mentioned in (12e), in May 1926 Heisenberg arrived in Copenhagen, at the ripe old age of 24, to succeed Kramers as lektor, a post he was to hold until June 1927. Twice a week he gave a one-hour lecture on theoretical physics, in Danish, for students working toward the *Magister* (M.Sc.) degree. At the end of his first lecture one student reportedly said that one wouldn't have believed he was so clever since he looked like a bright carpenter's apprentice just returned from technical school.[15] Quantum mechanics was not yet included in the syllabus: that happened only in 1928 after Klein had taken over from Heisenberg.[16]

This time Heisenberg lived in the new visitor's quarters in the institute's main building (12e), the Bohrs in the 'villa' next door. 'It was a considerable time we spent together every day ... After 8 or 9 o'clock in the evening Bohr, all of a sudden, would come up to my room and say, "Heisenberg, what do *you* think about this problem?" And then we would start talking and talking and quite frequently we went on till twelve or one o'clock at night.' At other times Bohr would call Heisenberg to come over to the villa for long evening discussions that would often end with a glass of port. Inevitably, Heisenberg was also enlisted to take Bohr's dictation of papers or letters.[17]

Right after arriving in Copenhagen (or perhaps slightly earlier) Heisenberg began an attack on an as yet unresolved problem that had caused so much trouble in the days of the old quantum theory: the spectrum of helium (10d). Already on 5 May he briefly informed Pauli of the essence of the answer.[18] In early June he wrote again to Pauli: 'For now I would like to go to Norway because of my well-known hay fever and there, along with some mountaineering, compute the helium spectrum quantitatively.'[19] By that time he had completed an article[20] on general aspects of the many-body problem in quantum mechanics. In his paper[21] on helium, submitted in July, he applied Schrödinger's methods. His results, the next great triumph of wave mechanics after Schrödinger's treatment of hydrogen, were obtained by incorporating both the exclusion principle and spin in quantum mechanics.

Recall (10e) that Pauli's analysis of atomic orbits had led him to state that no two electrons in an atom can have both the same three spatial quantum numbers, n, l, and m, and a same fourth quantum number which shortly afterward was interpreted to be the direction of the electron spin (11f). That is, in terms of the old quantum theory, two electrons cannot occupy the same orbit and have the same spin direction. Heisenberg translated this statement into wave mechanical language, as follows.* Let $\psi(1, 2)$ denote a two-electron wave function, where 1 and 2 denote the four coordinates, three for space and one for spin direction of electrons '1' and '2' respectively. Now, he says, the exclusion principle means that $\psi(1, 2)$ must be zero if the values of the two sets of four coordinates coincide: $\psi(1, 1) = 0$. This condition is obviously implemented by requiring that $\psi(1, 2) - = -\psi(2, 1)$ since then $\psi(1, 1)$ equals minus itself and thus equals zero. Thus the two-electron wavefunction must be antisymmetric for the exchange 1↔2.

---

* He made the good approximation of neglecting the small forces that couple spin to the angular momentum of orbital motion.

Consequently there are two sets of states, 'para-states' and 'ortho-states'. The former are symmetric under space-coordinate exchange, antisymmetric for spin coordinate exchange; and vice versa for the latter.

Heisenberg showed that spectral lines in helium can only arise from ortho→ortho and para→para transitions. This accounts for the two classes of spectral lines encountered in (10d), orthohelium and parahelium.

Starting from these general conceptions and after further detailed calculations, Heisenberg was able to show that 'quantum mechanics, also for systems with two electrons . . . allows us to determine approximately the behavior of the energy levels as a function of their quantum numbers.' [21] The approximate nature of his answers was inevitable. He was dealing with two electrons plus a nucleus, a three-body problem, for which to this day no general explicit solution exists, whether classically or quantum mechanically. Through later years the helium problem has been the subject of ever more refined computation.

(b) In which Schrödinger comes on a visit

In June 1926 Heisenberg wrote to Pauli: 'The more I reflect on the physical part of Schrödinger's theory the more gruesome [desto abscheulicher] I find it.' [19] Here he meant of course Schrödinger's attempts at reverting to a classical interpretation, see section (f) of the previous chapter. His reaction was reinforced after he had heard Schrödinger lecture in Munich, in July. 'I was really quite horrified [sehr entsetzt] by his interpretation . . . I simply could not believe it.' [22] After the talk, he has recalled: 'I went home rather sadly. It must have been that same evening that I wrote to Niels Bohr about the unhappy outcome of the discussion. Perhaps it was as a result of this letter that he invited[23] Schrödinger to spend part of September in Copenhagen. Schrödinger agreed,[24] and I, too, sped back to Denmark.' [25] It was to be the first time that Bohr and Schrödinger met personally.

On 4 October Schrödinger gave, at Bohr's invitation,[23] a lecture before the Danish Physical Society on 'Foundations of the undulatory mechanics'. Bohr had also asked[23] Schrödinger to 'introduce some discussions for the narrower circle of those who work here at the Institute, in which we can discuss more deeply the open questions in atomic theory'. According to Heisenberg:

The discussions between Bohr and Schrödinger began already at the railway station in Copenhagen and were continued each day from early morning until late at night. Schrödinger stayed in Bohr's house and so for this reason alone there could hardly be an interruption in the conversations. And although Bohr was otherwise most considerate and amiable in his dealings with people, he now appeared to me almost as an unrelenting fanatic, who was not prepared to make a single concession to his discussion partner or to tolerate the slightest obscurity. It will hardly be possible to convey the intensity of passion with which the discussions were conducted on both sides, or the deep-rooted convictions which one could perceive equally with Bohr and with Schrödinger in every spoken sentence . . .

. . . So the discussion continued for many hours throughout day and night without a consensus being reached. After a couple of days, Schrödinger fell ill, perhaps as a result of the enormous strain. He had to stay in bed with a feverish cold. Mrs Bohr nursed him and brought tea and cakes, but Niels Bohr sat on the bedside and spoke earnestly to Schrödinger: 'But surely you must realize that . . .'.[26]

Passions and strains there were, but no harshness, as is seen from what Schrödinger wrote a few weeks after his visit. A sketch of Bohr's personality, also included in that letter,[27] sheds light on both the subject and the writer:

In spite of everything I had already heard, the impression of Bohr's personality from a purely human point of view was quite unexpected. There will hardly again be a man who will achieve such enormous external and internal success, who in his sphere of work is honored almost like a demigod by the whole world, and who yet remains – I would not say modest and free of conceit – but rather shy and diffident like a theology student. I do not necessarily mean that as praise, it is not my ideal of a man. Nevertheless this attitude works strongly sympathetically compared with what one often meets in stars of medium size in our profession . . .

In spite of all [our] theoretical points of dispute, the relationship with Bohr, and especially Heisenberg, both of whom behaved towards me in a touchingly kind, nice, caring and attentive manner, was totally, cloudlessly, amiable and cordial . . . [Bohr] talks often for minutes almost in a dreamlike, visionary and really quite unclear manner, partly because he is so full of consideration and constantly hesitates – fearing that the other might take a statement of his [i.e. Bohr's] point of view as an insufficient appreciation of the other's (in this case, in particular, of my own work).

There exists no record of the discussions between Bohr and Schrödinger, but we do have an attempt at reconstruction by Heisenberg of 'two men . . . fighting for their particular interpretation of the new mathematical scheme with all the powers at their command'.[26]

The issues were sharply drawn. Bohr would have none of Schrödinger's attempts at interpreting quantum physics in classical terms. Schrödinger would have none of quantum jumps nor of Born's probability interpretation. Heisenberg has recalled[26] that at one point the following exchange took place.

'Schrödinger: "If all this damned quantum jumping were really here to stay then I should be sorry I ever got involved with quantum theory."

'Bohr: "But the rest of us are extremely grateful that you did; your wave mechanics has contributed so much to mathematical clarity and simplicity that it represents a gigantic advance over all previous forms of quantum mechanics." '

Heisenberg has given a succinct and most revealing summary of this debate:

No real understanding could be expected since, at the time, neither side was able to offer a complete and coherent interpretation of quantum mechanics.[26]

(c) Prelude to complementarity. The Bohr–Heisenberg dialog

In later years Bohr would often reminisce about those discussions with Schrödinger. I have listened quite a few times to him doing so. I must confess that on those past occasions I did not at all appreciate how very important to Bohr that encounter was. Now I look upon it as marking the beginning of a new phase in Bohr's scientific life: his struggles with the language of quantum physics that would lead him to the complementarity concept. As Heisenberg has recalled: 'After that time [with Schrödinger], of course, Bohr was then terribly anxious to get to the bottom of things.'[28] One finds a first inkling of Bohr's intentions in his letter[29] to Fowler, later in October 1926: 'We had great pleasure from the visit of Schrödinger ... After the discussions with [him] it is very much on my mind to complete a paper dealing with the general properties of the quantum theory.'

In a letter[30] to Kramers, sent two weeks later, Bohr referred for the first time to the need for care in use of language when expressing quantum mechanical concepts. After reporting what was happening at the institute: 'Heisenberg and Dirac move forward, as usual, with leaps and bounds ... ,' and on his own current activities: 'About myself, the main thing to report is that time passes with toil and drudgery due to holding the Institute together, both scientifically and materially,' he went on to write about

... How little the words we all use are suitable in accounting for empirical facts except when they are applied in the modest way characteristic for the correspondence theory. By that I mean a theory which allows for a consistent use of the theory in harmony with the fundamental postulates of the atomic theory. For some time I have had in mind an account of the more philosophical and axiomatic aspects of the quantum theory.

For later purposes I ask the reader to pay particular attention to Bohr's reference to the correspondence principle and to classical physics. I have pointed out earlier, in (10d), that already in 1923 he had made a similar comment, which I repeat here.

Every description of natural processes must be based on ideas which have been introduced and defined by the classical theory.'[31]

These two pronouncements can properly be considered as preludes to complementarity.

Plate 1 Niels Bohr and his mother, *ca.* 1902. (Niels Bohr Archive.)

Plate 2 Niels Bohr, brother Harald, and sister Jenny, *ca.* 1904. (Niels Bohr Archive.)

Plate 3 Signature of those attending the Cavendish Research Students' Annual Dinner at Cambridge, December 8, 1911. (Courtesy Professor Sir Sam Edwards.)

Plate 4 Niels Bohr and his wife, *ca.* 1920. (Niels Bohr Archive.)

Plate 5 Niels Bohr in the early 1920s. (Niels Bohr Archive.)

Plate 6 Niels Bohr and Werner Heisenberg, *ca.* 1925. (Niels Bohr Archive.)

Plate 7 Niels Bohr and Albert Einstein in Brussels, October 1930, during the Solvay Conference. (Niels Bohr Archive.)

Plate 8 Niels Bohr and his wife in the Carlsberg Gardens, *ca.* 1932. (Niels Bohr Archive.)

Plate 9 Margrette Bohr with (left to right) Ernst, Christian, and Hans in Tisvilde (1933). (Niels Bohr Archive.)

Plate 10 Niels Bohr in 1935. (Niels Bohr Archive.)

Plate 11 Niels Bohr and his wife in Japan 1937. (Niels Bohr Archive.)

Plate 12   Niels Bohr and his wife at Kastrup Airport on August 25, 1945, the day their foreign exile ended. (Niels Bohr Archive.)

Plate 13   Niels Bohr in the late 1940s. (Courtesy S. Rozental.)

Plate 14   Niels Bohr reads his open letter to the Danish Press, June 1950. (Niels Bohr Archive.)

Plates 15–19 Pictures taken at the Residence of Honor, Carlsberg, 1957. (Copyright: Larry Burrows Collection.)

Plate 15   In the Winter Garden.

Plate 16   In Mrs Bohr's study.

Plate 17   At the blackboard, with Aage Bohr.

Plate 18   In the living-room, with grandchildren.

Plate 19   In the study.

Plate 20 Niels Bohr in Greenland, July 1957. (Niels Bohr Archive.)

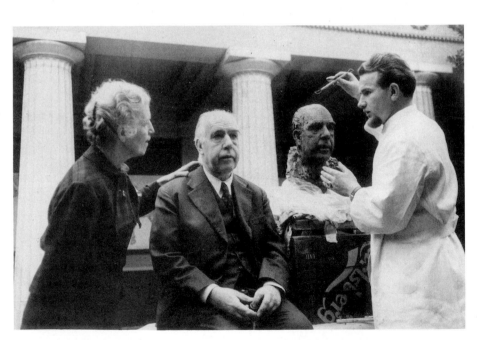

Plate 21 Posing for a sculpture by the Swiss artist Wolfram Riggenbach, 1957. (Niels Bohr Archive.)

Plate 23 'And now our honored guest will give his famous lecture on chain reactions.' Cartoon by B. O. Bøjensen in Politiken, 1958. (Copyright: Niels Bohr Archive.)

Plate 22 A moment of rest, Carlsberg, late 1950s. (Niels Bohr Archive.)

Plate 24 Churchill receives an honorary doctorate at Copenhagen University, October 10, 1950. Niels Bohr to his left. (Niels Bohr Archive.)

Plate 25 Niels Bohr with prime minister Nehru of India at Risø, 1957. (Niels Bohr Archive.)

Plate 26 Niels Bohr lecturing in Jerusalem, November 7, 1953. Martin Buber (with white beard) is in the front row. (Niels Bohr Archive.)

Plate 27 Niels Bohr (left) with Heisenberg (middle) and Dirac at a gathering of Nobel Laureates in Lindau (Bavaria) in June 1962. (Niels Bohr Archive.)

Plate 28 Niels Bohr with Ben Gurion in Copenhagen, 1962. (Niels Bohr Archive.)

Plate 29 Niels Bohr with King Fredrik IX of Denmark, 1959. (Niels Bohr Archive.)

Plate 30 Niels Bohr with Louis Armstrong, in Copenhagen. (Niels Bohr Archive.)

Plate 31   Royal visit to Carlsberg on May 22, 1957. From left to right, Queen Elizabeth, the Duke of Edinburgh, Niels Bohr, Crown Princess (later Queen) Margrethe, Mrs Bohr, King Fredrik IX. (Niels Bohr Archive.)

Plates 32, 33   Niels Bohr and his wife at Tisvilde, at the time of their golden wedding anniversary, August 1, 1962. (Niels Bohr Archive.)

'During the next few months [after Schrödinger's visit] the physical interpretation of quantum mechanics was the central theme of all conversations between Bohr and myself,' Heisenberg has recalled.[32] Their discussions focussed on the still undigested notion of particle–wave duality. Let us recall what had been said earlier on that subject.

For the case of light, duality had caused conceptual trouble ever since 1905, when Einstein had noted (see (5h)) that under certain circumstances light behaves as a set of particles, photons, while under other circumstances the long-familiar description of light in terms of waves continued to be irrefutable. In 1909 Einstein had conjectured[33] that 'a kind of fusion' of both particle and wave aspects should enter the picture in a future theory. In 1912, after the discovery that X-rays can exhibit diffraction (that is, wave) properties, the older Bragg had written: 'The problem [is], it seems to me, not to decide between the two theories of X-rays, but to find . . . one theory which possesses the capacities of both.'[34]

In 1923 de Broglie had proposed that the same kind of duality apply to matter (11e). In 1925 Heisenberg had discovered matrix mechanics by adopting the particle picture (13d). In 1926 Schrödinger had discovered *his* version of quantum mechanics by starting from the wave picture (13f). 'The connection [between Schrödinger and] de Broglie has not at all been discovered,' however, Heisenberg wrote[35] to Pauli in June of that year. Nor had the mathematical equivalence of the Heisenberg and the Schrödinger picture, established earlier in 1926 (13f) in and of itself led to any improved understanding of particle–wave duality.

When, in the fall of 1926, Bohr and Heisenberg began their discussions of duality for matter, they took the wave properties of matter seriously for only one reason: the successes of Schrödinger's wave mechanics. No direct experimental verification of de Broglie's hypothesis existed as yet. Definitive experimental proof only came in 1927, when Clinton Joseph ('Davy') Davisson, working together with Lester Halber Germer in the Bell Laboratories in New York City, demonstrated[36] that a beam of electrons generates diffraction patterns upon hitting a crystal – just as light does. A few months later the same result was obtained by George Paget Thomson (son of J. J.) with a quite distinct experimental arrangement.[37] In both experiments the electron velocity v and its 'de Broglie wavelength' λ were separately measured and the relation $\lambda = h/mv$ proposed by de Broglie was verified to good accuracy.

Neither in Bohr's writings, published or unpublished, nor in transcripts of interviews with him have I found any mention of his discussions with Heisenberg in late 1926 and early 1927 that yet turned out to be so manifestly important to him. Heisenberg on the other hand has on several occasions given accounts of their arguments. In what follows next I must therefore rely exclusively on his recollections which, as far as I can judge, are fair and impartial.

The behavior of electrons now as particles, then as waves, was still a grave paradox as Bohr and Heisenberg began their dialog. 'The trouble was, that to begin with, say in October or November [of 1926] . . . we were not able always to give the right answer because the thing was not worked out well enough . . . In spite of having a mathematical scheme both from Schröd- inger's side and from the matrix side, and in spite of seeing that these mathematical schemes are equivalent and consistent and so on, nobody could know an answer to the question: "Is an electron now a wave or is it a particle, and how does it behave if I do this and that and so on." [These] paradoxes became so much more pronounced in that time. That again was a gradual process. You couldn't pick out a definite time and say, "From then on the paradoxes were so important." But only by coming nearer and nearer to the real thing to see that the paradoxes by no means disappeared, but on the contrary got worse and worse because they turn out more clearly – that was the exciting thing . . . Like a chemist who tries to concentrate his poison more and more from some kind of solution, we tried to concentrate the poison of the paradox . . . [Bohr's] strongest impressions were the paradoxes, these hopeless paradoxes which so far nobody [had] been able to answer. These paradoxes were so in the center of his mind that he just couldn't imagine that anybody could find an answer to the paradoxes, even having the nicest mathematical scheme in the world[28] . . . Bohr would say "even the mathematical scheme does not help. I first want to understand how nature actually avoids contradictions . . . To this fundamental problem it looked as if the new mathematical tool[s] did give no clear answer yet. One just had no way of really talking about it. That was the stage in the autumn of '26 . . . We weren't so much worried about the experiment, but we were more worried about the theory . . . In '26 it was more or less clear that the experiment would come out as the theoreticians wanted it to come out if only the theoreticians knew exactly what to believe. That was just the point: "Do we know exactly what to predict?" ' [28]

As their discussion progressed, 'we discovered that the two of us were trying to resolve the difficulties in rather different ways.' [32] According to Heisenberg, Bohr thought like this: 'He was not so much interested in a special mathematical scheme. Especially he was not so willing to say, "Well, let us take for instance matrix mechanics and let's just work that out, then we must find all the right answers." He rather felt, "Well, there's one mathematical tool – that's matrix mechanics. There's another one – that's wave mechanics. And there may still be other ones. But we must first come to the bottom in the philosophical interpretation." Still, of course, it made an enormous impression on Bohr that one could now do the calculations. That was a definite proof that one had found, at least mathematically, the correct solution[28] . . . *Bohr was trying to allow for the simultaneous existence of both particle and wave concepts, holding that, though the two were mutually exclusive, both together were needed for a complete description of atomic processes* [my italics].'[32]

Heisenberg thought otherwise.

I disliked this approach. I wanted to start from the fact that quantum mechanics* as we then knew it already imposed a unique physical interpretation . . . so that it looked very much as if we no longer had any freedom with respect to that interpretation. Instead, we would have to try to derive the correct general interpretation by strict logic from the ready-to-hand, more special interpretation.[32]

I definitely wanted to keep always on the quantum mechanical side and not make any concession to the Schrödinger side which was not already contained in quantum mechanics. Perhaps this was just, psychologically, because I came from quantum mechanics. But at the same time I felt that whenever the people on the Schrödinger side would add something to it then I expected that it would probably be wrong . . . . That was my idea. Of course, this conviction came from the fact that I thought that now we have a mathematical scheme which is consistent, it can either be wrong or right, but if it's right then anything added to it must be wrong because it is closed in itself.[38]

The difficulties in the discussion between Bohr and myself was that I wanted to start entirely from the mathematical scheme of quantum mechanics and use Schrödinger theory perhaps as a tool sometimes . . . Bohr, however, wanted to take the interpretation in some way very serious and *play with both schemes* [my italics].[28]

However hard they tried, Bohr and Heisenberg could not come to a common opinion. 'We talked back and forth about these problems and sometimes got a bit impatient with each other about it. I would perhaps try to say, "Well, this is the answer." Then Bohr gave the contradictions and would say, "No, it can't be the answer," and so on . . . In the end, shortly after Christmas, we both were in a kind of despair. In some way we couldn't agree and so we were a bit angry about it[28] . . . Both of us became utterly exhausted and rather tense. Hence Bohr decided in February 1927 to go skiing in Norway, and I was quite glad to be left behind in Copenhagen, where I could think undisturbed about these hopelessly complicated problems.'[39]

Klein, who was close to Bohr in those days, has left us[40] his impressions of Bohr's state of mind as he left for Norway: 'He was very tired that time and I believe that the new quantum mechanics caused him both much pleasure and very great tension. He had probably not expected that all this would come so suddenly but rather that he himself perhaps might have

---

* In this and the next two paragraphs Heisenberg used the term quantum mechanics to mean matrix mechanics.

contributed more at that time. At the same time he praised Heisenberg almost like a kind of Messiah and I think that Heisenberg himself understood that that was a bit exaggerated.'

(d) The uncertainty relations, with a look back at the correspondence principle

Heisenberg discovered his uncertainty relations right after Bohr's departure for Norway: 'So I was alone in Copenhagen and then within a few days I thought that this thing with the uncertainty relations would be the right answer.' [28]

On 10 March 1927 Heisenberg wrote[41] to Bohr in Norway: 'I believe that I have succeeded in treating the case where both [the momentum] p and [the coordinate] q are given to a certain accuracy . . . I have written a draft of a paper about these problems which yesterday I sent to Pauli.' [42] Heisenberg's letter neither contains formulae nor further details about what he had done. Yet already on 23 February he had written[43] a fourteen page letter to Pauli in which the uncertainty relations appear. Why had he sent details to Pauli but not to Bohr? 'I wanted to get Pauli's reactions before Bohr was back because I felt again that when Bohr comes back he will be angry about my interpretation. So I first wanted to have some support, and see whether somebody else liked it.' [28]

Heisenberg's paper 'On the physical* content of the quantum theoretical kinematics and mechanics' [44] was received by the publishers on 23 March, after Bohr had returned – and had correctly criticized some substantial points in the manuscript (see below). All the same Heisenberg's work is on a par with his discovery paper of quantum mechanics and represents a most solid contribution to its interpretation. It is the first paper in which the question of what is observable and what is not is *quantitatively* discussed in the context of quantum mechanics. His work marks the beginning of a subject on which volumes have since been written: the measurement problem in quantum physics.

The question itself was not new. Already in October 1926 Pauli had written[45] to Heisenberg:

The first question is . . . why not the p's *as well as* [P.'s italics] the q's can be prescribed with arbitrary precision . . . One can look at the world with the p-eye and one can look at it with the q-eye but when one would like to open both eyes, then one gets dizzy.

Indeed, as Pauli well knew, it is a simple consequence of the non-commutativity of p and q that in a given experiment they cannot both be given a sharp value.

* Here I have taken some liberty in translating *anschaulich* by physical, since I believe that this best conveys Heisenberg's intent.

Heisenberg took right off in the first section of his paper, entitled 'The concepts of position, orbit, velocity, energy':

If one wants to be clear about the meaning of the words 'position of an object', for example an electron (in a given reference frame), one has to specify definite experiments with which one intends to measure the 'position of the electron'; otherwise these words have no meaning;

and likewise for the electron's velocity and energy.

An electron orbit, Heisenberg continued, is a time sequence of electron positions. One cannot give meaning to 'the orbit of a specific electron in a specific atom', however. Consider for example the orbit of an electron in the ground state of hydrogen which is supposed to have a radius of about 10^{-8} cm. In order to 'see' the electron's position (at a given time) one has to illuminate it with light with a wavelength small compared to this radius, hence also small compared to the wavelengths of visible light (see (4d)). That is, one has to observe the electron under a 'γ-ray microscope'. Illumination of that kind will scatter the electron (Compton effect) and knock it out of the orbit which one hoped to determine. In other words, Heisenberg said, when we look at the electron, we disturb its momentum, we lose its momentum. Although this argument goes in the right direction, it is in fact incorrect, as we shall see in the next section.

So much, for the moment, about electron orbits in atoms. One can observe electrons also under quite different circumstances, however, where it does make observational sense to speak of an electron in an orbit. For example, one can follow its path, its orbit, in a cloud chamber photograph in which one actually sees the orbit by the droplets of liquid created along its track. Thus, Heisenberg reasoned, 'The right question should . . . be: Can quantum mechanics represent the fact that an electron finds itself approximately in a given place and that it moves approximately with a given velocity, and can we make these approximations so close that they do not cause mathematical difficulties? A brief calculation . . . showed that one could indeed represent such situations mathematically.'[46]

This is what he found. Let Δq and Δp be the respective average imprecisions with which a certain coordinate q and its associated momentum p are known from some specific experiment. Then

$$\Delta p \Delta q \geqslant h$$

($\geqslant$ means 'larger than or equal to'). Let ΔE and Δt be the respective average imprecisions with which the energy E of a system and the time at which E is observed are known from some specific experiment. Then

$$\Delta E \Delta t \geqslant h.$$

These inequalities are the uncertainty relations. They express reciprocal limitations (the bigger Δp the smaller Δq, etc.) on the accuracies with which, in a given experiment, the various variables are knowable.

In deriving these relations Heisenberg stuck strictly to matrix methods and illustrated his answers for a few specific experimental arrangements. In the course of time his derivations have been improved and his results sharpened.*

In what follows (beginning with the next section) I shall expatiate on the physical contents of the uncertainty relations but note right away their most profound general consequence:

Quantum mechanics definitively establishes the non-validity of the law of causality,[44]

in the sense of classical physics. Consider the simple example of a particle moving in some field of force. Classical causality says: if at a given time you give me the precise initial position and velocity or (which amounts to the same) momentum of the particle, then I can give you its position and velocity at a later time. The uncertainty relations tell you, however, that you cannot give me precisely those initial data! In Heisenberg's words:

In the sharp formulation of the causality law: 'If we know the present, then we can predict the future,' it is not the consequence but the premise that is false. As a matter of principle we cannot know all determining elements of the present.[44]

We have seen in (13g) that the failure of classical causality had already been noted earlier by Born. That was in the context of the probability interpretation. The uncertainty relations are logically independent of probability considerations, however, and so therefore is the lack of causality.

Physicists, almost all of them, gladly pay the price of giving up causality for the tremendous gain of understanding atomic and molecular physics, and more, in terms of the new mechanics. Nevertheless they do not discard classical physics. Rather they now understand its limitations. In particular they appreciate that Bohr's concept of the correspondence principle, formulated prior to the arrival of quantum mechanics, was a good one. Let us briefly interrupt the story of the evolution of quantum mechanics in order to see, in terms of an example, how the correspondence principle emerges in the context of the new mechanics.

Consider once more the (non-relativistic) hydrogen atom in one of its eigenstates. According to Heisenberg we cannot assign a position to the electron in a classical orbit. According to Schrödinger we can describe the electron by a wavefunction $\psi(x, y, z)$ that depends on the three space

---

* By sharpening one means, in simplest terms, that h in the uncertainty relations appears multiplied with a coefficient less than one. See Ref. 47 for literature about better and technically more useful uncertainty principles.

coordinates x, y, z. According to Born (see (13g)) $|\psi|^2$ is the probability of finding the electron at a given place x, y, z. According to Bohr's correspondence principle the electron moves very nearly in a classical orbit when the principle quantum number n is large (see (8f)). Can this use of orbit as an approximate tool be justified by quantum mechanics?

Yes it can. In Fig. 9(a) we see the projection on a plane of $|\psi|^2$ for the ground state, $n = 1$, of hydrogen. The probability distribution fills a sphere with fuzzy edges. The circle indicates the size of the atom in the ground state. The figure does not represent the shape of the atom but rather the

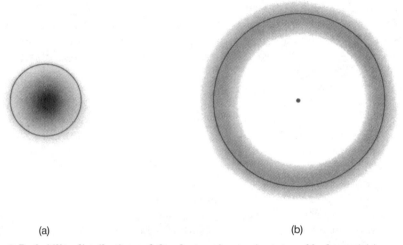

(a)   (b)

Fig. 9 Probability distributions of the electron in atomic states of hydrogen: (a) ground state; (b) $n = 10$ state.

projection of that shape on the plane of the paper. Here we see how drastically quantum mechanics changes the picture of an atom – from the classical flat pancake, the analog of the plane in which a planetary orbit around the sun is situated, to something three dimensional.

Consider next the case of large n, for example $n = 10$, shown (for the most nearly circular orbit) in Fig. 9(b).* For this case $|\psi|^2$ is (almost exactly) zero in the inner part, and is concentrated in a thin doughnut around the drawn circle. These simple pictures are meant to show that the classical description fails badly for low-lying atomic states but already begins to be a decent approximation for objects as small as high lying atomic states.

The uncertainty relations apply *in principle* also to much bigger, macroscopic, objects. For these the classical theory may nevertheless be

* This figure is not drawn to the same scale as Fig. 9(a), the size of the atom for $n = 10$ is actually about 100 times larger than for $n = 1$.

considered as *perfect in practice*. To illustrate this it is convenient to use the relation* $p = mv$ (m = mass, v = velocity) and to write the first uncertainty relation as $\Delta v \Delta q \geqslant h/m$. Using the numerical value of Planck's constant h, about 6×10^{-27} in units gram times (centimeter)^2 per second, one calculates that for an electron (m is about 10^{-27} gram) to be localized with a precision Δq of 10^{-8} cm, the size of a hydrogen atom, its velocity imprecision must be at least about 1000 miles per second. On the other hand, if you walk down the street and I want to measure your position at a given time with the same accuracy 10^{-8} cm, then, with due regard to the uncertainty relations, I can in principle still measure your velocity to an accuracy of a billionth of a billionth of a mile per second.

Nor is the renowned accuracy of astronomical observations in any way impaired by the uncertainty relations. Just remember that the earth, a lightweight body on the astronomical scale, weighs 55 powers of ten times the mass of an electron . . .

I now return to the spring of 1927.

When (around 18 March[48]) Bohr came back from Norway, Heisenberg showed him the paper he had written. According to Klein: 'Bohr read the paper and was at first very taken with it but when he began to look more closely he became very disappointed,'[40] because he saw that there was a serious error in the paper, not in its general conclusions but in the way Heisenberg had treated the example of detecting the electron's position with a γ-ray microscope. According to Heisenberg: 'Bohr tried to explain that it was not right and I shouldn't publish the paper. I remember that it ended by my breaking out in tears because I just couldn't stand this pressure from Bohr.'[28] Klein has remembered : 'About what Heisenberg said I know nothing but that in the discussions they both evidently were talking past each other and that there was evidently a lot of irritation at that time. And Heisenberg was very stubborn because Bohr would like him to refer to the paper [to be discussed in the next section] Bohr had begun to work on and at first Heisenberg did not want to do that.'[40] Heisenberg himself again: 'So it was very disagreeable [but only for] a short period of perhaps ten days or so in which we really disagreed rather strongly . . . [then] we agreed that the paper could be published if it was improved on these points and I had to agree that these were quite important improvements.'[28]

The published version[44] of Heisenberg's paper contains a note added in proof in which he does mention 'recent investigations by Bohr [that] have led to points of view that permit an essential deepening and refinement of the analysis of the quantum mechanical relationship attempted in this

---

* Here, effects of relativity are neglected, which is justified for the examples to be quoted next.

work', and does acknowledge Bohr's help in correcting his treatment of the γ-ray microscope.

In April 1927 Bohr sent Einstein a copy of the proofs of Heisenberg's paper, adding in an enclosed letter that it 'represents a most significant . . . exceptionally brilliant . . . contribution to the discussion of the general problems of quantum theory.'[49]

The autumn of 1926 and the early months of 1927 had been rough times, both for Bohr and for Heisenberg. Their relations had been severely strained – but that passed.

Letters from Heisenberg to Bohr, a bit later in 1927, show that in retrospect he felt quite uncomfortable with his recent comportment: 'I am very ashamed to have given the impression of being quite ungrateful.'[50] Shortly afterward: 'I have been so unhappy . . . that I have looked so ungrateful to you. I reflect almost every day on how that came about and am ashamed that it could not have gone otherwise.'[51]

In the fall of 1928 Heisenberg came to Copenhagen for a short visit. Afterwards he wrote to Bohr: 'My cordial thanks for the beautiful days in Copenhagen. It made me so happy that once again we understood each other so well and that everything was once again as in the "old days".'[52] Bohr replied, '. . . thanking you for the great pleasure you gave us all by your visit. Rarely have I felt myself in more sincere harmony with any other human being.'[53]

(e) Complementarity: a new kind of relativity

> Our interpretation of the experimental material rests essentially on the classical concepts.
>
> N. BOHR
> in his Como lecture (1927)[54]

Bohr and Heisenberg continued their discussions on the foundations of quantum mechanics during the two months following the submittal of Heisenberg's paper on the uncertainty relations. In May 1927 Heisenberg wrote to Pauli: 'Bohr wants to write a general paper on the "conceptual basis" of the quantum theory, from the point of view "there exist [es gibt] waves and particles" – when one starts like that, then one can of course make everything consistent . . . There are essential differences in taste between Bohr and me about the word "visualizable" [anschaulich].'[55] In 1963 Heisenberg explained[28] what these differences were:

The main point was that Bohr wanted to take this dualism between waves and corpuscles as the central point of the problem, and to say, 'That is the center of the whole story, and we have to start from that side of the story in order to understand it.' I, in some way would say, 'Well, we have a consistent mathematical scheme and this consistent mathematical scheme tells us everything which can be observed. Nothing is in nature which cannot be described by this mathematical scheme.' It was a different way of looking at the problem because Bohr would not like to say that nature imitates a mathematical scheme, that nature does only things which fit into a mathematical scheme. While I would say, 'Well, waves and corpuscles are, certainly, a way in which we talk and we do come to these concepts from classical physics. Classical physics has taught us to talk about particles and waves, but since classical physics is not true there, why should we stick so much to these concepts? Why should we not simply say that we cannot use these concepts with a very high precision, therefore the uncertainty relations, and therefore we have to abandon these concepts to a certain extent. When we get beyond this range of the classical theory, we must realize that our words don't fit. They don't really get a hold in the physical reality and therefore a new mathematical scheme is just as good as anything because the new mathematical scheme then tells what may be there and what may not be there. Nature just in some way follows the scheme.'

Having talked countless hours with Bohr on complementarity, I could imagine that to Heisenberg's 'our words don't fit' he would have replied: 'Our words *have* to fit, we have nothing else.' (More about that very shortly.) In any event a visit by Pauli to Copenhagen at the beginning of June 'played an important role in reconciling Heisenberg's with Bohr's point of view'.[56]

In the summer of 1927 Heisenberg's time in Copenhagen was up. In the autumn he assumed his professorship in Leipzig. Also thereafter he continued to make major contributions to physics, yet now he will begin to recede from the present story about Bohr, since while his influence on Bohr (and vice versa) continued, it would never again be as strong as in the period just described.

That influence was crucially important for the evolution of Bohr's own ideas in 1927. He must of course have reflected on his prior discussions with Heisenberg as, all by himself, he spent at least four weeks skiing in the Norwegian mountains around Guldbrandsdalen. It was there (as he often told) that the complementarity argument first dawned on him. Heisenberg remembered: 'When I discussed [my work] with Bohr after his return, we were unable to find at once the same language for the interpretation of the theory because in the meantime Bohr had developed the concept of complementarity.'[57] The result was 'a fresh round of difficult discussions'.[58] Klein has recalled: 'Both the results and the failures in Heisenberg's work became a source of inspiration to [Bohr], and from then on he worked almost day and night on these questions.'[59]

Much has been written on how Bohr was influenced in what he did next by his reading of various philosophers. I consider such speculations far fetched, to say the least. It was rather the physics discussions with Heisenberg that provided Bohr's prime stimulus. (I therefore see no reason for burdening this chapter with Bohr's relations to philosophy, but promise that I shall do so later (see (19a)).

After his return from Norway Bohr's ideas must have evolved rapidly. The letter to Einstein in mid-April already contains the gist of his new ideas: 'It has of course long been recognized how intimately the difficulties of the quantum theory are connected with the concepts, or rather with the words that are used in the customary description of nature, and which always have their origin in the classical theories . . .'[49]

The task of assisting Bohr in composing a paper on his new ideas fell to Klein. 'Bohr began eagerly . . . in April, and then we went to Tisvilde . . . and Bohr dictated and the next day all he had dictated was discarded and we began anew. And so it went all summer and after a time Mrs Bohr became unhappy . . . one time when I sat alone in the little room where we worked she came in crying . . . and then Bohr had to go to the Como meeting and then, under strong pressure by his brother Harald, he really tried to get an article written down.'[40]

Bohr presented his views on 16 September 1927 at the meeting held in Como on the occasion of the centenary of the death of Alessandro Volta. The manuscript of his lecture appears to be lost but many drafts of his paper have been preserved in the Niels Bohr Archives.* These give us a good picture of Bohr's struggles with the formulation of his ideas. Some samples: 'All information about atoms expressed in classical concepts . . . Prepared for difficulties with every single word . . . A few words about the relation with Heisenberg's work. Say that in essence the same endeavor. At the same time another spirit in that one stresses the visualizable and elementary character of the wave description.'

The term 'complementarity' appears for the first time in a draft from 10 July 1927.[60] In Bohr's correspondence it shows up for the first time in a letter to Pauli[61] in August. It is possible that Bohr decided to use that word during a sailing trip with friends. 'Ole Chievitz [Bohr's friend since his high school days; see (3)] and Bohr had long discussions about whether "complementarity" was the correct designation for the relation between the wave and the particle picture . . . and we flattered ourselves with the belief that the decision to use the word "complementarity" took place on one of our sailing trips.'[62]

It is also significant that a few drafts carry the title 'The philosophical foundations of the quantum theory', which differs from the one under which Bohr's paper finally appeared: 'The quantum postulate and the recent

---

* A selection from these have recently been published in CW, Vol. 6, pp. 57–88.

developments of atomic theory.' In what follows I use the version which appeared* in *Nature.*[63]

Ehrenfest, who only in the preceding July had complained to Bohr[64] about his great difficulties in understanding the physical interpretation of quantum mechanics, did not go to Como but was present at the Solvay conference (see the next section) where Bohr essentially repeated his Como lecture. After Solvay Ehrenfest wrote to his students that he was very enthusiastic about Bohr's ideas but less so about their rendering: 'Once again the awful Bohr incantation terminology. Impossible for anybody else to summarize.'[65] I have deep sympathy with Ehrenfest's sentiments but am nevertheless obliged to indicate Bohr's main points as well as I can. Before doing so, I should stress that in later years Bohr himself vastly improved his presentation of the complementarity concept. In subsequent chapters I shall come back to those later versions but confine myself at this point to the one given in 1927.

One of the prettiest points in the Como paper is Bohr's own derivation of the uncertainty relations, which goes like this. Consider a wave packet (a term defined in (13f)) of either light or material waves,** an object with finite extension. Introduce the following definitions: Δt, the time interval during which the bulk of the wave packet passes some fixed point; Δv, the frequency interval in which the bulk of the participating frequencies lie; $\Delta(1/\lambda)$, the similar interval for inverse wave lengths; Δx, the spatial extension of the packet. Then

$$\Delta t \Delta v \geqslant 1, \qquad \Delta x \Delta(1/\lambda) \geqslant 1.$$

These are *classical* relations, known from the theory of the resolving power of optical instruments.† Now use the Einstein–de Broglie relation

$$E = hv, \qquad p = h/\lambda,$$

and there you are. The beauty of this argument lies in its avoidance of all quantum mechanical technology.

A second main point first made by Bohr concerns the meaning of the conservation laws of energy and momentum in quantum mechanics. Does the appearance of ΔE's and Δp's mean that these laws are not precisely satisfied? No, he explains, one should rather put it as follows. They can only be sharply verified, hence sharply applied, under circumstances in which E and p are sharply measurable – at a loss of sharp information on 'space-time coordination' (to use Bohr's terminology). Under *other* circumstances one

---

* The paper appeared in English, French, German, and Danish. A list of references to these publications along with indications of main variants is found in CW, Vol. 6, pp. 110–12.

** Actually Bohr first considered light waves only and from there concluded to what happens with matter waves via the use of conservation laws.

† See, for example, Kramers' textbook[66] for their derivation.

should *not* say that the conservation laws are not valid, but rather that their validity cannot be verified.

That reasoning brings us to the heart of Bohr's concepts. In the very first sentence ever written on quantum mechanics, the abstract of Heisenberg's July 1925 paper (quoted earlier, in (13d)), it was stated that 'quantum mechanics should be founded exclusively upon relationships between quantities that are in principle observable'. By his uncertainty relations Heisenberg had shown that there exist limitations of principle on the precision of what is observable in the region where quantum effects are important. As noted before in this section, he had concluded from this that, to some extent, we have to abandon the concepts of particles and waves and that our classical words do not any longer fit in the quantum region.

At this point Bohr went beyond Heisenberg in taking the opposite view:

Our interpretation of the experimental material rests essentially upon the classical concepts.[54]

One may say that with the elaboration of that statement the logic of quantum mechanics reached its closure.

This phrase is almost identical with one that Bohr had used in 1923 and which I quoted at the beginning of the preceding section (c). While the context at that time, the correspondence principle, has no logical connection with what is at issue here, it nevertheless indicates once again that for reasons of physics rather than philosophy Bohr was prepared for the continued importance of classical language even before quantum mechanics had arrived. Bohr's expertise in classical physics made him ideally suited for the delicate and far from trivial 'interpretation of the experimental material', as he showed at Como by his improved discussion of Heisenberg's γ-ray microscope. In Heisenberg's example (see the preceding section), Bohr noted, one can calculate the change of the momentum of the electron kicked out of its orbit and therefore we can correct for that effect. Nevertheless there *is* an uncertainty in the determination of the electron's position. We observe that position by scattering a γ-ray off the electron, then sending that ray through a microscope and observing its momentum direction. The precision with which we can do this is limited, however. In order to observe that direction as well as possible one focuses the γ-ray beam by passing it through a lense, a familiar procedure for any kind of microscope. According to *classical* optics that lens diffracts the beam (the so-called finite aperture effect), hence makes its direction imprecise, hence makes the electron's position imprecise. A quantitative analysis of this imprecision shows that it is exactly in accord with the uncertainty relations.

I next enlarge on Bohr's general statement on the classical interpretation of experimental data. In the classical era one verified the validity of theories by comparing them with experimental observations made with balances, thermometers, voltmeters, etc. The theories have been modified in the quantum era but – and this was Bohr's point – their validity continues to be verified by the same readings of a balance's equilibrium position, a thermometer's mercury column, a voltmeter's needle, etc. The phenomena may be novel, their modes of detection may have been modernized, but detectors should be treated as classical objects; their readings continue to be described in classical terms.

'The situation thus created is of a peculiar nature,' Bohr remarked.[54] Consider for example the question: Can I not ask for the quantum mechanical properties of a detector, say a voltmeter? The answer is yes, I can. Next question: But should I then not abandon the limited description of the voltmeter as a classical object, and rather treat it quantum mechanically? The answer is yes, I must. But in order to register the voltmeter's quantum properties I need *another* piece of apparatus with which I again make classical readings. In Bohr's own rather cryptic words: 'The concept of observation is in so far arbitrary as it depends upon which objects are included in the system to be observed.'[54]

The language of science, more generally the ways in which we communicate – these were the themes on which Bohr focused in the Como lecture and for the rest of his life. Thus, he said (I paraphrase): The question of whether an electron is a particle or a wave is a sensible question in the classical context, where the relation between object of study and detector either needs no specification or else is a controllable relation. In quantum mechanics that question is meaningless, however. There one should rather ask: Does the electron (or any other object) *behave* like a particle or like a wave? That question is answerable, but only if one specifies the experimental arrangement by means of which 'one looks' at the electron. That is what Bohr meant in Como when he said:

An independent reality in the ordinary [that is, classical] physical sense can ... neither be ascribed to the phenomena nor to the agencies of observation.[54]

To summarize, Bohr stressed that only by insisting on the description of observations in classical terms can one avoid the logical paradoxes apparently posed by the duality of particles and waves, two terms themselves defined classically. Wave and particle behavior mutually exclude each other. The classical physicist would say: if two descriptions are mutually exclusive, then at least one of them must be wrong. The quantum physicist will say: whether an object behaves as a particle or as a wave depends on your choice of experimental arrangement for looking at it. He will not deny that particle and wave behavior are mutually exclusive but will assert that both are necessary for the full understanding of the object's properties. Bohr coined the term *complementarity* for describing this new situation:

The very nature of the quantum theory ... forces us to regard the space-time coordination [meaning: particle behavior] and the claim of causality [meaning: wave behavior], the union of which characterizes the classical theories, as complementary but exclusive features of the description ... complementary pictures of the phenomena ... only together offer a natural generalization of the classical mode of description.[54]

Relativity has taught us new ways of relating the experiences of one observer to those of another one. Quantum mechanics has taught us another kind of relativity, new ways in which one given observer relates one choice of experimental arrangement with which he intends to perform his experiments to another choice. Perhaps Bohr had that parallel in mind when he said: 'We find ourselves on the very path taken by Einstein of adapting our modes of perception borrowed from the sensations to the gradually deepening knowledge of the laws of Nature.'[54] These two kinds of relativity are the great new 'epistemological lessons' (another of Bohr's favorite terms) of twentieth century science.*

Bohr's lecture at Como did not bring down the house.

Léon Rosenfeld who attended the Volta conference later said: 'There was a characteristic remark by Wigner after the Como lecture, "This lecture will not induce any one of us to change his own meaning [opinion] about quantum mechanics."' Rosenfeld's own impression at that time was: 'This complementarity business was just a way of putting in words the situation that everybody knew. I suppose if you look at it now the Como lecture did not clinch the argument; all this question about defining the concepts came later.'[68] The editorial[69] with which the publishers of *Nature* saw fit to introduce Bohr's paper[54] was not very forthcoming either: 'The new wave mechanics gave rise to the hope that an account of atomic phenomena might be obtained which would not differ essentially from that afforded by the classical theories of electricity and magnetism. Unfortunately, Bohr's statement in the following communication of the principles underlying the description of atomic phenomena gives little, if any, encouragement in this direction ... It is earnestly to be hoped that this is not [the physicists'] last word on the subject, and that they yet may be successful in expressing the quantum postulate in picturesque form.'

It seems to me that Bohr, in spite of his own emphasis on the proper use of words, introduced terminology in his first presentation of complementarity,

---

* It is fitting to recall here a comment by Pauli from 1933: 'In analogy to the term "relativity theory" one might give the modern quantum theory also the name "complementarity theory".'[67]

at Como, which may have contributed to the considerable confusion that for so long has reigned around this subject. Thus he said: 'Our normal [classical] description of physical phenomena is based entirely on the idea that the phenomena may be observed without disturbing them appreciably' (which carries the implication that quantum effects do cause such a disturbance), and that quantum theory brings in an inherent 'irrationality' (the quotations are Bohr's). Later he himself would frown on expressions like 'disturbing the phenomena by observation', and 'irrationality'.

I have related earlier how all through the summer of 1927 Bohr struggled with committing his thoughts to paper. That was only the beginning. On 7 September, before Como, Bohr had sent a short article to *Nature*.[70] After Como he wrote to the Editor of *Nature*: 'I regret that I have not yet returned the proof of my article . . . [I was] led to rewrite the whole article, and I hope that in its present form it will be better suited to promote the mutual understanding of the advocators of the conflicting views.'[71] That new version was almost certainly the one on which Bohr and Pauli had worked during the week they spent together at Lake Como, after the Volta meeting.[72] In December 1927 Bohr wrote again to the Editor of *Nature*: 'I have found it most expedient to rewrite the whole article . . . I am much ashamed for all the trouble I am giving you . . .'[73] After more writing back and forth the Editor received Bohr's final version in the first days of March 1928.[74] It appeared in *Nature*[62] on 14 April.

We should next track back to October 1927, when the scene had shifted from Como to Brussels.

(f) Solvay 1927. The Bohr–Einstein dialog begins

From 24 to 29 October the fifth Solvay congress took place in Brussels. Neither before nor later would there again be such a gathering of all those who had participated in the creation of the old and the new quantum theory. Planck, Einstein, and Bohr, the founding fathers, were all there. (It was the first time that Bohr attended a Solvay meeting.) So were de Broglie, Dirac, Ehrenfest, Heisenberg, Kramers, Pauli, and Schrödinger. Lorentz (who died a few months later) was in the chair. Ehrenfest's strongest impression of the conference was of 'BOHR [his capitals] towering completely over everybody. At first not understood at all . . . then step by step defeating everybody.'[65]

The proceedings of that meeting[75] are a revealing document about the status of quantum physics in 1927. Here I shall only be concerned with the encounter of Bohr and Einstein at that Congress, which marks the beginning of their dialog on the fundamental principles of quantum mechanics. By way of introducing that subject I shall first sketch Einstein's reactions to the advances in quantum theory from early 1925 to the time he arrived in Brussels.*

I have already briefly mentioned (11e) that around the beginning of 1925 Einstein published important papers on quantum statistical mechanics. That work was his last constructive effort on the quantum theory, one among several reasons being that already then he was deeply immersed in the search for a unified field theory of gravitation and electromagnetism. Yet the great importance of the new developments in quantum theory was not lost on him. Thus he corresponded with Heisenberg soon after the discovery of matrix mechanics. Einstein's letters to Heisenberg have been lost but some of Heisenberg's are extant. In one of them, written in November 1925, he remarked that 'we have the hope that the validity of the energy and momentum laws in our quantum mechanics will one day make possible the connection with your [light quantum] theory'.[77] We know how important that connection was to Einstein from Bose's recollections of his next visit to Berlin that same November. 'Einstein was very excited about the new quantum mechanics. He wanted me to try and see what the statistics of light-quanta and the transition probabilities of radiation would look like in the new theory.'[78]

During the following months Einstein seems to have vacillated in his reactions to the matrix theory. In December he wrote to his friend Michele Besso: 'The most interesting recent theoretical achievement is the Heisenberg–Born–Jordan theory of quantum states. A real sorcerer's multiplication table, in which infinite determinants (matrices) replace the Cartesian coordinates. It is extremely ingenious, and thanks to its great complexity sufficiently protected against disproof.'[79] But in March 1926 he wrote to Born: 'The Heisenberg–Born concepts leave us all breathless and have made a deep impression on all theoretically oriented people. Instead of a dull resignation, there is now a singular tension in us sluggish people.'[80]

Meanwhile wave mechanics had arrived on the scene. Einstein's first response must have been positive. Schrödinger to Einstein: 'Your and Planck's approval are worth more to me than that of half a world.'[81] Einstein replied: 'I am as convinced that you have made a decisive advance with your formulation of the quantum condition as I am that the Heisenberg–Born route is a wrong track.'[82] In May 1926 Einstein wrote to Besso: 'Schrödinger has come out with a pair of wonderful papers on the quantum rules.'[83]

To the best of my knowledge that was the last time Einstein wrote approvingly on quantum mechanics.

The turning point was Born's work on the probability interpretation of

* In the following few pages I largely follow (in part verbatim) my earlier account about Einstein just before and during the Solvay meeting.[76]

quantum mechanics that appeared in the summer of 1926, and to which Einstein took unqualified exception. His earliest expression of dissent I know of dates from December 1926 when he wrote to Born: 'Quantum mechanics is very impressive. But an inner voice tells me that it is not yet the real thing. The theory produces a good deal but hardly brings us closer to the secret of the Old One. I am at all events convinced that *He* does not play dice.'[84]

Also at the Solvay meeting Einstein's position was that of a critic.

The happenings during that conference followed familiar patterns. First there were the official sessions, presentations of papers followed by discussions, during which 'Einstein said hardly anything beyond presenting a very simple objection to the probability interpretation . . . Then he fell back into silence.'[85] In addition Bohr and Einstein met for private discussions at which also Ehrenfest was present.[86] Then there were discussions in the dining room of the hotel in which all participants were housed, and here Einstein was much livelier. Otto Stern has given a first-hand account.*

'Einstein came down to breakfast and expressed his misgivings about the new quantum theory, every time [he] had invented some beautiful experiment from which one saw that [the theory] did not work. . . . Pauli and Heisenberg, who were there, did not pay much attention, *"ach was, das stimmt schon, das stimmt schon"* [ah, well, it will be all right, it will be all right]. Bohr, on the other hand, reflected on it with care and in the evening, at dinner, we were all together and he cleared up the matter in detail.'

There is no official record of Bohr's comments following Einstein's 'very simple objection'. From notes taken by Kramers at the meeting we know, however, that Bohr did reply. These notes, now in the Bohr Archives, show that Bohr began as follows: 'I feel myself in a very difficult position because I don't understand what precisely is the point which Einstein wants to [make]. No doubt it is my fault.'[87] The notes, though quite fragmentary, further show that Bohr did not directly address Einstein's remarks but rather spoke in general terms, making some of the same points he had raised in Como.** I shall therefore proceed by sketching Einstein's objection and one physicist's refutation.

Einstein discussed an experiment in which a beam of electrons hits a fixed screen with an aperture in it. The transmitted electrons form a diffraction

* In a discussion with Res Jost, taped on 2 December 1961. I am very grateful to Jost for making available to me the transcript of these discussions.
** Bohr wanted to get together with Kramers in order to write up his Solvay comments, and actually went for a few days to Utrecht for that purpose.[88] (Kramers had taken notes of what Bohr had said.) For one reason or another that did not work out. In the proceedings of the conference a French translation of Bohr's Como address was inserted 'at the request of the author, to replace his exposition in the course of the general discussions'.[89]

pattern, which is observed on a second screen. Question: Does quantum mechanics give a complete description of the individual electron events in this experiment? His answer: This cannot be. For let A and B be two distinct spots on the second screen. If I know that an individual electron arrives at A, then I know instantaneously that it did not arrive at B. But this implies a peculiar instantaneous action at a distance between A and B contrary to the relativity postulate. Yet (Einstein notes) in the Geiger–Bothe experiment on the Compton effect (see (11d)) there is no limitation of principle to the accuracy with which one can observe coincidences in individual processes, and that without appeal to action at a distance. This circumstance adds to the sense of incompleteness of the description for diffraction.

Quantum mechanics provides the following answer to Einstein's query. It does apply to individual processes, but the uncertainty principle defines and delimits the optimal amount of information obtainable in a given experimental arrangement. This delimitation differs incomparably from the restrictions on information inherent in the description of events in classical statistical mechanics. There the restrictions are wisely self-imposed in order to obtain a useful approximation to a description in terms of an ideally knowable complete specification of momenta and positions of individual particles. In quantum mechanics, the delimitations mentioned earlier are not self-imposed but are renunciations of first principle. It is true that one would need action at a distance if one were to insist on a fully causal description involving the localization of the electron at every stage of the experiment on hand. Quantum mechanics denies that such a description is called for and asserts that, in this experiment, the final position of an individual electron cannot be predicted with certainty. Quantum mechanics nevertheless makes a prediction in this case concerning the probability of an electron arriving at a given spot on the second screen. The verification of this prediction demands, of course, that the 'one-electron experiment' be repeated as often as necessary to obtain this probability distribution with the desired accuracy.

Nor is there a conflict with Geiger–Bothe, since now one refers to another experimental arrangement in which localization in space-time is achieved, but this time at the price of renouncing information on sharp energy–momentum properties of the particles observed in coincidence. From the point of view of quantum mechanics, these renunciations are expressions of laws of nature.

As we shall see in more detail in later chapters, what was and is an acceptable renunciation to others, was an intolerable abdication in Einstein's eyes. On that score he was never prepared to give up anything.

Einstein was not the only one to leave the Solvay conference with reservations about quantum mechanics, though such qualms were shared only by a minority. It is fair to say, however, that by October 1927 all the basic principles of (non-relativistic) quantum mechanics had been displayed, though not yet in perfected form. The Solvay meeting therefore provides a natural point for taking a break in the discussion of quantum mechanics. I shall come back later to more about complementarity and the ongoing arguments between Bohr and Einstein.

I conclude this chapter with a few comments by Heisenberg and Einstein. In 1963 Heisenberg said: 'The most important success of the Brussels meeting was that we could see that against any objections, against any attempts to disprove the theory, we could get along with it. We could get anything clear by using the old words and limiting them by the uncertainty relations and still get a completely consistent picture.' When asked who he meant by 'we', Heisenberg replied: 'I could say that at that time it was practically Bohr, Pauli, and myself. Perhaps just the three of us. That very soon spread out.'[90]

Einstein wrote in 1928: 'The soothing philosophy [*Beruhigungsphiloso-phie*] – or religion? – of Heisenberg–Bohr is so cleverly concocted that for the present it offers the believers a soft resting pillow from which they are not easily chased away. Let us therefore let them rest.'[91]

Heisenberg's lectures on quantum mechanics in Chicago, in 1929, have been published as a short book.[92] In its preface he introduced a term that aptly connotes the contributions he and Bohr had made to the interpretation of quantum mechanics: *Der Kopenhagener Geist* – the Spirit of Copenhagen.

References

1. P. A. M. Dirac, *Hungarian Acad. Sci. Rep.* KFK-62, 1977.
2. N. Bohr, letter to E. Rutherford, 27 January 1926, NBA.
3. N. Bohr, letter to E. Rutherford, 15 May 1926, NBA.
4. N. Bohr, letter to L. H. Thomas, 21 June 1926, NBA.
5. N. Bohr, *Nature* **119**, 262, 1927 (Abstract), CW, Vol. 6, p. 56.
6. N. Bohr, *Nature* **118**, 879, 1926.
7. N. Bohr, *Nature* **118** (Suppl.), 51, 1926.
8. P. A. M. Dirac, in *History of twentieth century physics*, p. 109, Academic Press, New York 1977.
9. Ref. 8. For other recollections by Dirac see NBR, p. 306.
10. N. Bohr, letter to M. Born, 22 January 1927, NBA.
11. P. A. M. Dirac, *Proc. Roy. Soc.* A **114**, 243, 1927.
12. P. A. M. Dirac, *Proc. Roy. Soc.* A **113**, 621, 1927.
13. N. Bohr, letter to C. W. Oseen, 29 January 1926, CW, Vol. 5, p. 238.
14. N. Bohr, letter to A. Heisenberg, 4 August 1926, NBA.
15. P. Robertson, *The early years*, p. 111, Akademisk Forlag, Copenhagen 1979.
16. Ref. 15, p. 112.

17. W. Heisenberg, interview by T. S. Kuhn, 19 February 1963, NBA.
18. W. Heisenberg, postcard to W. Pauli, 5 May 1926, repr. in *W. Pauli, scientific correspondence*, Vol. 1, p. 321, Springer, New York 1979.
19. W. Heisenberg, letter to W. Pauli, 8 June 1926, repr. in *Correspondence* (Ref. 18), Vol. 1, p. 328.
20. W. Heisenberg, *Zeitschr. Phys.* **38**, 411, 1926.
21. W. Heisenberg, *Zeitschr. Phys.* **39**, 499, 1926.
22. W. Heisenberg, unpublished lecture given in 1968, repr. in *Werner Heisenberg, Gesammelte Werke*, Vol. C IV, p. 22, Piper, Munich 1986; also W. Heisenberg, letter to W. Pauli, 28 July 1926, *Correspondence* (ref. 18) Vol. 1, p. 337.
23. N. Bohr, letter to E. Schrödinger, 11 September 1926, NBA.
24. E. Schrödinger, letter to N. Bohr, 21 September 1926, NBA.
25. W. Heisenberg, *Physics and beyond*, p. 73, Harper and Row, New York 1971.
26. Ref. 25, pp. 73–6, a much superior translation in CW, Vol. 6, pp. 11, 12.
27. E. Schrödinger, letter to W. Wien, 21 October 1926, NBA.
28. Ref. 17, interview on 25 February 1963, NBA.
29. N. Bohr, letter to R. H. Fowler, 26 October 1926, CW, Vol. 6, p. 423.
30. N. Bohr, letter to H. A. Kramers, 11 November 1926, NBA.
31. CW, Vol. 3, p. 458.
32. Ref. 25, p. 76.
33. A. Einstein, *Phys. Zeitschr.* **10**, 817, 1909.
34. W. H. Bragg, *Nature* **90**, 360, 1912.
35. W. Heisenberg, letter to W. Pauli, 8 June 1926, *Correspondence* (Ref. 18), Vol. 1, p. 328.
36. C. J. Davisson and L. H. Germer, *Nature* **110**, 558, 1927; *Phys. Rev.* **30**, 705, 1927.
37. G. P. Thomson, *Proc. Roy. Soc.* A **117**, 600, 1928.
38. Ref. 17, interview on 28 February 1963.
39. Ref. 25, p. 77.
40. O. Klein, interview by L. Rosenfeld and J. Kalckar, 7 November 1968, NBA.
41. W. Heisenberg, letter to N. Bohr, 10 March 1927, NBA.
42. Cf. W. Heisenberg, letter to W. Pauli, 9 March 1927, *Correspondence* (Ref. 18), p. 383.
43. W. Heisenberg, letter to W. Pauli, 23 February 1927, *Correspondence* (Ref. 18), p. 376.
44. W. Heisenberg, *Zeitschr. Phys.* **43**, 172, 1927, repr. in CW, Vol. 6, p. 514; English transl. in *Quantum theory and measurement*, p. 62, Eds. J. Wheeler and W. Zusek, Princeton University Press 1983.
45. W. Pauli, letter to W. Heisenberg, 19 October 1926, *Correspondence* (ref. 18), p. 340.
46. Ref. 25, p. 78.
47. E. Lieb, Uncertainty principle, in *Encyclopedia of physics*, p. 1078, Eds. R. Lerner and G. Trigg, Addison-Wesley, Reading, Mass. 1981; E. Arthurs and M. S. Goodman, *Phys. Rev. Lett.* **60**, 2447, 1988.
48. CW Vol. 6, p. 16.
49. N. Bohr, letter to A. Einstein, 13 April 1927, CW, Vol. 6, p. 418.
50. W. Heisenberg, letter to N. Bohr, 18 June 1927, NBA.
51. W. Heisenberg, letter to N. Bohr, 21 August 1927, NBA.

52. W. Heisenberg, letter to N. Bohr, 2 October 1928, NBA.
53. N. Bohr, letter to W. Heisenberg, late December 1928, CW, Vol. 6, p. 24.
54. N. Bohr, *Nature* **121** (Suppl.), 580, 1928, CW, Vol. 6, p. 147.
55. W. Heisenberg, letter to W. Pauli, 16 May 1927, *Correspondence* (Ref. 18), p. 394.
56. J. Kalckar, in CW, Vol. 6, p. 19.
57. W. Heisenberg, *Naturw.* **38**, 49, 1951.
58. W. Heisenberg, Ref. 25, p. 79.
59. O. Klein, NBR, p. 88.
60. CW, Vol. 6, p. 27.
61. N. Bohr, letter to W. Pauli, 13 August 1927, *Correspondence* (Ref. 18), p. 406.
62. N. Bjerrum, Erindringer om Niels Bohr som ven og kammerat, unpublished MS dating from 1955, NBA.
63. N. Bohr, *Nature* **121** (Suppl.), 580, 1928.
64. P. Ehrenfest, letter to N. Bohr, 24 July 1927, NBA.
65. P. Ehrenfest, letter to S. Goudsmit, G. E. Uhlenbeck, and G. H. Dieke, 3 November 1927, CW, Vol. 6, p. 37.
66. H. A. Kramers, *Grundlagen der Quantentheorie*, Chap. 1, Akad. Verlagsgesellschaft, Leipzig, 1938.
67. W. Pauli, *Handbuch der Physik* 24/1, p. 89, Springer, Berlin 1933.
68. L. Rosenfeld, interview by T. S. Kuhn and J. L. Heilbron, 1 July 1963, NBA.
69. *Nature* **121** (Suppl.), 579, 1928, CW, Vol. 6, p. 52.
70. N. Bohr, letter to the Editor of *Nature*, 7 September 1927, NBA; a draft of this article is found in CW, Vol. 6, p. 69.
71. N. Bohr, letter to the Editor of *Nature*, 13 October 1927, NBA.
72. See W. Pauli, letter to N. Bohr, 17 October 1927, CW, Vol. 6, p. 32.
73. N. Bohr, letter to the Editor of *Nature*, 27 December 1927, NBA.
74. N. Bohr, letter to the Editor of *Nature*, 28 February 1928, NBA.
75. *Electrons et photons*, Gauthier-Villars, Paris 1928.
76. SL, Chap. 25.
77. W. Heisenberg, letter to A. Einstein, 30 November 1925.
78. J. Mehra, *Biogr. Mem. Fell. Roy. Soc.* **21**, 117, 1975.
79. A. Einstein, letter to M. Besso, 25 December 1925, CW, Vol. 6, p. 8.
80. A. Einstein, letter to H. Born, 7 March 1926, repr. in *The Born–Einstein letters*, Ed. I. Born, Walker, New York 1971.
81. E. Schrödinger, letter to A. Einstein, 23 April 1926, repr. in *Letters on wave mechanics*, Ed. M. Klein, Philosophical Library, New York 1967.
82. A. Einstein, letter to E. Schrödinger, 26 April 1926, repr. in *Letters* (Ref. 81).
83. A. Einstein, letter to M. Besso, 1 May 1926, repr. in *Einstein–Besso Correspondance*, Ed. P. Speziali, Hermann, Paris 1972.
84. A. Einstein, letter to M. Born, 4 December 1926, repr. in *Letters* (Ref. 80).
85. L. de Broglie, *New perspectives in physics*, p. 150, Basic Books, New York 1962.
86. CW, Vol. 6, p. 37.
87. Cf. CW, Vol. 6, p. 103.
88. Letters by N. Bohr to H. A. Kramers, 17, 27 February 1928; and by H. A. Kramers to N. Bohr, 21 February, 12 March 1928, all in NBA.
89. Ref. 75, p. 215, footnote.

90. Ref. 17, interview on 27 February 1963.
91. A. Einstein letter to E. Schrödinger, 31 May 1928, repr. in *Letters* (ref. 81).
92. W. Heisenberg, *Die physikalischen Prinzipien der Quantentheorie*, Hirzel, Leipzig 1930.

15

Looking into the atomic nucleus

(a) Beginnings of a new direction for Bohr and his school

In August 1928 George Gamow, a native of Odessa (he became a US citizen in 1940), was about to conclude a postdoctoral fellowship in Göttingen. It was then and there that he obtained a result that marks the beginning of modern theoretical nuclear physics: the interpretation of α-radioactivity (also called α-decay) as a quantum mechanical effect.[1] In September the same result was obtained independently in Princeton by Ronald Gurney and Edward Condon, who wrote[2] in their letter to *Nature*: 'It has hitherto been necessary to postulate some special arbitrary "instability" of the nucleus; but in the following note it is pointed out that disintegration is a natural consequence of the laws of quantum mechanics without any special hypothesis.' *

Shortly after Gamow had submitted his paper on α-decay he ran out of money and decided to return to Leningrad. Fates willed otherwise, however.

I wanted to meet Bohr, and I probably had a return ticket [which] I changed to Copenhagen/Stockholm and Finland. And I had some $10 left, just enough for one day. And I came to Copenhagen and stayed in some cheap place . . . and went to [Bohr's] Institute and met *Frøken* [Miss] Schultz, Bohr's secretary . . . I told her I am only there for one day and could I see Bohr. *Frøken* Schultz first told me that the Professor was very busy and I'd have to wait probably a couple of days. I told her, "I have to leave tomorrow because I have no money to eat anywhere." And it was arranged and Bohr came to the library where I was waiting and asked what I had been doing. I told him about this [α-decay paper], it was not published yet . . . And then Bohr said, "My secretary told me you cannot stay more than one day because you have no money. Now if I organize for you a fellowship . . . would you stay for a year?" I told him, "Yes, I would." Right on the spot!'[3]

And so, supported by grants from the Rask–Ørsted fund and the IEB,

---

* In technical terms, the α-decay process is a quantum mechanical tunneling through a potential barrier, a mechanism described in most elementary textbooks on quantum mechanics. β- and γ-decay are also quantum mechanical processes but of different kinds (to be discussed in the next chapter). Note that γ-decay and atomic transitions from a higher to a lower state are generically similar.

Gamow became a research fellow at Bohr's institute from September 1928 to May 1929 and again from September 1930 to May 1931.[4]

During that last month Gamow completed his book on the constitution of atomic nuclei and radioactivity.[5] He was not the first to write a book on nuclear phenomena, but his was the first one ever on *theoretical* nuclear physics. Most of the people he thanked for valuable advice belonged to the Copenhagen circle: Bohr himself and also Gamow's friends and contemporary fellows at the institute, Hendrik Casimir from Leiden, Lev Davidovich Landau from Leningrad, and Nevill Francis Mott from Cambridge.

Thus did Niels Bohr commence the new task of directing the institute toward the young field of nuclear physics.

Bohr's interest in nuclear physics was of early vintage. In 1911 he had gone to Manchester in order 'to get to know something about radioactivity', where he had had good ideas about isotopes (7b). In 1913 he had been the first to demonstrate that β-decay is a nuclear process (8f). His next active personal involvement with nuclear physics began in the mid-1930s, a few years after major strides had been made in understanding nuclear structure. Bohr's main contributions during that period were threefold. He proposed a new theory of nuclear reactions. He moved the main thrust of experimental activities at his institute from atomic spectroscopy to nuclear processes. And he published a fundamental paper on the theory of nuclear fission.

In this chapter I shall only discuss the first of these topics, leaving the other two for later. I begin with a rather cursory account of how nuclear physics had developed up till the time that Bohr put his mind and energies to that subject.

In earlier chapters I have repeatedly stressed that this book is not meant to be a history of quantum theory. The same is true, only more so, with respect to nuclear physics. *Cognoscenti* will find whole chapters of that wonderful subject missing here. I had no other choice if I want to keep my main character in focus.

(b) Theoretical nuclear physics: the prehistoric era

Quantum mechanics is indispensable for an understanding of nuclear phenomena, as witness its successful application to the theory of α-decay, the solitary success of the new mechanics during the late twenties insofar as the nucleus is concerned. Quantum mechanics played another important role during those years, however, in showing that many speculations about nuclear structure that had preceded its discovery in 1925 were seriously flawed. Nevertheless several theoretical concepts – not to mention a large body of experimental facts – gathered during the first quarter of the

twentieth century have turned out to be of lasting importance. I therefore
begin the story of the atomic nucleus with a brief account of the good and
the bad about the nucleus as they emerged during that period, which I like
to call the prehistoric era of theoretical nuclear physics.

The earliest experimental findings of phenomena now known to be of
nuclear origin predate 1911, the year in which the nucleus itself was
discovered (7b). Those were the observations of radioactive processes
beginning with the work of Henri Becquerel in 1896.[6] He, Marie and Pierre
Curie,* and Rutherford made up the foursome that pioneered this new field
of study.[8]

Three advances from the pre-nucleus period are important for what
follows.

1. In the transition

$$\text{mother atom} \rightarrow \text{daughter atom} + \text{radioactive radiation}$$

(we would now write 'nucleus' for 'atom') the emitted radiation is either an
α- or a β- or a γ-ray eventually understood to be a helium nucleus, an
electron, and a photon, respectively.

2. A radioactive species has a characteristic half-life defined as the time it
takes for half a sample of mother atoms to turn into daughters. (This time
can vary from over a billion years (for uranium) to fractions of a second.)
The discovery and first determination of a half-life was made in 1900, by
Rutherford.[9] The half-life concept** was crucial for the unraveling of
frequently occurring sequential radioactive decays in which mother→
daughter is followed by daughter→granddaughter + radiation (often followed in turn by further generations). The theoretical analysis of these
sequences, the transformation theory of Rutherford and Frederick Soddy,[10]
'this great theory of radioactivity which these young men sprung on the
learned, timid, rather unbelieving, and, as yet, unquantized world of
physics of 1902 and 1903',[11] is one of the pre-nucleus theoretical contributions that has survived to this day.

The transformation theory did not explain *why* there is a half-life,
however. A moment's reflection shows that this is a profound question.
During the half-life, 50 per cent of the mother atoms disintegrate, the other
fifty per cent survive, to decay later. All atoms of a mother substance are
identical and likewise for the daughter. Then why should one mother atom
live longer than another? '[Suppose that] 500 million atoms are due to

* The term radioactivity was coined by the Curies in 1898. [7]
** Light emission by atomic transitions also has its half-life, which was in general too
short to be observable in the early days. In theoretical context the half-life concept was first
introduced by Einstein whose coefficient of spontaneous emission (see (10c)) is proportional
to one divided by the half-life constant.

disintegrate in the next second. What, we may inquire, determines which particular atom will fill the quota? . . . It seemed to remove causality from a large part of our picture of the physical world . . . The new laws merely tell that one of the atoms is destined to disintegrate today, another tomorrow, and so on. No amount of calculation will tell which atoms will do this . . .'[12]

The very existence of a half-life is a quantum mechanical effect. Quantum mechanics does *not* help us, however, in predicting which atom will decay in a given time interval and which one will survive. Rather, quantum mechanics tells us that as a matter of principle such a determination is out of the question, causality in the classical sense does not apply. At the price of this loss of information quantum mechanics helps us where classical physics is helpless, to wit in showing us how to compute (at least in principle) the magnitude of a given half-life – as was demonstrated so well by the 1928 theory of α-decay.

3. In 1905 Einstein derived from his theory of relativity[13] that mass (m) is a form of energy (E): $E = mc^2$, where c is the light velocity. In 1906 Planck pointed out[14] that this relation implies that a system of particles bound together weighs less than the sum of its constituents. The reason is this. Consider the particles unbound and at rest at large distances from each other. Now bring them together. The resulting bound state is more stable than the unbound one, or, which amounts to the same thing, it has less total energy. The energy difference between the two states is called the binding energy of the system. Planck's point was that, according to Einstein's relation, that energy can simply be determined by weighing.

As a first example Planck calculated the energy of binding two atoms of hydrogen and one of oxygen into a water molecule and found it to be extremely small. The binding effect is much larger for the case of binding inside a nucleus – not yet on the scene in 1906. In order to appreciate nuclear binding, one obviously has to know not only that a nucleus exists but also what its constituents are. As we shall see, it took twenty years between the discovery of the nucleus and the determination of what it is made of. (For more on binding energy, see (17b).)

(c) Great progress: the first artificial transmutation of chemical elements and the first signs of a new force. Great confusion: the proton–electron model of the nucleus

After Rutherford's discovery of the nucleus in 1911, it became obvious that the nucleus of hydrogen, the lightest of the atomic species, had somehow to play a fundamental role in the description of the structure of nuclear matter. This explains why in 1914 Rutherford referred to the hydrogen nucleus as the 'positive electron'.[15] In 1920 he proposed[16] to call it the proton, the name by which it has been known ever since.

Mainly as the result of the work by Rutherford (7b) and his school, especially Moseley (10b), the following nuclear parameters were known by 1914: the atomic number A, the nearest integer multiple of the nuclear mass in units of the mass of the hydrogen atom; the charge number Z, the charge of the nucleus in units $-e$, where e is the electron's charge; and the nuclear radius. It was further known at that time that there were two basic particles, the electron and the proton, the latter being about 1835 times as heavy as the former. It was natural to assume that the nucleus is made up out of these two building blocks. Thus Rutherford in 1914: 'It is to be anticipated that the helium atom [he meant the helium nucleus, the α-particle] contains four positive electrons [protons] and two negative.'[15] Why? Because $A = 4$ for helium, corresponding to a mass of approximately four protons. The charge $Z = 2$, so throw in two electrons to get the correct charge $(4 - 2 = 2)$. More generally it was assumed that a nuclear species (A, Z) is built up out of A protons and $A - Z$ electrons. It was an idea so inevitable – yet so wrong, as we shall see in the next section.

There was a further reason why an electron–proton model of the nucleus seemed appealing: β-radioactive nuclei emit electrons. Was it not obvious, therefore, that electrons are constituents of those unstable nuclei, waiting to be released? It was an idea so inevitable – yet so wrong, as we shall see in the next chapter.

Also in 1914, Rutherford expressed an opinion about the forces that hold together the particles inside the nucleus: 'The nucleus, though of minute dimensions, is in itself a very complex system consisting of positively and negatively charged particles, bound together by *intense electric forces* [my italics].'[17] In that same year he further wrote: '[The nuclear electrons] are packed together with positive nuclei and must be held in equilibrium by forces of a different [larger] order of magnitude from those which bind the external electrons.'[15] It must have been clear to Rutherford that it was not very obvious how to reconcile these two statements of his. It is true that the attractive electrical forces between particles of opposite electric charge increase in strength when they are close together, as in the nucleus. It would not have been difficult, however, to estimate that even so these forces are not sufficiently strong for nuclear purposes. Physicists in 1914 had, one might say, no choice but to ascribe electromagnetic origins to nuclear forces since, apart from the much weaker gravitational forces, no other forces were known. Thus Rutherford's idea was inevitable – yet so wrong, as we shall see next.

Rutherford was active in physics until his death in 1937, but his last contributions that deserve to be called seminal date from 1919. These are contained in the last papers he published from Manchester. In the course of that year he moved to Cambridge to succeed J. J. Thomson as director of the Cavendish Laboratory.

In 1919 Rutherford published a four-part article 'Collision of α-particles with light atoms' in which he reported results of experiments begun in 1917 and 'carried out at very irregular intervals, as the pressure of routine and war work permitted'.[18] The best-known result of this work[19] is the first observation of the artificial transmutation of elements. By means of α-particle bombardment he converted nitrogen into oxygen! This first nuclear reaction reads, in current notation,

$$\ _2^4\mathrm{He} + \ _7^{14}\mathrm{N} \rightarrow \ _1^1\mathrm{H} + \ _8^{17}\mathrm{O}.$$

The superscripts and subscripts are the values of A and Z respectively (both have to add up to the same totals right and left). $_2^4\mathrm{He}$ is the α-particle, $_1^1\mathrm{H}$ the proton, other symbols are in standard chemical use.*

How times have changed. These days experimental papers on particle physics with a hundred authors or more are not rare. By contrast, Rutherford founded nuclear chemistry all by himself, helped only by William Kay, the Manchester laboratory steward, whom he thanked 'for his invaluable help in counting scintillations.'[19]

Not as widely remembered but of profound importance as well is another result Rutherford reported in 1919: the scattering of α-particles on hydrogen does not always follow the law from which he had deduced the existence of atomic nuclei in the first place.[18]

Rutherford's α-particle energies were essentially the same as those used in 1909 by Geiger and Marsden (7b). The crucial difference between the new and the older experiments was that the earlier scattering targets had rather high Z values, whereas Rutherford's had the lowest possible Z. Correspondingly the electrostatic α-particle–target repulsion is minimal for hydrogen, so that, for the same energy, α-particles can come closer to this target nucleus and thus can be exposed to whatever forces act at relative distances smaller than for high Z.

What can be done with these deviations from Rutherford's scattering law? That law was derived on the assumption that the α-particle orbits are hyperbolae, as is the case for scattering under the influence of electrostatic forces between two objects both of which may be treated as points, that is, as having negligible spatial extension. Was the approximation by points the cause of the deviations? Or were there other than electrostatic forces at work? Rutherford initially opted for the first possibility: 'We have every reason to believe that the α-particle has a complex structure, consisting probably of four hydrogen nuclei and two negative electrons ... It seems

* He = helium, H = hydrogen, N = nitrogen, O = oxygen.

simpler [than a new force] to suppose that [the effect] is due to a deformation of its structure.'[18] In other words, he thought it more prudent to continue assuming the forces to be electromagnetic.

After settling in Cambridge, Rutherford set two of his boys, James Chadwick and Étienne Bieler, to continue work on α-hydrogen scattering. Using improved techniques they confirmed Rutherford's results but, unlike the master, opted for new forces. In their paper, published in 1921,[20] they wrote: 'No system of four hydrogen nuclei and two electrons could give an [electrostatic] field of force [as experiment demands] of such intensity . . . We must conclude that the α-particle is not made up of four hydrogen nuclei and two electrons [true!] or that the law of force is not [electrostatic] in the immediate neighborhood of an electric charge. It is simpler to choose the latter alternative . . . ;' also true!

That is the first statement I know to the effect that inside the nucleus a new force is at work, now called the nuclear force or more generally the strong force or strong interaction.

Already in 1919 Sommerfeld had ventured the opinion[21] that 'nuclear constitution is governed by the same quantum laws as the [periphery] of atoms'. As far as I have found, neither the statement about new laws nor the one on quantum laws initially caught much attention. I can see two reasons for this: the number of people actively concerned with the nucleus was still quite small; and even those interested could put neither statement to use for pushing physics further.

All that changed shortly after the advent of quantum mechanics.

(d) In which quantum mechanics reveals nuclear paradoxes and the neutron is discovered

In his opening remarks at a 'Discussion on the structure of atomic nuclei',[22] held at the Royal Society in February 1929, Rutherford noted: 'Bombarding hydrogen with α-particles the scattering is completely abnormal . . . the hydrogen and helium nucleus appears to be surrounded by a field of unknown origin,' and also 'probably in the lighter elements the nucleus is composed of α-particles, protons, and electrons.'

One might think therefore that not much had changed during the preceding fifteen years in regard to nuclear structure and nuclear forces. Actually, however, a crisis had developed, well diagnosed by Gamow in his 1931 book mentioned earlier: 'The usual ideas of quantum mechanics absolutely fail in describing nuclear electrons; it seems that they may not even be treated as individual particles.'[23] The general principles of quantum mechanics when applied to nuclei had scored one major success, the theory of α-decay (section (a)). But its application to electrons inside a nucleus had caused one perplexity after another. I name a few.*

1. Nuclear magnetic moments (1926). According to Bohr (8f) an electron has a magnetic moment of one Bohr magneton ($eh/4\pi mc$). Nuclei should therefore have a magnetic moment of similar magnitude 'unless the magnetic moments of all the nuclear electrons happen to cancel [the probability for which] seems a priori to be very small.'[25] From spectroscopical data it could be deduced, however, that magnetic moments of nuclei are smaller by several orders of magnitude than the magneton.

2. Nuclear spin (1928). The nitrogen nucleus $^{14}_{7}$N allegedly consists of 14 protons + 7 electrons, an odd total number of spin-$\frac{1}{2}$ particles. Quantum mechanics tells us that the total spin of a system consisting of an odd (even) number of spin-$\frac{1}{2}$ particles is half-integer (integer). Paradox: optical data showed that the spin of $^{14}_{7}$N is integer!

3. Nuclear statistics (1929). It was known that a system consisting of an odd (even) number of spin-$\frac{1}{2}$ particles follows Fermi–Dirac (Bose–Einstein) statistics (13a). Paradox: other spectroscopical data showed that $^{14}_{7}$N satisfies Bose–Einstein statistics!

In October 1931 Bohr summarized the situation like this: 'The experimental evidence regarding the charges and masses of atomic nuclei and their disintegrations finds, as is well known, an immediate explanation on the view that all nuclei are built up of protons and electrons . . . [However] according to experimental evidence, the statistics of an ensemble of identical nuclei is determined solely by the number of protons in each nucleus while the intranuclear electrons show in this respect a remarkable passivity.'[26] We can easily understand what Bohr had in mind in terms of our $^{14}_{7}$N example: if only protons count for determining the nuclear statistics, then their *even* number gives Bose–Einstein statistics! Also the $^{14}_{7}$N spin is integer if only protons count! Also the magnetic moment problem disappears if only protons count! But why would electrons in the nucleus not want to play along?

A few months after Bohr's address the beginnings, but only the beginnings, of the answer was at hand.

In February 1932 Chadwick submitted a paper[27] entitled 'Possible existence of a neutron' (symbol: n). It had been known for some time that bombardment of beryllium (Be) with α-rays produces neutral rays which had been assumed to be γ-radiation. Not so, said Chadwick. He showed instead that the neutral rays are neutrons, a new kind of particle with mass close to the proton mass. 'The capture of the α-particle by the Be nucleus may be supposed to result in the formation of a C [carbon] nucleus and the emission of a neutron':[27]

* A more detailed discussion is found in Ref. 24.

$$\alpha + {}^{9}_{4}Be \rightarrow {}^{12}_{6}C + n.$$

It was another major contribution of the Rutherford school.* The neutron is the last of the basic particles to be discovered in a table-top experiment. The main piece of apparatus Chadwick used (it is still on display at the new Cavendish Laboratory on Madingley Road) is contained in a metal cylinder 6 inches long, $1\frac{1}{2}$ inches wide, which can be held in one's fist. All basic particles discovered later were found either in cosmic radiation, or with accelerators, or with reactors. Naturally produced α-radiation, which had served Rutherford in discovering the atomic nucleus and artificial transmutation, and now Chadwick in discovering the neutron, had played out its major role.

It took another two years[30] before it became obvious that the neutron solves all three paradoxes mentioned above: electrons are banned as nuclear constituents. Instead, a nucleus consists of Z protons and $A-Z$ neutrons, hence there is no problem with nuclear magnetic moments. Neutrons have spin $\frac{1}{2}$, hence obey Fermi–Dirac statistics, so the spin and statistics problems vanish in one blow. Thus in the ${}^{14}_{7}N$ example this nucleus does not consist of 14 protons + 7 electrons, an odd number, but of 7 protons + 7 neutrons, an even number!

From the start Bohr had been intrigued with the neutron. In March 1932 he wrote to Heisenberg: 'Here we have begun to become very interested in the neutron problem.'[31] In April he gave a lecture in Copenhagen on the neutron's properties.[32] Heisenberg was not only interested but sat down and worked out a theory, primitive yet correct in several essentials, of a proton–neutron model of the nucleus. In June he wrote to Bohr: 'The basic idea is to shove all difficulties of principle onto the neutron and then apply quantum mechanics to the nucleus.'[33] Heisenberg could use the non-relativistic version of quantum mechanics, since both proton and neutron are heavy (compared to the electron) and have a low mean velocity while running around in a nucleus.

As Heisenberg noted in his letter the new nuclear model still contained 'difficulties of principle'. These centered on the process of β-radioactivity. Indeed, if electrons are scrapped as nuclear constituents, then how do they manage to appear in β-decay? This question will be discussed in the next chapter.

(e) In which the Bohrs move to the Residence of Honor

During the 11 December 1931 meeting of the *Videnskabernes Selskab*, Bohr spoke of his 'cherished memories'[34] of Harald Høffding, his teacher of

* The existence of a neutron-like particle had been conjectured by Rutherford already in 1920.[28] The term neutron had appeared in the literature long before Chadwick's discovery.[29]

philosophy in his student days (6b), who had died the previous 2 July. He recalled the intimate friendship between Høffding and his late father, the gatherings in his parental home during which he and his brother Harald would listen to discussions between these two men, of Høffding's constant endeavours at using points of view developed in particular branches of science for illuminating more general issues, and of his appreciation for the new conceptual developments in physics during recent years. 'To visit him in the last year of his life was every time a great and rich experience.'

Those last visits brought Bohr to the *Æresbolig*, the Residence of Honor, in the Carlsberg breweries, the erstwhile residence of brewer Jacobsen, left by him for use free for life by the Dane most prominent in science or literature or the arts (12d). Høffding had been the first recipient of that privilege and had lived in the *Æresbolig* since 1914. Now the *Videnskabernes Selskab* had to propose a new occupant. That choice was made at that same 11 December meeting.

The next morning the Danish newspapers reported[35] what had happened the previous evening. After Bohr had delivered his eulogy on Høffding, he left the hall. In his absence the members discussed and voted on the successor of Høffding at Carlsberg. Then Bohr was called back. All present rose when he reentered and, silently and solemnly, everybody turned from their chairs and bowed to him. After some seconds of complete silence, the president, Bohr's brother-in-law Niels Erik Nørlund, informed him that the *Selskab* had voted to propose him as successor to Høffding at Carlsberg. A subsequent letter[36] by Knudsen, Secretary of the Society, formally notified him that the vote had been unanimous. The necessary final approval by the board of the Carlsberg foundation followed forthwith.

In the summer of 1932 Niels and Margrethe and their five sons moved into their new home. In September Bohr wrote to Hevesy: 'We now live in Carlsberg ... it will be very moving for Margrethe and me to think that [Rutherford and his wife] will be our first guests in our new home.'[37] Baron Rutherford of Nelson (he had been elevated to the peerage in 1931) and Lady Rutherford stayed with the Bohrs from 12 to 22 September.[38] On the 14th and 15th Rutherford gave lectures. Afterwards Bohr wrote: 'We had immense pleasure of Rutherford's visit and not least to understand that they both felt themselves comfortable in our new home.'[39]

Carlsberg was to be Bohr's home for the rest of his life. It was there that he died.*

To reach the *Æresbolig* one enters at Pasteursvej the extensive grounds occupied by the Carlsberg Breweries, then follows a curved road marked

---

* The later inhabitants of the *Æresbolig* were the archaeologist Johannes Balthasar Brønsted (1963–5), the astronomer Bengt Strömgren (1966–87), and the orientalist Søren Egerod, the current occupant.

with signs '*Til Æresboligen*', until one reaches the residence. In Jacobsen's days it was called *Gammel Carlsberg's Hovedbygning* (old C.'s main building). In those times the brewery lay practically in the country, in the village of Valby, now part of metropolitan Copenhagen.

In 1846 Jacobsen had received royal permission to build his brewery. The residence was constructed in 1852–4 after his own designs. 'I have built this house not in order to acquire a magnificent home to live in but to make something beautiful,' he once said to his son, who remembered how H. C. Andersen, one of his father's frequent guests, would read his tales and poems to others present.[40] Right behind the house one finds one of Denmark's finest and largest botanical gardens, also laid out after Jacobsen's ideas. It spans nine acres, about the size of *Kongen's Nytorv*, Copenhagen's second main square. Many of the trees planted in Jacobsen's time have been preserved to this day, the most striking being a *platanus orientalis* near the house. To the particular delight of Margrethe Bohr, a hothouse provided flowers for the residence all year round. (Once, on the way home from China, she carried a water lily all the way on the trans-Siberian railroad.)

The house has two floors, a cellar in which the kitchen is housed, and an attic where the staff had its sleeping quarters – one of the great changes in the Bohr's lifestyle after they moved in was the number of servants now at their disposal. On the main floor one finds a living room, an elegant dining room, Bohr's study, Margrethe's room, and the 'winter garden', a large (35 × 35 ft) enclosed space filled with tropical and other plants, a small fountain in the middle, and comfortably upholstered wicker chairs in a corner, a favorite spot for cosy chats. The most impressive space in the house is the U-shaped 'Pompei Hall', 70 ft long, 40 ft wide, 30 ft high, which was added on in 1876. It is surrounded by a peristyle with columns copied after Athens' Erechtheion. In the Bohr era one wall was decorated with rubbings of Tang horses in relief, acquired in China. Along another wall were three small offices. In one of these Sophie Hellmann, Bohr's private secretary, held sway for many years. Another, containing the inevitable blackboard, was used by Bohr as an office.

The considerable amount of sculpture in Graeco-Roman style one finds both inside and outside the house are inheritances from Jacobsen, from the copy of Myron's famous discus-thrower in front to Hebe pouring nectar, in the dining room, to the copy of Venus de Milo that stands amid rose bushes behind the house. Sculptures in that same style by Bertel Thorvaldsen, considered by most Danes to be their most prominent sculptor, are found in several places inside.[41]

The Bohr's were ideal residents since they knew so well how to use their sumptuous quarters for receiving others. At dinners they would entertain not only the king and queen of Denmark, or the prime minister and other high officials, but also close friends and colleagues. They knew how to blend guests who were physicists with those from other professions, whether or not academic. The Pompei Hall was used for receptions, whether for the staff and visitors from Bohr's institute, or for Queen Elizabeth and Prince Philip of England, or other high dignitaries. Margrethe Bohr was in her element on all such occasions, officiating with great charm and dignity. She had the particular talent of knowing the names and some personal circumstances of all her guests. She came to be known as *Dronning* (Queen) Margrethe, with affectionate respect by some, with envy by others.

The Bohrs, of course, put their own stamp on the interior of their new home. Of their living room I remember most vividly a cosy corner sofa where they loved to sit, with or without guests. Of the many paintings in that room I recall one (dating from 1868) of Niels' maternal grandmother with her three daughters at a young age, one of Niels' mother in her mature years, and one of Christian, their oldest son. Several twentieth century paintings in more modern style hung in various places, including one by Jean Metzinger, a co-founder of cubism. Art objects, acquired at home or abroad, or presented them by friends and colleagues, were found everywhere.

On the wall behind the desk in Bohr's study hung three oils, one of his teacher Christiansen, one of his father, in the center, and one of Høffding, also some smaller paintings including one of his brother Harald. Also in that study one could note an antique Buddha figure, or an old lamp made of stone, a gift from the population of Greenland, or a small carved ivory figure given by Japanese colleagues on the occasion of his fiftieth birthday. It represents a chick that has just come out of the egg, symbolizing a man who has entered the company of mature adults.[41]

Happy memories of many hours spent at Carlsberg have remained with me through the years.

(f) In which Bohr takes nuclear matters in hand

The discovery of the neutron was most important not only because it led to the first sensible though primitive theoretical description of nuclei. In addition this new particle provided an extremely valuable new experimental tool for penetrating the secrets of nuclear matter. Since neutrons carry no electric charge, they can enter and explore the interior of the nucleus without being held back by electrostatic repulsion, as is the case for α-particles. Thus began a new chapter of experimental inquiry, neutron physics, the study of what happens when nuclei are bombarded by neutrons.*

* In what follows I focus on Bohr's activities in this new field and do not give references to many important contributions made by others, both in experiment and in theory. Guides to this extensive literature are found in two superb reviews, one[43] dealing with work up till mid-1937, the period of immediate interest to us next, the other[44] with a detailed history of neutron physics up till 1945.

Among the nuclear processes explored experimentally in the early days were the scattering of neutrons by nuclei, as well as nuclear reactions of the types neutron + nucleus → another nucleus + either a photon, or a proton, or two neutrons, or an α-particle, at neutron energies from a few million electronvolts down to 'thermal energies', a few electronvolts or less. Theorists did of course not wait long in trying to interpret the new data. I introduce their efforts with a general comment on the style in which theoretical nuclear physics was done in the early 1930s.

Electrostatic forces which mainly account for atomic structure are derived from an underlying fundamental theory, Maxwell's theory of the electromagnetic field. When Heisenberg introduced his theory of nuclear forces, he and his colleagues had no analogous underlying field theory to draw on. His approach was therefore necessarily phenomenological, that is, his only guide was what little there existed by way of experimental data, mainly the systematics of nuclear binding energies. For the rest he, and others who soon followed him, reasoned by analogy with atomic physics. Thus he assumed that the forces between nucleons, the collective name for protons and neutrons, act only between pairs of these particles (two-body forces). From the data he inferred that these forces must have a short range, that is, they weaken rapidly as the distances between nucleons increases; that they must be strong, since nuclear binding is about a million times stronger than atomic binding, and that the total nuclear binding energy is proportional to the atomic number A (saturation).

When neutron physics came along, the initial interpretation of data rested once again on analogies with atomic processes, such as the scattering of electrons by atoms or the ionization of atoms by electrons. A 'one-body model' was postulated, according to which the nucleus as a whole is represented by a rigid body that exerts a fixed overall average force on impinging neutrons. The general framework was of course quantum mechanical.

A few early results looked promising. The model could explain the observed large increase of neutron capture as the neutron moves ever more slowly. Large fluctuations of the capture probability from one element to another could be attributed, it was thought, to corresponding differences in the average force generated by the nucleus.

Very soon severe difficulties arose, however. The theory predicted that the probability for scattering of thermal neutrons should be larger than or comparable with the probability for their capture. Yet already in 1935 experiments showed that for certain elements capture was vastly more probable than scattering, by a factor of about 100 for cadmium for example. Also from that year date the discoveries of 'selective absorption'. These phenomena were discovered by means of experimental arrangements of the following kind. A continuous energy spectrum of neutrons first impinges on a layer of element X. Some neutrons are absorbed, some pass through. The latter hit a second layer, of element Y, in which further absorption can take place. This second absorption is much smaller if X and Y are the same substance than when they are different.

As a function of neutron energy the absorption exhibits a series of peaks and valleys whatever the absorbing nucleus may be.

All these observations were in conflict with the predictions of the one-body model according to which absorption should exhibit a smooth behavior, inverse proportionality to the neutron velocity, for any kind of absorbing nucleus.

At that stage Bohr came forth with a radically different approach.

There is some confusion regarding the time when Bohr first thought[45] of the 'compound nucleus', the central feature of his new theory.[46] It is certain, however, that he first unveiled these ideas at a *Videnskabernes Selskab*'s meeting in January 1936.[47] The next time he spoke publicly about this work was in London. According to *The Times* of London of 13 February: 'A new theory of the atom . . . was described by Professor Niels Bohr of Copenhagen when he lectured [on 11 February] before the Chemical and Physical Society of University College, London.' This article further reports that Bohr was introduced with these (not quite correct) words: 'It is a great honor, both to this country and to University College that Professor Bohr should have elected to make the first announcement of his new theory in this lecture here.' Bohr's first publication on the subject also dates from February. It is a clearly written brief communication which as usual contains no equations.[48]

Bohr's main point was that the idealization of the nucleus as a single rigid body is incorrect. Nuclear reactions should instead be treated, he suggested, as a many body problem of a special kind: a two-stage reaction.

In the first stage the incoming projectile – which may either be a neutron, or a proton, or an α-particle, with due regard of course to electrostatic repulsion in the last two instances – merges with the bombarded nucleus into a single unit, the compound nucleus. This compound has many properties in common with a stable nucleus, though it is not a stable body itself. Thus it has a discrete set of energy levels, as had been known to be the case for stable nuclei since the early 1920s, the time which marks the beginnings[49] of 'nuclear spectroscopy', the analog for nuclei of the long-familiar situation for atoms and molecules.

In the second stage the compound nucleus disintegrates, either into the particles from which it was formed (elastic scattering); or again into these same particles but the nucleus turning into one of its excited states (inelastic scattering); or into different particles (nuclear reaction). A similar two-stage description had been introduced earlier[50] for a limited set of chemical reactions via formation of a compound molecule. I do not know (nor does it matter much) whether Bohr knew this.

A crucial feature of this picture, Bohr continued,[48] is that the formation and the break-up of the compound nucleus are well separated in time (always reckoned on the scale of nuclear processes). This separability is a consequence, he thought, of the close packing of nucleons in nuclei. In an encounter between a neutron and a nucleus, 'the excess energy of the incident neutron will be rapidly divided among all the nuclear particles with the result that for some time afterwards no single particle will have sufficient kinetic energy to leave the nucleus . . . It is therefore clear that the duration of the encounter must be extremely long compared with the time interval, *circa* 10^{-21} sec, which the neutron would use in simply passing through a space region of nuclear dimensions.'[47] so long that, one might say, the compound nucleus has lost all memory of how it was formed by the time it breaks up. The only chance for break-up is a *rare* fluctuation in which a single particle gathers most of the available excess energy.

Bohr's new picture bears no resemblance whatever with what happens in close collisions between electrons and atoms. In that case the probability for elastic scattering is very large compared with that for inelastic scattering, which in turn is very large compared with that for emission of a photon, just the opposite of what was found in nuclear reactions, where, for heavy nuclei, photon emission is in fact the most probable process.

This brings us to the details of Bohr's model. Nuclear photoemission is so pronounced, he reasoned, because it does not depend on the complicated redistribution of energy among nucleons. Any nucleon can at any time get rid of extra energy by emitting a photon: 'The remarkable absence of selective scattering of slow neutrons is just what we would expect for small excess energy on account of the vanishing probability of neutron escape compared with that of radiative transitions.'[48]

Selective absorption, Bohr argued further, is a consequence of the quantization of the energy levels of the compound nucleus. Quantum mechanics teaches us that the probability of formation of a compound nucleus is quite large if the energy of the incident particle just fits with bringing the whole system into one of the energy levels of the compound nucleus, a phenomenon known as resonance excitation. The probability for compound formation is much smaller if the incident energy does not fit in that way.

Resonance excitation explains the absorption by elements X and Y mentioned before. Absorption by X principally occurs for those incoming neutrons which carry the specific resonant energies corresponding to the formation of the compound nucleus 'X + neutron'. If Y equals X then the neutron spectrum hitting Y is lacking in just those neutrons that can form a compound nucleus in the Y layer. If, on the other hand, Y is different from X, then the incoming continuous neutron spectrum has not suffered depletion of those neutrons that can form the compound 'Y + neutron'. In Bohr's words: 'The different selective absorbing elements [show] that the resonance is restricted to narrow energy regions which are differently placed for selective absorbers.'[48] Thus resonance excitation explains both the phenomenon of selective absorption and the general occurrence of peaks and valleys as a function of neutron energy.

By happy coincidence, Bohr's qualitative considerations of these phenomena were greatly helped along by simultaneous and independent quantitative studies of nuclear resonance phenomena undertaken by Gregory Breit and Wigner in Princeton. In their paper,[51] entitled 'Capture of slow neutrons' (submitted in February 1936), the authors do not use the compound nucleus model; in fact their main formulae do not depend on any model, and may therefore in particular be applied to Bohr's pictures. This work helped promote 'the profound reordering of the picture of nuclear dynamics implied by Bohr's ideas [which were] rapidly and widely accepted in the nuclear physics community; within months the literature is completely dominated by papers applying, testing, and extending the ideas of the compound nucleus'.[52]

During the next several years Bohr himself remained active in nuclear physics. He was fortunate to be assisted in these ventures by Fritz Kalckar, a brilliant young Danish physicist. The two men worked together through most of 1936, as witness the usual collection of unfinished draft manuscripts.[53] Their lengthy joint paper, dealing with collisions between either neutrons or charged particles and nuclei, was not completed until October 1937.[54] Its nine appendices summarize work meanwhile published by others on the main question they had been considering themselves: the energy spectrum of the compound nucleus.

It had, of course, been clear to Bohr that analogies with atomic spectra could not be of help in interpreting his picture of nuclear structure. Peripheral electrons, thinly spread within the atomic volume, can be compared to a dilute gas of particles interacting in pairs only. By contrast Bohr's picture of intranuclear motions of tightly bound nucleons should show 'essential collective aspects', he had said.[47] Now, together with Kalckar, he suggested that for nuclei a much more proper comparison would be with a drop of liquid.* That analogy should not be taken too literally, the dynamics of a true liquid drop is vastly different from that of nuclei. Yet the comparison, treated cautiously, was tempting and in the event proved fruitful in many respects, particularly in regard to collective

* In different context that same thought had occurred earlier to Gamow.[55]

motions. A liquid drop in equilibrium can be characterized by forces that would disperse it into smaller parts were it not counteracted by a surface tension. When the drop gets kicked, excited, it performs vibrations of various kinds: surface waves which do not change the drop volume, and volume waves, a sequence of compressions and dilations. These vibrations, Bohr and Kalckar, argued, give a good model for collective motions of nuclei. Vibrational energies, *when quantized*, should describe the spectrum of the compound nucleus. Since the surface waves have frequencies small compared with those of volume waves, the former should be representative of the nuclear spectrum at the relatively low energies at which the processes previously mentioned had so far been observed.

At lowest energies the spectrum so obtained consists of well separated levels. At higher energies the level density increases and eventually becomes so large that the levels overlap and practically form a continuous spectrum. (Note that the levels are not sharp lines but have each a finite width which also increases with increasing excitation.) Thus the number of excitable vibrational motions increases as the energy increases. Next question: What are the relative probabilities for the compound nucleus to occupy any one of these accessible excited states? Answer: These probabilities are given by the analog of the Planck formula for the probabilities of electromagnetic vibrations (see Chapter 5). Accordingly one considers the compound nucleus as a blackbody for which one can define a temperature in terms of its average excitation energy.[56] From there on one treats the compound nucleus with the help of statistical mechanical and thermodynamical concepts. In particular the break up of the compound nucleus into one or another final state can be looked upon as the analog of the evaporation of molecules from the surface of a liquid drop.

The collaboration of Bohr and Kalckar, so full of further promise, came to a sudden end when in January 1938 Kalckar unexpectedly died of a cerebral hemorrhage, at the age of not quite 28. Speaking at the funeral,[57] Bohr recalled Kalckar's maturity in spite of his youth, and how at one time they had agreed 'that there is no sorrow so great that does not find its background in joy'. In a newspaper obituary[58] Bohr wrote: 'That the collaboration, which we had looked forward so much to continue, should so abruptly come to an end is a thought which I find difficult to reconcile myself with . . .'

This concludes an outline of Bohr's model for nuclear reactions. During 1936–7 he lectured on this subject in Helsinki,[59] in various places in the United States,[60] Japan, and China, in Moscow, in Copenhagen,[61] and in Paris.[62] In 1938 he included a review of this work in a historical essay dedicated to Planck on his 80th birthday.[63] Later that year he applied the model to the nuclear photoeffect (photon + nucleus → neutron + other nucleus).[64] Also in that year he began a collaboration with Rudolf Peierls and George Placzek on an improved general treatment of nuclear reactions at higher energies (denser levels). Preliminary results were published in 1939.[65] Plans for a longer paper, interrrupted by the war and taken up again thereafter, were never executed. 'Copies of some draft circulated during [the war years] and as a result the paper was cited repeatedly in the literature, making it one of the most cited unpublished papers.'[66]

Meanwhile in 1939 Bohr had applied his model to nuclear fission. It was 'the compound nucleus' finest hour!'[52] As I have said, I will leave that contribution till later.

(g) Being a brief prelude to the war and the years thereafter

'In nuclear physics certainly the [nineteen] thirties were a very happy period.' So wrote Hans Bethe.[67] He should know since he was one of the leaders in theoretical nuclear physics in that period (and also later). The discovery of the neutron, the beginnings of a quantum mechanics of the nucleus as a neutron–proton system, and the Bohr theory of nuclear reactions were indeed reasons for rejoicing* (and there were more; see the next two chapters). Bethe further wrote: 'The compound nucleus dominated the theory of nuclear reactions at least from 1936 to 1954.'[67] One of the more shall we say spectacular chapters belonging under the heading of neutron physics was the development of the atomic bomb. There, too, Bohr's ideas played an important role. Bethe again: 'At Los Alamos when we tried to get [probabilities] we used the compound nucleus model and usually our predictions were quite reasonable. The compound model could explain many phenomena . . .'[67] He should know since in the War years he was the head of the theory division at the Los Alamos Laboratory.

Shortly after World War II the whole subject of nuclear models took an unexpected turn.

It began with the remark[68] that nuclei with a special number of protons (2, 8, 14, 20, 28, 50, 82) or neutrons (the same and also 126) have particularly stable ground states: their binding energies per nucleon are pronouncedly larger than those of neighboring nuclei. These peculiarities** were somewhat reminiscent of what happens in atoms with electron numbers $Z = 2, 10, 18, 36, 54, 86$, the noble gases, in which electrons fill closed shells (see (10e)). It took little time to realize that these 'magic numbers', 2, 8, 14, . . . , can be reproduced by assuming that nucleons inside the respective ground states of nuclei behave approximately as *independently moving*

* See Ref. 52 for a list of the most important developments connected with the compound nucleus.
** Some of which had been noted much earlier.

particles held together by a common overall force, just as is approximately true for peripheral atomic electrons moving in the electrostatic field of the nucleus, but with one important distinction. The nuclear magic numbers differ from the Z-numbers of noble gases principally because there exists a coupling between spin and orbital angular momentum of each participating particle which is strong in the nuclear, and weak in the atomic, case.[69] The independent particle model which so emerged – not surprisingly it came to be known as the shell model – soon booked many successes.[70]

Nuclear theory in the early 1950s therefore seemed at first glance to pose a paradox. On the one hand, since the mid-1930s the concept of collective motions of the nucleus, exemplified by the liquid drop model, and based on the assumption of strong forces between nucleons, had had one success after another. On the other hand, along comes the shell model with its opposite starting point of individual nucleon motions, exemplified by a gas rather than a liquid, implying relatively weak forces between nucleons, and claiming indisputable successes of its own. Can a nucleus behave both like a gas and like a liquid? Is there something wrong with Bohr's model?

It can and there is. Let us return to the way Bohr had deduced the compound nucleus picture. He had reasoned that strong forces between nucleons cause an incoming neutron to suffer so many collisions with other nucleons that its time of residence in the nucleus is very long compared with the time it would take for its unhindered traversal of the nucleus. In actual fact that residence time *is* (or rather can be) long but Bohr's explanation – though a logical possibility – is not. The alternative and true explanation for long residence times is wave mechanical: a slow neutron wave inside the nucleus can be reflected many times at the nuclear surface even if the forces between individual nucleons are not that strong.* Once that is clear a peaceful coexistence between the shell model and the compound nucleus becomes possible.

The next task was to find a theoretical framework from which both models and their respective ranges of applicability can be quantitatively deduced. There has been distinct progress in that direction,[71] but the final word has by no means yet been said. Research in nuclear models, including the compound nucleus,[72] is continuing. It is fitting to recall that these issues are but part of the large class of many-body problems that continue to be subjects of widely ranging studies, in which advances in one area often stimulate progress in another.

As to Bohr, almost from the very beginning he took a lively interest in the shell model, recognizing that it represented a genuine advance in nuclear theory.[73] In 1949 he began work on a paper provisionally entitled 'Tentative comments on atomic and nuclear constitution', which shows how the

---

* See further the more quantitative discussion by Mottelson.[52]

search for a synthesis of his earlier work with the shell model preoccupied him: 'As regards the excitation of nuclei we meet with analogies as well as with peculiar differences from the excitation of atoms.'[74] That manuscript was never completed.

The shell model and its ramifications belong to the post-Bohr era. To this day the Bohr institute remains an important active center of theoretical nuclear physics, however. Aage Bohr together with Ben Mottelson took over where Niels left off.[75]

References

1. G. Gamow, *Zeitschr. Phys.* **51**, 204, 1928.
2. R. W. Gurney and E. U. Condon, *Nature* **122**, 439, 1928; *Phys. Rev.* **33**, 127, 1929.
3. G. Gamow, interview by C. Weiner, 25 April 1968.
4. For more biographical details see G. Gamow, *My world line*, Viking Press, New York 1970. For the history of α-decay see R. H. Stuewer in *The kaleidoscope of science*, p. 147, Ed. E. Ullmann, Reidel, Boston 1986.
5. G. Gamow, *Constitution of nuclei and radioactivity*, Oxford University Press 1931.
6. IB, Chap. 2.
7. P. and M. Curie, *C.R. Acad. Sci. Paris* **127**, 175, 1898.
8. See IB, Chap. 3, for the early work of the Curies and Rutherford.
9. E. Rutherford, *Phil. Mag.* **49**, 1, 1900.
10. E. Rutherford and F. Soddy, *Phil. Mag.* **4**, 370, 569, 1902.
11. A. S. Russell, *Proc. Phys. Soc. London* **64**, 217, 1951.
12. J. Jeans, *Physics and philosophy*, pp. 149–150, Cambridge University Press 1943.
13. A. Einstein, *Ann. der Phys.* **18**, 639, 1905.
14. M. Planck, *Verh. Deutsch. Phys. Ges.* **4**, 136, 1906; also *Ann. der Phys.* **26**, 1, 1908.
15. E. Rutherford, *Phil. Mag.* **27**, 488, 1914.
16. E. Rutherford, see *Nature* **106**, 357, 1920.
17. E. Rutherford, *Scientia* **16**, 337, 1914.
18. E. Rutherford, *Phil. Mag.* **37**, 537, 1919; corr. in *Phil. Mag.* **41**, 307, 1921.
19. E. Rutherford, *Phil. Mag.* **37**, 581, 1919.
20. J. Chadwick and E. S. Bieler, *Phil. Mag.* **42**, 923, 1921.
21. A. Sommerfeld, *Atombau und Spektrallinien*, 1st edn, p. 540, Vieweg, Braunschweig 1919.
22. E. Rutherford, *Proc. Roy. Soc.* A **123**, 373, 1929.
23. Ref. 5, p. 5.
24. IB, Chap. 14, section (b).
25. R. de L. Kronig, *Nature* **117**, 550, 1926.
26. N. Bohr, contribution to a nuclear physics conference organized by the Volta foundation, CW, Vol. 9, p. 101.
27. J. Chadwick, *Nature* **129**, 312, 1932.
28. IB, p. 397.

29. IB, p. 398, esp. 2nd footnote.
30. See IB, Chap. 17, section (c).
31. N. Bohr, letter to W. Heisenberg, 22 March 1932, NBA.
32. CW, Vol. 9, p. 115.
33. W. Heisenberg, letter to N. Bohr, 20 June 1932, NBA.
34. N. Bohr, *Overs. Kong. Dansk. Vid. Selsk. Virksomhed 1931–1932*, p. 131.
35. *Politiken*, 12 December 1931.
36. M. Knudsen, letter to N. Bohr, 12 December 1931, NBA.
37. N. Bohr, letter to G. von Hevesy, 5 September 1932, NBA.
38. N. Bohr, letter to W. Heisenberg, 1 August 1932, CW, Vol. 9, p. 576.
39. N. Bohr, letter to R. H. Fowler, 28 October 1932, NBA.
40. Cf. D. Zanker-v. Meyer, *Die Bauten von J. C. und Carl Jacobsen*, Deutscher Kunstverlag, Berlin 1982. This book contains numerous architectural details concerning the *Æresbolig*.
41. For descriptions of the *Æresbolig* at the time the Bohrs moved in see *Politiken*, 11 December 1931; *Berlingske Aftenavis*, 12 December 1931.
42. For glimpses of the interior of the *Æresbolig* in the Bohr days see an interview with Margrethe Bohr in *Berlingske Tidende*, 22 September 1963.
43. H. A. Bethe and R. F. Bacher, *Rev. Mod. Phys.* **8**, 82, 1936; **9**, 69, 1937.
44. E. Amaldi, *Phys. Rep.* **111**, 1, 1984.
45. For an early draft, possibly from 1935, see CW, Vol. 9, p. 144.
46. For these and other historical details regarding Bohr's theory see especially an essay by Peierls, CW, Vol. 9, p. 3.
47. N. Bohr, *Dansk. Vid. Selsk. Virksomh. June 1935–May 1936*, p. 39; *Nature* **138**, 695, 1936, CW, Vol. 9, p. 150.
48. N. Bohr, *Nature* **137**, 344, 1936, CW, Vol. 9, p. 152; Editorial comment, *ibid.* **137**, 351, 1936, CW, Vol. 9, p. 158; German transl. in *Naturw.* **24**, 241, 1936.
49. IB, Chap. 8, section (g); Chap. 14, section (c).
50. M. Polanyi, *Zeitschr. Phys.* **2**, 90, 1920.
51. G. Breit and E. Wigner, *Phys. Rev.* **49**, 519, 1936.
52. B. Mottelson, in *The lesson of quantum theory*, p. 79, Eds. J. de Boer, E. Dal, and O. Ulfbeck, Elsevier, New York 1986.
53. CW, Vol. 9, pp. 179, 183, 191, 195.
54. N. Bohr and F. Kalckar, *Dansk. Vid. Selsk. Mat.-fys. Medd.* **14**, No. 10, 1937, CW, Vol. 9, p. 223. The content of that paper is summarized in CW, Vol. 9, pp. 27–32.
55. Ref. 5, p. 18.
56. Ref. 54, section 4.
57. N. Bohr, unpublished manuscript, NBA.
58. N. Bohr, *Politiken*, 7 January 1938. See also C. Møller, *Fysisk Tidsskr.* **36**, 1, 1938.
59. CW, Vol. 9, p. 161.
60. N. Bohr, *Science* **86**, 161, 1937, CW, Vol. 9, p. 207.
61. CW, Vol. 9, p. 213.
62. CW, Vol. 9, p. 265.
63. N. Bohr, *Ann. der Phys.* **32**, 5, 1938, English transl. in CW, Vol. 9, p. 318.
64. N. Bohr, *Nature* **141**, 326, 1096, 1938; CW, Vol. 9, pp. 297, 331.

65. N. Bohr, R. Peierls, and G. Placzek, *Nature* **144**, 200, 1939, CW, Vol. 9, p. 391.
66. CW, Vol. 9, p. 50.
67. H. A. Bethe, in *Nuclear physics in retrospect*, p. 11, Ed. R. Stuewer, University of Minnesota Press 1979.
68. See esp. M. G. Mayer, *Phys. Rev.* **74**, 235, 1948.
69. O. Haxel, J. H. D. Jensen, and H. E. Suess, *Phys. Rev.* **75**, 1766, 1949; M. G. Mayer, *ibid.*, 1969, 1949.
70. Cf. J. M. Blatt and V. Weisskopf, *Theoretical nuclear physics*, Chap. 14, Wiley, New York 1952.
71. Cf. G. E. Brown, *Unified theory of nuclear models*, Wiley, New York 1964; H. Feshbach, Nuclear reactions – a survey, in *Proc. Workshop Nucl. Phys.*, Torino, November 1987, Eds. A. Molinari *et al.*, World Scientific, Singapore 1988.
72. Cf. C. Mahaux and H. A. Weidenmüller, *Ann. Rev. Nucl. Sci.* **29**, 1, 1979.
73. Cf. CW, Vol. 9, pp. 76–83.
74. CW, Vol. 9, p. 523.
75. A. Bohr and B. R. Mottelson, *Nuclear structure*, 2 vols., Benjamin, Reading, Mass. 1969, 1975.

16

Toward the edge of physics in the Bohr style, and a bit beyond

(a) Particles and fields

The first international physics conference after World War II was held from 22 to 27 July 1946 at the Cavendish Laboratory. Its themes were 'Fundamental particles and low temperatures'. In the preface to the proceedings[1] one reads: 'The subject of Fundamental Particles is nowadays so wide that the arrangement of the programme was not easy.' The opening address was given by Bohr. It is entitled 'Problems of elementary particle physics'.[2]

What are fundamental or (which is the same) elementary particles? They are the ultimate building blocks of matter and radiation. Which, in 1946, were the entries on the list of fundamental particles? The electron and positron, the proton, the neutron, the meson, the neutrino, and the photon.* The positron, meson, and neutrino are new to this book. In this chapter I shall explain what they are and how they were found.

Knowing what we know today, how good is that list? No disrespect to the contributions of earlier generations, but it is now considered to be poor. The proton and neutron are no longer believed to be elementary but rather to be composites of a new breed of particles, quarks. That insight came only after Bohr's death and will therefore not be part of our present story. The meson on the list – since called the μ-meson – is a particle with mass intermediate between electron and nucleon. We now know that there is not one but that there are many kinds of mesons. Also, there are other kinds of particles (called hyperons) akin to the proton and neutron that are neither less nor more fundamental than those two are.

The only purpose of dumping all these facts into the reader's lap at this point is to explain why the post-war generations have become increasingly averse to using words like 'fundamental' or 'elementary' and have generally adopted the less pretentious and more cautious term 'particle physics' to denote the study of the objects on the 1946 list and its extensions.

---

* Another entry, the graviton, the gravitational field quantum, could have been, but was not, entered in that list.

In broad terms the great twentieth century successes in our understanding of the structure of matter can be listed under three headings: atomic and molecular physics; nuclear physics; and particle physics. In the course of time these areas have increased in importance in that order. That is not to say that one domain was closed when the next began. Thus particle physics began in 1897 with the discovery of the electron (7a), well before one had any inkling about the structure of atoms. Atomic and molecular physics continued to make major strides well beyond the 1930s, when nuclear physics began its rise.

Important results in nuclear physics had already been obtained before quantum mechanics had provided the necessary tools for a real understanding of atomic, molecular, and nuclear structure (15b). Quantum mechanics is likewise indispensable in particle physics, but there it is not sufficient, even in the simplest instances. One needs most especially an outgrowth of quantum mechanics called quantum field theory.

In order to indicate what is at stake, let us first reconsider a phrase by Heisenberg quoted earlier (13d) from his first paper on quantum mechanics: 'Even for the simplest quantum theoretical problem the validity of classical mechanics cannot be maintained.' Remember that mechanics is the discipline dealing with motions of particles. There is another area of classical theory which we have encountered earlier, Maxwell's theory of the electromagnetic field. The theory resulting from applying quantum mechanics to that field is called quantum electrodynamics (QED). It is the oldest example of a quantum field theory; others will be encountered later on.

To paraphrase Heisenberg, even for the simplest quantum theoretical problem the validity of classical electrodynamics (the theory initiated by Maxwell) cannot be maintained. That much was known long before the arrival of quantum mechanics. Indeed, let us never forget that the early quantum theory, the old quantum theory, originated from considerations of electromagnetic problems, leading in 1900 to Planck's quantum theory of blackbody radiation (5g) and in 1905 to Einstein's photon (5h). Let us further note that in 1909 Einstein, who had pondered further [3] on the peculiar particle wave duality of light, had written:

It is my opinion that the next phase in the development of theoretical physics will bring us a theory of light that can be interpreted as a kind of fusion of the wave and the [particle] theory . . . [The] wave structure and [the] quantum structure . . . are not to be considered as mutually incompatible.[4]

This statement allows us to consider Einstein as the godfather of complementarity, the fusion implemented by Bohr in 1927 (14e). Incidentally, Bohr had already read these Einstein papers by the time he wrote his doctor's thesis (as noted earlier (6d)).

Let us also remark that in 1917 Einstein had written, in the course of his rederivation of Planck's law (10c):

The properties of elementary processes ... make it almost seem inevitable to formulate a truly quantized theory of radiation.[5]

The development of that truly quantized theory, QED, began shortly after the discovery of quantum mechanics. Basically, QED and quantum mechanics obey the same quantum principles. Technically, that is, mathematically, QED is vastly more complex, however. Heisenberg, who himself played an important role in the earliest stages of its development, later said:

You know, it was not like quantum mechanics, in quantum mechanics everything came out much simpler and much better than what I expected. Somehow when you touched it and you had a disagreeable difficulty, at the end you saw, "Well, was it that simple?" Here in electrodynamics, it didn't become simple. Well, you could do the theory, but still it never became that simple.[6]

This statement, dating from the 1960s, is true to this day, nor will it ever be otherwise.

In order to give a first indication of why QED is so complex let us make a comparison with the simplest possible mechanical problem, discussed in Heisenberg's first paper on quantum mechanics (13d). It is the motion of one particle in one dimension characterized by one coordinate x and one velocity v, depending on one variable, time. What is the simplest possible electromagnetic problem? It is the case of electromagnetic radiation in otherwise empty space, that is, without interaction with matter. That situation is described by six fields, the three components of the electric field and another three of the magnetic field. Each of these fields is a function of four coordinates, three for space, and one for time. Field equations (Maxwell's equations) tell us how each field varies from one space-time point to another. Even in this simplest case Heisenberg's pair of variables x and v is replaced by an infinite set of variables at each given time, the electric and magnetic fields at each space point!

Heisenberg had assumed that his quantum variables x and v still obey the classical equations of motion but with the variables becoming matrices. Similarly in QED the fields are still assumed to obey the Maxwell equations but with all our fields at each point in space becoming matrices, so here we have an infinite set of those!

In spite of this proliferation of variables and matrices the problem of free radiation is exactly soluble. In particular it is not all that difficult to write down commutation relations for fields in different points in space and/or time. The real complexity starts when the interaction between free radiation and matter is taken into account. In that more general situation there does not exist any single problem amenable of exact solution. Approximate answers are all we have and all we can hope for. In the course of pushing these approximations to ever higher precision one encounters not only highly intricate technical problems but also certain still not fully clarified questions of principle. It is true that in the post–World War II period spectacular advances have been made in quantum field theory.* Yet it remains an area of physics about which we still do not know enough, and in which qualitative, intuitive arguments are and will remain lacking. As Feynman has written in a popular account: 'The theory of quantum electrodynamics describes Nature as absurd from the point of view of common sense. And it agrees fully with experiment. So I hope you can accept Nature as She is – absurd.'[8]

Rapidly following the beginning of QED, other quantum fields have made their appearance. The ultimate description of every species of fundamental particles – whatever these may be – is now in terms of a quantum field. Steven Weinberg has put it like this: 'The inhabitants of the universe [are] conceived to be a set of fields – an electron field, an electromagnetic field – and particles were reduced in status to mere epiphenomena. In its essentials, this point of view has survived to the present day, and forms the central dogma of quantum field theory: the essential reality is a set of fields, subject to the rules of special relativity and quantum mechanics; all else is derived as a consequence of the quantum dynamics of these fields.'[9]

As we shall presently see, theoretical particle physics and quantum field theory had their beginnings in the late 1920s. Bohr, then in his mid-forties, did some very useful work in this new area of physics, notably on the observability of electron spin (16c) and on the interpretation of QED (16d). Also his discussion (16e) of the general question of whether or not quantum mechanics is adequate for coping with nuclear and subnuclear phenomena is of interest, but only historically. A large part of the present chapter is devoted to setting these various issues in proper context.

Bohr's contributions are evidence of his deep interest in these new subjects. Yet he was no longer a director of research in this domain. There are two main reasons for this. First, he never felt quite comfortable with the very highly mathematical aspects of this area of theoretical physics. Secondly, he felt much more at home – as did many others – in other endeavors that developed in parallel, with hardly any overlap, with quantum field theory: issues of nuclear structure, to which he contributed importantly, as we already have seen (Chapter 15).

I now turn to QED.

---

* See Ref. 7 for a history of quantum field theory from its beginnings into the 1980s.

(b) QED(*)

QED made its entry in the paper by Born and Jordan[10] of September 1925, the second paper ever written on the new quantum theory: 'Electro-magnetic processes in the vacuum can be represented by a superposition of plane waves. We shall consider the electric and magnetic field strengths ... in such plane waves as matrices the elements of which are harmonically vibrating plane waves ... The Maxwell equations shall be retained as matrix equations.' The reference to the vacuum means that they did not include interactions with matter. As Heisenberg had done for classical mechanics (13d) they retained but reinterpreted the classical field equations but did not, however, give explicit expressions for their matrices. That was done in the Born–Heisenberg–Jordan paper[11] of November 1925. They applied to 'harmonically vibrating plane waves' the results obtained by Heisenberg in his first paper (13d) for a single harmonic oscillator. Derivations were therefore ready made, but the way they interpreted their result was new and most profound.

According to the quantum theory a harmonic oscillator with frequency v can only have the discrete energy values nhv, where $n = 0$ or 1 or 2, . . . That was known since Planck (5g) and Einstein (5h), though in those early days neither could derive that result from first principles, as Heisenberg had done. It was also known from classical times that a general field of electromagnetic radiation can be considered as a superposition of harmonic oscillators with varying frequencies, call those v_1, v_2, . . . In the absence of interaction with matter these oscillators vibrate independently with respective energies n_1hv_1, n_2hv_2, . . . , where each of the n's $= 0$ or 1 or 2 . . .

Now comes the new interpretation:* *'The quantum number [n] of an oscillator is equal to the number of quanta with the corresponding [v].'* [11] This reinterpretation is called field quantization, also sometimes second quantization. Its principal characteristic consists in making a transition from a one-oscillator problem (for each v**) to a problem of n bodies, where n is variable.

These bodies are Einstein's photons, which now appear for the first time in a logically tight scheme. The term 'body' should be taken with a grain of salt. The simplest general property of a body in the familiar sense of the word is that it has a characteristic mass. That is also true for the photon – but in that case the mass has the unfamiliar value zero.† We nevertheless call a photon a particle because, just like massive particles, it

---

* My italics. I slightly changed their phrase without changing its meaning.

** There are actually two oscillators for each v corresponding to the two states of polarization.

† It is probable that Einstein had realized that quite early, but he never wrote that.

obeys the laws of conservation of energy and momentum in collisions, with an electron say (Compton effect).

In this simplest of instances which does not include interactions of radiation with matter the numbers $n_1, n_2, \ldots$ of photons cannot jump in the course of time, nor can an atom emit a photon and jump from one of its quantum states to another.

Enter Dirac.

In August 1926 Dirac had completed a paper[12] in which Bose–Einstein as well as Fermi–Dirac statistics (13a) and also Planck's radiation law were given their quantum mechanical foundations – no mean feats.[13] In that same article he had also given a quantum mechanical derivation of Einstein's stimulated emission and absorption mechanisms (10c). That can be done without quantizing the electromagnetic field. Spontaneous emission (10c) was another story, however. 'One cannot take spontaneous emission into account without a more elaborate theory.'[12] That is why in the introduction to his next paper, written in Copenhagen in February 1927, Dirac observed: 'Hardly anything has been done up to the present on quantum electrodynamics . . . the production of an electromagnetic field by a moving electron and of the reaction of this field on the electron have hardly been touched.'[14]

So what did he do then? He used QED with its photon language. '[QED] is applied to the interaction of an assembly of light-quanta with an ordinary atom, and it is shown that it gives Einstein's laws for the emission [including spontaneous processes] and absorption of radiation.'[14] In a sequel[15] he gave the QED derivation of the Kramers–Heisenberg dispersion theory (13c). With these two papers QED started in earnest.

Let us return once more to the transition from the one-oscillator language to the n-photon language. If one oscillator goes from an energy $nh\nu$ to $(n+1)h\nu$ or $(n-1)h\nu$, it jumps from one state to another with higher and lower excitation respectively. In the photon language the jump is from n to $n+1$ or $n-1$ photons respectively. That is, a photon is respectively *created* or *annihilated*. That is precisely the content of the Bohr postulate $E_m - E_n = h\nu_{mn}$ for atomic transitions (8f). QED has taught us how to incorporate that postulate into quantum mechanics or, rather into quantum field theory.

Classical electromagnetism had provided the starting point not only for QED but also for the special theory of relativity, which, it will be recalled (4g), started out from new general postulates abstracted from classical electromagnetic radiation phenomena. What about their quantum counterparts?

That, in 1927, was a new type of question. Up to that time quantum mechanics had been couched in non-relativistic language. Nor was it at once obvious that QED satisfies all relativity requirements. The commutation relations for the variables of that theory, the electric and magnetic field strengths at one or another point in space and time, had been written down for fields at equal or different points in space but always at the same instant in time – in analogy with the relations for x and v, where both variables likewise are taken at the same time. This dissymmetry between space and time in QED is awkward from the point of view of relativity, since in that theory space and time must be treated on equal footing, as 'space-time coordinates'. That is not to say that the QED commutation relations violate relativity, but rather that their compatibility with relativity needs to be examined further. That was done in 1929–30 by Heisenberg and Pauli,[16] who, after surmounting serious initial difficulties, showed that all was in good order.

Thus the quantum equations for the electromagnetic field had been found to be in harmony with the postulates of relativity. What about the quantum equations for matter?

(c) Spin (continued). The positron. The meson (*)

Relativity requirements had played no role in Heisenberg's first work on quantum mechanics (13d), nor in Schrödinger's first treatment of the hydrogen atom and other problems by wave mechanical methods (13f), although in his first paper on wave mechanics[17] Schrödinger did mention that he had considered a relativistic version of his wave equation. A few months later he and several others all independently wrote down an equation of that type. For a number of technical reasons which I need not go into here, that equation (it goes by the name scalar wave equation) was not particularly popular[18] – until the mid-1930s when it turned out to be useful for the description of mesons.[19]

Meanwhile, in February 1928, Dirac had announced[20] his discovery of the relativistic wave equation for the electron, one of the marvels of twentieth century physics.

The great triumph of the Dirac equation is that it incorporates the electron spin. Recall (11f) that Uhlenbeck and Goudsmit had introduced spin in the context of the old quantum theory. Remember further (11f) that this intrinsic angular momentum orients itself either parallel or antiparallel to an external magnetic field. In 1927 Pauli had proposed[21] to describe the electron not by one but by two wavefunctions, one for each of the two spin orientations. That was an *ad hoc* recipe. By contrast the Dirac equation contains all spin properties in an ineluctable way.[22] In addition it yielded an intrinsic electron magnetic moment (11f) of the right magnitude, gave a correct account of the fine structure in the hydrogen spectrum (11f), automatically produced the factor two found by Thomas (11f), and reproduced the results of the non-relativistic Schrödinger equation for binding energies small compared with mc^2!

These results caused a sensation everywhere. Already in April 1928 Bohr wrote: 'Dirac has been able successfully to attack the problem of the magnetic electron.'[23]

This advance must have stimulated Bohr to raise the following question. The splitting of atomic spectral lines (fine structure) is due to the exposure of the spin to the magnetic field the electron experiences inside an atom (11f); the magnitude of the splitting is a measure for the size of its magnetic moment. Suppose now that electrons move in an external magnetic field but are otherwise free. In that case too the field splits the electron beam in two. Can one determine the magnetic moment also from that arrangement?

Already in the fall of 1928 that problem was on Bohr's mind.[24] In December he wrote: 'Continued discussions have given suggestive indications that such a situation should be principally [sic] unobservable.'[25] And shortly afterward: 'The possibility of [such an] observation would be inconsistent with the fundamental principles of quantum theory,'[26] that is, with Heisenberg's uncertainty relations. When Bohr reported his conclusions at a Copenhagen conference in April 1929, '[he] stunned us all (except Pauli) with the non-observability of the electron spin'.[27]

Bohr's argument which does not at all depend on the use of the Dirac equation is one of the nicest applications of the uncertainty relations I know. He asked: What happens to a beam of electrons when it passes through an inhomogeneous magnetic field? For neutral atoms that same question had been posed and experimentally answered in the early 1920s, in the famous experiment by Stern and Gerlach. If these atoms carry a magnetic moment, then the inhomogeneous magnetic field causes the atomic beam to fan out in various directions. Classically one should expect this fanning out to be continuous. Stern and Gerlach observed, however, that actually the beam splits into a discrete number of separated sub-beams. As became clear soon afterward this number equals $2j+1$, where j is the angular momentum of the atom (in units $h/2\pi$).

One might think that the same experiment performed with electron beams would yield two sub-beams, since here $j=\frac{1}{2}$. Not so, said Bohr. Remember that electrons carry not only a magnetic moment but also an electric charge! Since a moving electric charge is also acted on by a magnetic field (Ørsted! (4e)) the charge alone causes the beam to fan out. Using the uncertainty relations for position and velocity (14d), Bohr showed that this spread is large compared to the *additional* spread due to the electron's spin. Hence the magnetic moment of free electrons cannot be measured this way.

Bohr never published the details of his argument. He left that to an Englishman in his early twenties, Nevill (later Sir Nevill) Mott, who in May 1929 published this elementary calculation as an appendix to a paper[28] of his own, with due attribution to Bohr. Mott had arrived in Copenhagen in the autumn of 1928. 'Everyone wanted to go to Copenhagen.'[29] He was at once struck by Bohr's characteristic style of doing physics: 'When [Bohr] has a new idea ... he comes into the Institute and tells it to the first person he can find ... half one's work is discussing ... I do most of the mathematics, but Bohr provides the ideas[30] ... I wanted to get the answers ... I remember almost feeling sometimes, "Look I wish Bohr would let me get on with it without examining everything."'[31]

Back to Bohr himself, in 1934 he carefully stated his conclusion in these words: 'It is not possible to detect the magnetic moment of the electron by experiments based on the direct observation of its motion.'[32] Others (including Mott[33]) erroneously inferred that the magnetic moment of a free particle cannot be measured at all. It was not until 1954 that it was first noted[34] that the *shape* of the beam's velocity spread does contain observable information on the magnetic moment. Much more precise methods have since been devised and executed, such as the sequence: the electron scatters, then passes through a magnetic field, then scatters again.* Further refinements have since yielded extraordinarily precise magnetic moment measurements.[35]

Two other important Copenhagen contributions to Dirac's new theory and dating from 1928 must be mentioned.

In October, Klein and Yoshio Nishina applied the Dirac equation to the Compton effect, the scattering of light by electrons.[36] Because of some confusion about the experimental data,[37] it took a few years before it was appreciated that the 'Klein–Nishina formula' ranks among the great early achievements of the Dirac theory.

In a paper submitted[38] in December, Klein recorded what appeared to be a disastrous consequence of the Dirac equation. Consider a beam of electrons impinging on a potential barrier so steep that it varies by more than mc^2 (m = electron mass) over a distance of about h/mc. According to general quantum mechanics some electrons are reflected by the barrier, others penetrate it. Klein showed that more electrons are reflected than hit the barrier in the first place!

Already in November Bohr had commented on this so-called Klein paradox: 'In spite of the wonderful progress which we owe to Dirac, new

---

* Such 'double scattering' but without an interposed magnetic field was in fact the main subject of Mott's 1929 paper.[28]

difficulties are revealed every day ... A new particularly instructive example has recently been brought to light by Klein.'[39]

What were all these new difficulties?

Along with its manifest successes, the Dirac equation had created major confusion. Referring to the year 1928, Heisenberg later said: 'Up till that time I had the impression that in quantum theory we had come back into the harbor, into the port. Dirac's paper threw us out into the sea again.'[40]

This new disarray was caused by the fact that the Dirac equation necessarily implies that at each space-time point there are four wave-functions – not two, as Pauli had suggested for a particle with two spin orientations. What was the meaning of this further doubling, from two to four? As Dirac had at once noted,[20] the reason is that, along with two electron states à la Pauli, there appears another pair, also spin-doubled, but with negative kinetic energy. That is very bad: kinetic energy is essentially by definition always positive or zero. Nor can one simply ignore these negative energy states, since, according to the quantum theory, an accelerated electron with positive energy can jump into a state of negative energy, sinking ever deeper into this negative morass. This misery explains why Bohr referred to 'new difficulties ... revealed every day',[39] and why, also in 1928, Heisenberg wrote to Pauli: 'The saddest chapter of modern physics is and remains the Dirac theory.'[41]

There the matter lay until December 1929 when Dirac had a new idea: 'Let us assume ... that all the states of the negative energy are occupied except perhaps for a few of very small velocity.'[42] Pauli's exclusion principle (10e) implies that this occupation amounts to only one electron per state. In more precise detail Dirac's assumptions are these.[43]

1. In the absence of an external field all negative energy states with energies ranging from minus mc^2 to minus infinity are filled with electrons, so that no electron can jump into one of these occupied states.

2. The electrons filling up the negative energy states do not produce an external field and do not contribute to the electric charge, energy and momentum of the system. That may seem a bit rich. However, as was shown later all these three (infinite!) quantities can in fact be eliminated from the theory by simple mathematical tricks.

3. An external electromagnetic field can nevertheless act on the electrons in the negative energy states. What happens if such a field kicks a negative energy electron into a positive energy state? By assumption (2) the negative energy 'hole' so created behaves like a positive energy particle but with a charge opposite to that of an electron! The net result is *the creation of a pair of particles*: the negatively charged electron, kicked upward, and the positively charged hole. Dirac originally thought that the latter should be identified with the proton, but that led to other paradoxes.[44] Landau was not

off the mark when, after having listened to a lecture by Dirac on his current ideas, he sent a one-word telegram to Bohr: '*Quatsch*' [45] (Gibberish).

Another year and a half passed until, in May 1931, Dirac proposed: 'A hole, if there were one, would be a new kind of particle, unknown to experimental physics, having the same mass and opposite charge of the electron.' [46]

Another year went by until this hypothetical particle, now called the positron, was discovered. It was first seen by Carl Anderson from Cal Tech, in a cloud chamber exposed to cosmic radiation. [47] In early 1933 the first creation of electron–positron pairs was observed, also in cosmic radiation. [48]

Pair formation resolves the earlier mentioned Klein paradox: electrons impinging on steep potential barriers create electron–positron pairs.

It took Bohr a rather long time to accept Dirac's ideas. In a lecture given in October 1931, after the positron proposal, he referred to 'the peculiar difficulties which present themselves in the attempt to develop a proper relativistic treatment of atomic problems'. [49] In a paper published in 1932, after the discovery of the positron he wrote: '[Dirac's theory] would seem to trespass the limit of applicability of the correspondence argument.' [50] Bohr to Klein, April 1933: '[I] am afraid that it will take a long time before we can have any certain knowledge about the existence or non-existence of the positive electrons. Nor as regards the applicability of Dirac's theory to this problem do I feel certain, or, more correctly, I doubt it, at least for the moment.' [51]* And a month later, to Heisenberg: 'Regarding the positive electron I am still inclined to say, like Lord Rayleigh, "some of those who know me best think that I ought to be more convinced than I am. Perhaps they are right." ' [53] He finally became convinced when laboratory rather than cosmic ray experiments confirmed [54] electron–positron pair formation. 'I am enthusiastic about the possibilities for work which the discovery of the positrons have opened up, and about which any doubt had of course to be silenced as soon as it was clear that they could be produced under completely controllable conditions.' [55]

In the preceding section it was noted that a consistent description of the creation and annihilation of photons demanded the quantization of the electromagnetic field. Now we have encountered another creation process, the production of electron–positron pairs. As Dirac noted, his theory also implies the occurrence of pair annihilation, for example electron + positron→two photons. In his initial treatment of these processes no new quantum field theory concepts were introduced. It transpired soon, however, that an improved and systematic treatment does require a new

---

* The same was true for Pauli, who in 1933 wrote to Dirac: 'I do not believe in your perception of "holes" even if the [positron] is proved.' [52]

type of field quantization, a 'quantized Dirac wave field'. That is not a simple transcription of what had been done for the electromagnetic field, above all because electrons (and positrons) do, photons do not, obey the Pauli principle (10e) according to which at most one electron (or positron) can be in a given state. Already in 1927, before the Dirac equation, Jordan and Wigner had shown[56] how Pauli's principle can be incorporated in field quantization. The application of their method to the Dirac equation began in 1934.[57] I shall not discuss here these and later developments since Bohr did not participate in them. Interest in the subject remained strong in Copenhagen, however, as witness, for example, an important contribution to the Dirac theory by Weisskopf.[58]

QED and the quantized field theory of the Dirac equation changed the ways of treating particles and fields. So did another development of that period, the first attempts to formulate a quantum field theory of nuclear forces.

When in 1932 Heisenberg had made the first steps toward a theory of nuclear forces (15d), he had used what one may call the Coulomb analogy. Just as the interaction between a pair of slowly moving electrically charged particles is given by Coulomb's force, so the forces inside the nucleus should be given, he had argued, by a force between pairs of nucleons, but with several essential differences. In particular, Coulomb forces are long range, they decrease with the square of the distance, while nuclear forces should decrease much faster (15f).

Both the Coulomb forces and photons are manifestations of the electromagnetic field. QED teaches us that the zero mass of the photon is intimately related to the long-range nature of the Coulomb force. Suppose now that the nuclear force, more or less as conceived by Heisenberg, is also related to a field. What are its field quanta, the analogs of photons?

That was the question raised by Hideki Yukawa, a Japanese physicist in his mid-twenties. 'Is the new nuclear force a primary one? . . . It seemed likely that [it] was a third fundamental force unrelated to gravitation and electromagnetism . . . Perhaps the nuclear force could also find expression as a field . . . Let me not look for the [field quantum] that belongs to the nuclear force among the known particles . . . If I focus on the characteristics of the nuclear force field then the characteristics of the particle [i.e. the field quantum] I seek will become apparent.'[59]

Yukawa reported on his search in a series of papers the first of which was completed[60] in 1934. His main discovery was that the range of the nuclear force is inversely proportional to the mass of the quanta. From nuclear physics data he could obtain a rough estimate of that mass: about two hundred times that of the electron. Those quanta are now called mesons, more precisely π-mesons or pions.

Now it came to pass that in 1936 Anderson and his collaborator Seth Neddermeyer, using the same cloud chamber as employed in the discovery of the positron, and using the same source as before, cosmic radiation, discovered[61] a particle with a mass in the range Yukawa had predicted.

Bohr was pleased. 'It looks as if the "Yukon's" existence* is not only supported by various observations but also fits most conveniently with the theoretical treatment of nuclear problems.'[63]

Life was not that simple, however. It became clear in the 1940s that Anderson's particle (now called the μ-meson) and Yukawa's particle were different species of mesons! That wonderful story[64] need not concern us here. Let me only note that the Yukawa theory has been the subject of several investigations in Copenhagen in subsequent years.[65]

(d) Bohr on QED** (*)

As has been noted before (14e), in his 1927 Como lecture Bohr had expressed his central dogma regarding measurements of physical quantities like this: 'The interpretation of the experimental material rests essentially upon classical concepts.' Among the examples of a measurement he discussed was the observation of an electron in a γ-ray microscope. It was sufficient for his purposes to know the conservation laws for photon–electron scattering and classical optical properties of a microscope.

Strictly speaking this problem belongs to the realm of QED, which, however, had barely started its development at the time Bohr gave his talk. (His conclusions were nevertheless correct.) New measurability questions arose as QED began to take hold, such as: Given the commutation relations for electromagnetic fields, what are its uncertainty relations? What do these imply regarding measurability, in a given experimental arrangement, for the various field components?

The first sensible comment on these problems that I am aware of is found in a letter by Heisenberg to Bohr from 1929: 'As a matter of course, any measurement would yield not E and H [the electric and magnetic fields] at an exact *point* in space, but average values over perhaps very small spatial regions.'[66] One finds similar remarks, including the need for averaging over small time intervals, in Heisenberg's Chicago lectures (published in 1930), along with a preliminary account of uncertainty relations for fields.[67]

It was almost inevitable, one might say, that Bohr himself would turn to

* One of the several names initially proposed for Yukawa's particle. The term 'meson' appears to have entered the literature in 1939.[62]
** I am very grateful to Jørgen Kalckar for showing me a draft of his introductory essay to Volume 7 of Bohr's collected works, which has been of great help to me in writing this section.

issues of this kind, and in the event he did, but only after others had reached dramatic and incorrect conclusions on this topic.

In the draft of a letter to Heisenberg dated 8 December 1930, Bohr wrote 'about some questions that we have eagerly discussed here during Landau's visit concerning the possibilities of measuring electric and magnetic forces'.[68] Pauli to Klein, a few days later: 'Landau has brought with him from Copenhagen some interesting inequalities and the failure of many concepts, which have really interested me.'[69]

These communications referred to a paper by Landau and Peierls (LP), eventually submitted from Zürich on 3 March 1931.[70] Many of their results had been arrived at during their stays in Copenhagen, however.* They stated their general conclusions in these broad terms: 'The application of wave mechanical methods in the [relativistic] domain exceeds their range of validity ... there cannot exist predictable measurements of the fundamental quantities of wave mechanics in this domain.'[70] They claimed in particular that electromagnetic field strengths are not measurable where quantum theory *and* relativity play an essential role, as for the case of electromagnetic radiation.

These exceedingly drastic statements cannot be fully judged without attention to the time they were made. In 1931 the Dirac equation of the electron still suffered from, in LP's words, 'the meaningless solutions of negative energy'. LP also noted another apparent disease of QED: the electromagnetic energy of a charged pointlike particle is infinite.** In addition they mentioned unresolved paradoxes in the theory of β-radioactivity (see the next section). Thus the theory of particles and fields was suffering from malaise, to which LP erroneously believed to have added yet further trouble.

Browsing through correspondence between the masters, one gets the distinct impression that they were not at once clear what to make of LP's paper. For example, Heisenberg complained to Pauli: 'Nothing certain is at hand.'[73]† Bohr's early response is found in a later letter. 'Although I could not immediately find any error in Peierls' and Landau's arguments concerning the measurability of electromagnetic field quantities, I always felt uneasy about their criticism of the foundations of the formalism.'[73a]

* According to the institute records Landau was in Copenhagen 8 April–3 May and 20 September–20 November 1930, and 25 February–19 March 1931; Peierls 8–24 April 1930, and 24–28 February 1931.

** In this book I shall not discuss this so-called self-energy problem since Bohr, though well aware of this difficulty, only touched on it in passing.[71] The renormalization program developed shortly after World War II has made it possible to shunt this difficulty aside.[72] This is not an issue on which to this day the last word has been said, however.

† This is a poor rendering of Heisenberg quoting Ehrenfest's favorite dictum: *'Nichts Gewisses weiss man nicht.'*

Bohr's instincts were right but, as he wrote to Heisenberg in December 1930, he was not sufficiently at home with the finer points of QED. 'I do not quite understand the relationship between measuring relations and quantum electrodynamics as I am not able to survey the demands of the theory as regards the conditions for definition and measurement.'[74] He needed a helping hand – which was forthcoming.

In January 1931 O. Klein ended his five years' stay in Copenhagen as Bohr's closest collaborator, to assume a professorship in mechanics and mathematical physics in Stockholm. In February Léon Rosenfeld arrived, just after Peierls had left 'in a state of complete exhaustion'.[75] Rosenfeld has recalled: 'My first task was to lecture Bohr on the fundamentals of field quantization.'[75] In March Bohr wrote to Pauli: 'After Klein's departure I have found in Rosenfeld an excellent and understanding collaborator.'[76]

Rosenfeld, a native of Belgium, received his Ph.D. in 1926 at the University of Liège, then did postdoctoral work, first in Paris, next in Göttingen, finally in Zürich where he became thoroughly familiar with Heisenberg's and Pauli's work on QED. From 1930 to 1940 he held faculty positions in Liège, while in the same period he was Bohr's closest collaborator, visiting Copenhagen for periods lasting from a few days to half a year. For the rest of Bohr's life he remained in close contact with him. From 1940 to 1947 he was professor in Utrecht, where I got to know him well. (I received my Ph.D. with him in 1941.) I remember with gratitude the support he and his wife gave me during the war years. In 1947 he became head of theoretical physics in Manchester. In 1958 he was called to a chair in Nordita, the joint Nordic institute for theoretical physics in Copenhagen. There he spent the rest of his life until his death in 1974.

In their collaboration Bohr and Rosenfeld played complementary roles, Rosenfeld that of *savant*, Bohr that of intuitive. 'Rosenfeld was really just a help to Bohr. Bohr wanted somebody who knew mathematics and was willing to go through it; Rosenfeld sort of sacrificed himself.'[77] In the course of time Rosenfeld became the self-anointed defender of the complementarity faith, *plus royaliste que le roi*, managing at the same time to hold strong views on dialectical materialism. Pauli once called him 'the square root of Bohr times Trotsky'.[78]

The main result of the Bohr–Rosenfeld (BR) collaboration was their paper 'On the question of the measurability of electromagnetic field quantities'.[79] On 2 December 1932, after two years of labor, their manuscript was handed in to the *Videnskabernes Selskab*. Bohr to Heisenberg: 'We succeeded after many surprises to get to the bottom of the question, with the result that the possibilities of measurements are in every respect in the most beautiful agreement with the quantum mechanical formalism as I was convinced from the outset they should.'[80] Heisenberg replied: 'I consider it very important that you not only write but also publish this paper. Such problems cannot be treated by any physicist but you.'[81] Bohr to Gamow: 'I hope it will be a comfort to Landau and Peierls that the stupidities they have committed in this respect are no worse than those which we all, including Heisenberg and Pauli, have been guilty of in this controversial subject.'[82]

The printed version of the BR paper is dated April 1933. That, however, is undoubtedly not yet the date in which their article reached its final form. According to Rosenfeld[75] it took a year between the first submission in December 1932 and the completion of the reading of fourteen successive proofs. These kept changing. 'We did not hit upon a completely satisfactory answer until the very last proof correction.'[83] Bohr to Heisenberg, March 1933: 'New abysses were revealed every time we believed to have gotten it straight. After a visit from Pauli last week it became clear to me that our understanding still leaves much to be desired.'[84] Again to Heisenberg in May: 'The printing of the article took longer than I thought.'[85] And in August: 'I shall send you a second proof.'[86] In October Bohr reported[87] the BR results to the seventh Solvay conference in Brussels. But in November he wrote to Weisskopf, in response to a query: 'After your letter we shall of course try to formulate things still more clearly.'[88] In December Klein wrote to Bohr of his 'hope that the work with Rosenfeld is ready now'.[89]

I next comment on the content of the BR paper. Just as Bohr had done earlier (14e) for quantum mechanics, the assignment was now to verify that the consequences of QED, particularly its characteristic commutation relations,* are consistent with the *best possible* actual or idealized experiments aiming at measuring electromagnetic fields. Thus one employs 'the direct method of testing definitions of concepts by investigating the concrete measuring process they embody.'[75] The BR program was therefore to make clear the physical meaning of QED rather than to modify or extend that theory in any way.

As had been long familiar from classical days, one measures fields in a certain region and during a certain time interval by placing electric or magnetic test bodies in that space-time region and then observing how these are acted on by the fields. For example, one can measure an electric field by suitable emplacement of a body with known electric charge and mass and observing in what direction and with what speed it is displaced. For the purpose of measuring two fields in two either identical or distinct space time regions – necessary for an interpretation of field uncertainty relations – one needs to use two test bodies. In general terms, BR showed that in the

---

* BR use the commutation relations for *free* electromagnetic fields, which is all right to the approximation they consider.

latter case quantum *mechanical* properties of the test bodies lead to reciprocal limitations on field measurability which are exactly those derived from the field commutation relations. Thus 'quantum electro-dynamics and quantum mechanics form two inseparable parts of a single body of the quantum theory, both are logically connected and neither is consistent without the other. The quantum theory of the field can therefore be considered as the reasonable quantum theoretical extension of classical electrodynamics in the same way as quantum mechanics is the quantum theoretical extension of classical mechanics.' [90]

This statement makes evident the fundamental importance of the BR paper. From decades of involvement with quantum field theory I can testify that nevertheless it has been read by very very few of the *aficionados*. The main reason is, I think, that even by Bohr's standards this paper is very difficult to penetrate. It takes inordinate care and patience to follow Bohr's often quite complex gyrations with test bodies. In addition the main message of the article: in QED measurability is compatible with the commutation relations, just as in quantum mechanics, is cheered with enthusiasm – after which the pros continue with whatever calculation they are engaged in. As a friend of Bohr's and mine once said to me: 'It is a very good paper that one does not have to read. You just have to know it exists.' Nevertheless men like Pauli and Heitler did read it with great care.

If I next summarize the BR article only very briefly and qualitatively, it is not just because that fits best with the style of this book but also because I am not sure I have mastered all the fine points of this important paper. So here goes.

As Heisenberg had already noted, fields at definite space time points are idealizations without immediate physical meaning. BR systematically took as test bodies extended charge and current densities taken over finite time intervals. They emphasized that field measurements have nothing to do with the test body's atomic structure which therefore may be disregarded. The body may then be treated as a charge distribution which is uniform over its extension.

BR then showed that this procedure immediately disposed of one major criticism by LP. Using point charges as test bodies, LP had concluded that the inevitable emission of radiation of this particle, resulting from its acceleration in the field to be measured, perturbs its momentum to an extent that obviates the possibility of giving meaning to field measurements. Agreed, BR said, but a point charge does not provide the greatest possible accuracy of observation. Rather, they showed that for the purpose of measuring a *single* field, the radiation effect can always be rendered negligible by making the test bodies sufficiently heavy and their charge sufficiently high.

The higher the charge of the test body the stronger the electric field created by that body itself. Thus one must beware that the latter field perturbs as little as possible the 'external' field to be observed. For single field measurements this inaccuracy can be compensated by attaching the test bodies to suitable elastic contrivances (springs).

To take account of the finite time of propagation of the field through the test body – a relativistic effect – on the measurement of that body's momentum, one must imagine it to consist of a large number of independent elements, which, BR show, can all be taken to have the same momentum uncertainty.

The subtlest part of BR is the case of measurements of two fields in one experiment. Quantum mechanics is important here in that one must take into account the inevitable uncertainties (to be suppressed to the best *possible* extent) in the determination of the position and velocity for *two* test bodies. Relativity is important here in that the answers depend on whether or not the finiteness of the velocity of light permits a light signal from one test body to reach the other one. BR's conclusions are these. Two space averages of field components of the same kind (i.e. both electric or both magnetic) always commute if the time intervals coincide, while the time averages of two components of different kind always commute if the space domains coincide. It follows from this that all averages of components over the same space-time domain are independently observable with arbitrary sharpness. If the space-time intervals do not overlap, there occur complementary uncertainties in these mean values which are consistent with the field uncertainty relations.

Finally, there was 'one point [which] gave us much trouble to the very last'.[75] According to QED any electric or magnetic field intensity is subject to characteristic fluctuations. LP had claimed that this circumstance renders the very concept of electromagnetic field operationally meaningless in QED. BR showed that, on the contrary, these fluctuations are indispensable for the full logical consistency of the theory and that they in fact can be measured, at least in principle. QED does modify the classical connection between fields and their sources, but these changes do not contravene the observational possibilities of the theory as given by its formal content.

Thus was completed 'an arduous task which taxed all the resources of Bohr's ingenuity'.[83]

There is a sequel to this story. Shortly after BR had finished their last proofs Heisenberg had published a paper[91] on fluctuations of electric charge density caused by electron–positron formation according to the Dirac theory. This problem necessarily goes one step (or more) beyond the treatment of sources at the classical level. This work bestirred BR to turn their attention to the problem of measurability of electric charges and currents, the sources of the electromagnetic field.* They were encouraged in this new endeavor by Pauli's 'egging us on to continue'.[75]

Once again their main tools were electromagnetic field sources of finite space-time extent. On they went with their contraptions, shells of test bodies surrounding the sources, sets of levers that transmit to a single auxiliary body the total momentum of all the shell elements, etc.[75]

There exists an unpublished manuscript[92] dating, it is believed, from about 1936–7 in which their preliminary findings are recorded. Nothing was published until 1950, however. By that time QED had made major strides forward, as BR were, of course, aware. Their short paper[93] on charge measurements is essentially a brief summary of their findings,** including comments that not only electron–positron pairs but also pairs of other kinds of charged particles need to be included. The main tenor of their note is that their analysis indicated once again the consistency of the formal theory with the operational requirements of best possible observation.

(e) Bohr and the crisis of 1929. The neutrino

1929 was a crisis year in physics, perhaps not as grave as the years just preceding quantum mechanics (10d) but still pretty bad. The areas of trouble were relativistic quantum theory and nuclear physics.

First, it was the year of the Klein paradox (16c), and also the year in which Dirac had proposed the theory of holes but had wrongly identified a hole with a proton (16c). Hermann Weyl, the first to point out that the mass of a hole had to equal that of the electron, had written: 'I fear that the clouds hanging over this part of the subject will roll together to form a new crisis in quantum physics.'[95]

Secondly, 1929 was also the year in which the paradoxes concerning nuclear structure peaked. Nuclei were still considered to be built out of protons and electrons, but electrons refused to make their presence felt (15d).

Finally, 1929 was the first year in which it was fully appreciated that the energy spectra of electrons emitted in β-radioactivity posed a new mystery.

That last issue is the main topic of this section. Before plunging in let us

---

* They also reconsidered the measurability of fields if corrections to the *free* field commutation relations are taken into account.

** In 1946 I wrote a paper on the status of the theory of the electron, meant to serve as an introduction to a collection of papers on the Dirac theory. Rapid developments shortly thereafter caused the plans for the collection to be canceled. My paper was printed, as a pamphlet, however.[94] It contains as an appendix a contribution by Wheeler on the BR theory of charge measurement. According to Wheeler, his brief review is based on a BR version of 1939 which I have not seen, but which evidently differs both from the 1936–7 draft[92] and the 1950 paper.[93]

note that crises in physics are more easily identified after the fact than during their occurrence. 1929 was also a year in which many theoretical physicists, especially young ones, happily had their hands full with numerous applications of non-relativistic quantum mechanics, while the number of practitioners of relativistic quantum theory and of theoretical nuclear physics was still quite limited.

Experimental research on β-spectra had begun in 1906. Elsewhere[96] I have treated at length the fascinating evolution of those studies and the related theoretical conjectures from then until 1930. Here I give a capsule summary of that period.

It had been known since 1905 that in α-decay the α-particles emitted by any given species of atoms all have the same energy, as is to be expected for the disintegration mother→daughter + α. Indeed, in such a process the final two bodies emerge with equal and opposite momenta, and a unique α-particle momentum implies a unique energy. It seemed plausible that the same would be true for β-decay. That at any rate was the expectation when the experiments began. These were difficult for their time. The electron had been discovered only a decade earlier. Little was as yet known of its properties, for example about its behavior as it traverses a volume of gas between its points of production and detection. Nor was it yet known that in radioactive decays electrons are produced by two distinct mechanisms: first the primary β-decay process; secondly as a secondary effect accompanying γ-decay. In the latter case, a γ-ray comes out of the nucleus and is next absorbed by a peripheral atomic electron. This process, now called internal conversion, produces discrete electron energies corresponding to the discrete initial γ-energies.

By 1913 the picture concocted out of all this confusion was that electrons produced in β-decay exhibit a discrete spectrum of energies, carefully tabulated[97] in textbooks of that time. Thus seven years of experimentation had failed to reveal the most fundamental property of β-decay, to wit, that the primary β-spectrum, unlike the case of α-decay, is not discrete but continuous.

That startling discovery was announced in April 1914 by Chadwick, he of the neutron (15d). As a function of electron energy, the spectrum begins at zero for zero energy, then rises, passes through a maximum, then falls off again to zero at an upper energy limit characteristic for each β-radioactive substance.[98]

In the course of the next seven years – which included World War I! – nothing much new happened in regard to β-decay. In 1921 internal conversion was discovered.[99] During the next few years the continuous nature of the β-spectrum gained in acceptance but was thought by many to be caused by a smearing out of a discrete primary spectrum. The Compton effect (discovered in 1923!) was considered a candidate: a nuclear γ-ray scatters a peripheral atomic electron which is liberated with an energy that varies with the angle of ejection.[100] As became clear only years later, that process indeed occurs but far too infrequently to account for the data. In 1927 a difficult and ingenious experiment finally showed that in the *primary* process electrons are produced with a continuous range of energies.[101] It had taken twenty years of serious work by good people to establish that result, so crucial to particle physics.

What does that continuous spectrum mean? One could think of two possible explanations. Either β-decay, like α-decay, is a two-body process mother→daughter + electron. In that case, energy (and momentum) are not conserved – unlike in the α-case. That interpretation has turned out to be wrong. Or β-decay is not a two-body process, but rather of the kind mother→daughter + electron + another particle. In that case, the available energy is partitioned, in a continuous range, between the electron and the other particle, resulting in a continuous electron energy spectrum. That interpretation has turned out to be correct.

Bohr opted for energy non-conservation.

The first mention of Bohr's position I am aware of is in a letter to Fowler from February 1929: 'Lately I have been thinking a good deal of the possible limitations of the conservation theorems in relativistic quantum theory.'[102] Pauli too must have gotten wind of Bohr's thinking for that same month he wrote to Klein: 'With his considerations about a violation of the energy law Bohr is on a *completely wrong* track [P.'s italics].'[103] A few weeks later, Pauli to Bohr: 'Do you intend to mistreat the poor energy law further?'[104] In July Bohr sent Pauli 'a little piece about the β-spectra which I have had in mind for a long time', and asked his opinion, 'no matter how severe or how mild the expressions which you feel it appropriate to use'.[105] That little piece was never published but is presumably related to a draft manuscript[106] that has survived. This is a particularly interesting document because it shows how drastic Bohr's ideas were: 'While the quantum laws of propagation in free space offer no basis for a violation of the conservation principles ... the laws of interaction between particles ... may conflict with a simple identification of action and reaction, as that underlying the classical principles ... a departure from these laws might still result from the close interaction of the constituent particles of the nucleus ... remembering that the principles of conservation of energy and momentum are of a purely classical origin, the suggestion of their failure in accounting for β-ray emission can on the present state of quantum theory hardly be rejected beforehand.' In other words, Bohr was prepared for a possible failure of the conservation laws in regions where particles are closely packed, as inside nuclei. He was aware that the price was high: 'At the same time the loss of the unerring guidance which the conservation principles have hitherto offered would of course be a very disquieting prospect.'

Pauli's reaction to Bohr's manuscript was negative: 'The note about the β-rays . . . gave me very *little* satisfaction . . . *let this note rest for a good long time* [P.'s italics].'[107] Bohr, however, kept improving his draft. In October 1929 he wrote to Mott: 'I am preparing an account on statistics and conservation in quantum mechanics in which I also hope to give convincing arguments for the view that the problem of β-ray expulsion lies outside the reach of the classical conservation principles of energy and momentum.'[108] His reference to statistics clearly shows that he was after a resolution not only of the β-spectrum problem but also of the difficulties of the electron–proton picture of the nucleus (15d).

In November Rutherford sent Bohr a gentle warning: 'I have heard that you are on the warpath and wanting to upset the Conservation of Energy both microscopically and macroscopically. I will wait and see before expressing an opinion but I always feel "there are more things in Heaven and Earth than are dreamt of in our philosophy".'[109] Bohr could not be swayed, however. In a letter to Dirac, also in November, he asked his opinion as to whether 'the difficulties in relativistic quantum mechanics might perhaps be connected with the apparently fundamental difficulties as regards conservation of energy in β-ray disintegration and the interior of stars.'[110] Remember that November 1929 was the month of the Klein paradox (16c). Note further that at that time the mechanism of the energy production in stars posed yet another completely unsolved mystery.

We now see in its fullness why Bohr anticipated such drastic revisions of physics. He was looking for a comprehensive point of view that would all at once explain four puzzles: the β-spectra, nuclear structure, the Klein paradox, and the energy production in stars.

Dirac joined Pauli and Rutherford in expressing reservations: 'I should prefer to keep rigorous conservation at all costs.'[111] In his reply Bohr intimated that quantum mechanics might not apply at distances comparable to nuclear radii.[112] Dirac responded: 'Although I believe that quantum mechanics has its limitations . . . I cannot see any reason for thinking that quantum mechanics has already reached the limit of its development.'[113]

In May 1930 Bohr stated his current thinking for the first time publicly, in his Faraday lecture given in London. Since its text was not published[114] until 1932, 'due to unforeseen circumstances', it actually reflects Bohr's position up till that later date.* Here are Bohr's main points.

As soon as we inquire . . . into the constitution of even the simplest nuclei the present formulation of quantum mechanics fails completely.

---

* Some unpublished notes[115] written between November 1930 and February 1931 could possibly be partial drafts for the 1932 paper.

For example, Bohr points out, one cannot explain how four protons and two electrons are held together in the α-particle. Indeed! He goes on to note that 'the idea of spin is found not to be applicable to intranuclear electrons', and also the 'remarkable "passivity" of the intranuclear electrons in the determination of the statistics'. He concludes with his views on β-decay.

At the present stage of atomic theory we have no argument, either empirical or theoretical, for upholding the energy principle in the case of β-ray disintegrations, and are even led to complications and difficulties in trying to do so . . . Still, just as the account of those aspects of atomic constitution essential for the explanation of the ordinary physical and chemical properties of matter implies a renunciation of the classical idea of causality, the features of atomic stability, still deeper-lying, responsible for the existence and the properties of atomic nuclei, may force us to renounce the very idea of energy balance. I shall not enter further into such speculations and their possible bearing on the much debated question of the source of stellar energy. I have touched upon them here mainly to emphasize that in atomic theory , notwithstanding all the recent progress, we must still be prepared for new surprises.

In October 1931 Bohr expressed similar opinions at a physics conference in Rome.[116] The response was mixed.[117]

I believe it fair to characterize Bohr's position at that time like this. In 1925 the crisis at the atomic level had been resolved by quantum mechanics, a fundamental revision of earlier thinking. The crises of 1929 at the nuclear level might in turn demand a revision of quantum mechanics. In 1929 the thought of *one* new overarching framework was not all that far-fetched- – certainly less so than the ultimate resolution, *three* new particles, one for each puzzle: the neutron to explain nuclear structure, the positron to explain the Klein paradox, and the neutrino to explain β-spectra.

At least as early as December 1930 Pauli had adopted the second of the two possibilities mentioned earlier for explaining the continuous β-spectrum: β-disintegration is a three-body process. Some time later the third as yet hypothetical particle was baptized neutrino by Fermi.[118] In a letter[119] Pauli had correctly diagnosed some of the neutrino's expected properties: it is electrically neutral, has spin $\frac{1}{2}$, satisfies the exclusion principle, and has mass 'of the same order of magnitude as the electron mass'.[119] His ideas about nuclear structure were not right, however. At that time Pauli thought that nuclei are built up out of three constituents, protons, electrons, and neutrinos. Protons would mainly account for the nuclear mass, they and electrons for the nuclear charge, all three species for the correct nuclear spin and statistics.[120]

Initially Pauli considered his proposal to be 'a desperate way out',[119] and for some time remained reticent to discuss it in public.[119] All the same he soon began to heckle Bohr. 'It is of course clear to me that the [neutrino] hypothesis does not suit Bohr and the Bohrians. It gives me special pleasure just for that reason to discuss it.'[121] He did mention[122] his hypothesis at a symposium in Pasadena in June 1931, but at the Rome conference in October[116] neither he nor Bohr mentioned the new proposal publicly.

The discovery of the positron in December 1931 (16c) and of the neutron in January 1932 (15d) mark the beginnings of the unraveling of the 1929 crisis. The issue of the continuous β-spectrum remained unresolved all through 1932, however. Thus in May Bohr wrote to Rutherford of his hopes that 'it would perhaps be possible to settle this problem ... about the possible failure of energy conservation'.[123] In the latter half of 1932 Heisenberg, in his theory of nuclear forces (15d), considered the neutron to be a composite of a proton and an electron and had this to say about β-decay: 'It will be assumed that under suitable circumstances [the neutron] can break up into a proton and an electron in which case the conservation laws of energy and momentum probably do not apply[124] ... The failure of the energy law in β-decay proves the inapplicability of present quantum mechanics to the structure of the neutron.'[125]

The turning point came at the seventh Solvay conference in Brussels, October 1933. Pauli discussed the neutrino. '[Bohr's] hypothesis does not seem satisfactory nor even plausible to me.' He insisted on conservation of energy, momentum, angular momentum, and statistics 'in all elementary processes'.[126] Bohr's comments were rather muted. 'As long as we have no experimental data it is wise not to give up the conservation laws, but on the other hand no one knows what surprises may still await us.'[127] From a letter by Gamow, in his inimitable English, we learn that in early 1934 Bohr was looking for new ways out of the quandary: 'Bohr ... (well, you know that he absolutely does not like this chargeless, massless little thing!) thinks that continuous β-spectra is compensated by the emmition [sic] of gravitational waves (!!!) which play the role of neutrino but are much more physical things. It is ... very difficult to put through.'[128]

Meanwhile Fermi had found the right procedures. He too had been present at the Solvay meeting but there had kept his silence on β-decay. A few months later he was ready to publish his greatest discovery in theoretical physics: the language appropriate to β-decay is the language of quantum field theory. 'Electrons (or neutrinos) can be created and can disappear ... The [formalism for] the system consisting of heavy and light particles must be chosen such that to every transition from neutron to proton there is associated a creation of an electron and a neutrino. To the inverse process, the change of a proton into a neutron, the disappearance of an electron and a neutrino should be associated.'[129] The fundamental process of β-decay is

$$neutron \rightarrow proton + electron + neutrino.$$

Thus it was Fermi who formally banned electrons as nuclear *constituents*. For more details of the rich content of Fermi's 1934 papers I refer to the literature.[130]

Bohr's initial response to Fermi's theory was cautious. 'We have of course been very interested in Fermi's new paper which will undoubtedly have a stimulating effect on the work with electric [electron?] nuclear problems, even though I must admit that I do not yet feel entirely convinced of the physical existence of the neutrino.'[131] Some time later he fully accepted the theory as a great advance: 'It may be remarked that the grounds for serious doubts as regards the strict validity of the conservation laws in the problem of emission of β-rays from atomic nuclei are now largely removed by the suggestive agreement between the rapidly increasing experimental evidence regarding β-ray phenomena and the consequences of the neutrino hypothesis so remarkably developed in Fermi's theory.'[132] That comment marks the conclusion of Bohr's active involvement with β-decay.

Note finally that Fermi's theory implies that the coupling between electron–neutrino and proton–neutron is very weak. 'Seeing neutrinos', that is, observing them do something after creation is correspondingly difficult, it demands large fluxes of neutrinos. Only after those became available in the 1950s, using nuclear reactors, did it become possible to 'see neutrinos in action'. Only in the 1960s was it discovered that there is more than one kind of neutrino.[133]

References

1. The proceedings were published by Taylor and Francis, London 1947.
2. Ref. 1, p. 1.
3. See SL, Chap. 21, section (a).
4. A. Einstein, *Phys. Zeitschr.* **10**, 185, 817, 1909.
5. A. Einstein, *Phys. Zeitschr.* **18**, 121, 1917.
6. W. Heisenberg, interview with T. S. Kuhn, 28 February 1963, NBA.
7. IB, Chap. 15–21.
8. R. P. Feynman *Quantum electrodynamics*, p. 10, Princeton University Press 1985.
9. S. Weinberg, *Daedalus* **106**, No. 4, p. 17, 1977.
10. M. Born and P. Jordan, *Zeitschr. Phys.* **34**, 858, 1925.
11. M. Born, W. Heisenberg, and P. Jordan, *Zeitschr. Phys.* **35**, 557, 1925; English transl. in B. L. van der Waerden, *Sources of quantum mechanics*, Dover, New York 1968.
12. P. A. M. Dirac, *Proc. Roy. Soc.* A **112**, 661, 1926.
13. For details see IB, Chap. 13, section (d).
14. P. A. M. Dirac, *Proc. Roy. Soc.* A **114**, 243, 1927.
15. P. A. M. Dirac, *Proc. Roy. Soc.* A **114**, 710, 1927.
16. W. Heisenberg and W. Pauli, *Zeitschr. Phys.* **56**, 1, 1929; **59**, 168, 1930.

Electromagnetic commutation relations that are manifestly relativistic had been written down earlier by P. Jordan and W. Pauli, *Zeitschr. Phys.* **47**, 151, 1928, for the case of *free* fields.

17. E. Schrödinger, *Ann. der Phys.* **79**, 361, 1926, esp. p. 372.
18. For details see IB, pp. 288, 289.
19. See IB, pp. 387, 388.
20. P. A. M. Dirac, *Proc. Roy. Soc.* A **117**, 610; **118**, 351, 1928.
21. W. Pauli, *Zeitschr. Phys.* **43**, 601, 1927.
22. For textbook treatments see e.g. L. I. Schiff, *Quantum mechanics*, 2nd edn, McGraw-Hill, New York 1955.
23. N. Bohr, *Nature* **121**, 580, 1928; CW, Vol. 6, p. 147; esp. p. 158.
24. N. Bohr, letter to A. Joffé, 25 October 1928, NBA.
25. N. Bohr, letter to A. Joffé, 27 December 1928, NBA.
26. N. Bohr, unpublished MS dating from 1929, repr. in CW, Vol. 6, p. 333.
27. See *Selected papers of Léon Rosenfeld*, p. 306, Eds. R. S. Cohen and J. Stachel, Reidel, Boston 1979.
28. N. F. Mott, *Proc. Roy. Soc.* A **124**, 425, 1929.
29. N. F. Mott, letter to T. S. Kuhn, 27 March 1962, NBA.
30. N. F. Mott, *A life in science*, p. 27, Taylor and Francis, Philadelphia 1986.
31. N. F. Mott, interview with T. S. Kuhn, 13 May 1963, NBA.
32. N. Bohr, in *Introductory survey*, to *Atomic theory and the description of nature*, p. 13, Cambridge University Press 1934, CW, Vol. 6, p. 291.
33. N. F. Mott and H. S. W. Massey, *The theory of atomic collisions*, 3rd edn, pp. 214–19, Oxford University Press 1965.
34. W. H. Louisell, R. W. Pidd, and H. R. Crane, *Phys. Rev.* **94**, 7, 1954.
35. For a review up to 1972 see A. Rich and J. C. Wesley, *Rev. Mod. Phys.* **44**, 250, 1972; for more recent results see P. Schwinberg, R. S. van Dyck, and H. G. Dehmelt, *Phys. Rev. Lett.* **47**, 1679, 1981.
36. O. Klein and Y. Nishina, *Zeitschr. Phys.* **52**, 853, 869, 1929.
37. See IB, p. 348.
38. O. Klein, *Zeitschr. Phys.* **53**, 157, 1929.
39. N. Bohr, letter to C. W. Oseen, 5 November 1928, repr. in CW, Vol. 6, p. 189.
40. W. Heisenberg, interview with T. S. Kuhn, 12 July 1963, NBA.
41. W. Heisenberg, letter to W. Pauli, 31 July 1928, repr. in *W. Pauli, scientific correspondence*, Vol. 1, p. 466, Springer, New York, 1979.
42. P. A. M. Dirac, *Proc. Roy. Soc.* A **126**, 360, 1929.
43. P. A. M. Dirac, *Quantum mechanics*, Chap. 13, Oxford University Press 1935.
44. See IB, p. 351.
45. L. D. Landau, cable to N. Bohr, 9 September 1930, NBA.
46. P. A. M. Dirac, *Proc. Roy. Soc.* A **133**, 60, 1931.
47. First reported in *Science Newsletter*, 19 December 1931. First paper· C. D. Anderson, *Science* **76**, 238, 1932.
48. P. M. S. Blackett and G. P. S. Occhialini, *Proc. Roy. Soc.* A **139**, 699, 1933.
49. N. Bohr, in *Atti del Convegna di Fisica Nucleare*, October 1931, p. 119, CW, Vol. 9, p. 99, esp. p. 107.
50. N. Bohr, *J. Chem. Soc. (London)*, 1932, p. 349, CW, Vol. 6, p. 371, esp. p. 402.
51. N. Bohr, letter to O. Klein, 7 April 1933, NBA.

52. W. Pauli, letter to P. A. M. Dirac, 1 May 1933, *Correspondence* (Ref. 41), Vol. 2, p. 159.
53. N. Bohr, letter to W. Heisenberg, 19 May 1933, NBA.
54. Cf. I. and F. Joliot Curie, *C.R. Acad. Sci. Paris* **196**, 1105, 1581, 1933.
55. N. Bohr, letter to W. Heisenberg, 17 August 1933, NBA.
56. P. Jordan, *Zeitschr. Phys.* **44**, 473, 1927; P. Jordan and E. Wigner, *ibid.* **47**, 631, 1928.
57. See IB, Chap. 16.
58. V. Weisskopf, *Det Kongl. Dansk. Vid. Selsk. Mat.-fys. Medd.* **14**, No. 6, 1936.
59. H. Yukawa, *Tabibito*, transl. L. Brown and R. Yoshida, World Scientific, Singapore 1979.
60. H. Yukawa, *Proc. Phys. Math. Soc. Japan* **17**, 48, 1935.
61. S. H. Neddermeyer and C. D. Anderson, *Science* **84**, 1936, Suppl. following p. 404; *Phys. Rev.* **51**, 884, 1937.
62. *Rev. Mod. Phys.* **11**, 122, 1939.
63. N. Bohr, letter to O. Klein, 13 January 1938, NBA.
64. See e.g. IB, Chap. 18, section (b).
65. C. Møller and L. Rosenfeld, *Det Kongl. Dansk. Vid. Selsk. Mat.-fys. Medd.* **17**, No. 8, 1940; **20**, No. 12, 1943; S. Rozental, *ibid.* **18**, No. 7, 1941.
66. W. Heisenberg, letter to N. Bohr, 16 June 1929, CW, Vol. 7.
67. W. Heisenberg, *Die physikalischen Prinzipien der Quantentheorie*, Chap. 3, Hirzel, Leipzig 1930.
68. N. Bohr, draft of letter to W. Heisenberg, 8 December 1930, CW, Vol. 7.
69. W. Pauli, letter to O. Klein, 12 December 1930, *Correspondence* (Ref. 41), Vol. 2, p. 43.
70. L. Landau and R. Peierls, *Zeitschr. Phys.* **68**, 56, 1931.
71. See e.g. Ref. 1.
72. See e.g. IB, Chaps. 16 and 18.
73. W. Heisenberg, letter to W. Pauli, 12 March 1931. *Correspondence* (Ref. 41), Vol. 2, p. 66.
73a. N. Bohr, letter to W. Pauli, 25 January 1933, CW, Vol. 7.
74. N. Bohr, letter to W. Heisenberg, 25 December 1930, CW, Vol. 7.
75. L. Rosenfeld, in *Niels Bohr and the development of physics*, p. 70, Ed. W. Pauli, McGraw-Hill, New York 1955.
76. N. Bohr, letter to W. Pauli, 21 March 1931, *Correspondence* (ref. 41), Vol. 2, p. 69.
77. Felix Bloch, interview by T. S. Kuhn, 15 May 1964, NBA.
78. W. Pauli, letter to W. Heisenberg, 13 May 1954.
79. N. Bohr and L. Rosenfeld, *Det Kgl. Danske Vid. Selsk. Mat.-fys. Medd.* **12**. No. 8, 1933, CW, Vol. 7; English transl. in *Selected writings of L. Rosenfeld*, p. 357, Eds. R. S. Cohen and J. Stachel, Reidel, Boston 1979; also in J. A. Wheeler and W. H. Zuber, *Quantum theory and measurement*, p. 479, Princeton University Press 1983.
80. N. Bohr, letter to W. Heisenberg, 28 October 1932, NBA.
81. W. Heisenberg, letter to N. Bohr, 5 November 1932, NBA.
82. N. Bohr, letter to G. Gamow, 21 January 1933, CW, Vol. 9, p. 571.
83. L. Rosenfeld, NBR, p. 125.

84. N. Bohr, letter to W. Heisenberg, 13 March 1933, NBA.
85. N. Bohr, letter to W. Heisenberg, 19 May 1933, NBA.
86. N. Bohr, letter to W. Heisenberg, 17 August 1933, NBA.
87. N. Bohr, in *Proc. Seventh Solvay Conf.*, 22–9 October 1933, p. 216, Gauthier-Villars, Paris 1934, CW, Vol. 7.
88. N. Bohr, letter to V. Weisskopf, 10 November 1933, CW, Vol. 7.
89. O. Klein, letter to N. Bohr, 12 December 1933, NBA.
90. W. Heitler, *The quantum theory of radiation*, p. 81, Oxford University Press 1936.
91. W. Heisenberg, *Ber. Sächs. Akad. Wiss.* **86**, 317, 1934, repr. in J. Schwinger, *Selected papers in quantum electrodynamics*, p. 62, Dover, New York 1958.
92. N. Bohr and L. Rosenfeld, Field and charge measurements in quantum theory, unpublished MS, CW, Vol. 7.
93. N. Bohr and L. Rosenfeld, *Phys. Rev.* **78**, 794, 1950, CW, Vol. 7.
94. A. Pais, *Developments in the theory of the electron*, Princeton University Press 1948.
95. H. Weyl, *The theory of groups and quantum mechanics*, 2nd edn, preface, transl. H. Robertson, Dover, New York 1935; the original German version was completed in November 1930.
96. IB, Chap. 8, and Chap. 14, section (c).
97. Cf. J. Müller and C. Pouillet, *Lehrbuch der Physik*, 10th edn, Vol. 4, pp. 1272–4, Vieweg, Braunschweig 1914.
98. J. Chadwick, *Verh. Deutsch. Phys. Ges.* **16**, 383, 1914.
99. See IB, pp. 304, 305.
100. See IB, p. 307.
101. See IB, Chap. 14, section (c).
102. N. Bohr, letter to R. H. Fowler, 14 February 1929, CW, Vol. 9, p. 555.
103. W. Pauli, letter to O. Klein, 18 February 1929, *Corrspondence* (Ref. 41) Vol. 1, p. 488.
104. W. Pauli, letter to N. Bohr, 5 March 1929, *Correspondence* (Ref. 41) Vol. 1, p. 493.
105. N. Bohr, letter to W. Pauli, 1 July 1929, CW, Vol. 6, p. 443.
106. N. Bohr, β-ray spectra and energy conservation, unpublished MS, repr. in CW, Vol. 9, p. 85.
107. W. Pauli, letter to N. Bohr, 17 July 1929, CW, Vol. 6, p. 446.
108. N. Bohr, letter to N. F. Mott, 1 October 1929, NBA.
109. E. Rutherford, letter to N. Bohr, 19 November 1929, NBA.
110. N. Bohr, letter to P. A. M. Dirac, 24 November 1929, NBA.
111. P. A. M. Dirac, letter to N. Bohr, 26 November 1929, NBA.
112. N. Bohr, letter to P. A. M. Dirac, 5 December 1929, NBA.
113. P. A. M. Dirac, letter to N. Bohr, 9 December 1929, NBA.
114. N. Bohr, *J. Chem. Soc. (London)*, 1932, p. 349, CW, Vol. 6, p. 371.
115. N. Bohr, Space-time description and conservation principles, dated 16 November 1930 to 20 February 1931, unpublished, NBA.
116. N. Bohr, Atomic stability and conservation laws, *Proc. Rome Conf. Nuclear Physics*, 11–18 October 1931, p. 119, Reale Accademia d'Italia, Rome 1932, CW, Vol. 9, p. 101.

117. See letters to W. Pauli by P. Ehrenfest, 15 November 1931, and by M. Delbrück, 6 October 1958, quoted in *Correspondence* (Ref. 41), Vol. 2, p. 92.

118. W. Pauli, letter to P. M. S. Blackett, 19 April 1933, *Correspondence* (Ref. 41) Vol. 2, p. 158.

119. W. Pauli, letter to a physicists' gathering at Tübingen, 4 December 1930, repr. in Pauli's historical essay on the neutrino found in *W. Pauli, collected scientific papers*, Eds. R. Kronig and V. Weisskopf, Vol. 2, p. 1313, Interscience, New York 1964.

120. See also W. Pauli, letter to O. Klein, 12 December 1930, *Correspondence* (Ref. 41), Vol. 2, p. 43.

121. W. Pauli, letter to O. Klein, 8 January 1931, *Correspondence* (Ref. 41), Vol. 2, p. 51.

122. W. Pauli, *Phys. Rev.* **38**, 579, 1931.

123. N. Bohr, letter to E. Rutherford, 2 May 1932, NBA.

124. W. Heisenberg, *Zeitschr. Phys.* **77**, 1, 1932.

125. W. Heisenberg, *Zeitschr. Phys.* **78**, 156, 1932, esp. p. 165.

126. W. Pauli, in *Structure et propriétés des noyaux atomiques*, pp. 324–5, Gauthier-Villars, Paris 1934.

127. N. Bohr, Ref. 126, p. 328, repr. in CW, Vol. 9, pp. 139, 140.

128. G. Gamow, letter to S. Goudsmit, 8 March 1934.

129. E. Fermi, *Ric. Scient.* **4**, 491, 1934; *Nuov. Cim.* **11**, 1, 1934; *Zeitschr. Phys.* **88**, 161, 1934; repr. in *E. Fermi, collected papers*, Vol. 1, pp. 538, 559, 575 respectively, University of Chicago Press 1965.

130. See IB, Chap. 17, section (e).

131. N. Bohr, letter to F. Bloch, 17 February 1934, CW, Vol. 9, p. 541.

132. N. Bohr, *Nature* **138**, 25, 1936, CW, Vol. 5, p. 213.

133. For more on neutrino physics see IB, Chap. 21, section (c).

17

How Bohr orchestrated experimental progress in the 1930s, in physics and in biology

(a) Four fateful factors

The events described in the previous two chapters, progress in theoretical nuclear physics (Chapter 15), and the advent of new particles (Chapter 16), do not by any means exhaust the advances at the frontiers of physics during the 1930s. There were also important developments in experimental physics techniques which gave new impetus not only to physics but also to biology.

The present chapter deals with the resulting achievements in Copenhagen in both these areas. Four unrelated events would profoundly change the nature of these enterprises in Bohr's institute:

(1) The completion of the first particle accelerators in 1931 and 1932.

(2) The change in emphasis of the funding policies of the Rockefeller Foundation* resulting from the appointment of Warren Weaver as its director of the division of natural sciences, in 1932.

(3) The coming to power of the National Socialist Party in Germany in 1933.

(4) The discovery of induced radioactivity in 1934.

I begin with sketches, one by one, of these developments, confining myself as much as possible to those aspects which bear on the Copenhagen scene. Thereafter I turn to their combined influence on science in Denmark. We shall see how Bohr made use of these four diverse factors to orchestrate a major new emphasis in the experimental program at his institute.

(b) The first accelerators

An accelerator is a machine that speeds up electrically charged particles such as electrons or protons for the purpose of examining how they react at

---

* Also discussed in detail by Finn Aaserud. [1]

ever higher energies when they hit other particles. Such machines have two common characteristics. First, the speeding up is brought about by letting the particles traverse a voltage difference. The greater that difference, the greater the increase in energy of the particles. Secondly, this acceleration takes place inside a vacuum so that the particle's energy does not go to waste by collision with molecules in their environment. The (ongoing) development in this chapter of physics is a story of improvements in generating higher voltages, better vacua, greater beam intensities, and improved detectors – the tools with which one analyses the results of impacts by high-energy particles.

The first instruments that deserve – but were not given – the name accelerators date from the late nineteenth century. They consist of a closed straight evacuated cylindrical glass tube with a metal plate inserted at each end. These two 'electrodes' are linked to a generator that creates a voltage difference between them. That type of equipment served Röntgen[2] in discovering X-rays in 1895, and J. J. Thomson[3] in discovering the electron in 1897. In those days voltage differences were of typical order 100000 volts.

Interest in producing high voltages, also called high tensions, increased in the 1920s, for diverse purposes such as improved long-distance power transmission, the use of high-voltage X-ray tubes for medical applications, and also physics research with accelerated protons and electrons. For one reason or another several industrial and university laboratories in the United States participated in these efforts.[4] From these I select only the work of Charles Lauritsen since we shall meet him later on in Copenhagen (17j).

Lauritsen was a man of many parts. He was born in Denmark where he graduated in architecture. After emigrating to the US in 1917 he became involved in turn with the design of naval craft in Boston, professional fishing in Florida, building ship-to-shore radios in California, and radios for the home in St Louis. There a lecture by Millikan aroused his interest in high voltages, inducing him to move to Cal Tech, in 1926, where he stayed for the rest of his life, beginning as a student and ending as full professor.[5] In 1928 he published his first paper[6] on the construction of a high-tension X-ray tube of about a million volts.

The name accelerator dates from the early 1930s and refers to the new machines devised from that time on for the express purpose of studying nuclear processes at energies and intensities that exceed those of α-particles produced by radioactive substances. Accelerators come in various shapes and sizes. Let us have a brief look at the origins of the three kinds that were eventually set up in the Bohr institute.

(a) *The cyclotron.* The first major figure to emerge among the new breed of machine builders was Ernest Lawrence who will be remembered for his discovery of the cyclotron principle, for his rearing a new generation of distinguished American accelerator builders, and for his talents in obtaining funds for his enterprises during the economically diffcult years of the Great Depression: 'Lawrence's optimism, even his boosterism, engaged the willing belief of ordinary people sick of Depression . . . There was little money despite Lawrence's success at grant gathering; while the machines consumed tens of thousands, and then hundreds of thousands of dollars, the staff made do with small salaries, if any, and none of the fringe benefits now common: medical insurance, secretaries, and paid travel to meetings.'[7]

Lawrence's cyclotron concept rests on the application of resonance acceleration to circular orbits.* You yourself can make an accelerator of that type. Tie a massive ball to a string, hold the other end of the string in your hand, and make the ball move around in a horizontal circular orbit. Every time the ball is closest to you, kick it with one of your feet to speed it up. Clearly you must time your kicking frequency with the frequency of revolution of the ball. This matching process is called resonance acceleration.

Lawrence's principle is somewhat similar. The ball becomes an electrically charged particle injected in an evacuated horizontally placed hollow disk. The string becomes a homogeneous magnetic field perpendicular to the disk. It is known that our particle will describe a circular orbit in such a field with a frequency proportional to the magnetic field strength. The kicking (actually twice per revolution) is provided by an electric field that alternates with a frequency resonant with the revolution frequency. Of course one injects not one but a stream of particles with some given velocity. At a given time a particle will have a higher (lower) velocity the earlier (later) it was injected. Now comes the main joke: as the energy of a particle increases its revolution frequency in the magnetic field stays constant! Thus the *same* alternating field frequency will accelerate *all* particles in the stream – which makes it possible to achieve useful beam intensities and hence reasonable rates for collisions of the beam with a target interposed in its path.

The higher the desired energy the bulkier the cyclotron, the bulkiest part of equipment being the magnet. The first Berkeley cyclotron that worked was quite modest in size, however, its vacuum chamber had only a four-inch diameter. Its first results were reported in April 1931. '80000 volt hydrogen molecule ions have been produced using 2000 volt high frequency oscillators.'[12] Note the great virtue of resonance acceleration: repeated

---

* Resonance acceleration had been proposed earlier[8] for linear orbits by Gustav Adolf Ising, a Swedish physicist. The first practical application of Ising's mechanism had been made[9] by Rolf Wideröe, a Norwegian engineer, who has been called 'the first designer of accelerators'.[10] It was Wideröe's work that inspired Lawrence.[11]

application of a low voltage generates particles at a much higher voltage (energy).

So far so good. Unfortunately, however, no detectors had yet been built in Berkeley to do some nice physics with the accelerated particles. 'The planning of physics experiments had not paralleled the construction of instruments to perform them. This negative consequence of Lawrence's concentration on accelerator improvement was to recur throughout the thirties.'[7] As a result the honors for observing the first nuclear process produced with an accelerator did not go to Berkeley but, instead, to the Cavendish Laboratory.

(b) *The Cockcroft–Walton*. In the late 1920s Rutherford had expressed interest in new sources of high-energy particles: 'It has long been my ambition to have available for study a copious supply of atoms and electrons which have an energy far transcending that of the α- and β-particles from radioactive decay.'[13] Accordingly he was responsive to suggestions by his co-workers John Cockcroft and Ernest Walton for the construction of a device that now bears their names. In outline it consists of an ion source from which protons are pulled out and then accelerated in a linear vacuum tube. From the source at the top the protons are accelerated downward by a high voltage obtained from an alternating current which is converted into a direct current by a series of 'rectifiers'.

In June 1932, after some years of labor, Cockcroft and Walton could report the first observation of a nuclear process produced by artificially accelerated particles:

$$_1^1H + _3^7Li \rightarrow _2^4He + _2^4He + 17 \text{ MeV},$$

half of the seventeen million electronvolts being the kinetic energy carried by each of the two α-particles. By the time this experiment was performed the masses of all particles occurring in the above reaction were known to good accuracy. The value for the kinetic energy, due to a conversion of some mass into energy, therefore provided a test, the first one, for Einstein's $E = mc^2$. It worked just fine! These results drew the attention of the world press.[14] The reaction of physicists is well illustrated by a letter from Fowler in Cambridge to Bohr: 'Who would have thought that anything would happen at 100000 volts – except perhaps Rutherford?'[15]

(c) *The Van de Graaff*. In 1929 Robert Van de Graaff was in Princeton on a fellowship when he began his work on the belt-charged electrostatic generator since named after him. It works roughly like this. Electric charge is deposited on to one area of an endless belt made of insulating material and running around pulleys. The belt transports the charge into a hollow conducting sphere open at one end. The charge is now transferred on to the sphere. The whole contraption is somewhat analogous to luggage being deposited on one area of a conveyor belt and transferred to passengers at another area. The electric potential of the sphere rises as charge accumulates until a large spark liberates the charges. In later versions the potential is limited by controlling devices, and the charge removed by fine-toothed metal combs.

With his first model, made out of a tin can, a silk ribbon, and a small motor, Van de Graaff was soon able to produce an 80000 volt potential difference. Whereupon he went to the head of the physics department requesting about one hundred dollars for constructing an improved version. He did get the money, though not without difficulty.[16] By 1931 he could report 1.5 million volt potentials. 'The machine is simple, inexpensive, and portable. An ordinary lamp socket furnishes the only power needed.' [17]

It is of course important to optimize the charge density before insulation breakdown occurs and sparks fly. It was soon realized[18] that improvement could be achieved by enclosing the apparatus in a metal bell filled with gas under high pressure (thus preventing sparking to laboratory walls!).

Of later date is the 'tandem Van de Graaff'. *Negative* ions entering on one side are attracted to the high potential electrode, then move through gas which removes two or more electrons. The resulting *positive* ions, continuing downward, are now repelled by the electrode. This doubles the beam energy. The first tandem Van de Graaff was built in 1955–8 by High Voltage Engineering, an American company founded by Van de Graaff. In January 1959 it started operations at Chalk River, the Canadian atomic energy establishment. The next two, built in Harwell and Aldermaston, the British atomic energy laboratories, started up the next March. We shall see later how this variant of the classical Van de Graaff also came to play its role in the Bohr story (22f).

(c) Weaver at the helm

In 1917 Warren Weaver, native of a small Midwestern town, graduated in civil engineering at the University of Wisconsin in Madison. His favorite topics were mathematics and mathematical physics. Later that year he received appointment as assistant professor in mathematics at Throop College, better known since 1920 as Cal Tech. In 1920 he accepted an offer from Max Mason, his erstwhile teacher in mathematics, for a position in Madison. There he rose through the ranks, becoming head of the mathematics department in 1928. In 1929 he and Mason published an advanced textbook on electromagnetism[19] that was long used at universities. Mason had moved meanwhile, first to the University of Chicago as president, then to the Rockefeller foundation.

In 1928 the programs of the various foundations that together made up the

Rockefeller philanthropies had been reorganized. It had been decided that all programs relating to the advancement of knowledge should be concentrated in the Rockefeller foundation. Along with its existing division of international health and of medical sciences, three new divisions were to be formed: of the humanities, of the social sciences, and of the natural sciences.[20] The latter would include the support for science abroad handled earlier by the International Education Board – which had been such help to Bohr (12d). In 1928 Mason had been elected the first director of the division of natural sciences. In 1929 he became the foundation's president (until 1936).

In 1931 Weaver received a telephone call from Mason in New York, whose successor as division director had left. Would Weaver be interested in the vacant position? Weaver would, starting his new post in 1932, and holding it until 1952.[21]

From the very start Weaver had strong visions about the future direction of his division: 'Satisfied as I was with being immersed in the physical sciences, I was convinced that the great wave of the future in science, a wave *not yet* [my italics] gathering its strength, was to occur in the biological sciences. The startling visions that were just then beginning to open up in genetics [those were the days of Thomas Hunt Morgan and Hermann Muller], in cellular physiology, in biochemistry, in developmental mechanics – these were due for tremendously significant advances ... Despite my personal commitment to the physical sciences I strongly felt that the Rockefeller foundation ought to undertake a large and long-range support of quantitative biology.'[22] In 1933 he stated those views in a memorandum to the foundation's trustees:

'A highly selective procedure is necessary if the available funds are not to lose significance through scattering. In the past, this selection has consisted chiefly of a choice of scientific leaders, among both men and institutions, although there has always been some selection on the basis of fields of interest. It is proposed, for the future program, that interest in the fields play the dominant role in the selection process. Within the fields of interest, selection will continue to be made of leading men and institutions ... Science has made magnificent progress in the analysis and control of inanimate forces, but it has not made equal advances in the more delicate, more difficult, and more important problem of the analysis and control of animate forces. This indicates the desirability of greatly increasing the emphasis on biology and psychology, and on those special developments in mathematics, physics, and chemistry which are themselves fundamental to biology.'[23]

In the spring of 1933 this recommendation was accepted by the foundation's board which voted to make experimental biology the field of primary interest in the natural sciences.

That was just ten years after Rose had proposed a policy for the International Education Board in which physics, chemistry, and biology were treated on a par and the emphasis had been people oriented: 'Locate the inspiring productive men in each of these fields' (12c). By contrast, Weaver's policy emphasized biology, placed physics and chemistry in a secondary supportive position, and was mission-oriented. History has shown time and again that preference of missions over people can be dangerous. In 1933 Weaver could not have foreseen how very fruitful his new direction (to which he held throughout his tenure as division director) was nevertheless to become.

Within a few years after adoption of the new policy, major grants would be forthcoming, as far as Europe was concerned, to Oxford, Stockholm, Uppsala, and Utrecht.

And to Copenhagen.

(d) Troubles in Germany

In German history one commonly refers to the Holy Roman Empire as the first *Reich* and to the unification of German lands by Bismarck in 1871 as the beginning of the second *Reich*. In 1919 Adolf Hitler founded the National Socialist German Workers' Party. The third *Reich* can be dated to begin on 30 January 1933, when he became Germany's chancellor. At that time he was the head of a coalition cabinet elected (at least formally) by democratic process. Not long afterward he became Germany's *Führer*, dictator, and his party the only one allowed.

I need to discuss next the impact of these events on Denmark and more specifically on Bohr's institute. That of course gives but a pale reflection of the bestial cruelty and immense sufferings the Nazis caused during the next twelve years. Denmark's history does record personal tragedy, acts of heroism, and martyr figures. Nevertheless, of all countries eventually occupied by Germany, Denmark suffered least.

Already before 1933 some of those who saw what was coming had fled Germany for reasons of conviction, politics, or race, or a combination thereof. Their number grew steeply of course after the Nazis came to power. A further wave from Austria followed after its German occupation in 1938.

Denmark had its advantages as a refuge. In the beginning open emigration was simple. All one needed to leave Germany was a valid passport; a Danish resident permit was required only for a stay exceeding three months. Crossings for those who had reasons to fear arrest at the border were initially not too difficult either, for example with an illegally acquired 'Groschenpass', a document available to those living near the border for visits to the other side. For many it was hard to find employment, however. Also in Denmark the stock market crash of 1929 had caused a large rise in the number of unemployed. When an immigrant applied for a job the police would contact the relevant labor union to inquire how many Danes were jobless. Many refugees with special expertise were among those refused.

Several Danish committees were established for aid to refugees. The social democrats founded the 'Matteotti committee'; the Jewish community, the 'Committee of 4 May 1933'; the Lutheran state church, the 'churches' collection for non-Aryan Christian refugees' (on 30 August 1936 a collection was held in all the country's churches); academics, the 'Danish committee for support to refugee intellectuals' (including journalists, authors, and actors), directed by a board whose members included Niels and Harald Bohr. From 1934 on these committees collaborated as 'the joint Danish committees for help to emigrés'. The communist committee 'Red help' was never asked to join mainly because of suspicions that its activities were in part political. All these committees were sanctioned by the Danish government.

These various activities were hampered by the presence of spies among the immigrants, some known, some suspected, who were in touch with a small Danish Nazi party.[24]

A large fraction, about 4500, of the refugees who settled in Denmark for longer or shorter terms were Jews. Let us turn to those among them who were physicists.

According to the *Beamtengesetz* (civil service law), a German law of 7 April 1933, university authorities could fire academic staff on grounds of politics and/or race. On 13 April another law restricted membership in student organizations to Aryans only. On 10 May the infamous book burning took place. Thus began the destruction of German academic life, until then among the best of its kind in the world. One measure of the loss to German cultural life is the number of scientist Nobel laureates, some of them present but most of them future, mostly Jews but also some non-Jews, who left Germany in 1933 or shortly thereafter because they found the new situation unacceptable and intolerable: eleven in physics, four in chemistry, five in medicine.[25]

'Many of [the] colloquia [in Bohr's institute] were given in German. It was only after Hitler that we changed over to English completely.'[26] Danish physicists were deeply angered by the events in Germany. At that time Bohr himself had Jewish family there, a branch of the Adlers (Chapter 2). In 1936 his second cousin Paula Strelitz left Germany for Denmark and lived in Copenhagen for the rest of her life, always in close contact with the Bohrs.[27]

Our knowledge of Bohr's efforts on behalf of physicist and other refugees is limited by the fact that all pertinent correspondence was burned after the occupation of Denmark in 1940.[28] We can nevertheless form a picture of Bohr's considerable activities from other documents that have survived.

Because of close contacts with internationally oriented foundations, especially the Rask–Ørsted and the Rockefeller foundations, it was natural for Bohr to seek their financial support, mostly for younger physicists in trouble. The Rockefeller foundation would only award fellowships, however, to those who had a base to return to after the period of support had ended, clearly an obstacle at that time. Bohr managed to overcome that difficulty and thus was able to offer hospitality to a number of physicists including Guido Beck, Felix Bloch, Otto Frisch, Hilde Levi, George Placzek, Eugene Rabinowitch, Stefan Rozental, Erich Schneider, Edward Teller, Arthur Von Hippel,* and Victor Weisskopf. Not all of these were German citizens, but all of them were forced to leave junior academic posts in Germany. With the exception of Levi and Rozental, all moved on to other destinations – often helped by Bohr – where most of them rose to prominence.

(e) Bohr and the Rockefeller foundation's emergency program

In 1933 the Rockefeller foundation created a new form of support, its emergency program for European refugee scholars, designed to aid senior academics. During its existence – which ended with the cessation of World War II – it gave assistance to some 300 scholars. Until the outbreak of the war these were not selected by the foundation but were proposed by individuals or institutions in the US or in Europe.[29] In May 1933 Bohr had an opportunity to discuss the emergency program directly with Mason, during his visit to the US (18b). It was obviously a scheme of great interest to him and he made several proposals.[30]

The first of these concerned Lise Meitner, seven years older than Bohr, who had a distinguished career in research on radioactivity.[31] At that time she was working at the Kaiser Wilhelm Institut in Berlin, together with its director, her devoted 'Aryan' friend Otto Hahn. She had, relatively speaking, no difficulties yet in the first years after 1933 since she was Austrian, though her teaching privileges at the University of Berlin had been rescinded. In November 1933, after consultation with Meitner, Bohr applied to the Rockefeller foundation for one year support for her in Copenhagen. His request was granted. Meitner eventually declined this invitation, however, after being advised by Planck that acceptance might make it uncertain that she could return to Berlin afterward.

* Non-Jewish but married to a daughter of James Franck.

I indicate what befell Meitner thereafter, since she is to reappear later. Upon the German annexation of Austria in 1938 her situation in Berlin became critical. It was decided that she should leave Germany illegally – her Austrian passport was no longer a valid document. Hahn contacted Coster in Holland who traveled to Berlin to fetch her. A suitcase was hastily packed; Hahn gave her a diamond ring to be sold in case of emergency. The train trip to Holland, dangerous because of SS checks on illegal departures, went without incident.[32] After a short stay she moved on to Copenhagen, 'where for some weeks she enjoyed the hospitality of her good friends Niels Bohr and his wife'.[33] Then she went on to Stockholm where she had been offered a position; she was to stay there for the next 22 years.

Bohr's other two applications for senior support led to more positive results. Those concerned James Franck and Hevesy who both had visited Bohr briefly in Copenhagen after his return from the 1933 trip to the US. We have met both men earlier in this book. Let us catch up with them.

From 1917 to 1921 Franck (of the Franck–Hertz experiment (10b)) had held a post at the Kaiser Wilhelm Institut in Berlin. There he met Bohr for the first time during the latter's visit (11b), and again shortly afterward during a visit to Copenhagen. A lasting friendship resulted. 'Bohr's wisdom and his complete freedom from conceit . . . created such deep respect and admiration in the young physicists that Franck describes it as bordering on hero worship.'[34] In 1921 Franck accepted a professorship in Göttingen. In 1926 he shared a Nobel Prize with Hertz. Though Jewish he was at first exempt from the *Beamtengesetz* of 1933 since he had served in the German army during World War I. He was outraged, however, by demands that he fire some of his co-workers. In April 1933 he therefore resigned and published a protest in the German press.[35] After a short trip to the US Franck arrived in Copenhagen in April 1934 on a visiting professorship that Bohr had arranged via the emergency committee.

Bohr's friendship with Hevesy and respect for his oeuvre dated back to their Manchester days in 1912 with Rutherford (7b). Early in 1913 Hevesy spent some time in Vienna working together with Friedrich Paneth, who became his close confidant. In 1913 he was *privatdozent* at the University of Budapest. During World War I he was drafted in the Austro-Hungarian army where he served in technical capacities. In 1918 he was promoted to professor.[36]

Right after the war, Hungary went through a period of political chaos. In May 1919 Hevesy, in trouble in Hungary, managed to make a trip to Denmark, where Bohr offered him to come and stay in Copenhagen. In October Hevesy wrote to Bohr: 'The worst is the moral decay . . . politics also entered the University . . . two of my assistants, absolutely honest and able, have been deprived from their posts only because they are Jews.'[37] (He was to be fired himself shortly afterwards.[37a]) In November he wrote to Paneth: 'Bohr has cordially invited me to work in his laboratory, and I shall definitely not pass up the opportunity to work next to this unique human being.'[38] He arrived in Copenhagen in June 1920, before Bohr's institute was ready, as already noted (9c). Bohr had meanwhile secured financial support for him from the Rask–Ørsted foundation, which was extended to cover the six-year period Hevesy was to spend in Copenhagen. He liked the atmosphere: 'Bohr's institute is a very cosy one. Well buildt [sic], well equipped.'[39] Those were the years Bohr worked on the periodic table (10e). '[Bohr] reads the language of spectra like other people goes [sic] through a magazine.'[40] Hevesy's main contribution during that period was the discovery of hafnium (10e).

In the winter of 1926–7 Hevesy moved to Freiburg in Breisgau to assume a professorship at the university. This period lasted till 1934. Scientifically it was a relatively quiet time which he does not mention at all in his autobiographical essay.[41] He left Freiburg because of his disgust with the Nazi regime.

Hevesy was of Jewish descent from both parents' side. His mother's father was the first non-converted Jew to become a Magyar nobleman. His own father was ennobled in 1895. His family converted; Hevesy was educated in a Catholic monastic school in Budapest.[36] As a Hungarian he was at first not directly affected by the laws of 1933 but some of his co-workers were. Once again Hevesy went to see Bohr who offered him to come and work in Copenhagen. Hevesy once again accepted. In August 1933 he wrote to Paneth: 'Most people do not grow any more when they have reached the age of forty [but Bohr's] fantastic personality develops more and more . . . If one has the chance to live near to such a unique person one should not live somewhere else.'[42] In July 1934 he resigned from Freiburg. In October he and his family were back in Copenhagen where Bohr had arranged a visiting professorship for him.

The funds which Bohr had secured for Franck and Hevesy were mainly provided by the Rockefeller foundation's emergency program. In October 1933 he and Brønsted, the professor in physical chemistry, had written to the foundation's Paris office: 'We herewith allow us to apply to the Rockefeller foundation for a support which will enable us to connect Professor James Franck and Professor Georg von Hevesy from Freiburg with the institutes of theoretical physics and of physical chemistry at the University of Copenhagen as research professors for a period of three years . . . By help of a grant from the Rask–Ørsted Foundation and from a private Danish committee we reckon to dispose [in addition] of a total sum of 30000 Danish Kr which will allow to contribute 5000 Kr per year to each of the named scientists for the first three years . . . We allow us to apply to the Rockefeller foundation for a grant of $12000 to be paid in 3 rates [i.e. installments] . . .'[43] The request was granted.

Franck stayed in Copenhagen for not much more than a year. During that time he produced two papers[44] on the fluorescence of chlorophyl, in collaboration with Levi who had come from Germany as a fresh Ph.D. in experimental molecular spectroscopy. He also tried his hand at experimental nuclear physics, but without much success. In 1935 he left for the US having accepted a professorship at the Johns Hopkins University in Baltimore. In 1938 he moved on to the University of Chicago. These were, of course, tenured positions, a stability that must have appeared preferable to Franck compared with the temporary arrangement in Denmark. There is, however, at least one other reason why he left: then, as later, he had the greatest love and admiration for Bohr, yet he felt uncomfortable working in his vicinity:

Bohr was so superior that some people had difficulties with him, which I never understood. Never is not right. Which I understood only after Hitler came to power, and I was for one and a half years in [his] laboratory. Bohr did not allow me to think through whatever I did to the end. I made some experiments. And when I told Bohr about it, then he said immediately what might be wrong, what might be right. And it was so quick that after a time I felt that I am unable to think at all . . . Bohr's genius was so superior. And one cannot help that one would get so strong inferiority complexes in the presence of such a genius that one becomes sterile. You see? Therefore, I would like to say no one fitted really in that circle the whole time. But to be there for a time and to learn and to see this man and to understand the greatness of him and the goodness. He is really something.[44a]

Hevesy had no such compunction. He stayed on in Copenhagen until late 1943. We shall see presently what kept him busy during those years.

(f) The discovery of induced radioactivity

For nearly forty years after its first observation radioactivity remained a property of some thirty substances existing in nature, nearly all of them isotopes of lead or even heavier elements. After Rutherford's discovery of the nucleus, it was evident that radioactive processes are a particular class of spontaneous transmutations of nuclei. That class was vastly enlarged with the discovery of induced, also called artificial, radioactive processes, first observed in Paris by Marie Curie's daughter Irène and her husband Frédéric Joliot. Their discovery was made possible by Marie's gift of the world's strongest source of α-particles, produced in the decay of polonium, an element she had discovered and named after her native country.

In July 1933 the Joliot-Curies reported[45] that α-irradiation of aluminium

(Al) and boron (B) led in each case to two kinds of reactions:*

$$_2^4He + _{13}^{27}Al \rightarrow _{14}^{30}Si + p \quad \text{or} \quad \rightarrow _{14}^{30}Si + n + e^+,$$

$$_2^4He + _5^{10}B \rightarrow _6^{13}C + p \quad \text{or} \quad \rightarrow _6^{13}C + n + e^+.$$

In October 1933 they interpreted the second reaction in either case to be due to the disintegration of a proton: 'The transmutation with emission of a proton can sometimes lead to the latter's dissociation [into a neutron and a positron].'[46] Then, between October 1933 and January 1934, they made a great discovery. All nuclear reactions known till then had been instantaneous, but when an aluminium foil is irradiated by α-particles the emission of positrons does not cease immediately after the α-particle source is removed. Rather it continues, dropping off with a characteristic half-life (of about 3 minutes): 'These experiments demonstrate the existence of *a new kind of radioactivity* [my italics],'[47] β^+-decay, the counterpart of the long-familiar electron emission. Accordingly they abandoned their previous interpretation in favor of

$$_2^4He + _{13}^{27}Al \rightarrow _{15}^{30}P + n \quad \text{followed by} \quad _{15}^{30}P \rightarrow _{14}^{30}Si + e^+,$$

$$_2^4He + _5^{10}B \rightarrow _7^{13}N + n \quad \text{followed by} \quad _7^{13}N \rightarrow _6^{13}C + e^+.$$

That is to say, they had produced a hitherto unknown unstable isotope of phosphorus (P) and of nitrogen (N) which exhibit *induced radioactivity*. They were also able to detect[48] these new isotopes directly by radiochemical means – which is why in 1935 they received the Nobel Prize for chemistry (that year's physics prize went to Chadwick for the neutron).

The scene now moves from Paris to Rome. Fermi and his group there did not have a strong α-source – but they had neutrons. Their neutron intensity could not compare with that of the α-particle source in Paris – but neutrons are more effective than α-particles in penetrating nuclei and reacting with them. Already in March 1934 Fermi could announce induced radioactivity in fluorine and aluminium.[49] 'In rapid succession, 40 of the 60 elements the [Fermi] group irradiated revealed the existence of at least one new isotope. A new one was found every few days.'[50] With this work the Fermi group established Rome as one of the world's leading nuclear physics centers of the period.

We have now gathered the ingredients that caused experimental physics and experimental biology to flourish in Copenhagen in the 1930s.

(g) Four fateful factors fit

As noted earlier (15a), in the 1930s Bohr made three major contributions to

---

* Si = silicon, C = carbon, p = proton, n = neutron, e$^+$ = positron. They did not include neutrinos; these were not yet in vogue.

nuclear physics. He developed a new theory of nuclear reactions (15f). He steered the experimental program at his institute toward nuclear physics. And he made important contributions to the theory of nuclear fission. The remainder of this chapter is devoted to the second of these items. The preceding sections contain the materials concerning the four factors that jointly led to these new experimental developments.

The German catastrophe had caused a considerable number of physicists to come to Bohr (17d). His old friend Hevesy was one of the senior people who did so (17d). Induced radioactivity had been discovered shortly before his arrival. As we shall see, this advance enabled him, while in Denmark, to become the first to introduce the isotopic tracer methods in biology. Weaver's emphasis on biology (17c) made it possible for Bohr to obtain support for Hevesy's work. The new accelerators (17b) could produce the necessary artificially radioactive isotopes in amounts far exceeding anything possible earlier.

Bohr went after support from a variety of organizations for the construction of these new machines. Their purpose was not by any means confined to helping along a program in experimental biology, however. Bohr also had very much in mind that experimental nuclear physics should actively be pursued for its own sake.

All these various objectives given direction by Bohr, in physics, in biology, in fund raising, in machine construction, form a complex pattern of activities that evolved simultaneously. For ease of presentation I have chosen to treat these developments one by one. I begin with Hevesy and biology.

(h) How Hevesy introduced isotopic tracers in biology

Hevesy has recalled how his invention of the tracer method goes back to an event that occurred during his Manchester days (7b) with Rutherford. 'When I was in Manchester, Rutherford was much interested to come into the possession of a strong radium D sample. Large amounts of radium D were stored in the laboratory, but imbedded in huge amounts of lead . . . One day I met Rutherford in the basement of the laboratory where the lead chloride was stored. He addressed me by saying: "My boy, if you are worth your salt, you separate radium D from all that nuisance of lead." Being a young man I was an optimist and felt sure that I should succeed in my task . . . The result of my efforts was entire failure.'[41] No wonder. Radium D (RaD) is a radioactive isotope ($^{210}_{82}$Pb) of lead, a substance the bulk of which is inactive $^{207}_{82}$Pb – and isotopes cannot be separated by physical and chemical means (at least could not in those days), a fact that evidently was not yet clear at that time.

His negative result gave Hevesy the best idea he probably had in his whole life. 'And then I thought, if I put in such a lot of work, then I will have some pleasure and go the opposite way and take a milligram of lead nitrate and add some pure RaD and label it [that is, the lead nitrate], and follow with the aid of rate of measurements the pass of lead atoms through chemical reactions.'[51] In other words, since RaD and 'ordinary' lead are inseparable, then if you add a known amount of RaD to a known amount of lead you can determine how far and how fast lead salts move about in physico-chemical processes by measuring RaD radioactivity!

How to get sufficient pure RaD for observations? That was not too difficult. Radium decays into a gas, radon ($^{222}_{86}$Rn), which can be pumped off and enclosed in glass capillaries. These were an important tool in cancer therapy, since radon itself is radioactive – decaying into RaD! Thus 'old' radon sources were just what Hevesy needed, and he knew where most of these were found: in the Vienna radium institute. And that is why (17e) he got in touch with Paneth, who worked at that institution.

There, to his surprise, he learned that Paneth, too, had been trying in vain to separate RaD from lead. Hevesy suggested that the two collaborate on an experimental application of his labeling idea to studies of the solubility of certain lead salts. In their resulting joint paper[52] they state:

If one mixes the RaD with lead or lead salts, the former cannot be separated from the latter by any chemical or physical methods . . . Since RaD, as a result of its activity, can be detected in incomparably smaller amounts than lead, it can thus serve as a qualitative and quantitative proof of [the presence of] lead to which it is attached: *RaD becomes an indicator of lead* [my italics].[53]

These lines mark the beginning of the indicator technique. For many years Hevesy would use the term 'indicator'. Today we speak instead of 'tracers', a term which came in use after World War II and which I shall use in what follows (except for quotations).

A decade passed before Hevesy, then in Copenhagen, resumed his tracer work. 'In about 1922, while working on the chemistry of hafnium, I got interested in problems of botanics and tried to follow the path of lead in bean seedlings by using labeled lead.'[51] Using RaD and thorium B, a bismuth isotope ($^{212}_{83}$Bi), as tracers he also studied[54] the uptake as well as the loss of these elements, *the first application anywhere of tracers in the life sciences.* Shortly afterward dermatologists became interested in replacing arsenic by bismuth in syphilis therapy. This led Hevesy to tracer research (1924)[55] on the resorption, distribution,and excretion of labeled bismuth compounds administered to rats, *the first use of tracers in the study of animal metabolism.* Applications of this type were severely restricted, however, by the toxicity of the injected compound.

Another decade's pause followed in Hevesy's focus on tracer work. In the meantime he continued other researches, especially on rare earths, another of his favorite topics. His next involvement with tracers was the result of Harold Urey's discovery (at Columbia University) of deuterium (D), an isotope of hydrogen about twice as heavy as the proton. 'I approached Urey,* and he sent me a few liters of water containing half a percent of heavy water [D₂O]. Now half a percent is not very much, but it sufficed to place goldfish in this water and to study the interchange between water molecules of goldfish in the surrounding water.[56] . . . We determined also our own body water contents. It is quite easy to do: If you administer a known volume of water, of known heavy water content, wait for an hour or so for this water to distribute in the body, and then produce – for example from a blood sample – some water and determine its density, from this data you can determine how large is the total body water content which contributed to the dilution of the administered heavy water. In our case it was 67 percent for lean persons.'[51] It was also determined how long, on the average, water molecules stayed in the human body.[57]

These investigations, with a non-radioactive substance of low toxicity, were limited by the low concentration of heavy water. Also, 'deuterium is not an ideal indicator, its properties differing appreciably from those of hydrogen, and it must be used with discretion, a fact which, however, did not prevent the attainment of most important results with this tracer element.'[58]

After 1934 Hevesy left deuterium studies largely[59] to others.[60] Early in 1935, he resumed his researches, in Denmark. That was a year after the discovery of induced radioactivity.

In 1948 Hevesy wrote: 'During our early work with "natural" radioisotopes as indicators, we often mentioned what an attractive place that Fairyland must be where radioactive isotopes of all elements are available. This utopia became reality almost with a single stroke, when the Joliot-Curies made their most important discovery of artificial radioactivity. The path was thus paved for investigation of the fate of the atoms of the common constituents of the animal and plant organisms.'[58] His first important work in this Copenhagen period was not in biology, however, but in pure physics. In that project he was ably assisted by Hilde Levi, who, on Bohr's advice, had joined Hevesy after Franck had left. Fifty years later she would write[36] the finest biography of Hevesy, full of insight not only into his oeuvre but also into his personality.

The two of them began a systematic study of radioactivity induced in rare earth elements, Hevesy's favorite toys. A year went by before it dawned on them that one can use the variations in induced radioactivity from element to element for the purpose of detecting traces of one rare earth element

* Hevesy was very friendly with Urey since 1923, when both men had worked in Copenhagen.

admixed to another. Since they had discovered that dysprosium shows by far the strongest activity in this group, their natural first choice was to detect traces of dysprosium, present in an yttrium sample. 'The yttrium sample to be investigated was activated under exactly the same condition [of previous exposure of dysprosium to neutrons] and a comparison of the dysprosium activities obtained gave 1% as the dysprosium content.'[61] Since the 1950s this procedure goes by the name neutron activation analysis. It is widely applied today, in radiochemistry, chemical technology, studies of environmental contaminations, and elsewhere.

The Hevesy–Levi collaboration was greatly helped by the presence of Otto Frisch, the institute's great gadgeteer at that time, who taught Levi how to construct amplifiers as well as thin-windowed Geiger counters that could detect low-energy β-rays.[62] According to Hilde Levi, after they had built one of their first counters Frisch invited Bohr to have a look. Bohr came in, picked up the counter, and it imploded. 'Bohr was crushed – we laughed. It was no tragedy.' *

While this work was going on Hevesy had already turned his attention to biological applications of artificially produced radioisotopes.

At that time, 'he knew fundamentally very little about the biological and medical fields. He wanted to apply this method . . . he became more and more of a biologist and maybe within later years, as a matter of fact, first really knew what he was talking about.'[64]

It was Hevesy's good luck to find enormous support from August Krogh, Copenhagen's outstanding physiologist, a Nobel laureate since 1920. 'In a written statement, in 1934, Krogh . . . a man of unusual vision . . . drew the attention of the Copenhagen scientists . . . to the importance of the tracer methods . . . which he took up at once after Hevesy's arrival in Copenhagen.' ** One of Hevesy's first biological papers[59] was written together with Krogh.

Hevesy was 50 years old in 1935 when he turned his attention to applications of induced radioactivity. That year marks the beginning of the most important phase in his scientific career. From then on he very rarely published anything in physics; nearly all his further oeuvre, over 200 papers, deal with tracers in biology. That work was more influential than anything he had done before. I mention a few highlights.

First there was the question which artificially radioactive isotope to select that is biologically interesting and that has a suitable life time. The only choice was phosphorus-32 ($^{32}_{15}$P) which has the useful life time of 14 days.

---

* Frisch has told this story somewhat differently.[63] According to Levi, Frisch's recollections are not always reliable.

** Here I quote from Hevesy's obituary published by Cockcroft. Levi has told me that this document was actually written by Hevesy himself, Cockcroft only changed 'I' to 'he'; and that she prepared the Hevesy bibliography used by Cockcroft.[52]

According to Hevesy, as told in a lecture[51]: 'We took ten liters of carbon disulfide, put in the center of these the neutron source, and after a lapse of ten days or so we could [extract] . . . carrier free ^{32}P',* Its first use was described in a joint paper[65] with Bohr's old friend Chievitz, the professor of surgery, 'a most kind man of great character who put at Hevesy's disposal his technician who was in charge of rearing and dissecting mice'.[52] This paper dealt with a 'renewal problem': are the constituents of some parts of a biological system renewed or are they permanently present during a lifetime? The first experiments, on rats, showed that replacement of phosphorus of bone takes place incessantly, and that one-third of the phosphorus in the skeleton is replaced during life. In subsequent years Hevesy was to study renewal and exchange processes in other animals and other organs, from cell division to mature tissue, from the brain to the liver, from blood to teeth, in healthy and in cancerous tissue. Problems of plant growth were also examined.[66] Experiments of these types were soon performed in many places in Copenhagen. In 1938 an international 'physico-biological' conference was held in Copenhagen, the first one of its kind, focusing on applications of tracer techniques. By the early 1940s results were available on the formation of specific compounds like DNA and RNA; again Hevesy was among the pioneers.[67]

In the early days a main problem was to obtain sufficient quantities of ^{32}P. Hevesy, always enterprising and full of ideas hit upon the thought of remedying this shortage by arranging for a gift to Bohr of an amount of radium that could be used to produce a 'permanent' strong neutron source. He discussed this project with others who contacted Danish institutions with requests for contributions. So it came about that on 7 October 1935, Bohr's 50th birthday, he was handed a printed letter[68] signed by seven industrial concerns and ten foundations which read in part: 'A group of Danish businesses and foundations beg leave to express to you their high esteem and deep admiration on the occasion of your 50th birthday . . . We believe it could be of great importance for your and your institute's work if we could make available a large amount of radium . . . We beg you to accept today a pledge for 100000 Kr for the acquisition of radium for your institute . . .' And so Bohr could order 600 mg of radium,[69] which was ready for experimental use by the summer of 1936.[70] As to the birthday, it was celebrated in style with speeches in the morning in the institute's main lecture room and a great banquet in the evening in the Æresbolig. 'There were so many speeches . . . that dinner advanced exceedingly slowly . . . and it went on till eleven,'[71]

---

* Hilde Levi has counseled me to beware of Hevesy's recollections which occasionally are sloppy and incorrect. For example, in this case active phosphorus obtained was not carrier-free but extracted with non-active phosphorus – the amounts of active material were far too small to do otherwise.

Meanwhile Bohr was already on the warpath to arrange for the construction of accelerators, a main reason being that these could produce radioactive isotopes with activities much higher than available before, an evident great help for Hevesy's work (see the next two sections). In Berkeley, Lawrence and his people were, of course, far ahead in this respect. At Hevesy's request Lawrence generously sent him a few milligrams of active phosphate. According to Hevesy: 'This was sent in air mail letters. You couldn't see anything extraordinary in the letters, only the paper in which these active sodium phosphates were wrapped was brittle, pulverized: radiation produces ozone, and ozone attacks the paper, but otherwise nothing to see. I was fully convinced it hadn't done any harm to any passenger on the plane. But if you would today send an air-mail letter with a few milligrams of active phosphorus, this would be almost a capital offense'[51] – a wonderful but inaccurate tale. The paper would not get brittle; the tiny amount of active material sent would still not cause offense.

Hevesy certainly added to the life of Copenhagen. There is the story of the radioactive cat that had jumped out of a window of the institute for theoretical physics and was retrieved only after hours of hunting for it in the nearby park, when saliva tests on about a dozen captured cats showed one of them to be radioactive.[72] There are stories of his activities in other institutions. 'He made experiments on plants at the Carlsberg laboratory, on muscle at the physiology department, on teeth at the school of dentistry, and on membrane permeability with Krogh [at the laboratory of zoophysiology].'[70] The routine was: produce ^{32}P at Bohr's institute, take it to some other institute for biological experiments, then bring the samples back to the Bohr institute for analysis.

In the course of time Hevesy's widening field of operations could no longer fit into a physics institute. 'We had rats and we had cats and we had all sorts of strange things that didn't belong in the Bohr institute at all.'[64]

In the beginning of October 1943 Bohr escaped to Sweden by boat (see (21c)). In mid-October 1943 Hevesy too appeared in Stockholm. He had simply traveled by train on his Hungarian passport, and was eventually followed by his family.[73] 'Already before he left there was a feeling both in Hevesy and in Bohr and I have no doubt they talked about that even already at that time, that it was a little bit absurd and sort of out of place, that Hevesy tried to maintain a group working in biological work in an environment that was so utterly unbiological as the Bohr institute.'[64]

In 1944 Hevesy was awarded the 1943 Nobel Prize for chemistry 'for his work on the use of isotopes as tracers in the study of chemical processes'. Every laureate has the option of becoming a Swedish citizen – which Hevesy did. For personal and professional reasons he stayed on in Stockholm but commuted frequently to Copenhagen.[74]

After World War II the biological work moved from Bohr's to Krogh's institute. Hilde Levi obtained a position there which she held until her retirement in 1979. Now she is one of the principal figures at the Niels Bohr Archive.

In the post-war period the development of nuclear reactors provided for vastly enlarged production of radioisotopes. This in turn made possible much wider application of the tracer method in medicine. In hospitals all over the world one now finds special departments for nuclear medicine, a discipline which unquestionably was founded by Hevesy. Also from that period dates the use of numerous biological tracers with half-lives much longer than that of the popular ^{32}P, notably the carbon isotope $^{14}_{6}C$, discovered in 1940.[75]

In 1957 Bohr had received the first Atoms for Peace Award. In 1958 Hevesy became the second to be so honored. In his acceptance speech Hevesy said: 'I had the great privilege of working in the Copenhagen institute which was and is under the direction of Niels Bohr to whom I'm immensely indebted for an almost lifelong friendship and also for much help and encouragement.'[76]

After Bohr's death in 1962 Hevesy wrote to a friend: 'The shocking news of the death of Niels Bohr reached me this morning. What a loss. Centuries may elapse until a man like him will be born. The world became much poorer, very much poorer, by his death.'[77]

On 5 July 1966 Hevesy died of lung cancer.

(i) Bohr as fund raiser (continued)

We have met Bohr already twice as fund raiser, in the mid-1920s (12d), and in the early 1930s, in his efforts to help refugees from Germany (17d, e). We shall now encounter him again in this capacity as he goes after funds for construction, equipment, and operating expenses for the experimental program in the 1930s.[78] This time he pulled out all the stops.

Weaver first met Bohr in 1932 in Copenhagen, shortly after his appointment to division director (17c), when he went on a fact-finding trip to Europe, his first voyage overseas.[79] In May 1933 Bohr met Mason, this time in New York (18b). On that occasion Bohr suggested to attract to his institute 'able and thoroughly trained young men in mathematics, physics, and chemistry who under [his] direction turn their attention to some quantitative phase of important biological problems.'[80] That was before the discovery of induced radioactivity and Hevesy's return to Copenhagen. I could imagine that Bohr's mention of biology at that time was due both to his awareness of the Rockefeller foundation's new emphasis on biology and to his own interest in foundational biological questions (see (19d)). At any rate these first encounters with the foundation did not at once lead to concrete proposals from Bohr's side.

The next contact with the Rockefeller foundation occurred in April 1934 when two officials from its Paris office visited Bohr in Copenhagen. 'The conversation began in Bohr's institute, was continued the following evening at B.'s home, where Franck, Hevesy, Harald Bohr, and Pauli joined in . . . As a result of W.W.'s talk with B. about a year ago, he has apparently developed an active interest in biology, aided undoubtedly by the ramifications involved in the purification of the German race . . . B. worked up a very real enthusiasm but it was based on a very meagre knowledge of biology.'[81] Again, no specific proposals were made, yet Weaver was intrigued: 'The Bohr situation seems to me a most interesting one. It is undoubtedly true that some of the old line conservatives would consider the proposed development somewhat askance. On the other hand B.'s outstanding position will probably protect us from anything that would reach embarrassment. I think that we ought to adopt a pretty generous and broadminded attitude.'[82] Once again Bohr's prestige made itself felt.

By October 1934, when Franck and Hevesy had settled in Copenhagen, Bohr came forth for the first time with more concrete suggestions:

'N. Bohr and I discussed again the direction his thinking had taken since my talk with him in April on the possibilities of bringing physics or theoretical physics disciplines into biology. At that time Bohr's interests were mainly on the philosophical side, but in recent months he has come to feel that it may be possible to do more effective work at the present time in connection with definite problems. Due to the presence of von Hevesy in Copenhagen, Bohr has decided to undertake a cooperative problem with Krogh, von Hevesy, and himself . . . B. has decided to install high-tension equipment for the production of artificially stimulated radioactivity. With the elements so made radio-active, Krogh, von Hevesy, and Bohr are to enter upon the cooperative problem of the identification of the processes with which these elements are concerned.'[83] This is the earliest reference I have seen to Bohr's intent of having accelerator equipment in Copenhagen, specifically a Cockcroft–Walton.

In the year 1935 Bohr went into high gear.

January 1935. First reference[84] to the use of phosphorus-32. Also in that month Bohr applied to the Carlsberg foundation for a grant of 150000 Kr* to finance a high-voltage laboratory, noting the gradual shift from atomic to nuclear physics. Thus his motivation here was physics rather than biology. Acceptance of the proposal followed within weeks.[85]

February 1935. Bohr writes to the Rockefeller foundation, mentioning his

* At that time the exchange rate was about 5 Kr to the dollar.

Carlsberg grant and requesting support for yet another accelerator, a cyclotron.

'[Artificial radioactivity] has given [the] indicator method an almost unlimited range of application in biological research. Also deuterium gives ways to study circulation of water in organisms, studies on which Hevesy and Krogh are at present actively engaged.

'Our present plan is before all to follow up the great possibilities which the artificial radioactive indicators have opened for the cooperation between physicists and biologists.

'The discussion of the particulars of our plans which Hevesy and I have had in these days has convinced us . . . that the rate of progress in the physico-biological work would be much promoted if we beside high-tension generators . . . could also acquire a generator for multiple acceleration of the type designed by Professor Lawrence . . . To put our endeavor on a stable basis . . . it would be of the greatest importance if a . . . support . . . of $6000 per year . . . could be granted to us for 5 years.'[86]

The foundation contacted Hevesy. Where was the concrete biology motivation? Not to worry, Hevesy replied: 'This project . . . is in no wise an attempt on Bohr's part . . . to in any way compete with the Rutherfords, the Lawrences, and others who are working in the field of pure physics.'[87]

March 1935. Bohr applies[88] to the Nordic Insulin foundation for a grant of 15000 Kr 'for research in atomic physics in preparation for physiological experiments'. Granted. (The same foundation made another contribution[89] in July 1939.)

April 1935. Bohr receives word[90] from the Rockefeller foundation that favorable action is forthcoming. This was the first big money for his enterprises. The grant was divided[91] in four parts, each amount to be given annually for five years: $15000 for high-voltage equipment; 14000 Kr to provide assistants to Bohr and Hevesy; 14000 Kr for materials and equipment; and 3000 Kr for material and equipment for Krogh.

May 1935. Bohr to Rutherford: 'We are very busy here with our plans for a high tension laboratory.'[92] He is now 'so full of enthusiasm for the plans of physico-biological research that he can talk of nothing else. He says that he anticipates that in three years he will be giving all of his time to this work'.[93] Also in May Bohr requests[94] from the Carlsberg foundation 12000 Kr per annum for five years as salary for Hevesy. Granted.

August 1935. In 1934 Thomas Thrige and his wife had established a foundation with capital provided from the assets of his electrical manufacturing company, the largest of its kind in Denmark. Bohr applies to this foundation for an electromagnet 'for use in atomic research'.[95] The request is granted. A 40 ton magnet is produced at the Thrige factories and paid for by the foundation (44435.27 Kr). Bohr continued to tap this source for the rest of his life. In the foundation's archives donations between 1936–61 are recorded amounting to about 1710000 Kr. The same foundation also continued to make grants to the institute after Bohr's death.

October 1935. The radium gift mentioned in the preceding section, not Bohr's but Hevesy's high gear.

September 1936. Bohr applies to the Carlsberg foundation for 60000 Kr, for investigations of nuclear reactions. 'Most recently the so-called cyclotron constructed by Professor Lawrence has created a new supplementary tool . . . which can be anticipated to be of the greatest significance for demonstrating and extending the theoretical concepts about the mechanism of nuclear reactions which I have developed in the past year.' The reference to theoretical concepts concerns of course Bohr's own work of early 1936 (15f). The request is granted.

1937. From the Rockefeller foundation's Annual Report of that year: 'The University of Copenhagen is to receive $12500, payable during the two years beginning September 1, 1937, toward the construction and testing of a cyclotron.'[96] Weaver's comment on this grant: 'The position of Bohr in the scientific world is such that I think we would be entirely justified in considering this $12000 even if it were wholly outside of our program. Indeed I think this is the one place in the world where we would perhaps be willing to make an exception for support in pure atomic physics.'[97]

1938. In 1935 Bohr had been elected president of the *Landsforening til Kræftens Bekæmpelse* (National Association for Combatting Cancer). In 1938 he applied[98] to this association for 20000 Kr to be used for the Cockcroft–Walton, the specific purpose being exposure of cancerous tissue in humans to energetic X-rays. The request was granted. Documents in the Bohr Archive show that this association contributed an additional about 50000 Kr between 1939 and 1944.

1940. Bohr applies[99] to the Carlsberg foundation for 40000 Kr toward the construction of a Van de Graaff. Granted.

The preceding account is meant to give a picture of the range of Bohr's fund raising activities. No claim to completeness can be made, for example I have not tried to follow the various subventions by the Danish State. Bohr played the game in a manner familiar to all who have been involved with funding applications: go for the 'bread and butter', that is, give the motivation most appealing to the funding agency, and which shows reasonable prospects of some positive outcome, but do not hesitate to actually use some of the moneys also for other responsible purposes.

Bohr was of course first and foremost a physicist. One may therefore wonder how genuine his concern for biology was. In 1989 I asked Hilde Levi how Bohr responded to the biological work with tracers. She replied: 'He was exceedingly fascinated, electrified. That was an honest reaction – not one for the money.'

To conclude this section I record the action of the Rockefeller foundation in later years, as gleaned from their annual reports.

1940. 'The [cyclotron], completed in the fall of 1939, has assured quantity production of atoms tagged with high energy radiation for use in a number of studies which form part of a closely integrated research program. The foundation continued aid to the cooperating group during the past year by a grant of $8400.'[100]

1945. 'During the first three years of enemy occupation of Denmark, the program at the Institute was not interfered with ... After it became impossible for the Foundation to send funds to Denmark under its latest grant, the Carlsberg Foundation of Copenhagen advanced money at the approximate rate of 30000 Kr a year. The Rockefeller Foundation in 1945 appropriated $38400 to repay the Carlsberg Foundation for the advances made in support of the program in biophysics during the war.'[101]

1947. A grant of $17000 'specifically in biophysics ...'[102]

1949. 'The University of Copenhagen is building a new Institute of Nerve and Muscle Physiology, with one floor devoted to biomedical isotope teaching and research. Plans have also been made to add a full course of isotope techniques to the university curriculum.* The project had had Rockefeller foundation support since 1935. Aid was continued in 1949 with a two-year grant of $17000.'[103]

1951. 'This year's grant of $32000 from the Foundation is a tapering one for a period of five years and is intended as terminal support for a project which has shown its ability to function independently.'[104]

(j) Denmark's first accelerators and the fifth fateful factor

Nuclear physics experiments of high quality were being performed in Copenhagen well before the arrival of accelerators.

As has been indicated earlier (15d), certain types of precision data on atomic and molecular spectra contain information on atomic nuclei. One such category is the so-called hyperfine splitting of spectral lines, an effect due to the interaction between electron and nuclear magnetic moments. Experiments of this kind, which yield information on the magnitude of the spin of some or other nuclear species, had been performed[105] in Copenhagen in the mid-1930s, notably by the Danish physicist Ebbe Rasmussen.[106] At that time there was also in operation a budding experimental nuclear physics group led by Jacob Christian Jacobsen, who since the 1920s had been active in research on interactions of α-particles with matter and on radioactive lifetime determinations. (In 1941 Jacobsen became professor of experimental physics in Copenhagen.)

---

* This was Hilde Levi's initiative; she also did much of the teaching.

Also from that time date the first Danish experiments on nuclei themselves, not yet with accelerators but with tools of earlier vintage. As Hevesy had already done twenty years earlier (17h), physicists at Bohr's institute acquired old radon tubes, from Copenhagen's Radium Institute and Finsen Hospital. Frisch used their α-particles to discover new isotopes.[107] Mixing radon with beryllium one produces neutrons. He and co-workers used neutrons from a radon–beryllium source in a series of studies of absorption by various substances.[108] For neutron absorption in gold they could use (as Frisch has it) 'several Nobel Prize medals which some of Bohr's friends had left with him for safe keeping when the Nazis came to power. It was a source of great satisfaction to us that those otherwise useless medals should thus be employed for scientific purposes.'[109] Using the same radon–beryllium type source, the Dane Torkild Bjerge[110] made studies of induced radioactivity, discovering new unstable isotopes, notably[111] a rare species of helium ($^6_2$He). He also investigated[112] neutron processes by mixing beryllium with polonium.

Next came the much improved activities by means of the gift to Bohr of one-half gram of radium (17h). This new source was used by Frisch and collaborators, for instance in studies[113] of magnetic properties of the neutron. Incidentally, these were Frisch's last investigations prior to his work on fission (20a).[114]

As we have seen, by early 1935 Bohr had received grants for building both a high-tension generator and a cyclotron. He was now forced to create new space for these accelerators. In the fall of 1935 he wrote to Heisenberg about 'the rather significant extensions of the institute . . . especially in regard to a collaboration with the biological institutions.'[115] As was his wont he himself took active part in the architectural planning. Whether or not he once again overexerted himself, raising funds and planning buildings, he was not well in 1935. Bohr to Klein in August: 'I have in the last months suffered of rheumatism in the right shoulder which has bothered me rather much in my work. The doctors have urgently advised me to take a water cure in September in order to recover fully.'[116] Bohr to Rutherford in October: 'I have in the last year felt somewhat handicapped in my work by failing health, not only have I suffered rather severely from rheumatism, but during the summer I was unlucky to catch jaundice, of which we had quite an epidemic in the family, and afterwards, as one always does after that disease, I felt very tired and am not yet quite myself.'[117] No further such comments are found in the next few years, but in January 1938 Bohr wrote: 'I have been under much strain these past few months.'[118]

That was shortly before the inauguration of the new laboratory space, which took place on 5 April 1938. The date was chosen to commemorate the 25th anniversary of the day on which Bohr had completed his paper on the hydrogen atom, part I of his 1913 trilogy (8f). It was a busy day for him. During a festivity at the institute in the morning he gave a radio address to the English speaking world, on science and its international significance.[119] King Christian X honored him with the medal of merit 'in gold with crown', the highest Danish honor after the Order of the Elephant. Bohr and his colleagues led a number of distinguished visitors on a guided tour through the laboratory. Thereafter he gave his radio speech in the main auditorium in which he alluded to the difficult political times:

'The fruitful development that has occurred in science the world over is one of the most encouraging aspects of our civilization. We must hope that it will be possible to achieve equally peaceful and fertile conditions among countries in other domains.'

Whereupon, a newspaper wrote: 'The institute locks its doors again for publicity. One prefers to work unnoticed until results are available.'[120]

It was still a bit early for that, because in April 1938 none of the new accelerators was yet operational.

Design studies for the high-tension generator* had begun in 1935. Negotiations for the construction of key parts of the machine were taken up with an electrotechnical firm in Leipzig. Frisch was sent there to iron out a number of details. 'It gave me sardonic pleasure to be treated as an honored guest by the people who had sacked me under Hitler's race laws but who were willing to forget these laws when it was in their own financial interest.'[109]

Progress with the project was helped by the part-time presence of Charlie Lauritsen, the high-voltage specialist from Cal Tech (17b), who had become a prominent experimental nuclear physicist. I am not sure as to when Lauritsen first met Bohr but do know that in the early 1930s he and his family would visit the Bohrs in Denmark during several summer vacations.[121] In 1936 Lauritsen spent a number of months at the institute, assisting with the construction of various components of the high-tension apparatus. Several young Danes also participated, including Bjerge, Karl Brostrøm, and Jørgen Koch.[122]

'Erection of the building and installation of the generators took about two years . . . In the spring and summer of 1938 . . . the tube was set up and run for some time as an X-ray source in order to gain experience with the plant and, at the same time, to investigate its practicality as a therapeutically useful source of high voltage radiation.'[123]

In the fall of 1938 test work on accelerating deuterons was begun. In February 1939 this arrangement produced neutrons with energies of about one million electronvolts.

---

* Actually a variant of, not identical with, the Cockcroft–Walton design.

The construction of the cyclotron also began in 1935–6, under the direction of J. C. Jacobsen, 'an experimentalist of the old school ... who liked to build his own apparatus'.[124] The cyclotron equipment was largely built at Bohr's institute, with the exception of the Thrige magnet (17i) which upon arrival in Copenhagen from Odense caused a bit of commotion. 'When the magnet ... arrived we found that its largest piece was too big to go through the window into the room built for it, so a part of the wall had to be knocked out.'[109]* Among those in residence who assisted in the project was the Dane Niels Ove Lassen, who later would be in charge of the cyclotron's operations.[125]

In March 1937, when Bohr passed through Berkeley on his world tour, he had arranged with Lawrence that one of the latter's young men should come to Denmark to help with the construction of the cyclotron. Accordingly Jackson Laslett, 'a slim, bony, taciturn American',[109] arrived in Copenhagen in September 1937 for a stay that would last until November 1938. He used to "[spend] most of his time with his feet upon a table, his chair tilted back, and on his lap a drawing board on which he drew unperturbably one component after another of [the] cyclotron.'[126] In December 1937 Bohr wrote[127] to Lawrence: 'I can say that the whole laboratory every day has sent you thankful and admiring thoughts in connection with the work on the construction of the cyclotron in which we are most happy to have the invaluable help of Laslett. The work is going on quite well and we hope that the cyclotron will be working within a few months.'

That was a bit too optimistic. It was not until 1 November 1938 that the cyclotron produced a first weak beam of deuterons. On 11 November a four million electronvolt deuteron beam hitting a target produced an intense source of neutrons.[125] On that day Bohr cabled to Lawrence: 'Cyclotron working well stop whole institute wish express thanks and admiration.'[128] Four days later Bohr wrote Hevesy: 'The cyclotron is working and has already exceeded all expectations in that with one of the first attempts we obtained a neutron activity equivalent with a radium–beryllium source with one kilogram of radium.'[129] Be it remembered that the Copenhagen cyclotron ranks among the first in Europe, along with those at Cambridge, Leningrad, and Paris.[130]

In 1939 plans took shape for building a two million volt Van de Graaff. Its purpose was to make accessible the energy region between the high-tension machine (1 MeV) and the cyclotron (4 MeV). Brostrøm was put in charge of that project.[131] He was soon joined by a fresh Ph.D. from Cal Tech, Thomas Lauritsen, who together with Charles, his father, had just completed the construction of a Van de Graaff in Pasadena.[132] Tom knew the Bohrs from

* The Thrige firm also delivered the generator for the magnet current and several transformers, pumps, etc.

earlier family visits. Of Niels he has said: 'For [him] an experimental datum was the most precious thing in the world.' [121] His friend Aage Bohr has said: 'Tommy would ... always be at the center of activity. Whether in the laboratory or at a party, life around him would have a special quality because of his inexhaustible vitality and wit ... [He] launched our institute on a line of development that has continued to be of basic importance for nuclear research in Denmark.' [132] My own favorite story about Tom (I knew him and his father) concerns an occasion on which he had to fill out a security clearance form. One question was: Do you drink? With an answer to be chosen from: Never/Rarely/Occasionally/Frequently/To Excess. Tom marked off: Occasionally, and To Excess.

In early 1939 the political situation in Europe took another turn for the worse. It became increasingly risky for visitors from abroad to stay on at the Copenhagen institute. In July Frisch left for England. The war broke out on September 1. Tom Lauritsen stayed on till November 1940; he was the last foreign visitor to leave the institute. Construction of the Van de Graaff was still going on at that time. The machine was not used for scientific work until 1946.

This concludes an account of how accelerators came into being in Copenhagen. I have not yet discussed what kinds of physics was done with them. The early phase of those activities was dominated by a fifth fateful factor: the discovery of fission, first published in January 1939, just as two of the Copenhagen machines were ready to go. I shall come back in (20b) to the impact of this unexpected discovery on Danish physics.

References

1. F. Aaserud, *Redirecting science*, Cambridge University Press 1990; also *Physics Today*, October 1985, p. 38.
2. See IB, Chap. 2, section (a).
3. See IB, Chap. 4, section (d).
4. See especially E. M. McMillan in *Nuclear physics in restrospect*, p. 113, Ed. R. H. Stuewer, University of Minnesota Press, 1979.
5. For a biographical sketch of Lauritsen see W. A. Fowler, *Biogr. Mem. Nat. Acad. Sci.* **46**, 221, 1975.
6. C. C. Lauritsen and R. D. Bennett, *Phys. Rev.* **32**, 850, 1928.
7. J. L. Heilbron, R. W. Seidel, and B. R. Wheaton, *Lawrence Berkeley Laboratory News Magazine*, **6**, No. 3, 1981.
8. G. A. Ising, *Ark. Mat. Astr. och Fys.* **18**, No. 30, 1924.
9. R. Wideröe, *Arch. Elektrotechn.* **21**, 387, 1928.
10. M. S. Livingston, *Adv. Electronics Electron Phys.* **50**, 1, 1980.
11. E. O. Lawrence, in *Nobel lectures in physics 1942–62*, p. 430, Elsevier, New York 1967.

12. E. O. Lawrence and M. S. Livingston, *Phys. Rev.* **37**, 1707, 1931.
13. E. Rutherford, *Nature* **120**, 809, 1927; *Proc. Roy. Soc.* A **117**, 300, 1928.
14. See IB, p. 406.
15. R. A. Fowler, letter to N. Bohr, 13 May 1932, NBA.
16. For these early happenings see E. A. Burrill, *Physics Today* **20**, February 1967, p. 49.
17. R. Van de Graaff, *Phys. Rev.* **38**, 1919, 1931.
18. H. A. Barton *et al.*, *Phys. Rev.* **42**, 901, 1932.
19. M. Mason and W. Weaver, *The electromagnetic field*, University of Chicago Press 1929, Dover reprint, New York 1946.
20. R. B. Fosdick, *The story of the Rockefeller Foundation*, p. 137, Harper, New York 1952.
21. For these and more details about Weaver's life and career see W. Weaver, *Scene of change*, Scribner's, New York 1970.
22. Ref. 21, pp. 59, 60.
23. Ref. 20, pp. 157, 158.
24. For all these and many more details see S. Steffensen, *På flugt fra nazismen*, Reitzels Forlag, Copenhagen 1986.
25. A. D. Beyerchen, *Scientists under Hitler*, esp. p. 48, Yale University Press 1977.
26. C. Møller, interview by C. Weiner, 25 August 1974, NBA.
27. Ref. 24, p. 275.
28. S. Rozental, NBR p. 155.
29. Ref. 20, p. 276.
30. See also Ref. 1, Chap. 3.
31. Cf. IB, Chap. 8, sections (e) and (f), and Chap. 14, section (c).
32. O. Hahn, *Mein Leben*, p. 149, Bruckmann, Munich 1968.
33. See the biographical sketch by O. R. Frisch, *Biogr. Mem. Fell. Roy. Soc.* **16**, 405, 1970.
34. See the biographical sketch of Franck by H. G. Kuhn, *Biogr. Mem. Fell. Roy. Soc.* **11**, 53, 1965.
35. See Ref. 25, p. 15.
36. H. Levi, *George de Hevesy*, Rhodos, Copenhagen 1985.
37. G. von Hevesy, letter to N. Bohr, 25 October 1919, NBA.
37a. G. Palló, Periodica Technica, Budapest, **30**, 97, 1986.
38. G. von Hevesy, letter to F. Paneth, 27 November 1919, repr. in Ref. 36, p. 43.
39. G. von Hevesy, letter to E. Rutherford, 22 May 1921, NBA.
40. G. von Hevesy, letter to E. Rutherford, 26 May 1922, NBA.
41. G. von Hevesy, *Adventures in radioisotope research*, Vol. 1, p. 11, Pergamon, London 1962.
42. G. von Hevesy, letter to F. Paneth, 25 August 1933, repr. in Ref. 36, p. 71.
43. N. Bohr and J. N. Brønsted, letter to L. W. Jones, 11 October 1933, NBA.
44. J. Franck and H. Levi, *Zeitschr. Phys. Chem.* **27**, 409, 1935; *Nature* **23**, 229, 1935.
44a. J. Franck, interview by T. S. Kuhn, M. Mayer, and H. Sponer, 12 July 1962, NBA.
45. I. Curie and F. Joliot, *J. de Phys.* **4**, 494, 1933.

46. I. Curie and F. Joliot, *Proc. Seventh Solvay Conf.*, October 1933, p. 154, Gauthier-Villars, Paris 1934.

47. I. Curie and F. Joliot, *C. R. Acad. Sci. Paris*, **198**, 254, 1934; *Nature* **133**, 201, 1934.

48. I. Curie and F. Joliot, *C. R. Acad. Sci. Paris*, **198**, 559, 1934.

49. E. Fermi, *Ric. Scient.* **5**, 283, 1934, repr. in *E. Fermi's collected works*, Vol. 1, p. 645; English transl. *ibid.*, p. 674, University of Chicago Press.

50. G. Holton, *Minerva* **12**, 159, 1974.

51. G. von Hevesy, Radiation physics in the early days, unpublished MS of lecture before the Berkeley physics department, 23 May 1962, NBA.

52. J. D. Cockcroft, *Biogr. Mem. Fell. Roy. Soc.* **13**, 125, 1967; H. Levi, *Nucl. Phys. A* **98**, 1, 1967.

53. G. von Hevesy and F. Paneth, *Z. Anorg. Chem.* **82**, 223, 1913; also *ibid.* **82**, 322, 1913.

54. G. von Hevesy, *Biochem. J.* **17**, 439, 1929.

55. J. A. Christiansen, G. von Hevesy, and S. Lomholt, *C. R. Acad. Sci. Paris*, **178**, 1324; **179**, 291, 1924.

56. G. von Hevesy and E. Hofer, *Z. Physiol. Chem.* **225**, 28, 1934; *Nature* **133**, 495, 1934.

57. G. von Hevesy and E. Hofer, *Klin. Wschr.* **43**, 1524, 1934; *Nature* **133**, 879, 1934.

58. G. von Hevesy, *Cold Spring Harbor Symp. Quant. Biol.* **13**, 129, 1948.

59. See, however, G. von Hevesy, E. Hofer, and A. Krogh, *Scand. Arch. Physiol.* **72**, 199, 1935; G. von Hevesy and C. F. Jacobsen, *Acta Physiol. Scand.* **1**, 11, 1940.

60. Cf. G. von Hevsey, *Naturw.* **23**, 775, 1935.

61. G. von Hevesy and H. Levi, *Nature* **136**, 103, 1935; **137**, 185, 1936; *Kgl. Dansk. Vid. Selsk. Mat.-fys. Medd.* **14**, 5, 1936.

62. H. Levi, *Fysisk Tiddsskr.* **60**, 76, 1962.

63. O. R. Frisch, *What little I remember*, p. 86, Cambridge University Press 1979.

64. Hilde Levi, interview by C. Weiner, 28 October 1974, NBA.

65. O. Chiewitz and G. von Hevesy, *Nature* **136**, 754, 1935.

66. Ref. 36, p. 93.

67. L. Hahn and G. von Hevesy, *Nature* **145**, 549, 1940.

68. Copy in NBA.

69. Ref. 41, p. 26.

70. Ref. 36, p. 88.

71. Ref. 63, p. 98.

72. Ref. 36, p. 94.

73. Ref. 36, p. 100.

74. Ref. 36, pp. 101, 102.

75. S. Rubens and M. Kamen, *Phys. Rev.* **57**, 599, 1940.

76. G. von Hevesy, in *Proc. Atoms for Peace Awards 1957–1969*, MIT Press 1978.

77. G. von Hevesy, letter to C. Huggins, 17 November 1962, quoted in Ref. 36, p. 117.

78. See also Ref. 1, Chapter 4.

79. Ref. 21, p. 64ff.; N. Bohr, letter to W. Weaver, 13 April 1932, Rockefeller Archive Center.

80. W. Weaver, diary entry 10 July 1933, Rockefeller Archive Center.
81. Log on trip of W. E. Tisdale and D. P. O'Brien, entries 8–11 April 1934, copy in NBA.
82. W. Weaver, letter to W. E. Tisdale, 5 June 1934, copy in NBA.
83. W. E. Tisdale, diary entry 29 October 1934, copy in NBA.
84. H. M. Miller, diary entry 25 January 1935, Rockefeller Archive Center.
85. N. Bohr, letter to Carlsbergfondets Direktion, 26 January 1935, NBA.
86. N. Bohr, letter to W. E. Tisdale in Paris, 22 February 1935, copy in NBA.
87. W. E. Tisdale, letter to W. Weaver, 27 February 1935, Rockefeller Archive Center.
88. N. Bohr, letter to the Nordisk Insulinfond, 22 March 1935, NBA.
89. N. Bohr, letter to id., 7 July 1939, NBA.
90. W. E. Tisdale, cable to N. Bohr, 18 April 1935, NBA.
91. The Rockefeller Foundation, Annual Report, pp. 129, 130, 49 West 49th Street, New York.
92. N. Bohr, letter to E. Rutherford, 9 May 1935, NBA.
93. W. E. Tisdale, diary entry 24 May 1935, Rockefeller Archive Center.
94. N. Bohr, letter to the Carlsberg foundation, 8 May 1935.
95. N. Bohr, letter to the Thrige foundation, 19 August 1935, Thrige Foundation Archives.
96. Ref. 91, Report for 1937, p. 197.
97. W. Weaver, letter to W. E. Tisdale, 23 February 1937, copy in NBA.
98. N. Bohr, letter to the Landsforening, 5 October 1938, NBA.
99. N. Bohr, letter to the Carlsberg foundation, 30 September 1940, NBA.
100. Ref. 91, Report for 1940, p. 193.
101. Ref. 91, Report for 1945, p. 166.
102. Ref. 91, Report for 1947, p. 34.
103. Ref. 91, Report for 1949, p. 198.
104. Ref. 91, Report for 1951, p. 246.
105. For samples see E. Rasmussen, *Naturw.* **23**, 69, 1935; *Zeitschr. Phys.* **102**, 229, 1936; together with H. Kopfermann: *Naturw.* **22**, 291, 1934; *Zeitschr. Phys.* **98**, 624, 1936.
106. For biographical sketches see N. Bohr, *Fysisk Tidsskr.* **58**, 1, 1960; J. M. Lyshede, *ibid.*, p. 3.
107. O. R. Frisch, *Nature* **136**, 220, 1935.
108. O. R. Frisch and E. T. S. Sørensen, *Nature* **136**, 258, 1935; O. R. Frisch, G. von Hevesy, and H. A. C. McKay, *Nature* **137**, 149, 1936; O. R. Frisch and G. Placzek, *Nature* **137**, 357, 1936.
109. O. R. Frisch, NBR, p. 142.
110. For a biographical sketch see H. H. Jensen and F. Juul, *Fysisk Tidsskr.* **72**, 177, 1974.
111. T. Bjorge, *Nature* **138**, 400, 1936; **139**, 757, 1937.
112. T. Bjerge, *Proc. Roy. Soc.* A **164**, 243, 1938.
113. O. Frisch, H. von Halban, and J. Koch, *Nature* **139**, 1031, 1937; **140**, 360, 1937; *Phys. Rev.* **53**, 719, 1938.
114. For a biographical sketch and a bibliography of Frisch see R. Peierls, *Biogr. Mem. Fell. Roy. Soc.* **27**, 283, 1979.

115. N. Bohr, letters to W. Heisenberg, 5 September and 8 October 1935, NBA.
116. N. Bohr, letter to O. Klein, 9 August 1935, NBA.
117. N. Bohr, letter to E. Rutherford, 22 October 1935, NBA.
118. N. Bohr, letter to O. Klein, 19 January 1938, NBA.
119. N. Bohr, *Dan. Foreign J.* No. 208, p. 61, 1938.
120. *Politiken*, 6 April 1938.
121. T. Lauritsen, interview by B. Richman and C. Weiner, 16 February 1967, copy in Niels Bohr Library, New York.
122. For a biographical sketch of Brostrøm see T. Huus, *Fysisk Tidsskr.* **64**, 49, 1966.
123. T. Bjerge, K. J. Brostrøm, J. Koch, and T. Lauritsen, *Dansk. Vid. Selsk. Mat.-fys. Medd.* **18**, No. 4, 1940.
124. See the biographical sketches by N. O. Lassen, *Fysisk Tidsskr.* **63**, 145, 1965; *Nucl. Phys.* **85**, 1, 1966.
125. For the early history of the Copenhagen cyclotron see J. C. Jacobsen, *Dansk. Vid. Selsk. Mat.-fys. Medd.* **19**, No. 2, 1941; N. O. Lassen, *Fysisk Tidsskr.* **60**, 90, 1963.
126. Ref. 63, p. 106.
127. N. Bohr, letter to E. O. Lawrence, 20 December 1937, Lawrence papers, Bancroft Library, University of Calif. at Berkeley. Quoted by permission.
128. N. Bohr, cable to E. O. Lawrence, 11 November 1938. Copy in Bancroft Library. Quoted by permission.
129. N. Bohr, letter to G. von Hevesy, 15 November 1938, NBA.
130. Cf. J. L. Heilbron, *Rev. Stor. Sci.* **3**, 1, 1986.
131. For the early history of the Copenhagen Van de Graaff see K. J. Brostrøm, *Fysisk Tidsskr.* **53**, 255, 1955.
132. For a biographical sketch see W. A. Fowler and Fay Ajzenberg-Selove, *Biogr. Mem. Nat. Acad. Sci.* **55**, 385, 1985.

18

Of sad events and of major journeys

(a) Days of sorrow

The preceding three chapters have been devoted to Bohr's role in science in the 1930s. I now turn to more personal aspects of his life in that period. In broad terms, two facts stand out. In those years Bohr had to suffer the loss of several family members and close friends. Also, it was the decade during which he made more major journeys than before or after. I must begin with moments of deep sadness.

In the early morning hours of Sunday 30 November 1930 Niels' mother Ellen died. She had been suffering from cancer.

A newspaper obituary recalled[1] the cheerful and warm atmosphere of her home. How all who came in contact with her would grow fond of her. How she had friends among not only Danish but also foreign scientists who steadily came to Copenhagen to work with her sons. How in Göttingen she was referred to as *die Mutter* Bohr'. 'Her life was devoted to her daughter and her two sons and their children.'

Harald received the news in California, where he was guest lecturer at Stanford. In December Niels wrote to Heisenberg: 'A week ago we were greatly grieved to lose my mother, who preserved, in spite of illness and increasing frailty, to the very end her youth of mind and her warm interest in the younger and youngest in the family and in all our friends.'[2]

On 5 May 1933 Niels' sister Jenny died.

It has been mentioned (Chapter 3) that for many years she suffered from mental problems. Ellen's death caused Jenny to suffer some form of breakdown, whereupon she was placed in the mental hospital at Vordingborg, Oringe. It was there that her life came to an end.*

On that same 5 May Harald cabled or wrote to his brother Niels, who at that time was in the United States, on his way to Pasadena. Niels wrote back[4] to Harald – of Jenny's warm, inspiring disposition, and of the great relief that her death had been peaceful.

* The cause marked on the death certificate[3] is *psychosis manio depressiva in manitionem*, manic depression in the manic phase.

Harald spoke at the funeral, on 11 May. His words were profoundly moving. 'If Niels would have been home, it would for many reasons have been he who on behalf of the family would have spoken at Jenny's bier . . . In later years, not least after Mother's death, it was especially he to whom Jenny turned for support in difficult times . . . Now, at her death, we have had to reflect, as so often before, how much she could have meant and done, perhaps not only in narrower circles, if her health had been good. During nearly all her life, from her earliest youth on, she was hampered, often made powerless, by illness [which] took nearly all her strength.' Harald went on to recall how enthusiastically she began her university studies of history but had to give that up. How she went on to teach school but had to give that up also. How her ongoing search for a place in life tore at her. How in spite of everything her personality never broke nor changed, except for the last years so full of sorrow. How strong her ties had been to Niels and Margrethe. How their mother's mild yet strong personality had helped to keep her going, and how Ellen's death therefore had hit her more strongly than it had anyone else. How she had been full of love for others, and how 'she was strong in spite of her weaknesses, and healthy in spite of her illness'.*

On 25 September 1933 Niels' good friend Paul Ehrenfest committed suicide.
  Bohr's first contact with Ehrenfest had been by letter, in 1918.[5] '[Ehrenfest] and Bohr had much to talk about together – from the current problems of the quantum theory to the Icelandic sagas, from the stages of a child's development to the difference between genuine physicists and the others. Their exchanges ranged over heaven and earth as Ehrenfest showed his new friend the treasures of the Dutch museums and the brilliant colors of the bulb fields.'[6] After his return to Denmark Bohr wrote to Ehrenfest about 'my feeling of happiness over your friendship'.[7] Also in 1919 Ehrenfest had communicated at length with another good friend of his about Bohr's work. Einstein to Ehrenfest: 'You have shown me that there is a man [B.] of profound vision, one in whom great connections come alive.'[8]
  In 1921 Bohr could not attend the third Solvay conference, as originally planned, because he was overworked (9c). It was Ehrenfest who summarized Bohr's views at that meeting.[9] Later that year Bohr invited Ehrenfest to lecture in Copenhagen. Ehrenfest replied: 'Dear, dear Bohr, I would like so terribly much to be with you again.'[10] After his visit to Bohr in December 1921 – it was to be the first of many – Ehrenfest wrote to Einstein: 'I felt so happy in Bohr's house, happier than I have been for a long time.'[11] In 1922 he wrote to Kapitza that 'Bohr, Einstein, and Rutherford occupy the very first place among the physicists sent to us by God'.[11a]
  In December 1925 Ehrenfest arranged a personal meeting between Bohr

* I am grateful to Aage Bohr for letting me read a transcript of Harald's talk.

and Einstein in his home in Leiden (13e). Ehrenfest, deeply attached to both men, was much affected by the growing irreconcilable differences between them regarding the foundations of quantum physics. Once, in 1927, Ehrenfest, in tears, said that he had to make a choice between Bohr's and Einstein's position and that he could not but side with Bohr.[12]

Ehrenfest's attachment to Bohr explains why he would write to him in times he felt depressed. In May 1931 Bohr received a letter[13] from him that said in part: 'I have completely lost contact with theoretical physics. I cannot read anything any more and feel myself incompetent to have even the most modest grasp about what makes sense in the flood of articles and books. Perhaps I cannot at all be helped any more. Still I have the illusion that you could show me the way in a few days' encounter.'[13] In September he wrote[14] that he was too depressed to participate in conferences.

Ehrenfest was in his early fifties when he wrote those letters. It was a time when the outpour of papers on quantum mechanics made it difficult for him to pursue his relentless need for understanding the real point of an article or a lecture. *Was ist der Witz?* (What is the essence?) was one of his favorite questions.

It is not so uncommon that inability to keep up with developments causes depression. That, however, can explain only in part Ehrenfest's somber mood. All through life he had suffered from a sense of inadequacy, the high esteem in which he was held by the best of physicists notwithstanding. His personal life was troubled too. In particular he was heavily burdened by the fate of Wassik, one of his sons, who had serious mental or emotional problems (he was mongoloid).

One year later Ehrenfest sat down and wrote a letter dated 14 August 1932, part of which follow.[15]

My dear friends: Bohr, Einstein, Franck, Herglotz, Joffé, Kohnstamm, and Tolman!
I absolutely do not know any more how to carry further during the next few months the burden of my life which has become unbearable. I cannot stand it any longer to let my professorship here [in Leiden] go down the drain. I MUST vacate my position here. Perhaps it may happen that I can use up the rest of my strength in Russia . . .* If, however, it will not become clear rather soon that I can do that, then it is as good as certain that I shall kill myself. And if that will happen some time then I should like to know that I have written, calmly and without rush, to you whose friendship has played such a great role in my life . . .
In recent years it has become ever more difficult for me to follow developments [in physics] with understanding. After trying, ever more enervated and torn, I have finally given up in DESPERATION . . . This made me completely 'weary of life' . . . I did feel 'condemned to live on' mainly because of economic cares for the children . . . I tried other things . . . but that helps only briefly . . . Therefore I

---

* Ehrenfest had taught a number of years in St Petersburg.

concentrated more and more on ever more precise details of suicide . . . I have no other 'practical' possibility than suicide, and that after having first killed Wassik . . .

Forgive me . . .

May you and those dear to you stay well.

I have seen copies of this tragic letter in both the Bohr and the Einstein Archives, but could not find any response from either recipient. Upon consulting my friend Martin Klein, the Ehrenfest expert, I found out why. Ehrenfest never sent off this letter. It, and a similar one to some of his students, were found after 25 September 1933, the day on which in Amsterdam he first shot Wassik, then himself.*

On 28 September Dirac wrote to Bohr from Leningrad: 'I am afraid Ehrenfest was contemplating suicide at the time [earlier in September] when he left Copenhagen, as he was extremely agitated when I was saying goodbye to him and his last words to me referred to suicide. I saw him in the entrance hall of your house . . . and said to him that I hoped he knew how extremely useful he was at a conference . . . This seemed to give him a shock and he rushed into the house without saying anything . . . A little later he came out again and took me by the arm . . . He was then extremely agitated – quite bowed down and in tears. He said, in a very broken way, as nearly as I can remember, "What you have just said, coming from a young man like you, means very much to me, because, maybe, a man such as I feels he has no longer the force to live." (The last phrase I remember very well.) . . . He then remained holding my arm for a little while, as though struggling to find some more words to say, but then left me very abruptly without saying a word . . . I was very alarmed about it . . . I now cannot help blaming myself for not doing anything.' [17]

On that same day Margrethe Bohr wrote to Mrs Ehrenfest: 'I cannot find the words for expressing our sorrow and despair at the news of the death of your husband. It is almost impossible for us to comprehend that we shall not see him any more, we said goodbye to him only a few days ago and agreed to meet soon again in Brussels [at the seventh Solvay conference in October].

'Our thoughts and cares are first and foremost with you, dear Mrs Ehrenfest, and we wish so much that we could be with you. Niels would have liked best to journey right away to Leiden, but could hardly manage to do so and, since you are surrounded by so many friends, we thought it might also be more suitable for you to talk with us when next month we will pass through Leiden on our way to Brussels.

---

* This happened in the waiting room of the Professor Watering Instituut in the Vondelstraat in Amsterdam, where Wassik was under treatment. On 26 September Dutch newspapers merely reported Ehrenfest's sudden death, adding an extensive account of his career.[16]

'If only I could express better my love and care for you, dear Mrs Ehrenfest.' [18]*

The greatest grief in Niels' and Margrethe's lives was the loss of Christian, their oldest son, at the age of seventeen.

Already as a young boy Christian had been interested in the sciences. 'He [also] loved the arts, especially the theatre.' [20] After Niels had seen some poems Christian had written he suggested that they be shown to their friend Seedorff, the poet (12a), who after reading them urged Christian to continue. 'Seedorff had no doubt that Niels had hopes that Christian would develop into an artist.' [21]

Christan passed his *Studenterexamen* (final high school exam) in late June 1934. In those days 'he sometimes said that he would like to become a mathematician or possibly a physicist. But he also would say, when he was in the mood, that he would like to be a poet.' [20] Pictures of him from that time show him to be bright, vigorous, and good looking.

During the week thereafter, on 2 July, Christian joined his father and a few of the latter's friends in a sailing trip.

In 1926 Niels, together with Chievitz, his boyhood friend (Chapter 3), Bjerrum, the chemist, and Holger Hendriksen, a chemical engineer, had jointly bought a cutter, which they named Chita. In the course of the years they had made many sailing trips, some of them lengthy. 'With Bohr on board there were always discussions . . . [for example] when he saw the moonlight on the water the problem was to explain why the light showed itself as a band rather than as a patch.' [22]

That July day was their first outing in the summer of 1934. 'The weather had been rough the few days before . . . suddenly a tremendous breaker hit [the Chita] from port side. [Christian] was hurled overboard by the tiller. He was a good swimmer and kept himself afloat for a while. A lifebuoy was thrown out and was so near to him that one hoped he might reach it. The high seas made that impossible, however, and finally the young man disappeared in the waves.' [20]

'It must have been the most awful moment in the life of his friends when they had to hold Bohr back from jumping after his son . . .' [21]

That evening the Chita docked in the Swedish port of Varberg south of Gøteborg. From there Bohr hurried to Tisvilde where he had to face another gruesome moment: telling Margrethe . . .

It took until late August for Christian's body to be found. It was coffined and brought to Carlsberg, where, on 26 August, Niels addressed family and friends at the bier standing in the dining room. He spoke of the joy and hope that a first child brings to a young home. How Christian had been a loving

---

* A week later Margrethe replied to Dirac, to thank him for his letter. 'We have been almost heartbroken by Ehrenfest's death, it came as such a shock to us.' [19]

son, a chivalrous leader of his brothers, and like a ray of sunlight to his grandparents. How he harmoniously combined deep seriousness with infectious gaiety. How his purposeful pursuits, from science to art, had raised great expectations for his future.

Niels also spoke of pain and sorrow. 'It is harder for us than we can say to reconcile ourselves with the thought that we never again shall see Christian's warm smile and hear his cheerful voice, and that the rich promises for a productive manhood, delighting him and us, shall not reach fulfillment.'

Then, in words so characteristic for Niels' personality, he concluded by stressing that Christian's life and endeavors had not been in vain. 'He has given us precious memories purified by sorrow, which will bind us together and in which he, never aging, will always live with us ... On behalf of Christian and ourselves we express our deepest thanks for the loyalty you have shown to his memory, which in addition gives us the confidence that, also outside our small circle, he will continue to exert his influence in his own spirit, as truly as each of us lives his strongest life in the thoughts of his fellow beings.'

On 25 November 1934, the day on which Christian would have been eighteen, there was another gathering at Carlsberg, this time to attend the awarding of the first Christian Bohr memorial grant, established by aunt Hanna Adler, to Mogens Andersen, one of Christian's young friends, a painter who was to become prominent in the Danish art world. Niels spoke again in memory of his beloved son. Until recently this grant was awarded yearly.*

On 19 October 1937, in the evening, Rutherford died peacefully. He was 66 years old.

In his later years Rutherford had suffered from a slight hernia at the umbilicus for which he wore a truss harness.[23] After complaints of indigestion he was hospitalized in mid-October 1937. On the 15th he was operated for a strangulated hernia. There were brief hopes for recovery ...

From an authoritative medical account: 'The tragedy, if it can be called a tragedy to pass quickly from this world without forebodings and with powers undiminished, was heightened by the fact that his fatal illness was occasioned by a small mechanical, although notably dangerous, accident of an anatomical kind ... He was patient, courageous, and uncomplaining, still capable of a joke, still alert enough in his mind to take an interest in the mechanics of the relieving siphonage employed.'[24]**

Arthur Eve, Rutherford's principal biographer, has written of him:

---

* Bohr's talks on 26 August and 25 November have been privately printed as 'Mindeord over Christian Alfred Bohr'.
** See Ref. 25 for other responses at the time of Rutherford's death.

'People ask – what was the man like, how did he dress, did he really look like a farmer, what sort of accent did he have, did he believe in immortality? None of these things really matter. Here was a king making his way into the unknown. Who cares what his crown is made of, or what the polish of his boots?'[26]

The news of Rutherford's death reached Bohr in Bologna, where he was attending the Galvani bicentennial conference. On 20 October he gave a short address, one of his most eloquent ones I have seen in print. This, in part, is what he said:

With the passing of Lord Rutherford the life of one of the greatest men who ever worked in science has come to an end. For us to make comparisons would be far from Rutherford's spirit, but we may say of him as has been said of Galileo, that he left science in quite a different state from that in which he found it . . . Rutherford passed away at the height of his activity, which is the fate his best friends would have wished for him, but just on that account he will be missed more, perhaps, than any scientific worker has ever been missed before.'[27]

On 21 October Rutherford's remains were cremated. On the 25th his ashes were buried in the nave of Westminster Abbey, just west of Newton's tomb.[28] Among those present in the Abbey were his nearest family, a representative of the king, cabinet members, the High Commissioner of New Zealand, and a number of prominent scientists, including Dirac and Bohr, who had hastened to London. 'I attended his unforgetful dignified funeral in Westminster Abbey.'[29]

In November Lady Rutherford sent Bohr a silver cigarette box of Rutherford's as a memento.[30] Earlier that month Bohr had visited her. Bohr to Peter Kapitza:* 'In Cambridge, where I stayed with Dirac, I had a long talk with Lady Rutherford who was very brave and able to speak about everything in the most beautiful way.'[31]

Kapitza replied: 'From his [R's] words I always gathered that he liked you the most among all his pupils.'[32]

(b) Times of travel

Second trip to the United States. In May 1932 Bohr received an invitation[33] to attend and address a meeting of the 'triple-A S' (the American Association for the Advancement of Science) to be held in Chicago in June 1933, on the occasion of the centenary of the incorporation of the village of Chicago. An international exposition, with the theme 'A Century of Progress', was also planned for that time. Bohr accepted forthwith.[34]

No sooner did Bohr's intended visit to the States become known than a stream of invitations for him to visit other places started coming, from the

* Kapitza, the eminent Russian physicist, had worked in Cambridge from 1920 to 1934.

Franklin Institute in Philadelphia (accepted[35]), from Ohio State University in Columbus[36] (accepted[37]), from Cal Tech in Pasadena[38] (accepted[39]), from the University of Michigan in Ann Arbor[40] (accepted[41]), from the Johns Hopkins in Baltimore[42] (accepted[43]), and from Purdue University in Lafayette[44] (declined[45]).* In January 1933 Bohr was informed that he had been voted an honorary D.Sc. from Brown University in Providence, provided he would accept in person.[52] Bohr accepted.[53] In April he received a letter[54] from Nishina in Tokyo. Could professor Bohr perhaps extend his forthcoming trip so as to include a visit to Japan? Thus began a series of communications that would bring Bohr to the Orient four years later.

Bohr began his loaded schedule right on 1 May, the day he and Margrethe arrived in New York harbor on board the *Britannic*. That afternoon he visited with Mason at the Rockefeller foundation, a meeting Bohr had requested from Copenhagen.[55] That evening he gave a lecture at Columbia University. On 3 May he spoke at the Franklin Institute, on the 5th at Ohio State, both times on 'Explanation in natural science'. Then on they went to California – always by train, of course – with a stop to visit the Grand Canyon.

On 15 May they started their two-week stay at Pasadena, where a symposium on 'Nuclei and high energy transformations' had been organized. Other attendants included Anderson, Lauritsen, and Oppenheimer. Bohr gave a talk on 'The foundations of atomic mechanics'.[56]

On his arrival in Pasadena Bohr had found a letter on Metro–Goldwyn–Mayer stationery, written by Peter Freuchen, one of Denmark's great Greenland explorers.[57] Bohr had known him since their student days when both had played soccer in *Akademisk Boldklub*.[58] (I met Freuchen once in New York, in Bohr's company, a tall man with a red beard and a wooden leg. He cut a striking figure.) In his letter Freuchen explained that he and his wife were living in Hollywood at that time, 'involved in the filming of one of my books', and that they wanted to invite the Bohrs to their home. They accepted. The visit included a tour of the MGM studios, an event that has been immortalized in a photograph of Bohr, Freuchen, and an improbably handsome film actor.

From California the Bohrs traveled back, ending up once again on the East coast. In June they were at Brown University. '[Bohr] spent several days on our campus and gave two technical lectures on atomic theory.'[59] On the 17th he received his honorary degree and spoke at the graduate school convocation, once again on explanation in natural science.[60] 'It was unfortunately not a success.'[59]

From Brown they went to Chicago to attend the AAAS meeting. Its

* I have not been able to trace Bohr's replies to additional invitations, from McGill University in Montreal,[46] from the Carnegie Institution in Washington,[47] from Princeton,[48] from Berkeley,[49] from Harvard,[50] and from Stanford.[51]

session on physics had been organized jointly with the American Physical Society. According to the Society's records it was 'perhaps the most important scientific session in its history to date'.[61] Bohr chaired part of the proceedings. Cockcroft, one of the speakers, wrote to his wife that 'Bohr got up to open the discussion and talked for about an hour, thereby squashing any chance for a useful discussion, which is rather a pity'.[62] On 19 June Bohr gave a public lecture at the international exposition grounds.[63] Slater who was there has remembered: 'Most of the meeting was held at the University of Chicago, but there were a few talks given at the fairgrounds, including one by Fermi on hyperfine structure, and one by Niels Bohr on space and time in contemporary physics. These were open to the public, and it was an astonishing sight to see poor Bohr struggling with a balky microphone in a room with people standing up and filling all the seats, mothers with babies and others of the general public, hoping to be enlightened by a great man.'[64] According to Cockcroft not one per cent of the audience could comprehend him.[62]

On the occasion of Chicago's centenary an exposition had been arranged at the city's new museum of science and industry. Plans for a Danish contribution had been worked out by a committee of which Bohr was a member.[65] The Bohrs went to visit this exhibit which honored 21 Danish men of science. My faithful readers will recognize the names of several of these: Tycho Brahe, Bartholin, Steno, Rømer, Ørsted, Lorenz, Christiansen, Finsen, Knudsen, J. N. Brønsted, Bjerrum – and Bohr.[66]

After Chicago the Bohrs spent another month in the States, Niels fulfilling various obligations. They were back in Denmark by the beginning of August.

First visit to the Soviet Union. In the middle of May 1934 Bohr, accompanied by his wife and by Rosenfeld, arrived in Moscow on a visit arranged under the auspices of the Soviet Academy of Sciences. He lectured in Moscow, Leningrad, and Charkov. He visited scientific institutions, some factories, and some institutes devoted to social issues, and met notable personalities, among them Ivan Petrovich Pavlov, celebrated for his studies of conditioned reflexes. Right after his arrival Bohr gave a radio address in which he expressed his hopes for close scientific collaboration between Denmark and Russia.[67]

Danish newspapers gave accounts of interviews given by Bohr to Soviet newspapers. Samples of comments attributed to Bohr: 'Scientific institutions in Russia are astonishingly well organized. Practical and theoretical aspects are combined in extraordinarily felicitous manner.'[68] From an interview with *Izvestia*: 'The Soviet Union forces everyone to reflect, since one feels that here one is creating something extraordinary, something splendid ... everyone here feels that he does something that can improve the conditions of society as a whole.'[69]

These news items provoked strong Danish reactions. For example, from a letter one reader sent to his newspaper: 'Where does the professor get his information from on society as a whole – which so strongly contradicts experiences by seasoned observers . . .?' [70] One member of parliament called Bohr naïve and half-blind.[71] As best I know, there never was an occasion on which Bohr was publicly castigated more strongly.

Bohr was back in Copenhagen on 27 May. The next day an interview with him appeared in the Danish paper *Politiken* [72] in which he clarified his views. 'To my great astonishment I learned of a public discussion of my views on Russian conditions. I have of course not gone in for taking any kind of position on general political questions . . . One has taken one sentence from my interview, on scientific life, as a pronouncement in general on the position of workers in the Soviet Union.' Bohr had actually commented on what he had observed in one turbine factory. 'I am always very cautious concerning things I have not studied more closely.'

A few more letters to the Editor followed, whereafter everybody calmed down.

Journey around the world. In 1933 Bohr had been unable to accept Nishina's invitation (mentioned above) to visit Japan. In January 1934 he wrote to Nishina that perhaps he and his wife could come in the spring of 1935, and that they might try to take their son Christian along.[73] In September Bohr wrote again.[74] After Christian's death they did not wish to leave the other boys alone. He now proposed a visit in the spring of 1937, and to bring along his second son, Hans. So it came to pass.

A second fixed point of this new trip was settled in 1936 when Bohr received and accepted an invitation to give guest lectures in Berkeley.[75]

The journey began in January 1937 and lasted until late June. On 18 and 19 January Bohr lectured in Paris,[76] then joined Margrethe and Hans in Southampton, from where they sailed for the US on board the *Aquitania*.*

The Bohrs arrived in New York on the 28th. The by now familiar routine of lecturing began the next day with a talk at New York University. There followed a week in Princeton, with several more lectures. On to Toronto, with a stopover to visit Niagara Falls, lectures on 8 and 9 February.[77] Back to New York with lecture stops in Rochester and Cambridge. Southward, lectures in Washington and at Duke University in Durham. Then the trip west begins. Lectures in Pittsburgh on the 23rd, Ann Arbor on the 25th, Oklahoma City on the 27th. On March 2nd the Bohrs arrive in San Francisco for a month's stay in California. Niels gives the Hitchcock lectures, six of them, in Berkeley.[78] Also gives talks at Stanford and in Los Angeles.

One cannot fail but be impressed with Bohr's stamina – he was in his

---

* I have been privileged to have had access to a copy (deposited in NBA) of Hans Bohr's diary which gives a vivid account of this trip.

fifties now – in keeping up such a schedule, and with his evident urge to communicate. As to the subjects of these various lectures, they dealt with aspects of quantum physics, especially with complementarity, and with Bohr's newly developed theory of the compound atomic nucleus (15f).

While in Berkeley Bohr received a telegram from China: 'Chinese national educational and cultural institutions earnestly invite you visit our country,'[79] to which he responded after arrival in Japan. On 1 April the Bohrs boarded the *Asami Maru* bound for the Orient. On the 6th they visited Oahu. On the 15th they arrived in Japan for a two-week stay.

In Tokyo Bohr received a follow up letter[80] from China sent care of Nishina. It was signed by representatives from the Academia Sinica, the National Academy of Peiping (as Beijing was called those days), Tsing Hua University, the National Central University at Nanking, and the China Foundation for the Promotion of Education and Culture. In that letter the invitation to visit China was repeated, along with the 'request that you give some lectures at your convenience during your sojourn'. Bohr accepted, stating that he and his family would be able to stay in China for two to three weeks.[81]

While in Japan Bohr gave a series of eight lectures at the Imperial University of Tokyo, and also gave talks at Sendai, Kyoto, and Osaka. There was time for sightseeing and excursions, to Kamakura, Mount Fuji, Nara, and other places justly famed for their beauty. In addition Margrethe shopped energetically. Bohr had also an audience with the Emperor. On 19 May the family left Japan from Nagasaki, on board the *Shanghai Maru*, and arrived in Shanghai the next day.

Again there followed a mixture of lecturing, sightseeing, and shopping, in Shanghai, Hangchow, Nanking. On the 29th the Bohrs arrived in Peiping where they stayed, and Niels lectured, until 7 June – one month to the day before the oubreak of the Sino-Japanese war.

Then began the long trek homeward. The Manchuria railroad brought them to Siberia via Mukden and Harbin. The Siberia express led them past lake Baikal and Novosibirsk to European Russia. On the 16th they arrived in Moscow, where Landau and Kapitza met them at the railroad station. There they stayed until the 22nd, Bohr giving the last lectures of his trip. Then via Helsingfors (Helsinki), Stockholm, and Malmø they returned to Copenhagen where they arrived on 25 June.

References

1. *Politiken*, 1 December 1930.
2. N. Bohr, letter to W. Heisenberg, 8 December 1930, NBA.
3. Københavns Magistrat 1. Afd. Begravelsesprotokol, April–September 1933, No. 959.

4. N. Bohr, letter to H. Bohr, 15 May 1933.

5. N. Bohr, draft of letter to P. Ehrenfest, May 1918, CW, Vol. 3, p. 12.

6. M. Klein, in *The lesson of the quantum theory*, p. 325, Eds. J. de Boer *et al.*, North-Holland, Amsterdam, 1986.

7. N. Bohr, letter to P. Ehrenfest, 10 May 1919; also N. Bohr, letter to P. Ehrenfest, 22 October 1919, both in NBA.

8. A. Einstein, letter to P. Ehrenfest, November 1919, repr. in Ref. 6, p. 331.

9. P. Ehrenfest in *Atomes et électrons*, Proc. Third Solvay Conf., p. 248, Gauthier-Villars, Paris 1923, repr. in CW, Vol. 3, p. 381.

10. P. Ehrenfest, letter to N. Bohr, 3 July 1921, repr. in ref. 6, p. 334, also in NBA.

11. P. Ehrenfest, letter to A. Einstein, 27 December 1921, Einstein Archives.

11a. Quoted in A. Parry, *Peter Kapitza on life and science*, p. 130, McMillan, New York, 1968.

12. SL, p. 443.

13. P. Ehrenfest, letter to N. Bohr, 13 May 1931, NBA.

14. P. Ehrenfest, letter to N. Bohr, 19 September 1931, NBA.

15. P. Ehrenfest, letter to N. Bohr, A. Einstein, J. Franck, G. Herglotz, A. Joffé, Ph. Kohnstamm, and R. Tolman, 14 August 1932, NBA.

16. C. Duif, chief of press documentation of the municipal archives of Amsterdam, letter to A. Pais, 14 June 1989.

17. P. A. M. Dirac, letter to N. Bohr, 28 September 1933, NBA.

18. M. Bohr, letter to T. Ehrenfest, 28 September 1933, NBA.

19. M. Bohr, draft of letter to P. A. M. Dirac, 3 October 1933, NBA.

20. *Berlingske Aftenavisen*, 3 July 1934.

21. N. Blaedel, 'Harmony and unity', Springer, New York 1988.

22. Ref. 21, p. 178.

23. M. Oliphant, *Rutherford, recollections of the Cambridge days*, Elsevier, New York 1972.

24. A. S. Eve, *Rutherford*, pp. 425, 427, Cambridge University Press 1939.

25. IB, Chap. 17, section (h).

26. Ref. 24, p. 435.

27. N. Bohr, *Nature* **140**, 752, 1937.

28. Ref. 24, p. 427.

29. N. Bohr, letter to E. O. Lawrence, 20 December 1937, NBA.

30. Lady Rutherford, letter to N. Bohr, 24 November 1937, NBA.

31. N. Bohr, letter to P. Kapitza, 4 November 1937, NBA.

32. P. Kapitza, letter to N. Bohr, 7 November 1937, NBA.

33. J. J. Abel and R. C. Dawes, letter to N. Bohr, 15 May 1932, NBA.

34. N. Bohr, letter to J. J. Abel and R. C. Dawes, 27 May 1932, NBA.

35. H. McClenahan, letter to N. Bohr, 30 June 1932, NBA.

36. A. W. Smith, letter to N. Bohr, 7 October 1932, NBA.

37. N. Bohr, letter to A. W. Smith, 4 January 1933, NBA.

38. R. A. Millikan, letter to N. Bohr, 3 November 1932, NBA.

39. N. Bohr, letter to R. A. Millikan, 28 December 1932, NBA.

40. S. Goudsmit, letter to N. Bohr, 4 November 1932, NBA.

41. N. Bohr, letter to S. Goudsmit, 28 December 1932, NBA.

42. K. F. Herzfeld, letter to N. Bohr, 5 November 1932, NBA.

43. N. Bohr, letter to K. F. Herzfeld, 14 January 1933, NBA.
44. G. C. Brandenburg, letter to N. Bohr, 20 February 1933, NBA.
45. N. Bohr, letter to G. C. Brandenburg, 14 March 1933, NBA.
46. A. S. Eve, letter to N. Bohr, 27 January 1933, NBA.
47. J. A. Fleming, letter to N. Bohr, 10 March 1933, NBA.
48. R. Ladenburg, letter to N. Bohr, 15 March 1933, NBA.
49. R. Birge, letter to N. Bohr, 10 May 1933, NBA.
50. T. Lyman, letter to N. Bohr, 18 May 1933, NBA.
51. H. F. Blickfeldt, letter to N. Bohr, 22 May 1933, NBA.
52. C. A. Barbour, letter to N. Bohr, 18 January 1933, NBA.
53. N. Bohr, letter to R. G. D. Richardson, 14 March 1933, NBA.
54. Y. Nishina, letter to N. Bohr, 7 April 1933, NBA.
55. N. Bohr, letter to W. Weaver, 13 April 1933, NBA.
56. Science **77**, 505, 1933.
57. P. Freuchen, letter to N. Bohr, 13 May 1933, NBA.
58. N. Bohr, in *Bogen om Peter Freuchen*, p. 180, Eds. Pipaluk Freuchen *et al.*, Fremad, Copenhagen 1958.
59. R. B. Lindsay, in the *Brown Daily Herald*, 8 December 1962, supplement.
60. Science **77**, 423, 1933.
61. *Phys. Rev.* **44**, 313, 1933.
62. G. Hartcup and T. E. Allibone, *Cockroft and the atom*, p. 60, Adam Hilger, Bristol 1984.
63. Science **77**, 508, 1933.
64. J. C. Slater, *Solid state and molecular theory: A scientific biography*, p. 193, Wiley, New York 1975.
65. Cf. *Science* **77**, 206, 1933.
66. *Denmark and some Danish scientists of note*, published by the committee for the scientific exhibition at Chicago, Copenhagen 1933.
67. *Berlingske Tidende Aftenavis*, 15 May 1934.
68. *Ibid.* 14 May 1934.
69. Ref. 67 and *Dagens Nyheder*, 16 May 1934.
70. *Berlingske Tidende Aftenavis*, 19 May 1934.
71. *Arbejdsbladet*, 20 May 1934.
72. *Politiken*, 28 May 1934; also direct statement by Bohr in *Politiken*, 30 May 1934.
73. N. Bohr, letter to Y. Nishina, 26 January 1934, NBA.
74. N. Bohr, letter to Y. Nishina, 13 September 1934, NBA.
75. N. Bohr, letter to R. Birge, 22 October 1936, NBA.
76. L. de Broglie, letter to N. Bohr, 9 January 1937, NBA.
77. *Science* **85**, 117, 1937.
78. *Science* **85**, 195; **86**, 161, 1937; transcripts of the lectures are in the R. Birge collection, American Institute of Physics, New York.
79. Telegram to N. Bohr sent from Tsing Hua University, 11 March 1937, NBA.
80. Letter to N. Bohr signed by the president of the Academia Sinica and others, 27 March 1937, NBA.
81. N. Bohr, letter to Y. H. Woo, 30 April 1937, NBA.

19

'We are suspended in language'

(a) Bohr and philosophy: 'It was, in a way, my life'*

Se moquer de la philosophie c'est vraiment philosopher.

PASCAL,
Pensées, Pt. VII, No. 35.

After having encountered Bohr as creator of new physics, director of research, institute builder, fund raiser, helper of refugees, orchestrator of experimental science, and world traveler, we shall meet him next as one of the major twentieth century philosophers. In that respect Bohr came into his element from the late 1920s onward, when he began his elaboration of complementarity in physics and its extension to other disciplines. We shall see, however, that his strong interest in philosophical issues dates back as early as his student days.

What is a philosopher? According to the *Encyclopaedia Britannica*, philosophy (from the Greek φιλος, fond of, and σοφία, wisdom) is a general term whose meaning and scope have varied very considerably according to the usage of different authors and different ages. Reading the nine distinct definitions of philosopher in the OED is edifying but not necessary for what follows. I hope that this chapter will speak for itself regarding Bohr's views on philosophy.

Let us first see what Bohr thought about philosophy in general.

It has already been noted (14e) that a few drafts of Bohr's first paper[1] on complementarity, the Como lecture of 1927, carried the title 'The philosophical foundations of the quantum theory'. Also, when in November 1957 Bohr went to MIT to deliver the first Karl Taylor Compton lectures, he chose 'The philosophical lesson of atomic physics' for the overall title of his six talks.[2]

At the beginning of the first of these lectures Bohr cautioned his audience: 'From the title of these lectures you must not expect an academic philosophical discourse, for which I hardly possess the required scholarship.'

---

* I am grateful to David Favrholdt for discussions and correspondence, which, along with reading his papers, have greatly helped me in writing this section.

I know of no better illustration of Bohr's general attitude toward philosophy than the counterpoint of this title and the subsequent disclaimer. In my opinion he was first and foremost a physicist who, however, would not have objected to some of his thoughts being called philosophical as long as this would not be meant to identify him as a professional in that field.

Bohr's thoughts about philosophy need to be distinguished from his attitude toward philosophers. Numerous are ironic and critical comments by the latter concerning Bohr's contributions, even in Denmark where he was so especially revered. Favrholdt has shown me texts written by two philosophy professors who, in the 1950s, each taught philosophy courses at the University of Copenhagen in which students were told that Bohr was all wrong. These and other similar opinions go far toward explaining Bohr's opinions in his later years: 'There are all kinds of people but I think it would be reasonable to say that no man who is called a philosopher really understands what one means by the complementarity description ... The relationship between scientists and philosophers was of a very curious kind ... The difficulty is that it is hopeless to have any kind of understanding between scientists and philosophers directly.'[3] As he once said to my friend Jens Lindhard the day after he had attended a philosophers' meeting: 'I have made a great discovery, a very great discovery: all that philosophers have ever written is pure drivel [... *er det rene vaas*].'[4]

Bohr's own favorite definition of a philosopher, not found in the OED, goes as follows. What is the difference between an expert and a philosopher? An expert is someone who starts out knowing something about some things, goes on to know more and more about less and less, and ends up knowing everything about nothing. Whereas a philosopher is someone who starts out knowing something about some things, goes on to know less and less about more and more, and ends up knowing nothing about everything. I like to think that Pascal's words at the head of this section, 'To ridicule philosophy is truly philosophical', might have appealed to him. All the same it gave Bohr pleasure to be elected, in 1951, honorary member of the Danish society for philosophy and psychology.[5]

Among physicists, opinions about Bohr the philosopher range from a small minority who do not buy complementarity at all to Heisenberg's view that Bohr was 'primarily a philosopher, not a physicist',[6] a judgement of particular interest if one remembers how greatly Heisenberg admired Bohr's physics.

Bohr had published over fifty scientific articles by the time his Como lecture appeared in print. His oeuvre of later years consists of well over a hundred more contributions. About thirty of those deal with complementarity. One reason why that number is so large is that it includes printed versions of the numerous addresses on complementarity in physics as well as on possible applications in other domains which Bohr gave before a variety of audiences of non-physicists. That also explains why there is considerable repetitiveness in these articles. When someone would mention that to Bohr he would smile and on occasion tell the story of a Greek philosopher who had left his native Athens on a voyage. When he returned he found Socrates standing in a square, talking to his disciples. He said to him: 'Socrates, there you stand saying the same about the same things.' To which Socrates replied: 'You, who are so wise, you probably never say the same about the same things.'[7]

Bohr's eighteen most important philosophical papers, translated into English where necessary, have been collected in three slim volumes with the common title *The Philosophical Writings of Niels Bohr.*[8-10] (The selections for the first two volumes were made by Bohr himself.) A recent review[11] of these books may serve as a first impression of their impact: 'Against the sometimes maddening frustration brought about by a study of these ponderous essays is the indisputable fact that nobody has succeeded in saying anything better in the 60 years since Bohr started talking about the problem.' I can agree with much but not all of this opinion. If among the many inequivalent meanings of 'ponderous' one is supposed to pick 'dull, tedious', then I would dissent. I would understand the choice 'heavy, unwieldy, laborious', a widespread opinion which, however, I do not share either. To me it has not been all that frustrating to follow Bohr's thinking by reading these papers, an undertaking which does demand care and patience. I realize, however, my uncommon advantage of many discussions with Bohr about his philosophical ideas. It is the main purpose of this chapter to survey these. As an introduction to this subject I begin with a sketch of Bohr's philosophical background.

'Many of us [including this writer] remember how Bohr told that as far back as he could remember he had liked "to dream of great interconnections".'[12] Philosophizing was, one might say, part of Bohr's nature from boyhood on. 'Bohr's first preoccupation with philosophical problems did not arise from his physical investigations but from general epistemological consider-ations about the function of language as a means of communicating experience ... How to avoid ambiguity ... that was the problem that worried Bohr.'[13] Shortly before his death Bohr spoke about his youthful philosophical considerations. When asked how significant these were to him at that time, he replied: 'It was, in a way, my life.'[3]

An important impetus to Bohr's early thinking – he often reminisced about it – was the theory of the so-called Riemann surfaces with which he became acquainted in a mathematics course at the university. Briefly, this theory deals with multivalued functions, that is, functions that can take on various values in the same point in the complex plane (a term defined in (13h)). The resulting ambiguities can be avoided by introducing 'Riemann sheets', a set of superimposed complex planes arranged in such a way that the functions take on unique values by specifying not just a 'point' but rather 'a point on a given sheet'. It struck Bohr that this way of dealing with ambiguities could be transcribed to the use of 'planes of objectivity' applied to everyday language in which often one word can have multiple meanings.

So important to Bohr were these considerations that already as a student he contemplated writing a book on the subject. However, 'I did not write anything down, but I spoke to the various people that came here.'[3] The only glimpse in writing we have of these early thoughts is a line in a letter to his brother: 'Sensations, like cognition, must be analyzed in planes that cannot be compared.'[14] Some twenty years later Bohr toyed with another such plan, to start a journal for the philosophical implications of quantum physics. Nothing came of that either.[15]

At this point I make good on my earlier promise (14e) to comment on the influence of specific philosophers on Bohr's thinking.

First, Høffding, the Danish philosopher whom Bohr had met already as a young boy in his father's home and whose 'Filosofikum', an obligatory elementary course, he had to attend as a first-year student. Favrholdt has informed me that in this course Bohr became acquainted with philosophical problems such as the mind–body problem, free will–determinism, subject–object, and idealism–materialism, all in a very brief and popular version, but that we have no reason to assume that Bohr studied any of these topics for himself. As has been noted, while still a student Bohr had helped Høffding in editing a textbook on logic (6b). From this early acquaintance until Høffding's death in 1931 Bohr had great respect and affection for him (see (15e)). Toward the end of his own life Bohr said of him: 'I had very much to do with Høffding . . . [he] was really very interested [in complementarity], far more interested than any [other] philosopher who has been called a philosopher because he thought it was right. He had not too great an understanding of it, but he wrote an article[16] about these things, which is far better than any other thing which has appeared in philosophy since . . . He was a very fine person.'[3] Bohr admired Høffding's openness of mind and must have enjoyed discussing philosophical questions with him, but at no time did he make any comment to the effect that Høffding had influenced his own philosophical considerations. Also, as Favrholdt has noted,[17] in 1911 Høffding wrote: 'Of course we have no right to assume the presence of absolute leaps and gaps in nature' – hardly a source of inspiration to a quantum physicist.

Another Danish philosopher who, it is sometimes erroneously alleged, influenced Bohr was Kierkegaard. We know that in his student years Bohr read one of his books* and considered it 'something of the finest I have ever read',[18] noting, however, that he was 'not in agreement with Kierkegaard'.[19] In the 1930s he once said: 'His language is wonderful, often sublime [but] there is of course much in Kierkegaard that I cannot accept.'[20] Margrethe Bohr has recalled: 'He was not so deeply interested in Kierkegaard's thoughts, but he was an extreme admirer of his language.'[21]

One Dane whose influence Bohr acknowledged was Poul Martin Møller, an early nineteenth century poet and novelist, and at one time professor of philosophy in Copenhagen, whom he would often quote. More on this in (19d).

Regarding philosophers from other parts of the world, Bohr particularly admired William James: 'I thought he was most wonderful.'[3] Note that already in 1891 James had introduced the term 'complementarity' to denote a quality of consciousness in schizophrenics.[22] Since it is not clear how much of James Bohr had read, nor when he did so,[23] I do not know (but regard it neither as probable nor as interesting) whether Bohr took over that term from James.

In respect to Bohr's familiarity with the writings of other philosophers my knowledge is flimsy. I do know that once, when asked what kind of contributions he thought people like Spinoza, Hume, and Kant had made he replied evasively that that was difficult to answer.[3] As Favrholdt put it to me: 'He never *studied* philosophy: I mean sitting at his desk reading Kant or some other.' Bohr did refer with great respect to Buddha and Lao Tse, however.[24]

In summary, there is no evidence of any kind that philosophers played a role in Bohr's discovery of complementarity. The men who above all influenced him were his father,[25] Rutherford, Schrödinger during his visit in 1926, and Heisenberg in the struggle that followed (14b, c). His interests in philosophy in his student days were stimulated by mathematical analogies. The last picture Bohr drew on a blackboard before his death showed a curve on a Riemann surface . . .

I now turn to an attempt at giving an account of Bohr's philosophical contributions centering on complementarity. These fall into two groups.

First, improvements in the analysis of applications to quantum physics. Before plunging into section (b), where these matters are discussed, the reader may like to refresh his memory by reverting to (14b) where the beginnings of complementarity were outlined, in particular Bohr's insistence that measuring instruments must always be treated classically, that the choice of measuring instruments determines the extent to which objects to be observed exhibit particle or wave behavior, and that these two modes

---

* Entitled *Stages on Life's Way*.

of manifestation are not contradictory – but complementary. In section (c) I discuss Bohr's considerations on complementary relations between classical mechanics and thermodynamics, another kind of complementarity, having nothing to do with the quantum theory, but still in the domain of physics.

Secondly, Bohr's speculations on the possible applicability of complementarity arguments in disciplines other than physics, notably in psychology, biology, relations between human cultures, and language, see section (d). None of these applications can remotely compare in importance to complementarity in physics, some of them are in fact obsolete. I defer a more specific assessment to part 5 of section (d).

It seems proper to point out that the remainder of this chapter represents the point of view of a physicist who knows very little philosophy and whose knowledge of others' writings on the present subject is sparse. I believe that opinions expressed hereafter will on the whole agree with those of many but certainly not all of my physics colleagues.

(b) Complementarity (continued). More on the Bohr–Einstein dialog. A new definition of 'phenomenon'

From the autumn of 1927 onward – the time of his Como lecture[1] – Bohr was convinced he was on the right track for understanding what quantum physics was about. In May 1928 he wrote to Schrödinger[26] about the German version, just published,[27] of his Como talk: 'I am afraid to have greatly bored you with these many words. You must ascribe this to my enthusiasm. After years of struggle in the dark I feel perhaps particularly strongly the fulfillment of old hopes brought to us by your and others' new discoveries.'

Schrödinger did not share this optimism. His reaction to Bohr's paper was: 'Bohr wants to complement away [wegkomplementieren] all difficulties.'[28] Nor were his famous colleagues in Berlin enthused. Einstein to Schrödinger that same May: 'The Heisenberg–Bohr soothing philosophy – or religion? – is so finely chiseled that it provides a soft pillow for believers ... This religion does damned little for me.'[29] Planck to Sommerfeld, shortly afterward: 'In the battle between determinism and indeterminism I continue to side with the first, since it is my opinion that the difficulties are basically due to an inappropriate way of posing the question.'[30] Also from that time dates Einstein's dictum, more witty than profound, that God does not play dice.[31]

There exists no better record of the divergent opinions immediately following the birth of quantum mechanics than the proceedings of the fifth Solvay conference in October 1927 (see also (14f)). All the creators of both the old and the new quantum theory were in attendance. The general discussion was opened by the venerable Lorentz, president of the meeting, who asked: 'Could one not maintain determinism by making it an article of faith? Must one necessarily elevate indeterminism to a principle?'[32] All through the conference report one encounters unease if not outright opposition among the older generation, enthusiasm among the young, counting Bohr and Born along with the latter.

Bohr's first published paper on complementarity after the Como lecture appeared in 1929. It was a contribution to a *Festschrift* honoring Planck on the occasion of the golden jubilee of his doctorate.[33] As Bohr wrote to Pauli: '[This article] became too long and took so much time that I had to leave out all physics and confine myself to pure philosophy.'[34] I defer discussion of this article until section (d), noting here only that it contains a change of terminology, 'reciprocity' replacing 'complementarity'. Bohr briefly thought that this was more 'efficacious and pedagogical'.[34] A month later he declared the new name to be 'a blunder'[35] and never used it again. I also leave for later Bohr's next paper,[36] of particular interest because here for the first time he turned to possible applications of complementarity to biology.

In October 1931 Bohr went to Cambridge to 'pay a tribute of reverence to the memory of James Clerk Maxwell' on the occasion of the centenary of his birth.[37] His comments included reference to the measurement problem in quantum theory. 'It must not be forgotten that only the classical ideas of material particles and electromagnetic waves have a field of unambiguous application, whereas the concepts of photons and electron waves have not. Their applicability is essentially limited to cases in which, on account of the existence of the quantum of action, it is not possible to consider the phenomena observed as independent of the apparatus utilized for their observation.' Neither the inequivalence between particles and waves nor the relation between 'phenomenon' and 'apparatus' are stated in felicitous ways in this evidently hurriedly written paper. A few years later Bohr would do much better.

Cambridge provided the perfect setting for Bohr to restate (he had said it earlier in Como, but not as elegantly) his position regarding the language of physics.

The unambiguous interpretation of any measurement must be essentially framed in terms of the classical physical theories, and we may say that in this sense the language of Newton and Maxwell will remain the language of physicists for all time.

Later Bohr would express this position much more forcefully:

There is no quantum world. There is only an abstract quantum physical description. It is wrong to think that the task of physics is to find out how nature is. Physics concerns what we can say about nature.[15]

Meanwhile the debate between Bohr and Einstein on the foundations of quantum physics had entered its next phase.

You will recall (14f) that in 1927, at the fifth Solvay conference, Einstein had presented arguments to the effect that quantum mechanics was an inconsistent theory, and that Bohr had refuted these. Their next encounter took place in 1930 at the following Solvay meeting. That one was devoted to magnetism, which, of course, did not prevent the participants from discussing other subjects in the corridors. So it happened that Einstein told Bohr that he had found a counterexample to the uncertainty principle between energy and time.

His argument was quite ingenious. Consider a box having in one of its walls a hole that can be opened or closed by a shutter controlled by a clock inside the box. The box is filled with radiation. Weigh the box. Open the shutter for a brief interval during which a single photon escapes. Weigh the box again, some time later. From the weight difference one can deduce the energy of the photon by using $E = mc^2$. Thus (in principle) one has found to arbitrary accuracy both the photon energy and its time of passage, in conflict with the energy–time uncertainty relation.

Rosenfeld who was in Brussels at that time has recalled: 'It was quite a shock for Bohr ... he did not see the solution at once. During the whole evening he was extremely unhappy, going from one to the other and trying to persuade them that it couldn't be true, that it would be the end of physics if Einstein were right; but he couldn't produce any refutation. I shall never forget the sight of the two antagonists leaving [the Fondation Universitaire], Einstein a tall majestic figure, walking quietly, with a somewhat ironic smile, and Bohr trotting near him, very excited ... The next morning came Bohr's triumph.'[38]

The flaw Bohr had found was that Einstein had not taken into account that the weighing process amounts to observing the displacement of the box in a gravitational field, just like what happens when the grocery man uses his scales. The imprecision in the displacement of the box generates an uncertainty in the determination of the mass, and hence of the energy, of the photon. When the box is displaced, then so is the clock inside which therefore ticks in a gravitational field slightly different from the one in the initial box position. Now Bohr noted the well-known fact that the rate of a clock depends in a specific way on its position in a gravitational field. Correspondingly the imprecision in the box displacement generates an uncertainty in the determination of time. Using the position–momentum uncertainty relation as input, Bohr could show that the uncertainties in energy and in time are just linked by the energy–time uncertainty relation. All was well.*

Bohr's version of the clock-in-the-box experiment was not published until 1949 when it appeared in a volume[40] planned to be presented to Einstein on his 70th birthday. I know that article well. It happened that I was present when, at the Princeton University bicentennial in 1946, Paul Schilpp, the eventual editor, approached Bohr[40a] to ask him for a contribution to that book. During Bohr's stay in Princeton from February to June 1948 I assisted him with the preparation of that paper. From that time dates my story about Einstein wanting to steal his tobacco (1b).

It is generally agreed that Bohr's article of 1949 is his finest exposé on complementarity. Of particular interest in that paper is the drawing of the box and its content, reproduced in Fig. 10. Note the heavy bolts that fix the position of the scale along which moves a pointer marking the box position; the spring that guarantees the mobility of the box in the gravitational field; the counterweight underneath the box, needed to return the pointer to its initial position. None of these details were meant to be fanciful. Børge Madsen, who prepared this drawing told me of Bohr's insistence that the apparatus should look macroscopic, classical, that the clock should look like a real clock (in preparation for this drawing Madsen climbed a Copenhagen clock tower) etc. – all this to express pictorially that a physical measurement is a classical operation.

The episode just described seems to have convinced Einstein that quantum mechanics actually is a consistent scheme. In a nomination for a Nobel Prize to Heisenberg and Schrödinger he wrote (September 1931): 'I am convinced that this theory contains a part of the ultimate truth.' In 1933 he said of the Schrödinger wavefunctions: 'These functions are supposed to determine in a mathematical way only the probabilities of encountering those objects in a particular place or in a particular state of motion, if we make a measurement. This conception is logically unexceptionable and has led to important successes.'[41] None of that meant, however, that he now was happy with quantum mechanics. To him it was and remained part of the truth but not the whole truth. Thus in 1932 he wrote to Pauli: 'I do not say *"probabilitatem esse delendam"* but *"probabilitatem esse deducendam"*.'[42]**

---

* There are several subtleties to this reasoning. In this thought experiment one determines the *gravitational* mass of the photon, that is, the mass as it appears in the gravitational law of force between ponderable bodies. The mass m in $E = mc^2$ is the *inertial* mass, the proportionality factor in the relation between force and acceleration. These two masses are actually identical, a most non-trivial fact known as the equivalence principle. The rate of change of clocks in different gravitational fields also turns out to be a consequence of that principle, which, in turn, is one of the cornerstones of general relativity. It is not correct, however, (as is sometimes asserted) that that theory is used in its full force in Bohr's argument. Indeed it was shown by Kalckar[39] that actually one can devise an alternative clock-in-the-box experiment in which gravitation does not enter at all. This, of course, does not detract from Bohr's original reasoning.

** Probability should not be destroyed but derived.

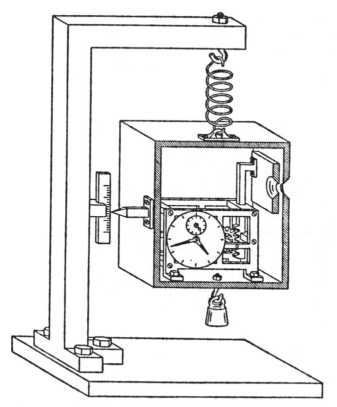

Fig. 10 Drawing of Einstein's clock-in-the-box experiment. (Reproduced with the kind permission of Professor P. A. Schilpp.)

In 1935 Einstein made what may be called a counter-proposal to complementarity. His alternative, which he named objective reality, was presented in a joint paper with Boris Podolsky and Nathan Rosen (the EPR paper).[43] Its main points follow.

1. Definition: 'If without in any way disturbing a system we can predict with certainty (i.e. with a probability equal to unity) the value of a physical quantity, then there exists an element of physical reality corresponding to this physical quantity. Every element of the physical [objective] reality must have a counterpart in the physical theory. We shall call this the condition of completeness.'[43]

2. Example: 'Two particles with respective momentum and position variables (p_1, q_1) and (p_2, q_2) are in a state with definite total momentum $P = p_1 + p_2$ and definite relative distance $q = q_1 - q_2$. This, of course is possible since P and q commute. The particles are allowed to interact. Observations are made on particle 1 long after the interaction has taken place. Measure p_1 and one knows p_2 without having disturbed particle 2. Therefore (in their

language), p_2 is an element of reality. Next, measure q_1 and one knows q_2, again without having disturbed particle 2. Therefore q_2 is also an element of reality, so that both p_2 and q_2 are elements of reality. But quantum mechanics tells us that p_2 and q_2 cannot simultaneously be elements of reality because of the non-commutativity of the momentum and position operators of a given particle. Therefore quantum mechanics is incomplete.'[43]

3. Their comment on the example: 'One would not arrive at our conclusion if one insisted that two . . . physical quantities can be regarded as simultaneous elements of reality *only when they can be simultaneously measured or predicted* [their italics].'[43]

4. Final remark which I have italicized in part:

This [simultaneous predictability] makes the reality of p_2 and q_2 depend upon the process of measurement carried out on the first system which does not disturb the second system in any way. *No reasonable definition of reality could be expected to permit this.*[43]

The only part of this article that will ultimately survive, I believe, is this last phrase which, paraphrased, expresses Einstein's opinion that quantum mechanics is not reasonable.

In 1949 Bohr recalled that the EPR paper 'created a stir among physicists and has played a major role in general philosophical discussions.'[40] When I asked George Uhlenbeck, who was an active physicist in his mid-thirties when EPR appeared, what he recalled about physicists' reactions, he replied that no one he knew paid any attention, that it was an issue that could safely be left to Bohr and Einstein. Bohr was certainly right, however, about the philosophers' response. Some of these continue to refer to the content of the paper as the EPR paradox. That to me seems inappropriate. EPR simply and correctly concluded that their definition of objective reality is incompatible with the assumption that quantum mechanics is complete, their paper is flawless from the point of view of logic. After I had written on this same subject in my Einstein biography,[44] a few people remarked that I had not treated this subject in sufficient detail. I therefore earnestly looked again into philosophers' comments but still have been unable to appreciate what all the fuss is about.

I should like therefore to confine myself to Bohr's response immediately after the appearance of EPR. Rosenfeld who was in Copenhagen at that time has remembered: 'This onslaught came down upon us as a bolt from the blue . . . As soon as Bohr heard my report of Einstein's argument, everything else was abandoned: we had to clear up such a misunderstanding at once.'[45] Rosenfeld has told me that Bohr was infuriated when he first was informed. The next day he appeared at his office all smiles, turned to Rosenfeld and said: 'Podolski, Opodolski, Iopodolski, Siopodolski, Asiopodolski, Basiopodolski.' Poor Rosenfeld was bewildered. Bohr explained: He was quoting from a Holberg play* in which a servant suddenly starts talking gibberish . . . When Rosenfeld remarked that Bohr had evidently calmed down, Bohr replied: 'That's a sign that we are beginning to understand the problem . . . They do it smartly but what counts is to do it right.'[45]

Three months later Bohr submitted his reply[46] to EPR. '[This] refutation of Einstein's criticism does not add any new argument to the conception of complementarity.'[45] Bohr did not believe that the EPR paper called for any change in the interpretation of quantum mechanics. *'We are, in the "freedom of choice" offered by [EPR], just concerned with a discrimination between different experimental procedures which allow of the unambiguous use of complementary classical concepts* [Bohr's italics].' Most physicists (myself included) agree with that judgement.

The 1935 papers mark the end of the Bohr–Einstein dialog insofar as it appeared in the scientific literature. There are a few who opine that Einstein concluded with a bang, while most consider it a whimper.

It is most fitting to let Einstein have the last word: 'Of the "orthodox" quantum theoreticians whose position I know, Niels Bohr's seems to me to come nearest to doing justice to the [EPR] problem.' Einstein remained forever opposed, however, to 'Bohr's principle of complementarity, the sharp formulation of which I have been unable to achieve despite much effort I have expended on it'.[47]

During the twenty years following the events just recounted, Bohr and Einstein met several times in Princeton. I have already described (1b) how Bohr reacted to Einstein's continuing dissent. As to Einstein, during that period he once said that Bohr thought very clearly, wrote obscurely, and thought of himself as a prophet.[48] On 19 March 1949 a symposium was held in Princeton to honor Einstein on his 70th birthday. I was present and recall that a tape containing Bohr's congratulations was played that afternoon.[49] Bohr used his reply to a thank-you letter from Einstein to comment once again on quantum mechanics: 'In my impudent way I would say that . . . no one – not even the dear Lord himself – can know what an expression like throwing dice means.'[50]

Einstein's last letter[51] to Bohr dates from March 1955 and begins as follows: 'Don't frown like that; this has nothing to do with our old controversy regarding physics but rather with a subject on which we fully agree.' The letter concerned an initiative out of which later grew the Pugwash conferences. One month later Einstein died – unconvinced.

Philosophy, at least natural philosophy, underwent a change which I would

* *Ulysses von Ithaca*, Act 1, Scene 15.

call dramatic – and which to my knowledge has not yet been digested by most professional philosophers – when in the late 1930s Bohr gave a new answer to an old question: *What does one mean by the word 'phenomenon?'* Next to complementarity, Bohr's new formulation is his most important contribution to philosophy.*

Let us first go back and consider Bohr's earlier views. As mentioned before (13e), in Como Bohr had said: 'Our normal [classical] description of physical phenomena is based entirely on the idea that the phenomena may be observed without disturbing them appreciably.'[1] which carries the implications that quantum effects do cause such a disturbance and that one should distinguish between a phenomenon associated with an object on the one hand and the mode of observation on the other. In 1929 he employed a similar usage of 'phenomenon'. *'The finite magnitude of the quantum of action prevents altogether a sharp distinction being made between a phenomenon and the agency by which it is observed* [his italics].'[53] He used a similar formulation (quoted earlier in this section) at the Maxwell celebration in 1931. In 1937 he still talked of 'aspects of quantum phenomena revealed by experience under mutually exclusive conditions',[54] which should be understood to mean, I think, that particle and wave properties refer to one and the same 'phenomenon'. I could well imagine that these various early statements may have added to misunderstandings of what complementarity is all about.

In 1938 Bohr abandoned all these formulations as inferior. He sharpened his own language, one might say, by *defining the term 'phenomenon' to include both the object of study and the mode of observation.* This is how he put it that year at an international conference in Warsaw:

> Speaking, as is often done, of disturbing a phenomenon by observation, or even of creating physical attributes to objects by measuring processes, is, in fact, liable to be confusing, since all such sentences imply a departure from basic conventions of language which, even though it sometimes may be practical for the sake of brevity, can never be unambiguous. It is certainly far more in accordance with the structure and interpretation of the quantum mechanical symbolism, as well as with elementary epistemological principles, to reserve the word 'phenomenon' for the comprehension of the effects observed under given experimental conditions.[55]

Thus, ten years after Bohr had begun talking about complementarity he had finally found the correct language in which to express what had been on his mind all that time. Another ten years later he slightly refined his Warsaw statement:

> Phrases often found in the physical literature, as 'disturbance of phenomena by observation' or 'creation of physical attributes of objects by measurements' represent a use of words like 'phenomena' and 'observation' as well as "attribute"

---

* This subject is discussed in detail in Ref. 52.

and 'measurement' which is hardly compatible with common usage and practical definition and, therefore, is apt to cause confusion. As a more appropriate way of expression, one may strongly advocate limitation of the use of the word *phenomenon* to refer exclusively to observations obtained under specified circumstances, including an account of the whole experiment.[56]

And, of course, he included this phraseology in the Schilpp book of 1949[40], his most readable account of the evolution of his ideas.

Bohr's usage of 'phenomenon', if not generally accepted, is the one to which nearly all physicists now subscribe.

The best known physicist to take exception was Einstein.

Having explained Bohr's concept of phenomenon, I can now state Einstein's objections to quantum physics in one brief phrase: Bohr's usage of *phenomenon* was unacceptable to Einstein. In contrast to the view that the notion of phenomenon *irrevocably* includes the specifics of the conditions of experimental observation, Einstein held that one should seek for a deeper-lying theoretical framework which permits the description of phenomena independently of these conditions. This is what he meant by the term *objective reality*, mentioned earlier in this section. It was his almost solitary conviction that quantum mechanics is logically consistent, but that it is an incomplete manifestation of an underlying theory in which an objectively real description is possible – a position he maintained until his death.*

This concludes my account of Bohr's philosophical contributions to quantum physics.

Whenever I teach quantum mechanics I include an account of complementarity. Invariably this leads to questions. What follows is a sort of composite of what I am asked (by Q) and how I (P) reply.

Q. All this about complementarity is very interesting. But of what use is it to me?

P. It will neither help you in your quantum mechanics calculations nor in setting up your experiment. In order to do physics you should not only assimilate and develop facts, however. In between you had better reflect on the meaning of what you are doing. In that respect Bohr's considerations are extremely significant. Don't you agree it ought to matter to you what, for example, a modern scientist means or should mean when he talks about 'a phenomenon'? Note also that insights like these may serve to explain to interested laymen and to remind scientists what our profession is about.

Q. You have told us what Einstein's objections were but not *why* he objected.

* See ref. 44 for more technical details of Einstein's position.

P. I have often wondered about that but have no good answer. It seems to me that this belongs not just to his intellectual but also to his emotional make up. His other oeuvre shows such flexibility, such daring, yet in regard to quantum mechanics he revealed such rigidity. I may add that to the end of his life he thought much and hard about quantum physics. He did not just say: 'I don't like what is happening.' He searched forever for alternatives.[57]

Q. I have read statements to the effect that the exchanges between Bohr and Einstein rank among the great intellectual debates of the century. You seem less effusive.

P. Yes and no. I do not think that these discussions affected the progress of physics in any way. I do believe, however, that they are fundamental to those concerned with epistemological issues.

In addition this debate is very revealing about the personalities of both men. There was Einstein, so wise, yet so incomprehensibly unyielding. There was Bohr, who just as well could have said: 'Einstein is a great man, I am fond of him, but in regard to quantum physics he is out to lunch. Let him.' Even so, I think Bohr would have put his stamp on quantum physics. But no, Bohr wanted so badly to convince Einstein. That is part of *his* emotional make up.

Q. There were and are those other than Einstein who were and are critical of quantum mechanics. How did Bohr react to their efforts?

P. I think he did not think these interesting. Neither, for that matter, did Einstein.[58] Nor did Pauli.[59] In any event, nowhere in his papers does Bohr enter into polemics on such matters as hidden variables or even more mind-boggling alternatives. Remember, however, that most of these activities occurred after Bohr's death. Also, Bohr's interests concerned the future, what new and exciting things were in store. By 1960 the non-relativistic quantum mechanics of a few particles in an external potential was a closed chapter to Bohr, as to most physicists.

Q. Some say that complementarity has introduced a subjective element in physics. Do you think so?

P. I would say: on the contrary. In his last published paper Bohr himself put it very succinctly: 'This development has essentially clarified the conditions for an objective account in atomic physics, involving the elimination of all subjective judgement.'[60]

Q. I have seen articles and books on the quantum theory of measurement. What did Bohr think about these?

P. I am glad you ask. Looking through old notebooks of my Princeton days I found the following entry.

16 November 1954. Lecture by Bohr. He thinks that the notion 'quantum theory of measurement' is wrongly put. What Bohr and Bohr–Rosenfeld [16d] did was to give examples which elucidate the mathematical contents of the quantum theory.

Bohr's reference to examples is important. He never wrote of complementarity as a theory or a theorem but rather in a case-by-case way as an illumination of measurement issues. That, I think, has added to the difficulties of the more mathematically minded in getting hold of what Bohr was after.

I do know, though, that when in Princeton Bohr would often discuss measurement theory with Johnny von Neumann who pioneered that field.[61] A little of those discussions has even appeared in print.[62] As I see it, these considerations have led to contributions, important ones, to mathematics[63] rather than to physics.

Q. I have often heard that in Copenhagen Bohr played the role of a sort of guru surrounded by worshipful disciples. What are your impressions?

P. I too have heard and also seen in print such utterances, for example: 'As a sage Bohr spoke in riddles and parables, both hard to grasp and hard to compose.'[64] Opinions like these show a complete misunderstanding of Bohr's personality. As I comprehend it, a guru is a person who has or believes he has possession of wisdom which he dispenses in oracular ways. Bohr was not like that at all. He tried as hard as he could to share his knowledge with others in simple and straightforward language. That it was not his forte to achieve this is quite something else than purposely speaking in tongues. As to worshipful disciples, we respected his ideas but certainly did not accept them, if at all, without often heated arguments, which Bohr in fact encouraged. As he would say from time to time, he had the good fortune to be surrounded by young critical people who liked to doubt and ridicule any new idea.

As antidote to that sage stuff I should like to note one more time what I consider the best characterization ever given of Bohr:

He utters his opinions like one perpetually groping and never like one who believes he is in possession of definite truth.

Hardly the guru style. Who wrote that? Einstein wrote it, shortly before his death.[65] That old man was not only a physics genius but also a keen observer of humanity – a trait he shared with Bohr.

Q. Do you think that Bohr's are the last words on the meaning of quantum mechanics?

P. I have seen too much to believe that anyone has the last word on any scientific issue, but I do think that Bohr's exegesis of the quantum theory is the best one we have to date. I should add, however, that Bohr never really went into the synthesis of quantum mechanics with general relativity theory and with cosmology. I do not at all feel comfortable with the current status of these issues.

(c) Bohr on statistical mechanics

Among physical questions of principle outside the quantum theory that particularly interested Bohr were those concerning the relations between thermodynamics and statistical mechanics at the classical level (5f). He thought for many years about this problem but published only twice on it, in a brief comment in his Faraday lecture[66] of 1932,* and in an even shorter one in his 1938 Warsaw lecture.[55] Those remarks are qualitative; I have nowhere seen anything quantitative by him on this subject.**

As early as when he was working on his doctor's thesis, we find Bohr brooding about statistical mechanics.[69] Increasingly his interest was drawn to the connection between *classical* mechanics and thermodynamics. Earlier Boltzmann had written at length about that problem, but Bohr believed that he did not have the right answer. (More about that anon.) In 1911 Bohr expressed himself critically about one of Boltzmann's results, but added: 'It is one of those problems that almost always slip away between one's fingers just at the moment that one really has caught it,'[70] an experience familiar to all who have struggled with these delicate and difficult issues. When in 1912 Bohr lectured in Copenhagen on the mechanical foundations of thermodynamics, he again expressed reservations about Boltzmann's views.[71]

Turning now to Bohr's Faraday lecture,[66] I note its main point regarding the issue at hand:

Notwithstanding the essentially new situation created by the discovery of the quantum of action, the characteristic feature with which we have here to do is not unfamiliar in atomic theory. A typical example is afforded by the statistical theory of heat, according to which the very concept of temperature stands in an exclusive relation to a detailed description of the behaviour of the atoms in the bodies concerned . . . In fact, in statistical thermodynamics, we have in the first place not to do with a failure of the mechanical concepts in accounting for the details of the events, but with the incompatibility of such a detailed account with a definition of temperature.

In explanation, let us remember (5f) that the use of statistical, probabilistic, techniques in the classical description of a system consisting of huge numbers of atoms is not a matter of first principles, as in quantum

---

* At that time Bohr was also interested in superconductivity. He actually wrote a paper on that subject which reached page proof but was withdrawn before publication.[67] See also his correspondence with Bloch.[68]

** Heisenberg's recollections of discussions with Bohr on this issue are of particular interest.[68a]

mechanics, but rather a matter of utmost convenience. For example, according to statistical mechanics the temperature of a gas, a thermodynamic concept, is proportional to the average, taken over all individual atoms in that gas, of the kinetic energy of each individual atom. Bohr's point about an exclusive relation is this. You can *either* ask for the energy of an individual atom, a mechanical notion, *or* for the temperature of a collection of atoms, a thermodynamic notion, but not for both at once. In 1938 he expressed this situation like this:

> Before [the] discovery [of quantum mechanics] statistical methods were of course extensively used in atomic theory but merely as a practical means of dealing with the complicated mechanical problems met with in the attempt at tracing the ordinary properties of matter back to the behaviour of assemblies of immense numbers of atoms. It is true that the very formulation of the laws of thermodynamics involves an essential renunciation of the complete mechanical description of such assemblies and thereby exhibits a certain formal resemblance with typical problems of quantum theory.[55]

Bohr expressed this formal resemblance by saying that energy and temperature are complementary. According to Rosenfeld: 'This question of complementarity here came in '31 when he was writing his Faraday lecture; it may have occurred to him before.'[72] Heisenberg has remembered how 'Bohr emphasized the complementarity between temperature and energy to the extreme'.[73] This new usage of the term complementarity remains qualitative (there are no underlying uncertainty relations!*) and is in no way related to quantum mechanics. One may say, it seems to me, that Bohr's views on complementarity between mechanics and thermodynamics are illuminating. They have made scarcely any impact, however. Correspondence in the late 1940s with Pauli[76] and with Stern[77] shows Bohr's continued involvement with the relations between mechanical and statistical pictures.

I conclude with a remark on Bohr's attitude toward Boltzmann and Gibbs, the two masters of statistical mechanics.

Boltzmann produced two distinct approaches to the theory of systems, particularly but not only gases, consisting of very many atoms. One of these is the 'kinetical method', in which he tried to deduce the overall behavior of a gas from the mechanics of two-body collisions between its constituent atoms. That approach seemed to Bohr to be a misunderstanding. 'He said that Boltzmann had spoiled things by insisting on the properties of mechanical systems.'[72**] This part of Boltzmann's work is relatively easily

---

* Rosenfeld has made an attempt at formulating uncertainty relations for energy–temperature.[74] It was shown by Lindhard and Kalckar that this work is not correct, however.[75]

** Nor did Bohr care for the relation, of later vintage, between thermodynamics and information theory.[78]

accessible in his two volume book *Lectures on Gas Theory*.[79] There Boltzmann touches only in passing on his alternative approach, the statistical method, in which there is no need to deal with collision mechanisms and collision frequencies. To appreciate this work one needs to consult Boltzmann's papers. These are long and sometimes obscure. He also had the habit of tucking away important conclusions amid lengthy calculations.* Maxwell said of his writings: 'By the study of Boltzmann I have been unable to understand him. He could not understand me because of my shortness, and his length was and is an equal stumbling block to me.'[81] Einstein once said to one of his students: 'Boltzmann's work is not easy to read. There are great physicists who have not understood it.'[82] One of these, I believe, was Bohr.

Bohr had the greatest admiration, expressed again and again throughout the years, for Gibbs' book, *Elementary Principles in Statistical Mechanics, Developed with Especial Reference to the Rational Foundations of Thermodynamics*, first published in 1902.[83] In particular he valued highly Gibbs' introduction to ensembles, large numbers of copies of the same system of atoms. The atomic motions in individual copies are not necessarily identical at a given instant, but all copies have either the same total energy and number of particles (micro-canonical ensemble), or only the same number of particles (canonical ensemble), or also the number of particles varies (grand canonical ensemble). Gibbs himself, however, acknowledged in the preface of his book that the first two types of ensembles are 'perhaps first found' in an 1871 paper by Boltzmann with the improbable title 'Relation between the laws of behavior of polyatomic gas molecules with Jacobi's principle of the last multiplier.'[84] (The grand canonical ensemble was Gibbs' own invention.) Thus Gibbs surely did read Boltzmann. Boltzmann in turn did read Gibbs. The introduction to Volume 2 of his *Gas Theory* opens with a quotation from an 1875 paper by Gibbs. Evidently the two men had great respect for each other's fundamental and independent contributions.

As to Bohr, I share Rosenfeld's conjecture: 'I don't think that he had ever read Boltzmann, or at any rate not Boltzmann's papers.** He had read, I think, and studied very carefully Boltzmann's lectures on gas theory.'[72]

(d) Complementarism

1. *Introductory.* Bohr had concluded his Como lecture[1] by suggesting that his new concepts might find applications outside physics as well: 'I hope . . .

* See especially M. Klein's essay[80] for an appreciation of Boltzmann's contributions and style.

** In his doctor's thesis Bohr did quote one paper (on another subject) by Boltzmann, however.[85]

that the idea of complementarity is suited to characterize the situation which bears a deep-going analogy to the general difficulty in the formation of human ideas inherent in the distinction between subject and object' – clearly an allusion to the ambiguities in psychological terminology which Bohr had thought so much about in his adolescence (19a). At that time the analogy between Riemann surfaces and 'planes of objectivity' had served him as a source of inspiration. Now the newly found tool of complementarity was, he hoped, much better suited to cope with his earlier quandaries. If since then the tools had changed, the purpose had not – which, I think, explains why in the late 1920s the psychologist Rubin, a friend since the Ekliptica days (6b), once said after Bohr had explained to him some point about complementarity: 'But Niels! You told us all of that twenty years ago!'[86]

I shall now try as well as I can to give some account of Bohr's thoughts about possible extended applications of complementarity. Unlike the situation in the quantum theory, these lack the quantitative support provided there by the uncertainty relations. In order to bear this distinction in mind, I shall refer to these reflections as 'complementarism', a term which may also serve to indicate that 'the epistemological lesson of the quantum theory' (one of Bohr's own favorite expressions) does not readily fit into the other isms with which philosophy abounds.

Bohr, well aware that these ideas were mostly preliminary (he often called them 'seeds for further thought'), had a story ready for the occasion. Once upon a time a young rabbinical student went to hear three lectures by a famous rabbi. Afterwards he told his friends: 'The first talk was brilliant, clear and simple. I understood ever word. The second was even better, deep and subtle. I didn't understand much, but the rabbi understood all of it. The third was by far the finest, a great and unforgettable experience. I understood nothing and the rabbi didn't understand much either.'[87]

I now turn to Bohr's wide-ranging considerations on complementarity, arranging them by subject.

2. *Psychology*. When in 1929 Bohr gave the opening address 'Atomic theory and the fundamental principles underlying the description of nature' before the congress of Scandinavian scientists, held in Copenhagen, he concluded like this:

The fact that consciousness, as we know it, is inseparably connected with life ought to prepare us for finding that the very problem of the distinction between the living and the dead escapes comprehension in the ordinary sense of the word. That a physicist touches upon such questions may perhaps be excused on the ground that the new situation in physics has so forcibly reminded us of the old truth that we are spectators as well as actors in the great drama of existence.[36]

This is perhaps the most succinct summary of Bohr's ideas on complementary aspects in psychology. A person contemplates, is spectator, when planning his action, and again when reflecting on its results. In between, when acting, he is, one hopes, also thinking but not in the contemplative mode. To be spectator is as necessary for executing and evaluating the role of actor as to perform the act itself. These two modes of engagement are both necessary elements in the person's mental content, yet they exclude each other – they are complementary. This is a new look at issues that one finds in ancient dramas, like the dialog between Arjuna and Krishna in the *Gita*, and also, to give a more recent example, in the story 'Adventures of a Danish student' by Poul Martin Møller, which made a strong impression on Bohr (19a) and from which he often quoted these lines:

My endless inquiries made it impossible for me to achieve anything. Moreover, I get to think about my own thoughts of the situation in which I find myself. I even think that I think of it, and divide myself into an infinite retrogressive sequence of 'I's who consider each other. I do not know at which 'I' to stop as the actual, and as soon as I stop, there is indeed again an 'I' which stops at it. I become confused and feel giddy as if I were looking down into a bottomless abyss, and my ponderings result finally in a terrrible headache.

Bohr's Copenhagen address was the second occasion, after his initial allusion in the Como lecture, in which he had turned to psychology. Earlier, in 1929, he had written: 'In order to describe our mental activity, we require, on the one hand, an objectively given content to be juxtaposed to a perceiving subject, while, on the other hand, no sharp separation between object and subject can be maintained, since the perceiving subject also belongs to our mental content.'[33] Bohr likened the resulting arbitrariness in the placement of the cut between object and subject in psychology, the actor describing his actions, with the arbitrariness (already discussed in (14e)) in the distinction between object and tool for observation in physics.

In that same paper[33] Bohr also entered 'the ongoing discussions going back to oldest times about the freedom of will'. Is our actor free to choose what act he wills to perform? Here too Bohr considers a complementary way of thinking to be liberating: 'The decisive point is here that the state of consciousness in the description of which words like 'I will' find application is complementary to a state in which we are concerned with an analysis of motives for our actions.'[88] In Bohr's view, 'I will' refers to a subjective emotional state, a *feeling* of freedom, complementary to a state of *reasoning* in which 'I will' is analyzed as a causal chain of objective acts. 'When we use the phrase "I will" we renounce explanatory argumentation.'[56] Bearing this distinction between feeling and reasoning in mind, 'the feeling of will finds its natural room for play'.[89]

In Bohr's writings on psychology the complementarity of emotion and reason is all-pervasive. 'The use of words like "thoughts" and "sentiment", equally indispensable for illustrating the diversity of psychical experience, pertains to mutually exclusive situations characterized by a different drawing of the line of separation between subject and object.'[56] This to him was old wisdom in new language. 'We know the old saying that, if we try to analyze our own emotions, we hardly possess them any more.'[90] Thoughts like these, pointing to 'the inseparability of epistemological and psychological analysis'[91] guided Bohr throughout his life. They found their final expression in Bohr's last paper, published posthumously: 'Words like thoughts and sentiments . . . have since the origin of language been used in a typically complementary manner.'[60]

3. *Biology*. Already in 1929 Bohr had noted,[36] but only in passing, that in the description of living organisms one might see a certain connection with the issues of the quantum theory. That brief remark developed into the main theme in the address 'Light and Life' which he gave in August 1932 at the opening session of an international congress of light therapists in Copenhagen.[92]

Here, for the first time, Bohr raised a question that was to preoccupy him, off and on, until his death: Would it ever be possible to push the analysis of living processes to the limit where they can be described in terms of pure physics and chemistry? 'The question at issue is whether some fundamental traits are still missing in the analysis of natural phenomena before we can reach an understanding of life on the basis of physical experience.'[92] He noted that some biologists held 'the belief that no proper understanding of the essential aspects of life is possible in purely physical terms, [but this] view, known as vitalism, can hardly be given an unambiguous expression by the assumption that a peculiar vital force, unknown to physics, governs all organic life'. It was obvious, Bohr continued, that one would find no 'features foreign to inorganic matter' by pushing the analysis of the constituents of a living organism to the molecular/atomic level. 'It must be kept in mind, however, that the conditions in biological and physical research are not directly comparable, since the necessity of keeping the object alive *imposes a restriction on the former* [i.e. living things] *which finds no counterpart in the latter* [my italics]. Thus we should doubtlessly kill an animal if we tried to carry the investigation of its organs so far that we could tell the part played by the single atoms in vital functions. In every experiment on living organisms there must remain some uncertainty as regards the physical conditions to which they are subjected, and the idea suggests itself that the minimal freedom we must allow the organism will be just large enough to permit it, so to say, to hide its ultimate secrets from us. On this view, the very existence of life must in biology be considered as an elementary fact, just as in atomic physics the existence of the quantum of action has to be taken as a basic fact that cannot be derived from ordinary mechanical physics. Indeed, the essential non-analyzability of atomic stability in mechanical terms presents a close analogy to the impossibility of a physical or chemical explanation of the peculiar functions character-istic of life,' [92]

This brings us to Bohr's new concept of analysis in biology: there exists an 'obvious exclusiveness between such aspects of life as the self-preservation and self-generation of individuals on the one hand, and the subdivision necessary for any physical analysis on the other hand. Due just to this essential feature of complementarity, the concept of purpose which is foreign to mechanical analysis finds a certain application in biology.' [92] Later Bohr expressed his views most succinctly like this: 'Mechanistic and vitalistic arguments are used in a typically complementary manner.' [93]

'When Bohr's address on "Light and Life" was published, it was not well received by the biologists.' [94] A positive response came from other quarters, however.

On the morning of the day Bohr addressed the light therapists Max Delbrück, a young physicist, arrived in Copenhagen from his native Berlin. He was 'met at the station [by Rosenfeld] with an outright summons that I should come at once to the *Rigsdag*, the Parliament building, where the opening session took place* . . . I am perhaps the only one of his associates of those days** who took [Bohr] so seriously that it determined [my] career, changing over into biology to find out whether indeed there was anything to this point of view.' [97] Delbrück's professional switch was Bohr's greatest contribution to biology. In an obituary of Delbrück[98] it has been written: 'Odd though these views [expressed in "Light and Life"] may seem to us now, in retrospect, this lecture confirmed Max's decision to turn to biology . . . It is fair to say that with Max, Bohr found his most influential philosophical disciple outside the domain of physics, in that through Max, Bohr provided one of the intellectual fountainheads for the development of 20th century biology.'

Actually Delbrück continued doing physics for a while, first in Copenhagen, where he spent the spring and summer of 1931. In 1932–4 he returned there for several short stays, during one of which he was the guiding spirit in the preparation of the famous Copenhagen Faust (1c). He also spent six months with Pauli in Zürich. His first papers in biology date from 1935. His celebrated work on bacteriophages began after his move to Cal Tech in 1937, where he became professor of biology in 1946. It is worthy of note that, in the 1963 meeting at Copenhagen commemorating the 50th anniversary of Bohr's first papers on atomic constitution, only one paper on complementarity was presented – by Delbrück, on biology.[97] He received a Nobel Prize in 1969.

---

* Among those attending were the Danish crown prince and prime minister.[95]
** Pascual Jordan was another physicist much interested at that time in Bohr's ideas on biology. His views diverged from those of Bohr, however.[96]

I return to Bohr. In a lecture given in 1937 he further elaborated. 'It is far from me to share the widely spread opinion that the new developments in atomic physics could help us to decide about questions like "mechanistic or vitalistic views" in favor of one or the other . . . already the definition of what life is contains epistemological problems . . . atomic physics yields no insight into the so-called holistic or finalistic characteristics of life activities . . . it is my purpose to avoid empty controversies by means of an analysis of the conditions and appropriateness of the pertinent concepts . . . [my opinions do not imply] any restriction on the physico-chemical methods in biology . . . I have endeavored to make clear that [my views] are no purely metaphysical speculations – as philosophers and biologists fear.'[99]

The next occasion on which I found Bohr commenting on biology was in his address 'Medical research and natural philosophy' to the second international poliomyelitis conference, in Copenhagen in 1951.[100] At that time he could point to the advances in biology due to the development of the isotopic tracer method (17h). He also returned to 'the old debate of what attitude to take to the explanation of life, or rather to the rational description of the position of living beings among the natural phenomena . . . According to the weight which in such discussions has been laid on words like cause and purpose, two viewpoints characterized as mechanicism and vitalism have often stood sharply against each other.' Once again Bohr presented his own opinion: 'We are here neither speaking of any such attempt of tracing an analogy to life in simple machinery, nor of the old idea of a mystic life force, but of two approaches which only together exhaust the possibility of increasing our knowledge.' As Bohr put it in the course of the Gifford lectures he gave in Edinburgh, this was 'the lesson derived from the recent progress in atomic physics concerning the logical aspects of man's position in existence'.[101]

Bohr's position had to change, of course, after the discovery in 1953 by Francis Crick and Jim Watson of the structure of DNA and of the physico-chemical processes of biological replication initiated by that specific molecule. All reference to vitalism now vanishes from Bohr's writings on biology – but complementarity persists. Thus, in 1958: 'A description of the internal function of an organism and its reaction to external stimuli requires the word *purposeful* [B.'s italics], which is foreign to physics and chemistry . . . attitudes termed mechanistic and finalistic are not contradictory points of view, but rather exhibit a complementary relation.'[102] Complementarity has shifted from mechanistic versus vitalistic to mechanistic versus teleological.* In 1959 Bohr said in addition: 'There appears to be no reason to expect any inherent limitation of the application of elementary physical and chemical concepts to the analysis of biological phenomena.'[104]

* A similar trend is found in Bohr's 1960 address to the international congress of pharmaceutical sciences in Copenhagen.[103]

Bohr's final verdict on biology was spoken on 21 June 1962 on the occasion of the opening of the Institute of Genetics at the University of Cologne. His address, entitled 'Light and Life revisited', contains no reference at all to complementarity:

In the last resort, it is a matter of how one makes headway in biology. I think that the feeling of wonder which the physicists had thirty years ago has taken a new turn. Life will always be a wonder, but what changes is the balance between the feeling of wonder and the courage to try to understand.[105]

Bohr was still at work on improving that manuscript at the time of his death. The posthumously published version was prepared under the supervision of Aage Bohr.

4. *Human cultures.* Bohr's 1938 address 'Natural philosophy and human cultures'[106] to the international congress of anthropology and ethnology, held at Helsingør, was the first occasion on which he publicly discussed questions regarding evolution and mutual interplay of cultures. These issues appear to have originated with Bohr as the result of his reflections on the complementarity of instinct and reason. 'The amazing capacity of so-called primitive people to orientate themselves in forests or deserts might justify the conclusion that such feats are only possible when no recourse is taken to conceptual thinking.' Those capacities are on a par, he thought, with those of animals who 'know' how to find their way over extraordinarily large distances.

Thoughts like these led Bohr to the issue of nature versus nurture. He emphatically sided with the latter.[107] 'Such considerations confront us at once with the question whether the widespread belief that every child is born with a predisposition for the adoption of a specific human culture is really well-founded, or whether one has to assume that any culture can be implanted and thrive on quite different physical backgrounds ... In characterizing different nations and even different families within a nation, we may to a large extent consider anthropological traits and spiritual traditions as independent of each other, and it would even be tempting to reserve by definition the adjective "human" for just those characteristics which are not directly bound with human inheritance.' Reading this lecture I find Bohr more provocative than were his usual tactful ways. One may well suppose that here his opinions were colored by aversion to racist ideology so prevalent in the 1930s.

Regarding the position of different human cultures relative to each other, Bohr had this to say: 'The main obstacle to an unprejudiced attitude towards the relation between various human cultures is the deep-rooted differences of the traditional backgrounds ... which exclude any simple comparison between such cultures ... In this connection the viewpoint of complementarity offers itself as a means of coping with the situation ...

Especially in the study of cultures of primitive peoples, ethnologists are, indeed, not only aware of the risk of corrupting such cultures by necessary contact, but are even confronted with the problem of the reaction of such studies on their own human attitude. What I here allude to is the experience, well known to explorers, of the shaking of their hitherto unrealized prejudices through the experience of the unsuspected inner harmony human life can present under conventions and traditions most radically different from their own ... We may truly say that different human cultures are complementary to each other ... Of course there cannot, in this domain, be any question of such absolutely exclusive relationships as those between complementary experiences about the behavior of well-defined atomic objects, since hardly any culture exists which could be said to be fully self-contained.' Bohr went on to note how the gradual fusion of traditions, for example by emigration or conquest, advances civilization by the creation of new cultures.

In 1948 Bohr returned to the relevance of complementarity 'in sociology ... where we have to cope with the element of complacency inherent in every national culture and manifesting itself in prejudices which obviously cannot be appreciated from the standpoint of other nations[56] ... This element of self-satisfaction inherent in every culture corresponds to the instinct of self-preservation characteristic for any kind of living organism.' [108]

During the last years of his life Bohr reflected on the 'typical complementary features in describing the relation between individuals and society ... every contact with social conditions other than our own makes us realize our prejudices which we hardly suspected we had'.[109] Such prejudices should be counteracted by all possible means: 'At the present moment, when the fate of all peoples is inseparably connected, a collaboration in mutual confidence, based on appreciation of every aspect of the common human position, is more necessary than ever before in the history of mankind.' [108]

5. *Conclusion: language.* One common thread weaving through all of Bohr's philosophical considerations, be it with respect to physics, psychology, biology, or human cultures, is the need for unambiguous use of words in communicating experience. From his earliest philosophical reflections in his student years to the last papers he wrote, language was forever his main concern. If Bohr may be said to have had 'a' philosophy, it is best expressed in these words of his:

What is it that we human beings depend on? We depend on our words. We are suspended in language. Our task is to communicate experience and ideas to others. We must strive continually to extend the scope of our description, but in such a way that our messages do not thereby lose their objective or unambiguous character.[15]

To this, by way of emphasis, he added at one time: 'Just because it is not yet awake to the use of concepts, a new-born child can hardly be reckoned as a human being.'[106]

'Bohr was not puzzled by ontological problems or by questions as to how concepts are related to reality. Such questions seemed sterile to him.'[15] In his opinion communicability was the be all and end all in our quest for knowledge:

Our task is not to penetrate into the essence of things, the meaning of which we don't know anyway, but rather to develop concepts which allow us to talk in a productive way about phenomena in nature.[110]

To Bohr, to be objective meant to give unambiguous expression to what one knows. Not surprisingly, therefore, he was averse to metaphysical speculation. There have been those who attempted to portray him as a mystic. Bohr summarily dismissed such opinions. He believed he could express his views 'without risking being misunderstood that it should be the purpose to introduce a mysticism which is alien to the spirit of natural science.'[37]

Communication of ideas was important to Bohr, but a great communicator he was not. Pauli has written of him: 'He knew what he wished *not* to say when he strove in long sentences to express himself in his scientific papers.'[111] It may be said, I think, that what stood in Bohr's way of expression was complementarity itself. How can a man talk and write in simple terms when he believes that 'the conscious analysis of a concept stands in an exclusive relation to its immediate application'[33]? Or that 'the practical use of every word stands in a complementary relation to its strict definition'[93]? As Rosenfeld has recalled: '[Bohr] felt that whenever you come with a definite statement about anything you are betraying complementarity . . .'[72]

What was the harvest of Bohr's philosophical reflections?

Without doubt Bohr's contributions to the foundations of quantum mechanics is the most important part. Complementarity, the use of classical language in quantum physics, the modern concept of 'phenomenon', all these are by now so ingrained in the way most physicists think that it seems hard to remember that someone had to say these things first.

As to Bohr's thoughts concerning other areas of knowledge, opinions about their value vary. To my own mind, his ideas about psychology, especially about free will, are of lasting value and deserve to be far more widely known than they actually are. Certainly they are new. His contributions to the general issues of human culture are not new and original, yet beautifully convey Bohr's position that complementarity carries lessons of tolerance and of openness toward all the world. His thoughts on biology have not borne fruit.

Finally, I hope that the spirit of this sketch on Bohr's philosophy reflects one of his examples of complementarity between reason and sentiment:

Though the closest possible combination of justice and love presents a common goal in all cultures, it must be recognized that in any situation which calls for the strict application of justice there is no room for display of love, and that, conversely, the ultimate exigencies of a feeling of love may conflict with all ideas of justice.[112]

This is just one of the many examples of the complementary style of thinking which have had such a lasting and liberating influence on my own life.

References

1. N. Bohr, *Nature* **121**, 580, 1928, CW, Vol. 6, p. 147.
2. N. Bohr, The philosophical lessons of atomic physics, lectures delivered at MIT on 5, 7, 14, 19, 21, 26 November 1957, unpublished, draft MS in NBA.
3. N. Bohr, interview by T. S. Kuhn, A. Petersen, and E. Rüdinger, 17 November 1962, NBA.
4. Also quoted in N. Blaedel, *Harmoni og enhed*, p. 232, Rhodos, Copenhagen 1985.
5. C. Jørgensen, Niels Bohr og filosofien, *Gads Danske Magazin*, 11 July 1951.
6. W. Heisenberg, NBR, p. 95.
7. H. Bohr, NBR, p. 328.
8. Volume I: Atomic theory and the description of nature, Ox Bow Press, Woodbridge, Conn. 1987.
9. Volume II: Essays 1932–1957 on atomic physics and human knowledge, same publisher.
10. Volume III: Essays 1958–1962 on atomic physics and human knowledge, same publisher.
11. D. Mermin, *Physics Today* **42**, February 1989, p. 105.
12. J. Kalckar, CW, Vol. 6, p. XIX.
13. L. Rosenfeld, *Physics Today* **16**, October 1963, p. 47.
14. N.Bohr, letter to H. Bohr, 5 July 1910, CW, Vol. 1, p. 512.
15. A. Petersen, *Bull. Atom. Sci.*, September 1963, p. 8.
16. H. Høffding, *Philos. Zeitschr.* **35**, 480, 1935. See also the letters by Bohr to Høffding, 11 July 1928, and by Høffding to Bohr, 1 August 1928, NBA, and most especially the comments on Høffding in CW, Vol. 10.
17. D. Favrholdt, *Danish yearbook of philosophy*, **13**, 206, 1976.
18. N. Bohr, letter to H. Bohr, 20 April 1909, CW, Vol. 1, p. 501.
19. N. Bohr, letter to H. Bohr, 26 April 1909, CW, Vol. 1, p. 503.
20. J. Rud Nielsen, *Physics Today* **16**, October 1963, p. 22.

21. M. Bohr, A. Bohr, L. Rosenfeld, interview by T. S. Kuhn, 23 January 1963, NBA.

22. W. James, *The principles of psychology*, Vol. 1, p. 206, repr. by Dover, New York. I learned of this usage from the book by K. M. Meyer-Abich, *Korrespondenz, Individualität und Komplementarität*, p. 154, Steiner, Wiesbaden 1965.

23. See Refs. 3, 13, 17, and also L. Rosenfeld, *Nucl. Phys.* A **126**, 696, 1969.

24. See e.g. N. Bohr, Biology and atomic physics, contribution to the Galvani conference, October 1937, Luigi Parma, Bologna 1938; repr. in Ref. 9, p. 13, and in CW, Vol. 10.

25. See (6b) and especially Bohr's Steno lecture 'Physical science and the problem of life' given in 1949, written text completed in 1957, Ref. 9, p. 94.

26. N. Bohr, letter to E. Schrödinger, 23 May 1928, CW, Vol. 6, p. 464.

27. N. Bohr, *Naturw.* **16**, 245, 1928.

28. C. Møller, *Fysisk Tidsskr.* **60**, 54, 1962.

29. A. Einstein, letter to E. Schrödinger, 31 May 1928, repr. in *Letters on wave mechanics*, Ed. M. Klein, Philosophical Library, New York 1967.

30. M. Planck, letter to A. Sommerfeld, 2 February 1929, Niels Bohr Archives, New York.

31. N. Bohr, letter to C. Oseen, 5 November 1928, CW, Vol. 6, p. 189.

32. H. A. Lorentz, *Proc. Fifth Solvay Conf.*, p. 150, Gauthier-Villars, Paris 1928.

33. N. Bohr, *Naturw.* **17**, 483, 1929, CW, Vol. 6, p. 203; in English: Ref. 8, p. 92.

34. N. Bohr, letter to W. Pauli, 1 July 1929, CW, Vol. 6, p. 443.

35. N. Bohr, letter to W. Pauli, 31 July 1929, CW, Vol. 6, p. 194.

36. N. Bohr, *Naturw.* **18**, 73, 1930; in English: Ref. 8, p. 102.

37. N. Bohr, *Nature* **128**, 691, 1931, CW, Vol. 6, p. 357.

38. L. Rosenfeld, in *Proc. 14th Solvay conf.*, p. 232, Interscience, New York 1968.

39. J. Kalckar, CW, Vol. 7.

40. N. Bohr, in *Albert Einstein: philosopher-scientist*, p. 199, Ed. P. Schilpp, Tudor, New York 1949.

40a. P. Schilpp, letter to N. Bohr, 7 October 1946, NBA.

41. A. Einstein, *Phil. Sci.* **1**, 162, 1934.

42. A. Einstein, letter to W. Pauli, 22 January 1932, repr. in *W. Pauli, scientific correspondence*, Vol. 2, p. 109, Ed. K. von Meyenn, Springer, New York 1985.

43. A. Einstein, B. Podolsky, and N. Rosen, *Phys. Rev.* **47**, 777, 1935.

44. SL, Chap. 25, section (c).

45. L. Rosenfeld, NBR, p. 128ff.

46. N. Bohr, *Nature* **136**, 65, 1935; *Phys. Rev.* **48**, 696, 1935, CW, Vol. 7.

47. A. Einstein in the Schilpp volume, Ref. 40, pp. 674, 681.

48. R. S. Shankland, *Am. J. Phys.* **31**, 47, 1963.

49. *New York Times*, 20 March 1949. Bohr's text was published in *UNESCO World Review*, March 1949; in Danish in *Politiken*, 15 March 1949.

50. N. Bohr, letter to A. Einstein, 11 April 1949, NBA.

51. A. Einstein, letter to N. Bohr, 2 March 1955, NBA.

52. H. J. Folse, 'The philosophy of Niels Bohr', Chaps. 5 and 6, North-Holland, New York 1985.

53. N. Bohr, *Introductory survey*, first published in Danish, see CW, Vol. 6, pp. 97, 257; in English: CW, Vol. 6, p. 279, and Ref. 8, p. 1.
54. N. Bohr, 'Biology and atomic physics', in *Proc. Galvani Congr.*, Bologna 1937, p. 5, L. Parma, Bologna 1938, repr. in Ref. 9, p. 13, see esp. p. 19; also in CW, Vol. 10.
55. N. Bohr, 'The causality problem in atomic physics', in *New theories in physics*, p. 11, Nijhoff, the Hague 1939, repr. in CW, Vol. 7.
56. N. Bohr, *Dialectica* **2**, 312, 1948, repr. in CW, Vol. 7.
57. See SL, Chap. 26.
58. A. Einstein, letter to M. Born, 12 May 1952, repr. in *The Born–Einstein letters*, Walker, New York 1971. For an exposé of views alternative to quantum mechanics see especially the important book by J. S. Bell, *Speakable and unspeakable in quantum mechanics*, Cambridge University Press 1987.
59. W. Pauli, letter to N. Bohr, 16 September 1952, NBA.
60. N. Bohr, *Naturw.* **50**, 725, 1963; in English: *ICSU Rev. World Sci.*, **5**, 194, 1963; Ref. 10, p. 23; CW, Vol. 10.
61. For a compendium of this subject see J. A. Wheeler and W. H. Zurek, *Quantum theory and measurement*, Princeton University Press 1983.
62. Ref. 55, pp. 30–45.
63. See e.g. S. Kochen and E. P. Specker, *J. Math. Mech.* **17**, 59, 1967.
64. J. L. Heilbron, *Rev. Hist. Sci.* **38**, 195, 1985.
65. A. Einstein, letter to B. Becker, 20 March 1954, Einstein Archives.
66. N. Bohr, *J. Chem. Soc. (London)*, 1932, p. 349. The part pertaining to statistical mechanics is reproduced in CW, Vol. 6, pp. 400, 401.
67. N. Bohr, Zur Frage der Supraleitung, *Naturw.*, unpublished proofs dated 11 July 1932, copy in NBA.
68. Letters by N. Bohr to F. Bloch, 15 June, 22 July, 7 September; by F. Bloch to N. Bohr, 12 and 26 July, all in 1932, NBA.
68a. W. Heisenberg, *Der Teil und das Ganze*, Chap. 9, Piper, Munich 1969.
69. See CW, Vol. 1, pp. 241–42, 352–54.
70. N. Bohr, draft of letter to C. W. Oseen, CW, Vol. 6, p. 324; this passage was deleted from the final letter sent 4 December 1911.
71. Cf. the fragment repr. in CW, Vol. 6, p. 320.
72. L. Rosenfeld, interview by T. S. Kuhn and J. L. Heilbron, 22 July 1963, NBA.
73. W. Heisenberg, interview by T. S. Kuhn, 12 July 1963, NBA. The part relevant here was reproduced in CW, Vol. 6, pp. 324–6.
74. L. Rosenfeld, Enrico Fermi school at Varenna, Course No. 14, p. 1, 1960.
75. J. Lindhard in *The lesson of quantum theory*, p. 99, Eds. J. de Boer *et al.*, North-Holland, New York 1986; J. Lindhard and J. Kalckar, *Fysisk. Tidsskr.* **80**, 60, 1982.
76. N. Bohr, letters to W. Pauli, 15 January and 16 May; W. Pauli, letter to N. Bohr, 28 January, all in 1947, CW, Vol. 6, pp. 440–51.
77. See CW, Vol. 6, pp. 467–73.
78. Cf. J. C. Slater, *Solid state and molecular theory*, p. 169, Wiley, New York 1975.
79. L. Boltzmann, *Vorlesungen über Gastheorie*, Barth, Leipzig 1898; English

transl.: *Lectures on gas theory*, transl. S. G. Brush, University of California Press, Berkeley 1964.

80. M. J. Klein, in *The Boltzmann equation*, p. 53, Eds. E. G. D. Cohen *et al.*, Springer, New York 1973.
81. J. C. Maxwell, letter to P. G. Tait, August 1873, repr. in C. G. Knott, *Life and scientific work of P. G. Tait*, p. 114, Cambridge University Press 1911.
82. C. Seelig, *Albert Einstein*, p. 176, Europa Verlag, Zürich 1960.
83. Repr. by Dover, New York 1960.
84. L. Boltzmann, *Wiener Ber.* **63**, 679, 1871, repr. in *Wissenschaftliche Abhandlungen von Ludwig Boltzmann*, Vol. 1, p. 259, Chelsea, New York 1968.
85. CW, Vol. 1, p. 353, footnote 2.
86. CW, Vol. 6, p. XXVI.
87. As retold by A. Petersen (Ref. 15).
88. N. Bohr, Medical research and natural philosophy, in *Acta Medica Scand.* **266** (Suppl.), 967, 1952, CW, Vol. 10.
89. N. Bohr, *Erkenntniss* **6**, 293, 1937; English transl. in *Philos. Sci.* **4**, 289, 1937; CW, Vol. 10.
90. N. Bohr, 'Natural philosophy and human cultures', text of an address, repr. in *Nature* **143**, 268, 1929, Ref. 9, p. 23, CW, Vol. 10.
91. N. Bohr, in *International Encyclopaedia of Unified Science*, Vol. 1, No. 1, 1938.
92. N. Bohr, *Nature* **131**, 421, 457, 1933; repr. in Ref. 9, p. 3, also in CW, Vol. 10; in German: *Naturw.* **21**, 245, 1933.
93. N. Bohr, in *Proc. Eighth Solvay Congr.* 1948, p. 9, Coudenberg, Brussels 1950.
94. L. Rosenfeld, NBR, p. 134.
95. For such and other details see the Delbrück biography by P. Fischer, *Licht und Leben*, Universitätsverlag Konstanz, 1985.
96. P. Jordan, letters to N. Bohr, 20 May, 22 June; N. Bohr, letters to P. Jordan, 5 and 23 June, all in 1931, NBA. See also P. Jordan, *Naturw.* **20**, 814, 1932.
97. M. Delbrück, in *Commemoration of the fiftieth anniversary of Niels Bohr's first paper on atomic constitution*, session of 12 July 1963, p. 41. Dittoed at the Institute for Theoretical Physics, Copenhagen.
98. W. Hayes, *Obit. Not. FRS* **28**, 59, 1982.
99. Ref. 89. Bohr spoke in a similar vein at the Galvani conference, also in 1937, Ref. 54.
100. N. Bohr, *Acta Medica Scand.* **142** (Suppl. 266), 967, 1952; CW, Vol. 10.
101. N. Bohr, the ten Gifford lectures, 21 October–11 November 1949. The quotation is taken from a synopsis delivered in the BBC, 16 January 1950, copy in NBA.
102. N. Bohr, *Daedalus* **87**, 164, 1958, CW, Vol. 10.
103. N. Bohr, address on 29 August 1960, repr. in Ref. 10, p. 17.
104. N. Bohr, 'Quantum physics and biology', contribution to the symposium on models in biology, Bristol 1959, repr. in *Light and Life*, Eds. W. D. McElroy and B. Glass, Johns Hopkins University Press 1961.
105. N. Bohr, *Naturw.* **50**, 725, 1963; in English: *ICSU Rev.* **5**, 194, 1963; Ref. 10, p. 23, CW, Vol. 10.
106. N. Bohr, *Nature* **143**, 268, 1931; repr. in Ref. 9, p. 23; CW, Vol. 10.

107. See also H. Bohr, NBR, pp. 328–29.
108. N. Bohr, 'The unity of human knowledge', repr. in Ref. 10, p. 8, CW, Vol. 10.
109. N. Bohr, *Politiken*, 20 April 1961.
110. N. Bohr, letter to H. P. E. Hansen, 20 July 1935, NBA.
111. W. Pauli, *Rev. Mod. Phys.* **17**, 97, 1945.
112. N. Bohr, in *Studia Orientalia Ioanni Pedersen*, p. 385, Munksgaard, Copenhagen 1953, CW, Vol.10.

20

Fission

The year 1939 changed many things. It witnessed the beginning of
the most destructive war in history. It has also changed science.

V. WEISSKOPF[1]

(a) The early days, including Bohr's discovery of the role of uranium 235

On 10 December 1938 Fermi received a Nobel Prize in physics 'for his
demonstration of the existence of new radioactive elements produced by
neutron irradiation, and for his related discovery of nuclear reactions
brought about by slow neutrons'.

I have already briefly mentioned that Fermi and his group had
immediately exploited the Joliot–Curie discovery of induced radioactivity
by finding a large number of new unstable isotopes. To repeat how one
proceeds (17f), irradiate a substance with neutrons, observe one or more
types of induced radioactivity radiations, each one characterized by a
specific lifetime. If that radiation consists of electrons (positrons), then the
isotope produced will have an atomic number Z (a measure of the nuclear
charge; see (7b)) one higher (lower) than the mother element. Whereupon
one uses radiochemistry to confirm the association of a specific radiation
with a specific element.

Among the results Fermi reviewed in his Nobel lectures were those
obtained by bombarding uranium (U). Already in June 1934, only half a year
after the Joliot Curies' first announcement, Fermi and his men had found
that neutrons hitting U produce several induced activities, one of which
'suggests the possibility that the atomic number of the [produced] element
may be greater than 92',[2] that number being the Z of U.

In his Nobel lecture Fermi summarized these and subsequent findings as
follows. 'The carriers of some of the activities of U are neither isotopes of U
itself nor of the elements lighter than U down to the atomic number 86. We
concluded that the carriers were one or more elements of atomic number
larger than 92; we, in Rome, use to call the elements 93 and 94 Ausenium and
Hesperium respectively.'[3] In early December 1938 Fermi's reasoning was
eminently reasonable. If an isotope does not lie in the region $Z=86$–92, then
it must lie above $Z=92$.

The work of the Rome group was confirmed and extended in other laboratories, notably in Berlin by Hahn, Meitner, and Strassmann, who in July 1938 published[4] preliminary evidence for elements with $Z = 93$–96, just before Meitner fled Berlin (17d). In that same paper the authors also announced the discovery of the new unstable isotope $^{239}_{92}U$, seen as a resonance (15f) of about 25 electronvolt (eV) neutrons. More about that isotope presently.

In 1938 Hahn lectured on these matters in Copenhagen, with Bohr in the audience.[5] Thus the realization grew in widening circles that a new chapter in physics and chemistry had begun, that of the transuranic elements.

Wrong.

In the fall of 1938 Hahn and Strassmann began a most careful radiochemical analysis of the elements produced in neutron–U collisions, a study that ranks among the finest work ever done in that field. Both its motivation and its execution have been summarized in later books by Hahn.[5,6] I must pass by all these fascinating details and turn directly to their results: among the products of neutron–U interactions they identified three isotopes of barium, which have $Z = 56$ – roughly half that of U!!

It was a discovery which can be called staggering. Nothing like it had either been seen or dreamed of before; up till that time nuclear reactions had never produced changes in Z larger than 2.

Their results appeared in print on 6 January 1939.[7] The authors were awed by their own findings: 'We publish rather hesitantly due to [these] peculiar results ... As chemists we should actually state that the new products are barium ... However as "nuclear chemists", working very close to the field of physics, we cannot bring ourselves yet to take such a drastic step which goes against all previous experience in nuclear physics. There could perhaps be a series of unusual coincidences which has given us false indications.'[7] Clearly they found their results hard to swallow, but as Hahn wrote later, 'our caution was not due to any mistrust of our results'.[8]

The first to hear the news was Lise Meitner, then in Stockholm. On 19 December Hahn wrote to her: 'I have agreed with Strassmann that we should first tell you.'[9] In her reply Meitner called the results 'startling, A slow neutron process that should produce barium!'[10]

Fermi first heard of the discovery in the United States.

In September 1938 the first anti-Semitic laws had been passed in Italy. Since Fermi's wife was of Jewish extraction, the family decided at once to leave Italy. The Nobel award presented the perfect opportunity for doing so. On 6 December Fermi, his wife, and their two children left Rome for Stockholm. From there they traveled to Copenhagen, where 'we spent most of our time in Professor Bohr's hospitable home'.[11] On 24 December they boarded the *Franconia* at Southampton. On 2 January 1939 they arrived in New York, where a visiting professorship had been arranged at Columbia University.

Meanwhile it had become clear how one had to interpret the Hahn–Strassmann results. From Frisch's recollections: 'Lise Meitner was lonely in Sweden and, as her faithful nephew, I went [from Copenhagen] to visit her at Christmas. There, in a small hotel ... I found her at breakfast brooding over a letter from Hahn.'[12] Frisch was sceptical until Meitner convinced him of Hahn's superior methods.

During the two or three days the two spent together that Christmas, 'the idea gradually took shape'[12] that Bohr's liquid drop model of a nucleus (15f) could explain what was going on. 'Perhaps a drop could divide itself into two smaller drops by first becoming elongated, then constricted and finally being torn.'[13] They realized that the key was an interplay between two opposing forces. There is an attractive nuclear force, represented in the drop model by a surface tension holding the drop together, similar to what happens to a drop of mercury. There is also a repulsive electrostatic force between protons, tending to pull the nucleus apart. Both forces increase with nuclear size but the repulsive force increases faster. They could estimate that the latter force would win for Z close to 100. Thus 'the uranium nucleus might be a very wobbly unstable drop ready to divide itself at the slightest provocation, such as the impact of a neutron.'[14] They estimated that the kinetic energy of the two fragments was huge: 200 million electronvolts, about ten times larger than in any nuclear reaction previously observed.

Meitner returned to Stockholm, Frisch to Copenhagen, where on 3 January 1939 he told Bohr. 'The conversation lasted only five minutes since Bohr immediately and in every respect agreed with us. He was only astonished that he had not thought earlier of this possibility.'[15] Bohr urged Frisch to write a short paper immediately. Frisch composed a letter to *Nature*, keeping in touch with Meitner by phone. On the evening of 6 January he and Bohr went over a draft.[16] The final version[17] was submitted on 16 January. Frisch had asked a biologist co-worker of Hevesy what term was used for cell division. 'Fission' was the answer. Fission it became, a name that first saw the light of day when on 11 February their Letter appeared.*

One week later a paper by Frisch alone came out.[19] It was a report of an experiment, performed in Copenhagen, which yielded direct evidence for the production of particles 'with an atomic weight of at least about seventy', by means of a study of ionization bursts resulting from bombardment of U by neutrons.

---

* For historical essays on fission see Ref. 18.

Meanwhile on 7 January Bohr had departed for the United States, accompanied by his son Erik and by Rosenfeld. They arrived in New York on 16 January and were met at the dock by several physicists and other friends, including Fermi and his wife who remembered: 'Of the words he spoke I grasped only the most familiar, "Europe . . . war . . . Hitler . . . Denmark . . . danger . . . occupation".' [11] Evidently Bohr was troubled by the gathering clouds of war, and for good reasons. Austria had been overrun by the Nazis the preceding 12 March. On 30 September the infamous Munich accord ('peace in our time') had been signed. Franco was about to enter Madrid. Two months to the day after Bohr's arrival Czechoslovakia would cease to be an independent state . . .

Bohr was headed for Princeton, having been invited on his previous visit to the US (18b) to spend a term at the Institute for Advanced Study. First, however, he had some things to do in New York. Rosenfeld went right on to Princeton and was asked the next day to say something at a journal club meeting of the university's physics department. 'So it was quite natural and quite obvious that I should talk about this note of Frisch . . . That created quite a sensation . . . When Bohr came and heard about that he was quite annoyed because, he said, "I did not want to talk about this Frisch business before Frisch's note had appeared in *Nature*." . . . Bohr tried to intervene at the *Physical Review* to stop the notes that were pouring in, but that was not quite possible.' [20] John Wheeler, who was present at Rosenfeld's talk has recalled: 'Isidor Rabi, who was at the journal club, carried the news to Columbia.' [21] That is how Fermi may first have heard the news.

Bohr was now becoming increasingly nervous about whether Frisch and Meitner would get their deserved priority. While American physicists were at work, he still had not heard from them about the status of their paper. By 20 January Bohr saw the Hahn–Strassmann paper in print, in Princeton.[22] On that same day he sent off a letter to *Nature*,[23] the main purpose of which was to establish priority for Frisch and Meitner. (It appeared in print on 25 February.) During the next ten days he sent letters and telegrams to Frisch asking what was happening.[24] (He finally received a copy of the two papers on 2 February.)

Bohr was particularly concerned because from 26 to 28 January he was going to attend a small theoretical physics conference in Washington, DC, and it was clear that under the circumstances he had to say *something* there about fission. On his way to Washington, he stopped off in New York to see Fermi, who, however, had already left for Washington himself. Bohr talked with Herb Anderson, a junior co-worker of Fermi's, who was at work on the same type of ionization experiment performed earlier by Frisch. On 25 January Anderson made essentially the same observations as Frisch. A telegram was sent to Fermi in Washington.[25] So it came about that on 26 January both Bohr and Fermi reported on fission. 'The whole matter was quite unexpected to all present.'[26] Word about fission immediately appeared in newspapers, for example in the 29 January issue of the *New York Times*.

It was shortly thereafter that a confrontation between Bohr and Fermi took place. As reported by Rosenfeld: 'Fermi gave a talk on the radio about fission . . . He did not mention Frisch . . . So Bohr was furious . . . Well, that was the only time in which I saw Bohr really angry and quite burning with passion, and that was because he was defending another . . . Bohr decided to go to see Fermi and thrash it out with him . . . I accompanied him . . . I did not witness the interview . . . I saw only their faces when they came out – it was a long time – and both of them were quite pale, harrassed, quite exhausted.'[20] Subsequent correspondence, though quite restrained, gives some inkling of their respective attitudes.[27]

The January meeting in Washington had marked the opening of the widespread hunting season for fission. A research group in Washington reported: 'At the conclusion of the conference on 28 January we were privileged to demonstrate [fission] to Professors Bohr and Fermi.'[26] In 1939 over a hundred papers on the subject were published.[28] Among the topics studied were the dependence of fission probability on the incoming neutron energy, the various modes of U fission – by the end of 1939 sixteen different elements had been identified as U fission fragments, some represented by several isotopes[29] – and the fissionability of other elements. All this was experimental. The only theoretical contributions in that period were made by Bohr and by Bohr and Wheeler.

When, one day in early February, Placzek came to Princeton, Bohr remarked to him that now all the confusion about transuranic elements belonged to the past. No, said Placzek, there is still a mystery: as a function of energy, neutron capture by U shows a sizable resonance peak at neutron energies of about 25 eV – the formation of the compound nucleus ^{239}U found earlier by Hahn, Meitner, and Strassmann.[4] One must therefore expect – said Placzek – that fission, a decay mode of ^{239}U, should also show a peak at 25 eV – of which, however, there was no sign. That discussion took place over breakfast at the Princeton Club. 'When Bohr heard that he became restless. "Let us go to Fine Hall,*" he said.'[30] During the five minutes it took to get there, Bohr was silent, deep in thought. When he came to his office, joined by Placzek, Rosenfeld, and Wheeler, he said: 'Now hear this, I have understood everything.'[21]

Bohr explained: the dominant U isotope with weight 238, has the resonance, but at that energy fission does not take place; the rare isotope with weight 235, making up only 0.7 per cent of natural U, becomes fissile at that energy but does not resonate.**

* The building on the Princeton University campus where physics and mathematics members of the Institute for Advanced Study had office space at that time.
** Still rarer isotopes of U do not play any role to speak of.

A short note to this effect was published[31] on 15 February. It is written in typical Bohr style: qualitative, no formulae whatever. It should be stressed that there existed as yet no experimental foundation for Bohr's idea of the role of 235. In fact, at that time 'very few physicists accepted Bohr's explanation. Fermi in particular disagreed strongly'.[32] A direct test would necessitate the enrichment of 235 in a natural U sample which then should exhibit an enhanced rate of fission by slow neutrons. That confirmation came only in March 1940.[33]

During the rest of Bohr's stay in the States he gave various lectures, in Princeton on observation problems in quantum mechanics,[34] at the Rockefeller Institute for medical research in New York on the physico-biological work done in Copenhagen,[35] on fission elsewhere. Most of his time was devoted, however, to a collaboration with Wheeler in which the theory of fission was worked out in much detail. In April Wheeler gave a short resumé of this work in Washington.[36] Their article was still unfinished when Bohr returned to Copenhagen in late May.[37] The collaboration continued by mail and telegram[38] until their main paper[39] was finished in late June, and a short sequel[40] in October.

In this work Bohr met with two old loves: the compound nucleus of 1936 (15f) and the study of the relation between surface tension and surface vibrations, the subject of his prize essay written in 1905–6 (6b). I summarize the main points.

A compound nucleus formed by a neutron incident on a U nucleus gains energy equal to the sum of the kinetic energy and the binding energy of the neutron. The compound system disintegrates when some fluctuation concentrates this excess energy either on a specific particle (a photon, a neutron, etc.) or on a vibrational mode of the compound nucleus as a whole. If the vibrational energy exceeds the critical energy for fission, then the compound nucleus is capable of deforming from its initial spherical shape to elongation, then to a dumbbell shape, then to fission into two big chunks. If the binding energy of the captured neutron is less than the critical fission energy, then the necessary additional energy, the 'activation energy', needs to be supplied by the neutron's kinetic energy. This is the case for the compound nucleus ^{239}U for which Bohr and Wheeler estimated a critical energy of 5.9 MeV and a binding energy of 5.3 MeV, so that at least 0.6 MeV neutron kinetic energy is called for to generate fission. (The experimental activation energy turned out to be more like 1 MeV.) For the compound ^{236}U, on the other hand, they found a critical energy 5.2 MeV and a binding energy 6.6 MeV, so no activation energy is needed at all: very slow neutrons can cause fission of 235!*

---

* The fact that the captured neutron binds more strongly to 235 than to 238 can be seen to be a simple consequence of the exclusion principle (10e) applied to nucleons.

Bohr and Wheeler discussed many other features: whether other nuclei can fission, the competition between fission and other possible fates of the compound nucleus, the fate of the fission fragments, the possibility of instantaneous neutron emission accompanying fission (see (20c) below), etc.[41]

The work with Wheeler was the last major novel contribution to physics by Bohr, now 53 years old. In later years the theory has been refined by others, for example by including shell model effects (15g). The liquid drop model has also remained basic to all later work, however (see also (15g)). A quarter of a century later it was fittingly written: 'Their work was rich in insights destined to aid many another scientist in the years ahead.'[42]

As a footnote to this episode I note that after the War Bohr proposed Frisch and Meitner for a Nobel Prize[43] – which they never received.

I began this section by describing failed attempts to identify transuranic elements. It is fitting to conclude by noting that the search for these has flourished since. Neptunium ($Z=93$) and plutonium ($Z=94$) – named after the two planets beyond Uranus – were discovered already in 1940[44] and 1941[45] respectively. Eleven more have been discovered and named since.[46]* There is evidence for still another four ($Z=106–109$),[47] which, as far as I know, have not yet been baptized.

(b) Fission in Copenhagen

Copenhageners had evidently been in the forefront of fission research: Frisch with his basic paper with Meitner and his experiment on the ionizing power of fission fragments, Bohr with his diagnosis of 235 as the source of U fission by slow neutrons. I have foreshadowed earlier (17j) that fission also played a central role in the early physics program of the new Danish accelerators. I turn next to a brief account of those activities. These do not include Frisch's first fission experiment. That one had been performed with neutrons produced by mixing beryllium with some of the radium that had been Bohr's 50th birthday present (17h).

One must marvel at the lucky timing of the completion of the high-tension accelerator (17j). In February 1939 (!) it had begun to produce an intense source of neutrons obtained by bombarding lithium with deuterons accelerated to 0.9 MeV. Meitner and Frisch at once went to work with this precious commodity, and on 6 March sent the first results to *Nature*,[48] a study of U fission fragments. In May, Bjerge, Brostrøm, and Koch

---

* The elements with $Z=95–105$ are, in this order, americium, curium, berkelium, californium, einsteinium, fermium, mendelevium, nobelium, lawrencium, kurchatovium or rutherfordium, nielsbohrium or hahnium. (In the last two cases there are conflicting claims to priority of discovery.)

completed[49] a search for differences in fission caused by fast and by slow neutrons, the purpose being to find experimental evidence for Bohr's proposal about the different fission properties of 235 and 238. Their results were inconclusive. In November, Brostrøm, Koch, and Tom Lauritsen published an important contribution[50] to the analysis of delayed neutrons in fission.*

Meanwhile a mishap had occurred in September: a high-voltage transformer had burned out and had to be brought back to the Thrige factory in Odense for repair. Its return to Copenhagen was considerably delayed because the Great Belt had frozen over, making ferry crossings impossible for some time. As a result the apparatus could not be turned back on until early 1940.[51]

After this delay the next use of the high-tension equipment was a study[52] of fission fragment tracks in a cloud chamber, made by Brostrøm and Lauritsen in collaboration with Jørgen Bøggild, the resident cloud chamber expert.[53]

The last experiment of that period was the first, performed by Jacobsen and Lassen, with the recently completed cyclotron (17j). It was a study[54] of deuteron-induced fission in U and in thorium, using deuterons in the energy range 7.5–9 MeV. That experiment was completed in the summer of 1940, when war had come to Denmark. The next experimental paper[55] on fission in Denmark did not appear until mid-1945 . . .

To complete this account of experimental nuclear physics work in Denmark in 1939–41 the construction of an isotope separator by Jørgen Koch needs to be mentioned. That project was no doubt in part inspired by Bohr's work on the differences between 235 and 238. Actually U separation was never performed with this apparatus, but important results were obtained for other elements.[56]

The various activities just described stimulated Bohr to further research of his own. The cloud chamber studies led him to extend his earliest postdoctoral studies, those on the scattering and stopping of charged particles traversing matter (7b). Here was a new area of application, the fission fragments being much heavier and having a much greater charge than the particles he had had at hand earlier. Therefore, he noted in a 1940 paper,[57] nuclear collisions play a much larger role here than before. Two further related papers followed, dealing with the velocity–range relations of fission fragments.[58] The experiments on delayed neutrons led to a study[59] of successive transformations in nuclear fission.** Finally, the cyclotron

---

* It was known by then that about one per cent of neutrons produced in fission emerge after the bombardment of U with neutrons has stopped. This is a secondary effect due to the instability of fission fragments.

** These are reactions of the type neutron + nucleus→compound nucleus→neutron + secondary nucleus, followed by fission of the latter.

experiment caused Bohr to analyze the interactions of deuterons with nuclei.[60] This was to be his last physics research paper until 1948 . . .

(c) Atomic energy? Atomic weapons?

Already in 1903 Rutherford and Frederick Soddy had reflected on the enormous energies locked inside the atom, as evidenced by the energy release in radioactive transformations.[61,62] They named this form of energy 'atomic energy'. They could, of course, not use the more appropriate term nuclear energy since the atomic nucleus had yet to be discovered (7b).

The issue of nuclear energy and its possible release entered a new phase after 1932 when the neutron had been discovered and the structure of the nucleus had become understood, at least qualitatively (15d). Even then it remained unclear whether nuclear energy would ever be useful in practice. Thus in his first paper (1936) on the compound nucleus (15f) Bohr remarked that, even if one could accelerate particles to much higher energies than so far possible, 'such effects would scarcely bring us any nearer to the solution of the much discussed problem of releasing the nuclear energy for practical purposes. Indeed, the more our knowledge of nuclear reactions advances the remoter this goal seems to become.'[63] That attitude may well have been influenced by Rutherford's remark[64] in 1933 that 'anyone who expects a source of power from the transformation of . . . atoms is talking moonshine.'[65] Most other physicists kept their own counsel, though I knew one overambitious chap who at that time erroneously believed he had found ways of producing nuclear energy in useful quantities.[66]

There matters lay until 1939, when fission came along.

It did not take profound wisdom to realize that this mechanism might well generate spectacular amounts of energy. Consider the bombardment of 235 with very slow 'thermal' neutrons, say with 0.02 eV kinetic energy. (General quantum mechanical principles tell us that the slower the neutron the greater the fission probability in this process.) Fission generates 200 million electronvolts (MeV) kinetic energy, so one has a ten-billion-fold return on investment!

That may sound impressive but in practical terms 200 MeV does not get you very far. It would take 25000 billion fissions per second to generate one horse-power. The real excitement began when it was realized that fission might possibly provide practical amounts of energy even vastly larger than that one miserable horse-power.

To see how this can happen, imagine that in the fission process not only two big chunks of nuclear matter but also two neutrons are produced. These neutrons could in turn fission two neighboring U nuclei. Now we have four neutrons – and on and on. We would have a snowballing effect, a chain reaction, which might produce most violent explosions. Elementary estimates show that one kilogram of 235 could generate an energy roughly equivalent to 20000 tons of TNT. Put otherwise, the fission of all uranium atoms in one cubic meter of natural U-oxide (U_3O_8) would release enough energy to lift one billion metric tons of water to a height of 17 miles. If one could control the energy produced by the kilogram of 235 so as to release it evenly in one day, then in that time one would generate one billion kilowatts of useful power.

Elementary knowledge of nuclear physics sufficed to realize that prompt neutron production in fission should in fact be a quite plausible occurrence. Consider, for example, the nucleus $^{238}_{92}U$ which consists of 92 protons and 146 neutrons. Why so many more neutrons? Because nucleons (protons and neutrons) attract each other by nuclear forces but only protons repel each other by electrostatic forces. The 'extra' neutrons fulfill the role of additional nuclear glue, serving to counteract that repulsion. Consider now, for the sake of argument, the fission of 238 into two equal parts, yielding two nuclei of palladium with charge 46 and mass 119. Now a palladium nucleus has less electric repulsion and therefore needs a lower percentage of glue. In fact the heaviest stable palladium isotope has mass only 110. Hence the palladium isotope produced in fission wants to get rid of nine 'excess' neutrons. That can happen in two possible ways. Either some of those neutrons convert into protons by β-decay, or some are simply ejected. And that is the way the cookie actually crumbles.

It is therefore not surprising that the possibility of neutron production was obvious to the experts from the start. Hahn has recalled about his experiment with Strassmann:[7] 'We suspected that a few neutrons might have been set free in the process. We also tried, with absolutely inadequate equipment and therefore without success, to prove the existence of such free neutrons.'[67] At the January 1939 meeting in Washington, 'Fermi mentioned the possibility that neutrons might be emitted during the process'.[68] As mentioned, Fermi worked at Columbia University at that time, where he shared an office with Uhlenbeck, another visiting professor. In February 1939 Uhlenbeck returned to Utrecht, where I was a graduate student at that time. I vividly recall Uhlenbeck telling me how one day Fermi had stood at the window of their office in Pupin Laboratory, looking out over the city, then had turned around and said: 'You realize, George, that one small fission bomb could destroy most of what we see outside?'

Experimental proof for the production of free neutrons was at hand by March 1939. An average value of 3.5 ± 0.7 neutrons* per fission was reported from Paris,[69] a value of about 2 from Columbia University;[70] the correct number is about 2.4 for 235. Later evidence has shown that, as has to be

---

* This number is not an integer because different fission modes may be accompanied by different numbers of neutrons.

expected, the neutrons are ejected from the fission fragments, and not from the compound mother nucleus.

All these early results were published in the open scientific press. So were speculations about their possible implications. To give but one example, in June 1939 there appeared a German article entitled 'Can the energy content of atomic nuclei be utilized in technology?'[71] The press also kept the general public informed from the start, as the following sample of headlines (all from 1939) illustrates. The *New York Times*, 5 February: 'Don't expect uranium atoms to revolutionize civilization.' The *New York Herald Tribune*, 12 February: 'In the realm of science: tempest in cyclotron isn't likely to smash earth'; 7 May: 'In the realm of science: practical development of atomic power is now just a matter of time.' The *Washington Post*, 29 April: 'Physicists here debate whether experiments will blow up 2 miles of the landscape.'

Headlines such as these may help sell newspapers. Scientists knew well, however, that manna was not about to fall from the heavens. As was written more soberly in the *Scientific American* in October 1939: 'Power production by means of nuclear fission would not be beyond the realms of possibility. But under present conditions the process is as inefficient as removing sand from a beach a grain at a time.'[72] Tom Lauritsen remembered how Bohr reacted in the fall of 1939: 'He was following quite avidly the measurements on the number of neutrons released. He would come bursting into the institute one day and say, "It can't be done!" The next day, "It can be done!" with equal enthusiasm . . . He thought of this, I'm sure, as something which might have a very significant effect on the war. I don't know in what detail he felt this, but I know he felt it to be very important.'[73]

Later in 1939 Bohr made up his mind: it can't be done, as is seen from a lecture he gave in December 1939, which was not published until 1941. 'Even if reaction chains can occur in [^{238}U] these will remain too short and rare for there to be any question of an explosion. The situation would be quite different if we had a sufficiently large quantity of ^{235}U available . . . With present technical means it is, however, impossible to purify the rare uranium isotope in sufficient quantity to realize the chain reaction.'[74]

As every civilized person knows today, chain reactions are possible.

Many many scientists and engineers contributed to this development which demanded some efforts in theoretical physics, more in experimental physics, but most in technology. Nearly all the work was done in the United States. Altogether it was a scientific/industrial effort on a scale never seen before. I have already noted (15g) that Bohr's liquid drop model played a crucial role in the theoretical analyses.

This fascinating story, well told several times, will not be part of what is to follow. I do need to add, however, just a few qualitative points to make clear that the issue of chain reactions is more complex than I have indicated so far.

1. Not every neutron produced in fission will ignite another fission. There are competing processes, such as the capture of a neutron followed by its rejection or by photon emission. A chain reaction will nevertheless occur if on the average at least one secondary neutron produces another fission.

2. Some neutrons may simply escape from the mass of uranium. The relative importance of this loss will decrease with increasing size of that mass. Clearly then there exists a minimal 'critical size' for obtaining an explosion.

3. The neutrons produced in fission need not have the optimal energy for producing further fission. One can control the energy dependence by judiciously mixing the fissioning substance with a 'moderator' element that slows down neutrons – at the price of some neutron loss by absorption in the moderator, and hence of an increase in critical size.

It should be abundantly clear from the foregoing that in 1939 the possibility of utilizing fission energy for peaceful and/or military purposes was openly and widely discussed. The advent of World War II made it imperative, however, that further developments – on either side – should be kept secret. Nevertheless, after the spring of 1939, 'publication continued freely for about another year, although a few papers were withheld voluntarily by their authors'.[75] In the spring of 1940 a 'Reference Committee' was organized by the US National Research Council 'to control publication policy in all fields of possible military interest . . . This arrangement was very successful in preventing publication . . . [it] was a purely voluntary [procedure]; the scientists of the [US] are to be congratulated on their complete cooperation.'[76]

In conclusion, it is useful to remember how much was in the public domain about the basic materials from which atomic bombs were made prior to this self-imposed censorship. There was the realization of the importance of ^{235}U, the substance of the bomb that was to destroy Hiroshima. There was the discovery[44] of neptunium (Np) produced in the sequence

$$n + {}^{238}_{92}U \rightarrow photon + {}^{239}_{92}U,$$

an instantaneous reaction, followed by the β-decay

$$^{239}_{92}U \rightarrow {}^{239}_{93}Np + electron + neutrino,$$

which has a half-life of 23 minutes. There were also intimations that Np would β-decay into plutonium (Pu):

$$^{239}_{93}Np \rightarrow {}^{239}_{94}Pu + electron + neutrino,$$

with a half-life of 2.3 days, and that $^{239}_{94}$Pu would α-decay into $^{235}_{92}$U with a half-life of 24000 years. This Pu isotope is the substance of the bomb that would devastate Nagasaki. The chemical isolation of Pu was achieved in early 1941[77] but not published until 1946,[45] when the following footnote was added to manuscripts* submitted earlier: 'This letter was received for publication on the date indicated, but was voluntarily withheld from publication until the end of the war . . .'

The secrecy was broken by a report entitled 'A general account of the development of methods of using atomic energy for military purposes under the auspices of the United States government 1940–5.'[68] When I asked its author, my late friend Harry Smyth, why he had used the term 'atomic energy' instead of 'nuclear energy' he replied that his original draft had indeed contained 'nuclear' but that he and other high authorities finally decided that 'nuclear' was either unfamiliar to the general public or else had primarily a biological flavor. So 'atomic' it became and 'atomic' it has remained.[62]

(d) Bohr as president of the *Kongelige Danske Videnskabernes Selskab***

On 17 March 1939 a meeting of the *Kongelige Danske Videnskabernes Selskab* (Royal Danish Academy for Sciences and Letters) was convened for the main purpose of discussing the election of a new president. Only one person was nominated: Niels Bohr. Whereupon Martin Knudsen, the Academy's secretary, sent a telegram to Bohr who was then in Princeton, asking if he would accept if elected. On 20 March Bohr cabled back, thanking him for the message and stating that he would accept with pleasure. On 31 March he was unanimously elected for the next five years, the standard period. The records state that 'special motivation for the proposal may be considered superfluous'. That same day Knudsen informed the king of Denmark and the minister of education by customary letters of the Academy's choice.

Bohr presided for the first time on 20 October 1939. In his opening words[78] he spoke of uneasiness about his country's future – World War II had broken out. King Christian X was present at the meeting of 15 March 1940. The president, in his speech of welcome to the patron of the Academy, expressed the hope that, under the leadership of the King, Denmark might come 'unscathed through the dangers of the time'.[78] That was three weeks before the German invasion of Denmark . . .

(In the 1740s King Christian VI had participated in an initiative that had

---

* There were two Letters: one dated 28 January 1941, the other 7 March 1941.

** Data in this section were culled from the archives of this institution, unless otherwise specified. For other reviews of Bohr's presidency see Refs. 78 and 79.

led to the founding of the Academy. He became the Academy's patron, a distinction held ever since by the monarch. For some years in the nineteenth century the reigning king actually was the Academy's president.)

Already much earlier Bohr had been considered for the presidency. Thus in 1927 Høffding had proposed Bohr's brother-in-law Niels Erik Nørlund as president, stating that he would rather have seen Bohr, who, however, had declined to accept election. Bohr was also nominated in 1934 but, the records show, 'Bohr wished for personal reasons not to accept election now even though a large number of members of both classes had appealed to him'. I can only speculate about why in 1939 Bohr finally accepted. Perhaps his growing interest in disciplines other than physics played a role. More probably it may have been his strong sense of responsibility which made him decide. Remember that the pre-war European crisis reached its height when Germany occupied all of Czechoslovakia, just two weeks before he was elected.

As president, Bohr continued to render certain services to the Academy which he had performed ever since his nomination to membership in 1917 (9c). He refereed physics articles submitted for publication in the Academy's *Meddelelser* (communications). Between 1917 and 1955 he took care of ninety such papers.[79]

Bohr himself published only a small fraction of his research papers in the *Meddelelser*. These are important contributions, however, including his three papers (1918–22) on line spectra (10b), the article with Rosenfeld on QED (16d), the paper with Kalckar on nuclear reactions (15f), and his last physics research paper[80] (1954), dealing with the transition of charged particles through matter, written in collaboration with his student Jens Lindhard, who himself was to be a later Academy president.

Through the years Bohr also often fulfilled the unwritten obligation of giving short addresses at Academy meetings on progress in his own research. In 1917 he reported on his theory of line spectra (10b), in 1918 on the foundations of the quantum theory. In 1921 and again in 1922 he gave talks on the periodic system (10e), in 1923 on hafnium (10e). In 1925 he spoke on the BKS theory (11d), and in 1926 and 1927 on the new quantum mechanics. Between 1937 and 1941 he made several communications on nuclear reactions (15f), including fission. He gave the last of these lectures, on 'Atoms and human knowledge', in October 1955, at a meeting held to celebrate his 70th birthday.[81] In all he spoke 29 times.[79]

Circumstances of war forced Bohr to be absent from Denmark from September 1943 until August 1945 (see the next chapter). He was still president when he departed. Following the rules, the chairmen of the two Academy sections (mathematics and natural sciences, and history and philosophy) divided the task of presiding over meetings. At the first such meeting (22 October 1943) the chairman began as follows: 'The first words that will be spoken tonight from this chair shall express the deep sorrow we all feel at having to meet without our president. The Academy has received no direct communication from the president, but we sincerely hope that he is safe.'[82]

By April 1944 the Academy was faced with an unprecedented situation: the end of the term of office of a president who could not be contacted. At the meeting of 31 March the chairman proposed and, at the next session, the membership accepted, that under the circumstances it would be best not to take any steps which would change the Academy's relations with its president, and to postpone the next election until further notice. At an extraordinary meeting on 21 September 1945 Bohr was unanimously reelected. Further reelections followed in 1949, 1954, and 1959, and so Bohr remained president until his death in 1962, holding this position for 23 years, the second-longest period of tenure in the Academy's history.

In Denmark, as in other countries, the Academy participates in numerous ceremonial functions, both at home and abroad. Many such undertakings belong to the more trivial specific obligations of its president. I give a few examples.

On 13 November 1942 Bohr gave an address at the celebration of the Academy's bicentennial in which he recalled that body's venerable traditions, its mission to further science and its applications, and its links with international scientific cooperation. 'What is specific for our own culture is the way in which we accept and transform the cultural movements originating in the larger countries. Its continued existence depends on its will to live which is true for individual living beings as well as for communities. Certainly in times like the present we have a vivid impression of how strong such a will can be.'[83]

When UNESCO was established after World War II and a national committee was established in Denmark, Bohr, on behalf of the Academy, served as its adviser. He also was a delegate to several meetings of the International Council of Scientific Unions.

In July 1946 Bohr represented Denmark in the Royal Society's celebrations of the tercentenary of Newton's birth. From 17 to 24 October the American Philosophical Society and the National Academy of Sciences organized meetings 'on the occasion of the visit of representatives of the Academies of Sciences of other Nations'. Bohr participated and on 21 October gave a talk in Philadelphia on 'Atomic physics and international cooperation'.[84]

On 17 October 1947 a ceremonial Academy meeting took place in memory of King Christian X, who had died the preceding April.[85] It was the first time that Frederik IX, his successor, was present. After Bohr had spoken words of welcome to the new king, Frederik thanked Bohr and announced that on that day he had conferred on Bohr the Order of the Elephant (9c), 'not merely to distinguish Niels Bohr personally, but also to honor Danish science, of which Niels Bohr was such an outstanding representative. The King called on the members to rise in honor to Niels Bohr who had lent lustre to the name of Denmark.'[86]

On 29 April 1955 Bohr spoke in memory of Einstein, who had died on the 18th.

Along with ceremonial duties Bohr also had to cope with numerous responsibilities regarding the organization and administration of Danish science. In preparing for these duties he was ably assisted by Asger Lomholt, the Academy's archivist,* who would often come to Carlsberg prior to a meeting in order to brief Bohr. Most of these activities were routine, but two events are of interest.

In January 1947 August Krogh, Nobel laureate, one of the most distinguished senior Academy members, made the sensible proposal to the science section that the Academy ought to act more efficiently toward promoting the role of science in Danish society. This could be achieved, he argued, by significantly extending and rejuvenating the membership. More new members should be elected at a younger age, while those over 70 should be declared passive non-voting. On 28 November 1947 Krogh's concepts were formally presented to the Academy. On 12 December a modest increase in the size of the membership was accepted but, in Krogh's words, 'the question of working conditions was completely left aside, emphasis was rather placed on the very special honor to be elected to the Academy', whereas, Krogh felt, 'the Academy ought to emerge from the deep shadows of high distinction'.[88]

Nothing happened further in this affair until the meeting of 14 January 1949 during which the secretary read aloud an 'open letter' by Krogh, received immediately before that meeting, stating that he resigned from the Academy from the moment of receipt of the letter. At the same time Krogh had sent to the press a copy of this letter as well as a further motivation for his resignation. 'The president expressed the Academy's regrets for August Krogh's step.'[89]

On 15 January Krogh's letter appeared in the Danish papers under headlines such as 'First resignation in 200 years'.[88] On that day Krogh gave an interview to one paper[90] in which he explained that he had made up his mind to resign when an outstanding young physiologist, unable to find a position in Denmark, had accepted a position in the United States. It was 'evidently inconceivable that the Academy would clear up this situation'. When asked whether he could not have been more effective by remaining a

* Lomholt also was the author of the Academy's authoritative history.[87]

member he replied: 'I am too old. The young should take action.' Was he a personal friend of Bohr? 'Yes. That has nothing to do with it. I did not say anything to him in advance, nor to anyone else.' I have not seen any public comments by Bohr but have been told by eyewitnesses that he was not amused.

A second, more positive, matter of Danish scientific policy arose as the result of an initiative in 1946 by the minister of education for establishing a committee of inquiry into conditions of scientific research. Lengthy studies resulted, of institutions of higher learning, libraries, museums, and research facilities. On 18 January 1951 Bohr took up the issue in a radio address to the Danish people and its authorities.[91] He began by expressing the gratitude of the scholarly community to the Carlsberg foundation* and the Rask–Ørsted fund (12d), but stressed that post-war developments demanded more extensive support. 'It is urgently necessary that also here at home greater support than hithertofore shall be given to the advancement of science if our country shall not be left behind and lose a position among nations important for the progress of our society and the safeguarding of our culture . . . It should be stressed most strongly that this does not concern an issue that can wait because of our country's economic difficulties.'

At the Academy meeting the next evening Bohr's suggestion that the Academy should approach the government in these matters met with unanimous approval.

On 2 February Bohr's appeal was followed by a demonstration of academics and students.[92] Participants, about 10000 according to police estimates, from institutions all over the country, especially from Aarhus, met at Vor Frue Plads, in front of Copenhagen University's main building. From there they marched to the Parliament building in a two-mile long procession, carrying posters and banners. 'It was for a serious purpose but spirits were cheerful. Onlookers from all sections of the population expressed sympathy.'[92] At the Parliament building the rector of Copenhagen University handed a petition to government officials.

That same evening Bohr (who had not participated in the demonstration) reported to the Academy the content of a letter he and the Secretary had handed to the minister of education on behalf of all members. This document is in substance identical with Bohr's radio speech, but emphasized in addition the need for supporting subjects not represented in the Academy, such as technology and agricultural and medical research. The letter ends as follows: 'In presenting this appeal the Academy expresses its

---

* In 1894 the Carlsberg foundation had offered the Academy permanent premises free of charge in a planned new building that was also to house the foundation's main offices. A few years later the Academy moved into these quarters, located on what is now called H. C. Andersen's Boulevard. The Academy has further benefited from later rebuilding and modernization and from annual financial support by the foundation.

obligation, under present circumstances, to suggest to the state authorities that a proper solution shall be sought for this pressing matter so vital for our nation.'[93]

The initiative was of decisive importance for the establishment in 1952 of *Statens almindelige Videnskabsfond* (National Science Foundation).

It will be obvious that Bohr's presidential activities were manifold and energy consuming, especially when one remembers how much else was on his mind.

I have been told that some academicians were critical of Bohr's handling of affairs. There were those who found him too high-handed, or favoring physics too much over other disciplines, or of teaming up too much with his brother Harald (a member since 1918) and his brother-in-law N. E. Nørlund. (This threesome was called 'the troika' by some.) Was this criticism justified? Was it envy? I cannot say, but would be surprised if Bohr would not be even-handed. As my own contribution I can tell a pertinent story, which I have from the best possible source. At a meeting of the university science faculty the matter arose of distributing stipends allotted to the faculty as a whole. Bohr had a physics candidate who, however, he withdrew in favor of an ethnographer on the grounds that the latter was more worthy and that something ought to be done for that field.

In any event the Academy honored Bohr on several occasions.

On 5 October 1945 a festive meeting was held to celebrate Bohr's forthcoming 60th birthday. In an address one speaker referred to Bohr's many scientific contributions, including those in nuclear physics, 'which in recent times have [led to the release of] sources of energy of such gigantic power that mankind has been seized by fear and must unite in the hope, which you yourself recently expressed, that the right course can be found to enable science ... to make ... a decisive contribution to harmonious cooperation between nations ... We trust that you will be the person to succeed in making a decisive contribution to this end.'[94]

That meeting was further informed that 'the Carlsberg Foundation has decided to grant the sum of 100000 Kr for the establishment of an endowment bearing Professor Bohr's name which shall serve as an aid to research in a subject to be determined by himself'.[95] The foundation also granted money for a portrait of Bohr. For a number of years that handsome oil painting[96] was placed in Bohr's home. After his death it was moved to the Academy, where it now hangs in the reading room.

On 14 October 1955 the Academy celebrated Bohr's 70th birthday in the presence of the king who announced that he had bestowed on Bohr the Grand Cross of the Order of Dannebrog with diamonds. 'At the King's invitation the Academy rose to honor the president.'[97] Bohr also received a *Festschrift*[98] and (as mentioned) gave a lecture himself.

After Bohr's death in 1962 the Academy received expressions of sorrow from the numerous sister societies abroad, many of which counted Bohr among their foreign members. On 14 December 1962 a memorial meeting was held. Mrs Bohr, her four sons and their wives, and the king and queen were among those present. Several memorial speeches were held. The last one concluded as follows.

We felt secure and comfortable having as leader a man of his cast of mind, excelling equally in intelligence and character. His memory will forever live in our hearts, his name will for all times honor our Academy.'[99]

(c) References

1. V. Weisskopf, *Physics Today* **20**, October 1967, p. 39.
2. E. Fermi, *Nature* **133**, 898, 1934.
3. E. Fermi, in *Nobel lectures in physics, 1922–1941*, p. 414, Elsevier, New York 1965.
4. O. Hahn, L. Meitner, and F. Strassmann, *Naturw.* **26**, 475, 1938.
5. O. Hahn, *Mein Leben*, p. 150, Bruckmann, Munich 1968.
6. O. Hahn, *A scientific autobiography*, Scribner's, New York 1966.
7. O. Hahn and F. Strassmann, *Naturw.* **27**, 11, 1939; Engl transl. by H. G. Graetzer, *Am. J. Phys.* **32**, 9, 1964; see further *Naturw.* **32**, 9, 1939.
8. O. Hahn, *Sci. Am.* **198**, February 1978, p. 76.
9. O. Hahn, letter to L. Meitner, 19 December 1938, Ref. 5, p. 151.
10. L. Meitner, letter to O. Hahn, 21 December 1938, Ref. 5, p. 152.
11. L. Fermi, *Atoms in the family*, p. 154, University of Chicago Press 1954.
12. O. R. Frisch, *Physics Today* **20**, November 1967, p. 43.
13. O. R. Frisch, NBR, p. 144.
14. O. R. Frisch, NBR, p. 145.
15. O. R. Frisch, letter to L. Meitner, 3 January 1939, CW, Vol. 9, p. 53.
16. O. R. Frisch, letter to L. Meitner, 8 January 1939, CW, Vol. 9, p. 53.
17. L. Meitner and O. R. Frisch, *Nature* **143**, 239, 1939.
18. R. H. Stuewer, *Physics Today* **38**, October 1985, p. 49; L. Badash *et al., Proc. Am. Philos. Soc.* **130**, 196, 1986.
19. O. R. Frisch, *Nature* **143**, 276, 1939.
20. L. Rosenfeld, interview by T. S. Kuhn and J. L. Heilbron, 22 July 1963, NBA.
21. J. A. Wheeler, *Physics Today* **20**, November 1967, p. 49.
22. R. H. Stuewer, Ref. 18.
23. N. Bohr, *Nature* **143**, 330, 1939, CW, Vol. 9, p. 341.
24. CW, Vol. 9, pp. 556–564.
25. H. L. Anderson, *Bull. Atom. Sci.* **30**, September 1974, p. 56.
26. R. B. Roberts *et al., Phys. Rev.* **55**, 416, 1939.
27. N. Bohr, letters to E. Fermi, 1, 2, 17 February, 2 March; E. Fermi, letter to N. Bohr, 1 March, all 1939, CW, Vol. 9, pp. 550–4.
28. Reviewed by L. A. Turner, *Rev. Mod. Phys.* **12**, 1, 1940.
29. Ref. 28, p. 23.

30. L. Rosenfeld, *Selected papers*, p. 335, Eds. R. S. Cohen and J. Stachel, Reidel, Boston 1979; also *Fysisk Tidsskr.* **60**, 65, 1962.
31. N. Bohr, *Phys. Rev.* **55**, 418, 1939, CW, Vol. 9, p. 343.
32. CW, Vol. 9, p. 66.
33. A. O. Nier *et al.*, *Phys. Rev.* **57**, 546, 748, 1940.
34. CW, Vol. 8, p. 301.
35. J. Kidd, letter to N. Bohr, 14 February 1939, NBA.
36. N. Bohr and J. A. Wheeler, *Phys. Rev.* **55**, 1124, 1939, CW, Vol. 9, p. 359.
37. N. Bohr, letter to A. Flexner, 31 May 1939, NBA.
38. CW, Vol. 9, pp. 72, 73, 657–62.
39. N. Bohr and J. A. Wheeler, *Phys. Rev.* **56**, 426, 1939, CW, Vol. 9, p. 363.
40. N. Bohr and J. A. Wheeler, *Phys. Rev.* **56**, 1056, 1939, CW, Vol. 9, p. 403.
41. For a summary see Ref. 21.
42. R. G. Hewlett and O. E. Anderson, *A history of the U.S. Atomic Energy Commission*, Vol. 1, p. 13, Pennsylvania University Press 1962.
43. N. Bohr, letter to O. Klein, 21 January 1947, NBA.
44. E. McMillan and P. H. Abelson, *Phys. Rev.* **57**, 1185, 1940.
45. G. T. Seaborg *et al.*, *Phys. Rev.* **69**, 366, 367, 1946.
46. G. Herrmann and K. E. Seyl, *Naturw.* **56**, 590, 1969.
47. P. Ambruster, *Ann. Rev. Nucl. Sci.* **35**, 135, 1985.
48. L. Meitner and O. R. Frisch, *Nature* **143**, 471, 1939; more details in *Danske Vid. Selsk. Mat.-Fys. Medd.* **17**, No. 5, 1939.
49. T. Bjerge, K. J. Brostrøm, and J. Koch, *Nature* **143**, 794, 1939.
50. K. J. Brostrøm, J. Koch, and T. Lauritsen, *Nature* **144**, 830, 1939.
51. T. Bjerge, K. J. Brostrøm, J. Koch, and T. Lauritsen, *Danske Vid. Selsk. Mat.-Fys. Medd.* **18**, No. 1, 1940; see also CW, Vol. 8, p. 232.
52. K. J. Brostrøm, J. K. Bøggild, and T. Lauritsen, *Phys. Rev.* **58**, 651, 1940; in more detail in *Danske Vid. Selsk. Mat.-Fys. Medd.* **18**, No. 4, 1940; see also J Bøggild, *Phys. Rev.* **60**, 827, 1941.
53. For biographical details about Bøggild see CW, Vol. 8, p. 235.
54. J. C. Jacobsen and N. O. Lassen, *Phys. Rev.* **58**, 867, 1940; *Nature* **148**, 230, 1941; *Danske Vid. Selsk. Mat.-Fys. Medd.* **19**, No. 6, 1941.
55. N. O. Lassen, *Phys. Rev.* **68**, 142, 1945.
56. See e.g. J. Koch, *Phys. Rev.* **69**, 238, 1946. For biographical details on Koch see N. O. Lassen, *Fysisk Tidsskr.* **70**, 97, 1972.
57. N. Bohr, *Phys. Rev.* **58**, 654, 1940, CW, Vol. 8, p. 319. See also an unpublished manuscript, CW, Vol. 8, p. 307.
58. N. Bohr, J. Bøggild, J. Koch, and T. Lauritsen, *Phys. Rev.* **58**, 839, 1940, CW, Vol. 8, p. 323; N. Bohr, *Phys. Rev.* **59**, 270, 1941, CW, Vol. 8, p. 327.
59. N. Bohr, *Phys. Rev.* **58**, 864, 1940, CW, Vol. 9, p. 475.
60. N. Bohr, *Phys. Rev.* **59**, 1042, 1941, CW, Vol. 9, p. 483.
61. E. Rutherford and F. Soddy, *Phil. Mag.* **5**, 576, 1903.
62. See further IB, Chap. 6, section (c).
63. N. Bohr, *Nature* **137**, 344, 1936, CW, .Vol. 9, p. 151.
64. See e.g. *New York Herald Tribune*, 12 September 1933.
65. See further IB, Chap. 17, section (h).

66. *L. Szilard: His version of the facts*, p. 38ff. Eds. S. R. Weart and G. Weiss, MIT Press 1978.
67. Ref. 6, p. 159.
68. H. D. Smyth, *A general account of the development of methods of using atomic energy for military purposes under the auspices of the United States government 1940–1945*, p. 15, United States Government Printing Office 1945.
69. M. Dodé, H. von Halban, F. Joliot, and L. Kowarski, *C.R. Acad. Sci. Paris* **208**, 995, 1939; *Nature* **143**, 470, 680, 1939.
70. H. L. Anderson, E. Fermi, and H. B. Hanstein, *Phys. Rev.* **55**, 797, 1939; L. Szilard and W. H. Zinn, *Phys. Rev.* **55**, 799, 1939.
71. S. Flügge, *Naturw.* **27**, 492, 1939.
72. J. Harrington, *Sci. Am.* **161**, October 1939, p. 214.
73. T. Lauritsen, interview by B. Richman and C. Weiner, 16 February 1967, NBA.
74. N. Bohr, *Fysisk Tidsskr.* **39**, 3, 1941; English transl. in CW, Vol. 9, p. 443.
75. Ref. 68, p. 26.
76. Ref. 68, p. 27. For many details about the secrecy issue in the US and elsewhere see S. R. Weart, *Physics Today* **29**, February 1976, p. 23.
77. For the histories of the discoveries of Np and Pu see E. M. McMillan in *Nobel lectures in chemistry 1942–1962*, p. 314, Elsevier, New York 1964; G. T. Seaborg, *ibid.*, p. 325.
78. J. Pedersen, NBR, p. 266.
79. B. Strømgren, in *The lesson of quantum theory*, p. 3, Eds. J. de Boer *et al.*, North-Holland, Amsterdam 1986.
80. N. Bohr and J. Lindhard, *Danske Vid. Selsk. Mat.-Fys. Medd.* **28**, No. 7, 1954, CW, Vol. 8, p. 593.
81. N. Bohr, *Danske Vid. Selsk. Oversigt, 1955–1956*, p. 112.
82. J. Hjelmslev, see Ref. 78, p. 271.
83. Ref. 78, p. 270.
84. N. Bohr, *Proc. Am. Philos. Soc.* **91**, 137, 1947.
85. See also Bohr's speech to the Academy on 25 April 1947, *Oversigt over Selskabets Virksomhed, 1946–47*, p. 53.
86. *Oversigt, 1947–48*, p. 26.
87. A. Lomholt, *Det Kongelige Danske Videnskabernes Selskab 1742–1942*, 3 vols., Munksgaard, Copenhagen 1942–60.
88. *Berlingske Tidende,* 15 January 1949.
89. *Oversigt 1948–1949*, p. 39.
90. *Berlingske Aftenavis*, 15 January 1949.
91. Printed in *Politiken*, 19 January 1951.
92. *Politiken*, 3 February 1951.
93. *Oversigt 1950–51*, p. 41.
94. J. Hjelmslev, see Ref. 78, p. 273.
95. J. Pedersen, see Ref. 78. p. 273.
96. By the Norwegian painter H. Sørensen.
97. Ref. 78, p. 279.
98. *Danske Vid. Selsk. Mat.-Fys. Medd.*, **30**, 1955.
99. J. Pedersen, *Oversigt 1962–63*, p. 99.

21

Bohr, pioneer of 'glasnost'

(a) Introduction

World War II will be remembered above all for the human suffering it caused. On a more abstract level it was the physicists' war,[1] won by radar and ended by the atomic bomb.[2] This chapter deals with Bohr's experiences during those bitter years.

Some physicists had obviously been aware of the threats and promises of atomic energy well before these became common knowledge, as they have been since 1945. Niels Bohr was the first among the scientists to bring these prospects to the attention of political leaders. As we shall see, he had already in 1944 pleaded with Churchill and Roosevelt the case for openness between the Western Allies and the Soviet Union. It seems fitting, therefore, to consider Bohr as the pioneer of glasnost. Efforts towards the creation of an open world were to remain his dominant preoccupation throughout the last twenty years of his life.

The war had lasted for more than three years before Bohr became seriously involved with these issues. The hostilities had touched his life already during that early phase, however. The German occupation of his country in 1940 affected him as a Dane and a half Jew. The safety of his family and his institute and its members concerned him deeply.*

In order to set the stage for that episode, I begin in the next section with a glance at the Danish predicament. In the section thereafter, (c), I relate Bohr's own war experiences in Denmark, which came to an end in October 1943 when he fled to Sweden and thence voyaged on to England. In section (d) I discuss Bohr's connections with the Anglo-American atomic weapons program. Section (e) deals with Bohr's efforts at promoting political openness. The chapter ends with Bohr's return to Denmark in August 1945.

---

* His activities during 1933–40 on behalf of Jewish refugees have been mentioned earlier (17d, e).

(b) Denmark and Germany, from 16 November 1864 until 4 May 1945

On 16 November 1864 King Christian IX of Denmark signed the peace treaty with Prussia and Austria that brought to a formal end the war concerning the possession of Slesvig and Holstein (Chapter 3). From then to the times now under consideration Denmark's military and diplomatic postures were largely determined by one overriding factor: fear of Germany, in particular concern for the Danish population under German rule in North Slesvig. National defense policy became a matter of striking a balance between sufficient strength to resist violations of Denmark's neutrality and to maintain its strategic position at the entrance to the Baltic on the one hand, and not provoking their southern neighbor on the other.

Attention focused on Copenhagen and Sjaelland, the island on which this capital is situated, since it clearly made no sense to try and defend the whole Danish archipelago. Two schools of thought emerged. Either concentrate on fortifying Copenhagen toward land and sea, in the hope that this redoubt could withstand a German attack long enough for possible help to bring relief. Critics stressed that the landward defense could be considered as specifically being aimed against Germany. Or establish defenses, mainly seaward, of Sjaelland as a whole, a more neutral posture. Debates about these alternatives moved to and fro between Danish factions, and changed emphasis as the relations between the great powers created one tension after another. The hybrid solution eventually adopted was never put to the test.[3]

On 1 August 1914 World War I broke out. On the 4th England declared war on Germany. On the 5th Germany requested that Denmark mine the Great Belt, part of Danish territorial waters and the main link between the Baltic and the North Sea. Denmark acceded and maintained mine fields in the Belt throughout the war from which it, as all of Scandinavia, emerged with its neutrality intact.

Rarely, if ever, in its history did Denmark experience less the threat of foreign intervention than in the years right after World War I, when North Slesvig had been regained. Germany lay in shambles; Russia (forever interested in the Baltic) was torn by revolution. The League of Nations, still young, appeared to carry the promise of settling arguments between nations by arbitration. Accordingly, the Danish government reduced the standing army by one-third and ordered the dismantling of land fortifications around Copenhagen.

All such rosy visions faded as the National Socialists in Germany grew stronger and eventually took over power in January 1933. In March of that year the Danish foreign minister called representatives of the Danish press into his office to demand a softening of their criticisms of developments in

Germany, especially in regard to their choice of pictures and headlines.[4] In 1935 Denmark abstained from voting on a League of Nations resolution condemning Germany's breach of the peace Treaty of Versailles. On 25 July 1938, the Danish government saw fit to confer on Hermann Goering one of Denmark's highest distinctions, the Grand Cross of the Order of Dannebrog with diamonds. The tepid reactions of the Western powers to the overrunning of Austria and Czechoslovakia did not increase Denmark's faith in support if ever their own turn might come, and must have added to their willingness to submit to a German demand for concluding a non-aggression pact with Germany, signed in May of 1939. This document begins as follows: 'The German Reich and the Kingdom of Denmark will under no circumstances resort to war or any other form of violence against each other.'[5]

On the following 1 September German forces invaded Poland. Two days later Britain and France declared war. During that September month Bohr's institute became the unusual scene of certain preparations aimed at protecting the Danes against possible hostile actions.

'Remembering the experience of the First World War, one could not exclude the possibility of gas attacks, and responsible circles in Denmark were concerned with the question of organizing help for the population.'[6] This led to an initiative by Bohr's long-time friend Chievitz (Chapter 3), now a professor of surgery. 'His plan was based on providing all the hospitals in the country with apparatus for treating cases of gas-poisoning by passing a stream of oxygen through the nose. But no factory would undertake the speedy delivery of "nose catheters", and so Chievitz turned to Niels Bohr for help and advice. Bohr promised that the institute should produce the required number of nasal tubes, admittedly in rather primitive form, but on the other hand within a very short time.

All the personnel of the institute, including the theoretical physicists, donned overalls, and in the following days activity developed on the best mass-production lines. After a week 6000 tubes with accessories were lying packed and ready to be sent off to the hospitals of the country. Fortunately they were never needed.'[6]

The period between late September 1939, when Germany had completed its conquest of Poland, and April 1940, when hardly any military activity occurred in Western Europe, became known as the 'phony war'. In the meantime armed conflict had developed in the East, however.

After Finland had refused to accept a Russian ultimatum demanding cession of part of its territories, war between the two countries broke out on 30 November 1939. This furious and short encounter became known as 'the winter war' because of the exceptionally bitter cold in which the armies did battle. In Scandinavia indignation was widespread. Help in the form of money, clothing, and food came streaming in to the Finns. On the day the war broke out, Chievitz, that remarkable man, contacted the Danish Red Cross to ask if there was interest in sending an ambulance to Finland. With characteristic Danish fear of acts that might appear lacking in neutrality the Red Cross responded by inquiring if Chievitz planned to send an ambulance to Russia as well. Chievitz reacted by organizing on his own a field hospital with a staff of 120 men and women.[7] At Chievitz's funeral in 1946 Bohr said of him: 'He won many Finnish hearts in that country's grievous hour . . . by relieving the lot of the wounded.'[8]

In January 1940 Bohr himself donated his gold Nobel medal to the Finnish cause[9] (so did Krogh). In March he also gave his gold Franklin medal,[10] asking Lewis Strauss to sell it for the Finnish relief. In 1946 Bohr received a letter from Strauss that said in part: 'I return to you the Medal presented to you by the Franklin Institute . . . which did not reach me until after your country had been invaded, and Finland and Russia were at peace. I am glad to have been its custodian during these years and I am happy now to return it to you.'[11]

As to the winter war, on 6 March 1940 Finland sued for peace; an accord was signed on 12 March.*

Meanwhile Germany had started planning a strike northward, the major military target being not so much Denmark as the Norwegian Atlantic coast. During that period, on 2 February 1940, Churchill met with Scandinavian journalists and said[12] in part: 'I could not reproach Denmark if she surrendered to Nazi attack . . . Denmark is so terribly near Germany that it would be impossible to bring help. Personally I would in any case not undertake to guarantee Denmark . . . The question for Denmark is to find a balance . . . We get some bacon and butter and the Germans get some . . . That is perhaps the best way. Denmark has a pact with Germany but I do not doubt that Germany will overrun Denmark on the day that it will suit them.'

That is exactly what happened. On 9 April 1940 at 4:15 a.m. German forces began the occupation of Denmark. During a few hours of scant resistance Danish casualties were 16 killed, 23 wounded. 'In those few hours of fighting the Danish army put up just enough resistance to escape complete dishonor.'[13]** At 6:20 the Danish capitulation was broadcast to all military units. The Germans pledged respect for Danish neutrality (!), non-interference in internal Danish affairs, and maintenance of the Danish army and navy on active duty status. The positions of parliament and king were to remain unaltered.

Life in Denmark did not at once change drastically after the occupation. There was not even a ban on listening to the BBC. Rationing had been

---

* On 28 June 1941 Finland joined Germany in its war against Russia.

** It is regrettable that documents which could clarify the role of some high Danish government officials in these events are, 50 years later, still kept under lock and key.

introduced earlier, but throughout the war the food situation remained incomparably better than in any other occupied country. The inevitable small band of Danish National Socialists was more a nuisance than a threat, as the following minor incident may illustrate. In the autumn of 1942 a new rector of the University of Copenhagen had to be elected. Many newspapers reported Bohr to be among those prominently mentioned for the position. Whereupon a Danish Nazi newspaper, in an article[14] headlined 'The days of the Jews should be past', referred to 'the Jew Niels Bohr', and wondered: 'Should it not be possible to find a *Dane* [their italics] for this post?' To which another Danish newspaper could retort[15] with impunity: 'If Bohr is not Danish then who is?' Perhaps this may seem a rather trivial comment to those unaware of the dire consequences a similar public remark might have had elsewhere in occupied Europe.

As to foreign policy, two events of note occurred in 1941. The first: On 9 April Henrik von Kauffmann, Danish envoy to Washington signed a pact 'on behalf of the King of Denmark'[16] giving the United States the right to establish air bases and other military facilities on Greenland. Kauffmann had not consulted with Denmark, however, and by royal resolution was promptly ousted from his post.[17] After the war the agreement was renewed within the framework of NATO, and Kauffmann, who had meanwhile acquired the nickname 'King of Greenland', was promoted to Ambassador. (I recall meeting him in New York at Aage Bohr's wedding in 1950. He was a strikingly handsome man.) The second: On 25 November, Denmark, along with Bulgaria, Croatia, Finland, Rumania, and Slovakia, joined the Anti-Comintern Pact initiated by Germany, Italy, and Japan. It may be noted that on 1 October 1941 the Danish government saw fit to confer on Joachim von Ribbentrop, Germany's minister of foreign affairs, the same order Goering had received earlier.*

The Danes became restive as Germany began to experience major military setbacks. Anti-German demonstrations and strikes increased in number, as did acts of sabotage, from ten in 1940 to over 100 in 1942, to over 1000 in 1943.[18] In August 1943 the German authorities demanded that the Danish government declare a state of emergency and impose capital punishment for acts of sabotage. The government rejected this ultimatum, then resigned. On 29 August at 4 a.m. the Germans declared martial law, attacked Danish military installations, interned its personnel, and arrested influential Danish personalities. Most notable among Danish responses were the navy's scuttling of most of its ships and the founding, on 16 September, of the Frihedsråd, the Council for Liberty that successfully

---

* By royal decree of 10 October 1946, after the final verdict at the Nürnberg trials, both gentlemen were struck from the roll of knights of Dannebrog. I thank Professor Tage Kaarsted, the kongelige ordeners historiograf, for information on these two cases.

coordinated activities of various resistance groups with each other and with activities directed from London.

The position of the Jews in Denmark now became perilous.[19] By August 1943 there were 8000 of them, 6500 native born, of which 1500 were half Jewish, and 1500 refugees (all in round numbers.) Their problems up till that time had been no more severe than those of other Danes. Their civil rights had remained protected under Danish law, they had retained their jobs and had continued to conduct religious services. This situation, idyllic compared to what was happening elsewhere, came to an end on 28 September when a direct order from Hitler for the deportation of all Danish Jews reached Copenhagen. On that very day Georg Ferdinand Duckwitz, a high German official, informed two Danish political leaders that the rounding up of Jews was to begin at nine o'clock on the evening of 1 October. For this act his name will live in the history of the Danes and of the Jews. (He also helped prevent catastrophic action by the Germans during the last days of the war.[20] From 1955 to 1958 he was the first West German ambassador to Denmark. The Bohrs knew him personally at that time.)

On the evening of 29 September two German freighters docked in the port of Copenhagen for the purpose of transporting the Jews to Germany. On that same day Bohr fled Denmark, as will be related in the next section. Most of the war events that took place in Denmark after his departure are less directly relevant to our story. A few concluding remarks on the subsequent fate of the Jews from Denmark are not too much out of place, however.

On the evening of 28 September the information about impending deportations was transmitted to three Jewish leaders. On the next day, 'the news ... spread by word of mouth throughout the Jewish community: relative warned relative; friend warned friend; Jew warned Jew; non-Jewish Danes warned their Jewish acquaintances ... Many Jews walking the streets ... or riding the trams ... were startled at the approach of strangers who offered them keys to their apartments or cottages "where you can hide until it is safe" ... So widespread was the willingness of the average Dane to help that by the evening of 1 October most Jews had found safety somewhere,'[21] in homes, churches, and in hospitals, where they became lost among the patients. One Dane later wrote: 'In the midst of all the tragedy we underwent a great experience for we saw how that same population which had hitherto said to itself, in awe of German power, "What can we do?" – how this same population suddenly rose as one man against the Germans and rendered active help to their innocent brethren.'[22] The German roundup which began at 9 p.m. on 1 October, as planned, netted only 284 men, women, and children, and about 200 more later that month. Of the 474 Jews deported (to Theresienstadt) only an astonishingly low fraction, ten per cent, did not survive.[23]

Next followed the greatest mass rescue operation of the war: the transportation of all those in temporary hiding to Sweden, where 7220 of them arrived safely. It is a tale of improvisation and great courage from the side of the resistance movement, only slightly marred by occasional greed of some fishermen who asked for too much money. Help also came from unexpected quarters. 'The German naval commander of the port of Copenhagen took his coastal patrol vessels out of operation during the very period when the illegal sailings were most frequent; he reported to his superiors that his vessels were in need of repairs and unable to put to sea.'[24]

The rescue raised Danish morale. 'For non-Jewish Danes, October 1943 marked a rebirth of hope and dignity through action ... Denmark did manage to save the bulk of its Jewish population, the only country of Europe which succeeded, for whatever mix of reasons, in accomplishing this life saving task.'[25]

At 8:35 on the evening of 4 May 1945 the BBC broadcast to Denmark the news that the German High Command had surrendered all German forces in Denmark to Field Marshall Montgomery. The next day the first British troops arrived at Copenhagen airport.

There can be little doubt that three factors eased the subsequent acceptance of Denmark among the victorious allies: Kauffmann's pact with the US, the rescue of the Jews, and Bohr's role (to which I shall of course turn shortly) in atomic weapons projects.

(c) Bohr's war years, the Scandinavian episode

1. *Keeping the work going.* On 5 April 1940 Bohr was in Oslo in order to lecture before the Norwegian Engineering Society on the problem of exploiting atomic energy. At that time he was still doubtful about workable applications (20c). 'The possibility of a practical use of atomic energy via fission processes cannot be completely excluded. For the present this question must be considered completely open, however,'[26]

'The evening before his return to Denmark Bohr had dinner with King Haakon. He later told us of the gloomy atmosphere prevalent on this occasion in Norwegian circles, where the coming German attack was foreseen.'[0] Late that evening, it was 8 April, Bohr boarded the night train from Oslo to Copenhagen. On the ferry between Helsingborg in Sweden and Helsingør he was awakened by airplane noise. An officer of the Danish state police informed him that meanwhile Denmark had been occupied by the Germans.

Bohr's immediate concern was the safety of his co-workers. 'One of the first things he did was to contact the Chancellor of the University and other Danish authorities to protect those of the staff at the institute whom the Germans might be expected to persecute.'[6]

Hevesy recalled another early concern – less grave to be sure – of Bohr. 'I found Bohr worrying about Max von Laue's Nobel medal, which Laue had sent to Copenhagen for safe-keeping. In Hitler's empire it was almost a capital offense to send gold out of the country and, Laue's name being engraved into the medal, the discovery of this by the invading forces would have had very serious consequences for him. I suggested that we should bury the medal, but Bohr did not like this idea as the medal might be unearthed. I decided to dissolve it. While the invading forces marched in the streets of Copenhagen, I was busy dissolving Laue's and also James Franck's medals. After the war, the gold was recovered and the Nobel Foundation generously presented Laue and Franck with new Nobel medals.'[27]

Almost at once after the occupation of Denmark Bohr received several invitations to visit the United States. These further intimated that he could sit out the war over there if he so desired. Bohr declined. More than ever he felt that his place was in Denmark, that he should strive toward keeping research at the institute going, including his own. Increased isolation created problems of course. Bohr in May 1940: 'At the moment we feel very much cut off from the world and are not least missing American periodicals. Thus we have not seen any issue of *Physical Review* since 1 February [1940].'[28] Nevertheless research remained a source of solace. Bohr in September 1940: 'Such interests [physics] are indeed the only way sometimes to forget the great anxieties under which all people in Europe are living at present.'[29]

And so, under restrictive conditions (including rationing of heat and electricity), the work somehow continued. Bohr published on fission until well into 1941 (20b). Fission experiments with the high-tension generator and the cyclotron also continued until that time. The Hevesy group managed to keep biology research going through the war years.* 'The palpable lack of materials, especially of metals, was relieved by the Carlsberg breweries, who loaned to the Institute a large quantity of metals from their stores.'[6] The Carlsberg foundation advanced funds (reimbursed after the war) covering grants which, under the circumstances,** the Rockefeller foundation could not remit directly (17i).

'For a long time Bohr succeeded in keeping the work going, even if events made dramatic claims on time, strength, and nerves. The staff shrank in

---

* In the years 1941–4 the number of published papers from the institute was 25, 15, 7, 12, respectively.

** Because of US Treasury Department restrictions on the export of money.

numbers, no foreign visitors could come; and the few who remained gradually left the country. But mainly it was the pressure of world events which weighed heavily on people's minds. Wherever Bohr was – at home, at the Institute, or with friends – he listened to every single news bulletin, both from Denmark and from the British radio. The general war situation and what was happening closer at hand occupied his thoughts and gave rise to long conversations and speculations about the progress of the war,'[6]

The last foreign visitor to depart was Tom Lauritsen (17j). On 9 November 1940 he and his recent bride (a daughter of Chievitz) left by plane to Berlin, Barcelona, then by train to Madrid and Lisbon, where they boarded a ship to New York. On his arrival he visited the offices of the Rockefeller Foundation to report on the news from occupied Denmark.[30] A memorandum[31] summarizing this information reads in part: 'The German occupation of Denmark has not touched educational and scientific institutions directly . . . There has been no interference with the policy of the University of Copenhagen . . . No race laws have been enacted . . . Threatened or actual shortages has made rationing necessary . . . Men of courage and persistence are sticking to their posts, driving their work forward with more vigor than ever before, in the expressed hope and conviction that the culture to which they are contributing will outlive the invaders and help to rebuild Denmark at a time when thought and conscience are again considered to be respectable concepts.'

As to Bohr's activities between 1941 and his escape from Denmark in 1943, in regard to research he busied himself with questions concerning the transition of charged particles through matter (see section (b) of the next chapter). That work was not published until after the war. Apart from his papers on fission his only writings in those years are a newspaper article[32] on 'The university and research' (the text of an address in the Danish radio), and his contribution to 'Danish culture in the year 1940' (Chapter 2), which took up a good deal of his time.

It was during that period, in October 1941, that Heisenberg came to Copenhagen and visited Bohr.

2. *Heisenberg's visit.* Heisenberg had been a professor in Leipzig since 1927 (12c). In 1933, the year Hitler came to power, he had received the Nobel Prize. From then on he was a man of stature in Germany.

Rozental (of Polish Jewish extraction), who off and on until early 1938 spent time in Leipzig has told me that people at Heisenberg's institute spoke freely in contempt of Hitler and his hordes, that there was no doubt about Heisenberg's negative attitude toward Nazism, and that on several occasions he (H.) helped Jewish physicists to get positions outside Germany.

In the summer of 1939 Heisenberg lectured in the US (in Ann Arbor and

Chicago). During that trip he met Fermi with whom he discussed issues of atomic energy, including the possibility of atomic weapons.[33] When Fermi suggested that Heisenberg might like to stay in America, the latter replied that such a step would be a betrayal of those young Germans for whom he felt responsible.[33] He returned to Germany in August 1939.

In September, a few weeks after the outbreak of war Heisenberg wrote to Bohr that a trip by a colleague to Denmark 'gives me one more possibility to write to you. You know how the whole development has made me sad ... Since I do not know if and when fate will bring us together again, I should like to thank you once more for your friendship, for everything I learned from you and you have done for me.'[34]

In that same month Heisenberg was ordered to the army weapons command in Berlin. 'There I learned that, together with a group of other physicists, I had to work on the question of technical use of atomic energy.'[35] Heisenberg and some of his colleagues were, of course, fine theorists, but nuclear physics instrumentation in Germany was still quite primitive at that time. Only two small high-tension accelerators were in use in all of Germany; the first cyclotron did not become operational until 1944.[36]

In 1946 Heisenberg published a paper[36] containing a summary of the German atomic energy effort. It has the advantages of being brief and concise, and written with memory still fresh. He himself had contributed a series of papers, which have been in the public domain since 1989.[37] These will be of interest to experts. Here it suffices to list a few qualitative points.

Most of Heisenberg's articles, 21 in all, deal with properties of an *Uranbrenner*, a uranium burner, or what we call a reactor. Already his first two papers (dated 6 December 1939 and 10 February 1940[38]) contain important elements of reactor theory. There is only sporadic reference to atomic weapons, but nothing I have seen on how to build or detonate these. It is of particular interest that at least as early as 1942 the Germans were aware of the possible use of plutonium (not so named then, of course) as an explosive.[39]

By all accounts the crucial German decisions regarding atomic weapons were the result of a meeting on 6 June 1942 attended by Albert Speer, minister of armaments, Field Marshall Erhard Milch and other high military officers, and by Heisenberg and other scientists. Heisenberg gave a briefing.* According to Heisenberg: 'After this meeting Speer decided that the effort should be continued on the present small scale ... External circumstances took the difficult decision whether atomic bombs should be made out of the hands of the physicists.'[36] According to Speer: 'On the suggestion of the nuclear physicists we scuttled the project to develop an

---

* Dr Rechenberg kindly informed me that in his opinion, shared by other Heisenberg experts, this briefing was a simplified version of Ref. 39.

atomic bomb by the autumn of 1942 ... It would have been impossible – given the strain on our economic resources – to have provided the materials, priorities, and technical workers.' [40]*

After these orienting remarks on the German atomic efforts in wartime I turn to Heisenberg's visit to Denmark which took place before Speer had made his decision.

After the occupation of Denmark the Nazis established a German Cultural Institute, situated on the Nørrealle in Copenhagen. In October 1941 this institute arranged an astrophysics meeting during which Heisenberg and another colleague were each to give a public lecture. Letters of invitation for these two talks were sent to Bohr and others at his institute. None of them went.

Rozental remembers: 'During that week Heisenberg came several times to our institute and had lunch with us. He spoke with great confidence about the progress of the German offensive in Russia** ... He stressed how important it was that Germany should win the war. To Christian Møller for instance he said that the occupation of Denmark, Norway, Belgium, and Holland was a sad thing but as regards the countries in East Europe it was a good development because these countries were not able to govern themselves. Møller's answer was that so far we have only learned that it is Germany which cannot govern itself.' [42]

During that week Bohr and Heisenberg had a private conversation. Neither made an immediate record of what was said. Their later recollections are conflicting to some extent.

According to Aage Bohr: 'Heisenberg brought up the question of the military applications of atomic energy. My father was very reticent and expressed his scepticism because of the great technical difficulties that had to be overcome, but he had the impression that Heisenberg thought that the new possibilities could decide the outcome of the war if the war dragged on.' [43]

According to Rozental: 'I can only remember how excited Bohr was after that conversation and that he quoted Heisenberg for having said something like, You must understand that if I am taking part in the project then it is in the firm belief that it can be done.' [42] In a private conversation also Aage Bohr confirmed to me that it was his father's clear impression that Heisenberg was engaged in atomic war work.

According to Heisenberg (in his autobiography, published after Bohr's death). 'Since I had to fear surveillance of Bohr by German authorities I

* German equipment for atomic energy research was captured by American troops on 22 April 1945.[41]

** German forces in Russia were advancing rapidly at that time. Their debacle at Stalingrad had not yet occurred.

spoke with extreme caution . . . I tried to indicate to Niels that in principle one could make atomic bombs, that this demanded an enormous technical effort, and that as a physicist one might well ask oneself, if one should work on this problem.' [44] Heisenberg later wrote that he had meant to point out that physicists were in a position to convey to their governments that in the course of the war atomic bombs could either not be readied at all or else only after extreme exertion. Again according to Heisenberg: 'After my first intimations about the possibility in principle of building atomic bombs, Niels became so frightened that he no longer grasped the part of my information that was most important to me, to wit that it would take a quite enormous technical effort to do so.' [44]

Much has been written about Heisenberg's role in this meeting, some of it unnecessarily defensive, [45] some unnecessarily aggressive. [41] Much distortion has crept in, notably the assertion [45] that 'the German physicists submitted a secret plan to my father, aimed at preventing the development of atomic weapons through a mutual agreement with colleagues in the Allied countries. This account has no basis in the actual events.' [46]* Some time after the war Heisenberg said to Rozental that such a proposal would, of course, not have made sense.

Heisenberg's own recollections are not always consistent. In 1969 he wrote [33] that in 1939 he had told Fermi that Germany could not win the war. In 1941 he claimed the opposite. According to Heisenberg [44] his talk with Bohr took place during a walk near Bohr's home. Several Danes have assured me that it happened in Bohr's office at the institute. In 1947 a visit by Heisenberg to Bohr was arranged [47] during which, according to Heisenberg, [48] the two men spent an evening trying to reconstruct without success their discussion in 1941.** In a 1967 interview [49] Heisenberg said: 'Bohr told me in 1947 that he was enormously frightened [*wahnsinnig erschrocken*] by my remark that we now knew that one could make atomic bombs.' There is no confirmation that Bohr had shown fright. It may be, however, that he was taken aback, because, as has been noted (20c), in 1941 he himself was by no means certain yet of the practical applicability of atomic energy for whatever purpose. It could perhaps also be that he was shaken by the prospect of an atomic arms race between Germany and the Western Allies.

What is one to make of this unfortunate episode? All I have heard and read leaves me without doubt that Heisenberg was neither a Nazi nor a Nazi

---

* *Added in proof.* Very recently the German author of ref. 45 has published a frank retraction: 'That I have contributed to the spreading of the myth of passive resistance by the most important German physicists is due above all to my esteem for those impressive personalities which I have since realized to be out of place.' [45a]

** I have been unable to obtain confirmation by others of what was said during that evening's discussion.

sympathizer, yet that he had tied his fate to that of Germany. Note also that in 1942 he was elected member of the *Mittwochsgellschaft* (Wednesday Society), founded in 1863, a small group of intellectuals that met regularly on Wednesday evenings for discussions and a meal in the home of one or another of its members.[50] In Heisenberg's day some of these were anti-Nazi activists who were executed after the failed 20 July 1944 plot to kill Hitler – the time when the Society disbanded for good.* It is inconceivable that this group would have invited Heisenberg to join had he had sympathies with the other camp.

It has been written,[51] and I am persuaded, that Heisenberg was an apolitical figure. In my opinion that does not help to explain all his actions, however. Why should he have chosen to come to Denmark in 1941 under the auspices of an organization that most Danes detested? Why should he have visited Bohr at all to talk about atomic weapons? Why should he believe 'that the war and the occupation of Denmark by German troops would not change anything in his relation to Bohr and be astonished that this was not the case'?[52] Why did he not realize that it would be preferable to keep his convictions of a German victory to himself rather than alienate others?**

I do not see evil in all this, but rather a glaring insensitivity in regard to human relations, which on occasion Heisenberg also exhibited after the war.[54] 'Mrs Bohr [has] said that it had made Niels very very sad that Heisenberg, whom he admired and who had in many ways been a close friend, should have so little understanding of the feelings of the Danes.'[55]

The relations between Bohr and Heisenberg in the post-war years were no longer as close as they had been in earlier times. Neither Bohr nor anyone else would ever forget the tremendous debt owed to Heisenberg for his scientific labors, however. As Bohr wrote[56] in a contribution to the Festschrift for Heisenberg's 60th birthday (in 1961), Heisenberg's role in the development of physics will be remembered as a superior one.

3. *A letter from England.* Were I asked to name the time when Bohr's contact with the Allied atomic weapons program began, I would choose the day early in 1943 when he received a visit from Captain (later Colonel) Volmer Gyth.

The reason for Gyth's call was this. A courier from Stockholm had arrived in Copenhagen with a communication from England to the Danish general staff to the effect that an important message for Professor Bohr was to come via the general staff offices. It was requested to ascertain whether Bohr would be willing to receive that message which was to be written on a piece of ultramicrofilm hidden in a hollowed-out section of a key attached to a

---

* The last meeting took place on July 1944 – in the Berlin home of Heisenberg, who himself did not participate in the plot.

** I do not find it plausible that he did so in order to protect his safety, as camouflage.[53]

bunch of other keys. Only after receipt of a signal that Bohr would accept the message would the bunch of keys be sent to Copenhagen.

Gyth was charged with contacting Bohr. He was a figure in the style of the Scarlet Pimpernel, an officer in the information division of the Danish general staff who at the same time was deeply involved with the Danish resistance movement. Thus came about Gyth's visit to Bohr, the beginning of a secret operation code named '213'. Bohr declared himself willing to accept the message, but asked if Gyth could help him by copying the content of the microfilm on paper. Gyth could and would and did.* It took another three weeks before a sufficiently well qualified courier was found to bring the material from Stockholm to Copenhagen.

After receipt of the keys Gyth managed to locate the microdot which was the size of a pinhead. He put it under a microscope and transcribed it, then brought it right away to Bohr, who read it carefully. This is what it said.

> The University of Liverpool
> Physics Laboratories
>
> 25th January 1943.

I have heard in a roundabout way, that you have considered coming to this country if the opportunity should offer. I need not tell you how delighted I myself should be to see you again; and I can say to you, there is no scientist in the world who would be more acceptable both to our university people and to the general public. I think you would be very pleased by the warmth you would receive. A factor which may influence you in your decision is that you would work freely in scientific matters. Indeed I have in my mind a particular problem in which your assistance would be of the greatest help. Darwin and Appleton are also interested in this problem and I know they too would be very glad to have your help and advice. You will, I hope, appreciate that I cannot be specific in my reference to this work, but I am sure it will interest you. I trust you will not misunderstand my purpose in writing this letter. I have no desire to influence your decision, for you alone can weigh all the different circumstances, and I have implicit faith in your judgement, whatever it should be. All I want to do is to assure you that if you decide to come, you will have a very warm welcome and an opportunity of service in the common cause. With my best wishes for the future and my deepest regards to Mrs Bohr,

> Yours sincerely,
> (sign.) J. Chadwick

Gyth has remembered that Bohr told him of the invitation, and that he would not accept, because it was best for Denmark that he stay and also because he still could continue his own work. (In March 1943 Bohr wrote to

---

* These details as well as others to be mentioned below of Gyth's activities are recorded in a memorandum he later wrote about his contact with Bohr.

a colleague: 'In spite of the times it was possible to continue undisturbed both the experimental and the theoretical work.'[57]

At Bohr's request Gyth returned the next day to pick up a reply to Chadwick.He saw to it that this letter was reduced to 2×3 mm size. Next it was wrapped in metal foil and handed to a courier. The latter went to a dentist who inserted the message in a hollow tooth of the courier, then covered it with a filling.

In Bohr's answer (undated) he stated the above-mentioned reasons for not accepting the invitation, adding that 'I have to the best of my judgment convinced myself that in spite of all future prospects any immediate use of the latest marvelous discoveries of atomic physics is impracticable'. Two weeks later he called Gyth again. Further reflection had led him to believe he saw a method for practical uses of fission. He had committed his idea to paper and asked Gyth if he could help him once again to get his message to the British. Gyth obliged and this time the letter was sent in secret but less dramatic ways. Its content is not too interesting; the method Bohr had in mind was not used.

As to the fate of Chadwick's message, Bohr himself buried the key and a copy of the transcript, everything enclosed in a metal container, in the garden of Carlsberg, where it stayed safely until after the war. The key and the message now hang, framed, in Aage Bohr's office.

4. *The Swedish interlude.* It has already been mentioned in the preceding section (b) that on 29 September 1943 Bohr fled Denmark. How little time he had to decide to escape can perhaps be seen from the fact that only two weeks earlier he had written to Kramers 'How much all of us here, and especially myself, are happy in the thought that it might be possible to see you soon.'[58] (That visit never took place.)

In mid-September Bohr was informed by Swedish diplomatic sources in Copenhagen that arrest of refugees was imminent. In the following days it became increasingly clear that Bohr's own fate was also at risk. All this led him to contact the Danish underground, especially Chievitz and the biochemist Kaj Linderstrøm Lang. The latter arranged for an escape route to Sweden. On 29 September Bohr and his wife left Carlsberg on foot to walk to a *Kolonihavehus***** in the *Musikby*,**** part of the *Sydhavn* quarter, where they arrived in the early evening. That was the place of assembly for about a dozen people who, together with the Bohrs, were to make the illegal crossing over the Øresund in the same boat. Others included Niels' brother Harald, the latter's son Ole, and Edvard Heiberg, a well-known architect and communist, who had to get out for political reasons. In 1988 Judge Ole

* One of the tiny houses situated on a plot of land, used by Copenhagen families for planting flowers and vegetables.
** The 'music town', so called since all streets are named after musicians.

Bohr told me how that evening Niels, Harald, and Heiberg got into a lively political discussion.

Toward ten o'clock everyone left the little house, crawling on all fours part of the way, to get to the beach. 'Bohr looked a bit embarrassed as if he felt that the trip was a little too dramatic.'* Linderstrøm Lang, who kept an eye on the Bohrs[60] all the way from Carlsberg to the boat, now departed. Everybody boarded a little fishing boat that brought them on to the Øresund. A good hour later all passengers were transferred to a large trawler. In the early hours of 30 September they were safely delivered in the harbour of Limhamn. From there they were transported to Malmø, three miles to the north, where everyone was bedded down in the detention rooms of a police station.[59] Bohr immediately contacted the rector of the University of Lund asking him to request an interview with the Swedish minister of foreign affairs in Stockholm.

In the early afternoon of the same September day Bohr arrived by train in Stockholm. His wife stayed behind to await the arrival of the sons who came over shortly afterward with their families. At the station he was met by Professor and Mrs Klein, who would be the Bohr's hosts, by an intelligence officer of the Swedish general staff – and by captain Gyth.

For his own reasons Gyth had had to flee to Sweden earlier in September. A few hours after Bohr's arrival he had been told what had happened. At once he arranged for a communication to England of Bohr's escape. Almost immediately he received word that the British wanted Bohr to come over as soon as possible and that the next day an unarmed Mosquito bomber would be at Bohr's disposal at Stockholm's airport.

Gyth brought Bohr to the Kleins by taxi. In high Le Carré style they first drove to a building used by the Swedish intelligence service, went up to the roof, walked over roofs to another building, then went down and took another taxi. Soon after arrival at the Klein home a police officer arrived with whom Gyth arranged security measures: one policeman in khaki to be present at all times in the home, one to be stationed in front of the house, one to patrol nearby streets. That done, Gyth told Bohr of the British desire to have him come quickly.

Bohr did not want to leave at once, however. First he intended to intervene with the Swedish government on behalf of the Jews in Denmark. As it happened, for a few days bad weather over the British Isles made his departure impossible anyway. Beginning that same evening and lasting through 3 October Bohr proposed modes of action to the Swedish minister of foreign affairs and other high officials in the foreign office, had an audience with King Gustav V, another with the crown prince, and discussed the issue with a number of other prominent Swedes. The actions of the Danish

---

* According to an account by another fellow escapee[59]

population, described in section (b), overtook the course of events, however.

Meanwhile Gyth had arranged for Bohr and his wife (who had arrived in Stockholm) to move to more spacious quarters provided with great hospitality by a member of the Danish embassy staff. Surveillance continued, now also including an armed Danish officer who during the night guarded the bedroom.

The time had now come for Bohr to fly to England. At ten o'clock on the evening of 4 October Bohr said goodbye to his family (without any drama, Gyth observed). After he had left, Gyth and the host and hostess broke open a bottle of champagne to celebrate the successful conclusion of this part of the adventure. Shortly after midnight the bell rang. There stood Bohr. His plane had taken off all right but after a short while had to return because of engine malfunction. Bohr had taken a taxi back.

What was to be done now? All security personnel had been dismissed. Gyth decided to guard the bedroom himself armed with the host's old revolver. All was peaceful until in the early morning hours he heard soft steps on the stairs. Somebody approached the apartment door. Gyth stood at the ready, the revolver in one hand, a heavy candelabrum in the other. Then, to his great relief, the morning newspaper dropped through the mail slot. Looking out of the window some moments later Gyth saw an old newspaper lady wearing felt slippers so as not to wake her customers.

That evening Bohr took off again and this time reached his destination.

5. *The fate of the institute.* On 6 December 1943 at 7:30 a.m. a squad of military police marched into the institute and declared it occupied. Jørgen Bøggild and Holger Olsen, the head of the institute machine shop (I remember him well, he was a feisty little chap), who each had living quarters at the institute, were sent to a Copenhagen prison, where they were held but not considered prisoners and could receive visitors without special permission. Both men were interrogated several times and eventually released unharmed, Olsen on 12 December 1943, Bøggild on 26 January 1944.

On the afternoon of 6 December the university rector called a meeting in which the physics professors Jacobsen and Møller participated. He reported that he had protested the occupation to the German authorities.* It was decided to inform Heisenberg of what had happened without, however, requesting specific action from his side.

Meanwhile Jacobsen had asked for and was granted an interview with German authorities which took place on 11 January. He was asked if Bohr worked with the cyclotron. No, he did not. Did he know anything about Bohr's activities in England? No, he did not.

* These and other details are given in a report, present in the NBA, on the events during the institute's occupation.

While all this was going on, the Danish resistance had become concerned that the institute might actually be of military importance, so they started preparations to blow it up. 'It was mined through the sewers, and the plan would certainly have been carried out, had not Professor Chievitz, who was very active in the resistance movement, got wind of it. He persuaded the initiators of the plan to wait until a statement could be obtained from Bohr whether the demolition of the institute was desirable. A message was sent to Stockholm, and passed on to Bohr by the quickest possible route.' [61] Bohr got word directly to Copenhagen to do nothing of the sort.

On 24 January Heisenberg appeared in Copenhagen. He had not heard of the events until the message from Denmark had reached him. He told Møller that he had managed to be included in a committee of German scientists that was to be sent to Copenhagen to examine whether secret war work was done at the institute. Before meeting Møller he had already talked with local Gestapo officials who had made three proposals. Either Germans take over the institute; or it is given back with a pledge that Danish physicists collaborate with German colleagues; or it is given back after Germans remove some instruments for their own use. Only this last choice seemed perhaps acceptable to the Danes.

On 25 January Heisenberg and some others made the inspection tour of the institute. The next day Heisenberg showed Møller their report. Its main point was that it would benefit Germany if research would continue and be published as before. That same day the rector was informed by the Danish Foreign Office that the institute would be unconditionally released. On 3 February the institute was formally returned to Copenhagen University. Only a few minor objects were found missing.

'After the war, more details of the planned arrest of Bohr and the occupation of the institute came to light at the Nürnberg trials. Originally Bohr was to have been arrested and taken to Germany soon after 29 August 1943 [when the Germans declared martial law in Denmark; see (21b)]. The order for the arrest was, however, not carried out because of internal conflicts between German officials, and it was decided to put off the move until the proposed deportation of the Jews. The Germans were hoping that in the general confusion an order for Bohr's arrest would then attract less attention.The occupation of the institute took place at the instigation of a member of the Gestapo, living in Copenhagen, who wanted to curry favour with his superiors.' [61]

(d) Bohr's war years, the Anglo-American episode

1. *On to Britain.* Bohr's plane flight to Britain had its hairy moments. He talked almost incessantly while he was given his swimming vest and oxygen

mask at Stockholm's Bromma airport and probably did not pay sufficient attention to the instructions the pilot gave him. When the plane reached the Kattegat near occupied Denmark it increased altitude and it became necessary to use the mask. By intercom the pilot instructed Bohr, who was lying in the bomb bay separated from the cabin, to turn on the oxygen but got no response, although the phone system had been checked at Bromma. So the pilot took the plane down to near sea level. When it landed at a military airport in Scotland, in the early hours of 6 October, Bohr was in fine shape, telling that he had slept most of the way – which meant that he had been unconscious because of lack of oxygen.*

Bohr spent the rest of that night in the home of the airport commander. The following morning he was flown to London's Croydon airport where he was met by Chadwick and the secret service officer who had supervised his escape to Britain. They saw to it that Bohr was installed in the Savoy hotel.

All this was of course meant to be hush hush. Nevertheless the *New York Times* of 9 October carried the following news item.

Scientist Reaches London

Dr N. H. D. Bohr, Dane, Has a New Atomic Blast Invention

LONDON, Oct. 8 (AP)—Dr Niels H. D. Bohr, refugee Danish scientist and Nobel Prize winner for atomic research, reached London from Sweden today bearing what a Dane in Stockholm said were plans for a new invention involving atomic explosions.

The plans were described as of the greatest importance to the Allied war effort.

It was the last time until after the war that news about Bohr appeared in the *New York Times*.

Back to 6 October: that evening Bohr was received by Sir John Anderson, who had been appointed chancellor of the exchequer in 1943. Anderson had begun his career as a physical chemist and had actually done research on the chemistry of uranium.[62] He had been interested in fission physics since the fall of 1939.[63] When Bohr met him in 1943 he had been for some time the cabinet minister who, at Prime Minister Churchill's request, had assumed the responsibility for supervising the British atomic bomb project, code named Tube Alloys.

Aage Bohr, who came over to England a week after his father and who was his personal assistant during nearly all the time from 1943 to 1945 that Bohr was to spend in England and the US has told me how profoundly surprised Niels was by what he was told that day about the status of the Anglo American atomic weapons effort.

Let us have a brief look at how those matters had developed up till that time.

---

* This account was given by Gyth who later also went to England, where he saw Bohr a few times.

2. *Anglo-American efforts up till October 1943.** On 2 August 1939 Einstein signed a letter addressed to President Roosevelt in which he drew attention to the military implications of atomic energy. That document reached the president on 11 October.[69] Allegations sometimes made that this letter was the initial stimulus for the atomic bomb project are without substance. In response to the letter the president did authorize the formation of an Advisory Committee on Uranium consisting of four undistinguished men but did not start a governmental program.[70] As to Einstein, he was excluded from wartime nuclear development.[71] After the war he said more than once that he regretted having written to Roosevelt. 'Had I known that the Germans would not succeed in producing an atomic bomb, I would not have lifted a finger.'[72]

The man primarily responsible for getting the American project going was Vannevar Bush, 'a shrewd, spry Yankee of fifty – plain spoken, but with a disarming twinkle in his eye and a boyish grin – [who] was well known for his original work in applied mathematics and electrical engineering'.[73] He had close contact with both science and government after he moved to Washington in 1939, as president of the Carnegie Institution. It was Bush who pushed the creation of the National Defense Research Committee (NDRC), created by executive order on 27 June 1940. Roosevelt defined as its objective to generate 'experimental investigations and reports, as may be found desirable in order to accelerate the creation or improvement of the instrumentalities of warfare'.[74] Bush saw to it that prominent scientists became involved with the Uranium Committee which was now placed under control of the NDRC.

The NDRC was a research organization 'not well adapted to fill the gap between research and procurement orders that engineers called development'.[75] To remedy this Bush proposed to the president to create the Office of Scientific Research and Development. The OSRD, established by executive order of 28 June 1941 'was to serve as a center for mobilizing the scientific resources of the nation and applying the results of research to national defense'.[75] Bush became OSRD director. The NDRC, now chaired by James Bryant Conant, president of Harvard, became part of OSRD. The Uranium Committee became the 'S-1 Section' of OSRD. Bush and Conant became the two principal United States statesmen of science in the war effort.

By the time the OSRD went into operation important laboratory work related to fission had been done, most notably the chemical isolation of plutonium in early 1941 (20c), in Berkeley, where its fission cross-section

---

* What follows next is only the merest outline of a few events of interest for what comes later. For detailed accounts see histories of the British,[62] the American,[64] and the combined[65] atomic bomb projects, and of Los Alamos Laboratory.[66] See especially Ref. 67 for the related political developments, and Ref. 68 for a useful list of primary sources.

had also meanwhile been measured. Fermi had proposed plans for building a uranium–graphite reactor. Numerous scientific reports had been written. No authorization had yet been given, however, for US engagement in an industrial effort to produce atomic weapons. That decision was made on 9 October 1941 at a meeting between Roosevelt, Vice-President Henry Wallace and Bush. Roosevelt named at once a policy board for handling the matter, consisting of those present, Conant, army chief of staff George Marshall, and secretary of war Henry Stimson – who up till that time had never even heard of atomic bombs![76]

Of these events on 9 October it has been written: 'The second world war is marked by many lonely decisions . . . but in its speed, its loneliness, and the magnitude of its eventual consequences, Franklin Roosevelt's decision of 9 October stands alone.'[77] In order to comprehend the abruptness of his step, it is necessary to appreciate what the British had meanwhile been up to.

Early in 1940, Frisch and Peierls (then both in Birmingham) had set out to estimate how much pure U235 was needed to make a bomb. Their conclusion was startling. Frisch has written: 'To my amazement it was very much smaller than I [and others] had expected; it was not a matter of tons, but soemthing like a pound or two . . . we [F. and P.] came to the conclusion that . . . one might produce a pound of reasonably pure U235 in a modest time . . . At that point we stared at each other and realized that an atomic bomb might after all be possible.'[78] Their work was based on theoretical arguments and inspired guesswork. Their results were eventually seen to be quantitatively incorrect (the amount of U235 needed is something like ten times larger). Nevertheless, their results, reported in the renowned 'Frisch Peierls memorandum'[79] (in which reference is made to Bohr's 'strong arguments' for slow neutron fission being ascribed to U235) were the first time anyone had stated that atomic weapons were feasible; also the first time in which it was stated that a bomb 'should be made in two (or more) parts which are brought together first when the explosion is wanted . . . [This] assembling should be done as rapidly as possible'[79] (to avoid fizzling).

That memorandum 'triggered [as Frisch put it[80]] the formation of a committee', the British counterpart of the Uranium Committee, named the Maud Committee, a name due to Bohr – unbeknownst to him.*

Scientific liaison between Britain and the US had begun in the autumn of 1940.[81] The initial focus was on radar, but 'in the spring of 1941 this practice was extended to the work of Maud'.[82] American physicists in the know were

---

* 'The reason for that name was a telegram which had arrived from Niels Bohr, ending with the mysterious words "and tell Maud Ray Kent". We were all convinced that this was a code . . . The mystery was not cleared up until after the war when we learned that Maud Ray used to be a governess in Bohr's house and lived in Kent.'[80]

permitted to attend sessions of the Maud Committee. In the summer of 1941 the committee completed a detailed report on a U235 bomb.[83] (Plutonium was mentioned only in passing.) It is an assertive document. 'We have now reached the conclusion that it will be possible to make an effective uranium bomb ... [which is] likely to lead to decisive results in the war.' This document contains an outline for a concrete practical program.

Bush first heard of the report in July, when Bohr's friend (17j) Charlie Lauritsen told him of a discussion of the draft report he had attended in London. Shortly thereafter Bush received a copy of the draft and became convinced. On 3 October Conant received the official final version.[84] That was the document Bush had with him on that 9 October meeting. He outlined its content to President Roosevelt, who immediately grasped its importance, 'understood that a great deal of money would be required and said he could make it available ... Bush was to expedite the work in every possible way.'[85] That was two months before the US entered the war ...

The year 1942 marked the beginning of major practical decisions.

(a) In July Anderson sent a Minute[86] to Churchill in which he proposed, reluctantly, that the bomb project be a joint Anglo-American effort, to be executed in the United States. 'We now have a real contribution to make a merger. Soon we shall have little or none.' On 31 July Churchill approved.[87] Details were worked out in first instance by Anderson and Bush. During the following year the collaboration did not work out smoothly and at one point broke down completely.[88] It became effective again after the secret agreement 'governing collaboration between the authorities of the USA and the UK in the matter of Tube Alloys',[89] signed on 19 August 1943 by Roosevelt and Churchill at the first Quebec Summit Conference.

(b) A special US army office for controlling procurement, construction of plants and other practical matters was created. Its headquarters was initially in New York City, whence the code name it acquired and kept: Manhattan Engineering District or Manhattan Project. In September 1942 Colonel Leslie Groves, deputy chief of construction, US Corps of Engineers, was appointed its commanding officer and promptly promoted to brigadier general. A military colleague has described him as 'the biggest sonovabitch I've ever met in my life, but also one of the most capable officers'.[90] It turned out to be a very good choice.

(c) On 2 December 1942 at 3:20 p.m. the first man-made sustained chain reaction was achieved in Chicago, under the direction of Fermi, a major experimental achievement without immediate practical implications, however. The Chicago pile* would have had to operate for thousands of

---

* Consisting of very pure natural uranium, uranium oxide, and graphite piled upon each other layer by layer, whence the name pile. A number of cadmium strips, strong neutron absorbers, kept the chain reaction in check.

years to accumulate sufficient plutonium for a weapon.[91] For such purposes major plants were required. Since it was not clear at that time whether a U235 or a plutonium plant would achieve the quickest results, a typically American decision was made: build both.

(d) In October 1943 the U235 plant in Oak Ridge, Tennessee (which also delivered the first batch of plutonium) was well under way but had not yet reached production stage.[92]

(e) In January 1943, Hanford, State of Washington, had been chosen as the location for the plutonium plant. Construction of piles could not begin until the basic design drawings were released – which happened in October 1943.[93]

(f) Meanwhile, in November 1942, the site had been chosen for the atomic weapons laboratory, the nerve center of the entire operation: Los Alamos in New Mexico. Its planning board began to meet there in March 1943. By October 1943 activities were in the early stages.[94] Its director was an old acquaintance of Bohr: Robert Oppenheimer.

Bohr had met Oppenheimer for the first time during a visit to Cambridge in 1925, when the latter was doing postgraduate work there, hoping to be taken on by Rutherford, 'but Rutherford wouldn't have me'.[95] Oppenheimer remembered his first meeting with Bohr: 'When Rutherford introduced me to Bohr he asked me what I was working on. I told him and he said, "How is it going?" I said, "I'm in difficulties." He said, "Are the difficulties mathematical or physical?" I said, "I don't know." He said, "That's bad."'[95]

The two men met again during Bohr's visits to Pasadena in 1933 and to Berkeley in 1937 (18b). After the second of these encounters Bohr wrote to Oppenheimer: 'It was a very great pleasure to me indeed to get an opportunity of coming in still closer connection with you and to feel how, in spite of all differences as regards points of approach, we sympathize with each other so thoroughly in physics as well as in many other things . . . I remember so clearly the first time I met you, when as a quite young man you came into Rutherford's office in the Cavendish Laboratory, while I was sitting and talking to him there. When you went out, I remember that Rutherford said some warmly appreciating words regarding his expectations about you.'[96] These recollections show differences worth a moment of reflection.

3. *From London to New York.* It will now be clear what were the main points Bohr learned during his first briefings in London. First, that the project was under way but that no definitive results had yet been obtained. Secondly, that it had turned into a joint Anglo-American venture.

Anderson asked Bohr to join the British organization and then to proceed to the US. Soon thereafter Bohr received a letter[97] offering him appointment as scientific adviser to the directorate of Tube Alloys. Meanwhile the American physicist Tolman, who was in London at that time, brought Bohr an invitation from Groves to become member of the American organization. Bohr felt that his close connections with US science might make a joint appointment preferable. Anderson agreed. On 9 November Bohr received a modified letter of appointment[98] from the British. Concurrence from the American side followed sometime later.

Before leaving for the US Niels and Aage did a good amount of traveling in Britain, visiting sites where work related to Tube Alloys was in progress and visiting colleagues and friends, among them Chadwick, Dirac, Peierls, and Lady Rutherford. Bohr also called on Danish diplomats and resistance leaders in London; and on King Haakon of Norway, whom he had last met the night before their countries were invaded, and who had stuck it out until June 1940 before fleeing to London. In Anderson's home he met Jan Smuts, distinguished statesman, commander of the South African forces during the war, field marshall in the British army, with whom he discussed general philosophical issues, in which Smuts was very interested. In November he gave a speech[99] at the Royal Society on international scientific relations, including a brief account of recent events in Denmark.*

In a meeting with Churchill's personal scientific adviser Lord Cherwell the latter expressed concern that the project would come under the complete domination of the US army. Bohr conveyed this to Anderson, offering to report on his own impressions. Anderson authorized Bohr to do so via Lord Halifax, the British ambassador in Washington.

On 28 November Niels and Aage took the night train to Glasgow where in the early morning they boarded the *Aquitania* bound for New York. From Aage's recollections: 'On our arrival in New York [on 6 December] my father was requested to assume the pseudonym Nicholas Baker, while I became James Baker. We were issued with papers in these names, and at the beginning there was constantly an armed detective at our side. When we travelled around in the States, we were always accompanied by a bodyguard; over long distances the guard was changed, and the one who assumed responsibility for us had to sign a receipt for our delivery in good condition.'[100] It had further been agreed that, whenever necessary, Bohr would state by way of cover that the purpose of his stay in the US was to prepare for post-war scientific cooperation.

4. *Bohr's role in the weapons program.* When Bohr once said after the war: 'They did not need my help in making the atom bomb,'[101] he did not only mean to pay a well-deserved compliment to all the physicists, engineers, and technical personnel who had done the work, but also to indicate that his

---

* During his hectic few days in Stockholm Bohr had already found time to prepare a draft for such a talk.

own focus of attention had shifted. While the physical and technical aspects of atomic weapons continued of course to be of great interest to him, his overriding concern had turned to their political implications, as I am about to relate. That is why in what follows very little will be mentioned about actual weapons development.

Nevertheless Bohr did play a role also in this last respect, albeit a modest one. Oppenheimer has recalled: '[Bohr] did not take up residence at Los Alamos but made several extended visits [during which] he showed a vigorous interest in both theory and design, and acted as a scientific father confessor to the younger men[102]* . . . Bohr at Los Alamos was marvelous. He took a lively technical interest . . . His real function there was that he made the enterprise which looked so macabre seem hopeful . . . His own high hope was that the outcome would be good and that the cooperation that science had established would play a helpful part.'[104] The only concrete contribution by Bohr I know of was his help with work on initiators.** 'This device remained a stubborn puzzle . . . but in early February 1945 Niels Bohr clarified what had to be done.'[105]

While in Los Alamos Bohr found time to enjoy nature. He went hiking with friends. When he had to cross a stream, 'he never stopped to consider its width, or the best place to cross it. He jumped it. And while he did so his body straightened, his eyes glowed with pleasure.'[105a] He went skiing. 'He gave himself to elegant curves, to expert snowplows, to dead stops at fast speeds, and to stylish jumps that no one else could perform. He quit only when the sun went down.'[105a]

(e) Bohr, Churchill, Roosevelt, and the atomic bomb†

1. *Glasnost 1944.* The information about the Manhattan project which Bohr had first received upon his arrival in London had come as a revelation to him. The more he saw for himself the more he admired the energy and efficiency devoted to its development. 'He had no trouble, then or later, with the wartime effort and its wartime purpose.'[106] Remember that Bohr and others were still greatly troubled by the possibility of German atomic weapons.

From the very start Bohr's thoughts were less concerned with the current

---

* Bohr got along particularly well with Feynman. See Ref. 103 for Feynman's recollections of Bohr in Los Alamos.

** Two methods for setting off an atomic bomb were considered: the gun method (used in the U235 bomb on Hiroshima) in which two bomb halves are literally shot against each other; and the implosion method (used in the plutonium bomb on Nagasaki) in which the active material is shot inward by surrounding explosives. An initiator is the little neutron source that starts the chain reaction in an implosion bomb.

† I was enormously helped in the writing of this section by discussions with Aage Bohr and by his permission of access to confidential documents.

war effort, however, than with the enormous changes the new weapons would create in the post-war world. He foresaw that the unparalleled new threats to the security of nations caused by atomic bombs might lead to terrifying new arms races unless unparalleled new efforts were made to create trust and confidence between the West and the Soviet Union. Otherwise their alliance would not endure after the war – already then turning clearly in favor of the Allies – was over.

Bohr became increasingly convinced that the only way to maintain world stability was to engage at once, and at the highest level, in consultations with the Russians, to inform them of the Western military preparations without initially divulging technical details, and to offer them full future cooperation in scientific progress and industrial exploitation. In a word, Bohr's aim was glasnost. Every possible threat to security should be openly – though not necessarily publicly – discussed by all concerned. Bohr realized that nothing could be lost but very much could be gained by such an initiative.

Bohr was, of course, well aware of the enormous difficulties that stood in the way of effecting such an approach. He had visited the Soviet Union. He had learned about the state of affairs from newspapers and accounts by Russian friends. When in 1938 the Russian physicist Landau had been imprisoned he had personally intervened with Stalin, without success,* with an 'urgent request to instigate an investigation about the fate of Professor Landau'.[108] Thus Bohr did not need to be told that openness did not remotely fit with the Soviet political style of the day. That he nevertheless put his energies behind pursuing the need for an open world shows how strongly convinced he was that atomic weapons would radically change the world situation and that their very existence, far from only posing new threats, might actually hold a promise for improved intercourse between nations.

I turn to Bohr's efforts to promote glasnost.

2. Meetings with Ambassador Halifax and Justice Frankfurter. On 8 December 1943 Bohr arrived in Washington, DC. There he met Groves for the first time, and called on Ambassador Kauffmann, officially dismissed from his post (21b), yet still in place. On December 21 he was received by Lord Halifax to whom he reported on his discussions with Anderson and, in general terms, on weapons development. The next day was spent in Princeton, where Bohr met Einstein and Pauli, who was spending the war years at the institute.

A week later Bohr wrote[109] to Halifax, thanking him for his kind

---

* After having made an equally unsuccessful approach to the president of the Soviet Academy of Sciences.[107]

reception. This is the first document I know in which Bohr refers to a possible bright side of atomic weapons development. 'The unique hopes and peculiar dangers involved in this project are, of course, fully appreciated by the responsible statesmen, but nevertheless it must be the duty of a scientist . . . to call to their attention any detail of this development which may have a bearing on the realization of such hopes and on the elimination of such dangers.' On the 28th Niels and Aage left for their first visit to Los Alamos.

In February 1944, after his return to Washington, Bohr met his old friend Felix Frankfurter, a Supreme Court justice and confidential adviser to President Roosevelt. When Frankfurther indicated his awareness of the Manhattan Project, Bohr told him of his hopes that this effort might eventually be for the better of mankind, carefully omitting all secret technical details. Frankfurter took Bohr's point and said that Roosevelt might be responsive to these ideas.

At about that same time Bohr wrote[110] to Anderson in London about his experiences. After discussing technical issues he went on to reflect on atomic arms control which demand 'openness about industrial efforts including military preparations which would hardly be conceivable unless all partners were assured of . . . common security against dangers of unprecedented acuteness . . . Such an initiative, aimed at preventing future competition about the formidable weapon should in no way impede the importance of the project for immediate military objectives.' This letter was accompanied by a letter from Halifax who wrote Anderson that 'it is urgent that you and the Prime Minister give the matter most thorough attention'.[111] Anderson replied[112] to Bohr that he understood his points which also were much on his own mind.

In March Frankfurter told Bohr that he had reported the substance of their earlier discussions to Roosevelt, who had expressed deep concern about the political consequences of atomic weapons, adding that he and Churchill ought to take up this issue. Roosevelt authorized Frankfurter to write out a message for Bohr to take to London for Anderson, Bohr's link with the British government. Bohr next informed Halifax, who on 6 April cabled Anderson: 'I think it is important that Bohr returns to London to discuss the latest developments.'[111] On 8 April Anderson cabled back that he would welcome very much a visit from Bohr, whom he would receive immediately after his arrival. Accordingly Bohr returned to London on 14 April.

3. *The Kapitza letter.* On 28 October 1943 Kapitza had sent a letter from Moscow to Bohr in Stockholm which had been forwarded to the Soviet Embassy in London. A letter from the Embassy to Bohr (c/o the Danish Council in London) had advised that a communication from Kapitza was waiting for him.[113] On 20 April Bohr called on the embassy. After being

handed the letter he engaged in some friendly conversation on international scientific cooperation.

Kapitza's letter[114] contained an invitation to Bohr and his family to come
to the Soviet Union, 'where everything will be done to give you shelter'.
Kapitza also remarked that 'we scientists have done everything in our
power to put our knowledge at the disposal of the war cause'.

It is not simple to decode that statement. Note, however, that it is now
known[115] that as early as 1942 Stalin had called in some leading Soviet
physicists, Kapitza among them, to inquire about the possibilities of
developing an atomic weapon.

Bohr drafted a cordial but non-committal reply to Kapitza. 'I am hoping
that I shall soon be able to accept your kind invitation.' Otherwise he
mainly wrote about prospects for international scientific cooperation. Both
Kapitza's letter and Bohr's draft reply were sent to the British Secret
Service. Upon their approval Bohr's answer[116] was delivered by messenger
to the Soviet Embassy.

4. *Bohr meets Churchill.* After Anderson had met with Bohr upon the
latter's return, he arranged for the message Bohr had brought to be
conveyed to Churchill and for Bohr to meet Cherwell to discuss arrangements for a meeting with the prime minister. Cherwell intimated that
Churchill was extremely occupied with current military problems and
would probably not be receptive to discussing future plans. Nevertheless
Bohr felt, as he wrote to Anderson, that 'I cannot help feeling that the only
way in which I can carry out my mission is if I can be given the opportunity
to see Mr Churchill ... The aim of my delicate mission was to convey ...
that the President is deeply concerned with the unique hope the situation
inspires, and eager to receive any suggestion ... from Mr Churchill.'[117]

Meanwhile, Sir Henry Dale, president of the Royal Society had written to
Churchill: 'It is my serious belief that it may be in your power even in the
next six months to make decisions which will determine the future course of
human history. It is in that belief that I dare ask you, even now, to give
Professor Bohr the opportunity of brief access to you.'[118] On 16 May 1944
Bohr was received by Churchill in the presence of Cherwell.

Let us briefly interrupt the story to catch a glimpse of the status of the
bomb project at that time. On the preceding 4 February Groves had written
to Roosevelt that it was still unknown how much fissionable material was
needed to produce a bomb.[119] The discovery during the following June/July
that the plutonium-240 isotope fissions spontaneously (i.e. without the need
for prior bombardment with neutrons) led to a serious revision of
detonation methods for plutonium bombs.[120]

The point of all this is that at the time of the Bohr–Churchill meeting
scientists did not yet have the means for constructing a testing device, let

alone a deliverable weapon. Yet even then Bohr was urging the case for an open world.

The meeting was a disaster. Here was the War Lord, desperately preoccupied with immense responsibilities, used to incisive decisions, three weeks before D-day. There was Bohr, hard to follow as always, failing to make any impact. Much of the time was taken up by Churchill arguing with Cherwell about side issues. Bohr never got his points across. When right afterward he met a colleague in the know on a London street who asked how it had gone, Bohr replied: 'It was terrrible. He scolded us [B. and Cherwell] like two schoolboys.' [121]

As he was leaving, Bohr asked Churchill if he might send him a memorandum on his ideas. Churchill replied that he would always be honored to receive a letter from Professor Bohr but hoped it would not be about politics.[122] Bohr did write: 'The lead in the efforts to master such mighty forces of nature . . . which by good fortune has been achieved by the two great free nations, entails the greatest promises for the future . . . [these achievements] might perhaps influence the judgement of the statesmen as to how the present favourable situation can best be turned to lasting advantage for the cause of freedom and world security.' [123]

Shortly thereafter Bohr had a discussion with Smuts which caused the latter to write to Churchill: 'The discovery [is] the most important ever made by science. I have discussed its possibilities with the scientific expert [B.] who saw you also . . . Something will have to be done about its control . . .' [124]

Thus Bohr had not convinced Churchill but had won over important allies: Anderson, Cherwell, Frankfurter, Halifax, and Smuts.

5. *Bohr meets Roosevelt.* Meanwhile, on 8 June, Bohr had left London and was back in Washington on the 16th. He at once reported his London adventures to Frankfurter, who in turn informed Roosevelt. Shortly afterward Frankfurter told Bohr that the president thought it was good that Bohr had tried to talk with Churchill and that he himself wished to see Bohr too. Frankfurther advised Bohr to collect his ideas in a short memorandum, which Bohr did, and which Frankfurter forwarded to the president. The key phrase of this document[125] is the following:

[We must seek] an initiative aiming at forestalling a fateful competition about the formidable weapon, [an initiative which] should serve to uproot any cause of distrust between the powers on whose harmonious collaboration the fate of coming generations will depend . . . Of course, the responsible statesmen alone can have the insight in the actual possibilities.

Because Roosevelt had to journey to the Pacific the meeting could not be arranged until 26 August.[126] They talked for more than an hour. This time Bohr got his points across. Roosevelt sounded promising and expressed trust in Stalin's wisdom. (Bohr later heard that Roosevelt had said to a mutual friend that he found Bohr to be one of the most interesting men he had ever met.)

Two weeks later Bohr wrote[127] to the president, thanking him for the honor of receiving him, 'for the wish you expressed to see me again at some later occasion' – that never happened – and summarizing the main points of their discussion. That letter reached Roosevelt on the eve of his departure for Quebec, where on 11 September he began another meeting with Churchill.

On 18 September, after the conclusion of the Quebec conference, Churchill and Roosevelt met privately at the president's residence in Hyde Park, New York. An *aide-mémoire* of that encounter contains three points.[128] First, the bomb project shall be kept strictly secret for the time being. Secondly, the US and the UK shall continue their collaboration on these projects after the war. Thirdly, 'enquiries should be made regarding the activities of Professor Bohr and steps should be taken to ensure that he is responsible for no leakage of information, particularly to the Russians.' The next day Churchill sent a note[129] to Cherwell: 'The President and I are much worried about Professor Bohr. How did he come into this business? He is a great advocate of publicity. He says he is in close correspondence with a Russian professor, an old friend of his in Russia, to whom he has written about the matter and may be writing still. The Russian professor has urged him to go to Russia in order to discuss matters. What is all this about? It seems to me Bohr ought to be confined or at any rate made to see that he is very near the edge of mortal crimes. I had not visualized any of this before, though I did not like the man when you showed him to me, with his hair all over his head, at Downing Street. Let me have by return your views about this man. I do not like it at all.'

Bohr had gotten nowhere.

6. *Coda.* Why not? Bohr's meeting with the prime minister may have failed in part because Churchill was 'abnormally impenetrable to most kinds of insight'.[130] Far more importantly, however, 'it failed because the prime minister had already made up his mind and did not want to hear any further argument'.[131] Prior to the Bohr–Churchill meeting, Anderson and Cherwell, inspired by Bohr, had attempted to convey to Churchill the merits of early broad-based discussions of atomic issues. Churchill had disapproved.[132]

It also appears that Roosevelt had second thoughts of his own after having met Bohr. In a meeting on 22 September with Bush and Cherwell he wondered how Frankfurter knew about the bomb, and whether Bohr was trustworthy.[133] In regard to rejecting the open world idea, 'on balance one is led to guess that here Roosevelt acquiesced, without much thought, in a sentiment pressed upon him by his friend,'[134] Churchill.

As to Bohr, he had been scrupulously careful in his dealings both with Frankfurter and Kapitza. It is regrettable that he had to spend many subsequent conversations in making that clear, with Anderson, Bush, Frankfurter, Groves, and Tolman. Perhaps one should not exclude the possibility that Churchill and Roosevelt used the issue of Bohr's reliability as a means for evading the main issue.

As if Bohr did not have trouble enough, in December 1944, while in Washington, he received a letter[135] from Einstein. The latter was alarmed by visits from Stern, who had said to him that after the war a secret arms race would develop that necessarily would lead to worse wars than ever before. Einstein proposed that leading scientists suggest to the political leaders to internationalize military forces, and asked Bohr to join. Bohr hastened to Einstein (also in December) to make clear to him that such a *démarche* might have the most deplorable consequences if anyone with confidential information would participate. Einstein replied that he understood, that he himself would refrain from action, and that he would urge other colleagues to do likewise.

Bohr continued to hope for another meeting with Roosevelt. With that purpose in mind he wrote an addendum, dated 24 March 1945, to his earlier memorandum to Roosevelt. Of particular interest is the reason he gives there for early action.

A postponement to await further developments might, especially if preparations for competitive efforts in the meantime have reached an advanced stage, give the approach the appearance of an attempt at coercion in which no great nation can be expected to acquiesce.

While discussions were in progress regarding the best way of bringing this document to the president's attention, Roosevelt died, on 12 April . . .

Some final questions: Was Bohr's attempt naïve? Did Churchill's and Roosevelt's lack of response show lack of wisdom and foresight? My own answer to these questions would be no. Times were simply not yet ripe.

Did Bohr's failure to win over the West's two leading statesmen cause him to drop his proposal for glasnost? Others might have given up. Not Bohr. Stay tuned for Chapter 22, section (c).

7. *Going home.* After the events just recounted Bohr went back and forth several times between Washington and Los Alamos and between the US and Britain. In June 1945 he was in London again, after his last wartime visit to the US. Denmark had been liberated and Margrethe could join her husband in England.

Atomic bomb developments were now reaching their climax. On 16 July the test explosion at Trinity near Los Alamos took place, the first detonation of a nuclear device, made of plutonium. (U235 was never tested prior to use.) On 6 August, at 8:15 in the morning, Japanese time, Hiroshima was destroyed by a U235 bomb. On 9 August, at 11:02 in the morning, Japanese time, Nagasaki was hit by a plutonium bomb.

On 11 August *The Times* of London published an article 'Science and civilization', written by Bohr with Aage's help. It is his first public statement about the need for an open world.

The formidable power of destruction which has come within reach of man may become a mortal menace unless human society can adjust itself to the exigencies of the situation. Civilization is presented with a challenge more serious perhaps than ever before ... We have reached the stage where the degree of security offered to the citizens of a nation by collective defense measures is entirely insufficient ... No control can be effective without free access to full scientific information and the granting of the opportunity of international supervision of all undertakings which, unless regulated, might become a source of disaster ... The contribution which an agreement about this vital matter would make ... can hardly be exaggerated.

At Frankfurter's suggestion Bohr published shortly afterward a similar article in *Science*.[136]

On 25 August Bohr returned to Denmark. On the evening of that day he made a short radio address in which he expressed his happiness to be back home. On the 26th he arrived by bike at his institute. That evening he spoke again over the radio, at somewhat greater length.[137] On 21 September he was reelected president of the *Videnskabernes Selskab* (20d). On 7 October Bohr celebrated his 60th birthday. That evening Copenhagen students marched in a torchlight parade to Carlsberg where they serenaded the Bohrs. On New Year's Eve Bohr gave another address on the Danish radio,[138] which concluded as follows.

At this year's end mankind has reached a watershed. We have received the most serious lesson about the dangers that can lead all of us into the abyss if each of us continues blindly as before, but at the same time we see prospects that give greater hope than ever before for creating together happier conditions for man's life.

References

1. D. J. Kevles, *The physicists*, Chap. 20, Vintage Books, New York 1979.
2. As L. DuBridge put it, see J. S. Rigden, *Rabi*, p. 164, Basic Books, New York 1987.
3. For an account of the period of 1864–1914 see T. Fink, *Deutschland als Problem Dänemarks*, Christian Wolff Verlag, Flensburg 1968; also C. R. Woodhouse, *Scand. Stud.* (Lawrence, Kansas), **46**, 201, 1974; H. Brems, *ibid.* **51**, 428, 1979.
4. H. Haue, J. Olsen, and J. Aarup-Kristensen, *Det ny Danmark*, p. 187, Munksgaard, Copenhagen 1979.
5. *New York Times*, 31 May 1939.

6. S. Rozental, NBR, p. 149; also S. Rozental, *Erindringer om Niels Bohr*, p. 20, Gyldendal, Copenhagen 1985.

7. H. Lefèvre, in *Ole Chievitz*, p. 49, Nordisk Boghandel, Copenhagen 1956.

8. N. Bohr, Ref. 7, p. 7.

9. *New York Times*, 26 January 1940.

10. *New York Times*, 9 March 1940.

11. L. Strauss, letter to N. Bohr, January 1946, NBA.

12. Fink (Ref. 3), p. 116.

13. R. Petrow, *The bitter years*, p. 49, Morrow, New York 1974.

14. *Fædrelandet*, 16 August 1942; see also *National Socialisten*, 10 September 1942.

15. *Frederiksborg Amtsavis*, 26 August 1942.

16. *New York Times*, 10 April 1941.

17. *New York Times*, 17 April 1941.

18. Ref. 4, p. 219.

19. For a detailed account of the fate of the Danish Jews see e.g. Ref. 13, Chaps. 14 and 15.

20. See *Besaettelsens hvem hvad hvor*, Politikens Forlag, Copenhagen 1965.

21. Ref. 13, pp. 208, 211.

22. Ref. 13, p. 212.

23. Ref. 4, p. 218.

24. Ref. 13, p. 226.

25. Ref. 13, pp. 220, 290.

26. N. Bohr, address to the Norsk Ingeniörforening, 5 April 1940, MS of an unpublished abstract in NBA.

27. G. von Hevesy, *Adventures in radioisotope research*, Vol. 1, p. 27, Pergamon, New York 1962.

28. N. Bohr, letter to J. A. Wheeler, 27 May 1940, CW, Vol. 8, p. 233.

29. N. Bohr, letter to Y. Nishina, 14 September 1940, CW, Vol. 8, p. 233.

30. W. Weaver, letter to N. Bohr, 26 December 1940, NBA.

31. T. Lauritsen, memorandum in File 713D, Box 4, Folder 46, Rockefeller Archive Center, Tarrytown, N.Y.

32. N. Bohr, *Politiken*, 3 June 1941.

33. W. Heisenberg, *Der Teil und das Ganze*, p. 231 ff., Piper, Munich 1969.

34. W. Heisenberg, letter to N. Bohr, 14 September 1939, NBA.

35. Ref. 33, p. 235.

36. W. Heisenberg, *Naturw.* **33**, 325, 1946; in English (abridged): *Nature* **160**, 211, 1947.

37. W. Heisenberg, *Collected works*, Vol. AII, pp. 365–601, Springer, New York 1989; see also *ibid.*, Vol. B. p. 419.

38. Ref. 37, Vol. AII, pp. 378, 397.

39. Ref. 37, Vol. AII, p. 517.

40. A. Speer, *Inside the third Reich*, p. 227, Macmillan, New York 1970.

41. S. A. Goudsmit, *Alsos*, Schuman, New York 1947.

42. S. Rozental, letter to M. Gowing, 6 September 1984, quoted with permission.

43. A. Bohr, NBR, p. 191.

44. Ref. 33, pp. 247–8.

45. For example, R. Jungk, *Heller als tausend Sonnen*, Goverts Verlag, Stuttgart 1956; in English: *Brighter than a thousand suns*, Harcourt Brace, New York 1958.

45a. R. Jungk, preface to *Die Uranmaschine*, Siedler, Berlin 1990, the German translation of M. Walker, *National Socialism and the quest for nuclear power 1939–1949*, Cambridge University Press 1989.

46. Ref. 43, p. 193, footnote.

47. R. Fraser, letter to N. Bohr, 15 July 1947.

48. Ref. 33, p. 233.

49. *Der Spiegel*, 3 July 1967, p. 79.

50. See K. Scholder, *Die Mittwochsgessellschaft*, Severin and Seidler, Berlin 1982. Also Ref. 33, p. 258.

51. E. Heisenberg, *Das politische Leben eines unpolitischen*, Piper, Munich 1980.

52. As told by C. Møller to R. Jost in 1946, R. Jost, letter to A. Pais, 14 September 1989.

53. For example, Ref. 45, p. 110.

54. See e.g. N. F. Mott and R. Peierls, *Biogr. Mem. Fell. Roy. Soc.* **23**, 213, 1977, esp. p. 236.

55. H. Casimir, *Haphazard reality*, p. 210, Harper and Row, New York 1983. The account of the Bohr–Heisenberg meeting by C. F. von Weizsäcker, *Bewusztseinswandel*, p. 377, Carl Hanser Verlag, Munich 1988, strikes me as rather convoluted.

56. N. Bohr, Die Entstehung der Quantenmechanik, in *Werner Heisenberg und die Physik unserer Zeit*, Vieweg, Braunschweig, 1962.

57. N. Bohr, letter to H. Wergeland, 2 March 1943, NBA.

58. N. Bohr, letter to H. A. Kramers, 16 September 1943, NBA.

59. H. Høgsbro, in *Berlingske Tidende*, 8 August 1945.

60. Private communication by Dr C. F. Jacobsen.

61. S. Rozental, NBR, p. 145.

62. M. Gowing, *Britain and atomic energy, 1939–1945*, p. 107, Macmillan, New York 1964.

63. Ref. 62, p. 39.

64. R. G. Hewlett and O. E. Anderson, *The new world 1939–1946*, Pennsylvania State University Press 1962.

65. R. Rhodes, *The making of the atomic bomb*, Simon and Schuster, New York 1986.

66. D. Hawkins, *Project Y: The Los Alamos story*, Tomash, Los Angeles 1983.

67. McG. Bundy, *Danger and survival*, Random House, New York 1988.

68. M. J. Sherwin, *A world destroyed*, p. 273, Knopf, New York 1975.

69. Ref. 64, pp. 15–17.

70. Ref. 67, pp. 34–8.

71. Ref. 65, p. 635.

72. A. Vallentin, *The drama of Albert Einstein*, p. 278, Doubleday, New York 1954. See also SL, p. 454.

73. Ref. 64, p. 24.

74. F. D. Roosevelt to V. Bush, quoted in Ref. 68, p. 31.

75. Ref. 64, p. 41.
76. H. Stimson, *On active service in peace and war*, Chap. 23, Harper, New York 1947.
77. Ref. 67, p. 45.
78. O. R. Frisch, *What little I remember*, p. 126, Cambridge University Press 1979.
79. Repr. in Ref. 62, p. 389.
80. Ref. 78, p. 131. See also the obituary of Frisch by R. Peierls, *Biogr. Mem. Fell. Roy. Soc.* **27**, 283, 1981.
81. Ref. 62, p. 64.
82. Ref. 67, p. 49.
83. Repr. in Ref. 62, pp. 394–436.
84. Ref. 65, pp. 368, 377.
85. Ref. 64, pp. 45, 46.
86. Repr. in Ref. 62, p. 437.
87. Ref. 62, p. 145. For a different version see Ref. 64, p. 261.
88. Ref. 62, Chap. 9; Ref. 64, Chap. 8.
89. Text published by Her Majesty's Stationary Office, London 1954; repr. in Ref. 62, p. 439.
90. Quoted in Ref. 65, p. 426.
91. Ref. 64, p. 174.
92. Ref. 64, Chap. 5.
93. Ref. 64, pp. 212–16.
94. Ref. 64, pp. 230–5.
95. J. R. Oppenheimer, interview by T. Kuhn, 18 November 1963, transcript in American Institute of Physics, New York. See also IB, pp. 366–7.
96. N. Bohr, letter to J. R. Oppenheimer, 20 December 1937, NBA.
97. Letter to N. Bohr from the Department of Science and Industrial Research (DSIR), 25 October 1943.
98. Letter to N. Bohr from the DSIR, 9 November 1943.
99. N. Bohr, lecture at the Royal Society on 4 November 1943, brief preparatory notes written by A. Bohr in NBA.
100. A. Bohr, NBR, p. 191.
101. J. Rud Nielsen, *Physics Today*, October 1963, p. 22.
102. J. R. Oppenheimer, quoted in Ref. 64, p. 310.
103. R. P. Feynman, in *Reminiscences of Los Alamos, 1943–1945*, pp. 129–130, Eds. L. Badash et al., Reidel, Boston 1980.
104. J. R. Oppenheimer, third of the Pegram lectures given at Brookhaven National Laboratory, September 1963, revised excerpt published in *New York Review of Books*, 17 December 1964.
105. Ref. 64, p. 317.
105a. L. Fermi, *Atoms in the family*, pp. 224–5, University of Chicago Press, 1954.
100. Ref. 07, p. 114.
107. N. Bohr, letter to V. L. Komarov, 27 August 1938; V. L. Komarov, letter to N. Bohr, 15 September 1938.
108.. N. Bohr, letter to J. Stalin, 23 September 1938.
109. N. Bohr, letter to Halifax, 28 December 1943.

110. N. Bohr, letter to J. Anderson, 16 February 1944.
111. Approximately as told to Bohr by Sir Ronald Campbell, counsellor at the British Embassy in Washington.
112. J. Anderson, letter to N. Bohr, 30 March 1944.
113. C. Zinchenko, letter to N. Bohr, 11 March 1944.
114. P. Kapitza, letter to N. Bohr, 28 October 1943.
115. *Moscow News*, 8 October 1989.
116. N. Bohr, letter to P. Kapitza, 28 April 1944.
117. N. Bohr, letter to J. Anderson, 9 May 1944.
118. Quoted in Ref. 62, p. 354.
119. Ref. 64, p. 243.
120. Ref. 64, p. 251.
121. R. V. Jones, in the obituary of Churchill, *Biogr. Mem. Fell. Roy. Soc.* **12**, 35, 1966, esp. p. 88.
122. Ref. 62, p. 355.
123. N. Bohr, letter to W. Churchill, 22 May 1944.
124. J. Smuts, letter to W. Churchill, 15 June 1944.
125. N. Bohr, memorandum to Roosevelt, 3 July 1944.
126. See Ref. 100 for further details.
127. N. Bohr, letter to Roosevelt, 7 September 1944.
128. Ref. 67, p. 117.
129. Ref. 62, p. 358.
130. C. P. Snow, *Variety of men*, p. 120, Macmillan, London 1967.
131. Ref. 67, p. 120.
132. Ref. 62, pp. 350–2; also Ref. 131.
133. Ref. 67, p. 117.
134. Ref. 67, p. 119.
135. A. Einstein, letter to N. Bohr, 12 December 1944.
136. N. Bohr, *Science* **102**, 363, 1945.
137. *Politiken*, 27 August 1945.
138. N. Bohr, speech on the Danish radio, 31 December 1945, MS in NBA.

22

In which Bohr moves full steam into his later years

(a) Prolog

As the curtain rises for the final act, we see Bohr at age 60, still holding center stage, still in full vigor, still running up steps two at a time.

Bohr has now reached the zenith of his influence. He has become a public figure of the first rank, he and Margrethe often being called Denmark's second royal family. High dignitaries visit his home. From Denmark, the king and queen, cabinet ministers, and ambassadors come for dinner. On his 70th birthday (1955) the king and queen come to congratulate him, and the prime minister addresses the Danish people by radio to honor him.[1] Foreign notables visit Carlsberg, among them Queen Elizabeth II and Prince Philip of England, the queen of Siam, the crown prince (now the emperor) of Japan, Jawaharlal Nehru, prime minister of India, David Ben Gurion, prime minister of Israel, Adlai Stevenson. On 10 October 1950 Bohr meets Churchill for the last time, in Copenhagen, as the latter is in town to receive an honorary doctorate.

Along with all these consuming events the Bohrs still find time and take pleasure in receiving physicists, junior and senior, in their home.

Denmark's population looks up to him. In 1959, when the newspaper *Politiken* celebrated its 75th anniversary, its readers were asked to vote on which men and women had put the greatest stamp on developments in Denmark during that era. Among the thousands of answers Bohr topped the list with a sizable majority.

After the war Bohr continues earlier activities. Beginning in 1946 building is resumed of further extensions of his institute. New apparatus is installed.* Bohr continues to tap foundations, some old sources (17i), some new ones, among the latter the Ford Foundation,** which awards grants of $200000 (1956) and $300000 (1959) 'for study and consultation at the Institute

---

* A new five story building was added. A subterranean hall was constructed to house the renovated cyclotron.[2]

** Founded in 1936; separated from the Ford family's control in 1950, when its modern charter was enacted.[3]

by young and senior physicists outside Denmark.'[4] Once again (12d) this news catches the attention of the world press.[5]

On 1 April 1955 Bohr reaches the mandatory retirement age as university professor but continues as institute director. On 1 April 1956 his son Aage succeeds him in the professorship.[6]

For some of the post-war years Bohr continues to be active in research, but more and more he assumes the roles of elder statesman and senior philosopher. This is reflected in his published papers of the period, about 50 items, roughly one-third of his lifelong oeuvre. Only three of these are research articles. Bohr's main activities in his later years lie less in his writings, however, than in other ways of promoting science, as we shall see later in this chapter.

I turn next to a survey of Bohr's later publications. Most of these have already been discussed in earlier chapters. At this point a brief synopsis will therefore suffice, which is aimed less at describing their contents than at driving home the variety of topics covered, of audiences addressed, and of places of delivery. Section (c) deals with Bohr's efforts to convey to the world at large his views on political openness. Sections (d) and (e) describe his efforts at establishing international physics centers. Section (f) concerns Bohr's most important contributions to science in his late years. It is a two-part story. Part 1 tells how Bohr initiated a project that grew into Denmark's finest multipurpose research center. Part 2 is the tale of the fifth accelerator, or Bohr's last initiative. Section (g) contains a laundry list of his later travels. Section (h) deals with Bohr's last months.

As I reflected on Bohr's activities in his later years, the differences with Einstein struck me. Einstein spent the last twenty years of his life in Princeton, lecturing only quite rarely, traveling little, and going abroad only once, to Bermuda, in order to arrange for his immigration papers. As to Bohr – just wait and see.

(b) The later writings, 1945–1962

> Some things are so serious that one can only jest about them.
>
> NIELS BOHR

1. *Physics, research*. As has been noted before (20b), the discovery of fission had caused Bohr to return to a topic that had already engaged him during his first Manchester period in 1912: the stopping and scattering of electrically charged particles in matter. His war and post-war work on this subject were meant to enlarge considerably on his short papers[7] of 1940. The earliest draft of a detailed paper dates from November 1940.[8]

Bohr had much else on his mind during those years. A few weeks before his escape to England he wrote to Kramers: 'Due to many disturbances I still haven't finished the paper on penetration problems.'[9] (7b, 20b). When in September 1943 Rozental fled to Sweden he took along a copy of the paper as it stood then, but lost it in the commotion.[10] Another copy reached Bohr while in the US. From January 1946 on he was busy again with the penetration problems. In October 1946 his paper was sent in for printing.[11] Bohr lectured on his work in 1947.[12] As had happened so often before, he kept making changes in the page proofs, however. The final version,[13] dated 17 December 1948 has become a standard reference on penetration theory.

Bohr's final paper on stopping theory, written jointly with Lindhard, likewise took them a number of years to complete.[14] This work, on electron capture and loss by heavy ions traversing matter, was begun in the summer of 1949. The final version,[15] sent off in January 1954, is Bohr's last research publication.

The only other post-war physics article by Bohr is his joint paper[16] with Rosenfeld on QED, a sequel to their long article of 1933 (see (16d)).

2. *Physics, discussions of complementarity.* These include Bohr's finest writings on philosophical issues. The most important items are his paper[17] of 1948 on the definition of the concept of phenomenon and his account[18] (1949) of discussions with Einstein, both discussed in (19b). He also wrote several shorter articles on these same topics.[19]

3. *Complementarity outside physics*, discussed in (19d). Most of these papers[20] touch on issues in biology, the last one being posthumous.

Bohr on still other subjects. In a 1949 interview he discussed 'jest and seriousness in science'.[21] When asked: What is complementary to truth? He replied: Clarity – a response that tells more about him than many a lengthy essay. So does one of his favorite sayings on the same subject to be found at the head of this section. In 1953 Bohr wrote a brief note – not too interesting – on science and religion.[22] In an address in 1960 Bohr discussed language as a tool for communication.[23]

4. *Occasional addresses.*

October 1945. In a lecture to the Danish Engineering Society Bohr said[24] that plutonium can be produced at the rate of 1 kilogram per day, causing allegations that he was giving away atomic secrets. This led him to send a clarification to the press[25] stating that he did not know technical details about the production of active materials.

July 1946 Address on Newton's principles and atomic mechanics at the Newton tercentenary celebrations in London;[26] and in Cambridge on problems of elementary particle physics, at the first post-war international physics conference.[27]

September 1946. Address at[28] the Princeton University centennial celebrations, where Bohr received an honorary degree.

October 1946. Address in Philadelphia on atomic physics and international cooperation.[29]

October 1948. Address to the eighth Solvay conference in Brussels on causality and complementarity.[30]

February 1949. Lecture to the Danish medical society on physical science and the problem of life.[31]

April 1949. Radio address to Danish and Norwegian high school students on atoms and human understanding.[32]

October–November 1949. Gifford lectures in Edinburgh.[33]

February 1951. Radio address to the people of Denmark on the role of science in their country (20d).

March 1951. Address to the Danish Physical Society on the occasion of the centenary of Ørsted's death.[34]

October 1954. Address on the unity of knowledge delivered during the bicentennial of Columbia University[35] (where Bohr picked up another honorary degree). Also in that month: an address on atomic energy in industry, given in New York.[36]

March 1955. Address to the Danish industrial organization, again on the last mentioned topic.[37]

August 1955. At the personal invitation[38] of Dag Hammarskjöld, secretary general of the United Nations, Bohr addressed the first international conference on peaceful uses of atomic energy, held in Geneva. He spoke on complementarity in physics, biology, and psychology.[39]

Autumn 1955. Address in Lund at the Rydberg centennial conference.[40]

October 1955. Address to the Danish Academy on the occasion of his 70th birthday (20d).[41]

November 1957. Address on atoms and human knowledge[42] at a panel meeting of the American Academy of Arts and Sciences in Cambridge, Massachusetts; also Compton lectures at MIT (19a).

Spring 1958. Address to a symposium in Belgrade commemorating Rudjer Bošković.[43]

August 1960. Address to the international pharmacological conference in Copenhagen on the connection between the sciences.[44]

October 1960. Address to the congress of the *Fondation Européenne de la Culture* on the unity of human knowledge.[45]

April 1961. Address in Copenhagen on atomic science and the crisis of humanity,[46] on the occasion of his receiving an award.

October 1961. Address to the twelfth Solvay meeting in Brussels on 'The Solvay meetings and the development of quantum physics'.[47] It was the 50th anniversary of the first of these meetings. I was present and remember Bohr asking permission to give this talk while seated. He was tiring quickly by then.

Also in 1961 Bohr contributed an article 'On the genesis of quantum mechanics' to a *Festschrift* for Heisenberg's 70th birthday.

Reference to a few other addresses will be found later in this chapter.

5. *Writings in memoriam.* Bohr has written movingly on occasions of passing of friends and colleagues: in 1946 at the death of Ole Chievitz, friend ever since his youth[48] (Chapter 3), in 1949 to commemorate Martin Knudsen, teacher and colleague since his twenties[49] (6b), in 1960 in memory of his colleagues and friends H. M. Hansen[50] and Ebbe Rasmussen.[51]

In 1952 Kramers, Bohr's first collaborator and trusted friend through the years, died a painful death.[52] At the memorial meeting in Leiden, organized by the Netherlands Physical Society,[53] Bohr spoke of Kramers' Copenhagen days. 'I still remember his radiant youth so singularly combined with a maturity of mind ... the greatest achievement of Kramers in the Copenhagen years was his general dispersion theory,'[54] (13b).

In 1949 Bohr had saluted Einstein on his 70th birthday. 'Our entire generation owes him admiration and gratitude.'[55] After Einstein's death in 1955 he wrote: 'With the death of Albert Einstein, a life in the service of science and humanity which was as fruitful as any in the whole history of our culture has come to an end ... He gave us a world picture with a unity and harmony surpassing the boldest dreams of the past.'[56]

Bohr's memorial lecture on Rutherford, delivered in 1958, is the best source of insight into the relations between these two men.[57]

The unexpected death of Pauli in 1958, after a brief severe illness, must have been a blow to Bohr. No one understood both Bohr's physics and his philosophical views better than Pauli. Bohr's only interesting scientific correspondence in all the post-war years is in fact the exchange of letters between these two men. 'I will miss him most deeply,' Bohr wrote to Pauli's widow.[58] Niels and Aage flew to Zürich to attend the funeral. Afterward Mrs Pauli wrote to Niels: 'I was deeply touched by the tribute you accorded to Wolfgang's work and personality ... Your presence at the funeral put Wolfgang's life and death right.'[59] I do not know what Bohr said on that occasion. We do have the in memoriam that he wrote shortly afterward.[60]

The most grievous personal loss to Bohr in his later years was the death due to cancer of his brother Harald in 1951, at the age of 63, who was, after Niels' wife, his closest confidant. The only glimpse I can get of Bohr's feelings at that time is a letter in reply to condolences by Einstein: 'Your expressions of warm sympathy and your beautiful words at the death of my brother have deeply moved me. As you know, my brother and I were very close from early childhood on. At this moment of sad loss I am grateful, however, to know how much he was esteemed and loved in wide circles, and how many faithful friends he had made.'[61]

(c) Glasnost 1950: Bohr's open letters to the United Nations

On 29 April 1989 the *New York Times* carried an editorial that began as follows. 'The cold war of poisonous Soviet–American feelings, of domestic political hysteria, of events enlarged and distorted by East–West confrontation, of almost perpetual deadlock, is over.' At the time of writing it looks that way. Let us pray that it stays that way.

It is debatable whether the cold war began before or after the hot war ended in 1945. Events like Churchill's iron curtain speech in 1946, or the Soviet blockade of Berlin in 1948 certainly underscored the hostile atmosphere between the superpowers.

In those early years the Western camp considered the unique possession of atomic bombs as their primary weapon in the struggle against Communism. It would be a threat if not treason to imagine giving information about those weapons to the Russians. At that time most estimates about how long it would take them to produce such bombs on their own, unaided, were generally too high.

That was the atmosphere in which the atom entered the arena of public international affairs. In January 1946 the General Assembly of the United Nations adopted a resolution establishing the UN Atomic Energy Commission. (Its scientific and technical subcommittee was chaired by Kramers.) Bernard Baruch became the US representative on the Commission, a choice that was soon realized to be a disaster even by those who had proposed him.[62] I have been told that in 1946 Baruch once said to Bohr that he preferred an honorable war over a dishonorable peace.

On 14 June 1946 Baruch presented to the Commission a US proposal for international control of atomic energy. Subsequent discussions were not helped by the 1 July US weapons test at Bikini. (Some may remember the pun of that year: it doesn't Bikini difference atoll.) The Baruch proposal never got anywhere.* The international control issue had reached a deadlock. On 17 May 1948, the UN Atomic Energy Commission recommended suspension of its activities.

Bohr was, of course, fully aware of the political climate. Rather than being resigned to failure, he reached the decision to pursue once again his ideas of an open world, this time not in private consultations with world leaders (21d), however, but in public.

At one time – my best guess is the autumn of 1947 – the US ambassador to Denmark received a visit from John Jay McCloy, who had been the US assistant secretary of war from 1941 to 1945 and who was now president of the World Bank. The ambassador took McCloy to see Bohr. The two discussed world affairs, Bohr explaining his views on openness. A second meeting followed in New York, in March 1948,** during which McCloy suggested that Bohr talk to Secretary of State George Marshall, and asked him to prepare a brief memo for the Secretary, describing his ideas. Bohr did

* See Ref. 63 for a detailed history of these events.
** Bohr was spending the spring term of 1948 in Princeton.

so.[64] In May McCloy asked Bohr to write more explicit comments, which Bohr also did.[65] In that document Bohr noted the failure of UN efforts and the increasing distrust and suspicion between nations, then made his own proposal:

Under the circumstances it would appear that most careful consideration should be given to the consequences which might ensue from an offer, extended at a well-timed occasion, of immediate measures towards openness on a mutual basis. Such measures should in some suitable manner grant access to information, of any kind desired, about conditions and developments in the various countries and would thereby allow the partners to form proper judgement of the actual situation confronting them.

An initiative along such lines might seem beyond the scope of conventional diplomatic caution; yet it must be viewed against the background that, if the proposals should meet with consent, a radical improvement of world affairs would have been brought about, with entirely new opportunities for cooperation in confidence and for reaching agreement on effective measures to eliminate common dangers.

After having read Bohr's comments, Marshall met with him in private in McCloy's home in Washington. During their long and frank talk, Marshall entered on difficulties in preparing the American public and Congress for a policy of openness.[66] In a letter to Marshall following this meeting[67] Bohr reiterated his position 'to make a stand for free access on a mutual and world wide basis, and to make this a paramount issue.' He also raised questions regarding 'observers admitted to the various territories' (*verification!*), and the dangers of bacteriological and biochemical warfare.

I find this letter of particular interest because of Bohr's expressed hope that his suggestions might lead the US government to take an initiative which 'would serve the true interests of this country as well as of humanity at large . . . Your country possesses the strength required to take the lead in accepting the challenge with which civilization is confronted.' *

Bohr did not meet Marshall again but did have some discussions with State Department officials. It must have become clear to him that the US government was not willing to speak for his suggestions.

The next few years witnessed rapid developments in regard to atomic weapons. In August 1949 the Russians exploded their first test bomb. In January 1950 it was publicly announced that the US would proceed to determine the technical feasibility of a hydrogen bomb.

Meanwhile Bohr had decided to make a personal public appeal via the UN.

When in February 1950 Bohr arrived once again in Princeton, the first

* I am grateful to Aage Bohr for permitting me access to the documents on the McCloy–Marshall episode. For his own account see Ref. 68.

subject he wanted to discuss with me was a draft he had brought along of an Open Letter to the UN. Would I help him to work further on this manuscript? I would. I have vivid memories of many discussions that showed Bohr's deeply serious engagement concerning these matters.

A story told to me by Oppenheimer dates from those days.

At one point during this time Bohr called on Secretary of State Dean Acheson to discuss with him the content of his planned Letter. The meeting began at, say, two o'clock, Bohr doing the talking. At about two thirty Acheson spoke to Bohr about as follows. Professor Bohr, there are three things I must tell you at this time. First, whether I like it or not, I shall have to leave you at three for my next appointment. Secondly, I am deeply interested in your ideas. Thirdly, up till now I have not understood one word you have said. Whereupon, the story goes, Bohr got so enraged that he waxed eloquent for the remainder of the appointment.

In May Bohr returned to Copenhagen. Helped by his brother Harald and by Hans Henrik Koch, permanent undersecretary in the Foreign Office, the Letter was now nearing its final version. The plan was to have a copy handed to Trygve Lie, secretary general of the UN in New York, at the same time that Bohr would call a press conference in Carlsberg. Concerned about premature leakage to the press Bohr made the final preparations in a special room. On 9 June at 10 a.m. New York time Aage, who had been at Columbia University for some time, handed the Letter to Lie's secretary.* At 4 p.m. Danish time Bohr received the press. He refused to take questions afterward.**

The Open Letter,[71] Bohr's first public statement about the atomic age since his note to *The Times* of London[72] of August 1945 (21b), was written 'without consultation with the government of any country'. It contains the first published version of essential parts of Bohr's memoranda to Roosevelt of 3 July 1944 and 24 March 1945 (21e). Also included are parts of his May 1948 memorandum[65] to Marshall (in particular the lines I quoted above), about which Bohr commented:

The considerations in this memorandum may appear utopian, and the difficulties of surveying complications of non-conventional procedures may explain the hesitations of governments in demonstrating adherence to the course of full mutual openness. Nevertheless, such a course should be in the deepest interest of all nations, irrespective of differences in social and economic

---

* See Ref. 69 for more details leading up to this moment.

** Nevertheless a reporter from the communist Danish newspaper *Land og Folk* managed to ask Bohr what he thought of the Stockholm appeal, a current proposal to ban all atomic weapons, with which Bohr was not yet familiar at that moment. The next day the paper published a blistering attack on Bohr, who replied that he could not sign the appeal since it did not include demands for access to information and free exchange of ideas.[70]

organization, and the hopes and aspirations for which it was attempted to give expression in the memorandum are no doubt shared by people all over the world.

The key phrases in the Letter are these.

The situation calls for the most unprejudiced attitude towards all questions of international relations. Indeed, proper appreciation of the duties and responsibilities implied in world citizenship is in our time more necessary than ever before. On the one hand, the progress of science and technology has tied the fate of all nations inseparably together, on the other hand, it is on a most different cultural background that vigorous endeavours for national self-assertion and social development are being made in the various parts of our globe.

An open world where each nation can assert itself solely by the extent to which it can contribute to the common culture and is able to help others with experience and resources must be the goal to be put above everything else . . . The arguments presented suggest that every initiative from any side towards the removal of obstacles for free mutual information and intercourse would be of the greatest importance in breaking the present deadlock and encouraging others to take steps in the same direction.

'The Open Letter produced very little reaction in the public outside Denmark and the other Scandinavian countries.'[68] Trygve Lie, acknowledging receipt, wrote: 'I shall, of course, give it the most careful consideration,'[73] but 'no step was taken on the part of the UN towards any further promulgation of, or debate about the views contained in it',[68] one of the early indications of the shabbiness and futility of that world organization, especially of its leaders.

Right after his press conference Bohr delivered a copy of the Letter to the prime minister, another to the US ambassador. At his own expense he had thousands of copies printed. Some were sent to diplomats, politicians (one went to Churchill), physicists, friends.* Others went to foreign newspapers. Some press reactions were sympathetic. The *New York Herald Tribune*: 'The open world is an idea of such simplicity, such power and such potential effect that it is not lightly to be dismissed.'[75] The *Washington Post*: 'The letter . . . is not to be dismissed as impractical idealism.'[76] Others were neutral if not negative.[77]

Within weeks Bohr's initiative was overshadowed by dramatic developments.

On 24 June the Korean war broke out.

On 1 November the US exploded its first thermonuclear device in the Pacific.

Bohr was defeated by overwhelming historical forces.

And that is why Frankfurter and I chatted about how bittersweet a day in Bohr's life the 24th October 1957 had to be (1a).

---

* I was in Israel at that time and was supposed to brief President Weizmann, but my copy of the Letter reached me too late to do so.[74]

Bohr nevertheless persisted. From Aage's recollections:[68] 'My father continued throughout the years to work tirelessly for the understanding of the views he had put forward in the Open Letter. He often discussed with Danish and Scandinavian government circles what possibilities the existing situation might contain for promoting a development in the direction of greater openness and understanding.* He also had opportunities to discuss these problems with many of the leading statesmen of the time whom he met on his journeys, or who visited Denmark. In 1956, during the crisis caused by events in Hungary and Suez, my father made a new approach to the UN in an open letter[79] to [Secretary General] Hammarskjöld, pointing out how much an initiative within the UN for the furtherance of openness in the world could contribute to an easing of the prevalent divergences.' In a memorandum[80] Bohr noted that his second Open Letter does not contain new points of view and expressed the hope that it might be debated in the UN General Assembly – which did not happen. This Letter, too, was privately printed and distributed. Comments in the press were quite brief and factual.

Even then Bohr did not give up. 'However difficult the situation might be, my father always saw new hopes and possibilities, and his optimism, which was founded on a deep conviction, made a strong impression on practically everybody he talked to. In his attitude to political problems, as in all other matters, any differentiation between "opponents" and "supporters" was foreign to him, and he had a particular gift for entering into the spirit of the various points of view, and with this background working for a cause which he was convinced was in the deepest interest of all.'[68]

In Bohr's lifetime his noble cause never received the public attention it deserved.

On 11 March 1985 Gorbachev came to power and the era of glasnost began. In October 1985 the centenary of Bohr's birth was celebrated with several conferences in Copenhagen. In the course of one of these, devoted to the challenge of nuclear armaments, a three way TV hookup was arranged, linking speakers in Copenhagen, Moscow, and Cambridge, Massachusetts. The proceedings of the conference are recorded in a book of essays 'dedicated to Niels Bohr and his appeal for an open world'.[81] A follow-up meeting took place in 1989.[82]

Of all the centennial tributes paid to Bohr those he himself would have appreciated most are, I think, the public discussions during international symposia of his pleas for openness.

---

* In July 1951 Bohr issued a plea for better international understanding, on behalf of about a hundred scientists gathered in Copenhagen.[78]

(d) CERN

Shortly after World War II it became evident to some of the leading European physicists that European science and technology would only be able to keep in step with developments elsewhere and that the brain drain could only be slowed down by pooling European manpower and material resources.

These considerations eventually led to the establishment of CERN, the European Organization for Nuclear Research, to this day the finest example of what Europe can achieve if its states join forces. CERN's official birth date is 15 February 1952. On that day an agreement was signed constituting a 'Council of Representatives of European States for Planning an International Laboratory and Organizing Other Forms of Cooperation in Nuclear Research'. The task of the Council was to draw up a Convention, choose a site, settle on equipment, etc. The Convention entered into force on 29 September 1954. CERN's governing body comprises one eminent scientist and one senior science administrator from each member state. At the time of writing fourteen countries have joined.

CERN is a high-energy laboratory, an institution devoted to experimental and theoretical studies of the smallest constituents of matter and of the forces that act between them. High-energy physics, also called particle physics, is the next chapter in science beyond nuclear physics. Its main experimental tools are new generations of the kinds of accelerators already in use in the 1930s (17b). These new machines aim at reaching higher, much higher, energies than were accessible in that earlier period. They are not only bigger and better but also much costlier than their ancestors.

The high price of accelerators was an important practical reason why Europe could only participate in particle physics by cost-sharing between states. No individual nation could afford any longer to pay for this kind of equipment by itself, except perhaps Britain. A similar situation had developed in the United States, where the price of the big machines had grown beyond the means of individual universities. As a result, laboratories have been established in the US that are run by university consortia and are financed with Federal funds, the oldest one being Brookhaven National Laboratory, authorized in January 1947.*

The problems facing the CERN planners were new and awesome. How were they to strike a balance between physics done at an international center and at home? Where, in which country, should the laboratory be located? Should it be an extension of some existing facility or should it be a

---

* See Ref. 83 for an account of these historical developments and brief descriptions of postwar accelerators.

completely new institution? What types of equipment should be selected? How should the budget be divided between member states?

This section is devoted to an account of Bohr's role in these decisions. Nearly all my information is taken from the admirable volume[84] on the history of CERN through 1954, where many additional details will be found.

Bohr did not participate in early planning meetings organized by the distinguished French physicist Pierre Auger. When asked later why neither Bohr nor Heisenberg had been invited to those sessions Auger replied that both were far too important to trouble them with preliminary proceedings.[85]

The first occasion I know of when Bohr took part in preparatory discussions was in September 1950, when a number of those involved got together during a physics conference at Oxford. At that time Bohr apparently suggested to center the future laboratory around a big instrument with energy no less than 6 GeV* (higher than anything available as yet). That proposal was unanimously[86] adopted in a meeting held the following December (not attended by Bohr).

In August 1951 Kramers came to Copenhagen with a quite different plan. He suggested to Bohr to try and place the European laboratory in Denmark, using Bohr's institute as a nucleus.[87] Their discussions gradually evolved into a proposal that ran counter to everything that the planners had discussed and agreed upon previously. Briefly stated, Kramers and Bohr, concerned about the cost of a large accelerator and the drain on manpower of member states, proposed to proceed much more cautiously, for example by adopting a pilot project for a machine in the 0.5 GeV region.

Auger was not amused. In private discussions he remarked that Bohr, in spite of his vast experience, was a little too old to undertake a big international project; and that the Copenhagen institute was an old one, now past its prime.[88] Another physicist commented that they were prepared to have Bohr as president of a democracy but not as absolute monarch.[89]

Thus began a tense period. Young Turks were pitted against the establishment, traditional science against the new 'big science'. Sweden and Britain tended to side with Kramers and Bohr; Belgium, France, and Italy were opposed. Complex negotiations ensued, described in detail in the CERN history.[90] I state only the main events.

In October 1951 the plan for a high-energy machine was reaffirmed.[91] It was further decided to establish four study groups, including one for theoretical aspects of the project.

A few days before the signing of the February 1952 agreement Bohr pledged his Copenhagen institute in support of CERN.[92]

In May 1952 it was decided to place the theory group at Copenhagen. Bohr

* 1 GeV = 1 gigaelectronvolt = 1 billion eV.

became its director, Rozental its administrative director. In September 1954 Møller took over from Bohr.

In June 1952 it was decided to build two machines, one with energy about 0.5 GeV (the synchrocyclotron or SC), the other at 10–15 GeV (the proton synchrotron or PS); later developments pushed the planned PS energy to 25 GeV.

In October 1952 Geneva was chosen as the CERN site. Construction started in May 1954.

In 1957 the SC came on the air at 0.6 GeV. On 1 October of that year the CERN theory group in Copenhagen was closed down and a new group set up in Geneva.

In 1959 the PS started operations. At 28 GeV it held for a short time the world record as the highest-energy machine.

Weisskopf, one of the later directors general of CERN has written: 'There were other personalities who started and conceived the idea of CERN. The enthusiasm and the ideas of the other people would not have been enough, however, if a man of his stature had not supported it.'[93] As the preceding has shown, that does not fully convey Bohr's role. The evolution of the planning for CERN had undeniably caused him moments of disappointment. Nonetheless he became a strong supporter. It was Bohr who in February 1960 formally inaugurated the PS.

(e) Nordita

Early in 1953, after the CERN theory group had been installed in Copenhagen, and after it had also become certain that Copenhagen would not be the definitive site for CERN, the first steps were taken to secure the future of Bohr's institute by other means.

On 17 January 1953 physicist members of the CERN council from Denmark, Norway, and Sweden met in Göteborg, Sweden, to discuss the possibility of forming a joint Scandinavian theoretical physics institute in Copenhagen. Bohr, who participated in this meeting, insisted that such a plan should not be considered as a threat to CERN.[94]

That gathering was the first step toward the founding of the *Nordisk Institut for Theoretisk Atomfysik*, Nordita for short.*

Joint Scandinavian scientific undertakings have a long history. The first of a series of joint meetings of Scandinavian natural scientists was held in 1839, as it happened also in Göteborg. Bohr had hanging in his office the reproduction of a painting (6a) showing Ørsted addressing the second meeting, in 1840. These gatherings continued periodically for a century.

---

* See Ref. 95 for the early history of Nordita.

In 1945, after the interruptions caused by World War II, the Swedish government made it known that it was prepared to contribute sizable funding, 100 million Swedish Kronor, toward establishing and maintaining a Scandinavian institute for theoretical and applied nuclear physics, to be directed by Bohr. The obvious intent of this proposal was to start preparing for industrial applications of nuclear power. Such a project was not timely, however, largely because of the secrecy still surrounding all aspects of atomic energy.

The physicists who had met in Göteborg did not have applied physics in mind. Their idea was rather to start a new regional institute for pure theoretical research. Several factors favored their plan. The Copenhagen institute had had long experience with theorists from other countries. The CERN theory group had begun its activities in Copenhagen in the autumn of 1952; therefore the planners need not hurry, since it clearly made no sense to start a new institute before the CERN group had moved to Geneva. In addition there was growing governmental interest in establishing increased cooperation between the Nordic states. Efforts to proceed together with economic and defense planning had not borne fruit. Nevertheless the governments had decided to establish a joint *Nordisk Raad* (Nordic council of ministers), which was convened for the first time in February 1953(!), in Copenhagen. This council provided the perfect instrument for negotiations between scientists and politicians.

The physicists continued their preparatory discussions. At their meeting in Stockholm in November 1955 the Danes, Norwegians, and Swedes were joined by Finnish colleagues. In the next meeting in Copenhagen in January 1956 Iceland also participated. On 21 February 1957 the Nordic council, meeting in Helsinki, approved the formation of the five nation Nordita, 'a Nordic Institute for Nuclear Research in Copenhagen, and to appoint a Board of Governors of the Institute, the Board being also the body responsible for Nordic cooperation in nuclear physical science.' It is the oldest of some thirty research institutes currently maintained by the council.

Nordita started its activities on 1 September 1957, one month before the CERN theory group left Copenhagen for Geneva. Bohr was the first chairman of its governing board. Møller and Rozental continued in the positions they had held in the CERN group.

Nordita, still going strong, has been a success.

Its beginnings were marked by customary birth pangs. A core of permanent scientific staff had to be appointed. Administrative apparatus had to be put in place. Arrangements had to be worked out for the selection and financing of the about fifteen stipends awarded annually to young Scandinavians. Tax problems had to be resolved. And so on.

Two important changes date from the 1960s.

The initial focus on nuclear physics has been widened to include, as time went by, condensed matter physics, particle physics, and astrophysics. This is entirely in Bohr's spirit: he had in fact suggested that the institution's name should contain the word atomic rather than nuclear, so as to leave room for new options.

In 1964 the mathematicians left the Mathematical Institute, part of the Blegdamsvej complex, for new quarters. The building was taken over by Nordita. Research at Nordita is performed in close collaboration with the Niels Bohr Institute. These days Nordita's activities look like this.*

Awards of stipends to Scandinavians remains central. Research fellows are assisted in making short visits to their home base in the course of their tenure. The permanent staff consists of six professors, not all of Scandinavian birth. Nordita invites foreign scientists for longer stays as well as for short visits. It helps arrange visits by these guests to other Scandinavian centers. Conferences, colloquia, and other meetings are organized, all with worldwide participation. In 1987 about 70 papers were published under Nordita by-line. In 1987 each member state contributed about $2 million to the overall budget.

Bohr was almost 72 when Nordita started its activities. He was understandably quite pleased with this addition to theoretical physics in Copenhagen. The time was past, however, for him to participate much in its research activities. The widening of Nordita's research program and its move to new quarters occurred only after his death.

Nordita is an important part of the legacy Bohr left to the world of physics in general and of Denmark in particular.

(f) Risø

1. *The National Laboratory.* Roskilde, Denmark's largest city in the late middle ages, lies at the southern end of a fjord, twenty miles west of Copenhagen. Four miles from Roskilde a peninsula juts into the fjord. It is called Risø. Two laboratory complexes are situated there, the results of Bohr's last major initiatives.

In December 1953, President Eisenhower gave an address to the UN in which he proposed to end the atomic arms race and to institute international cooperation in the peaceful uses of atomic energy. He implied that countries not possessing uranium might obtain supplies of that material.

---

* According to Nordita's annual report for 1987.

The Danes were interested. In February 1954 a committee was formed, chaired by Bohr, to explore the issue. This was a semiprivate move, initiated by the Danish Academy of Technical Sciences and financially supported by the Thrige foundation. After some deliberations the committee decided that work on industrial application of atomic energy ought to be taken up in Denmark.*

In the autumn of 1954 Bohr called on Denmark's prime minister to lay this suggestion before him. As a result of further discussions the government constituted in March 1955 a Preparatory Atomic Energy Commission, again chaired by Bohr.

It was obvious that important components for atomic reactors and power stations had to be bought abroad. Bohr, having excellent personal relations with experts in the US and the UK, was the best imaginable counsel on how to proceed. In April 1955 he again called on the prime minister to request permission for making cooperation agreements with those countries. After consultations in May with the Parliamentary Finance Committee Bohr received the go-ahead.[97] In June 1955 an agreement was signed between the US and the Danish governments, stipulating that the US would supply information on the construction and operation of reactors. A similar agreement was signed with the UK.

Times were ripe by now to give more formal structure to the committee's activities. Accordingly, by Act No. 312 of 21 December 1955, the Danish Parliament approved that 'an Atomic Energy Commission shall be appointed for the promotion of peaceful use of atomic energy for the benefit of the community,' to be answerable to the minister of finance. 'The government asked Bohr to take over the chairmanship, and he readily accepted, even though he was already carrying a heavier burden of work than most people and had reached the age [70] when many of us begin to reduce our commitments.'[98] The first steps toward organizing the Commission were guided by an official of the Ministry of Finance, working in a small room next to Bohr's study on Blegdamsvej.[99] The Commission held its first meeting in February 1956. 'Bohr enjoyed his work in the Commission. He directed its work with a firm hand and common sense.'[98]

The first steps toward realization of the plans had meanwhile been taken in August 1955. In that month tender offers were received from a number of American firms; and the search began for an appropriate site. 'To this search Niels Bohr devoted himself with the same unflagging zeal as to all other tasks he took upon himself. He studied the map of Sealand to find a suitable island, peninsula, or headland, and drove about discretely and unobtrusively to inspect the localities . . . Bohr was happy when one day he came to the Ministry to tell me about his discovery of Risø.'[97]

---

* See Ref. 96 for the early history of atomic energy in Denmark.

A group of Commission members took a trip to inspect the area. First they had a look at Bolund, a tiny island in the Roskilde fjord, almost linked to the mainland at low tide. 'We went down to the beach. From there it seemed evident that it did not suit the purpose. Bohr was not content with guesses, however. We should have a look. Off with shoes and socks, up with pants, out into the water, Bohr ahead, over sharp stones, then up the slope to Bolund's top – our guess was correct, we could in good conscience drop Bolund and concentrate on other possibilities – in the meantime we had learned something about Bohr's working style.'[100]

The choice fell on nearby Risø peninsula, where the Commission eventually acquired three farms and some undeveloped area, over 600 acres in all. Construction of the laboratories began in the autumn of 1956.

Meanwhile contracts had been signed for the acquisition of three reactors. The first one (code named DR1), designed by an American firm, was to have a core of 5 kilograms of enriched uranium containing 1 kilogram of 235, provided by the US government. It was intended to be an instrument for education and scientific and technical experiments, aims upon which Bohr had insisted from the outset. The second one (DR2; closed down in 1975), also American, was to generate power up to 5000 kW. The total contract price for both reactors was about half a million dollars (ah, the good old days) to which the US government would eventually contribute $350000. A third reactor (DR3) was contracted for with a British firm. Danish industry was to participate in the various constructions to the greatest possible extent.*

By May–June 1957 the machine shop, a meteorology and an agriculture station, as well as laboratories for physics, chemistry, reactor development, and electronics were in use. On 15 August DR1 reached criticality.[101] Other equipment was still under construction when on 6 June 1958 the Risø research center was formally inaugurated in the presence of the king and queen and of Danish and foreign officials. 'Niels Bohr extended a warm welcome to all in the beautiful lecture theatre.'[97] In his short address Bohr noted that in Risø 'the past and the future meet harmoniously'.[102] By 1960 all reactors were in operation.

On 26 August 1960 a small ceremony took place in Risø during which a bust of Bohr was unveiled. The director expressed to Bohr the gratitude of the Danish industry.[103] During his last years Bohr much enjoyed showing colleagues and other prominent personalities around the research center. He was also much pleased by the international contacts created as the result of Risø's activities.[103]

2. *A new part of the Niels Bohr Institute.* I turn to Bohr's final initiative. As mentioned earlier (17j), in 1939 plans had taken shape for building a Van de

---

* I have not found it necessary to give all the reactor parameters. For these see Ref. 96.

Graaff accelerator, the characteristics of which were outlined in (17b). Work on that machine had proceeded during the war; it came in use in 1946 at an energy of 2 MeV. After a fire had destroyed some of its parts it was decided not to patch it up but rather to build a new one. That one came on the air in 1955.[104] Both machines produced some very good physics.*

The second Van de Graaff was the last of the four accelerators to find a place on Blegdamsvej and one of two still in use today. The high-tension machine, the first to be completed (17j), had become obsolete and was dismantled. The first Van de Graaff still stands today, a silent relic of the past.

The second Van de Graaff has been taken over by the Department of the Environment and is currently used for measuring what elements are present as pollutants in air samples taken from various places in Denmark. The cyclotron is still in operation, producing isotopes for medical and industrial purposes. When a batch is ready it is placed in a container shielded with lead which then is picked up either by a porter who comes with a dolly and transports it to the *Rigshospital* (University Hospital) next door, or by a cab for transportation to users farther away.

Next came the fifth accelerator.

As experimental nuclear physics moved into new areas of exploration in the 1950s, it became desirable for the Danish physicists to acquire a tandem Van de Graaff, a tool whose properties have been sketched in (17b). This machine offers several advantages over the earlier ones. It operates at higher energies; and it can accelerate heavy ions (the standard type only worked for hydrogen and helium ions).

The first question that arose was whether this new gadget should be built at Bohr's institute, as had been done successfully with the two earlier versions. After careful consideration it was decided that this time it would be better to buy the accelerator and to confine in-house construction to detection apparatus.

Next question: Where should such a new machine be placed? Existing space was inadequate. Plans for extension of the institute into the park behind it met with objections from the community.

The problem was solved when the Atomic Energy Commission offered Bohr space near the Risø center. The advantages were obvious. At relatively modest cost one could extend existing facilities for heat, water, sewage, roads, and share others such as a cafeteria and a library. Bohr accepted of course. In 1958 he went after funds for acquisition and construction. As usual his requests were granted. In May 1959 Bohr signed

---

* Including studies of level densities in light nuclei, Coulomb excitation, and isobaric analog states.[105,106]

a contract with the American High Voltage Engineering Company for delivery of an accelerator producing protons at 10–12 MeV. Building started in April 1960. Operations began by the end of 1961, less than a year before Bohr's death.*

The new laboratory is now called the Niels Bohr Institute, like the one on Blegdamsvej. The two institutions have a common overall administration, though each has of course its local management. Both are part of Copenhagen University, unlike the Risø center.

3. *Risø in* 1989. The two institutions at Risø have developed into vibrant parts of the Bohr legacy. Risø National Laboratory has gradually moved from its initial focus on atomic energy to a multipurpose laboratory. The Energy Policy Measures Act of 28 April 1976 abolished the Danish Atomic Energy Commission and redefined Risø's purpose to cover research, development, and consultancy concerning nuclear energy and energy in general. In 1986 this act was amended; Risø's goals are now defined to be scientific and technological research and development, mainly energy. It is authorized to contract for outside industrial projects. It currently has a staff of about 800 people of whom 200 have had higher education.

Officially Risø is not an educational institution, it resides under the Ministry of Energy. Nevertheless the center is, of course eminently suited for educating Ph.D. students; more than 30 of these are presently attached.

Risø now houses nine divisions, for physics (including a plasma and solid state section), energy technology, health physics, information technology, chemistry, agriculture, metallurgy, meteorology and wind energy, and systems analysis. It has rendered advisory services on wind energy projects in developing countries; it participates in national and European programs for fusion, reactor safety, ceramic cells for high-temperature systems, pollution problems, radioecology, high-temperature superconductors, and others. It also considers it part of its task to educate the general public, especially schoolchildren. Guided tours through the laboratories are conducted every Saturday.

The Niels Bohr Institute at Risø ranks among the best of its kind. It has become more and more an international center. On a recent visit I was shown a γ-ray detector constructed and operated jointly by Denmark, Finland, Germany, Holland, Italy, Japan, Norway, and Sweden. Collaborations with institutions abroad are part of its program, for instance with the Saturne laboratory in Paris.

Nowhere have I found Niels Bohr's spirit more alive than on that little peninsula in the Roskildefjord.

---

* See Ref. 106 for the history and a description of the tandem laboratory.

(g) The later travels

The purpose of the following brief account of Bohr's travels is to emphasize once again the breadth and intensity of Bohr's post-war activities.

Visits to the United States. These were numerous, Bohr nearly always making his headquarters at the Institute for Advanced Study in Princeton, where he had a standing membership invitation.*

Visit to Iceland, 2–10 August 1951. Bohr gave a lecture at Háskóli Islands (the University of Iceland**) on atoms and human understanding. He met with the president and the prime minister.

First visit to Israel, 2–12 November 1953, to attend a memorial to Chaim Weizmann, the first president of Israel, who had recently died. Bohr had known him since his early Manchester days (9b). Bohr lectured on physics and philosophy, on atoms, molecules and atomic nuclei, and on observational problems in quantum mechanics.[107]

First visit to Yugoslavia, 10–12 July 1956. Bohr spoke at the meeting commemorating the 100th anniversary of Nikola Tesla, inventor of electrical equipment. He was received by President Tito.[108]

Visit to Greenland, 9–23 July 1957, together with other members of the Danish Atomic Energy Commission, for the purpose of examining the availability of uranium ore, potentially important for the Risø projects. (No adequate deposits were located.) Bohr was elected honorary citizen of the town of Narssaq.

Second visit to Yugoslavia, spring 1958, to attend the Bošković symposium (22b).

Second visit to Israel, 18–25 May 1958. Bohr was the guest of honor at the dedication of the Weizmann Institute for Nuclear Science in Rehovoth.[107] On the way he stopped in Athens (16–17 May) to receive an honorary degree.

Visit to India, 3–27 January 1960, to attend the Indian Science Congress in Bombay, where Bohr gave two lectures, on atoms and human knowledge, and on principles of quantum physics. He also visited Madras, Calcutta, Delhi – where he was the personal guest of Nehru – and Agra, as well as the famous caves at Elephanta, Elora, and Ajanta.

Visit to Geneva, February 1960, to inaugurate the PS at CERN (22d).

Second visit to the USSR, (see also (18b)), 3–19 May 1961. In the early 1950s Bohr had not been popular with the Soviet leadership, as witness a *New York Times* headline: 'Einstein and Bohr scored as bourgeois reactionaries.'[109] All that disappeared after Stalin's death. On this tour Bohr visited institutions in Moscow and Dubna, and spent three days in Georgia.

Visit to Brussels, to attend his last Solvay meeting (22b).

---

* After the war Bohr was in residence in Princeton during February–June 1948, February–May 1950, September–December 1954, and December 1957–February 1958.
** Founded in 1911 by merging three existing colleges.

(h) The final half year

From 4 to 7 June 1962 Bohr paid his final visit to the US in order to collect the last of his more than thirty honorary doctorates, this one from The Rockefeller Institute (now University) in New York.

Later that month Bohr and his wife drove by car to Germany. On the 21st he gave a talk on biology in Cologne (19d), his last public address. From there they moved on to attend one of the annual gatherings of Nobel laureates traditionally held in the Bavarian city of Lindau on the Bodensee (Lake Constance). While there Bohr became unwell. A minor cerebral hemorrhage was diagnosed. He was transported to Frankfurt and from there flown to Copenhagen, where he was immediately brought to the *Rigshospital*. After his release he and his wife went to Tisvilde for rest and recuperation.

On 1 August the Bohrs celebrated their golden wedding anniversary at Carlsberg, surrounded by their children and grandchildren.

During August Bohr began again to do some work. In particular he busied himself with revisions of his Cologne lecture. Also from that month dates a letter about his 'great hope which inspired me that the atomic energy project . . . might provide a unique opportunity for the establishment of a harmonious cooperation between nations'.[110]

On 30 September Niels and Margrethe left for Italy. They spent a happy vacation in Amalfi, during which Bohr celebrated his 77th birthday.[111] They returned to Copenhagen on 27 October.

On the evening of 16 November Bohr presided for the last time over a meeting of the Danish Academy.

On 17 November Bohr gave the last of a series of interviews on the history of quantum physics.[112] Listening to the tapes of these talks one can hear deep fatigue in his voice.

After lunch on Sunday 18 November, Bohr went upstairs for his by then customary nap. Shortly afterward his wife heard him call 'Margrethe'. She rushed upstairs where she found him unconscious next to his bed. A doctor was called, but nothing more could be done. According to the death certificate the diagnosis was heart failure.[113]

Shortly thereafter Bohr's remains were cremated at Søndermarken's crematorium. During a private ceremony his ashes were interred in the family grave in Assistens Kirkegaard in Copenhagen, where they now rest next to those he loved most: his wife (who died 22 years later), his parents, his brother Harald, and his son Christian.

References

1. *Berlingske Tidende*, 8 October 1955.
2. S. Rozental, *Erindringer om Niels Bohr*, Chap. 7, Gyldendal, Copenhagen 1985.

3. R. Magat, *The Ford Foundation at work*, Plenum Press, New York 1979.
4. Letters by Ford Foundation officials to N. Bohr, 14 May 1956 and 17 December 1959 (signatures on my copy unreadable), Ford Foundation Archives, New York.
5. *New York Times*, 22 December 1959.
6. *Yearbook of Copenhagen University 1953–1958*, pp. 202–4.
7. N. Bohr, *Phys. Rev.* **58**, 654, 839, 1940, CW, Vol. 8, pp. 319, 323.
8. Repr. in CW, Vol. 8, p. 369.
9. N. Bohr, letter to H. A. Kramers, 16 September 1943, CW, Vol. 8, p. 246.
10. Ref. 2, p. 47.
11. S. Rozental, letter to N. Bohr, 11 October 1946, CW, Vol. 8, p. 250.
12. A. Bohr, letter to A. Pais, 4 March 1947, CW, Vol. 8, p. 250; lecture notes in NBA.
13. N. Bohr, *Danske Vid. Selsk. Mat.-Fys. Medd.* **18**, No. 8, 1948, CW, Vol. 8, p. 425.
14. For the vicissitudes of this and the previous paper see CW, Vol. 8, pp. 240–61.
15. N. Bohr and J. Lindhard, *Danske Vid. Selsk. Mat.-Fys. Medd.* **28**, No. 7, 1954, CW, Vol. 8, p. 595.
16. N. Bohr and L. Rosenfeld, *Phys. Rev.* **78**, 794, 1950.
17. N. Bohr, *Dialectica* **2**, 312, 1948.
18. N. Bohr, in *Albert Einstein: philosopher-scientist*, p. 199, Ed. P. Schilpp, Tudor, New York 1949; in German, in *Albert Einstein als Philosoph und Naturforscher*, p. 115, Kohlhammer, Stuttgart 1955.
19. N. Bohr, *Matem. Tidsskr.* B, 163, 1946; contribution to *Philosophy in midcentury*, p. 308, Ed. R. Klibansky, La Nuova Italia, Florence 1958; *Naturw. Rundschau* **7**, 252, 1960.
20. N. Bohr, in *Proc. 8th Solvay Conf.* 1948, p. 9, Coudenberg, Brussels 1950; *Acta Medica Scand.* **142** (Suppl.), 266, 1952; *Daedalus* **87**, 164, 1958; Address to international congress on pharmaceutical science, 29 August 1960, MS in NBA; in contributions to the symposium on models in biology, repr. in *Light and Life*, Eds. W. D. McElroy and B. Hass, Johns Hopkins University Press, 1961; *Naturw.* **50**, 725, 1963, in English, *ICSU Rev.* **5**, 194, 1963.
21. *Politiken*, 17 April 1949.
22. N. Bohr, in *Studia Orientalia Ioanni Pedersen*, p. 385, Munksgaard, Copenhagen 1953.
23. N. Bohr, address to the second international Germanist congress, 22 August 1960, in *Spätzeiten und Spätzeitlichkeit*, p. 9, Francke, Bern 1962.
24. *Politiken*, 3 October 1945.
25. *Politiken*, 4 October 1945.
26. N. Bohr, address at the Royal Society meeting in London, July 1946, MS in NBA; see also *Nature* **158**, 90, 1946.
27. N. Bohr, in *Proc. Int. Conf. Fundamental Particles and Low Temperatures*, p. 1, Taylor and Francis, London 1947.
28. N. Bohr, Observation problems in atomic physics, transcript of dictograph record in NBA.
29. N. Bohr, *Proc. Am. Philos. Soc.* **91**, 137, 1946.

30. N. Bohr, in *Les particules élementaires*, Ed. R. Stoops, Coudenberg, Brussels 1950; repr. in *Science* **111**, 51, 1950.
31. Repr. in *The philosophical writings of Niels Bohr*, Vol. 2, p. 94, Ox Bow Press, Woodbridge Conn. 1987.
32. Printed in *Berlingske Tidende*, 2 April 1949; also in *Vor Viden*, No. 33, p. 123, 1950.
33. MS in NBA.
34. N. Bohr, *Fysisk Tidsskr.* **49**, 6, 1951.
35. *Writings* (Ref. 31), Vol. 2, p. 67.
36. Minutes of a conference held from 13 to 15 October 1954 in New York.
37. N. Bohr, *Tidsskr. Industri*, No. 7/8, p. 168, 1955.
38. N. Bohr, letter to J. R. Oppenheimer, 23 May 1955, NBA.
39. N. Bohr, *Ingeniören* **64**, 810, 1955.
40. N. Bohr, *Kungl. Fysiogr. Sällsk. Handlinger*, **65**, 15, 1955.
41. Repr. in *Writings* (Ref. 31), Vol. 2, p. 83.
42. N. Bohr, *Daedalus* **87**, 164, 1958.
43. N. Bohr, in *Extrait des actes du symposium Boškovič*, p. 27, Belgrade 1954.
44. Repr. in *Writings* (Ref. 31), Vol. 3, p. 17.
45. Repr. in *Writings* (Ref. 31), Vol. 3, p. 8; in Danish in *Berlingske Tidende*, 22 October 1960.
46. *Politiken*, 20 April 1961.
47. Repr. in *Writings* (Ref. 31), Vol. 3, p. 79.
48. N. Bohr, *Ord och Bild* **55**, 49, 1946.
49. N. Bohr, *Oversigt Dan. Vid. Selsk. 1949–50*, p. 7.
50. N. Bohr, *Fysisk Tidsskr.* **54**, 97, 1956.
51. N. Bohr, *Fysisk Tidsskr.* **58**, 1, 1960.
52. W. J. de Haas, letter to N. Bohr, 25 April 1952, NBA.
53. C. J. Bakker, letter to N. Bohr, 12 June 1952, NBA.
54. N. Bohr, *Ned. Tydsschr. Natuurk.* **18**, 161, 1952; also *Politiken*, 27 April 1952.
55. N. Bohr, in *Politiken*, 15 March 1949.
56. N. Bohr, *Sci. Am.* **192**, June 1955, p. 31.
57. N. Bohr, *Proc. Phys. Soc. London* **78**, 1083, 1961.
58. N. Bohr, letter to Franca Pauli, 16 December 1958, NBA.
59. F. Pauli, letter to N. Bohr, 15 January 1959.
60. N. Bohr, in *Theoretical physics in the twentieth century*, p. 1, Eds. M. Fierz and V. Weisskopf, Interscience, New York 1960.
61. N. Bohr, letter to A. Einstein, 14 February 1951, NBA.
62. McG. Bundy, *Danger and survival*, p. 161 ff., Random House, New York 1988.
63. R. G. Hewlett and O. E. Anderson, *A history of the U.S. Atomic Energy Commission*, Vol. 1, Chap. 16, Pennsylvania State University Press 1962.
64. N. Bohr, letter to J. J. McCloy, 22 March 1948.
65. N. Bohr, MS entitled 'Comments', dated 17 May 1948.
66. N. Bohr, draft of letter (not sent) to Sir John Anderson, 23 July 1948.
67. N. Bohr, letter to G. Marshall, 10 June 1948.
68. A. Bohr, NBR, p. 191.
69. Ref. 2, p. 70 ff.

70. N. Bohr, statement dated 14 June 1950 published via the office of Ritzau's press services.
71. N. Bohr, Open Letter to the United Nations, dated 9 June 1950, printed as pamphlet by Schultz, Copenhagen.
72. N. Bohr in *The Times*, London, 11 August 1945.
73. T. Lie, letter to N. Bohr, 16 June 1950.
74. A. Pais, letter to N. Bohr, 4 July 1950, NBA.
75. *New York Herald Tribune*, 14 June 1950.
76. *Washington Post*, 15 June 1950.
77. See e.g. *New York Times*, 14 June 1950; *The Times* of London, 21 June 1950.
78. *New York Times*, 10 July 1951.
79. N. Bohr, open letter addressed to D. Hammarskjöld, dated 9 November 1956.
80. N. Bohr, untitled and unpublished memorandum, dated 11 November 1956.
81. *The challenge of nuclear armaments*, Eds. A. Boserup, L. Christensen, and O. Natan, Rhodos, Copenhagen 1986.
82. *The challenge of an open world*, Eds. N. Barfoed *et al.*, Munksgaard, Copenhagen 1989.
83. IB, Chap. 19, section (a), and Chap. 21, section (c).
84. A. Hermann, J. Krige, U. Mersits, and D. Pestre, *History of CERN*, Vol. 1, North-Holland, New York 1987; referred to below as C.
85. C, p. 106.
86. C, p. 367.
87, C, p. 148.
88. C, p. 154.
89. C, p. 171.
90. For what follows see esp. C, Chap. 7.
91. C, p. 161.
92. *New York Times*, 12 February 1952.
93. V. Weisskopf, NBR, p. 261.
94. C, p. 286, Ref. 31.
95. *Nordita 1957–1982*, pamphlet issued by Nordita; T. Gustafson, Nordita prepr. 86/24, 1982; Ref. 2, pp. 117–21.
96. *Report on the activities of the Danish Atomic Energy Commission up to 31 March 1957*, published by the DAEC, January 1958.
97. V. Kampmann, NBR, p. 281.
98. H. H. Koch, NBR, p. 310.
99. S. Rozental, NBR, p. 64.
100. H. H. Koch, quoted in N. Blaedel, *Harmony and Unity*, pp. 250–1, Springer, New York 1988.
101. H. H. Koch, *Nationalökon. Tidsskr.* **96**, 117, 1958.
102. N. Bohr, *Elektroteknikeren 1958*, No. 13, p. 238.
103. T. Bjerge, *Fysisk Tidsskr.* **60**, 173, 1962.
104. For the history and design of these two machines see K. J. Broström, *Fysisk Tidsskr.* **53**, 225, 1955.
105. See e.g. T. Huus and Č. Zupančič, *Danske Vid. Selsk. Mat.-Fys. Medd.* **28**, No. 1, 1953.

106. S. Holm, *Fysisk Tidsskr.* **60**, 120, 1962.

107. N. Zeldes, letter to H. Levi, 14 January 1983, NBA.

108. *Berlingske Aftenavis*, 17 July 1956.

109. *New York Times*, 17 January 1953.

110. N. Bohr, letter to Sir Henry Dale, 15 August 1962, NBA.

111. N. and M. Bohr, letter to G. von Hevesy, 19 October 1962, NBA.

112. N. Bohr, interview by T. S. Kuhn, A. Petersen, and E. Rüdinger, 31 October, 1, 7, 14, 17 November 1962, NBA.

113. Begravelsesbog, City Hall, Copenhagen.

23

Epilog

Physicists and other friends, young and old, sent expressions of sorrow and sympathy to Margrethe Bohr and her family.* So did dignitaries from various parts of the world.

President Kennedy wrote to Mrs Bohr: 'I am deeply saddened by Professor Bohr's death. American scientists, indeed all American citizens who knew doctor Bohr's name and his great contributions, have respected and venerated him for more than two generations ... We are forever indebted to him for the scientific inspiration he brought along on his many visits to the United States, and especially for his great contribution to the atomic center at Los Alamos. Please accept my condolences and deep sympathy.'[1] Other messages included those from the prime minister of Israel, the king of Sweden, and the chancellor of West Germany.[2]

Editorials in memory of Bohr appeared in the world press.

The *New York Times*: 'With the passing of Niels Bohr the world has lost not only one of the great scientists of this century but also one of the intellectual giants of all time.'[3] Felix Frankfurter, in a letter to the same paper: 'However great a scientist he was, he was even a rarer phenomenon as a noble character.'[4] The *Christian Science Monitor:* 'For physicists throughout the world, Niels Bohr, the gentle genius of Denmark, has long embodied the heroic image of a scientist.'[5] The *Washington Post Times Herald*: 'Niels Bohr was one of the seminal thinkers of the present age ... He was a humanist no less than a scientist.'[6] *Time Magazine*: 'He was a gentleman who helped create the world's most deadly weapon; a humble man who collected as many honors as almost any man in his time.'[7] Sir Henry Dale, president of the Royal Society during the war years, in *The Times* of London: 'I believe that the memorial which he would have wished for most himself would have been a renewed and really determined effort, even now, to follow where he tried to give a lead, to get back to a policy which might have been tried before the bombs were dropped.'[8]

A number of memorial events took place.**

---

* Many other condolences were addressed to the Danish Academy (20d).
** I have already mentioned the memorial meeting of the Danish Academy (20d).

All members of the *Folketing* stood as, on 20 November, their president expressed 'the sorrow over the loss of Denmark's great son.'[9] It is believed to be the first time in the centuries-long history of the Danish parliament that a non-member was thus memorialized.[2]

At CERN the flags of all member nations flew at half-mast.

Bohr was eulogized at the United Nations in New York.[10] At a UNESCO meeting in Paris a minute of silence was observed.[2]

It is an Israeli custom to plant one or more trees in honor of a person, living or dead, who has helped promote in whatever way the cause of the state. On 27 October 1967 a ceremony was held at Kibbutz Palmachim near Rehovoth, during which a ten thousand tree forest, to be known as the Niels Bohr Memorial Forest, was dedicated. Mrs Bohr expressed her deep gratitude for the honor.[11]

A tribute which I have found particularly touching was a recollection published in the Danish press by a Danish diplomat.[12] One day in the 1950s Bohr came to tell him that he had read in the paper of Prime Minister H. C. Hansen's need for a recreational journey to Italy after having undergone a major operation. 'A Danish politician could not afford such a trip, Bohr said, and therefore asked his host to take 5000 Kroner to Hansen and to let him, Bohr, know if that was not enough. He also asked for a promise that nobody should be told of their meeting. When asked if Hansen himself could be told, Bohr replied, "Not a word to anyone." Now that donor and recipient are both gone and I feel released of my promise, I may lay at Bohr's grave this remembrance as an additional testimony to the man's greatness – a greatness that matched his goodness.'

A conference had been planned in Copenhagen for 1963 to celebrate the 50th anniversary of Bohr's first papers on the quantum theory of atomic structure (8f). After Bohr's death it was decided to hold this meeting anyway, but now as a memorial.* It was held from 8 to 15 July 1963. Many earlier and later Copenhagen co-workers had come from all over the world. Only few talks dealt with the past, the others were devoted to current developments.** A number of the old guard got together to prepare a present to Mrs Bohr, a silver tray with our autographs.

During that conference week I called on Mrs Bohr, who at that time was still living in Carlsberg. I felt uneasy as I went on my way. Margrethe and Niels had been so close. Would she now feel lost, downcast? It turned out to be quite otherwise. She was in very good spirits and exuded even more energy than I had been used to noting in earlier years. (I was of course not

* On 21 November 1963 both Denmark and Greenland issued a pair of stamps commemorating 50 years of atomic theory. They depict a handsome portrait of Bohr.
** For example, Heisenberg, Pais, and Wick discussed the status of particle physics.

surprised when others told me that on other occasions she would miss Niels very much.)

Not long after these events I visited my old friend the psychoanalyst Theodor Reik in New York. I told him of my visit and expressed puzzlement about Mrs Bohr's demeanor. Reik smiled. If one partner in a good marriage dies, he said, the other will feel a sense of fulfillment because she or he has brought a vital task to good conclusion. If, on the other hand, the marriage had been bad, then the survivor is ridden with guilt and a sense of failure . . .

In March 1980 Margrethe's 90th birthday was celebrated with a big dinner attended by more than fifty guests, family, scientists, artists, politicians. In reply to my own letter of felicitation, Margrethe wrote how much she had enjoyed that evening. 'The grandchildren were singing and performing a splendid long song.'[13] Jørgen Kalckar, one of the dinner guests, recently told me that dessert was not served until toward midnight, after which Margrethe gave an impromptu speech. She was still going strong when Kalckar left several hours later.

Afterward: 'I am now beginning to get over all the different kinds of festivities and am back into daily life.'[13] She lived another four years.

A few weeks before the end she had a stroke which paralysed her right side and the speech center. During her last days she slept nearly all the time. She died peacefully just before Christmas 1984. Her remains rest close to her beloved Niels.

Bohr's brief speech[14] in memory of Rutherford, his second father, included these words.

His untiring enthusiasm and unerring zeal led him on from discovery to discovery and among these the great landmarks of his work, which will forever bear his name, appear as naturally connected as the links in a chain.

Those of us who had the good fortune to come in contact with him will always treasure the memory of his noble and generous character. In his life all honours imaginable for a man of science came to him, but yet he remained quite simple in all his ways. When I first had the privilege of working under his personal inspiration he was already a physicist of the greatest renown, but nonetheless he was then, and always remained, open to listen to what a young man had on his mind. This, together with the kind interest he took in the welfare of his pupils, was indeed the reason for the spirit of affection he created around him wherever he worked . . . The thought of him will always be to us an invaluable source of encouragement and fortitude.

I know of no better way of concluding this book than applying these words to Niels Bohr himself.

Snip, snap, snude,
Saa er historieen ude.

References

1. Repr. in *Berlingske Tidende*, 21 November 1962.
2. *Politiken*, 21 November 1962.
3. *New York Times*, 20 November 1962.
4. *New York Tmes*, 27 November 1962.
5. *Christian Science Monitor*, 20 November 1962.
6. *Washington Post Times Herald*, 22 November 1962.
7. *Time Magazine*, 30 November 1962.
8. *The Times*, London, 26 November 1962.
9. Parliament *Fortryk* of 21 November 1962.
10. *New York Times*, 2 December 1962.
11. N. Zeldes, letter to H. Levi, 14 January 1983, NBA.
12. Sigvald Kristensen, letter in *Aktuelt*, 22 November 1962.
13. M. Bohr, letter to A. Pais, 10 April 1980.
14. N. Bohr, *Nature* **140**, 752, 1937.

Appendix

A synopsis of this book in the form of a chronology

A number and letter in parentheses refer to the chapter and section in which the subject is discussed. A date refers to time of receipt by a journal, unless indicated otherwise. B stands for Niels Bohr.

1690   Christiaan Huyghens suggests that light consists of waves propagating through an ethereal medium (4c).

1704   Isaac Newton suggests that light consists of extremely small particles (4b).

1740   (c.) Birth of Christian Baar, B's great great grandfather, in the duchy of Mecklenburg, now part of Germany (d. 1800), (2).

1776   Christian becomes burgher of Helsingør (Elsinore). Birth of his son Peter Georg, registered under the surname Bohr, B's great grandfather (d. 1846), (2).

1813   Birth of Henrik Georg Christian Bohr, B's grandfather (d. 1880), (2).

1855   Birth of Christian Harald Lauritz Peter Emil Bohr, B's father (2).

1856   Birth of Joseph John Thomson (d. 1940).

1860   Birth of Ellen Adler, B's mother (2).

1860s   Beginnings of quantitative spectral analysis (8d).

1868   Birth of Arnold Sommerfeld (d. 1951).

1871   Birth of Ernest Rutherford.

1879   Birth of Albert Einstein.

1881   Marriage of B's parents (2).

1883   9 March. Birth of Jenny Bohr, B's elder sister (2).

1885   1 August. Birth of Georg von Hevesy (d. 1966).

1885   7 October. Birth of Niels Henrik David Bohr (B) at Ved Stranden 14, a Copenhagen mansion (2).
Balmer publishes his formula for the frequencies of the hydrogen atom's spectral lines (8d).

1886   Christian Bohr is appointed lektor (associate professor) in physiology at the University of Copenhagen. He and his family move into an apartment at the *Kirurgisk Akademi* (Academy of Surgery), where B will live until after he receives his Dr. Phil. degree (3).

1887   22 April. Birth of Harald August Bohr, B's younger brother (3). Birth of Erwin Schrödinger (d. 1961).

1890   Christian Bohr is promoted to professor (3). 7 March. Birth of Margrethe Nørlund.

1891   1 October. B starts school at *Gammelholms Latin og Realskole* (3). 6 October. B, his sister, and his brother are all baptized in *Garnisonskirken*, a Lutheran church (3).

1895   Röntgen discovers X-rays.

1896   First observations of radioactive radiations, by Henri Becquerel.

1897   J. J. Thomson discovers the electron (7a).

1900   Max Planck's discovery of his law of blackbody radiation marks the beginning of the quantum theory (5g). Birth of Wolfgang Pauli.

1901   Birth of Werner Heisenberg (d. 1976).

1902   Birth of Paul Dirac (d. 1984).

1903   B graduates from the Gammelholm school and enters Copenhagen University (3; 6b).

1905   Einstein introduces the light-quantum (later called the photon) (5h) and discovers the special theory of relativity (4g).

1905–6 Christian Bohr is rector of Copenhagen University (2).

1907   23 February. The *Kongelige Danske Videnskabernes Selskab* (KDVS) (Royal Danish Academy of Sciences and Letters) announces that B has won a gold medal for a prize essay on the determination of the surface tension of liquids from the surface vibrations of liquid jets (6b). Christian Bohr is proposed for the Nobel Prize in physiology or medicine (also in 1908) (2).

1909   First meeting of B and Margrethe Nørlund, his future wife. They are engaged in 1910 (6e). 2 December. B receives his masters degree (6d).

1910   Harald Bohr receives his Dr. Phil. in mathematics (6d).

1911   3 February. Death of B's father (6e). 7 March. Rutherford presents his discovery of the atomic nucleus (7b). 13 May. B receives his Dr. Phil. on a thesis dealing with the electron theory of metals (6d). September. B leaves for England to do postdoctoral research with J. J. Thomson (7a). 8 December. B and Rutherford arrange for B's transfer to work with him in Manchester (7b).

1912   March. B arrives in Manchester. First meeting of B and Georg von
          Hevesy. Research on the stopping of α-particles in solids (7b).
          March or April. B applies for a vacant professorship in physics in
          Copenhagen. The application is denied (8a).
          16 April. B resigns as member of the Lutheran Church (8b).
          24 July. B returns to Denmark (7b).
          1 August. B and Margrethe Nørlund are married in the town of Slagelse
          (8b).
          September. B becomes assistant to Martin Knudsen and also *privatdo-
          cent*. His office is in the *Polytekniske Læreanstalt* (Institute of Tech-
          nology) (8a).

1913   January. Van den Broek proposes that the place of an element in the
          periodic table is determined by the electric charge of the nucleus (10b).
          February. B hears for the first time of Balmer's formula (8e).
          5 April. B completes his paper on the quantum theory of the hydrogen
          atom. It appears in July (8f).
          August. B gives the first proof that β–radioactivity is a nuclear process
          (8f).
          12 September. B's new theory is presented for the first time to an
          international audience, in Birmingham (8g).
          20 November. Announcement of the splitting of spectral lines when
          atomic hydrogen is exposed to a static electric field (Stark effect) (10b).
          20 December. In a lecture before the Danish Physical Society, B presents
          the germs of the correspondence principle (8f).
          December–April 1914. Moseley's experiments bring definitive order in
          the periodic table of elements (10b).

1914   13 March. B petitions the Danish government to create a professorship of
          theoretical physics for him (9b).
          April. The Franck–Hertz experiment confirms B's idea of quantum jumps
          (10b).
          1 August. World War I breaks out.
          October. B returns to Manchester, assuming a position of lecturer
          (associate professor) (9b).

1916   January. Sommerfeld's theory of the fine structure of the spectral lines in
          hydrogen (10b).
          March. Epstein and Schwarzschild independently give the theory of the
          Stark effect, a great success for the Bohr theory (10b).
          5 May. B receives a professorial appointment in Copenhagen (9b).
          July. Sommerfeld introduces the magnetic quantum number (10b).
          Early summer. B and his wife return to Denmark (9b).
          Autumn. Kramers, B's first collaborator, starts work in Copenhagen. He
          will stay until 1926 (9c).
          November 25. Birth of Christian, B's first son.

1916–17   Einstein introduces probabilities in quantum dynamics (10c).

1916–22   Vain efforts to understand the atomic spectrum of helium (10d).

1917   April 18. B petitions the physics faculty to work for establishing an institute for theoretical physics (9c).
        April 27. B is elected to the KDVS (9c).

1918   April 7. Birth of Hans, B's second son.
        April. B formulates the correspondence principle in more detail (10c). He and Rubinowicz independently introduce the first selection rules in quantum theory (10c).

1919   January 2. Betty Schultz starts work as B's secretary, a post she will keep throughout B's life (9c).
        Rutherford observes the first artificial transmutations of elements and finds the first indications that nuclear forces are not purely electromagnetic (15c).

1920   March. Sommerfeld introduces a fourth quantum number (j) (10d).
        April. On a visit to Berlin B meets Planck and Einstein for the first time (11b).
        June. Hevesy arrives in Copenhagen for a stay that will last until 1926 (17e).
        23 June. Birth of Erik, B's third son (d. 1990).
        August. First visit by Einstein to Bohr in Copenhagen (11b).
        September. First visit by Rutherford to Copenhagen (9c).

1920–2 B develops a theoretical foundation for the periodic table of elements (10e).

1921   3 March. The Institute for Theoretical Physics in Copenhagen is officially opened (9c).
        Summer. B is overworked and needs to take a rest (9c).
        December. First visit by Ehrenfest to Copenhagen (18a).

1922   June. B gives a series of lectures in Göttingen, the 'Bohr Festspiele' (9a), where he meets Heisenberg (12e) and Pauli (10d) for the first time.
        19 June. Birth of Aage Niels, B's fourth son.
        10 December. B receives the Nobel Prize, 'for his investigations of the structure of atoms and of the radiation emanating from them'.

1923   January. From Copenhagen Coster and Hevesy announce the discovery of the element hafnium (10e).
        July. Second visit by Einstein to Bohr in Copenhagen (11b).
        10 September. De Broglie associates waves with electrons (11e).
        September–December. B's first trip to the US and his first personal contacts with the Rockefeller philanthropic institutions (12c).
        6–15 November. B's Silliman lectures at Yale bring the quantum theory of the atom for the first time to the attention of a wider audience (12c).

1924   February. B, Kramers, and Slater propose that in atomic processes energy is only conserved statistically; experimental refutation in April, May, 1925 (11d).
        7 March. Birth of Ernest, B's fifth son.
        Easter. Heisenberg comes to Copenhagen for a first brief visit (12e).
        July. First papers on quantum statistics, by Bose and by Einstein (13a).

First application of isotopic tracers to the life sciences, by Hevesy in Copenhagen (17h).

Summer. B is overworked and needs to take a complete rest (12e).

September–April 1925. Heisenberg works at the Copenhagen institute (12e, 13c).

B is permanently relieved of obligations to teach students (12e).

B buys *Lynghuset*, a country house in Tisvilde (12a).

Beginning of construction of two additional buildings at B's institute; completed in summer of 1926 (12e).

1925   January. Pauli enunciates the exclusion principle (10e).

25 July. Heisenberg's first paper on quantum mechanics (13d).

16 November. First comprehensive treatment of matrix mechanics, by Born, Heisenberg, and Jordan (13d).

20 November. Uhlenbeck and Goudsmit announce the first theory of electron spin (11f).

1926   17 January. Pauli derives the Balmer formula from matrix mechanics (13d).

26 January. Schrödinger's first paper on wave mechanics (13f).

February. Fermi's first paper on 'Fermi–Dirac statistics' (13a).

May–June 1927. Heisenberg's second long stay in Copenhagen. In July 1926 he resolves the mystery of the helium spectrum (14a).

25 June. Born introduces for the first time the quantum mechanical probability concept (13g).

August. Dirac gives the quantum mechanical foundations of quantum statistics and of Planck's radiation law (16b).

October. In Copenhagen Schrödinger discusses the foundations of quantum mechanics with B and Heisenberg (14b).

December. Dirac's paper on the transformation theory of quantum mechanics, written in Copenhagen (14a).

Together with friends B buys 'Chita', a sailboat (18a).

1926–32. The application of quantum mechanics to atomic nuclei poses serious paradoxes (15d).

1927   February. Dirac's first paper on quantum electrodynamics, written in Copenhagen (14a).

23 March. Heisenberg's paper on the uncertainty principle, written in Copenhagen (14d).

16 September. B's first statement of the complementarity concept, at the Volta meeting in Como (14e).

24–29 October. Fifth Solvay congress in Brussels. Beginning of the B–Einstein dialog on the foundations of quantum mechanics (14f).

1928   January. Dirac discovers the relativistic wave equation of the electron (16c).

12 March. Birth of Harald, B's sixth son (d. c. 1938) (11a).

Autumn. B shows that it is impossible to detect the magnetic moment of the electron by observation of its motion in a magnetic field (16c).

October. In Copenhagen Klein and Nishina apply the Dirac equation to Compton scattering (16c).

December. In Copenhagen Klein diagnoses an apparent grave inconsistency of the Dirac equation ('Klein paradox') (16c).

1929   April. First of a series of international physics conferences at B's institute in Copenhagen (1c).

B applies complementarity to psychology (19d).

1930   8 May. In his Faraday lecture B expresses doubts on the applicability of quantum mechanics to nuclear processes and suggests that energy may not be conserved in β decay (16e). He also mentions a new kind of complementarity in classical statistical mechanics (19c).

20 June. B receives the Planck medal.

October. Sixth Solvay conference. Einstein's 'clock-in-the-box' experiment. B's refutation (19b).

30 November. Death of B's mother (18a).

1931   March. The Landau–Peierls paper on limitations of quantum electrodynamics (QED) (16b).

April. First report on a functioning cyclotron, in Berkeley (17b).

May. Dirac postulates the positron (16c). In Copenhagen Gamow completes the first textbook on theoretical nuclear physics (15a).

September. Van de Graaff's electrostatic generator surpasses 1 MeV (17b).

December. First experimental evidence for the positron (16c).

1932   February. Discovery of the neutron (15d).

June. First nuclear process produced by an accelerator (17b).

August. B's lecture 'Light and Life', his first detailed attempt to apply complementarity to biology (19d).

B and his family move into the *Æresbolig* (Residence of Honor) (15e).

Warren Weaver, the newly appointed director of the natural science division of the Rockefeller foundation, focuses its direction toward biology (17c).

1933   7 April. The *Beamtengesetz* authorizes German universities to fire staff on grounds of politics and/or race (17d). B becomes board member of the Danish committee for support of refugee intellectuals. He obtains funds enabling junior refugee physicists to stay temporarily at his institute (17d).

April. Date of publication of the Bohr–Rosenfeld paper on QED (16d).

May–August. B's second visit to the US (18b).

5 May. Death of B's sister Jenny (18a).

25 September. Death of Paul Ehrenfest (18a).

1934   January. Discovery of induced radioactivity (17f).

8 February. Opening of the Mathematics Institute, under the directorship of B's brother Harald, situated next to B's institute (1c).

May. B's first trip to the Soviet Union. He lectures in Moscow, Leningrad, and Charkov (18b).

2 July. Christian, B's oldest son, drowns in a sailing accident (18a).
Two senior refugees join B's institute: James Franck (arr. April, dep. 1935), and Hevesy (arr. October, dep. 1943).

1935   B begins a series of grant applications for building accelerators at his institute (17i).
At B's institute Hevesy, together with Levi, develops the neutron activation analysis method, and starts a major program of isotopic tracers in biology (17h).
Publication of the Einstein–Podolsky–Rosen paper and of B's reply (19b).
B is elected president of the Danish cancer society (17i).
7 October. On his 50th birthday B receives a gift enabling him to order 600 mg of radium (17h).
B is in poor health for some months (17j).
Beginning of extension of B's institute to create space for accelerators; completed in 1938 (17j).

1936   B's theory of the compound atomic nucleus (15f).

1937   January–June. B makes a trip around the world and lectures in the US, Japan, China, and the Soviet Union (18b).
19 October. Death of Rutherford (18a).

1938   5 April. On the 25th anniversary of B's completion of his paper on the hydrogen atom (8f) the accelerator section of the B institute is formally inaugurated (17j).
Summer. The high-tension accelerator begins operations (17j).
November. The cyclotron begins operations (17j).
B gives a new definition of the concept 'phenomenon' (19b).
B on complementarity and human cultures (19d).

1939   6 January. Publication of Hahn and Strassmann's discovery that irradiation of uranium with neutrons yields barium (20a).
16 January. Frisch and Meitner interpret this result as uranium fission. B arrives in the US for a stay that will last till May (20a).
26 January. B's and Fermi's reports on fission at a physics meeting in Washington, DC, mark the beginning of widespread activities in fission physics (20a).
7 February. B proposes that uranium fission by slow neutrons is due to the presence of the rare isotope 235. Experimental confrmation follows only a year later. Bohr–Wheeler theory of fission (20a).
31 March. B is elected president of the KDVS, a position he will hold until his death (20d).
1 September. World War II breaks out (21b).

1940   January. B donates his Nobel medal to Finnish relief (21b).
9 April. German military forces occupy Denmark (21c).
The Frisch–Peierls report on feasibility of atomic weapons (21d).

1941   October. Heisenberg visits Denmark (21c).
9 October. After a briefing by Vannevar Bush, President Roosevelt decides to go ahead with the atomic weapons project (21d).

1943 February. B receives a letter from Chadwick inviting him to England. He declines (21c).
29 September. B and his wife flee Denmark (21c).
30 September–5 October. B in Stockholm (21c).
6 October. B arrives in London. His son Aage follows him a week later (21d).
9 October. The *New York Times* reports B's presence in London (21d).
28 October. Kapitza writes to B inviting him to Moscow (21e).
28 November. B and Aage leave for the US (21d).
8–28 December. B in Washington, DC. Meetings with General Groves, Ambassadors Kaufmann and Halifax, and Einstein. Active beginnings of B's concern with an open world (21d, e).
28 December. B leaves for first visit to Los Alamos (21d).

1944 February. B meets with Justice Frankfurter (21e).
March. Frankfurter informs B that President Roosevelt is interested in B's ideas for an open world (21e).
16 May. In London B is received by Prime Minister Churchill (21e).
3 July. B memorandum to Roosevelt (21e).
26 August. B is received by Roosevelt (21e).
18 September. In an *aide-mémoire* Churchill and Roosevelt reject B's proposals (21e).
December. Einstein writes to B proposing internationalization of military forces (21e).

1945 24 March. Second B memorandum intended for Roosevelt (21e).
12 April. Death of Roosevelt (21e).
4 May. German forces in Denmark capitulate (21b).
6 August. Bombing of Hiroshima (21e).
11 August. *The Times* of London publishes an article 'Science and civilization' by B, his first public appeal for an open world (21e).
25 August. B returns to Denmark (21e).

1947 7 October. The king of Denmark confers on B the Order of the Elephant, the highest Danish order (1c, 9c, 20d).

1948 Spring. B meets with US Secretary of State George Marshall (22c).

1950 9 June. B's open letter to the United Nations (22c).

1951 22 January. Death of B's brother Harald (22b).
August. B visits Iceland.

1952 24 April. Death of Kramers (22b).
Autumn. The theory division of CERN starts work in Copenhagen. B is its first director (22d).

1953 November. B's first visit to Israel (22g).

1955 1 April. B retires as university professor (22a).
18 April. Death of Einstein (22b).

1956 9 November. B's second letter to the UN (22c).

1957 July. B visits Greenland (22g).

1 September. Nordita starts operations in Copenhagen. B is the first director of its board (22e).

1 October. The CERN theory group at Copenhagen is dissolved (22d).

24 October. In Washington B receives the first Atoms for Peace award (1a).

1958   6 June. B formally opens the Risø research center, of which he had been the prime mover (22f).

15 December. Death of Pauli (22b).

1960   January. B visits India (22g).

1961   May. B visits the USSR (22g).

Opening of a second branch of Bohr's institute, at Risø (22f).

1962   4–7 June. B's last visit to the US (22h).

21 June. B's last public address, in Cologne (22h).

Late June. B suffers a minor cerebral hemorrhage (22h).

1 August. B celebrates his golden wedding anniversary (22h).

18 November. B dies of heart failure. Shortly afterward his remains are cremated. His ashes are interred in the family grave in Copenhagen (22h).

1963   8–15 July. B memorial conference in Copenhagen (23).

1965   The Institute for Theoretical Physics in Copenhagen is renamed the Niels Bohr Institute (9c).

1984   21 December. Death of Margrethe Bohr (23).

Index of Names

Note: An asterisk (*) after a name indicates that it receives fuller treatment in the Index of Subjects

Aaserud, Finn (1948–) 377
Acheson, Dean Goodenham (1892–1971) 516
Adler, Baruch Isak (1789–1843) 36
Adler, Bertel David (1851–1926) 38
Adler, David Baruch (1826–1878) 32, 36, 37, 38, 42, 47
Adler, Ellen, see Bohr (-Adler), Ellen
Adler, Hanna (1859–1947) 4, 37, 38, 44, 164, 412
Adler, Isaac David (1760–1812) 36
Adler (-Raphael), Jenny (1830–1902) 32, 36, 37, 38, 39, 47, 335
Alexander III (Tsar of Russia 1881–1894) (1845–1894) 42
Alexandra (Queen of England 1901–1910) (1844–1925) 42
Ampère, André Marie (1775–1836) 63, 64, 69, 95, 151
Anaxagoras (500 BC(?)–428 BC(?)) 104
Andersen, Hans Christian (1805–1875) 25, 39, 97, 111, 334
Andersen, Mogens (1916–) 412
Anderson, Carl David (1905–1991) 356, 358, 414
Anderson, Herbert Lawrence (1914–1988) 455
Anderson, Sir John (1882–1958) 491, 494, 495, 496, 498, 499, 500, 501, 502, 503
Ångström, Anders Jonas (1814–1874) 141, 143
Appleton, Edward (1892–1965) 486
Aquinas, Thomas (1225(?)–1274) 93
Aristotle (384–322 BC) 52, 74, 93, 94, 104
Arrhenius, Svante (1859–1927) 215
Aston, Frances William (1877–1945) 211
Auger, Pierre (?) 520
Aurivillius, Christopher (1853–1928) 214

Baar, Christian Friderich (1771–?) 33
Baar (later Bohr), Christian (c. 1740–1800) 32, 33, 538
Bacon, Roger (1214–1294) 94
Balmer, Johann Jakob (1825–1898) 142, 143, 215, 538, 540

Barkla, Charles Glover (1887–1944) 267
Bartholin, Rasmus (1625–1698) 54, 60, 94, 415
Baruch, Bernard Mannes (1870–1965) 514
Beck, Guido (1903–1988) 383
Becquerel, Antoine Henri (1852–1908) 52, 122, 326, 539
Ben Gurion, David (1886–1973) 509
Bendix, Dagmar (1868–1954) 249
Bendix, Victor (1851–1926) 249
Bergner, Elisabeth (1897–1986) 225
Berlème, Aage (1886–1967) 169, 258
Besso, Michele Angelo (1873–1955) 317
Bethe, Hans Albrecht (1906–) 161, 341
Bieler, Etienne Samuel (1895–1929) 330
Bismarck, Otto von (1815–1898) 42
Bjerge, Torkild (1902–1974) 399, 400, 458
Bjerrum, Niels Janniksen (1879–1958) 146, 411, 415
Bjørnson, Bjørnsterne (1832–1910) 25
Blixen, Karen, see Dinesen, Isak
Bloch, Felix (1905–1983) 383, 436
Bøggild, Jørgen Kruse (1903–1982) 459, 489
Bohr, Aage Niels (1922–) 4, 9, 27, 249, 343, 402, 444, 477, 483, 487, 491, 496, 497, 504, 510, 513, 515, 516, 518, 541, 545
Bohr, Christian Alfred (1916–1934) 26, 168, 226, 249, 335, 411–12, 416, 429, 540, 544
Bohr, Christian Fredrik Gottfried (1773–1832) 33, 34
Bohr, Christian Harald Lauritz Peter Emil (1855–1911) 15, 16, 25, 35, 36, 39, 42, 43, 44, 46, 47, 98, 99, 100, 102, 111, 226, 333, 335, 424, 529, 538, 539
Bohr (-Adler), Ellen (1860–1930) 26, 36, 38, 39, 43, 44, 46, 102, 107, 111, 120, 229, 335, 407, 408, 529, 538, 543
Bohr, Erik (1920–1990) 4, 249, 455, 541
Bohr, Ernest David (1924–) 4, 249, 541
Bohr, Hans Henrik (1918–) 4, 249, 250, 416, 541

Bohr,* Harald August (1887–1951) 4, 15,
    19, 45, 46, 47, 48, 99, 102, 107, 108, 109,
    112, 120, 128, 132, 134, 135, 151, 154, 155,
    164, 167, 226, 311, 333, 335, 382, 395, 407,
    408, 469, 487, 488, 513, 516, 529, 539, 543,
    545
Bohr, Harald (1928–c. 1938) 226, 249, 542
Bohr, Henrik Georg Christian (1813–1880)
    34, 35, 538
Bohr, Jenny (1883–1933) 26, 39, 44, 46,
    407–8, 538, 543
Bohr (-Nørlund), Margrethe (1890–1984)
    4, 6, 10, 16, 24, 29, 43, 47, 48, 103, 111,
    112, 120, 133, 134, 143, 153, 165, 166, 168,
    226, 227, 229, 250, 262, 299, 311, 333, 334,
    335, 384, 408, 410, 411, 414, 415, 416, 417,
    424, 470, 485, 487, 488, 503, 509, 529, 534,
    535, 536, 539, 540, 545, 546
Bohr, Niels Erdmann (1795–1823) 33
Bohr, Niels Henrik David (1885–1962)
    passim
Bohr, Ole (1922–   ) 487
Bohr, Peter Georg (1776–1846) 34, 250,
    538
Boltzmann, Ludwig (1844–1906) 52, 60,
    76, 77, 78, 79, 80, 82, 83, 85, 98, 104, 109,
    110, 189, 436, 437
Bomholt, Johanne Engelka (c. 1749–1789)
    3
Born, Max (1882–1970) 14, 21, 22, 155,
    162, 178, 180, 191, 198, 237, 270, 271, 272,
    278, 279, 282, 284–9, 299, 306, 307, 317,
    350, 426, 542
Bose, Satyendra Nath (1894–1974) 269,
    317, 541
Bošković, Rudjer (1711–1787) 513
Bothe, Walther (1891–1957) 237, 238, 239,
    272, 319
Boyle, Robert (1627–1691) 36
Bragg, William Lawrence (1890–1971)
    213, 301
Brahe, Tyge (Tycho) (1546–1601) 93, 94,
    415
Brandes, Georg Morris Cohen (1842–1927)
    25
Breit, Gregory (1899–1981) 339
Bridgman, Percy (1882–1961) 14, 253
Broglie, Louis de (1892–1987) 16, 239–41,
    269, 281, 283, 289, 301, 316, 541
Brøndal, Vigo (1887–1942) 99
Brønsted, Johannes Balthasar
    (1890–1965) 333
Brønsted, Johannes Nicolaus (1879–1947)
    260, 385, 415

Brostrøm, Karl Jakob (1905–1965) 400,
    401, 458, 459
Browne, Sir Thomas (1605–1681) 255
Bruno, Giordano (1548–1600) 94
Bunsen, Robert Wilhelm (1811–1899) 140,
    141, 215
Bush, Vannevar (1890–1974) 492, 494,
    503, 544

Carlheim-Gyllensköld, Vilhelm
    (1859–1934) 213
Carnegie, Andrew (1835–1919) 256
Casimir, Hendrik (1909–   ) 190, 289,
    325
Chadwick, James (1891–1974) 330, 331–2,
    365, 387, 486, 487, 491, 496, 545
Cherwell, Lord (1886–1957) 496, 500, 501,
    502
Chievitz, Johann Henrik (1850–1903) 50
Chievitz, Ole (1883–1946) 44, 50, 311, 392,
    411, 475, 476, 487, 490, 513
Christian I (King of Denmark 1448–1481)
    (1426–1481) 92
Christian III (King of Denmark
    1536–1559) (1503–1559) 93
Christian VI (King of Denmark
    1730–1746) (1699–1746) 464
Christian VII (King of Denmark
    1766–1808) (1749–1808) 33
Christian IX (King of Denmark
    1863–1906) (1818–1906) 42, 474
Christian X (King of Denmark 1912–1947)
    (1870–1947) 166, 167, 400, 464, 466
Christiansen, Christian (1843–1917) 98,
    99, 101, 106, 107, 108, 109, 132, 133, 144,
    335, 415
Churchill, Winston Leonard Spencer
    (1874–1965) 28, 226, 473, 491, 494, 496,
    499, 500–1, 502, 503, 514, 517, 545
Chwolson, Orest, Daniilovich (1852–1934)
    213
Clausius, Rudolf Julius Emmanuel
    (1822–1888) 80, 81, 83, 104
Cockcroft, John Douglas (1897–1967)
    378, 391, 415
Cohn, Einar (1885–1969) 99
Compton, Arthur Holly (1892–1962) 2,
    234, 237, 238
Compton, Karl Taylor (1887–1954) 87,
    162
Conant, James Bryant (1893–1978) 492,
    494
Condon, Edward Uhler (1902–1974) 324
Cooper, James Fenimore (1789–1851) 49

Copernicus, Nicholas (1473–1543) 92, 94

Cornell, Ezra (1807–1874) 256

Cornu, Alfred-Marie (1841–1902) 198

Coster, Dirk (1889–1950) 208, 210, 214, 216, 258, 541

Coulomb, Charles Augustin de (1736–1806) 63

Courant, Richard (1888–1972) 112, 135

Crick, Francis Harry Compton (1916–) 443

Curie, Marie (1867–1934) 52, 257, 326, 386

Curie, Pierre (1859–1906) 52, 326

Cusanus, Nicolaus (1401–1464) 74

Dagmar (Tsarina Maria Feodorovna 1881–1894) (1841–1910) 42

Dale, Sir Henry Hallett (1875–1968) 500, 534

Darwin, Charles Galton (1887–1962) 126, 127, 128, 129, 136, 163, 234, 238, 486

Darwin, Charles Robert (1809–1882) 127

Davisson, Clinton Joseph (1881–1950) 301

Debye, Peter Joseph Wilhelm (1884–1966) 160, 161, 199, 213, 234

Delbrück, Max Ludwig Henning (1906–1981) 442

Democritus (late fifth century BC) 104, 107

Dennison, David Mathias (1900–1976) 295

Descartes, René (1596–1650) 54, 104

Dickens, Charles (1812–1870) 25

Dinesen, Isak (Karen Blixen) (1885–1962) 25, 42

Dirac, Paul Adrien Maurice (1902–1984) 14, 18, 52, 216, 269, 279, 280, 295–6, 300, 316, 331, 351, 352–3, 354–7, 364, 367, 410, 411, 413, 496, 539, 542, 543

Dresden, Max (1918–) 238

Drude, Paul Karl Ludwig (1863–1906) 109

Duckwitz, Georg Ferdinand (1904–1973) 478

Eckart, Carl (1902–1973) 284

Eckhart, Johannes (?1260–?1327) 75

Edward VII (Kind of England 1901–1910) (1841–1910) 42

Edwards, Sir Samuel Frederick (1928–) 125

Egan, Maurice Francis (1852–1924) 43

Egerod, Søren Christian (1923–) 333

Ehrenfest,* Paul (1880–1933) 26, 178, 189–90, 192, 193, 195, 196, 198, 225, 228, 237, 243, 253, 280, 312, 316, 318, 359, 408–11, 541, 543

Einstein,* Albert (1879–1955) 3, 7, 8, 10, 11, 12, 13, 15, 16, 21, 52, 56, 63, 68, 69, 70, 71, 76, 77, 84, 86, 87, 109, 138, 146, 153, 154, 160, 176, 178, 179, 188, 189, 190–2, 196, 200, 207, 211, 212, 213, 214, 215, 216, 224–32, 234, 236, 237, 238, 239, 240, 241, 243, 252, 257, 269, 271, 274, 280, 281, 287, 288, 301, 309, 311, 315, 316, 317, 318, 319, 320, 327, 347–8, 350, 351, 408, 409, 425, 427, 428, 429, 430, 431, 433, 434, 435, 438, 467, 492, 498, 503, 510, 513, 528, 538, 539, 540, 541, 542, 543, 544, 545

Einstein, Hans Albert (1904–1973) 68

Eisenhower, Dwight David (1890–1969) 1, 2, 523

Elizabeth II (Queen of England 1953–) (1926–) 335, 509

Elsasser, Walter (1904–) 281

Epstein, Paul Sophas (1883–1966) 182, 183, 188, 196, 213, 540

Euler, Leonhard (1707–1783) 57

Eve, Arthur Stewart (1862–1948) 153, 412

Faraday, Michael (1791–1867) 63, 64, 95, 97, 179

Favrholdt, David (1931–) 420, 421, 423, 424

Fermi, Enrico (1901–1954) 76, 269, 331, 368, 369–70, 387, 415, 452, 453, 455, 456, 457, 461, 482, 484, 493, 494, 542, 544

Feynman, Richard Phillips (1918–1988) 14, 349, 497

Finsen, Niels Ryberg (1860–1904) 52, 415

Fokker, Adriaan (1887–1968) 10, 11

Ford, Henry (1863–1947) 52

Fowler, Alfred (1868–1940) 149, 280, 366, 378

Franck, James (1882–1964) 4, 155, 178, 183, 184, 205, 209, 216, 288, 383, 384, 385, 386, 390, 395, 409, 480, 540, 544

Frankfurter, Felix (1882–1965) 2, 499, 501, 502, 503, 504, 517, 534, 545

Franklin, Benjamin (1706–1790) 255

Franz, Johann Carl Rudolph (1826–1902) 110

Fraunhofer, Joseph von (1787–1826) 139

Frederik VIII (King of Denmark 1906–1912) (1843–1912) 42

Fredrik IX (King of Denmark 1947–1972) (1899–1972) 466, 467, 469

Fresnel, Augustin Jean (1788–1827) 57, 59, 60, 87
Freuchen, Peter (1886–1957) 414
Frisch, Otto Robert (1904–1979) 26, 383, 391, 399, 400, 402, 454, 455, 456, 458, 493, 544

Galileo Galilei (1562–1642) 94, 413
Gamow, George (1904–1968) 324, 325, 330, 361, 369, 543
Gauguin, Paul (1848–1903) 52
Geiger, Hans Wilhelm (1882–1945) 122, 123, 124, 237, 238, 239, 272, 319, 329
George I (King of Greece), see Vilhelm
Gerlach, Walther (1889–1979) 199, 353
Germer, Lester Halber (1896–1971) 301
Gibbs, Josiah Willard (1839–1903) 52, 437, 438
Goering, Hermann (1893–1946) 475, 477
Goethe, Johann Wolfgang von (1749–1832) 9, 25, 97, 275
Gorbachev, Mikhail Sergeyevich (1931–   ) 28, 518
Goudsmit, Samuel Abraham (1902–1978) 21, 241–2, 243, 244, 295, 352, 542
Grimaldi, Francesco Maria (1618–1663) 55, 60, 61
Groves, Leslie Richard (1896–1970) 494, 496, 498, 500, 503, 545
Gurney, Ronald Wilfrid (1898–1953) 324
Gustav V (King of Sweden 1907–1950) (1858–1950) 215, 229, 488
Gyth, Volmer (1902–1965) 485, 486, 487, 488, 489, 491

Haakon VII (King of Norway 1906–1957) (1872–1957) 42, 479, 496
Haas, Arthur Erich (1884–1941) 144, 145, 148
Hahn, Otto (1879–1968) 122, 383, 384, 453, 454, 455, 456, 461, 544
Halifax, Lord (1881–1959) 496, 498, 499, 501, 545
Hammarskjöld, Dag (1905–1961) 512, 518
Hansen, H. C. (1906–1960) 535
Hansen, Hans Marius (1886–1956) 144, 163, 164, 167, 513
Heiberg, Edvard (1897–1958) 487, 488
Heine, Heinrich (1797–1856) 37
Heisenberg,* Werner Carl (1901–1976) 14, 18, 21, 24, 27, 29, 52, 99, 161, 162, 163, 177, 178, 179, 196, 197, 198, 205, 216, 236, 243, 244, 251, 260, 262–4, 267, 270, 272–9, 280, 281, 288, 295, 296, 297–8, 299, 300,

301–6, 308, 309, 311, 313, 316, 317, 318, 320, 332, 336, 347, 348, 350, 352, 355, 356, 357, 358, 359, 360, 361, 362, 363, 369, 399, 407, 421, 424, 428, 436, 437, 481–5, 489, 490, 512, 520, 535, 539, 541, 542, 544
Heitler, Walter (1904–1981) 362
Hellmann, Sophie (1894–1979) 334
Helmholtz, Hermann von (1821–1894) 98
Hendriksen, Holger Simon (1878–1955) 411
Henriksen, Kai (1888–1940) 99
Herglotz, Gustav (1881–1953) 409
Herschel, William (1738–1822) 62
Hertz, Gustav Ludwig (1878–1975) 183, 184, 540
Hertz, Heinrich (1857–1894) 65, 67, 78, 79, 84
Hevesy,* Georg Charles von (1885–1966) 27, 126, 127, 129, 144, 154, 170, 210, 214, 216, 251, 258, 333, 384, 385, 386, 388–94, 395, 396, 399, 454, 480, 538, 540, 541, 542, 544
Hilbert, David (1862–1943) 154, 177
Hitler, Adolf (1889–1945) 381, 477, 480, 481, 485
Høffding, Harald (1834–1931) 99, 170, 257, 260, 332–3, 335, 423, 465
Holberg, Ludvig (1684–1754) 25, 431
Holm, Emma Ottine Sophie (1862–1962) 112
Holst, Hans Peter (1811–1893) 43
Hooke, Robert (1635–1703) 57
Hopkins, Johns (1795–1873) 256
Hoyt, Frank C. (1898–1977) 264
Hulthén, Lamek (1909–   ) 7
Huyghens, Christiaan (1629–1695) 56, 57, 60, 61, 70, 87, 88, 538

Ibsen, Henrik (1828–1906) 25, 49
Ishiwara, Jun (1881–1947) 186
Ising, Gustav Adolf (1883–1960) 377

Jacobsen, Carl Christian Hilman (1842–1914) 257, 334
Jacobsen, Jacob Christian (1811–1887) 256–7, 333, 334
Jacobsen, Jacob Christian (1895–1965) 398, 401, 459, 489
James, William (1842–1910) 424
Jeans, James Hopwood (1877–1946) 84, 120, 154, 252
Joffé, Abram Feodorovich (1880–1960) 409
Johansson, Johan Erik (1862–1938) 36

Joliot-Curie, Irène (1897–1956) 216, 386, 390, 452

Joliot-Curie, Jean Frédéric (1900–1958) 216, 386, 390, 452

Jordan, Pascual (1902–1980) 243, 278, 279, 282, 288, 317, 350, 357, 442, 542

Jost, Res (1918–1990) 318

Kaarsted, Tage (1928–   )

Kalckar, Fritz (1910–1938) 288, 339–40

Kalckar, Jørgen (1935–   ) 25, 358, 428, 465, 536

Kant, Immanuel (1724–1804) 23, 75, 424

Kapitza, Pyotr Leonidovich (1894–1984) 413, 499–500, 503, 545

Kármán, Th. von (1881–1963) 162

Kauffmann, Henrik Louis Hans von (1888–1963) 477, 479, 498, 545

Kay, William (1879–1961) 329

Kayser, Heinrich Gustav Johannes (1853–1940) 141

Kelvin, Lord (1824–1907) 68

Kemble, Edwin Crawford (1889–1984) 235

Kepler, Johann (1571–1630) 54, 200

Kierkegaard, Søren Aaby (1813–1855) 25, 97, 423, 424

Killian, James Rhyne (1904–1988) 1, 2, 3

Kirchhoff, Gustav Robert (1824–1887) 76, 77, 78, 79, 80, 82, 83, 140, 141, 215

Klein, Martin Jesse (1924–   ) 410

Klein, Oskar Benjamin (1894–1977) 18, 45, 170, 171, 193, 237, 251, 295, 297, 303, 310, 311, 354–5, 359, 360, 361, 364, 366, 399, 488, 543

Knudsen, Martin Hans Christian (1871–1949) 98, 132, 133, 135, 143, 163, 213, 333, 415, 464, 513, 540

Kobylinski, Hanna (1907–   ) 24

Koch, Hans Henrik (1905–1988) 516

Koch, Jørgen (1909–1971) 400, 458, 459

Kohnstamm, Philipp Abraham (1875–1951) 409

Kossel, Walther Ludwig (1888–1956) 162, 181, 202, 203, 204

Krack (or Krak), Elias Christian Thorvald (1830–1908) 40

Kragh, Helge (1944–   ) 204

Kramers,* Hendrik Antonie (1894–1952) 21, 167, 168, 171, 179, 183, 185, 190, 193, 195, 197, 198, 202, 204, 205, 210, 234, 235, 238, 239, 244, 251, 253, 263, 270–2, 273, 274, 275, 276, 280, 288, 295, 296, 300, 312,

316, 318, 487, 510, 513, 514, 520, 540, 541, 545

Kratzenstein, Christian Gottlieb (1723–1795) 95

Krogh, August (1874–1949) 260, 391, 393, 394, 395, 396, 467, 476

Kronig, Ralph de Laer (1904–   ) 243, 244, 272, 285

Landau, Lev Davidovich (1908–1968) 325, 355, 358, 361, 498, 543

Landé, Alfred (1888–1975) 154, 155, 162, 200, 201, 204, 205

Langmuir, Irving (1881–1957) 216

Larmor, Joseph (1857–1942) 120

Laslett, Laurence Jackson (1913–   ) 401

Lassen, Niels Ove (1914–   ) 401, 459

Laue, Max von (1879–1960) 11, 213, 480

Lauritsen, Charles Christian (1892–1968) 376, 400, 401, 414, 459, 481, 494

Lauritsen, Thomas (1915–1973) 401, 402, 462

Lawrence, Ernest Orlando (1901–1958) 216, 376–8, 393, 396, 401

Leacock, Stephen (1869–1944) 25

Leibnitz, Gottfried Wilhelm (1646–1716) 57, 74

Lessing, Gotthold Ephraim (1729–1781) 37

Levi, Hilde (1909–   ) 383, 386, 390, 391, 392, 394, 397, 544

Lie, Trygve (1896–1968) 516, 517

Lilienfeld, Julius Edgar (1882–1963) 213

Linderstrøm Lang, Kaj (1896–1959) 487, 488

Lindhard, Jens (1922–   ) 128, 421, 465, 511

Lindman, Karl (1874–1952) 213

Locke, John (1632–1704) 75

Lomholt, Asger (1901–1990) 467

Lorentz, Hendrik Antoon (1853–1928) 69, 76, 78, 108, 109, 189, 198, 228, 240, 242, 280, 316, 426

Lorenz, Ludwig Valentin (1829–1891) 65, 96, 98, 108, 415

Ludwig, Carl Friedrich Wilhelm (1816–1895) 46

Lundsgard, Christen (1883–1930) 258–9

Mach, Ernst (1838–1916) 52, 200

McCloy, John Jay (1895–1989) 514–15

Madsen, Børge (1918–   ) 428

Mann, Thomas (1875–1955) 25

Marconi, Guglielmo (1874–1937) 121
Maria Feodorovna (Tsarina), see Dagmar
Marsden, Ernest (1889–1970) 122–3, 329
Marshall, George Catlett (1880–1959)
  493, 514, 515, 516, 545
Mason, Max (1877–1961) 379, 380, 383,
  394, 414
Massey, H. S. W. (1908–1983)
Maxwell, James Clerk (1831–1879) 53, 56,
  63, 64, 65, 66, 67, 69, 76, 96, 103, 104, 105,
  107, 117, 118, 142, 179, 233, 336, 347, 426,
  438
Mehra, Jagdish (1937–   ) 180, 281
Meitner, Lise (1878–1968) 26, 383, 384,
  453, 454, 455, 456, 458, 544
Melvill, Thomas (1726–1753) 139
Mendeléev, Dimitri Ivanovitch
  (1834–1907) 203
Merton, Robert King (1910–   ) 94
Metzinger, Jean (1883–1956) 335
Meyer (-Bjerrum), Kirstine (1861–1941)
Meyer, Leopold (1852–1918) 36
Meyer, Stefan (1872–1949) 213
Michelson, Albert Abraham (1852–1931)
  67, 68, 184, 253, 254, 261
Milch, Erhard (1892–1972) 482
Millikan, Robert Andrews (1868–1953)
  213, 230, 233, 376
Mittag-Leffler, Magnus Gustaf
  (1846–1927) 212
Møller, Christian (1904–1980) 483, 489,
  490, 521, 522
Møller, Knud Max (1922–   ) 47, 111
Møller, Poul Martin (1794–1838) 25, 424,
  440
Moffelson, Ben Roy (1926–   )
Montgomery, Bernard Law (1887–1976)
  479
Morgan, Thomas Hunt (1866–1945) 380
Morley, Edward William (1838–1923) 67,
  68, 184
Mörner, Karl Axel Hampus (1854–1917)
  36
Moseley, Henry Gwyn Jeffreys
  (1887–1915) 152, 154, 180, 181, 182, 183,
  184, 328, 540
Mott, Nevill Francis (1905–   ) 288,
  289, 325, 354, 367
Mottelson, Ben Roy (1926–   ) 342, 343
Muller, Hermann Joseph (1890–1967) 380
Myron (middle 5th century BC) 334

Nadolny, Rudolf (1873–1953) 215
Nagaoka, Hantaro (1865–1950) 137

Nagel, Bengt (1927–   ) 212
Neddermeyer, Seth Henry (1907–1988)
  358
Neesen, Friedrich (1849–1923) 213
Nehru, Jawaharlal (1889–1964) 509, 528
Nernst, Hermann Walther (1864–1941)
  146, 214, 234
Newton, Isaac (1642–1727) 3, 4, 10, 55, 56,
  57, 61, 63, 66, 76, 77, 87, 87, 88, 104, 139,
  141, 185, 413, 426, 466, 511, 538
Nicholson, John William (1881–1955)
  145, 150, 184
Nielsen, Jens Rud (1894–1979) 133
Nishina, Yoshio (1890–1951) 258, 354,
  416, 417, 543
Nørlund, Alfred Christian (1850–1925)
  112
Norlund, Margrethe, see Bohr (-Norlund),
  Margrethe
Nørlund, Niels Erik (1885–1981) 99, 112,
  333, 465, 469
Nørlund, Poul (1888–1951) 99, 112

Olsen, Holger (1889–1958) 489
Oppenheimer, J. Robert (1904–1967) 1,
  414, 495, 497, 516
Ørsted, Anders Sandøe (1778–1860) 97
Ørsted, Hans Christian (1777–1851) 63,
  64, 95, 96, 97, 98, 108, 111, 251, 257, 258,
  353, 415, 512, 521
Oseen, Carl Wilhelm (1879–1944) 132,
  163, 184, 214, 296

Pais, Abraham (1918–   ) 1, 2, 4–13,
  142, 201, 249–50, 258, 296, 360, 428, 461,
  516, 517, 535
Palmerston, Henry John Temple
  (1784–1865) 42
Paneth, Friedrich Adolf (1887–1958) 384,
  385, 389
Panum, Peter Ludvig (1820–1885) 46
Pascal, Blaise (1623–1662) 420, 421
Paschen, Friedrich (1865–1947) 154
Pauli,* Wolfgang (1900–1958) 12, 21, 29,
  52, 151, 161, 162, 180, 199, 200–1, 208–9,
  224, 237, 238, 241, 243, 244, 258, 262, 268,
  270, 272, 275, 278, 279, 280, 283, 284, 288,
  297, 298, 301, 304, 309, 310, 311, 315, 316,
  318, 320, 352, 353, 355, 359, 360, 361, 362,
  364, 366, 367, 368, 369, 395, 426, 428, 434,
  437, 442, 446, 498, 513, 539, 541, 542, 546
Pavlov, Ivan Petrovich (1849–1936) 415
Peierls, Rudolf Ernst (1907–   ) 341,
  359, 360, 361, 493, 496, 543, 544

Peltier, Jean Charles Athanase
 (1785–1845) 110
Philip (Prince, Duke of Edinburgh)
 (1921–   ) 335, 509
Picasso, Pablo (1881–1973) 52
Pickering, Edward Charles (1846–1919)
 149
Pissarro, Camille (1830–1903) 52
Placzek, George (1905–1955) 341, 383, 456
Planck,* Max Karl Ernst Ludwig
 (1858–1947) 3, 15, 16, 78, 79–80, 81,
 82–8, 104, 108, 109, 138, 144, 146, 160,
 161, 177, 186, 212, 213, 227, 228, 229, 230,
 231, 233, 252, 281, 285, 316, 317, 327, 340,
 347, 350, 383, 425, 426, 539, 541
Plato (c. 428–c. 347 BC) 56, 255
Pliny the Younger (62–c. 113) 255
Plücker, Julius (1801–1868) 141
Podolsky, Boris (1896–1966) 429, 544
Pohl, Robert Wichard (1884–1976) 154
Poincaré, Henri (1854–1912) 69, 108, 109
Prytz, Peter Kristian (1851–1929) 98, 101

Rabi, Isidore (1898–1988) 285, 455
Rabinowitch, Eugene (1911–1973) 383
Raman, Chandrasekhara Venkata
 (1888–1970) 216, 274
Ramus, Petrus (1515–1572) 94
Raphael, John (1802–1877) 36
Raphael, Nathan (?1726–1808) 37
Raphael, Raphael (1763–1845) 37
Rask, Rasmus Kristian (1787–1832) 258
Rasmussen, Knud (1879–1933) 398, 513
Rayleigh, Lord (1842–1919) 84, 101, 108,
 117, 153, 356
Rechenberg, Helmut (1937–   ) 180, 281
Reik, Theodor (1888–1969) 536
Rhodes, Cecil (1853–1902) 256
Ribbentrop, Joachim von (1893–1946) 477
Richardson, Owen Willans (1879–1959)
 216
Rimestad, Caroline Louise Augusta
 (1817–1896) 35
Ritter, Johann Wilhelm (1776–1810) 62
Ritz, Walter (1878–1909) 149, 215
Rockefeller, John Davison Jr. (1874–1960)
 258
Rockefeller, John Davison (1839–1937)
 256
Rømer, Ole Christensen (1644–1710) 54,
 55, 64, 94, 415
Röntgen, Wilhelm Conrad (1845–1923)
 62, 122, 213, 376, 539

Roosevelt, Franklin Delano (1882–1945)
 28, 226, 473, 492, 493, 494, 499, 500,
 501–2, 503, 516, 544, 545
Rose, Wickliffe (1862–1931) 258, 259, 381
Rosen, Nathan (1909–   ) 429, 544
Rosenfeld, Léon (1904–1974) 11, 15, 315,
 360, 361, 415, 427, 430, 431, 437, 438, 442,
 446, 455, 456, 465, 511, 543
Rosseland, S. (1894–1985) 170, 171
Rozental, Stefan Szymon (1903–   ) 24,
 383, 481, 483, 484, 511, 521, 522
Rubens, Heinrich (1865–1922) 213, 227
Rubin, Edgar (1886–1951) 99, 439
Rubinowicz, Adalbert (1889–1974) 170,
 194, 258, 541
Rutherford,* Ernest (Lord R. of Nelson)
 (1871–1937) 11, 17, 26, 52, 76, 106,
 121–7, 128–9, 134–5, 136, 144, 145, 146,
 150, 152–3, 163, 164, 165, 168, 170, 171,
 172, 180, 181, 182, 185, 191, 196, 197, 202,
 205, 209, 213, 229, 252, 254, 259, 261, 280,
 295, 326, 327–30, 332, 333, 367, 369, 378,
 384, 386, 388, 396, 399, 408, 412–13, 424,
 460, 495, 513, 536, 538, 539, 541, 544
Rutherford, James (1838–1928) 121
Rutherford (-Thompson), Martha
 (1843–1935) 121, 333, 413, 496

Sandal, Birgitte Steenberg (1784–1846)
 34
Scharff, Niels William (1886–1959) 249
Schiff, Emma (1803–1844) 37
Schiller, Friedrich von (1759–1805) 9, 25
Schilpp, Paul Arthur (1897–   ) 428,
 433
Schmauss, August (1877–1954) 213
Schneider, Erich Ernst (1911–   ) 383
Schrödinger,* Erwin (1887–1961) 7, 21,
 22, 52, 206, 216, 237, 280–4, 285, 286, 288,
 289, 297, 298–9, 300, 301, 303, 306, 316,
 317, 352, 424, 425, 428, 539, 542
Schultz, Betty (1898–1980) 5, 171, 324,
 541
Schwarzschild, Karl (1873–1916) 182, 183,
 188, 213, 540
Seedorff, Hans Hartvig (1892–1986) 25,
 249, 411
Sellmeyer, W. 98
Shakespeare, William (1564–1616) 25
Silliman, Augustus Ely (1807–1884) 253
Simon, Alfred 237
Sixtus IV (Pope) (1414–1481) 92
Skov, Peter (1883–1967) 99

Slater, John Clarke (1900–1976) 234, 235,
    236, 238, 239, 240, 241, 268, 415, 541
Slomann, Vilhelm (1885–1962) 99, 100
Smekal, Adolf Gustav (1895–1959) 274
Smithson, James (1754–1829) 256
Smuts, Jan Christiaan (1870–1950) 496,
    501
Smyth, Henry De Wolf (1898–1986) 464
Socrates (c. 470–399 BC) 99, 422
Soddy, Frederick (1877–1956) 122, 126,
    211, 326, 460
Sommerfeld,* Arnold Johannes Wilhelm
    (1868–1951) 110, 145, 154, 155, 161–2,
    163, 164, 178, 180, 182, 184, 186, 187, 188,
    189, 193, 194, 196, 198, 199, 200, 202, 204,
    205, 208, 213, 214, 215, 227, 228, 229, 234,
    241, 242, 243–4, 262, 263, 268, 269, 272,
    330, 425, 538, 540, 541
Speer, Albert (1879–1953) 482, 483
Stalin, Joseph (1879–1953) 498, 500, 502,
    528
Stanford, Leland (1824–1893) 256
Stark, Johannes (1874–1957) 142, 144,
    182, 183, 184, 185
Steensen (Steno), Niels (1638–1686) 94,
    415
Stefan, Josef (1835–1893) 77
Stern, Otto (1888–1969) 199, 201, 216, 243,
    318, 353, 437, 503
Stevenson, Adlai (1900–1965) 509
Stimson, Henry (1867–1950) 493
Stokes, George Gabriel (1819–1903) 141
Strassman, Fritz (1902–1980) 453, 454,
    455, 456, 461, 544
Strauss, Lewis (1896–1974) 476
Strelitz, Paula (1892–1963) 44, 382
Strömgren, Bengt Georg Daniel
    (1908–1987) 333

Tallqvist, Hjalmar (1870–1958) 213
Teller, Edward (1908–   ) 383
Tesla, Nikola (1856–1943) 528
Thiele, Thorvald Nicolai (1838–1910) 99
Thomas, Llewellyn Hilleth (1903–   )
    243, 268, 353
Thompson, Benjamin (Count Rumford)
    (1753–1814) 255
Thomsen, Julius (1826–1909) 209
Thomsen, Vilhelm Ludwig Peter
    (1842–1927) 99
Thomson, George Paget (1892–1975) 301
Thomson,* Joseph John (1856–1940) 16,
    52, 105–6, 109, 117–21, 122, 123, 124, 125,
    136, 139, 142, 149, 153, 165, 252, 295, 329,
    376, 538, 539
Thorvaldsen, Bertel (1768–1844) 32, 334
Thrige, Thomas Barfoed (1866–1938) 396
Tito (Josip Broz) (1892–1980) 528
Tolman, Richard Chase (1881–1948) 409,
    496, 503
Tomonaga, Sin-itiro (1906–1979) 14
Tordenskjold, Peder (1691–1720)
Trotsky, Leon (1879–1940) 360
Twain, Mark (1835–1910) 25

Uhlenbeck, George Eugene (1900–1988)
    21, 241–2, 243, 244, 285, 295, 352, 430,
    461, 542
Urbain, Georges (1871–1938) 209, 210
Urey, Harold (1893–1981) 390

Van de Graaff, Robert Jemison
    (1901–1967) 378, 379, 543
van den Broek, Antonius Johannes
    (1870–1926) 180, 181, 540
Van Vleck, John Hasbrouck (1899–1980)
    180, 235
Victoria (Queen of England 1838–1901)
    (1819–1901) 42
Vilhelm (Prince, King George I of Greece
    1863–1913) (1845–1913) 32, 42
Villard, Paul (1860–1934) 62
Volta, Alessandro (1745–1827) 63, 311
Von Hippel, Arthur (1898–   ) 383
von Neumann, John (1903–1957) 435

Wallace, Henry Asgard (1888–1965) 493
Walton, Ernest Thomas Sinton
    (1903–   ) 378
Warburg, Emil Gabriel (1846–1931) 154,
    182
Watson, James Dewey (1928–   ) 443
Weaver, Warren (1894–1978) 375, 379–81,
    388, 394, 395, 397, 543
Weinberg, Steven (1933–   ) 349
Weisskopf, Victor (1908–   ) 357, 361,
    383, 452, 521
Weizmann, Chaim (1874–1952) 165, 517,
    528
Westfall, Richard Samuel (1924–   ) 3
Weyl, Hermann (1885–1955) 364
Wheeler, John Archibald (1911–   ) 2,
    364, 455, 456, 457, 458, 544
Whewell, William (1794–1866) 94
Wick, Gian Carlo (1909–   ) 535
Wideröe, Rolf (1902–   ) 377

Wiedemann, Gustav Heinrich (1826–1899) 110

Wien, Wilhelm (1864–1928) 78, 79, 84, 85, 212, 213

Wiener, Norbert (1894–1964) 285

Wigner, Eugene Paul (1902–   ) 178, 285, 287, 315, 339, 357

Wildenvey, Hermann (1886–1959) 25

Wilhelm II (Emperor of Germany 1888–1918) (1859–1941) 42

Willumsen, Jens Ferdinand (1863–1958) 111

Wilson, William (1875–1945) 186

Wodehouse, Pelham Grenville (1881–1975) 25

Wollaston, William Hyde (1766–1828) 139

Wood, Robert Williams (1868–1955) 216

Wright, Orville (1871–1948) 52

Wright, Richard (1908–1960) 25

Wright, Wilbur (1867–1912) 52

Young, Thomas (1773–1829) 57, 59, 60, 87, 104, 105

Ysaye, Eugène (1858–1931) 11

Yukawa, Hideki (1907–1981) 357, 358

Zeeman, Pieter (1865–1943) 198

Index of Subjects

accelerators 26, 388, 399–402, 519
  Cockcroft–Walton 378, 395, 400
  first 375
  high-tension 399, 400, 458, 526
  Van de Graaff 378–9, 397, 401–2, 525–6
    tandem 379, 526
  see also cyclotrons
activation energy 457
adiabatic principle 189, 190
aether 56, 66–8, 69, 70, 71
alkalis 203
α-decay 324, 331, 365
α-particles 123, 127, 180, 368, 386, 387,
    398, 399
  scattering of 329
  stopping of 184
  structure of 328, 329, 330
α-rays 106, 122, 126, 127, 326
Ampère's law 64, 69
angular momentum 145, 150
arms race 498, 503, 523
astronomy 93
atomic bombs 463–4, 484
  consequences of 498, 501
  development of 341
    Anglo-American efforts 492–5, 500
    Bohr's role in 496–7
    in Germany 482–3
    in Soviet Union 500, 514, 515
    hydrogen 515
atomic energy 52, 460, 464, 473, 482
  international control of 514
  peaceful uses of 512, 523, 524
atomic number (A) 181, 328
atomic orbits 270
atomic physics 347
atomic power 462
atomic spectra 139
atomic states 147, 179
  stationary 147, 153
  transitions between 179
atomic structure 118, 119, 129, 135–9,
    182, 196, 202, 215
  quantum theory of 144, 153
atomic weights 180
atomism 103, 104

Balmer formula 142, 143, 144, 146, 147,
    148, 151, 182
  corrections to 184, 185
  Pauli's derivation of 279, 280, 283
  Schrödinger's derivation of 283–4
beryllium 331
β-decay 324, 332, 365, 366, 367, 368
  Fermi's theory of 369–70
β-particles, stopping of 184
β-radioactivity 17, 332, 364, 540
  origin of 150
β-rays 106, 122, 126, 127, 152, 326
β-spectra 365, 366, 368
binding energy 327, 457
biology 375, 380
  emphasis on 380–1
  experimental 380
BKS proposal 234–9, 270, 271, 281
blackbody radiation 76, 77, 78, 86, 109
Bohr, Harald August
  boyhood 45, 47, 48
  correspondence with Niels 128, 151,
    154, 155
  death of 513, 545
  on death of mother 407, 408
  as director of Mathematics Institute
    19, 543
  master's degree 107
  relationship with Niels 15, 45, 226
  as soccer player 108, 167
  other references 4, 46, 99, 102, 112, 120,
    132, 134, 135, 164, 311, 333, 335, 382,
    395, 469, 487, 488, 516, 529, 539
Bohr, Niels
  acquisition of Institute for Theoretical
    Physics 168–72
  addresses, post-war 511–13
  assistant to Knudsen 133, 135, 143, 540
  Atoms for Peace Award 2
  baptism of 48
  and biology 397, 441–4, 511
  birth of 33, 538
  births of sons 168, 249, 540–1
  boyhood of 42–51, 539
  at Cambridge, England 117, 119–21,
    125

as CERN director 521, 545
in China 417
chronology of 538–46
coat of arms 24
Como lectures 311–16, 420, 421, 432, 438
compound nucleus model 336–41
concentration 4, 224
and culture 24–6, 39, 225
death of 29, 333, 470, 529, 546
death of Christian (son) 26, 411–12
death of father 111, 539
death of Jenny (sister) 407–8, 543
death of mother 407, 543
dictation, preference for 102
as 'director of atomic theory' 267–70
docentship 135
doctor's thesis 107–11, 117
Ehrenfest and 243, 253, 280, 408–10
Einstein and, see under Einstein
engagement to Margrethe 111, 112
family history 32–9
family life 226, 249–51
Faraday lecture (1932) 436, 437, 543
fiftieth birthday gift to 392
fund raising by 19, 20, 256, 257, 258–60, 382–6, 394–8, 509
and glasnost 497–503, 518
Göttingen lectures (1922) 201, 204, 205, 206, 209, 262
Heisenberg and 262–4, 273, 279–80, 308–11
  dialog between (1926–7) 301–4
  meeting between in 1941 481–5
international recognition 251 2
in Japan 417
and language 445–6, 511
lecture courses by 167, 171
and literature 24–5, 49
in Manchester 17, 125–9, 164, 165–6, 540
marriage to Margrethe 133–4, 541
master's thesis 107
and mathematics 178–9
in memoriam tributes to 534–5
and music 25, 225
and Nobel Prize 18, 97, 210–16, 229, 250
  nominations by 216–17
  nominations for 212–14
and Nordita 521–3, 546
open letters to the United Nations 12, 28, 516–18, 545
open world ideas 28, 29, 473, 501, 504, 513–18, 545

Order of the Elephant conferred on 166, 468, 545
Ørsted and 97
overwork 172, 225, 261
and painting 25
and periodic table of elements 202–10
and philosophy 24, 97, 420–33, 438–47, 511
  philosophers influencing 423–4
  philosophical papers by 422
  see also complementarity
postulate for atomic transitions 147, 351
professorship 163, 164, 166
and psychology 439–41, 446
as public speaker 11
and QED 349, 358–64
and religion 24, 134, 225, 511
Residence of Honor 20, 26, 333–5, 543
and Rockefeller Foundation emergency program 383–6
Rosenfeld and, see Bohr–Rosenfeld (BR) collaboration
Rutherford and, see under Rutherford
Rutherford memorandum 135–9
schooldays 48–51
Schrödinger and 22, 298–300, 424
scientific papers by, see Bohr's scientific papers
Silliman lectures at Yale 253–4, 541
sources of personal data on 40
and sports 100, 120, 225, 249
student days 98–103, 107
theory of the hydrogen atom 10, 17, 146–52, 540
  reactions to 152–6
  refinements to 185
in Soviet Union 415–16, 417, 528
in Tisvilde 249–51, 529
travels, later 528
as UNESCO adviser 466
in United States
  first trip (1923) 253–4
  second trip (1933) 413–15
  third trip (1937) 416–17
  in World War II 496, 498–500, 501–3
  post World War II 528
and Videnskabernes Selskab (KDVS)
  member of 167
  president of 464–70, 504
in World War II 27–8, 473, 475, 478, 479–504
  in Britain 491, 495–6, 500–1, 503
  concern for Jews 488–9
  escape from Denmark 481, 487–8

Bohr, Niels—*cont.*
  in World War II—*cont.*
    return to Denmark 504
    in Sweden 488–9
    in United States 496, 498–500, 501–3
  writings 29, 422
  in memoriam 513
'Bohr effect' 36
Bohr magneton 151
Bohr radius 145, 148
Bohr relation 184
Bohr–Rosenfeld (BR) collaboration
    360–4
Bohr–Rutherford model 136, 213
Bohr's scientific papers 225, 261
  1912 146
  1913 128, 146, 149, 161, 180
  1914 182, 185
  1915 128, 182, 184
  1916 182
  1918 183, 192, 202, 204
  1921 203, 232
  1922 192, 195, 204
  1923 196, 208
  1924 236, 273
  1925 239
  1926 243
  1928 309, 312, 315, 420, 425
  1929 426
  1930 426
  1932 356, 367
  1933 360
  1935 431
  1936 338, 339, 460
  1937 339, 340
  1938 340, 341
  1939 341, 457
  1940 128, 459, 510
  1941 128, 460
  1948 128, 511
  1950 364, 511
  1954 128, 465, 511
  1963 434
Boltzmann's principle 82, 86
Bose–Einstein statistics 269, 331, 351
Broglie, de, wavelength 240
Brownian motion 105
building up principle 205–6

Carlsberg foundation 19, 117, 256–7, 260,
    261, 333, 395, 396, 397, 398, 468, 469,
    480
cathode rays 105

causality 22, 23, 82, 191–2, 236, 237, 287,
    315
  non-validity of law of 306, 327
Cavendish Laboratory, Cambridge 117,
    121, 122, 252
central field model 204
CERN 29, 519–21, 522
charge number (Z) 328
classical physics, *see* physics, classical
clock-in-the-box experiment 427–8
c-numbers 279, 290
color 55, 60–3
commutation relations 361, 362
complementarism 439
complementarity 8, 14, 22, 29, 109, 310,
    347, 417, 425–31, 511, 512
  applied outside physics 24, 29, 425,
      438–47, 511
    biology 441–4, 511
    human cultures 444–5
    psychology 439–41
  between temperature and energy 437
  Bohr–Einstein dialog on 425, 427–31
  first presentation of concept of 312–16
  formulation of concept of 97, 311, 424
  preludes to 300–4
  questions and answers on 433–6
complex numbers 289–90
Compton effect 234, 237, 238, 365–6
continuity 74–5
conversion, internal 365
Copenhagen, University of
  founding of 92
correspondence principle 20, 152, 178,
    193, 194, 195–6, 206, 268, 300
cosmic radiation 63
crystal lattices 162
crystals 202
cyclotrons 26, 216, 376–8, 396, 397, 398,
    401, 459, 526

Denmark
  decline of (19th century) 42–3
  German occupation of 381, 473, 476–9
  and Germany before 1940 474–6
  rescue of Jews from 478–9
deuterons 459
deuterium 390
diffraction 56, 318–19
Dirac equation 352, 353, 354

Ehrenfest, Paul
  on adiabatics 189–90, 193

Bohr and 243, 253, 280, 408–10
and complementarity 312
death of 26, 408–11, 543
other references 178, 192, 195, 196, 198, 225, 228, 237, 316, 318, 359, 541
eigenstates 283
Einstein, Albert
on atomic energy implications 492
Bohr and 13, 224–44, 280, 467, 498, 545
comments by E on B's work 154, 179, 207, 408
comparisons between B and E 224–7, 510
correspondence 309, 311, 503
disagreements between B and E 12, 230–2, 237, 238, 425, 427–8, 431, 435
and Ehrenfest 408–9
first encounters between B and E 21, 227–9, 231, 541
at Solvay (1927) 316–20, 542
as sparring partners 8
tributes to E by B 513
on Bohr's theory of the atom 154
Born and 288
clock-in-the-box experiment 427, 543
on complementarity 109
counterproposal to complementarity, see EPR paper
death of 467, 545
early life 68
on general relativity 178
on guiding fields 287–8
on heat capacities 138, 160
light quantum discovery by 3, 87, 153, 160, 539
Nobel Prize 211, 212, 213, 214, 215, 216, 229
on Maxwell's theory 63
objection to quantum mechanics 318–19, 431, 433
on particle–wave duality 16, 287, 301, 347–8
Pauli and 200
on Planck's law 86
on probabilities 190–2, 236, 274, 540
on quantum gases 281
on radiation theory 231, 239, 241, 287
relativity theory discovery by 15, 176
on special relativity 69, 71, 327
on spin 243
on statistical mechanics 146, 269, 281, 317
other references 7, 10, 11, 52, 56, 70, 76, 77, 84, 138, 188, 189, 196, 240,

252, 257, 271, 315, 350, 351, 430, 438, 528, 538, 541
see also entries beginning Einstein; Rayleigh–Einstein–Jeans law
Einstein–de Broglie relation 312
electrical revolution 97
electrodynamics, classical theory of 155
electromagnetic waves 63, 65, 66
electromagnetism 64, 95
electrons
creation of 369
discovery of 52, 105, 117, 376
valence 201, 206
wave properties of 240
electron orbits 305, 306
electron–positron pairs 356
electron rings 202
electron shells 202, 203, 207, 208
electron spin 197
see also spin
electron theory of metals 107, 109, 110
emission, spontaneous 191, 195, 351
energies, quantized 277
energy, conservation of 233, 234, 237, 278, 312–13
in relativistic quantum theory 366, 367, 369
energy states, negative 355
ensembles 438
entropy 80, 81, 82, 86
EPR paper 429–31
equivalence principle 428
exclusion principle 197, 208–9, 268, 269, 297, 457

Fermi–Dirac statistics 269, 351
field quantization 350, 357
fine structure 353
see also under hydrogen atom; helium
fission 26
discovery of 402, 452–6
research in Copenhagen 458–60
theory of 456–8
Ford Foundation 509
Franck–Hertz experiment 183–4, 196, 540
Frisch Peierls memorandum 493

γ-decay 324, 365
γ-rays 62, 63, 106, 127, 313, 326, 365, 366, 527
Germany, troubles in 381–3, 388
ghost fields 287, 288
Göttingen
Bohr Festspiele in 162, 172

Gottingen—*cont.*
  pursuit of quantum theory in 161, 162,
    163
ground states 147, 150, 204, 342

hafnium 209–10, 389, 541
half-life concept 326–7
Hall effect 110
halogens 203
heat capacities 138, 162
Heisenberg, Werner
  in Copenhagen
    first arrival 272–3
    as lektor 296
    in 1943 490
  correspondence with Bohr 332, 356,
    358, 359, 360, 399, 407
  dialog with Bohr (1926–7) 301–4
  early years 262–4
  Einstein and 428
    correspondence 317
    meetings 318
  on electric charge density fluctuations
    363
  on helium spectrum 196, 197, 198,
    297–8
  Kramers and 274, 276
  on matrix mechanics 21
  Nobel Prize 161, 216
  nuclear force theory 336, 357, 369
  obituary of Bohr by 14
  on polarization 273
  probability interpretation by 288
  on QED 348, 352
  quantum mechanics discovery by 267,
    275–9
    Bohr's reaction to 280
  visit to Bohr (1941) 27, 481–5, 544
  other references 18, 24, 29, 52, 99, 162,
    163, 177, 178, 179, 205, 236, 243, 244,
    251, 260, 270, 281, 295, 299, 300,
    304–6, 308, 309, 311, 313, 316, 320,
    347, 350, 355, 361, 362, 421, 424, 436,
    437, 489, 512, 520, 535, 539, 541, 542
  see also entries beginning Heisenberg's
Heisenberg's uncertainty relations 22,
    304–8, 312, 313
  applied to electron spin 352
  applied to hydrogen atom 306–7
  applied to macroscopic objects 307–8
helium
  discovery of 140
  spectrum of 196–8, 297–8, 540
    4686 line 242, 246

fine structure of 194
  orthohelium 298
  parahelium 298
  see also α-particles
Hevesy, Georg von
  Bohr and
    correspondence 144, 333
    friendship 126
  at Bohr's institute 170, 385, 386, 388,
    480, 541
  discovery of hafnium by 210, 216
  and isotopic tracer methods 27,
    388–94, 542, 544
  Nobel Prize nomination 214
  other references 127, 129, 154, 251, 258,
    384, 395, 396, 399, 454, 538, 540
holes, theory of 364
human cultures 444–5
hydrogen atom
  including relativity effects 187–8
  neglecting relativity effects 186–7
  probability distributions of atomic
    states 307
  spectrum of 141, 142, 192–3, 268
    fine structure of 184, 187, 192, 196,
      244
    H_α-line 242, 244
hydrogen molecule 139
hyperons 346

initiators 497
Institute for Advanced Study in
    Princeton 2, 11, 528
Institute for Theoretical Physics at
    Copenhagen 2, 97
  accelerators at 399–402, 525–7, 544
  biology at 27
  CERN theory group at 520–1
  expansion of 258–60, 261–2, 399, 509
  German occupation of 489–90
  international theoretical physics
    conferences at 18
  new part at Risø 525–7, 546
  nuclear physics at 26, 388
  opening of 17, 171
  proposal for 168, 169, 170
  renamed Niels Bohr Institute 171, 546
Institute of Mathematics, Copenhagen
    19
Institute of Technology, Copenhagen 17
International Conference on
    Fundamental Particles in
    Cambridge, England 7

International Education Board (IEB) 258–60, 324, 381
ionization potentials 202
irradiation 271
isotopes 126, 150, 399
    unstable 452
    see also radioisotopes; uranium

Kirchhoff's law 16, 75–7, 83, 140
Klein paradox 354, 355, 365, 367, 543
K_x-line 181
K radiations 181
Kramers, Hendrik
    Bohr–Kramers–Slater (BKS) paper 234, 235, 238, 541
    book on quantum mechanics by 288, 312
    collaboration with Bohr 21, 168, 179
        start of 167, 540
    on correspondence principle 193
    death of 513, 545
    on dispersion of light 270–2, 273
    Heisenberg and 274, 276
    on spectral intensities 183, 185, 195
    in Utrecht 263
    other references 171, 190, 197, 198, 202, 204, 205, 210, 239, 244, 251, 253, 275, 280, 295, 296, 300, 316, 318, 487, 510, 514, 520
    see also entries beginning Kramers
Kramers' dispersion relation 271, 274
Kramers–Heisenberg dispersion theory 351
Kramers–Kronig relations 272

Landau–Peierls (LP) paper (1931) 359, 362, 363
language, ambiguity in 22–3
light
    dispersion of 271
    emission of 141
    infrared 62, 84
    interference of 57, 59–60, 88
    monochromatic 61
    nature of 53, 54, 232, 538
        corpuscular theory of 56, 57, 59, 87, 230, 231
        semicorpuscular theory of 230
        wave theory of 56, 57, 59, 87, 230, 231
        see also particle–wave duality
    velocity of 54, 56, 64, 67–8
        see also velocity, universal

light-quanta 87, 230–2, 233, 234, 287, 351, 539
    see also photons
liquid drops 339–40
Los Alamos Laboratory 341, 495, 497, 499, 503

magnetic moment measurements 354
magnetism 151
Manhattan Project 494, 497, 499
mathematics in physics 176–9
matter, particle–wave duality of 240, 241
matrices 278, 279, 290
    coordinate 278
    energy 278
    momentum 278
    square 278
matrix mechanics 21, 22, 275, 279, 284, 289, 302, 317, 542
Maud Committee 493–4
Maxwell–Lorentz theory 106
Maxwell's equations 63–6, 69, 70, 75, 106, 233, 348
Maxwell's theory of the electromagnetic field 336, 347
measurement theory 435
mechanicism 443
mechanics, statistical 79, 80–2, 86, 146, 281, 317, 436–8
mercury 183, 184
mesons 346, 352, 357
    μ-mesons 346, 358
    π-mesons 357
Michelson–Morley experiment 67–8, 69, 70
microwaves 63
molecular physics 161, 347
molecules 103, 145, 146, 191
    properties of 105
momentum, conservation of 233, 234, 237, 312–13, 367, 369
Munich
    pursuit of quantum theory in 161–2

National Science Foundation 469
neptunium 463
neutrinos 346, 368, 369, 370
    observation of 370
neutron physics 335, 336
neutrons 369, 387
    discovery of 26, 331–2, 368, 369, 460
    free 461
    selective absorption of 336–7, 338

Newton's laws of mechanics 69, 75, 96,
    185
nitrogen 329, 331
noble gases 202, 203, 342
Nordita 20, 29, 521–3
nuclear energy 460, 464
nuclear fission 325, 341
  discovery of 122
nuclear forces 330, 357, 461
  Heisenberg's theory of 336
nuclear magnetic moments 331, 332
nuclear medicine 27, 394
nuclear physics 26, 152, 347
  crisis in (1929) 364
  theoretical 325, 336
nuclear radius 328
nuclear reactions 337, 453, 454
  chain reactions 462–3
  at higher energies 341
nuclear reactors, development of 394
nuclear spin 331, 332
nuclear spectroscopy 337
nuclear statistics 331, 332
nucleons 336, 457, 461
nucleus
  compound 337, 338, 339, 341, 342, 417,
    457, 544
    energy spectrum of 339, 340
  discovery of 123, 180, 326, 327
  liquid-drop model of 339–40, 454, 458,
    462
  one-body model of 336, 337
  protein–electron model of 328, 367
  proton–neutron model of 332
  shell model of 342, 343, 458

objective reality 429
observability 313
observation 314, 316
optics 54
  classical 313
orbits 276
oscillators, harmonic 350, 351
  quantum numbers of 350

particle physics 8, 29, 347, 519, 523
  definition of 346
particles, fundamental (elementary) 346
particle–wave duality 22, 287, 301, 347
Pauli, Wolfgang
  Balmer formula derivation by 279, 280,
    283
  β-spectrum explanation by 368

correspondence with Bohr 311, 360,
    426, 437
  death of 513, 546
  early life 200–1
  Einstein and 200
  and energy conservation 366, 367
  Heisenberg and 262
    correspondence 275, 278, 297, 298,
      301, 304, 309, 355
  Nobel Laureate 161
  at Solvay 316, 318, 320, 369
  on Zeeman effect 199
  other references 12, 21, 29, 52, 151, 162,
    180, 208–9, 224, 237, 238, 241, 243,
    244, 258, 268, 270, 284, 310, 352, 353,
    355, 359, 361, 362, 364, 395, 428, 434,
    442, 446, 498, 539, 541, 542
  see also exclusion principle
Pauli exclusion principle, see exclusion
    principle
Peltier effect 110
penetrating orbit effect, see Tauchbahn
    effect
penetration theory 511
periodic table of elements 103, 150, 154
  explanation of 179, 180–2
perturbation theory 193
phase integrals 186
phenomenon, definition of 23, 432–3
philanthropy 255–60
philosopher, definitions of 420, 421
phosphorus-32 391–2, 395
photoelectric effect 215, 230, 233, 234
photoelectric equation 230
photons 87, 230, 233, 238, 301, 347, 350–1
  emission of 338
  see also light-quanta
physics
  at start of twentieth century 53
  classical 16, 300, 310, 313
    definition of 66
    end of universal validity of 79, 86,
      177
    indispensability of 196
  in Denmark, development of 92–7
  high-energy 518
    see also particle physics
  language of 426
  mathematics in 176–9
  statistical 189
Pickering lines 149
pions 357
Planck, Max
  binding energy calculations 327

early life 79–80
meetings with Bohr 227, 252, 541
and Nobel Prizes 212–13
quantum rule formulation by 186
quantum theory discovery by 3, 82–8,
    160, 539
other references 15, 16, 78, 81, 104, 108,
    109, 138, 144, 146, 161, 177, 228, 229,
    230, 231, 233, 281, 285, 316, 317, 340,
    347, 350, 383, 425, 426
see also entries beginning Planck
Planck length 83
Planck's constant 85, 86, 128, 138, 145,
    160
Planck's radiation law 85, 87, 138, 152,
    191, 224, 230, 348, 351
plutonium 463–4, 482, 492, 495, 503, 511
polarization 195
of fluorescent light 273
polonium 386
positrons 346
discovery of 356, 368, 369, 543
precession 243, 268
probability
    and entropy 82
    in quantum dynamics 191
    quantum mechanical 286, 317–18, 319
    of a state 287
    transition 287
protons 328, 369
    magnetic moment of 216
psychology 439–41

q-numbers 279, 290
quantization
    field 350, 357
    rules 176
    second 350
quantum chemistry 137, 152, 268
quantum dynamics of atoms 17
quantum electrodynamics (QED) 15, 29,
    296, 347, 350–2, 542
    complexity of 348
    measurability in 358–64
        of charges and currents 363–4
        of fields 358–63
quantum field theories 347, 349, 351
    of the Dirac equation 357
    of nuclear forces 357
quantum gas 110
quantum jumps 191
quantum law, first 15
quantum mechanics 14, 88, 231
    birth of 16, 21, 148, 160, 267, 276

consistency of 427, 428
display of basic principles of 320
early development of 296
emergence of 275–9
meaning of 23
of molecules 295
quantum numbers 148
    auxiliary 187, 204, 242
    fourth 199–200, 241, 297
    magnetic 268
    new 184–8
    orbital 268
    principal 204, 242, 267
    spatial 297
quantum physics 138, 160, 161
    between 1913 and 1924 176
    general principles underlying 189
    measurement problem in 304, 426
quantum postulate 86
quantum rules, general formulation of
    186
quantum statistics 268
quantum theory 3, 71
    discovery of 82–7
    of electrodynamics 5, 6–7
    first law 85
    and Nobel Prizes 211
    old 20–1, 29, 160, 161, 190, 197, 198,
        199, 243, 275
        1913–1916 179–88
        to 1925 267–70
    origins of 15, 75
    of radiation 231
    relativistic, crisis in (1929) 364–70
    of the solid state 138
quarks 346

radar 63
radiation
    emission and absorption of 191
    free 348
radiation field, virtual 236, 238
radiative instability 136, 137, 147
radioactive decay 191
radioactive displacement law 126, 127
radioactive transformation theory 122,
    326
radioactivity 106, 122, 383
    experimental studies in 125
    induced 216, 390, 543
        applications of 391
        discovery of 375, 386–7, 452
radioisotopes 390, 394

radio waves 63, 121, 122
radium D (RaD) 388, 389
Raman scattering 274
rare earths 203, 207, 209, 390
Rask–Ørsted foundation 258, 324, 383, 385, 468
Rayleigh–Einstein–Jeans (REJ) law 84, 85, 86, 152
reciprocity 426
refraction
  double 54, 55, 60
  laws of 55
relativity, general 178, 200, 436
relativity, new 315
relativity, special, theory of 15, 16, 68–71, 176, 351, 352
  and hydrogen fine structure 185–6, 187–8
renormalization program 7
resonance 456
resonance acceleration 377
resonance excitation 338–9
Riemann surfaces 422, 424
Risø 29, 523–7
  National Laboratory 29, 523–5, 527
  new part of Niels Bohr Institute at 525–7
Rockefeller foundation 27, 256, 258, 260, 379–80, 383, 394–5, 396, 397, 398, 414, 480, 481
  divisions of 380
  emergency program 384, 385
rotation, hidden 201
Rutherford, Ernest
  and accelerators 378
  artificial transmutation of elements by 327–30, 541
  on atomic energy 460
  on β-radioactivity 150
  Bohr and
    correspondence 145, 146, 152, 163, 164, 168, 170, 171, 172, 182, 185, 196, 197, 205, 254, 261, 280, 295, 367, 369, 396, 399
    friendship 134–5, 333, 513, 536
    influence of R on B 17, 129, 424
  on causality 153
  death of 26, 412–13, 544
  early life 121–2
  move to Cambridge by 252
  nucleus discovery by 121–7, 136, 180, 539
  on radioactive decay 191, 326
  war effort by 165

other references 11, 52, 76, 106, 134, 181, 202, 209, 213, 229, 259, 386, 388, 408, 495, 538
  see also entries beginning Rutherford's
Rutherford's nuclear model 123, 125

scattering
  elastic 337, 338
  inelastic 337, 338
Schrödinger, Erwin
  discussions with Bohr 22, 298–300, 424
  early life 280–1
  Nobel Prize nomination 428
  paper on Tauchbahn effect 206
  wave mechanics discovery by 21, 281–4, 301, 542
  other references 7, 52, 216, 237, 285, 286, 288, 289, 297, 303, 306, 317, 352, 425, 539
scientists, first 94
selection principles 195
selection rules 199, 244, 268
Solvay conferences in Brussels
  1911 125, 145, 186
  1921 172, 195, 408
  1927 316, 318, 319, 320, 425–6, 427
  1930 427, 543
  1933 361
  1946 512
  1961 13, 512
Sommerfeld, Arnold
  Bohr and
    correspondence 154, 205
    meetings 164
  as mathematical physicist 162
  on energy conservation 234
  on fine structure 184, 186, 187, 189, 242, 243–4, 540
  Nobel Prize nominations 214
  on nuclear constitution 330
  quantum numbers introduced by
    fourth 199–200, 541
    third 188, 199
  as teacher 161
  other references 110, 145, 155, 163, 178, 180, 182, 193, 194, 196, 198, 200, 202, 204, 208, 213, 215, 227, 228, 229, 241, 262, 263, 268, 269, 272, 425, 538, 539
sound waves 60
space–time coordination 312, 315
spectra
  absorption 139
  band 141
  emission 139, 140

rotational 146
    studies of 160
    vibrational 146
spectral density 76, 77, 79, 85
spectral frequencies 142, 146, 149, 194
spectral function 78, 84
spectral numerology 142
spectroscopy 61, 140, 149
spectrum, visible 61, 62
spin 241–4, 268, 297, 352
Spirit of Copenhagen 320
stability 136
Stark effect 182–3, 185, 188, 194, 196, 540
    linear 182, 183
Stefan–Boltzmann law 77
stopping theory 511
strings, vibrating 282–3
strong forces 330, 342
strong interaction 330
surface tension in liquids 101, 102

Tauchbahn effect 206
telescope 54–5
temperature 76, 77, 436, 437
thermal equilibrium 81
thermodynamics 77, 78, 80, 81, 436–8
    first law of 81
    second law of 80, 81, 83, 85, 104
Thomson, J. J.
    as director of Cavendish Laboratory
        117–20, 252, 329
    discovery of electron by 52, 105–6, 376,
        539
    on quantum theory 153
    relationship with Bohr 120, 121, 122,
        125
    on spectra 142
    other references 109, 123, 124, 136, 139,
        149, 165, 295, 538
    see also entries beginning Thomson
Thomson atom 137
Thomson effect 110
Thomson scattering 119
Thrige foundation 524
tracers, isotopic
    introduction of 388–94
transition frequencies 271
transuranic elements 453, 456, 458

unified field theory 178
uranium 452–3, 454, 456–7
    fission of 26, 456
        deuteron induced 459

fission fragments 458, 459, 462
    separation 459
    uranium 235 456–7, 458, 459, 461, 463,
        493–4, 495, 503–4
    purification of 462
    uranium 238 456, 459, 461, 462, 463
    uranium 239 453, 456, 463
Uranium Committee 492, 493

velocity
    relativistic sum 70
    universal 70
vibrations 340
vitalism 441, 443

wave amplitude 58
wave equations 283
    relativistic 352
    scalar 352
wavefunctions 428
    as complex functions 290
    interpretation of 288
wavelength 57, 61
wave mechanics 21, 197, 241, 281, 282,
        284, 286, 301, 317, 352
wave motion 57–9
wave packets 285, 312
waves
    frequencies of 61, 62–3
    longitudinal 60
    surface 340
    transverse 60
    volume 340
    water 60
    see also entries beginning wave
Wiedemann–Franz law 110
Wien's displacement law 78, 79, 83, 84,
        85, 87

X-rays 62, 119, 122, 162, 202, 208, 210, 272
    discovery of 376
    secondary 181
    theories of 301
X-ray spectra 149, 154, 180
X-ray tubes 376

Young experiment 59

Zeeman effect 198–9, 200, 208, 242, 268,
        272
zirconium 209, 210
Zweideutigkeit 201